MAP LIBRARIANSHIP:
Readings

compiled by

ROMAN DRAZNIOWSKY

Map Curator,

American Geographical Society

The Scarecrow Press, Inc.

Metuchen, N.J.   1975

Library of Congress Cataloging in Publication Data

Drazniowsky, Roman, comp.
  Map librarianship: readings.

  Bibliography: p.
  1. Map collections. 2. Cartography. I. Title.
Z692.M3D73   025.17'6   74-19244
ISBN 0-8108-0739-4

PREFACE

Graphic representation of the earth's surface is not a recent discovery. From the earliest times men prepared maps, although not necessarily in familiar forms, to show and understand space relationships. That simple function has since been multiplied, and now, in modern life, the map is used in many disciplines and has no substitute. To realize the importance of maps today, it would be sufficient to mention only a few vital subjects such as density and distribution of population, geographical location of diseases, land use, geology, distribution of minerals and industries, transportation, planning and many other subjects, which could not be better represented, understood or studied than on a map. According to Professor Salishchev, "maps find their use in all spheres of scientific, economic and cultural activities. They are indispensable for a detailed registration, analysis and objective evaluation of natural conditions and resources, labour resources and productive forces, as well as the multiform service system (education, public health services, trade etc.). ... Many works from cartography are among the outstanding achievements of the world of science; they are cultural values of non-transient significance."*

In this age of intense and sophisticated investigations of the environment, the map as a medium for information storage and as an analytical tool is of a great importance. How to prepare, search, order, catalog, store, preserve and retrieve them is a complicated task. Satisfactory service in these areas can be provided only by properly trained map librarians. It is surprising that, although the value of maps

---

*"The Present-day Thematic Cartography and the Task of International Collaboration," Institution of Surveyors. (India). New Delhi: 21st International Geographical Congress, New Delhi, Nov.-Dec. 1968; 7-8.

has been long recognized, the fundamentals of map librarianship are only beginning to be considered. There has been very limited professional training in map librarianship. Map curators, or if you prefer, map librarians, have indicated that their collections could be improved in both service and care, if professionally trained personnel were available. Realizing the present needs and future demands in map librarianship, the Columbia University School of Library Service initiated a course in map resources and map librarianship in 1969.

Although numerous articles on the subject of map librarianship have been published--mostly in specialized journals--a systematic and sequential description of map collection operation has heretofore not been available. The present work is intended by presenting a compilation of selected articles on seven specific subjects, to provide at least some guidance for map librarians. At the end of the book will be found a bibliography, arranged by chapter, of further readings related to each area of interest. Taken together, these represent an extensive listing of articles related to the processing and care of maps and the running of map libraries.

This publication was possible only because so many writers have contributed to the knowledge of map librarianship. They made possible the selection of 48 excellent articles herein reprinted; to them I express my thanks and appreciation. Also, I would like to thank the many authors, organizations and editors who granted permission to reprint the selected articles, and the many persons who helped prepare this book. Special thanks I would like to express to Dr. Walter W. Ristow, Chief of the Geography and Map Division, Library of Congress, for very useful suggestions and professional advice.

Roman Drazniowsky
New York City
August 1973

TABLE OF CONTENTS

4. MAP BIBLIOGRAPHIES/ACQUISITIONS

5. MAP PROCESSING AND CATALOGING

6. MAP STORAGE AND PRESERVATION

7. MAP LIBRARIANSHIP / MAP COLLECTIONS

1. INTRODUCTION TO MAPS

MILESTONES OF MAPPING*

E. D. Baldock

The origin of maps is unknown, but their genesis must have been associated with man's need to record his surroundings in some graphic form. Primitive man drew pictures on the walls of his cave; many of these drawings probably represented a pictorial map of the area where he lived. Because early nations based their wealth on land and as taxation was levied upon its produce, it was necessary to mark land boundaries for assessment purposes. The earliest recorded cadastral surveys were made in Babylonia about 2300 B.C. and a very accurate system of land survey was developed in Egypt during the 14th century B.C., with permanent boundary markers to find land holdings after the annual flooding by the Nile.

The oldest map in existence today was found in the ruins of ancient Babylon. It was carved on a small clay tablet about the year 3500 B.C. It is interesting to note that the positions of north, east and west are shown by circular symbols. The Babylonians were possibly the first to divide the circle into 360 degrees.

To the Greeks we owe the foundation of our present system of cartography. Many of the ancient scholars recognized the earth as a sphere with its poles, equator and climatic zones; they developed the latitude and longitude system and calculated the earth's size. Philosophers of this pre-Christian era were slowly producing the key to our

*Reprinted by permission from The Canadian Cartographer [formerly The Cartographer], vol. 3, no. 2 (1966), 89-102. Published by B.V. Gutsell, Department of Geography, York University, Toronto.

knowledge of mother earth; it was contained in their many
writings, which had fortunately been gathered together in the
magnificent libraries of Alexandria.   Twenty-five years before the birth of Christ, Strabo, a young Greek scholar, decided to compile man's knowledge of geography.   He took
up residence in Alexandria and commenced the gigantic task
of sorting cartographic knowledge, often submerged in the
most unlikely works of the philosophers.   Strabo was a confirmed stoic, exemplifying a philosophy well suited to the task
he was to perform.   After some five years of intensive study
he produced a history of cartographic knowledge which had
been advanced to his time.   It is not the intention to deal in
detail with Strabo's work but simply to establish a few basic
facts and his influence on cartographic development.   Strabo
traced man's knowledge of the heavenly bodies which, from
earliest times, had provided the calendar for events.   By
the 7th century B. C. a great wealth of data had been
gathered and Strabo rightly concluded that man's knowledge
of the Universe was an important factor in developing his
understanding of earth geography.

When the Greek philosophers were delving into the
nature of things, it was natural that the earth was a much
debated subject.   Anaximander, a pupil of Thales of Miletus,
founder of the Ionian School of Philosophy, advanced the
theory that the earth was a thick section of a cylinder suspended in the circular vault of the heavens, supported by
whirling balls of fire; this idea was possibly based on an
early Babylonian concept.   A pupil of Anaximander, by the
name of Anaximenes, rejected his teacher's theory for that of
a rectangular shaped earth supported in the heavens by the
air it compressed, the habitable world being surrounded by
a great ocean flowing into the Mediterranean.

Many philosophers followed, but Pythagoras the Ionian,
founder of a school of philosophy at Crotona in the 6th century
B. C., is credited with the nearest approach to the truth regarding the earth's shape.   He argued against the generally
accepted theory that the earth was disc-shaped and offered
his theory that the earth was spherical; how he arrived at
such a revolutionary idea is not known.   Aristotle later came
to the same conclusion when in summing up the various
theories he stated that "the Universe is finite and it is
spherical. "   From about the time of Pythagoras the earth
began to take its rightful shape in the minds of a few men,
and mathematicians endeavoured to calculate its size.   Aristotle stated the mathematicians of his day estimated the

circumference of the earth to be between 30, 000 and 40, 000 miles.

The first detailed account of how the earth's circumference was measured comes from the Greek scholar Eratosthenes of Cyrene in the 2nd century B. C.   Having observed at Syene that the sun shone down a deep well, with no shadow at mid-day on the summer solstice, he assumed that the well was situated on the Tropic of Cancer.   Using the measurements available from the Egyptian land surveys he estimated the distance between Syene and Alexandria to be 500 miles (expressed in stadia) and assumed that Alexandria was directly north of Syene, therefore on the same meridian. With the sun at its zenith on the summer solstice he measured the angle of a shadow cast by a pole in Alexandria as 1/50th of a circle.   By applying Proposition 29 of Euclid, who lived in the 3rd century B. C., Eratosthenes concluded than an angle of 1/50th of a circle subtended an arc of 500 miles making the earth's circumference 25, 000 miles.   This was a remarkable achievement, taking into account that not all of his assumptions were correct.   (The earth's circumference at the equator is approximately 24, 899 miles.)

Eratosthenes produced a map based on a parollelogram having seven irregular meridians and seven parallels passing through specific places such as Meroe, Alexandria, Rhodes, etc.   Topographical content was normal for this time, covering from the west coast of Africa to India across the Equator and from Scandinavia in the north to Libya in the south.   This map remained in use despite its many errors until 30 A. D.

Hipparcus, the famous astronomer of the 2nd century B. C., criticized Eratosthenes' map, maintaining that the parallels and meridians should be equally spaced at intervals of one half-hour, and that all geographical information should be positioned by using latitudes and longitudes reduced from astronomical observations.   Posidonius, who conducted a school on the island of Rhodes in the 2nd century B. C., made the second recorded attempt to measure the earth's circumference.   He observed that the star Canopus just grazed the horizon at Rhodes; measuring the meridian height of the star as 1/48th part of a circle at Alexandria, which was accepted as 500 miles to the south and on the same meridian as Rhodes, he concluded the difference in latitude of the two places was 1/48th of a circle; therefore his calculation of the circumference of the earth was 500 X 48 =

24,000 miles.   Posidonius also made certain assumptions
which were not correct.

Crates of Mallus, a Stoic philosopher, constructed
a globe in 140 B.C., reasoning that the spherical earth
described by geographers did not comply with the Greek
laws of symmetry.   He added balancing land masses in the
four quarters of the sphere.   This globe was later to become a symbol in the regalia of Kings.

Strabo, in summarizing these calculations, attempted
to fill in details assumed to be in error and established a
revised measurement of 18,000 miles around the earth's
circumference.   He described the habitable world as a
spherical quadrilateral washed on all sides by the sea.   To
construct such a map, he said one would require a very
large sphere, so that the small area representing the
habitable world would be large enough to show the required
detail.   Strabo also recognized the difficulties of representing
the spherical co-ordinates of the sphere on a flat surface;
he offered no solution of his problem, but maintained that
for practical purposes meridians and latitudes could be
drawn as straight lines.

Independent of the cartographic knowledge being developed by western philosophers, China was producing maps,
reference being made in their early literature to one produced in the 3rd century B.C.   Some of these maps followed the circular concept, China occupying most of the circle.
Pei Hsiu in the 2nd century A.D. actually laid down the guiding principle for drawing maps.   Local governors were required to have maps made covering their areas, these being
drawn on paper.

Roman cartography differed considerably from that of
the contemporary Greek.   The Romans required maps for
military and administrative purposes and were not concerned
with any mathematical consideration.   Their map of the
habitable world was circular (Orbis Terrarum) with the
Roman Empire occupying the greater portion of the map;
Asia, much reduced in size, occupied the top segment (this
is apparently where our term "orientation" is derived).
These circular maps, often referred to as "T-O maps,"
were destined to be used extensively by early Christian cartographers.   Roman topographical maps were actually diagrams of places and routes with little attention being given
to actual latitude, longitude or scale.

Most cartographers after Eratosthenes were endeavouring to portray a more accurate map of the habitable world. Information was gathered from travellers, latitudes and longitudes were estimated, then plotted on maps. In the 2nd century A. D. a noted geographer Marinus of Tyre attempted to bring the mapping of the habitable world up-to-date, placing the northern extremity at the parallel of Thule designated as 63° north of the equator. This distance was approximately 3,150 miles according to his acceptance of 1° = 50 miles. He extended the southern limit to 24° below the equator. The east-west distance was one over which considerable controversy existed; however, Marinus extended the habitable world over 15 hours of longitude or about 11,250 miles at the equator. The map Marinus produced was crude and followed the early concept of parallels and meridians being straight lines intersecting at right angles. A copy of this map was reported as being seen in the 10th century A. D.

In the 2nd century A. D., Claudius Ptolemy was appointed curator of the library in Alexandria where he had access to Strabo's records. Ptolemy's influence was to be felt in cartography for many centuries to come. He was a prolific writer, more inclined to science than philosophy, delving into astronomy, optics, cartography and music. As a map compiler his topographic detail was not highly rated, but he laid down the foundations for an orderly system in the practice of cartography. If Ptolemy's geographic interpretation of the habitable world left much to be desired, his cartographic knowledge far surpassed his predecessors. His writings contained detailed instructions on how to construct the stereographic, orthographic and conic projections of a sphere to a flat surface. He produced a gazetteer listing all important places by latitude and longitude and made considerable studies on distances between places.

Ptolemy's map of the habitable world was constructed on a conic projection, recognizing the convergency of meridians towards the north pole. He estimated the habitable world to be about 180° around the equator, but accepted Strabo's figure of 1° = 50 miles thus reducing the equatorial circumference to 18,000 miles. As reports of travellers were received map-makers extended Asia eastwards until only 50° separated the Indies from Spain. This error persisted to the 14th century and possibly inspired Columbus to venture westward to the Orient and thus a new continent was discovered. After the collapse of the Roman Empire, the

Arabs became the heirs of Ptolemy's works, which they translated into Arabic. The Arabian mathematicians continued to add precision to earth measurements and although accepting a spherical earth, their world maps were crude and followed the circular concept.

With the growth of the Christian Church, monastic orders became established as seats of learning from which some of the great universities developed. We often hear the middle ages referred to unjustly as the Dark Ages, but one must consider conditions that existed at that time. The average person could neither read nor write, nations and states waged perpetual wars, and intrigue among the ruling classes was rampant. The monasteries provided the scholar with peace and quiet where he could pursue both religious and secular studies. These monks developed the skill of better writing, produced books on many subjects and drew maps. To them we owe the preservation of the sciences and the foundation for future development of knowledge.

There developed during this mediaeval time three distinct types of maps mostly all hand-drawn on vellum, some beautifully illuminated; like books, they were scarce due to the tremendous amount of time consumed to draw and write by hand. These maps might be classified as symbolic, topical and practical. In the last type is included the famous Portolano navigation charts, produced solely by sea captains. Their accuracy was extremely good and in time formed the basis for better knowledge of shorelines and distances.

Symbolic maps were developed from the Roman circular maps and were designed by ecclesiastics to instruct the faithful in church dogma. Jerusalem was usually shown at the centre. We are reminded that the ordinary person could not conceive of the earth as a sphere and the circular concept was a compromise. Some symbolic maps did attempt to become theoretical as explained by a 6th-century monk, Cosmas, in his Christian Topography. His habitable world was based on the biblical description of the tabernacle. Fortunately, these maps were not numerous and were soon forgotten.

Topical maps of this period were designed for specific purposes such as illustrating estates, routes of pilgrims, locations and place names. They were artistically drawn on parchment, often with illuminated text. These early map makers had to have a detailed knowledge of the map area, and the artistic skill to produce it. Many problems must have faced them: for example, the size of available parchment would affect the scale; how features were to be symbolized and which colours were to be used. The latter was based on nature; green for trees, blue for rivers, brown for roads, black for outlines and names. Such application of colours has not changed to any extent on our modern maps.

Let us pause at this point in the story of maps to consider what materials were available to the map maker on which to record his work. As already stated, the earliest known map was incised on a clay tablet about the year 3500 B.C.; more portable maps and diagrams were most likely produced long before this on skins of animals which have not survived the ravages of time.

Papyrus, which was processed by the Egyptians, was the first material that had good qualities for drawing and writing, records indicating its use as early as 3500 B.C. The papyrus plant flourished along the banks of the Nile. The portion used was the stalk, being cut into 16" lengths. The centre marrow was cut into thin strips and laid side by side with another layer placed at right-angles over the first, then treated with a gum solution, pressed and smoothed, the resulting sheets being approximately 12" X 16". If extra length was required in a roll, the sheets were pasted together.

Parchment made from splitting the skins of sheep or calves was known to exist by 500 B.C.; the calf skin produced the best writing surface and became known as "vellum." Due to the availability of papyrus, parchment did not come into general use until about 200 B.C. and then only due to an Egyptian embargo being placed on the export of papyrus to the King of Pergamum (Asia Minor) who was then forced to manufacture skins for writing. The process of splitting and curing skins had by this time been much improved, producing a more durable and better surface than the fragile papyrus. When these writing skins were exported to the Romans they called it pergamena from which the name parchment is derived. Parchment became the main medium for writing in Europe by the 4th century A.D. and had far-reaching effects on the development of writing techniques, due to its smooth surface allowing the easy movement of the quill pen in all directions.

Due to the skill and labour required for the manufacture of writing materials, it is little wonder that very
few maps and records existed in early times. A more
economical and simplified method of producing a writing
material would have to be developed if dissemination of
knowledge was to be extended to more people than the few
learned scholars who were unfolding the nature of things.
The manufacture of paper finally solved this problem, but
from the time of its invention until its use in Europe many
centuries elapsed.

The Chinese developed a system of bookmaking from
engraved wood blocks nearly six centuries before printing
was introduced into Europe. The reason for this amazing
development was the invention of paper-making about 105 A.D.
in central China credited to a man named Ts'ai Lun. By
the 5th century A.D. paper had become the general medium
for written documents in China. Examination of this original paper has proven it to be pure rag paper. The movement of the use of paper towards the Western World was
slow, influenced by the powerful military and religious
forces of Islam. Records reveal that paper was used in the
following locations in its movement westward.

Central China	105 A.D.	Chinese use
Tun-huang	150 A.D.	"
Lou-lan	200 A.D.	"
Turfan	399 A.D.	"
Gilghit (Kashmir)	500-600 A.D.	
Samarkand	751 A.D.	Moslem
Baghdad	793 A.D.	"
Egypt	900 A.D.	"
Fez (Morocco)	1100 A.D.	"
Jativa (Spain)	1150 A.D.	"
Fabriano (Italy)	1270 A.D.	Christian
Nuremberg (Germany)	1390 A.D.	"
England	1494 A.D.	"
North America	1690 A.D.	"

Long before paper provided the impetus to printing books in
Europe, it was playing an important role in Asia. The
Arabs, inflamed with religious zeal to conquer the world for
Islam, gained the knowledge of paper-making from prisoners
captured in a campaign in Russian Turkestan. Their con-
quest denied Europe free access to the established trade
routes from the east, and the Moslem world controlled the
paper-making industry exclusively. Paper derived its name
from papyrus, which it completely replaced by 950.

The invasion of Spain by the Moors introduced paper-making for the first time into Europe; a paper mill, operated by the Moors, was erected in the town of Jativa about 1150. Paper then became available to Christian Europe and was used for block printing and writing. Paper-making was established in Italy about 1270 at Fabriano which is still an important centre in the manufacture of high quality paper. The largest size of paper produced in these early mills was about 19" X 25", which naturally restricted the size of maps produced by printing methods that developed in the 15th century. Early in that century, the printing press was destined to change man's knowledge of the world in which he lived. Illustrations engraved on wood were being printed on paper on a press adapted from the wine presses of the Rhine. With the invention of moveable type by Johanne Gutenburg in 1440, it was not long before books dealing with scientific subjects were printed.

No record of man's ability to write and print would be complete without some mention of ink. The ancient scribes of Egypt used a reed pen-brush to apply an ink which was mixed when needed. For black ink, lampblack was mixed with an aqueous solution of vegetable gum, and for carmine ink, red oxide of iron was used; the red being used for initial words. This practice was later adopted by the Greeks and Romans, surviving in the rubrics of early manuscripts. This method of preparing ink remained in use as a writing medium, even being used to pull impressions from early woodcuts. Iron-gall ink was described by Theophilus about 1100 and often resulted in a brownish cast noted in many early woodcut prints. While this watery ink was excellent for writing it was of little use with the new metal moveable type introduced in 1440. However, at the turn of the 14th century, painters had commenced using drying oils and varnishes for colour pigments. It was a natural step for printers to use the oil paint developed by artists with certain modifications to suit the new art of printing.

The demand for cartographic knowledge had caused the works of Ptolemy to be translated into Latin by 1410 and, in the first 60 years of printing, several elaborate folio editions of his geography were published, spanning a period of little cartographic advance. Ptolemy's acceptance of Strabo's figures for the earth's measurement was again in evidence and Christopher Columbus, a dealer in maps and charts, became convinced that the quickest route to the Indies--so richly proclaimed by Marco Polo after his journey

there in 1485--could be made by sailing from Spain across
the western sea; he made his first voyage of discovery in
1492. The period following this epic event saw explorations
to distant places, extending man's knowledge of the earth;
old theories and traditions were slowly discarded and separate
scientific disciplines emerged.

From the beginning of printing, maps required in
quantity were reproduced from copper engravings, a skill
developed by the goldsmiths of Italy who had for some time
made records of their designs engraved on goblets, plates,
etc. by rubbing a greasy ink into the incisions, then pressing
an image to paper; it was a natural step to use their skill
to engrave maps on flat sheets of copper and print impressions on paper.

Not all maps produced during this period were engraved on copper; many maps were still being hand drawn
or wood engraved. Two examples come to mind: the first,
produced by Juan de la Costa on an oxhide in 1501, showing
the Western discoveries of Christopher Columbus; the other,
a map produced by Martin Waldseemüller in 1507, engraved
on 12 wood blocks (18" X 24 1/2") which when assembled
measured 36 sq. ft. in size; records show that some 1,000
copies were printed. The latter map illustrated the Western
discoveries and was the first to name the New World as
America after Amerigo Vespucci, who was possibly the first
man to recognize it as a separate continent after his voyage
to South America in 1499. This map should never fail to
intrigue the cartographer as to the method used to engrave
the wood. Was it cut intaglio or were the non-printing areas
cut away? The former would seem more likely due to the
great number of intersecting lines and the large amount of
fine lettering which might have been stamped with a die.

The skill of map engraving soon became a prerequisite of the map maker. Gerard Mercator (1512-1594), the
famous cartographer, engraved four map sheets of Flanders,
which he published in 1540, having first surveyed the country
to obtain the entire compilation of data. The tremendous
skill and patience required to engrave a map is so often overlooked as we examine maps produced during this period of
cartographic renaissance. All work on the engraved plate
was reverse reading; corrections were difficult to make, requiring hammering out from the back of the plate then re-
surfacing the work side. All colours had to be added by
hand on the printed copy; over two centuries were to elapse

before a solution to the problem of reproducing colours was
to be found.

The method of printing engravings was also destined
to advance slowly from simply rubbing ink into the incisions,
polishing off the surplus ink and then placing dampened paper
over the plate and rubbing or squeezing it in a Rhine-type
screw press.   William Jansjoon Blaeu (1571-1638), a printer
and map maker of Amsterdam, developed a press which
eliminated a lot of the back-breaking pressure required to
print a copperplate impression.   This press employed moveable parts which allowed the plate to be moved by a crank-
ing handle under a stationary block that applied a constant
pressure, the paper being protected by a metal tympan
greased for easy movement.   Copperplate engraving was used
as a map making method well into the 20th century, being
combined with other reproduction methods for quantity printing.

The 16th and 17th centuries witnessed a flourishing
trade in maps and charts.   They generally had a definite
similarity in cartographic expression irrespective of their
origin, due no doubt to the itinerant fraternity of map
makers during this period.   The great amount of detailed
ornamentation of titles and borders was quite possibly engraved by non-cartographic artisans retained for that purpose.   The introduction of conventional map symbols began
to appear on maps towards the end of the 16th century, replacing to some extent descriptive notes and miniature pictures; however, few map makers considered the necessity
of supplying the map reader with a reference.

A completely new system of printing was developed
by Alois Senefelder about 1805, destined in time to provide
the map maker with a much improved method of reproducing
his maps.   Senefelder was an amateur writer who, finding
the cost of printing his works too excessive, began experimenting with a "do-it-yourself" method based on contemporary printing systems.   He began experimenting with copper
etching, which involved lettering in reverse with a scribing
point through a waxy acid resist coated over the copper.
His ability to reverse letter was not good and, having many
corrections, he developed a correcting ink made of wax,
soap and lampblack formed into sticks; when needed, it was
rubbed down in a little water and applied with a brush.   The
high cost of copper for practicing his reverse lettering
prompted him to look for a substitute which happened to be

a highly polished flooring tile of kellheimer sandstone mined
near his home in Bavaria.   By mere chance he wrote a
laundry list for his mother on a clean stone with his correcting ink stick and before cleaning the stone poured acid
over it; the result was a raised image of the lettering which
would print.

Having succeeded in producing a printing method
which was not new, but one he could do himself, he set out
to develop a method to eliminate reverse lettering.   Using
a thin paper coated with gum, he lettered right reading with
his correcting ink.   Wetting the finished work and rubbing
it face down to a new stone, he transferred a greasy image
in reverse which could be etched.   He observed when wetting
the work that water adhered only to the gummed areas and
any grease on water adhered only to the inked letters.
This observation was the birth of lithography.   His next
step was to transfer an image to a new stone and treat it
with a mild acidulated gum solution that would not lower
the non-image surface.   Keeping the stone moist, he found
that greasy ink applied with a roller would adhere to only
the image area from which a reproduction on paper could
be made.

Senefelder had now discovered a completely new technique by which an image could be printed that was neither
above nor below the surface of the stone, based on the principle that grease and water will not mix.   Lithography developed very rapidly, and, by 1845, lithographic prints in
colour were appearing in many countries.

One might ask what all this has to do with mapping.
The simply answer is that lithography provided the map
maker with many advantages.   As printing presses were designed to afford registration, the heretofore hand-coloured
maps could now be printed in colour.   In addition, quantity
printing was cheaper and faster than copperplate reproduction.   Maps and charts continued to be engraved on copper
and were transferred to lithographic stones for printing.
A precise date cannot be ascertained but, towards the end of
the 19th century, line engravings were being colour separated,
using blue for water features, brown for contours and black
for culture.

The method of obtaining tint colours was to pull a
paper impression of the engraving, dust it with ox-blood--
a red powder--which adhered to the wet ink; this was then

pressed to a clean stone, leaving a chalky non-printing image as a guide to draw the colours. The ink used was precisely the same as developed by Senefelder but referred to as "touch." Stipples and rulings could also be applied to the lithographic stone by gumming a mask and using transfer paper on which an image from an engraved ruling or stipple had been pulled. When pressed to the stone it left a printable image on the exposed areas. The stone then was washed with water to remove the gum mask.

These techniques naturally gave rise to a new type of map maker, and many maps were produced at the turn of the 19th century by lithographic draftsmen who drew maps directly onto stone, pulling transfers from one stone to another to provide keys for colour.

Photography may well be called the hand-maiden of cartography as its development provided the cartographer with many advantages in the reproduction of maps. During its early development in the 18th century, photographic images could be made by exposing nitrate of silver to light, but no way was known to "fix" the image. Joseph Niepce, a printer living in Paris, had become interested in lithography. Being an indifferent artist, he commenced experimenting in 1814 to produce transferable images by photography. By 1824, he actually produced proofs from photo-etched plates. His process was to coat a pewter plate with asphaltum and expose it to light under an etching, or in a camera. The asphaltum became insoluble when exposed to light in its normal solvent (oil of lavender) leaving an acid resist coating of hardened asphaltum allowing the plate to be etched.

By 1848, photographic coatings and processes were developing rapidly and glass was becoming the accepted medium for negative support. John Hershall had discovered sodium thiosulphate (Hypo) as a fixing agent for silver salts. Frederic Scott Archer describes in 1851 a process being used in London, employing wet collodian on glass sensitized by immersion in a silver nitrate bath and exposed while the plate was wet. This became known as a "wet plate" which was used by map makers well into this century and replaced only after stable base films became available about 1949.

Col. Sir Henry James, R. E. of the British Ordnance Survey, saw the advantages of photo-mechanical methods in map making, and from 1855 conducted experiments resulting in the photo-zincography which was perfected by Capt. A. de Courcy Scott in 1860.

The actual process of photo-zincography by which many maps were printed has not been too clearly documented. From available sources it appears this was a zinc etching following the Niepce process but using a wet plate negative to expose the prepared zinc plate (emulsion to emulsion); after etching, the line work would be in positive (right reading) relief from which a double transfer would be made to give a reverse reading image on a printing stone. However, as the wet plate process developed it was possible to strip the negative from the glass support which allowed the etching of a reverse relief reading image requiring only one transfer to the printing stone. This might appear to be an involved process but power-operated stone presses (capable of printing several hundred copies per hour), were available about 1860.

The use of grained zinc in place of stone commenced about 1889 with the introduction of rotary litographic presses. Up to the turn of the century all lithographic plates and stones had to be reverse reading in order to print, which was a definite disadvantage to photo-mechanical processes connected with map reproduction. In 1904, the first offset press was developed allowing the use of right-reading images on zinc printing plates; however, stone flat bed presses continued to be used well into the first quarter of the 20th century.

Map makers during the first quarter of the 20th century employed a variety of methods to reproduce maps. Copper engraving continued to be used but pen and ink drawings were being produced in greater quantities and by 1920 had become a standard practice. The introduction of type for map nomenclature was a natural step and by 1925 most map makers were employing some method of preprinted lettering.

The great demand for maps after World War II forced the cartographer to develop faster reproduction methods in order to keep pace with the advancement made in both equipment and method employed by surveyors and photogrammetrists. An average map draftsman employing the pen and ink method could produce only two or three maps per year. The development of thin stable base plastic sheets provided the impetus to studies being conducted in the United States

and Canada on faster map reproduction methods. The first
step in utilizing plastic sheets was to eliminate the making
of map tints on metal printing plates. Using a blue line
image on vinyl plastic the tint areas were filled in with water soluble opaque. When dyed and washed, an open-window
negative was obtained. The map maker could now provide
all reproduction material and eliminate long delays when
colour tint plates broke down during printing. This development occurred about 1949.

By 1952, map makers commenced map scribing on
plastic sheets (which is the removal of a surface coating
with a scribing tool). This was a breakthrough in the history of map making in Canada and, for the record, was first
developed and used in this country by map makers in the
Map Compilation and Reproduction Division of the Surveys
and Mapping Branch, Department of Energy, Mines and Resources, Ottawa, Canada. The overall advantages of this
new technique are many. To enumerate a few:

(a) the average draftsman doubled his annual output of
    finished maps.
(b) the instruments are simple, line weights can be main-
    tained and difficult symbols can be easily drawn with
    templets.
(c) the basic tools are the rigid scriber and the swivel
    scriber; scribing cutters in single and double lines
    are commercially made to rigid specifications.
(d) draftsmen can be trained, in less than a year, to
    perform acceptable work under supervision.
(e) the idiosyncrasies of individual penmanship are
    eliminated, permitting more than one person to work
    on a specific map.

To describe the various scribing materials and methods in
detail would be impossible in this paper. They have, however, given the cartographer the greatest flexibility he has
ever had in map design and production.

The advancement in photo-mechanical processes has
provided the very necessary support to these new techniques.
It has also eliminated a considerable amount of hand drawing.
What the future holds for map-making in this age of automation only time can tell, but whatever transpires, printed
maps will require the artistic skill of the cartographer to
present a readable and attractive product to the map user.

Map Librarianship

SELECTED REFERENCES

Lloyd A. Brown, The Story of Maps (1949), Map Making; The Art that Became a Science (1960); Erwin Raisz, General Cartography (1938); G. R. Crone, Maps and Their Makers (1953); Leo Bagrow, Die Geschichte der Kartographie (1951), Eng. trans., ed. R. A. Skelton, The History of Cartography (1964); Alois Senefelder, Vollstandiges Lehrbuch der Steindruckery (1818), Eng. trans. by J. W. Muller, The Invention of Lithography (1911); E. D. Baldock, Manual of Map Reproduction Techniques (1964); W. Gamble, Line Photo-Engraving (1909).

OLD MAPS RECORDED HISTORY*

Arthur B. Carlson

The following advertisement appeared in The New-York Gazette for August 30-September 6, 1731:

JUST PUBLISHED

A Plan of the City of New-York from an actual survey made by James Lyne, being curiously engraved on a copper plate and printed on a sheet of demy Royal Paper, wherein is laid down the situation of his Majesty's Fort, and Chappel, all the Churches and Meeting-Houses, City Hall, Custom House, Weigh House and other remarkable places, shewing also the names and Boundaries of the Six wards in said City with all the Streets, Lanes and Allyes therein [here follows a list of all the street names].
Printed and sold by William Bradford Pr. 4s
Pr. 4s 6d

This is the earliest known public announcement for James Lyne's Survey or as it is more popularly known The Bradford Map, the first plan of the City of New-York, engraved and printed locally. Though advertised as "just published," it should be noted that Governor John Montgomerie, of the Provinces of New-York and New-Jersey, to whom the plan is dedicated, had died on July 1, 1731, two months prior to the notice, which would seem to indicate that the

*Reprinted by permission from Library Journal, vol. 75, no. 6 (1950), 461-463, 465. Published by R. R. Bowker (a Xerox Company). Copyright 1950, R. R. Bowker Company.

plan was in existence before his demise. Further evidence
of this may be found in the fact that in the inventory of the
Governor's estate (in the manuscript collections of The New
York Public Library) there appears the following entry:
"6 Black Tye Wiggs and 3 plans of New-York.", these plans
may well have been the Bradford Map.

The surveyor of the Bradford Map, James Lyne, first
appears on the New York scene in 1730 with an announcement that he would open an evening school for instruction
in mathematics, surveying and navigation on September 15th
of that year in a room in the Custom House. He was appointed Constable of the West Ward in 1737 but refused this
office in favor of an appointment as Adjutant in the Militia.
He next appears at New Brunswick, N.J., where he was
active as a surveyor and attorney-at-law from 1741 to 1750.
In 1748 he was one of four managers of a lottery for the
benefit of Christ Church, New Brunswick. His will dated
March 3, 1753, is recorded at Trenton, N.J., under date
of December 10, 1761. It is hoped that further search will
reveal information on the activities of Mr. Lyne in the last
10 years of his life. His one contribution to New York City
history, the Bradford Map, has been and still is a great aid
in the study of the development of the city in that formative
period two hundred and twenty years ago.

The printer and publisher of the map, William Bradford, was born in England, May 20, 1663. He established
the first printing press in the Middle English Colonies, at
Philadelphia in 1685. With others he built the first paper
mill in America in 1690 at Germantown, near Philadelphia.
Bradford came to New York in 1693 and was appointed Printer to King William and Queen Mary. From 1703 to 1733
he was official Printer to the Province of New-Jersey. The
first paper currency issued in New York was printed by
Bradford in 1709. On November 8, 1725 he published the
first issue of The New-York Gazette, New York City's first
newspaper. This weekly paper continued until November 19,
1744. Bradford retired in that year being succeeded by his
apprentice James Parker. William Bradford died on May 23,
1752 at the age of 89 years. He was buried in Trinity
Churchyard, Broadway at the head of Wall Street in New
York City.

In addition to its historical importance the Bradford
Map is also one of the rarest of American Maps. Not more
than three impressions from the original copper plate have

ever been located. The illustration accompanying this article
[not included in this reprint] was made from a photograph of the
copy presented to The New-York Historical Society in 1807 by
John Pintard, one of the founders of the Society in 1804.

A Historical Guide

The copy now in The New York Public Library was
formerly in the collection of William Loring Andrews, a well
known collector of rare Americana who died in 1920. In his
book "The Bradford Map" 1893, Mr. Andrews tells of finding this copy of the map in a scrap book, with several
other scarce engravings, about 1863. This copy is a later
impression since it depicts two additional buildings not shown
on the New-York Historical Society copy, --namely--The
Dutch Free School erected in 1748 and The English Free
School erected in 1749. It is fair to assume that the Andrews copy was printed not earlier than 1749.

A third copy was until early in 1922 in the Bureau
of Engineering, President of the Borough of Manhattan.
This probably was the copy from which a lithographic reproduction was made in 1834 by George Hayward with the
following title. "Facsimile of an Original Map in the possession of G. B. Smith Street Commissioner."

Many copies of the Bradford Map have been issued
in facsimile, the earliest in the same size as the original
being that of 1834, mentioned previously. The earliest reduced copy is one that appeared as an insert on a Guide
Map of New York City, published by David Longworth in 1817.
The copper plate from which this map was printed is in the
collections of The New-York Historical Society.

The map itself has many guide points for historical
research, just a few can be mentioned here. Of the 37
streets shown more than one half retain the same names
and locations today. Street names derived from English
Royalty were changed after the American Revolution, for
example, King Street became Pine Street, Queen Street became Pearl Street, Little Queen Street became Cedar Street
and Crown Street became Liberty Street, etc.

Of the houses of worship shown on the map only one,
Trinity Church, retains its original location. The first
church building was erected in 1697 and this is the edifice
shown on the map, this structure was enlarged in 1735 and

again in 1737. It faced the North River with grounds sloping
down to the water edge at what would be Greenwich Street
today. This building was destroyed in the great fire of 1776.
A second church was completed in 1788, facing Broadway.
This was demolished in 1837 and the present or third building of Trinity Church was completed in 1847.

To Be One of Series

On the plan is shown Bayard's Sugar House on the
north side of Wall Street between Nassau Street and William
(or Smith Street as it was named at that time). Mr. Bayard
announces his new establishment in The New-York Gazette
for August 10-August 17, 1830 as follows:

> Public Notice is hereby Given that Nicholas
> Bayard of the City of New-York has erected
> a Refining House for Refining all sorts of
> Sugar and Sugar-Candy and has procured
> from Europe an experienced artist in that
> mystery. At which Refining house all Per-
> sons in City and Country may be supplied by
> Wholesale and Re-Tale with both double and
> singel-Refined Loaf-Sugar as also Powder and
> Shop-Sugars and Sugar-Candy, at Reasonable
> Rates.

Mr. Bayard appears to have been the pioneer Sugar refiner
of New York City.

EARLY ATLASES*

R. A. Skelton

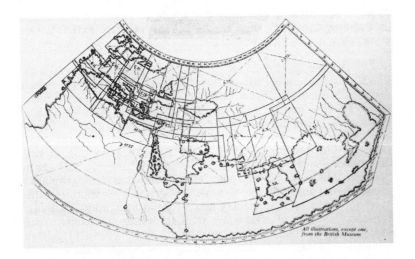

(Fig. 1) Ptolemy's world map, showing the coverage of his twenty-six regional maps. (Reproduced from A. E. Nordenskiöld's Facsimile Atlas, 1897)

THE BIRTH OF THE ATLAS: 16TH CENTURY

The atlas published in 1570 by Abraham Ortelius, under the title Theatrum Orbis Terrarum, is often described as the "first modern atlas." This is true only in a narrow sense, for there had been many earlier manuscript and printed works which satisfied the dictionary definition of an

*Reprinted by permission from The Geographical Magazine (London), vol. 32, no. 11 (1960), 529-543.

atlas as "a collection of maps bound in a volume." In the
14th and 15th centuries, for instance, a group of portolan
charts embracing the known or navigable world was often
gathered by its author into a codex or bound volume. Some
of the Greek manuscripts of Ptolemy's Geographia, brought
to Italy at the beginning of the 15th century, were accompanied by a world map and twenty-six regional maps (ten for
Europe, four for Africa, twelve for Asia) compiled from
his tables of co-ordinates. These maps were copied in the
Latin version and, after being redrawn at Florence about
1460, were engraved on copper and first printed with Ptolemy's text in 1477. Drawn on a uniform projection, they provided a systematic cover of the whole habitable world known
to Ptolemy (Fig. 1), and in this sense may be called a world
atlas--but not a "modern atlas."

       To the 1482 edition of the Geographia (the first with
woodcut maps) were added five tabulae modernae, or modern
maps, of European countries and the Holy Land; and in successive 16th-century editions of Ptolemy the number of such
maps was gradually increased by editors who grafted the new
geography of the great discoveries on the old stock of Ptolemy. The Strassburg edition of 1513, with a section of twenty tabulae modernae by Martin Waldseemüller, is the earliest
that can claim to be an index of contemporary geographical
knowledge. In 1528 the German geographer Sebastian Münster appealed to his countrymen to send him maps of their
regions "so that all Germany with its villages, towns, trades,
etc., may be seen as in a mirror." This was a primitive
attempt at a national atlas of composite authorship; and many
of the maps received by Münster were printed by him in
his edition of Ptolemy (1540) and in his Cosmographia (from
1545).

       The expansion of the "modern" section in the Ptole-
my editions of the 16th century led by an easy transition to
the comprehensive atlas of wholly modern maps. Soon after
the middle of the century the map-sellers of Venice and
Rome, who then dominated the European market, developed
the practice of assembling in a volume, to the order of their
customers, collections of "modern maps of the greater part
of the world, by diverse authors, gathered and arranged in
Ptolemy's order." About seventy collections of this kind are
known; made up from maps in stock at the time, they are not
uniform in contents. They have been given the name "Lafreri Atlas," from Antonio Lafreri, a Burgundian engraver
and map-seller who was in business at Rome from 1544 to

1577 and produced a number of these collections. About
1570 he engraved a title-page for them (Fig. 2); and here
we see, for the first time, the figure of the Titan, Atlas,
supporting the universe on his shoulders, as a symbol for a
collection of maps covering the world.

The origin of Ortelius's celebrated atlas recalls that
of the Italian collections. About 1560, at the request of the
merchant Aegidius Hooftman, Ortelius (then in business at
Antwerp as an illuminator and seller of maps) brought together a set of maps of Europe "not larger than a sheet of
paper," that is, of convenient size for handling. This bound
volume of thirty-eight maps (about thirty engraved in Rome,
the rest in the Netherlands), the prototype of the Theatrum,
still existed in a somewhat battered condition in 1604, but is
now lost. Hooftman's commission brought home to Ortelius
the public need for bound sets of maps of uniform size, which
would be more convenient in use, less greedy of storage
space, and less expensive than the contemporary sheet maps
of varied size and style.

Unlike the Italian map sellers, Ortelius set about the
compilation of his atlas for general sale in no haphazard way.
He consulted geographers about the most suitable projections,
and engravers about problems of reduction; and through his
correspondents in many countries he made a critical selection of the best maps available, to be re-engraved by his
own artists. When the first edition of the Theatrum Orbis
Terrarum came from the press of Aegidius Coppens on May
20, 1570, it was therefore a true conspectus of contemporary
knowledge; and to it Ortelius prefixed a catalogue of no
fewer than eighty-seven cartographers whose work he had
consulted or adapted. The folio volume contained seventy
maps on fifty-three plates, most of them engraved "by the
cunning hand of Frans Hogenberg"; and its title-page bore
symbolic figures of the three parts of the Old World (Fig.
3).

Ortelius's friend Mercator wrote with enthusiasm of
the Theatrum: "... you deserve no small praise, for you
have selected the best descriptions of each region and have
digested them in a single manual, which ... may be bought
for a low price, kept in a small space, and even carried
about whither we wish ... I am certain that this work of
yours will always remain saleable." Three more editions
were called for in the same year, and before Ortelius's
death in 1598 twenty-seven further editions had been printed

(from 1579 at the famous Antwerp house of Christopher
Plantin), with a steadily increasing number of maps and with
text in three European languages besides Latin. The only
English edition was published by Ortelius's successor in 1606,
and the last edition, with Latin text, in 1612.

Gerard Mercator, the greatest geographer of the
Renaissance, whom Ortelius called "the Ptolemy of our day,"
had met Ortelius at the Frankfort book fair in 1554, and
gave him help and encouragement in the preparation of the
Theatrum. Mercator himself had formulated, and in 1569
described, his scheme for a world atlas; this he conceived
as only one part in a grandiose fivefold treatise of the whole
creation. The slow progress of Mercator's Atlas and his
failure to complete it were in the 17th century ascribed to
his desire to avoid competition with his friend Ortelius; but
they are more easily explained by the sweeping scale of his
project, by his method of work, and by the practical difficulties which, as both craftsman and scholar, he encountered.
His combination of talents was singled out by a map-engraver
of the next generation, Jodocus Hondius, who wrote that
Mercator "to his knowledge of geography and chronology
added a quality exceedingly rare in scholars--a skill in
drawing, engraving and elegant illuminating." Unlike the
maps of Ortelius, those of Mercator were compiled, drawn
and (for the most part) engraved by himself or by members
of his family in his Duisburg workshop.

While Ortelius exercised much care in the choice of
maps to be copied or reduced by his engravers, little was
done to "edit" them or to bring them into consistency with
other maps in the Theatrum. Mercator, on the other hand,
envisaged each sheet of his Atlas as a section of a whole
map, ensured that it was correctly placed in relation to the
others by the graduation in latitude and longitude, and submitted every detail to rigorous criticism before admitting it
(Fig. 5). This process gives the maps from his hand an individual character, a fineness of execution, and an air of
authority which those of the Theatrum often lack, and which
(as we shall see) account for the much longer life enjoyed by
Mercator's plates; but Mercator's method of work called for
more time than that of Ortelius.

In Mercator's cosmographical scheme, geography
formed one of the five divisions and was again subdivided into
three parts: modern maps, Ptolemy, and ancient geography.
The third of these remained unaccomplished; the second,

GEOGRAFIA

TAVOLE MODERNE DI GEOGRAFIA
DE LA MAGGIOR PARTE DEL MONDO
DI DIVERSI AVTORI
RACCOLTE ET MESSE SECONDO L' ORDINE
DI TOLOMEO
CON IDISEGNI DI MOLTE CITTA ET
FORTEZZE DI DIVERSE PROVINTIE
STAMPATE IN RAME CON STVDIO
ET DILIGENZA
IN ROMA

(Fig. 2) Title-page engraved by Antonio Lafreri in Rome, c. 1570, for collections of maps published by him. By courtesy of the Royal Geographical Society.

(Fig. 3) The title-page of Abraham Ortelius's Theatrum Orbis Terrarum, published in 1570.

ATLAS
SIVE
COSMOGRAPHICÆ
MEDITATIONES
DE
FABRICA MVNDI ET
FABRICATI FIGVRA.

Gerardo Mercatore Rupelmundano,
Illustrissimi Ducis Iuliæ Cliviæ & Mõ
tis &c Cosmographo Auctore.
Cum Privilegio

(Fig. 4)   The title-page of Mercator's <u>Atlas</u>, 1595 (the title
may be translated: Atlas, or Meditations of a Cosmographer
on the Creation of the World and on the Form of Created
Matter)

Mercator's edition of the Geographia with the maps re-engraved, was completed and published in 1578; and the modern atlas was never finished, although two parts of it appeared before Mercator's death in 1594 and a third, edited
by his son Rumold, posthumously. In 1585 the maps of
"Gallia" (France, Switzerland, the Netherlands) and "Ger-
mania" were printed at Mercator's press at Duisburg, each
with its own title-page and so forming a national atlas; and
in 1589 followed those of "Italia, Slavonia et Graecia."
Finally, in 1595 Rumold Mercator brought out a great folio
volume, the title of which indicates the broad sweep of his
father's cosmographical thought (Fig. 4); the first part contains the text of Mercator's essay on the creation of the
world, the second the 107 maps. The maps now added
comprised those of the British Isles and of Northern and
Eastern Europe, with maps of the world and the four continents by Mercator's son and grandsons: The regional
maps of Spain and Portugal and of countries outside Europe
were never executed.

The magnificent torso of Mercator's work not only
introduced the word Atlas into common currency, but also

(Fig. 5) Mercator's map of Guernsey, in the Atlas of 1595.

provided the model and framework for the great undertakings
of this kind projected in the next century.

THE CENTURY OF ATLASES

The atlas was to become the dominant cartographic
form of the 17th century, and its history exemplifies both
the supplanting of Antwerp by Amsterdam as the principal
centre of map production and the commanding position a-
chieved by the Dutch in the international map trade. The
Amsterdam houses owed their success to their control of
capital, derived largely from a strong and prosperous home
market, and to their highly developed workshop organization.
Thus the maps of John Speed's Theatre of the Empire of
Great Britain (published 1611-12), the earliest large-scale
map-publishing venture in this country, were sent to be engraved in the Amsterdam shop of Jodocus Hondius.   Hondius
had already, in 1604, purchased the plates of Mercator's
Atlas, and its expansion and frequent republication were to
be the staple of his firm and of its successors in business
for three-quarters of a century.   In the first edition issued
by him, in 1606, Hondius added thirty-six maps to those of
Mercator; and over the successive imprints of his son Henricus Hondius and his son-in-law Jan Jansson the Atlas
Novus, as it came to be called, grew to four volumes (with
over 350 maps) by 1646, and to six volumes (with nearly
500 maps) by 1658, with text in five languages; and finally
to ten or eleven volumes.

This expansion was largely stimulated by the competition of a powerful rival, the scholar-cartographer Willem Jansz.   Blaeu entered the field of atlas-publication,
late but effectively, with his Atlantis Appendix, which appeared in 1630 with sixty maps (including thirty-seven plates
purchased from Henricus Hondius!).   This was followed in
1631 by Blaeu's Appendix Theatri A. Ortelii et Atlantis G.
Mercatoris, with ninety-nine maps; by 1634 the collection
was styled Novus Atlas; and in 1635 it was extended to a
two-volume work of 207 maps under the title--still recalling
its two great predecessors--Theatrum Orbis Terrarum, sive
Atlas Novus (Fig. 6).   After Blaeu's death in 1637, his sons
gradually enlarged the Atlas Novus in step with--and often
in advance of--the Hondius-Jansson publication.   By 1655 it
had reached six volumes with over 400 maps, and in 1662
came the magnificent Atlas Maior sive Cosmographia Blaviana, of eleven volumes and nearly 600 maps.

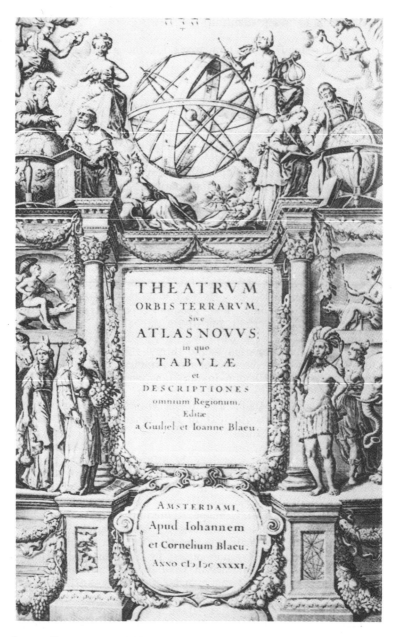

THEATRVM
ORBIS TERRARVM,
Sive
ATLAS NOVVS;
in quo
TABVLÆ
et
DESCRIPTIONES
omnium Regionum,
Editæ
a Guiljel. et Ioanne Blaeu.

AMSTERDAMI,
Apud Iohannem
et Cornelium Blaeu.
Anno cIↄ Iↄc xxxxi.

(Fig. 6) Engraved title-page used by W. J. Blaeu and his sons in editions of their Atlas Novus from 1635. Left and right are figures symbolizing the four continents; above is an armillary sphere constructed on Ptolemy's system.

Like Ortelius, but with less discrimination, the Hondiuses and Jansson copied into their atlas such maps by other cartographers as they could acquire--sometimes even those of Blaeu--to depict regions still unrepresented. The Blaeus, father and son, were their superiors both in selection and in presentation of their materials. Their official appointment as hydrographers to the Dutch East India Company and to the States-General placed at their disposal much first-hand cartographic work, some of it secret; and their enterprise in bringing regional surveys into print is illustrated by their publication of the first atlas of Scotland (in 1655, as vol. V of the Atlas Novus), from Timothy Pont's manuscript surveys, and of the atlas of China by the Jesuit father Martino Martini (as vol. VI of the Atlas Novus, in the same year). As a scientific cartographer, trained by the Danish astronomer Tycho Brahe, the elder Blaeu was fastidious in his choice of projections and in setting out the geographical apparatus of his maps. Like Mercator, Blaeu and his sons were accomplished craftsmen, who controlled every stage in the production of their maps and books. A German visitor to Amsterdam in 1663 described "the far-famed printing house of Johan Blaeu, " with its "nine type presses, named after the nine Muses, six presses for copper-plate printing, and type foundry"; storage cases for the plates "from which the atlases ... and other choice books are printed"; and rooms for washing type, drying sheets, and proof-reading. On the same premises were carried on the drawing, engraving and colouring of maps, the making of fine paper with Blaeu's own mark, and the binding. The superb craftsmanship of the house is apparent in its vellum-bound atlases, often stamped with the arms of the collector for whom they were prepared and illuminated.

In the second half of the 17th century other family firms of Amsterdam--Visscher, De Wit, Danckerts--published world atlases, none on the ambitious scale of Jansson and Blaeu; and the plates of the older businesses were dispersed among such firms after the destruction of Blaeu's printing-house by fire in 1672 and the sale of Jansson's stock by auction in 1694.

In the atlases of this period the engraved maps were commonly backed by text, although separate impressions of the maps with blank backs were also on sale. The conflicting demands of printing in one volume from type, which must be quickly distributed, and from copper plates, from which (to reduce wear) no more impressions should be taken than

were needed for immediate sale, were neatly reconciled.
A very large number of sheets were printed from type on
the text side; the type was distributed; and the maps were
added only to so many sheets as were called for by each
successive edition of the atlas, in which the text was therefore usually a reissue and the maps new impressions. The
plates could be, and were occasionally, revised, and these
alterations are sometimes the only evidence for dating an
edition when (as often) the engraved title-page date is uncorrected.

Regional cartography in atlas form had been initiated
in the 16th century, and national atlases of many countries
appeared in the 17th, either separately or incorporated in
the larger world atlases. By the end of the century map-
publishers in other countries had established themselves
with sufficient substance and commercial organization to
produce world atlases modelled on the Dutch prototypes. In
France, particularly, an independent map industry developed
as a productive unit, enjoying royal patronage, under the
direction (in turn) of Nicolas Sanson of Abbeville, his sons,
and A. H. Jaillot. Sanson's maps were first collected into
atlases about 1645, and were re-engraved by Jaillot in a
series of splendidly decorated world atlases from 1689.

In Italy, at the end of the century, there appeared
the isolated but commanding figure of the Franciscan V. M.
Coronelli, Cosmographer to the Republic of Venice. Coronelli combined sound geographical scholarship and judgment
with a taste for baroque decoration and grandiose design.
These qualities found expression both in his globes, which
ranged from two inches to fifteen feet in diameter, and in
his immense Atlante Veneto in twelve volumes published in
1697.

SEA-ATLASES

The earliest modern sea-atlas to be printed was De
Spiegel der Zeevaerdt, by Lucas Jansz. Waghenaer of Enk-
huizen, the first part of which came from Plantin's press at
Antwerp in 1584 (Fig. 7). Here, as in the manuscript pilot-
books from which it descended, but for the first time on engraved charts, the seaman found many features necessary
to navigation laid down by conventions still in use today--
soundings, reefs and other hazards, leading lines and landmarks, channels and buoys. Since the charts were printed,

(Fig. 7) The title-page of Part I of Waghenaer's sea-atlas,
Spiegel der Zeevaerdt, Latin edition, 1586; with instruments
for navigation represented in the border.

(Fig. 8) The title-page of <u>Le Neptune François</u>, engraved
by Jan van Vianen, 1693.

the danger of copyist's errors was greatly reduced and the pilot could use them with the more confidence. For over a century such sea-atlases accompanied by sailing directions were familiarly known, from the name of their progenitor, as "waggoners. "

During the 17th century, when Dutch maritime activity reached its highest level, the Netherlands led the field in hydrography and chartwork. Up to the middle of the century Blaeu's two sea-atlases, Het Licht der Zeevaert (1608) and De Zeespiegel (1623), met with little competition, but thereafter many handsome works of this kind, with titles as flamboyant as the decoration of their title-pages, were produced by rival firms vying for the native and foreign markets. Such atlases were (to give them the titles of their English editions) The Upright Fyrie Colomne of J. A. Colom, The Sea Atlas or the Watter-World of P. Goos, and The Lightning Colomne or Sea Mirror of T. Jacobsz. ; and their technique of chart construction and drawing was conservative, showing little advance on Waghenaer. Yet Blaeu had occasionally made use of the Mercator projection; and the first sea-atlas with charts drawn entirely on this projection, the Arcano del Mare of the Englishman Sir Robert Dudley, had been engraved and published at Florence in 1646-7.

The reformation of cartography in the late 17th century was the work of French geodesists directed by the Académie Royale des Sciences. After the foundation of the Paris Observatory in 1671, under J. D. Cassini, French scientists were active in determining the latitude and longitude of places by astronomical methods. In the great sea-atlas Le Neptune François, published at Paris in 1693, the coasts of Western Europe were laid down from accurately fixed positions supplemented by a thorough land survey; and its charts, drawn on the Mercator projection, were all graduated in latitude and longitude (Fig. 8). This marked an epoch in hydrographic publication; and its pattern was followed by the official French charts gathered in 1756 in the atlas L'Hydrographie Française.

In the 18th century, an age of intense activity in seaborne commerce and warfare and in the publication of maps and charts, a multitude of "Pilots" and "Neptunes" delineated the coasts and navigations (or ocean routes) of the world. The noblest of these in presentation was The Atlantic Neptune (1777-81), the first cartographic work to be published by the Admiralty; its charts, superbly drawn

by J. F. W. Desbarres, covered 1000 miles of the North
American coasts from British surveys. Atlases of charts
were also published with numerous accounts of voyages of
discovery, notably those of Captain Cook, the most accomplished hydrographer of his day.

TOWARDS THE MODERN ATLAS

By the beginning of the 19th century the seeds of the
modern atlas had already been sown. New techniques of
observation and analysis introduced a wealth of data which,
with improved methods of cartographic representation, enabled the mapmaker to record, more precisely than ever
before, not only the topography of land surfaces but also
the materials of special sciences in their geographical relationships. The typical products of the new age were the
general atlases, such as Stieler's Hand-Atlas, the successive editions of which (from 1817 to 1930) formed an index
to the current state of world cartography, and the special
or thematic atlas, exemplified in the Physikalischer Atlas
of Heinrich Berghaus, completed in 1848. These are the
prototypes of the atlases of today.

A CHRONICLE OF MAPPING*

Kenneth R. Stunkel

[Part I:] Undoubtedly, man was drawing maps of
one sort or another long before the advent of recorded history. Many so-called primitive peoples know that verbal
descriptions are inferior to even a crudely executed representation of the earth's surface. Marshall Islanders of the
last century, for example, made serviceable navigation
charts from shells and the midribs of palm leaves; the
shells symbolized islands, while the palm ribs formed a
network marking the open sea and the pattern of wave fronts
encountered when approaching the islands. Eskimo maps,
some covering several thousand square miles, compare
favorably with accurate hydrographic charts produced today.
Just as these primitive people have attempted to organize
their geographical knowledge, so it is likely that sketches
in earth or sand, stone, hide, or bone enabled prehistoric
man to relate himself more effectively to his surroundings.

The most ancient map extant was found in the ruins
of Ga Sur, a Mesopotamian city which flourished about
2500 B. C. Incised on a clay tablet, it depicts the location
of a rich man's estate. Except as a relic of great antiquity
the map has no cartographic significance. Many Babylonian
city plans have survived, including one dating from the 7th
Century B. C. A clay tablet of the 5th Century B. C. shows
the world as the Babylonians knew or imagined it, and indicates the limits of their geographical knowledge. The known
world is contained in a circle surrounded by an ocean.

*Reprinted by permission from The Military Engineer, Pt.
I: vol. 57, no. 375 (1965), 1-5; Pt. II: vol. 57, no. 376
(1965), 110-115; Pt. III: vol. 57, no. 377 (1965), 180-182.
Copyright 1965 by The Society of American Military Engineers.

"Hecataeus' Map of the World, 6th Century B.C."

Beyond the circle are seven islands forming a link with the
Heavenly Ocean, which is the habitat of the banished ancient
gods, and at the center of this Cosmos is Babylon.   The
Babylonians contributed nothing of value to the technique of
map making, but they did succeed in advancing cartography
in other respects.   They originated the sexigesimal system,
dividing the circle into 360 degrees, the degree into minutes,
and the minute into seconds.   They also divided the day into hours, minutes, and seconds, and thus the basis was
laid for relating the motions of the earth to the sky in a
constant and calculable manner.   Also, they invented the
gnomon, a measuring device for determining latitude.   The
philosopher Anaximander (c. 580 B.C.) is credited with

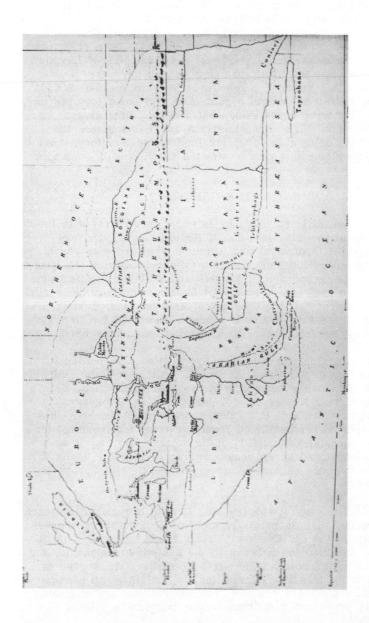

Map of the world according to Eratosthenes, 3rd Century B.C. This, and map on previous page, from E. H. Bunbury, History of Ancient Geography (1879).

introducing the instrument to the Greeks, who used it to
better advantage than had its inventors.

Although the Egyptians are known to have practiced
surveying in ancient times, very few examples of Egyptian
mapping have survived, and those which have are of no
cartographic interest. The Turin Papyrus (c. 1320 B. C.)
is the oldest; it depicts a gold mine and some features of
the neighboring countryside, but gives no firm clue as to
the location. Like the Sumerians and Babylonians, the
Egyptians seldom ventured far from home territory, and
consequently had a very restricted knowledge of geography.

THE GREEKS

Scientific cartography is encountered first with the
Greeks of the Classical and Hellenistic Ages, who established a theoretical and practical standard that was to
remain unequaled until the 16th Century. During the time
between Anaximander of Miletus and Ptolemy of Alexandria
(A. D. 90-168), the resourceful Greeks conceived the earth
as a sphere; distinguished poles, tropics, and equator; devised the latitude-longitude system; developed the first projections; and calculated the circumference of the earth.

Anaximander is generally credited with putting together the first map of the world. Although nothing of his
work remains, some notion of his achievement may be
gleaned from a later improvement of it by the geographer
Hecataeus (c. 500 B. C.), also a resident of Miletus. His
map can be reconstructed from surviving fragments of his
comprehensive description of the world. He saw it as a
flat disc ringed by an ocean, and he divided the habitable
world into two regions--Europe and Asia, with Europe the
larger.

The eager, wide-ranging Greeks brought geographical
knowledge to a surprisingly high level of coverage and accuracy in the 5th Century. Their world extended from the
Indus River to the Atlantic in the east-west dimension, but
was much narrower from north to south. The voyage of
Pytheas of Massilia (Marseilles) to Britain is an example of
Greek exploratory courage, for superstition and fear generally prevented men from sailing beyond the Pillars of
Hercules.

One of the greatest geographers of antiquity was
Eratosthenes of Cyrene (276-196 B. C.) who directed the
Library at Alexandria, the center of learning in the Hellenistic Age. His writings and maps summed up Greek geographical knowledge to his time, and included the discoveries
of Xenophon and Alexander, the results of Megasthenes' mission to India, and information accumulated by Hellenic
colonists throughout the Mediterranean and Black Sea areas.
Eratosthenes' most remarkable achievement, however, was
to measure the circumference of the earth with an error of
only 14 percent. Believing that Syene (Aswan) lay on the
same north-south meridian as Alexandria, that the two
places were 500 miles apart, and that Syene lay directly
on the Tropic of Cancer, he made simple measurements
and calculations during the summer solstice and estimated
the earth's circumference at 28, 000 miles. All his major
assumptions were incorrect, as well as his measurement
of the sun's angle at Alexandria, but the four factors balanced out unusually well. A hundred years later, Posidonius
(c. 130-50 B. C.) repeated the measurement and ended with
a value of 1800 miles, which was accepted by Ptolemy.
This underestimate of the earth's size was accepted by
geographers until the era of exploration in the 16th Century.
The Alexandrian geographer also compiled a map of the
world which had seven parallels and seven meridians. Although the map included many new geographical data, such
as the island of Ceylon (known as Taprobana), it still cut
India and Africa short on the theory that the southern ocean
was too hot for navigation. Subsequently, the astronomer
Hipparchus proposed a new parallel-meridian system of
eleven exactly located and evenly spaced parallels supported
by longitude measurements derived from simultaneous observations of the moon in eclipse, but his program was not
carried out. To compensate for the disturbing lack of proportion between the size of the earth and the known habitable world, the globe-maker Crates (c. 150 B. C.) put three
additional continents over the empty seas. One of these
continents was known as the Antipodes, the great southern
land of Terra Australis, although, of course, Crates had no
basis for believing in its existence. Greek cartography and
geography reached its height with Ptolemy. For 1500 years
his work dominated western cartography, and his influence
is still felt after more than eighteen centuries. Ptolemy's
Geographia, in eight volumes, contains discussions of projections, mathematical geography, globe construction, astronomical observation, cartographic principles, and other
important topics. This was intended to revise and correct

a previous work by Marinus of Tyre (A.D. 70-130), whose
pioneer geography has been lost. The Geographia was accompanied by the first atlas ever produced. It was in the
form of a world map and twenty-six detailed maps; more
than 8000 place names, with their longitude and latitude,
were listed. The major defects of his world map are most
evident in the eastern and southern regions, where the Dec-
can peninsula is shrunk to almost nothing, while Ceylon is
proportionately huge, and the eastern coast of Africa sweeps
around to join Asia, thus converting the Indian Ocean into
an enclosed sea. While he underestimated the size of the
earth (following Posidonius), he exaggerated the length of
the Mediterranean Sea. These errors were profoundly influential. After Ptolemy, geography and cartography went
into a decline, and the scientific achievements of the Greeks
were either forgotten or ignored until the Renaissance.

THE ROMANS AND THE DARK AGES

        The characteristic bent of the Roman mind was to-
ward the concrete and the practical, and there are few aspects of Roman civilization that exemplify this tendency better than mapping and geography. Although Roman authority
spread from the British Isles to the Persian Gulf and from
the Rhine to North Africa, their interest in the geography
of the conquered lands was almost nil. Students of geography were a rarity in the Roman Empire, and even the few
of note were either lost in obscurity or had serious faults.
The great Strabo (63? B.C.--A.D. 24?), for example, was
practically unknown outside the remote province in Asia
Minor where he was born, and Pliny the Elder (A.D. 23-79),
author of the concise Natural History, made few original
contributions to geographical knowledge, and was misleading,
since he was often more concerned with unnatural than
natural events. In general, Roman utilitarianism impeded
scientific inquiry and dulled normal curiosity. In particular, it had no use for Greek ideas about projections, astronomical observation, latitude and longitude, and other matters relating to mathematical cartography. Desiring a type
of map that would serve in warfare and government, the
Romans ignored Greek projections and relied upon the disk
map, which gave the impression of a flat earth. This Orbis
Terrarum showed practically the entire world as part of the
Roman Empire, and was divided into three conventional re-
gions--Asia, Africa, and Europe, with great prominence
being given to the provinces of Rome. China, India, Scythia,
and Russia were reduced to mere fringe areas.

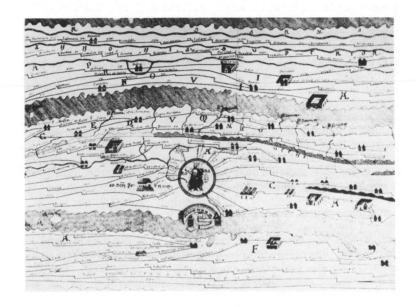

Parts of Sections 5 and 6 of the Peutinger Table, 3rd Century A. D., attributed to Castorius (Rome at the center).

        The most important surviving example of Roman car-
tography is the Peutinger Table, a map of military roads
in Southern Europe and the Western Roman Empire in about
A. D. 250.   The extant manuscript was copied from the
original in 1265 by a monk at Colmar.   The Peutinger
Table is 21 feet long and 1 foot high.   No attempt was
made to include the entire known world or to show the features depicted in correct proportion, but merely to set
down highways, mileages, and military posts as they existed
in a limited portion of the Empire.   This map is a rich
source of information about the geography of the time, particularly as it includes some 5000 place names.

        Roughly in the period A. D. 500-1000, Europe was in
the Dark Ages.   This was the time of social, political, economic, and cultural decline following Rome's dissolution as
a great empire.   There was widespread disorder and a
breakdown in trade and communication which constricted
horizons and interests.   These circumstances created an
atmosphere of insecurity and narrowness unsympathetic to

geographical exploration and scholarship. The leading scholars of the period--Orosius, Isidore of Seville, Cassiodorus,
the Venerable Bede, Dicuil, Gregory the Great, Raban
Maur--produced vast digests of knowledge culled from classical sources. But their compilations were almost wholly
from other compilations, and were not, in many cases,
based on the most reliable sources of the ancients. For
example, one can search the works of Orosius and Isidore
in vain for evidence of personal observation of natural phenomena, and nowhere is there a suggestion that their authorities can be corrected or questioned. The past was
drawn upon without supplementation or comment. Geographical knowledge degenerated as a result of this unscientific
attitude. Geographical descriptions were often unrelated
to realities, and maps reflected neither descriptions nor
realities. Land masses were distorted beyond recognition;
place names were commonly arbitrary or fictitious; there
was a bias in favor of the conception of a flat world, and
theological interests clearly overshadowed strictly empirical
ones. The learned Irish monk Dicuil (c. A. D. 825) stated
that the Alps are a mere 50 miles high, and that the entire
world comprises 40 mountains, 2 seas, 65 countries, 281
towns, 55 rivers, 72 islands, and 116 peoples. The 9th
Century scholar, Scotus Erigena, was not so exact in his
judgments, but the few chapters on geography and natural
science in his De Divisione Naturae were extracted almost
entirely from Pliny's Natural History. The most extreme
theological interpretation is in the Christian Topography of
Cosmas Indicopleustes (Indian traveler), who would have
nothing to do with pagan learning. Writing in the 6th Century, he used the Scriptures to substantiate his views about
geography as did, to a greater or lesser extent, all the en-
cyclopedists of the Dark Ages. Thus he argued against a
round earth by pointing out that when the apostles were
ordered to preach the Gospel to all creatures throughout the
world, it is not recorded that they went to a place called
the Antipodes, a land presumed to be on the other side of
a round earth, and since the place was not mentioned in the
Scriptures, it did not exist, proving the world to be flat.
Ideas of this sort were included in maps of the period.

During the Dark Ages the scholars preserved and
transmitted the geographies and maps of the Classical and
Hellenic ages. The Arabs performed the same service, and
at the same time produced a view of the world which was
broader and more accurate than that of Europe.

THE ARABS

When the Roman world split and collapsed in the West, it was Islam that became the heir of the Greek achievement in science. For about three centuries, from A. D. 750 to 1050, the development of geography and mapping was in the hands of Moslem scholars.

Inspired by the prophet Mohammed, who died in A. D. 632, the Arabs built an empire in less than a half century. At the height of its power, the Moslem world extended from Spain to Central Asia, and since all Moslems were obliged by their religious beliefs to make at least one pilgrimage to Mecca, travelers and scholars from all regions of the empire passed through the centers of Arab learning. The result was an intermixing of ideas and a wide diffusion of geographical knowledge. Of the numerous Moslem geographers of note, only a few can be mentioned in this summary of Arabic geography and mapping.

An impetus was given to scientific studies when the Seventh Abbasside caliph, al Mamun (A. D. 786-833) organized a scientific academy known as the House of Wisdom, which had a library and observatory. His astronomers compiled tables of planetary motions and found the inclination of the ecliptic to be equal to 23 degrees 33 minutes. The size of the earth was measured as 20,400 miles in circumference and 6500 miles in diameter. A large map of the world was prepared for the caliph.

Ptolemy's Geographia was translated into Arabic in the 8th Century and formed the basis for Arabic cartographic development. Arabic maps were crude, more like diagrams, and showed little true understanding of Ptolemy's co-ordinate system. Their world view was generally along classical lines. The earth was shown as circular in form, and the habitable portion was encircled by an ocean. Al-Khwarizmi (A. D. 780-850), one of the greatest Moslem scientists, probably assisted in making geodetic measurements under al-Mamun. He made an important revision of Ptolemy's Geographia, both in the text and the maps.

About eleven outstanding Moslem geographers flourished in the 10th Century. Among them were al-Hamdani, who wrote a geography of Arabia; ibn-Fadlan, who visited the region of the Volga and composed the first reliable description of Russia; abu-Dulaf, who wrote a first-hand

account of Tibet, India, and Pakistan; al-Masudi, who was
author of a massive historical and geographical encyclopedia
that indicated a wide knowledge and a deep scientific curiosity; al-Muqaddasi, who visited most of the countries of
Islam and wrote a careful study of them, Best of Divisions
for Knowledge of the Climates; and al-Biruni, who determined latitudes and longitudes and made geodetic measurements. From the work of al-Biruni it is possible to sum
up the state of Moslem geographical knowledge in the 11th
Century. The Arabs knew something about the east coast
of Africa as far as 20 degrees south; and although most
ideas about the southern part of the world were conjectural,
they seemed to have some second-hand knowledge of the
Mozambique channel. In spite of Ptolemy's authority, and
with no confirming evidence, they believed the African continent to be peninsular in nature, and did not question the
existence of an antipodal land mass. There was very little
Arab knowledge concerning Northern Europe and Eastern
Asia. Al-Biruni also discussed the rotation of the earth on
its axis, and correctly analyzed the origin of the Indus Valley as an ancient sea basin filled with alluvium.

The work of al-Idrisi (1100-1166) was the climax of
creative Arabic geography. He described the earth as a
globe, computed the circumference at 22, 900 miles, and
gave a long account of the earth's various regions. He
divided each of the Ptolemaic "climata" (latitudinal zones)
into ten longitudinal sections, and then treated each of these
seventy sections in great detail. His account of each section was accompanied by a map, and when all of them were
joined, they formed one large rectangular world map in the
fashion of Ptolemy. Although his divisions are arbitrary,
al-Idrisi's analysis of them is based on wide sources of
information used with scientific discrimination.

In the Arabic maps Africa was foreshortened and
elongated toward the east, but it did not completely seal in
the Indian Ocean as on Ptolemy's map. To the west was
the "Green Sea of Darkness. " Inland seas and ocean gulfs
were commonly out of proportion, and geographical locations on the maps often disagreed with their texts. The
authorship of the maps is questionable in most cases, for
they cannot be attributed reliably to the men in whose writings they are found. The Arabs were better geographers,
mathematicians, and astronomers than cartographers.

After the 12th Century, Europe recaptured its

intellectual leadership and the Arab influence declined because of the traditional ideas in geography which stifled
independent observation and thought.   Latin Christendom
revived and continued the advance of geographical knowledge
that had been made by the Arabs through three centuries.

[Part II:] MEDIEVAL EUROPE

The scope of geographic exploration and knowledge
grew enormously in the middle ages from A.D. 1000-1400
through the efforts of numerous pilgrims and wayfarers.
The greatest achievements of the age were daring journeys
into Asia by such travelers as the Franciscan monk Gio-
vanni Piano de Carpini, who reached the Mongol capital of
Karakorum: John Montecorvine, founder of the first Catholic
missions in China and India; and Niccolo, Maffeo, and
Marco Polo, whose adventures in the China of Kublai Khan
are well known.   However, new geographical knowledge as
it became available was not reflected in maps or in commonly used texts.   The uncritical reverence for tradition
and authority was a handicap to the advancement of cartography and geographical scholarship.   Of course, there
was improvement over the accomplishments of the preceding
five centuries, but the scientific flame shone fitfully.
Medieval conservatism and resistance to change preserved
the status quo in both fields.

This reactionary attitude is evident in the surviving
maps of the period.   Before 1400, no European map indicated the true extent of contemporary knowledge.   Lands
that were familiar and accurately described in texts suffered
hopeless distortion in graphic portrayals of the world.
There appear to have been three cartographic traditions
during the Middle Ages, which must have influenced the
average student in arriving at his notions of the world:
they were the "mappae mundi" or "maps of the world";
sketches of the sort that often accompanied guide books for
pilgrims; and the portolanos.

Some of the 600 "mappae mundi" that are still in
existence date from the 8th to the 15th Centuries and indicate their aesthetic and instructive purpose.   Most of them
emphasized the supernatural and fantastic, having little
scientific value, although they were believed to be representations of the earth.   The strong ecclesiastical influence
was plainly visible.   A common format was to depict the

world as a wheel, with Jerusalem at the hub and the ocean streaming around the rim; another was to show the three major land masses--Europe, Asia, and Africa--arranged in a highly schematic design.

In three examples of monastic maps, the Psalter (c. 1250), Hereford (c. 1275), and Ebstorf (c. 1284) maps, there is seen the influence of Biblical stories and topography, and the persistence of traditional ideas long discarded by advances in knowledge. The Hereford map shows the Terrestrial Paradise encircled by a wall of flame. As late as about 1436, Andrea Bianco showed the Paradise on his world map along with four westward flowing rivers.

A favorite subject was about the lands of Gog and Magog, whose nonexistent inhabitants were thought to be a terrible menace to Christendom. Biblical places were portrayed, greatly exaggerated in relation to the surrounding lands. In the circular Psalter map they cover a third of Asia, with Jerusalem in the center, a practice that often characterized world maps as late as the 15th Century.

Classical influences are apparent, but usually are drawn from more secular sources such as Pliny and Macrobius. Distorted versions of Greek concepts are seen in the portrayal of the earth's surface as flat and projectionless, encircled by the "ocean river," and in the inclusion of monsters borrowed from Greek and Roman mythology: the Sciapodae, a race of men with feet large enough to serve as sunshades; the Monoculi, one-eyed men; and the Cynocephalae, dog-headed apes. This lively interest in the classics was accompanied by a remarkable ignorance of the geography of the ancient world. Delphi is confused with Delos, and Cadiz is shown as an island in the middle of the Gibraltar Straits. In spite of the classical allusions, Ptolemy's world map remained in obscurity. The Arabs recognized it, and al-Idrisi's was one of the few maps before the 15th Century that bowed to the Ptolemaic tradition. Although the trend of mappae mundi was ever further from reality, a few maps had some practical value. In the Este world map (1400), an effort to balance fictitious and religious themes with actual geographical information is apparent.

Sketches and drawings which often supplemented pilgrim handbooks did not become important until the last quarter of the 15th Century. Good early examples are the Matthew Paris maps of Great Britain (c. 1250). Compared

with the average mappae mundi they have obvious merit.
One of Paris's maps, the earliest known detailed map of
England, shows more than 100 places, mostly inland towns
along the route from Dover to St. Albans, and thence to
Durham. But in spite of its informational value, the map
is crude and reveals the powerful monastic influence that
caused map makers to choose the safe expedient of imaginative design rather than verifiable facts.

The finest cartographic achievement of the Middle
Ages in Europe was the portolano, a type of mariner's
chart based on experience and observation. The earliest
extant copies date from about 1300, but they are known to
have existed before that time. The Arabs made them and
there are references to such charts in the writings of
Marco Polo, Ramon Lull, and other medieval sources.
The portolano is often called a compass chart to distinguish
it from the symbolic mappae mundi and the theoretical maps
in the Ptolemaic tradition. Such examples were the accounts of voyages in the ancient world by sailors who kept
a sort of logbook, such as the Periplus of Seylax of Cary-
anda, 6th Century B. C. Many of these old manuals were
revised and brought up to date with fresh coastal information and determinations of distance and direction from compass and log readings. Medieval portolanos do not indicate
latitude or longitude, but they are crisscrossed with loxo-
dromes, or rhumb lines, which radiate from various foci
scattered over the map. Although there is a certain uniformity in the geographical features pictured on portolanos,
there is great variety in the colors and symbols used. The
crudeness of the portolano was offset by its accuracy. On
the length of the Mediterranean, Ptolemy's map was off by
20 degrees; portolanos are seldom off by more than 1 degree.

The oldest portolanos were made in Italy, usually at
Genoa or Pisa. Those from the latter half of the 14th
Century are of Catalan origin. They were more than seaman's charts, having more the characteristic of a world
map organized around a portolano. In general, the Catalan
school of cartography practiced its craft with a critical
spirit. Weak factual data were balanced against sound
theory in a way that produced good results. The Catalan
Atlas of 1375 depicts Asia better than any other known map
of the time.

Portolanos were often collected into atlases of four

to twelve charts. An atlas of Petrus Vesconte, dated 1320, contained a world map, plans of Jerusalem, a map of Palestine, and six charts covering the normal portolano area. While in the beginning very little was done to delineate anything but coastal features, later charts gradually provided more information about the interior of Europe, Africa, and, finally, America.

The Laurentian Portolano (1351) shows a remarkable conception of Africa which suggests the possibility of circumnavigating the continent long before the Portuguese actually achieved the feat. Catalan speculations about unexplored regions of the earth were generally restrained and responsible, and occasionally were borne out by later discoveries. However, this critical restraint did not prevent the Catalans from believing in the Terrestrial Paradise and in a hydrographic system that was thought to stretch from sea to sea, in spite of accessible evidence to the contrary. The western portion is a portolano, while the eastern portion is based on Ptolemy, with supplementary material culled from the works of Marco Polo (a rare instance of Polo's mine of information being tapped by responsible cartographers).

After 1400, with the growing pressure of discovery, the problem of harmonizing old assumptions and new facts grew so acute that cartographers could no longer ignore inconsistencies, absurdities, and gross inaccuracies. The relatively scientific outlook of the Catalan school was to become more and more the outlook of all map makers as the tension between fact and fancy mounted to a level impossible to tolerate.

THE 15TH AND 16TH CENTURIES

In the two centuries from 1400 to 1600 a more scientific approach to geography and cartography was made than at any time since the high point of the Greco-Roman civilization. This advance was due mainly to the revival of secular interest in the natural world, which weakened the hold of theology on scientific thought and led to a greatly expanded outlook. A step in this secular revival was the recovery of classical learning through the diligence of scholars like Petrarch and Boccaccio, who made available for study the scientific works of the past. Of greatest significance was the invention of movable type and the subsequent

The "Borgia" map (c. 1410-1458). This world map (orbit terrae), engraved on iron, is an example of the 15th Century decorative map showing some Catalan influence.

distribution of printed books which stimulated learning in all fields.

     With improvements in ships and navigational instruments, intensive geographical exploration was undertaken. The traditional fear of unknown seas was somewhat dispelled by the School of Sagres, founded in about 1416 by Prince Henry the Navigator, which promoted the empirical study of nautical lore. Travel was further encouraged by the publication of sailing manuals in the first decade of the 16th Century. They were Portuguese in origin and were based on carefully recorded observations. With new confidence, explorers like Vespucci, Magellan, Cabot, and Columbus set out to find legendary lands and to circumnavigate the globe.

In Europe, geography and cartography received fe-
verish attention. Map making became so prodigious that
only the most important developments can be included here.

Italy's contribution began with Fra Mauro's world map,
assembled in 1457-1459 near Venice. It resembles the medieval "mappae mundi" in form, but differs from them greatly
in content. The map, over 6 feet in diameter, is replete
with geographical detail, which includes corrections for
western Europe and the Mediterranean and shows some information from the Portuguese discoveries. Other Italian
manuscripts comprise about five hundred surviving portolanos, many of which were collected into atlases. From
coverage of the Mediterranean area they were extended to
western Europe and finally to discoveries in Africa and
America. Italy was a leader in the printing of maps, the
first being Ptolemy's Geographia (Bologna, 1477) produced
by copperplate engraving. The maps in this and subsequent
editions were made with a minimum of ornamentation and
mythological figures. Italian craftsmen depended upon
quality of material and delicate workmanship to achieve
beauty of effect.

The printing of the Geographia was of greatest importance, for it served as the prototype of nearly all geographical atlases from the time of the invention of printing
to the advent of modern cartography. Its disadvantage was
that cartographers tended to copy it too closely. The
surest way to sell an atlas was to print on the cover "After
Claudius Ptolemy," a reverence for the past which to some
extent held back the development of mapping.

Of special note in Italy was Giacomo Gastaldi, who
served as Cosmographer to the Republic of Venice, and to
whom one hundred nine separate map publications have been
attributed. His maps were widely used by map makers in
other lands. The outstanding cartographic work in Italy was
the Lafrere Atlas (Rome, 1556-1572), a collection of maps
by experts like Gastaldi, Bertelli, and Zaltieri. Italian
maps generally were made from original surveys, the accuracy of which was more or less sufficient for the needs
of the time. Maps of countries north and west of the Alps
were based on the work of foreign cartographers. In
mapping, a great deal had to be taken on faith and blended
with the known facts.

German cartography was creative and prolific in the

great cultural centers at Nuremberg and Cologne, under
such leaders as Etzlaub, Behaim, Schoner, Zundt, Münster,
and Waldseemüller. Although emphasis was placed on separate publications rather than on atlases as in Italy, the
German atlases were superior to the Italian ones. In the
first German edition of Ptolemy (Ulm, 1482) five maps
based on contemporary sources were added to the original
twenty-seven. A later edition (Strassburg, 1513) included
twenty additional contemporary maps which were the best
presentation of the world's geographical features since the
Classical era. These "modern" maps were made by Martin
Waldseemüller, who was also famous for a large map of the
world (1507) that was widely copied and imitated. For the
first time in an atlas the North American continent was delineated separately [Martin Behaim's globe had been the last
important representation of the world prior to the discovery
of America, besides being a summation of geographical
knowledge at the close of the 15th Century.]. Sebastian
Münster introduced a separate map for each of the four
known continents (Africa, Asia, Europe, and America), an
innovation that became standard, and his Cosmographia
(1544) was a major source of information for half a century.
His edition of Ptolemy (1540) contained the first separately
printed map of England. It was probably based on the Gough
or Bodleian Map of 1335, and showed unusually good detail
for England, but less for Scotland and Wales. The Germans
produced the world's finest globes and compasses, and in-
sisted usually on high critical standards for source material.
They also developed a new type of map--the road map--such
as Etzlaub's map of Central Europe, Der Rom Weg (The
Way to Rome).

The large map of England and Wales (1583) by the
English cartographer Saxton is considered by some scholars
to be the finest map of the 16th Century. Bearing the title
Britannia Insularum in Oceano Maxima, it was engraved on
twenty-one sheets at a scale of 8 miles to the inch. It
made such an impression that for 200 years it was used as
a source by map makers throughout Europe. In the latter
half of the 16th Century world maps were published, usually
through foreign agents, by Thomas Best, Robert Thorne, and
John Blagrave, the latter an Oxford mathematician. The
most important, however, was by Edward Wright, whose
book, Certain Errors of Navigation (1599), revolutionized
nautical science. The projection used in his maps of the
world and four continents was so excellent that it was pla-
giarized by the Dutch publisher Hondius as a basis for his

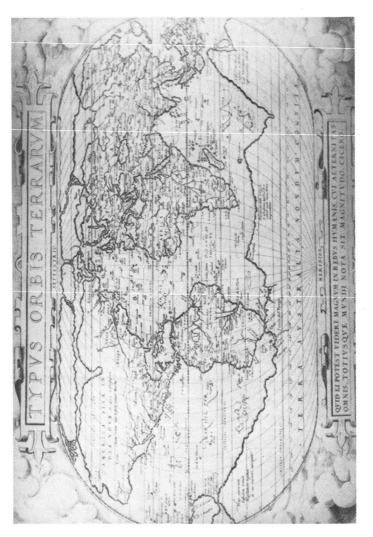

The world, by Ortelius, from his Atlas, 1575.

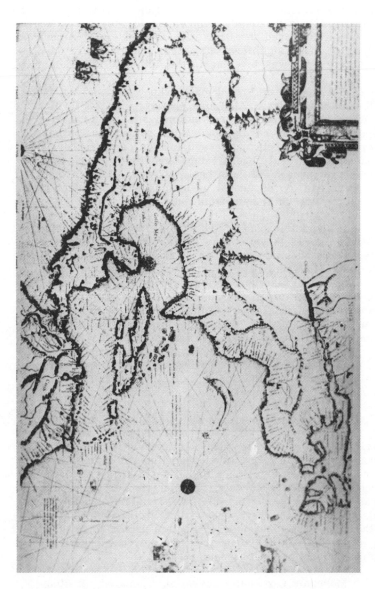

Section of world chart by Mercator, 1569, showing eastern part of North America.

maps. Mercator charts to the present time are drawn from
a modified version of Wright's projection. Also to the credit
of the English is Wytfleet's Supplement to Ptolemy's Geography, which contained the first atlas exclusively of America.
In spite of these significant advances, the great era of English cartography was to come in the 18th and 19th Centuries.

The heyday of French cartography also did not come
until a later century. At Tours, however, in 1594, Maurice
Bouguereau produced the first national atlas of France,
based on numerous cartographic studies made in the course
of the century by both native and foreign cartographers. It
consisted of several general maps and fifteen maps of
French provinces. At their best, however, French maps
were drab and too dependent on antiquated source material,
particularly the Ptolemaic tradition.

In the latter part of the 16th Century, cartographic
leadership began to shift away from Italy to the Low Countries. The transition was marked by the publication of
Ortelius's Theatrum Orbis Terrarum (Atlas of the Whole
World) in 1570. It was a systematic collection of maps,
of uniform size, of all the countries of the world, based
on the soundest available contemporary knowledge, as well
as on all sources since Ptolemy. In format and critical
outlook, the Theatrum may be considered as the first modern atlas. During the next hundred years it was distributed
all over Europe in various editions and many languages.
Ortelius documented the sources of his information and kept
his maps abreast of new surveys and discoveries.

Perhaps the most eminent geographer after Ptolemy
was Gerard Mercator (1512-1594), friend and advisor of
Ortelius, surveyor, map maker, engraver, and scientist.
It was he more than any other map who raised cartography
to the level of exact science and freed it from the dominance of Ptolemy. Mercator's projection was a fine example of geometry, being a system of parallels and meridians
whose relationships were true to one another on all parts
of the map. The Mercator Projection proved to be ideal
for navigation charts, since it is the only one on which
compass direction lines appear straight.

Mercator personally surveyed, compiled, drafted,
and engraved an accurate map of Flanders. The names
"North America" and "South America" were used for the
first time on his world map of 1538. This map also went

contrary to the popular idea that Asia and North America
were joined at some point, but did propose the possibility
of a northwest passage from one continent to the other.
His large-scale map of Europe (1554) was the most accurate of the day. On the basis of his scientific study and
integrity, he corrected Ptolemy. For example, he reduced
Ptolemy's estimate of the length of the Mediterranean from
62 degrees to 53 degrees. In an age when many maps were
still drawn more from imagination and art than from science, Mercator set a standard that inspired cartographers
to look forward rather than backward. There were many
other important cartographers in this period, such as
Hondius and de Jode, who contributed to the development
of surveying and mapping.

SCIENTIFIC TECHNIQUES

This period can hardly be reviewed without some
discussion of the scientific techniques involved in the production of the beautiful 15th and 16th Century maps. The
question arises as to just how accurate a map of a large
area could be, given the tools and knowledge then available.
The answer is, not very accurate by the highest standards,
but probably accurate enough, in the best maps, for the
ordinary needs of the time. The most basic feature of
maps is the location of points on the earth's surface in relation to each other and the determination of relative elevations. It is hard to realize the difficulties that faced even
such masters as Mercator with the little geodetic control
that existed in those days. For the purposes of comparison,
imagine the globe intersected by parallels of latitude and
meridians of longitude spaced 1 degree of arc apart, and
assume that each intersection represents a point firmly
established by astronomic observations. Leaving out the
poles and those points located on water (about three-fourths
of them), there would be left 16,020 points on land, which
represent the minimum geodetic control necessary to draw
the earth to scale within an accurate framework. Yet the
German astronomer and mathematician Johann Doppelmayr
estimated as late as 1740 that not more than 116 points had
been accurately fixed by astronomic observation. This was
the problem facing cartographers of the 15th and 16th centuries.

The surveyor's tools were simple but effective. In
the field he used a box compass with alidade (a ruler with

sighting vanes which can be raised or lowered), a plane
table equipped with compass and alidade, perhaps a per-
ambulator or odometer, for measuring irregular lines such
as the course of a river, and a semicircle for measuring
angles. By means of these instruments, a skilled surveyor
could determine distance and direction, and measure horizontal and vertical angles. Latitude was determined with
the astrolabe or cross staff, used to measure the angular
height of the sun or a star above the horizon as well as
star angles of various kinds. Longitude could be measured
by the angle (expressed in degrees up to 180 degrees in
either direction) which the meridian passing through a particular place made with the standard or prime meridian, or
by the difference in time between the two meridians. The
latter method became possible only with the invention of a
reliable chronometer around 1770. Before that time the
measurement of longitude was a serious problem for navigators and surveyors. On the other hand, the determination of latitude by means of astrolabe and mathematical
tables giving corrections had been known since antiquity.
Even with the best astrolabe under the best conditions at
a stationary observation point, angle measurement before
the 17th Century was subject to serious error.

     With the basic flaws in geodetic control added to the
primitive standards of the geographical science of the time,
it is no wonder that the content of even good maps was often
as questionable as the co-ordinate framework. Nevertheless,
a Mercator map or an atlas of Ortelius was better than anything that had come before, and was a relatively sound and
useful legacy for cartographers of the next century.

[Part III:] 17TH AND 18TH CENTURIES

     In a review of the whole range of mapping activity in
the 17th and 18th Centuries, three characteristics stand out.
First, great families of cartographers dominate the compilation and production of maps, charts, and atlases: the Blaeus
in Holland, the Sansons and Jaillots in France, and the Ho-
manns in Germany. Second, the quantity of cartographic
material which poured into the world market seems staggering even by modern standards. And third, the scientific
aspect of mapping, exact measurement and observation, as
opposed to the decorative aspects, was greatly emphasized
and entailed the development and extensive use of new techniques and instruments.

At the close of the 16th Century the Dutch were preeminent in map production. The former glory of Italy had
faded as the trade routes shifted from the Mediterranean
area to the Atlantic seaboard, thus depriving Italian cartographers of their source of wealth and information. But
the same high quality of execution remained, and one important work bears mention, the atlas Arcano del Mare
(1646-1647), which was put together by an Englishman, Sir
Robert Dudley, who lived in Florence. The Dutch continued
the Italian tradition of superb artistry and became leaders
in the quantity of maps and atlases produced. In some
cases, atlases comprised ten or twelve large folio volumes,
were published in many editions, and were translated into
all important European languages. The establishment of
Willem Blaeu (1571-1638), master surveyor, globe maker,
and publisher, was a producer of many such works of high
quality. The plant was equipped with nine flat-bed presses
for letterpress printing and six presses for copperplate
printing, all of which embodied the elder Blaeu's improvements in the operation of moving parts, the first since the
invention of printing. The firm also had the best engravers,
artists, scribes, and pressmen to be found in the Netherlands. The beauty of the Blaeu product can be judged
from the famous Atlas Major in twelve volumes, which in
many respects is the most superb geographical work ever
published, and also is largely typical of what map makers
offered in the 17th Century. Although the atlas did not contain the latest available geographical data, it made up for
the absence of facts by its artistic magnificence and fine
production. Bleau apparently made artistic maps for the
decorative-minded clientele, and more accurate, utilitarian
ones for persons engaged in navigation. Since the maps in
the latter category would probably be worn out with use,
those that remain are chiefly the artistic works.

The French school of cartography, under Nicholas
Sanson (1600-1667), gave France the leadership in that field
by the latter decades of the 17th Century, and she held this
position for the next hundred years. Sanson published some
three hundred maps, and his sons produced atlases covering the four continents of Asia, Africa, Europe, and America. These works were less ornamental than those of the
Dutch school and were printed in a handier format, usually
20 by 16 inches. After the Sansons came Alexis Jaillot
(1632-1712) and his family, whose publishing operations continued until 1780. The Jaillot maps were based largely on
the work of the younger Sansons, except that they were much

more ornate, thus reverting to the Dutch tradition. However, ornament was conbined with science in a way that had not been done before, and the French maps of the 18th Century were the most beautiful as well as the most accurate to be found.

This emphasis on accuracy was especially evident in the work of Guillaume de l'Isle (1675-1726), who became Royal Geographer to the King of France in 1718. He issued over a hundred maps in which many errors were corrected. Continents were changed in size, islands were shifted in position, doubtful place names were removed or corrected, and, for the first time, the Mediterranean was given its true length of 41 degrees. Guillaume's brother, Nicolas (1688-1768), was an astronomer who spent many years in Russia at the invitation of Peter the Great, training geographers, astronomers, and surveyors, and going on many journeys of exploration into the country. His Atlas Russicas was published in 1745 with twenty maps, the first clear geographical account of a land virtually unknown to Western Europe. China also received its due with the Nouvelle Atlas de la Chine, compiled by Jean Bourguignon (1679-1782) and published in 1737 with forty-two maps.

Scientific developments that had been taking place during this period had greatly aided the cartographers. It was some one hundred years earlier that the scientific approach to mapping had been spurred by the establishment of the Académie Royale des Sciences (1666), now the Institute de France. The Dutch mathematician Snellius had discovered triangulation in 1617 (actually triangulating part of the coast of Flanders), and provided a method of measurement that was taken up by members of the Académie and applied to the systematic mapping of France. In surveying, the old cross and back staffs were replaced by the reflecting octant, quadrant, and sextant which could measure celestial angles with fair accuracy. Angle measurement was refined still further with the invention of the telescopic theodolite. Scientists at the Académie, such as the physicist Christian Huygens, the astronomer Jean Picard, and Jean Cassini, the Italian astronomer who had been lured to France from Italy in 1669, set to work on a method of determining the longitude on land by observing eclipses of the moons of Jupiter. Pendulum clocks for keeping solar and sidereal time and powerful telescopes were developed. Thus terrestrial longitude was finally conquered (the determination of longitude at sea had to await the invention of Harrison's chronometer

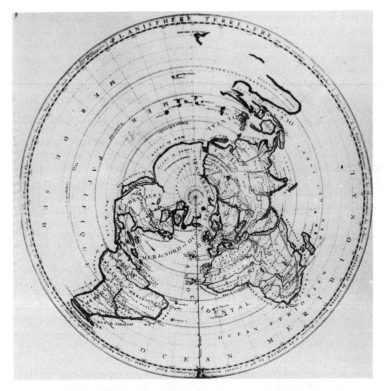

World map by Jean Cassini, 1696.

nearly a century later). Teams of surveyors were sent to
remote parts of the world to make observations, and data
were exchanged freely between them and many scientists in
other countries. The results were so favorable that Cassini
was able to lay out a new world map on the floor of the
Paris Observatory in 1682, a map with an accurate network
of latitude and longitude that immediately made obsolete the
maps of the past.

A survey of France was one of the eventual objectives when the Académie Royale was established. With the
advances that were being made in the theory and technique
of terrestrial measurement, the project became one of the
major preoccupations of the members of the Académie.
After many delays and difficulties, an outline map of France
containing all the triangles surveyed by the Académie up to

1740 was published in 1744. The map showed 18 base lines, more than 2,000 triangles, and was accompanied by a table of latitudes and longitudes. A year later, eighteen sheets were joined to form a map of France at 1:878,000 scale, which included surveys made between 1740 and 1744. This map showed 900 triangles and 19 measured base lines. From this point the work continued under the direction of César Cassini (1714-1784), grandson of the great Jean Cassini, and terminated in 1789 with the publication of the Carte Géométrique de France, or, as it is sometimes called, the Carte de Cassini. This was the finest expression of French cartographic achievement and was a high point in the history of mapping. For the first time, an entire country had been mapped by genuine topographic surveys. The guesswork was gone and the basic principles of geodesy had been formulated and tested. The world had a trustworthy model to follow.

The English had also made contributions in the mapping field. Edmund Halley (1656-1742), for example, originated the meteorological and magnetic chart and the methods of representing the geographical distribution of the earth's features. English maps did not come up to the general standards of the Dutch in the 17th Century and French in the 18th Century. The first atlas published by an Englishman was John Speed's Prospect of the Most Famous Parts of the World (1627). There were translations of Ortelius and Mercator, and in 1646, as noted above, the first English sea atlas, Arcano del Mare, was published by Sir Robert Dudley. In the 18th Century, English maps were similar to those of the French in style and composition. It is surprising that the British government took so long to appreciate the utility of a national survey based on scientific principles developed by the French Académie Royale. British activity seemed to lag until César Cassini suggested that astronomy would be benefited if the difference in latitude and longitude between the Greenwich and Paris Observatories were known. This difference could be worked out, he said, if a precise line were triangulated from London to Dover. The Royal Society took up this project and enlisted the services of Maj. Gen. William Roy to conduct it. A base line was measured in 1784 on Hounslow Heath (near London) and Greenwich, and three years later the survey was made with the aid of Ramsden's new theodolite. The results convinced General Roy that English maps were fraught with error, and he became the champion of a general survey of England. The idea finally received royal approval in 1791, after Roy's death.

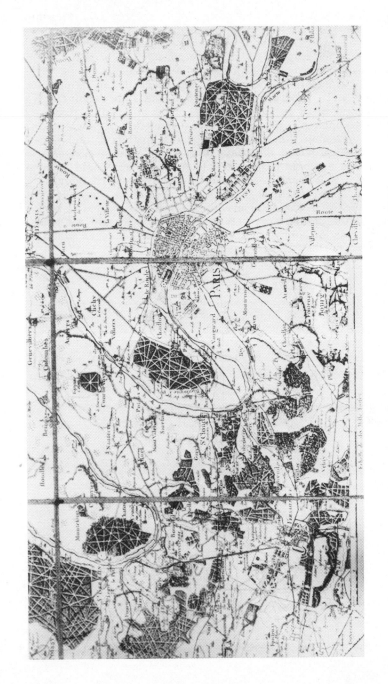

A section of César Cassini's Map of France, 1744.

The work of the French and British inspired other
European governments to make comprehensive surveys of
their own countries, the Scandinavians being among the
first to take action. The value and necessity of national
surveys were generally recognized in the 19th Century,
while good maps became essential tools of national power
and development. The world was indebted to the scientists
of the Académie Royale, whose genius, patience, and tire-
less labor provided the basis of geodetic science and gave
a detailed example of how a scientific survey should be conducted. The French even made a gesture toward international cooperation through Cassini's project to link the
Greenwich and Paris Observatories. However, extensive
cooperation of that sort between the nations would not take
place until the 20th Century, when national surveys would
be more or less consolidated.

2. THE ELEMENTS OF MAPS

THE ELEMENTS OF A MAP*

Richard E. Dahlberg

The function of this article is to provide the basis
for a better understanding of maps. Its strategy is to dis-
sect the map so that the elements may be viewed separately
or simply before turning to more complex questions of map
interpretation and use considered elsewhere in this series.
Attention will be directed to the following topics: (1) the
earth's address system, (2) transformations of the earth's
address system to a flat surface, (3) address systems for
maps, (4) map scale, and (5) map symbols.

THE EARTH AND ITS ADDRESS SYSTEM

Basic to any work with maps is an understanding of
the earth's address system.[1] Commonly referred to as the
earth grid, this system is displayed on most maps and
globes and provides a simple and unique address for any
point on the earth's surface. By this means the reader
is able to determine the location of specific features, to
add information to the map, or to transfer information
from one map to another.

The address system is based upon distance measures
of latitude and longitude and is marked upon maps by the
familiar lines called parallels and meridians. The distance
called latitude is measured in degrees either north of south
of the equator reaching a maximum value of 90° at the
poles. The lines on the map marking points of equal distance from the equator are parallels.

Intersecting the parallels at right angles are the

*Reprinted by permission from The Journal of Geography,
vol. 68, no. 9 (1969), 527-534.

meridians which extend from pole to pole as great circle
arcs. These lines mark points of equal longitude or distance east or west of the prime meridian. The numbering
of the meridians begins at the prime or Greenwich meridian
and proceeds east and west to the 180th meridian, also
known as the International Date Line.

Because the spacing of grid lines on maps is generally broad, often it is necessary to read between the lines,
or to interpolate, to find a specific value.[2] This process
is made more complicated because the sexagesimal system
is used to divide degrees into 60 minutes and the minutes
into 60 seconds. Along the meridians these subdivisions
are nearly equal and it is useful to remember that 1° of
latitude equals ca. 69 statute miles. One minute of latitude equals 1.15 statute miles or 1.0 nautical miles. The
convergence of the meridians toward the poles produces a
corresponding decrease in the length of degrees of longitude. Thus, 1° of longitude diminishes from 69.2 miles
at the equator, to half that value (34.7 miles) at latitude
60°, and to zero at the poles. From these data one notes
that the 60th parallels are half the length of the equator.

TRANSFORMATION OF THE EARTH
ADDRESS SYSTEM TO A PLANE

Underlying the map is a plane-surface representation
of the earth's grid called a projection.[3] It serves precisely
the same function on the map as on the globe and thus constitutes the structure for controlling locations on a map.
Conversion or transformation of the spherical grid is required for the obvious reason that the surface of a sphere
cannot be flattened without an intolerable degree of shrink-
ing, stretching, or tearing. In performing such a transformation it is the cartographer's task to keep such changes
within acceptable limits. It falls to the map user, on the
other hand, to judge what these changes are and to interpret the resulting arrangement of grid and features accordingly.

The number of transformed grids, or map projections,
that have been created is indeed vast and the possibilities of
additional transformations are limitless. However, the user
can cope with this variety because the number of projections
commonly used is small and the selection is a relatively
logical process. Although the selection of a projection is
clearly the cartographer's task, the map user is called upon

to interpret the results of such a transformation and therefore has a vital interest in the projection choice. Further,
the user at times has a need to choose among similar maps
based upon different projections.

Grid Classes

Sometimes it is helpful to visualize the kinds of surfaces on which the grid might be projected readily from the
globe, i. e., plane, cone, or cylinder. As one imagines
this transformation, it seems clear that those areas of the
grid on or near the point or line of contact between globe
and projection surface will be subject to the least distortion. Further, those portions of the globe remote from
this contact will be most distorted.

These observations provide the basis for a very
simple but useful regionalization of grid quality. Thus it
is clear that projections of the plane class afford good representation to areas situated at or near the center of the map
as well as to areas of generally circular shape. Such projections are ideal for maps of the polar regions and of
hemispheres. Since the point of tangency that constitutes
the center of the area of best representation can be positioned anywhere on the globe, it follows that oblique cases
of these projections are highly useful for areas of continental
size. It should be noted that changing the location on the
globe of the projection center changes the appearance of the
grid but not the quality of representation. Projections of
the conic class are used principally for mapping areas of
predominantly east-west extent located in the mid-latitudes.
Since the height of the cone can be adjusted, the zone of
best-fit can be centered readily on the region of maximum
interest.

Projections of the cylindric class readily encompass
most or all of the globe though the zone of best representation usually is centered on the equator. Such projections
are ideal for equatorial areas such as the East Indies as
well as for world maps on which the interest centers upon
low latitude areas. Because the parallels in higher latitudes
on cylindric projections are stretched so greatly, many projections have been devised that depart from the strict cylindric model. On these so-called pseudo-cylindric projections the poles are shortened to one-half or one-third the
length of the equator or even to a point. This causes the
meridians to become curves that converge in higher latitudes.

This results in improved shapes that are more pleasing to
the eye and many of the most popular projections fall in this
class.   As in the case of projections of the plane class, the
projection may be centered upon different points of the globe
giving rise to oblique cases characterized by more complex
grids.

Projection Properties

A major consideration in choosing or evaluating a
map projection is the extent to which properties of the grid
as it exists on the globe are preserved in the transformation
to a plane. [4]   Some of the chief properties of concern here
are areas, shapes, distances, and directions.   Projections
of the equal-area or equivalent class preserve areas in constant ratio to those on a globe of the same scale.   This
one-to-one correspondence of area is extremely important
for many geographic purposes in that it frees the user from
having to make rather complex mental adjustments as he
compares features in different parts of the map.   Clearly
this equal-area property is essential on many types of statistical maps.

In Table 1 selected map projections have been cross-
classified according to grid class and property.   In the equal-
area row are listed several important projections widely
used for geographic education, viz., Lambert azimuthal
equal-area, Albers' conic equal-area, sinusoidal, Mollweide's, and Goode's homolosine.   Many of the equal-area
projections of the pseudo-cylindric subset are used principally in interrupted form.   This means that the little distorted region centered upon the principal meridian is used
repeatedly for each major land mass and the much distorted
margins of the grid are discarded.   The improvement in
overall shape representation thereby achieved comes at the
cost of internal interruptions of the grid. [5]

A second property of importance is that of shape.
Unfortunately no transformations exist that preserve shapes
except for local areas.   The merit of conformal projections is that angles, and therefore shapes, are preserved
provided that one limits his field-of-view to a small segment of the map.   Such projections are characterized by a
right-angle intersection of the grid lines, even in oblique
cases.   Conformal projections are of great importance in
navigation, topographic mapping, coastal and aeronautical
charting but of only modest importance for world or

continental maps in textbooks and atlases. The reason for
this is mainly that areas on such maps become greatly enlarged, especially near the projection margins.

The preservation of distance on projections is not
possible except in a very limited sense. The common
azimuthal equidistant projection represents correct distances
but only along straight lines extending from or to the center
of the projection. Thus, on an oblique case of the projection centered on Chicago one could measure distances from
Chicago readily to any other point on the map. To measure
distances from London to various other cities would require
another development of the projection centered on London.
On world or hemispheric maps long distance measurement
is complex and one is better off to use a suitable globe or
distance tables. On maps of smaller areas, viz., topographic quadrangles, distance errors are generally negligible
for most purposes.

The preservation of directional relationships on map
projections is similarly limited. Within small areas, such
as that covered by a topographic quadrangle, errors of direction or azimuth are negligible so that azimuths can be
measured readily by means of a protractor. [6] As the separation of points referred to increases to global dimensions
measurement of azimuth becomes much more complex. On
projections of the azimuthal group it is limited to directions
measured from the center of the map. The projection most
widely used for this purpose is the azimuthal equidistant.
On large scale maps, such as city plans or topographic
sheets, directions are keyed to a north arrow or compass
rose. However, on smaller scale maps the presence of
meridians obviates the need for a compass rose. Indeed,
it is inappropriate to include a north arrow on a map having
anything other than straight, vertical meridians.

Several of the world projections used in teaching fall
into a group called compromise projections. This term implies that certain requirements have been relaxed in order
to produce a more useful projection on which shape distortion and areal exaggeration are reasonably balanced. Common examples are the Van der Grinten and Denoyer semi-
elliptical projections.

Role of the Grid

In addition to its function for locational control noted

TABLE 1
SELECTED MAP PROJECTIONS CROSS-CLASSIFIED BY PROPERTY AND GRID CLASS

GRID CLASS / PROPERTY	PLANE	CONIC		CYLINDRIC	
		REGULAR CONIC	PSEUDO-CONIC***	REGULAR CYLINDRIC	PSEUDO-CYLINDRIC**
CONFORMAL	STEREOGRAPHIC (polar regions, hemispheric weather maps, air navigation)	LAMBERT CONIC CONFORMAL (air navigation U.S. and middle latitudes)		MERCATOR (navigation; in transverse case much used for topographic maps. All cases considered is the world's most widely used projection. But the world case not to be used in schools)	
EQUAL AREA	LAMBERT AZIMUTHAL EQUAL AREA (hemispheres, continents in atlases and school texts)	ALBERS' CONIC EQUAL AREA (official projection for U.S. atlases, dist. maps)	BONNE (continents, esp. Europe)	LAMBERT'S CYLINDRIC EQUAL AREA	SINUSOIDAL* MOLLWEIDE* GOODE'S HOMOLOSINE* ECKERT IV* FLAT POLAR QUARTIC IV* BRIESEMEISTER+ HAMMER (world dist. maps in atlases, textbooks, etc.)
AZIMUTHAL	ORTHOGRAPHIC (lunar maps) GNOMONIC (navigation) STEREOGRAPHIC LAMBERT AZIM. EQUAL AREA AZIMUTHAL EQUIDISTANT				
EQUIDISTANT	AZIMUTHAL EQUIDISTANT+ (atlases and text books to show distances and international air routes; communication)	SIMPLE CONIC (atlas maps of small areas)			
COMPROMISE	GLOBULAR (obsolete-Nat. Geog. Soc. emblem)		POLYCONIC (topographic maps of U.S.)	MILLER CYLINDRIC, GALL'S STEREOGRAPHIC (General purpose, world reference or dist. maps)	VAN der GRINTEN, DENOYER'S SEMI-ELLIPTICAL WINKEL III HÖLZEL (General purpose, world reference or dist. maps)

Projections in italics are commonly used in school atlases, wall maps, and text books. + Usually in oblique case. * Often used in interrupted form. ** Meridians other than central meridian are curved. Parallels straight or gently curved. Zone of best representation either in low latitudes centered along equator or two zones centered along standard parallels located in middle latitudes. *** Meridians other than central meridian are curved.

previously, the grid also serves as an important visual clue to
the organization of the map. The grid helps the user to
judge the class of projection and certain of its properties.
It enables the user to relate the map to the globe and to his
spatial image of the earth or to his "mental map."[7] This
visual guidance is especially important on maps having grid
lines that change their form across the maps of that are
interrupted.[8] If the grid lines are deleted in the final presentation the user can be misled badly.

Other Transformations

In the case of all the projections noted above spherical distances on the globe are transformed to distances on
a plane according to some specified scheme. Similarly,
areas on the globe correspond with areas on the projection.
However, it is feasible to relate map distance or area to
other characteristics of places on the earth such as population or income. Such maps are called cartograms and present the user with a different view of a distribution, one
that commands a "second look."[9] A fairly common example
is a map showing a New Yorker's view of the U.S. on which
areas are distorted according to the importance he attaches
to them. More pertinent perhaps is the type of cartogram
on which the areas of countries are proportional to their
populations.

ADDRESS SYSTEMS FOR MAPS

In addition to the geographic or earth grid described
above, other types of address systems called map grids are
applied to particular maps for greater convenience of location. The two chief types of map grids will be discussed
below.

Alpha-Numeric Grids

Perhaps the simplest map grid is the so-called alphanumeric grid employed so commonly on road as well as on
atlas maps on which places are designated simply by a letter and a number. These letter and number designations
ordinarily appear along the margins of the map and refer to
the intersection of a column and a row. The columns and
rows may be straight or curved depending upon the projection and design of the map.

Rectangular Coordinate Systems

 For quite a number of technical purposes the sometimes complicated grid comprised of meridians and parallels
is replaced by a strictly rectangular grid system. It is
important to note that such grid systems are drawn upon the
map and thus bear no relationship to features of the earth's
surface. They possess the advantage of uniformity and simplicity of use.

 One of the most widely used rectangular grid systems
of today is the Universal Transverse Mercator (U. T. M.)
grid, a military system which appears on large- and medium-scale topographic maps of the U. S. 10 On the sheets
published by the Geological Survey, this grid is indicated by
blue marginal ticks together with a brief note of identification at the bottom of the map. Another grid that appears on
our domestic topographic sheets is that of the state coordinate systems. This grid also is indicated by marginal ticks,
in this case black, which enable the user to extend the grid
across the map if and when its use is required. 11 Such
grids are useful to the military forces as well as to surveyors. They are proving to be useful to many others including planners and those concerned with the locational coding of information for data banks.

MAP SCALE

 Surely one of the most significant characteristics of
a map is its scale. The scale defines the size of the map
or of map features in relation to the earth. As the map
user becomes familiar with scales he is able to judge distances readily and, very significantly, to form his expectations of map distance and feature size. 12 Users commonly
categorize scales into three classes for ease of reference.
These classes are named small, medium, and large. Small
scale maps are relatively small in size and therefore rather
highly generalized. They are used for maps of major regions, countries, or continents. Classroom wall maps, atlas maps, and ordinary state road maps are examples.
Medium scales are much used by the armed forces for planning operations in areas between county and state size. The
widely used 1:250, 000 scale map series covering the U. S. is
an example of a medium scale series. Large scale maps
require so much space to cover a state that they characteristically are divided into sheets or quadrangles of manageable size.

Ordinarily the scale of a map is displayed in a conspicuous place. It is defined as the relationship of map distance (MD) to ground distance (GD) and may be expressed in numerous ways. One of the most popular is as a fraction called the representative fraction or R. F. This is expressed as RF = MD/GD and is reduced to a pure fraction so that it can be applied to any system of distance measurement. An example, RF = 1/24, 000, is a commonly used scale for topographic maps of the U. S. This scale may be expressed also as a ratio, or 1:24, 000, a form popular because it is simpler to set in type. Yet another form of the same scale is a verbal statement, vis., one inch represents 2000 feet. It may also be expressed as a graphic or bar scale conveniently subdivided for ease of measurement.

Table 2 provides some useful data for seven popular map scales. It gives the ground distance in statute miles represented by one inch on the map, and the distance on the map required to represent one mile on the earth. It also gives the map area required to represent the U. S. at each of these scales. A study of these data suggest the significant relationship between map scale and the quantity of information that the map can display. Of particular interest is the last column which clearly reveals the reason that smaller scale maps have such a severely limited information carrying capacity. The one square mile that maps as a 2. 64-inch square on a 1:24, 000 scale topographic map is reduced to a square measuring only 0. 0013 inches on a textbook map at the 1. 50, 000, 000 scale.

TABLE 2
SELECTED SCALES: LINEAR AND AREAL COMPARISONS

Typical Use	Scale	Scale Class*	Miles/In.	Inches/Mi.	Map Area U.S. (48 states) Sq. In.
Topographic maps	1: 24,000	L	0.38	2.64	21,065,000
	1: 250,000	M	3.95	0.25	194,130
Aeronautical charts	1: 1,000,000	S	15.78	0.06	12,133
School atlases	1: 5,000,000	S	78.91	0.01	485
	1:12,500,000	S	197.29	0.005	78
Textbook maps	1:25,000,000	S	394.57	0.003	19
	1:50,000,000	S	789.14	0.001	5

* L - large scale; M - medium scale; S - small scale.

Symbols on Maps

The use of symbols to portray characteristics of the earth's surface is one of the most distinctive qualities of the map. It distinguishes a map from an aerial photograph. By means of symbols the cartographer is able to present the user with simple but useful interpretations of complex information in a universal language. One of the first observations to be made is that a map is an incomplete portrayal of an area. Although this is an obvious characteristic of small and medium scale maps, it is not always appreciated that it applies to large scale maps as well. However, a comparison of a topographic map with a matching aerial photograph makes the selective nature of the map apparent. Not only is the photograph more detailed than the map but also it records many types of data that the cartographer feels he must omit when compiling the map.

It is through the use of symbols that the cartographer generalizes information when making a map. Generalization is essential to the purpose of a map and will be discussed briefly.[13] The simple omission of information is one important aspect. Also, features to be represented must be categorized so that they can be represented by a limited number of symbols. Thus, roads of a given capacity, whether concrete or blacktop, heavily traveled or remote, lined with trees or automobile cemeteries are all shown by the same symbol. Minor deviations in the course of the road are ignored for they would complicate the map without adding useful information. As map scales diminish, linear features, such as roads and coastlines, must be simplified accordingly. Part of the art of cartography lies in judgment exercised to preserve the distinctive shape or pattern of features as their delineation is simplified.

In addition, it generally is necessary to exaggerate the size of map symbols relative to the features they represent. For example, the width of the Mississippi River near Vicksburg is one-half mile. On a representative school atlas map it appears to be 1.9 miles wide. On a classroom wall map it appears to be 3.6 miles wide. Because of the need to use symbols large enough to be seen and to give desired emphasis, oversize symbols are required. It is clear that in areas of symbol congestion it is necessary to relax the position or alignment of symbols to preserve their legibility.

TABLE 3

REPRESENTATIVE SYMBOL USES CROSS-CLASSIFIED
ACCORDING TO SYMBOL FORM AND MEASUREMENT SCALES

Symbol Form	Measurement Scales		
	Nominal[a]	Ordinal[b]	Interval-Ratio[c]
Point	City	Large city	City with population in 50,000–99,999 size class
Line	Road	Major road	Road having average commercial traffic flow 2000–2999 vehicles per 24-hr. period
Area	Inhabited area	Densely populated area	Area having a population density of 256–512 persons per sq. mi.

[a] Nominal scaling, sometimes called qualitative, classifies but does not rank.
[b] Ordinal scaling involves classification and ranking.
[c] Interval or ratio scaling involves classification, ranking plus information on distance between ranks.

One very important requirement in the proper interpretation of map symbols is that the user develop a set of
expectations of symbol meaning that takes cognizance of both
the complexities of the earth's surface and of the cartographer's coding practices.   To identify and characterize the
manifold variations in features of the earth, including man
and his works, the map maker is limited to three symbol
forms that may vary in size, shape, or color.   In Table 3
these symbol forms are related to scales of measuring
phenomena and several examples of symbol use are provided.
Exposure to newspaper maps or topographic sheets serves to
acquaint map users chiefly with the use of symbols for the
nominal and ordinal measurement scale categories.   The use
of symbols for more quantitative characterizations, involving
the interval or ratio scales, is less familiar.   Space limitations preclude the further exploration of this topic here,
but the reader may find the references useful. [14]   The important point is that map users need to appreciate the inter-
relationships among symbol forms, feature forms and characteristics, and scales of measurement.   Then they will be
"tuned in" to read the cartographic message.

NOTES

1.   David Greenhood, Mapping, Phoenix Science Series, rev.
     with assistance of Gerald L. Alexander.   (Chicago
     and London: University of Chicago Press, 1964), 6-
     11.
2.   U. S. Department of Army, "Map Reading, " Field Manual
     21-26.   (Washington, D. C. :   Government Printing Of-
     fice, March 1965), 11-16.

3. Greenhood, op. cit., 113-171; Arthur N. Strahler, Phys-
    ical Geography (3rd ed.; New York: John Wiley,
    1969), 19-41.
4. Arthur H. Robinson and Randall D. Sale, Elements of
    Cartography (3rd ed.; New York: John Wiley, 1969),
    199-248; Wellman Chamberlin, The Round Earth on
    Flat Paper ... (Washington, D.C.: National Geo-
    graphic Society, 1947), 37-104.
5. Howard F. Hirt, "Reducing Distortions: A Useful Ap-
    proach in Augmenting the Understanding of Map Pro-
    jections," Journal of Geography, LIX, 7 (October
    1960), 308-314.
6. U.S. Department of Army, "Map Reading," op. cit.,
    52-62.
7. John E. Dornbach, "The Mental Map," Annals of the
    Association of American Geographers, XLIX, 2
    (June 1959), 179-180 (abstract); Peter R. Gould,
    "On Mental Maps," Discussion Paper No. 9, Michigan
    Inter-University Community of Mathematical Geogra-
    phers, University of Michigan, September 1966, 53 pp.
8. Richard E. Dahlberg, "Maps Without Projections,"
    Journal of Geography, LX, 5 (May 1961), 213-218.
9. Chauncy D. Harris and George B. McDowell, "Distorted
    Maps, A Teaching Device," Journal of Geography,
    LIV, 6 (November 1955), 286-289; Erwin Raisz,
    Principles of Cartography, (New York: McGraw-Hill,
    1962), 215-218; John M. Hunter and Jonathan C.
    Young, "A Technique for the Construction of Quanti-
    tative Cartograms by Physical Accretion Models,"
    Professional Geographer, XX, 6 (November 1968),
    402-407.
10. Strahler, op. cit., 56-58; U.S. Department of Army,
    "Map Reading," op. cit., 16-28.
11. Greenhood, op. cit., 21-22; Hugh C. Mitchell and Lan-
    sing G. Simmons, "The State Coordinate Systems,"
    Coast & Geodetic Survey, Special Publication No. 235,
    1945, vii + 62 pp.
12. U.S. Department of Army, "Map Reading," op. cit.,
    29-33, 129-130.
13. John K. Wright, "Map Makers are Human. Comments
    on the Subjective in Maps," Geographical Review,
    XXXII (1942), 527-544. Bobbs-Merrill Reprint Series
    in Geography, G-258; Robinson and Sale, op. cit.,
    52-60.
14. Robinson and Sale, op. cit., 95-101; William L. Schaaf,
    Basic Concepts of Elementary Mathematics (2nd ed.;
    New York: John Wiley, 1965), 292-294; C. Board,

"Maps as Models," in Models in Geography, ed. by
Richard J. Chorley and Peter Haggett (London:
Methuen, 1967), 690-692; G. C. Dickinson, Statistical Mapping and the Presentation of Statistics (London: Edward Arnold, 1963), 160 pp.; F. J. Monkhouse and H. R. Wilkinson, Maps and Diagrams ...
(2nd ed.; London: Methuen, 1966), xix + 432 pp.

THE TEACHING OF CONTOURS*

Ling Chu Poh

Many eminent geographers have tried to explain the nature of geography. [1] In all these attempts it is always stated that the map is the geographer's unique and basic tool. [2] It is one of the important focuses which seems to integrate and collate the work of geographers.

Teachers of geography, therefore, have the responsibility to help children understand the nature of maps and to equip them with map reading skills. Of all the different types of maps, the large scale topographical map is probably the most useful one for studying the pupil's immediate environment, the planning and execution of field work, the examination of sample studies, and the detailed study of the physical and cultural landscape.

Before the pupil can use the large scale topographical map effectively, he has to be taught the concept of contours. It is the common experience of most teachers that this is one of the most difficult concepts to teach in geography.

PROBLEMS OF CONTOUR TEACHING

The teaching of contours has been found to be difficult because many teachers are not clear about the important and basic concepts underlying this topic. It is, therefore, necessary that these concepts be identified so that more light may be thrown on the problem of why students find this a difficult topic to understand and why teachers find the concepts

*Reprinted by permission from The Journal of Geography, vol. 68, no. 8 (1969), 484-490.

difficult to teach.

The basic concepts involved in contour teaching are:

1. The understanding of the nature of maps. Children must be taught that maps are basically a bird's-eye-view of the land below. The map is a reduced drawing or a drawing to scale of the landscape from this vantage point. The landscape, however, from this view has been squashed or pressed down to form a two-dimensional plane. Mapmaking is, therefore, fundamentally the translation of the three-dimensional landscape to a two dimensional drawing to scale. In this process the map has lost the quality of height through its two-dimensional nature. Various methods of expressing heights on maps through shading, hachuring, and coloring have arisen because of this problem.

2. The visualization of the landscape or the three-dimensional reality. When the children are required to read contour maps, we are in fact assuming that they are able to visualize the landscape or relief from the two-dimensional drawings. This operation is the reverse of the process in map-making. In map-making the three-dimensional is transformed into the two-dimensional, but in this case we ask them to mentally reconstruct the three-dimensional from the two-dimensional. The reconstruction in the children's minds of the three-dimensional landscape involves the ability to visualize or mentally recapture the lost quality of height (lost in the process of map-making or pressing the landscape down to a two-dimensional plane). In this task of visualizing the three-dimensional landscape, the children are often aided only by the contour lines drawn on the map. Most of the difficulties of the pupils or their failure to grasp the nature of contours stem from their inability to visualize. The skillful teacher can help children learn to visualize by using diagrams and models. He can also reduce the big task into small and gradual steps.

3. The meaning of height. Children also must be taught what is meant when places are referred to as 1000' or 3000' or 5000' high. They have to be helped to realize that a line can pin points of equal height. To achieve this end, heights and contour lines have to be related to sea-levels. The possibility that different contour lines can be different sea-levels is a useful concept to convey.

4. Other related concepts. Besides these three

basic concepts, there are other related concepts which arise
from them and they are:

(a) The meaning of the horizontal equivalent and vertical
     interval.
(b) The idea behind the drawing of cross-sections of the
     landscape from contour maps.
(c) The concept of how different degrees of distortion of
     the cross-sectional drawing can result with the vary-
     ing of the vertical scale.
(d) The relationship between the different types of land-
     forms and their corresponding contour patterns.
(e) The relationship of slopes and the spacing of contour
     lines.

                    SUGGESTIONS FOR THE TEACHING OF
                              CONTOURS

          The Nature of Maps--Preliminary Exercises. Chil-
dren in the primary grades have been taught how to draw
plans of their classrooms and school buildings. Just before
the topic of contours is introduced it would be profitable to
revise this aspect of their work. The teacher should explain that in doing these exercises, they are, in fact, making simple maps. Certain other exercises can also be
planned to reinforce this basic idea of the nature of maps.
Children can be asked to draw the plans of cones, pyramids,
and blocks of different shapes. They should be reminded
that they are drawing from a bird's-eye-view. Later concentric lines can be drawn on the cone and the children required to draw the plan of the cone with these lines. The
teacher should, in particular, point out how the lines on
the cones have been translated into concentric circles in
the plan.

          B.   The Immersion Method and the Glass-Planes
Method. Of the many methods that can be used to teach
contours, the immersion and the glass-planes methods,
when combined, seem to be able to present all the relevant
and related concepts most lucidly and simply.

          In the immersion method, the following things are
needed:

          1.   A tank with glass sides.
          2.   A simple plasticine or plaster of paris model

of an island or a mountain.
3.   A piece of glass big enough to cover the tank.
4.   Some drawing materials.

The model is first put into the tank.   After that,
water is poured in.   The children are told to imagine that
the model is an island in an ocean.   The subsequent steps
are:

1.   A pupil is asked to draw a line around the model
to mark the sea-level.   Colored thread is laid over the line
of the model.

2.   The water in the tank is increased by regular
intervals.   The children are told that each increase is a
rise of the sea-level by 1000 feet.   Colored thread is used
to mark these levels on the model.   After four or five lines
have been drawn on the model, corresponding to the different sea-levels, the water in the tank is drained to its
former level.

3.   The teacher will then draw on the blackboard a
diagram showing what has happened.   Points X, Y, Z are
located on sea-level$_2$.   The children are asked about the
height of these different points, keeping in mind the fact
that the sea-level in the tank is now at sea-level$_1$.   This
step will help them to understand the relationship of height
and sea-level.   Following this step, S. L. $_2$, S. L. $_3$, S. L. $_4$,
S. L. $_5$ are represented as lines joining places of equal height
about S. L. $_1$.   Therefore, these lines are described as contour lines.   From these steps, the children will then be able
to see the relationship between sea-levels, equal heights,
and contour lines.

4.   Next, a glass plane is used to cover the tank.
Students are invited to look down at the tank and model.
Some of these students are asked to draw with a felt pen
on the glass plane the outline of each colored thread found
on the model.   After they have done this, the teacher will
hold up the glass plane and tell the children that the lines
on it are contour lines depicting the height of the model.
They are asked to draw these contour lines in their exercise books.   The children have, therefore, seen and participated in the transference of the contour lines on a three-
dimensional model to a two-dimensional plane.   These learning tasks have given them the experience of making a simple
map of the model.

5. Lastly, the model with the contour lines is left at a convenient place so that the students can compare what they have drawn with what is on the model. In this way, they can see the relationship between the three-dimensional and the two-dimensional.

In the glass-planes method, the following things are needed:

1. Several pieces of glass planes.
2. A wooden box with three sides open.
3. A simplified contour drawing of a hill, spur, and valley.
4. Drawing materials.

This glass-planes method is meant to supplement the immersion method. The following steps are suggested for the execution of this method:

1. The contour lines on the simplified contour drawing are transferred one at a time on to each glass plane. Each glass plane will, therefore, have on it a particular contour line.

2. The glass-plane with the lowest contour line is then inserted into the lowest groove in the box. Similarly, according to this principle, the other glass-planes are put into the grooves in that order.

3. After the glass-planes are in place, the children are invited to look down at the box. They will see the contour lines in vivid relief representing the three-dimensional landscape. This stage will show very clearly how contour lines can represent height.

4. The intervals between the glass-planes can be varied. As the intervals are increased or decreased uniformly, the emerging model in the box suffers from varying degrees of corresponding distortion. This is an example of the effect of varying the vertical interval or the vertical exaggeration.

This method, therefore, can help the student to visualize the three-dimensional landscape from a contour drawing. It could also be used in the upper grades to explain the related concepts of vertical exaggeration, vertical interval, vertical scale, and distortion.

This method could be used in conjunction with the cross-section drawing method. Using the same contour drawing, different cross-sections are drawn. The cross-section in its finished form shows the configuration of the land. The pupil drawing the cross-section has reconstructed a view of the three-dimensional landscape from the contour drawing. He had, in the process, recaptured the lost quality of height because the cross-section shows height.

In the drawing of the cross-section, the pupils have to choose the vertical and horizontal scales for the vertical and horizontal axes of the cross-sectional drawing, respectively. The problem of the choice of the vertical scale is related to the concepts of vertical exaggeration and vertical interval, introduced earlier through the glass-planes method.

In the two methods outlined earlier, different types of models and contour drawings of different landforms are used. As the pupils use these varied examples, they will come to associate certain landforms with certain contour patterns. They will also begin to understand, for example, why the contour lines representing spurs go outward and why those for the valleys go inward.

C.   The Relationship of Slope and the Pattern of Contour Lines. The simple concept that contour lines are closer together for steep slopes than for gentle slopes is taught with the help of two wedges of different inclinations. On the vertical sides of the wedges, uniform and regular intervals representing heights of 100 feet are marked. The corresponding contour lines are drawn on the slopes. With this illustration, it should be quite evident to the pupils why the gentler slopes have their contour lines farther apart, and, conversely, why the steeper slopes have their contour lines closer together.

This illustration is also helpful in pointing out to the pupils why contour lines for uniform slopes are relatively straight and uniform. The smooth surfaces of the wedges with the contour lines show this clearly.

The relationship between undulating terrain and contour patterns is best shown on a sand tray. This sand tray is a shallow box filled with fine sand. The fine sand is first made a bit damp. After that, it is molded to represent an undulating terrain. Colored thread showing the major contour lines is laid out carefully on the sand model.

The pupils are then asked to view the model from above.
Consequently, they will begin to associate that type of terrain with the irregular and looping contour lines.

       D. <u>The Horizontal Equivalent and the Vertical Inter-</u>
<u>val.</u> The concepts of the horizontal equivalent and the ver-
tical interval are two concepts which are often not clear to
the children in the lower grades. One simple way of making
these concepts clear is to use a simple wooden model. The
skeleton of the model is made of wood, i.e., AB, BC, CD,
ED, EF, EG, GF, FD, AG. The contour lines are colored
thread stretched and pinned to the wooden skeleton. The
different heights are marked on the central beam EF. This
model is placed on a big sheet of paper. On this piece of
paper the points A, C, D, F, and G are marked. The
points N, O, P, Q, R, S, and the corresponding points on
the other side of the model are also marked. After this
has been completed, the respective points on the paper are
joined. The result is a contour drawing of that model.

      The children are asked, in particular, to note the dis-
tances between the contour lines on the slopes of the model
and the corresponding distances on the contour drawing.
They are asked to measure these distances on the slope and
on the contour drawing. They will then come to the conclusion that there is a difference in lengths. The distance on
the contour drawing is the "horizontal equivalent." Referring
to the model, it could also be explained that FP or XZ is
the horizontal equivalent of EZ. The teacher should relate
the concept of the horizontal equivalent with the concept of
the landscape squashed down. This will help to explain the
discrepancy in lengths.

      The teacher also points out that EX is the vertical in-
terval between the 300 ft. and 400 ft. contour lines. The
other vertical intervals are simply shown on the vertical
beam EF. The children are, therefore, led to associate the
differences in height between contour lines with "vertical"
height.

      The children can be organized in groups. The dif-
ferent groups are given the tasks of identifying the vertical
intervals and horizontal equivalents on the wooden model
and contour drawing. They are also asked to draw diagrams of the model and the contour drawing in the exercise
books.

OTHER METHODS IN THE TEACHING OF
CONTOURS

Besides the methods that have been explained in some detail, there are other methods that could be used to teach contours. They are:

1. **Sectioned Model Method.** A model made of wood or of any other materials is sliced into pieces of equal height. The slices are assembled to form a model. At the points where the model is cut, lines are drawn to represent contour lines. The outline of each successive piece is drawn on a piece of paper. The outcome is a series of contour lines drawn on the piece of paper. This drawing is then compared with the model.

2. **Locus Tracing Method.** The retort stand with the sharp instrument is moved around the model with the sharp instrument in contact with the model. The level of the clamp is varied to draw other contour lines. This method is useful because it explains why valleys and spurs are represented by certain contour patterns. For the valleys, the sharp instrument is pushed inward to come into contact with areas of equal height. It also shows clearly the concept that contour lines are lines joining places of equal height.

3. **Layered Method.** The teacher first has a simplified contour drawing. Pieces of cardboard are cut out corresponding to the outline of each contour line. These pieces of cardboard representing the different contour lines are then piled up to form a model of the contour drawing. The comparison of the resulting model and the contour drawing will help the students see the relationship of the two-dimensional and the three-dimensional.

4. **Interpolation of Contour Lines Between Spot Heights.** Pupils are given exercises with spot heights. They are taught how to interpolate certain chosen heights. These chosen interpolated heights are subsequently joined to form contour lines. This brings out clearly that contour lines are boundaries between "regions" at different levels.

5. **Field Work Method.** A suitable cleared sloping ground is chosen. Children are asked to put pegs on the ground marking spots of equal height above an observation point. From this observation point, the leader will guide and correct his classmates so that they place the pegs at

the right places. Pegs representing a certain height are
joined by a rope or a line of white chalk. This method
has the advantage of associating contour lines with practical
field work.

Finally, other methods using aerial photographs and
sand trays are also used to advantage to help the pupils
understand the meaning of contours.

CONCLUSION

An attempt has been made to identify and analyze
some of the difficult concepts in the teaching of contours.
Suggestions have also been offered as to how these difficulties may be overcome. Some of the more useful methods have been explained in detail.

Very little, however, has been said about the develop-
mental-psychological problems involved in the teaching of this
topic. Research needs to be done to throw more light on the
levels of difficulty of the different concepts that can be taught
to children at different grade levels. As we learn more a-
bout these problems, contour exercises designed to teach certain concepts can be graded to suit the pupils of different
ages and stages of intellectual development.

NOTES

1. R. Hartshorne, Perspective on the Nature of Geography
   (Chicago: Rand McNally, 1959). G. Taylor, Geography in the Twentieth Century (Toronto: Methuen,
   1953).
2. F. Debenham, The Use of Geography (London: English
   Universities Press, 1950).

BIBLIOGRAPHY

Briault, E. W. H., and Shave, D. W. Geography In and Out
    of School. London: George C. Harrap, 1960.
Clarke, J. D., Practical Geography for the Primary School.
    London: Macmillan, 1953.
Garnett, O. Fundamentals in School Geography. London:
    George G. Harrap, 1949.

Gopsil, G. H. The Teaching of Geography. London: Macmillan, 1962.

Incorporated Association of Assistant Masters in Secondary Schools. The Teaching of Geography in Secondary Schools. London: George Philip, 1958.

Long, M. , and Roberson, B. S. Teaching Geography. London: Heinemann Educational Books, 1966.

Thralls, Z. A. The Teaching of Geography. New York: Appleton-Century-Crofts, 1958.

Walker, J. Aspects of Geography Teaching in School. London: Oliver & Boyd, 1963.

WHAT IS A MAP?*

Paul D. McDermott

What is a "map"? This simple question can evoke
many answers. These will differ according to one's past
experiences with maps--especially the type and amount of
use that has been made of them. In this article the following topics are discussed in order to provide an answer:
(1) the definition and analysis of the word "map," (2) map
classification, (3) types of maps, with an emphasis on
topographic, nautical, aeronautical, and road maps, (4) map
value and uses, and (5) future demands for maps.

THE MAP DEFINED AND EXPLAINED

The word "map" is derived from the Latin mappa,
signifying a "napkin or cloth (on which maps were painted)."
In turn, the term mappa can be traced back to ancient
Carthage where it meant "signal cloth."[1]

Today a well-known definition of a "map" is "a representation usually on a flat surface of the whole or part of
an area."[2] Although this is a reasonable definition, it is
lacking in its ability to describe the reality of the product.
It fails to indicate that a map is an abbreviated representation of the earth's reality. Furthermore the definition does
not indicate that the representation is based upon the use of
abstract symbols which vary in form, size, or color from
the real objects they portray. Therefore a more appropriate
definition of the word would be: a map is an abstract, abbreviated representation of a part or whole of an area, usually the earth's surface.

*Reprinted by permission from The Journal of Geography,
vol. 68, no. 8 (1969), 465-472.

Why is the map an abbreviated abstraction of the real earth? In order to function as an effective communication tool, the map must represent a large unit of the earth's surface upon a manageable sheet of material, usually paper. In transferring information from the earth to the map, an attempt is made to preserve four important properties: (1) true distance, (2) true shape, (3) true area, and (4) true direction. One of the problems the cartographer faces is that no singular map projection can possess all four of these properties at the same time.[3] Therefore, the map projection and the map scale chosen should be the ones that best preserve reality while, at the same time, they suit the purpose for which the map was designed.

Since the area being mapped contains a mixture of natural and/or cultural features of varying size and importance, the process of representing these features on the map becomes highly selective.[4] Only those features that are the most significant are used. Because of the vast reduction in size that takes place, abstract symbols are chosen and many details are lost in the process of representing natural and cultural features on the map. For instance, settlements (e. g., cities and towns are shown on smaller-scale maps via squares, dots, and spheres bearing little visual resemblance to the objects they represent). Rivers and coastlines lose some of their intricate idiosyncrasies. Land masses (e. g., continents and islands) often change in shape or area. Therefore, the map becomes an abbreviated abstraction of the earth's reality.

MAP CLASSIFICATION

Normally, maps are classified according to their scale and content.[5] As far as scale is concerned, there are three broad categories of maps: large-scale, medium-scale, and small-scale maps.[6] However, the primary method of classifying maps is by content. Using this method, maps fall into two basic categories: general and special purpose maps. In the former grouping, the maps contain symbols representing various types of physical and cultural features, none of which are purposely planned to dominate the graphic. The special purpose maps differ significantly. Their content and design reflects a specific theme or subject (e. g., land-use maps) or fulfills a function (e. g., navigation). Only information pertinent to the theme or function is shown; all else is subdued or eliminated. One important

type of special purpose map is the thematic map, which
deals with only one factor. Statistical maps, cartograms
(or diagrammatic maps), and qualitative maps such as those
concerned with geology or vegetation are all examples of
thematic maps. [7]

TYPES OF MAPS

There are many different types of maps. These vary
from topographic, atlas, and geologic maps to highway and
city maps, just to mention a few. [8] The types that follow
are some of the most commonly encountered and have considerable value in the classroom, if used correctly. One
of the purposes for using them as examples here is to reveal how content varies from one map to the other. Other
purposes are to provide information about the maps produced by various agencies and to explain how they can be
obtained by the general public.

Topographic Maps

The topographic map is a good example of a general
purpose map. Although it presents general natural and cultural features, the topographic map is distinguished by its
portrayal of the shape and elevation of the terrain. Various
methods are used to represent this terrain. However, the
most common method (and the most accurate) is by contour
lines. In the United States topographic maps are largely
compiled and published by the United States Geological Survey (USGS). [9] Frequently, they are produced by the Survey
in conjunction with other federal or state agencies concerned
with geologic or topographic mapping. These agencies help
to gather and check information as well as provide revenue
for the development of the maps--a significant help, indeed!

Today one of the major functions of the USGS is the
production of a series of topographic maps which will eventually cover the entire United States at selected standard
scales. [10] Two of the most common maps series published
are the 7 1/2-minute and 15-minute series at scales of
1:24,000 and 1:62,500 respectively. [11] A section of a 1:
24,000-scale map is illustrated in Figure 1. Both series
use the same basic type of symbols with natural features
portrayed in blue (hydrography), brown (terrain), and green
(vegetation), and cultural features in black or red.

At present, the USGS has been able to publish topographic coverage for approximately 72 percent of the United States at scales of 1:62,500 or 1:63,360 (Alaska only) and about 37 percent of this same area at a scale of 1:24,000. [12] In recent years the average topographic mapping cost for the 7 1/2-minute series has ranged from $175 to $350 per square mile, depending on such factors as terrain and population density. [13] Unfortunately, some of this coverage is outdated, especially in urban areas where changes are taking place at a very rapid pace. [14]

Nautical and Aeronautical Charts

The word "chart," originally derived from the Greek chartos meaning "leaf of paper," is commonly defined as a "map used for navigation in air or in water." [15] The nautical chart is one example of this type of product; the other being the aeronautical chart. In either case, information printed on charts is selected on the basis of simplifying navigation as much as possible. Hence, they serve a special purpose. In most instances, charts are continually updated or revised as additional navigational information is accumulated.

Nautical charts contain a wide variety of information valuable to navigators. Such features are stressed as the depth of water; port facilities for handling cargo, passenger freight, and repairing ships; and the location of channels. [16] In the United States nautical charts are produced by both federal and state agencies along with local organizations. However, the primary authority for the production of nautical charts of the coasts of the United States and its possessions is the United States Coast and Geodetic Survey. Charts of foreign coasts are prepared by the United States Naval Oceanographic Office. Both agencies make their charts available to the general public at a nominal cost and the index maps for United States coastal waters are free. [17]

In the United States aeronautical charts are produced chiefly by the Aeronautical Chart and Information Center (ACIC) in St. Louis, Missouri. Because of their special use certain features are emphasized on these small-scale charts such as the elevations of mountain peaks, the outlines of lakes and cities, landmarks, and landing fields. Relief is represented usually by bright colors. However, most of the maps are sold and distributed to the public through the United States Coast and Geodetic Survey. [18]

The Road Map

The most popular special purpose map in the United States is the familiar road map. Its main purpose is to help motorists to locate places. Therefore, it emphasizes road types and systems as well as the cities, towns, and villages that link them together. The typical road map also shows the location of important terrain and hydrographic features, airports, buildings, and special points of interest. However, in varying degrees, this information is considered subordinate to the road detail and is, therefore, subdued either by the use of less intense colors or a reduction in symbol size. The amount of de-emphasis is usually determined by the significance of the information for road use.

Two hundred and fifty million copies of road maps are published and distributed to the public each year.[19] The majority of these are published for the oil companies by three major concerns: Rand McNally & Company, H. M. Gousha Company, and General Drafting Company, Inc.[20] While the total cost of these maps to the public is nil, the cost to the sponsoring oil corporations is 18 million dollars a year (at a rate of five cents to fifteen cents per map).[21]

As the cost of providing road maps has increased, oil corporations have sought various means to reduce or eliminate this expense. In fact, one corporation tried to initiate a distribution program by selling the maps through vending machines. To their dismay, the public not only rejected the idea, but the company's products as well! The machines were removed promptly.[22] Another means used to reduce expenses has been to include advertisements on the road maps.

THE VALUE OF THE MAP AND
ITS MANY USES

Each year millions of maps are published and distributed throughout the world. One of the most common uses of maps is to locate places. Atlas and road maps are good examples designed for this purpose.

Topographic maps can also be used for a variety of purposes. They are employed by serious outdoorsmen as a guide for hunting and fishing expeditions. They are also used as base maps for plotting land uses, geologic structures, historic sites, and scenic attractions. The quadrangles are suitable for supplementing the teaching of map reading in elementary and secondary school classrooms. They can also serve as the basis for exercises in map interpretation in either physical geography or geology. [23]

Many maps are designed to be used as tools to translate into visual form the verbal results obtained from various fields such as planning, teaching, research, and exploration. The information on these maps is designed to be more rapidly assimilated in a shorter period of time than verbal material which must be consumed in a sequential and longer process. Much of the information portrayed by maps generally makes a greater impression upon the reader and is usually retained for a greater length of time than verbal material. [24] However, maps can achieve these values only if the persons using them can read and understand them.

In teaching, maps have considerable value in that they can be used to fulfill a variety of roles: as motivation devices to create interest in a subject or concept, as tools for testing purposes, as sources for geographic information and as vehicles for transmitting primary and secondary information. [25]

As tools for transmitting basic concepts in geography classes, maps possess many uses. They are helpful in enabling students to perceive distribution patterns of various geographical elements on the earth's surface (e.g., as tools in drawing conclusions about the type and degree of spatial relationships between geographical elements.

Road maps can be used to reveal important clusters of population and to study relationships between these clusters and physical features such as rivers, mountains, and plains. In addition, by using road maps of the same area but published in different years, it is possible to examine changes that have occurred in the highway systems, place names, and settlement patterns. Questions could be asked of the students such as: Why have these changes occurred? What factors have accounted for them?

FUTURE DEMANDS FOR MAPS

As the population of the world is increasing and a greater pressure is being placed upon the earth's land and water resources, there is an increasing demand for more

and better maps. There is also a rising need for more cartographers. Concurrently, the number of people using maps
today is greater than ever before.

In order to provide the requisites for man's existence,
more definitive information has to be acquired about: the
location and availability of resources in terms of their type,
quantity, and quality; the intricate character of the earth's
surface including geological structures, surface structures,
and hydrography; and present and potential land uses. 26 Unfortunately, mapping programs, which provide the basis for
a considerable proportion of this information, have thus far
proved unable to meet demands; and as long as a significant
portion of the world remains unmapped at scales larger than
1:250, 000, they will be unable to do so. 27

Since there is a growing need to be able to read and
understand maps, it is hoped that steps will be taken, especially in the United States, to assure that all students are
given a sufficient exposure to them. It is also hoped that
they will learn to comprehend and appreciate more the role
and value of the map in today's world. 28 Perhaps, then,
cartographers will be provided with the personnel needed to
adequately map the world and to obtain the data necessary to
solve some of its complex problems.

NOTES

1. David Greenhood, Mapping (Chicago: University of Chicago Press, 1964), xi.
2. Webster's Seventh New Collegiate Dictionary (Springfield,
   Mass.: G. & C. Merriam, 1967), 516.
3. Greenhood, op. cit., 114. The nature, employment,
   and construction of map projections are discussed in
   full detail in the following basic cartography text by
   Arthur H. Robinson, Elements of Cartography (2nd
   ed. ; New York: John Wiley, 1960), 50-120.
4. Natural features refer to those that are physical in nature (e. g., terrain, rivers, lakes); cultural features
   to those that are man-made (e. g., cities, roads).
5. Erwin Raisz, Principles of Cartography (New York:
   McGraw-Hill, 1962), 9. For a detailed classification
   of maps, see pp. 9, 10.
6. Raisz, op. cit., 32. Large-scale maps are concerned
   with representing a small area of the earth's surface,
   usually with a great amount of detail. Their scale is

larger than 4 miles to the inch. City maps are one
example. Medium-scale maps are concerned with a
greater area of the earth's surface. Their scale
ranges from 4-16 miles to the inch. An auto road
map is one example. Small-scale maps portray a
relatively greater amount of the earth with lesser
detail than the other two types. Their scale is
smaller than 16 miles to the inch. Many atlas maps
are small-scale maps. Classification, according to
map scale, is somewhat of a subjective process, in
that authorities frequently disagree on the specific
scale ranges for the three categories of maps (large,
medium, and small-scale).

7. Ibid., p. 10.
8. For a more complete list of map types, see Erwin
    Raisz, Principles of Cartography, op. cit., 9, 10.
9. U. S. Dept of the Interior, Geological Survey. Topo-
    graphic Maps (folder distributed by Geological Survey;
    no date), 1, 8.
10. U. S. Dept. of the Interior, Geological Survey. U. S.
    Geological Survey (brochure; Washington, D. C. : U. S.
    Government Printing Office, 1964), 4.
11. U. S. Dept. of the Interior, Geological Survey, Topo-
    graphic Maps, op. cit., 7. A 7 1/2-minute series
    is a group of maps where each map possesses a
    quadrangle area bounded by 7 1/2 minutes of longi-
    tude and 7 1/2 minutes of latitude; in a 15-minute
    series each map would contain 15 minutes of longitude
    and 15 minutes of latitude. On a scale of 1:24, 000,
    one inch on the map represents 2, 000 feet on the
    ground and on a 1:62, 500-scale map, one inch repre-
    sents nearly one mile. Topographic maps also avail-
    able include a series at scales of 1:250, 000 (one inch
    represents nearly four miles) and 1:1, 000, 000 (one
    inch represents nearly 16 miles). However, the
    amount of detail portrayed is reduced in the smaller-
    scale representations.
12. Letter from R. H. Lyddan, Chief Topographic Engineer,
    Geological Survey, U. S. Dept. of the Interior, Wash-
    ington, D. C., July 10, 1969.
13. Ibid. Cost includes publication of maps.
14. Ibid. If one considers only those maps published during
    the last ten years, 35 percent of the U. S. is covered
    at a scale of 1:24, 000 and 8 percent of the scales of
    1:62, 500 or 1:63, 360. The average length of time to
    complete a 1:24, 000-scale quadrangle in its published
    form is about four years.

15. Raisz, op. cit., 293. This is only one use of the word.
    It can also be used to describe large layouts and
    maps dealing with one subject.
16. U. S. Army Map Service, Map Intelligence, AMS Train-
    ing Aid No. 6 (2nd ed.; Washington, D. C.: U. S.
    Government Printing Office, 1954), p. 213.
17. Nautical charts can be purchased from the Director,
    United States Coast and Geodetic Survey, Environ-
    mental Science Services Administration, Rockville,
    Maryland 20852. Hydrographic charts of foreign
    coasts are available to persons living west of the
    Mississippi River from the United States Naval Ocean-
    ographic Distribution Office, Clearfield, Utah 84016.
    For those living to the east of the river, send to
    Naval Oceanography Distribution Office, Naval Supply
    Depot, 5801 Tabor Avenue, Philadelphia, Pennsyl-
    vania 19120.
18. Some ACIC charts which can be purchased by the public
    from the Coast and Geodetic Survey are as follows:
    Global Navigation Charts at a 1:5, 000, 000 scale, Jet
    Navigation Charts at a 1:2, 000, 000 scale, Operation-
    al Navigation Charts (ONC) at a scale of 1:1, 000, 000,
    and the older World Aeronautical Charts (WAC) at
    the same scale. The latter are slowly being replaced
    by the ONC.
19. The New York Times, March 3, 1968, Sec. X, p. 9,
    col. 1.
20. Gwen M. Schultz, "New Developments in American Road
    Maps," Professional Geographer, XV (May 1963), 15.
    In 1963 state highway departments throughout the
    United States published approximately 18, 000, 000
    road maps.
21. The New York Times, loc. cit.
22. Ibid.
23. Information pertaining to USGS topographic map cover-
    age for each state can be obtained by writing for a
    free index map for that particular state to one of
    the following addresses: Washington Distribution
    Section, United States Geological Survey, 1200 South
    Eads Street, Arlington, Virginia 22202 or Distribu-
    tion Section, United States Geological Survey, Fed-
    eral Center, Denver, Colorado 80225. The state in-
    dex maps contain addresses of federal map distribu-
    tion centers, local map dealers, and libraries where
    collections of USGS maps are maintained for public
    reference. To purchase USGS topographic maps by
    mail, use the Virginia address listed above for maps

east of the Mississippi River and the Colorado one
for those to the west. For full information concerning maps published by the federal government, write
to the Map Information Office, United States Geological Survey, Washington, D. C. 20242. Some very
well illustrated and interesting workbooks on the application of maps in the elementary grades are written by Susan Marsh, Teaching About Maps Grade by
Grade (Darien, Conn.: Teachers Publishing Corporation, 1965). The workbooks progress from Grades
One to Six.

24. Raisz, op. cit., p. 1. For information pertaining to
basic geographic uses for maps, see William W.
Elam, et al., "Equipment, Materials, and Sources,"
A Handbook for Geography Teachers, ed. by Robert
E. Gabler (Geographic Education Series No. 6;
Normal, Ill.: National Council for Geographic Edu-
cation, 1966), p. 26.

25. Linnie B. James and La Monte Crape, Geography for
Today's Children (New York: Appleton-Century-
Crofts, Division of Meredith Corporation, 1968),
p. 98.

26. H. Arnold Karo, Maps as Requisites for Economic Development. A paper presented at the United Nations
Regional Cartographic Conference for Africa (July
1963), p. 1. Mr. Karo states that in 1949 the
United Nations "... could not proceed intelligently in
the solution of world problems when adequate information is lacking for three-fourths of its surface."
He further indicated that the statement was still
valid in 1963.

27. Arthur J. Brandenberger, "The Impact of Surveying and
Mapping on the National and International Economy,"
Papers of 34th Annual Meeting, American Society of
Photogrammetry (Falls Church, Va.: American
Society of Photogrammetry, 1968), p. 69. In a recent survey, it was revealed that only 35 percent of
the world's surface has been mapped at scales of
1:250,000, 15-20 percent at scales of 1:100,000 or
larger, and about 5 percent at scales of 1:25,000.

28. Arthur Robinson, "The Potential Contribution of Cartography in Liberal Education," The Cartographer
[now known as The Canadian Cartographer], II (May
1965), 3.

PSYCHOLOGICAL ASPECTS OF COLOR IN CARTOGRAPHY*

Arthur H. Robinson

INTRODUCTION

Of all the elements of map making, color probably has the distinction of being among the most frustrating to the cartographer. Just as the process of generalization requires the map maker to balance a variety of substantive aspects in his graphic communication, the selection of color calls for a similar weighing of psychological and mechanical aspects. These are very complex and, as yet, many of the variables are not completely known. These aspects are not only complicated by well established conventions in cartography, but they are frequently contradictory. Color in mapping is a subject that is and will remain controversial for a long time. In spite of its complexity it is much sought after. It is a rare cartographer, indeed, who would decline the opportunity to use color on a map, or if offered black and one color, would not ask for two.

Color on a map is worth all its costs and frustrations, as is evident from the widespread practice of hand-painting maps before the days of common color printing, in spite of the fact that hand painting was ordinarily very expensive and time consuming. Whether these earlier cartographers understood the fact as well as we do today is difficult to judge, but even a little color "added" to a map has remarkable consequences. It functions in several ways. Firstly, color is a great simplifying and clarifying element. By even sparing use of it one can markedly increase the number of "visual

*Reprinted by permission from International Yearbook of Cartography, vol. 7 (1967), 50-59. Published by the Bertelsmann Verlag/Kartographisches Institut Bertelsmann, Gütersloh.

levels" upon which the reader can focus. For example, one can easily limit his attention to all the green areas on a map, or to the complex of red boundaries, even though the map may be heavily loaded with lettering and line work in black. In similar fashion color acts as a unifying agent in the Gestalt structure of a communication. By brightness difference, and by its function toward producing closed forms and enhancing the similarity of areas, color markedly affects the ease with which a cartographer can develop that most important element of cartographic design, the figure-ground relationship.

A second reason why color is of extreme importance in cartography is that its use seems to have remarkable effects on the subjective reactions of the map reader. It is very difficult for most people, cartographers included, to separate clearly their rational thinking from their emotional reactions. Accordingly, everyone, upon looking at a colored map, usually instinctively likes it or dislikes it, quite apart from any understanding of what the map is supposed to be communicating. He may, quite unconsciously, associate the colors with bitter, frightening, or joyful experiences in his past, and the map may call up in his mind all sorts of reactions, gay or somber, handsome or ugly, boring or interesting.

Thirdly, the use of color has a marked effect in the general perceptibility of a map. In several ways the colors affect the legibility of the lettering used on the map, a very important element indeed. Furthermore, several aspects of color are significant factors in visual acuity, the ability of the observer to distinguish fine detail. Color is also often employed to define the limit separating disparate areas on maps, such as land and water or national territories, and the nature of the colors will have a noticeable effect on the clarity of the distinction as well as the degree of difference implied.

Quite apart from the psychological-perceptual complications which arise from introducing color in the design framework of a map, color is important simply because of the increased technical problems associated with its use, to say nothing of the financial. When color is involved registry problems are made more difficult, press time is increased, and quality control becomes a major factor. Nevertheless, color in cartography is eagerly sought after, and its use never fails to be an exciting experience for the cartographic designer.

DEFINITION OF TERMS

When one considers the various aspects of color it is
necessary always to pause at the beginning and define one's
terms. In map making and map reproduction there are many
aspects of inks and colors that have a profound effect on the
cartographic process. In this paper, however, I am restricting myself to the psychological aspects and accordingly I will
define only those terms having to do with the perception of
color.

Psychologically color is a sensory or perceptual reaction, received by way of the eye, to the physical stimuli
occasioned by various aspects of the small, visible portion
of the electromagnetic spectrum. There are three basic psychological dimensions of color. These are:

1. The reaction to the stimulus provided by a single wave
   length, or to mixtures of wave lengths, or to the absence of any wave lengths emanating from a colored
   area. This I shall call a reaction to hue. Thus red is
   a different hue than brown, and in the sense of this definition black and white are hues.

2. The reaction to the stimulus provided by the total amount
   of reflectance from a colored area, that is, its lightness
   as rated in relation to a standard scale of reflectances
   to the grey scale. This I shall call a reaction to value.
   White is high value, black low value, and a tone composed of 50% black and 50% white would be a middle
   value. Every colored area regardless of hue has a value
   rating that can be ascertained by comparing it with a
   grey scale.

3. The reaction to the stimulus provided by the degree of
   apparent saturation of a color area by some hue other
   than black or white compared to an area having the same
   value composed of only black and white, that is, grey.
   This, sometimes called chroma, saturation, or purity,
   I shall refer to as a reaction to intensity. Thus a bright
   red is more intense than that same red when mixed with
   a grey of the same value.

It is important to bear in mind that these dimensions
of color do not exist alone; every color area has its hue,
value and intensity.

These terms--hue, value, and intensity--are artist's
terms. The physicists, when working with light, use closely
analogous terms such as dominant wave length, percent reflectance of brightness, and saturation. The spectrophoto-
meter, graphs of reflectance plotted against wave length, and
tristimulus data are very useful for precise specification and
the management of data in research. But since, for cartographic purposes color, like beauty, is solely in the eye of
the beholder, it is more appropriate that we use terms that
depend upon the characteristics of sensation for their definition.

PSYCHOLOGICAL ASPECTS OF COLOR

Color surrounds us and everyone reacts to it both
consciously and unconsciously. Each individual, since his
infancy, has acquired and stored away in his subconscious
an incredible array of associations with color which show up
as likes and dislikes. Through repetition he has learned to
accept some uses of color as being "normal" or the "right
way of doing things, " and most cultures have developed and
perpetuated symbolic associations with color. Because color
is a physical stimulus, we respond to its dimensions with
physiologic-perceptual reactions. All these factors promote
complexity, and make the subject of the psychological aspects
of color in cartography a fascinating study.

In this paper I have tried to compile, from a variety
of courses, the more important of the perceptual aspects of
color and to list them in a logical structure. I have chosen
to arrange them according to the psychological dimensions of
color--hue, value, and intensity--under the following general
headings:

I.   Physiologically Based Perceptual Aspects of Color
II.   Connotative and Subjective Aspects of Color
III. Conventional Aspects of Color.

The first of these includes those ways in which the appreciation of hue, value, and intensity differences are affected by what seem primarily to be factors stemming from the
physiological mechanisms involved in perception. The second
recognizes that the intellect significantly modifies the elementary response to the physical stimuli of color. The third
takes into account the fact that since color is used as a symbol in cartography its use has become conventionalized in

many ways. Together they comprise the psychological aspects
which the designer must keep in mind when manipulating the
color elements of his cartographic communication.

The reader will note that there is no place in this outline for a consideration of the aesthetic aspects of color, such
as harmony. The aesthetic is not susceptible to objective
testing and analysis except on a group basis with some of the
recently devised psychophysical methods. In any case, the
preferences of an individual are his and any attempt to urge
them upon another is a form of missionary activity that seems
inappropriate in the scholarly-scientific context. This is not
to say that there is no place for color harmony in cartography; quite the opposite is the case. The harmonious and
tasteful use of color in a map can certainly lead to most
pleasing compositions, and such are greatly to be desired.
A recent publication on "Arts in Society" has observed that
the artist can be taught his craft, but not his art. He can
learn the characteristics of his materials, the objects and
tools with which he works, but he cannot be taught the talent
to create. So it is with the cartographer; he can be taught
his craft but his creativity as an artist must come from within himself. The psychological aspects of color in cartography
are elements based upon the more or less complete scientific
study of its dimensions, and they are important characteristics of one of his most versatile tools.

When the objective of a map is to communicate geographical data and concepts then the use of color, like the
use of line, must be based upon precepts and understandings
of how color affects communication. It is with that objective
in mind that I have compiled the following, admittedly incomplete, list. In most instances the application of the principles to cartography is self-evident and I shall not spell it
out except when not to do so might lead to misunderstanding.

When considering many of these particular reactions
to hue, value, or intensity it is difficult to discuss them separately because each color inherently always has all three
dimensions. One ordinarily would introduce each precept or
principle with caeteris paribus. But this is cumbersome and
the reader is requested to add it himself whenever a comparison is made. For example, if I observe that, in general,
brown is a poorer defining hue than green the reader must
assume that the brown and the green are of the same value
and intensity.

IA. Physiologically Based Perceptual Aspects of Hue

      1. Sensitivity. The human animal is not very sensi-
tive to hues in several respects. For example, it is easy
enough for an ordinary person to recognize a difference in
hue when two are side by side, but his ability to recall hues
upon demand, such as from a legend to the body of a map or
to conjure up a precise mental image of bistre or beige, is
apparently quite limited. Sensitivity appears to improve markedly with training, but unfortunately there is little room made
for such training in today's schools. The relative insensi-
tivity of man to differences among hues is both absolute and
relative:

    a) In absolute sensitivity, man is not very sensitive.
        What sensitivity he does have varied with area,
        that is, the smaller the area the more difficult
        it is to distinguish the hue.

    b) In relative terms man seems to react faster and
        to a greater degree to some hues than to others.
        Man appears to be most sensitive to red followed
        in order by green, yellow, blue, and purple. Un-
        fortunately there is, I believe, no data which tell
        us how they compare within the ranking.

      2. Advance and Retreat. Because light, when pass-
ing through a transparent medium, is refracted in inverse
relation to its wave length, when entering the eye red is refracted the least and blue the most. This chromatic aberration has the effect of causing the eye to bring red to a focus
nearer the lens than it does blue. When seen side by side
red sometimes appears "above" or "closer" and the blue "below" or "farther" in relation to one another. Chromatic
aberration is apparently not the only factor involved. In any
case, the effect is generally weak, is by no means universal,
and it appears largely to occur when the hues are side by
side. On occasion the effect can be very startling. Its utility in hypsometric representation seems to have been more
theoretical than practical.

      3. Acuity or Definition. Hue seems to have a notice-
able effect upon the ability of a reader to distinguish fine detail. For the lack of a better term I use "acuity" although
the recognition of fine cartographic detail is of a different
order than the usual discrimination threshold employed for
the technical term "visual acuity." At any rate, hue affects
the map reader's perception in three important operations:
(a) when he is attempting to follow a colored line, (b) when

he is reading linear elements against a colored background, and (c) when he is perceiving the line formed by different colors being placed on either side of an edge such as a coastline or a boundary. Monochromatic light is superior to polychromatic for definition. Therefore, by extension, hues that combine fewer wave lengths should be superior to those that combine more. For example, a brown, which combines many wave lengths, would not be as efficient a color for line or background as would a pure green. Among the monochromatic hues yellow stands at the top as a defining color and blue at the bottom. I know of no statement of the magnitude of the range between the two, but I am sure that many map readers have had trouble following coastlines printed in blue or which were edged by a blue ocean.

4. Simultaneous Contrast. Hues adjacent to one another are modified by the eye from their appearances when separate. The effects are quite varied and their origin is complex. In cartography it is most noticeable when the reader is required to match colors from the legend to a map or from one part of the map to another. The general rule is that discrimination of matching hues is reduced by variations in background or surroundings.

IB. Physiologically Based Perceptual Aspects of Value

1. Sensitivity. As is the case with hue the human eye is not very sensitive to value differences. Because of simultaneous contrast effects even the discrimination of values side by side is difficult.
   a) In absolute terms the average untrained eye can apparently distinguish, that is recognize, from six to eight value steps from the highest (white) to the lowest (black). The discrimination is even less when one is limited by a hue that does not have a very large value range; yellow is an extreme example.
   b) In relative terms sensitivity to value appears to be greater in the middle range than near the extremes. In other words, if this be true, then for equal discrimination one should provide a greater value difference near the dark or light ends of the value scale.

2. Simultaneous Contrast. This psychological-percep-

tual phenomenon is as significant in connection with value as
it is with hue. Without hue the effect is commonly called in-
duction, a remarkable response of the eye and mind to adjacent areas of different value wherein the contrast between
the areas is enhanced. The lower value appears even darker
and the higher even lighter. (The phenomenon is greatly
lessened or disappears when separation occurs by way of an
extreme value such as a black or white line.) The importance
of this phenomenon in the design of maps of graded series of
geographical phenomena, such as temperature, is obvious.

3. Acuity or definition. The effect of value contrast
upon the ability of the eye and the mind to distinguish, perceive, or read cartographic detail is probably the single most
important element in cartographic design, when the objective
is to communicate. Two aspects seem important:
- a) The basic precept is that the greater the value
  contrast the greater the definition and, accordingly, the greater the perceptibility and legibility.
  (There seems no doubt that this relationship is
  far more important from a communicative point
  of view than is hue contrast.)
- b) Because of some complex visual reactions, such
  as "halation," which are not well understood,
  dark line on a light ground may be better defined
  than the reverse.

IC. Physiologically Based Aspects of Intensity

1. Sensitivity. Man's reaction to differences in intensity, like his response to differences in value or hue, is
apparently not strong, and there is some evidence that his
discrimination with respect to intensity is relatively less than
with either hue or value. At least two very minor complications may be observed:
- a) The more extreme the value the less the discrimination of intensity.
- b) As one proceeds toward the extreme of the visible
  portion of the spectrum the discrimination of intensity differences decreases.

2. Variation with Size. The larger the area of a
given hue the more intense it will appear, as many amateur
painters of home walls and colorers of maps have learned to
their sorrow. Many a color which looked good in a small
chip or in a tiny legend box becomes brilliant and intense
when used to cover a larger area. The complications this
can provide for the map reader are apparent.

IIA.   Connotative and Subjective Aspects of Hue

     1.   Preference for Hues. It is a rare person indeed
who does not have his unique set of preferences for the various dimensions of color. In spite of this individuality there
seem to be group preferences as well. For example, given
an unbiased test a majority of persons in the western culture
would probably rank hues on a scale of "pleasingness" with
blue first, red next, then several with no clear rank, and
then would place yellow at the bottom. Although precise data
are lacking, so far as I know, it appears reasonable to expect that yellow would rank high in the oriental culture areas
since that hue is widely employed there. It is very likely
that there are many refinements that could be made of these
very gross assertions, but to my knowledge there is little or
no data available as yet.

     2.   Symbolic Connotations. There seems to be an al-
most unlimited number of symbolic connotations with respect
to color, largely in connection with hue. Some of these may
seem far removed from cartography, yet they may partially
account for the conventional employment of hues in cartography. Furthermore, disregard of them may well produce a
cartographic composition that is inherently unpleasant or, conversely, one conceivably might wish to employ colors to that
end. These aspects of hue are not easy to catalog because
many are emotional or rooted in cultural experience. There
are a variety:

    a)   Hue is closely associated with moods and feelings.
        I am not familiar with this phenomenon in other
        language areas but in English language and culture
        there are many examples such as, in the pink,
        see red, feel blue, brown study, blue Monday, red-
        letter day, black Friday, and so on. I assume
        other language areas and culture groups have sim-
        ilar associations.
    b)   In the world of art, hues bear a connotation of tem-
        perature. Thus there are warm and cool hues and
        they seem almost to be instinctive. Thus the reds,
        yellows, and oranges are warm like sunlight, blood,
        fire, etc. , while the blues and greens are the cool
        colors of ice, snow, shadow, twilight, etc. Their
        employment in cartography in dealing with land-
        scape, the light and darks of terrain representation,
        the geographical variations associated with latitude,
        elevation, ocean currents, etc. , seems obvious

even to the neophyte.

c) In Gestalt psychology colors have "dimension" and thus, for example, yellow is "large, " black is "small, " and green is "fresh" and "soft. " Polychromatic magazine advertising, at least in America, has adopted this aspect of hue as well as the other symbolic reactions mentioned above and their uses of them are made with careful calculation. For example, I have no recollection of ever seeing an advertisement for a menthol cigarette that was not largely done in green and white. (The white is no doubt for the purpose of connoting purity!)

3. Individuality. One of the curious phenomena regarding hue is the fact that some hues appear to the observer as mechanical mixtures of other hues, retaining some of the identity of the apparent components, while some appear to be pure, that is, not mixtures. For example, neither red nor yellow looks to have another hue involved, but orange looks like red and yellow put together, just as violet looks like a mixture of red and blue, and gray like a mixture of black and white. The individual appearing hues are blue, green, yellow, red, brown, white, and black.

IIB. Connotative and Subjective Aspects of Value

1. Implication of Magnitude. The assignment of magnitudes to relative values seems to be a generally accepted practice.

a) The basic precept is: the darker or lower the value the greater the magnitude. Thus in a graded series high value is assigned the least numerical magnitude and vice versa. Of course one may become involved in difficulties when the relations are complementary; for example high literacy is the same as low illiteracy.

b) A secondary precept is: the darker or lower the value the more unfavorable. Thus to use the example above, if one were expressing grades of illiteracy by a value series one would normally assign the lower values to the higher magnitude of illiteracy.

2. Dominance of Extremes. It is generally acknowledged that in graphic compositions the extreme values dominate the viewer or reader. This precept is, of course,

complicated by the many other perceptual responses, especially by the figure-ground phenomenon. Thus, white is an
extreme value, yet when it is the paper that is the ground
upon which a figure is clearly apparent, then that extreme
value subsides and does not dominate. If we discount that
obvious example wherein an extreme does not dominate because it is not really a part of the composition, then in
other instances I think the phenomenon of the dominance of
extremes is a common experience. A black or dark blue
ocean on an otherwise line and white map or the area of
heavy precipitation on a rainfall map are common examples.

IIC.   Connotative and Subjective Aspects of Intensity

        1. Implication of Magnitude. As is the case in con-
nection with the dimension of value there seems to be an
assignment of magnitudes to relative intensities. The basic
precept is: the more intense the color the greater the magnitude. Needless to say, variations in intensity are usually
accompanied by concomitant variations in value, and of the
two the implication of magnitude associated with value is
probably much the stronger, although I know of no actual
tests.

        2. Age Relationship. Although it is not well docu-
mented there seems to be a relation between intensity and
age in that the young prefer more intense colors than the
more mature. Bright colors and gaudiness are commonly
associated with immaturity and lack of sophistication.

IIIA.   Conventional Aspects of Hue

        1. Hypsometric Representation. Early in this century
the convention of representing successively higher elevations
more or less according to the progression of wave lengths
in the spectrum became established. Following the work of
Karl Peucker, this occurred largely by reason of the action
of the committee charged with the design of the International
Map and the use by commercial organizations thereafter of
its "international" character.

        2. Blue Water. This is a very old and very strong
convention readily accepted by most map readers.

        3. Connotative Hues. There are a number of conven-
tional uses of hues to suggest qualities and elements of physical and economic geography. Some of these are:

a) Red is associated with warm and blue with cool temperatures, such as in the representation of climates or ocean currents.
b) Yellow and tan are associated with dryness and paucity of vegetation.
c) Brown is associated with the land surface as in the representation of uplands or contours.
d) Green is associated with lush or thick vegetation as opposed to sparse vegetation. Thus true forests would be green and shrubland would be tan.
e) On maps showing positive and negative values red usually represents positive and blue negative.

4. Denotative Hues. There is one well established color scheme in which the hues, by convention, signify a particular phase of the data. I refer to the scheme for geological maps wherein the rocks of various periods are given distinctive hues, as established in 1881 at the Geological Congress at Bologna.

IIIB. Conventional Aspects of Value

1. Magnitude Representations. Generally the convention follows the connotative and subjective precept of the darker the more. It is used this way in all aspects of geography for representation by magnitude classes of everything from precipitation to population density. In one element of physical geography a conflicting view arose during the past century and has apparently never been resolved one way or another. I refer to the proposals to represent hypsometric classes on relief maps, in the one instance by "the higher the darker," and in the other, "the higher the lighter."

IIIC. Conventional Aspects of Intensity

1. Magnitude Representation. Although not nearly so marked as it is in connection with the dimension of value, intensity is usually graded the same way, namely the greater the magnitude the more intense the color.

GENERAL CONCLUSIONS

The study of the various ways in which the use of color in cartography is affected by the psychological elements of its physiologic-perceptive aspects, its connotative and subjective aspects, and its conventional aspects is obviously

extremely complicated. Indeed, it is because of these very
psychological aspects that it is unlikely that the cartographer
will ever be able to approach his design exercise in a purely
technical fashion. Because the "map reader" for whom we
design, both individually and collectively, is an incredible
mixture of perceptual complications there will always be that
more sensitive cartographic designer who can erect a design
structure that is more appropriate than that of other designers. That designer is blessed with "taste," "understanding,"
"talent," or whatever one wishes to call it; he has the cartographic equivalent of the ability of the truly great communicative artists in other fields, be it speaker, writer, painter,
or what you will. Cartography, as Max Eckert observed fifty
years ago, is both an art and a science and good cartography
will continue to be that mixture.

But being in part an art does not mean that it is impossible for the average cartographer to learn his craft. He
may never reach the stature of a cartographic artist of first
rank, but he can surely design his maps so that they are
thoroughly acceptable graphic communications. He can best
do this by understanding the perceptual complications involved
in the use of his graphic media. For this he needs the results of research in cartographic perception. It is with the
hope that more of this kind of basic research will be undertaken that this tentative outline of the psychological aspects
of color in cartography has been compiled. The reader will
note that many of the psychological characteristics lead to
precepts which are not solidly based since the assertions lack
the desirable authority provided by experimental evidence.
Nevertheless, they do provide some assistance in the complicated area of color use in cartography.

From them we may distill several important generalizations that are helpful in the general approach to cartographic design.

1. The psychological reactions to the various dimensions of
    color are quite varied and are, by no means, on a par
    with one another. We can recognize three of fundamental
    significance.
    a) We find hue to be perceptually the most interesting,
        by far. We love to talk about it, everyone con-
        siders himself an expert, and it leads to a variety
        of conventions and is generally controversial.
        Therefore, the cartographer must put his greatest
        "creative" effort in the design process on matters
        of hue.

b) We find value to be much the most important in
terms of fundamental perceptual behavior of the
map reader, ranging from his reactions to figure-
ground to simple legibility. Value is basic to the
recognition of form. If the whole world were color-
blind, that is hue blind, we would find it no real
handicap in cartography. The contrast provided by
value differences should have the highest priority
in cartographic design.

c) Intensity is the least significant of the psychological
dimensions of color.

2. There exist a variety of kinds of responses to color:
physiological--perceptual, connotative--subjective, and
conventional, and these lead to basic conflicts and problems. For example: there is a complete disregard for
the importance of value contrast to legibility in the "international" spectral progression of hues with elevation
classes; if blue connotes cold and yellow connotes dry
what hue can we employ for a cold desert? Conventionally, green is used for lowland and green suggests fer-
tility, but what then do we do with a barren lowland or a
fertile upland? The existence of contradictory precepts
is not unusual and certainly not in cartography. One can
only proceed with "good judgement" when faced with the
conflict, as Professor Imhof so clearly pointed out in
connection with the parallel circumstances that arise when
one is carefully positioning the lettering on a map.

3. An understanding of the complexity of our perceptual response to color and of the variety of ways we need to
use color in cartography leads one to be wary of establishing additional conventions for the use of color in cartography. It is improbable that we will ever be able to
rid ourselves of the ones we already have. To para-
phrase Keates slightly: green is likely to spring eternal
on our cartographic lowlands, be they Midlothian or Sa-
haran, to the confusion of all those innocent map readers
who have not learned that in cartography we use color
abstractly.

SELECTED BIBLIOGRAPHY

1. Arnheim, Rudolf. Art and Visual Perception. Berkeley: University of California Press, 1954.
2. Bevan, W. and W. F. Dukes. "Color As a Variable in

the Judgment of Size," American Journal of Psychology, 66 (1953), 285-288.

3. Birren, Faber. The Story of Color. Westport, Conn.: The Crimson Press, 1941.

4. Birren, Faber. Color, Form and Space. New York: Reinhold Pub. Co., 1961.

5. Brueckner, Eduard and Arthur. "Zur Frage der Farbenplastik in der Kartographie," Mitt. der K. und K. Geographischen Gesellschaft (1909), 186-194.

6. Crewdson, Frederick M. Color in Decoration and Design. Wilmette, Ill.: F. J. Drake and Co., 1955.

7. Dorcas, Roy M. "Color Preferences and Color Associations," Journal of Genetic Psychology, 33 (1926).

8. Eckert, Max. Die Kartenwissenschaft, 2 vols. Berlin: Walter de Gruyter, 1921, 1925.

9. Edwards, A. S. "Effect of Color on Visual Depth Perception," Journal of General Psychology, 52 (1955), 331-333.

10. Evans, Ralph M. An Introduction to Color. New York: John Wiley, 1948.

11. Graves, Matiland. The Art of Color and Design. New York: McGraw-Hill, 1951.

12. Imhof, Eduard. Gelände und Karte. Erlenbach-Zürich: E. Rentsch, 1950.

13. Imhof, Eduard. Kartographische Geländedarstellung. Berlin: Walter de Gruyter, 1965 (large bibliography).

14. Kartographische Studien (Haack-Festschrift). Gotha: VEB Hermann Haack, 1957.

15. Keates, John S. "The Small-Scale Representation of the Landscape in Colour," International Yearbook of Cartography, 2 (1962), 76-84.

16. Keates, John S. "The Perception of Color in Cartography," Proceedings of the Cartographic Symposium, Edinburgh, 1962.

17. Luckiesh, M. Color and Its Applications. New York: D. Van Nostrand, 1915.

18. Luckiesh, Mathew. The Language of Color. New York: 1918.

19. Munsell, Albert H. A Color Notation, 10th ed. Baltimore: Munsell Color Company, 1946.

20. Ostwald, Wilhelm. Colour Science., 2 parts (trans. by J. Scott Taylor). London: 1933.

21. Robinson, Arthur H. The Look of Maps; An Examination of Cartographic Design. Madison: University of Wisconsin Press, 1952.

22. Sargent, Walter. The Enjoyment and Use of Color. New York: Dover Publications, 1964.

23. Thomas, Edwin N. "'Balanced' Colors in Use on the Multi-Color Dot Map, " The Professional Geographer, 7 (1955), 8-10.

24. Tobler, Waldo R. "An Empirical Evaluation of Some Aspects of Hypsometric Colors" (unpublished MA thesis, University of Washington, Seattle, 1957).

A CLASSIFICATION OF MAP PROJECTIONS*

Waldo R. Tobler[1]

The desire for a classification of map projections stems from the fact that an infinite number of distinct projections are possible. Hence, the fundamental problem in classifying map projections is the partitioning of this infinite set into a comprehensible and useful finite number of all-inclusive and preferably non-overlapping classes.

Several classifications of map projections are to be found in the cartographic literature. The advantages and disadvantages of each, of course, depend on the purpose, just as the properties by which classes are to be distinguished depend on the purpose. The classification based on geometric models (perspectivities) separating projections into conic, cylindric, planar, polyconic, polycylindric, etc., is convenient and is often used. The major shortcoming of this system is that it is not all-inclusive. Another most important method of classification, based on the preservation of certain geometric properties of the surface of the referent object, separates the conformal projections from the equal-area projections, leaving a third class which is neither. Preservation of additional properties yields further classes; e.g., geodesic maps (for the sphere there is the gnomonic projection and all linear transforms thereof), azimuthal projections, equidistant projections (including polar isometries such as the azimuthal equidistant), and many more. In fact, Felix Klein, the German mathematician, defined a geometry as the study of properties preserved by a particular group of transformations. From this point of view, a classification according to properties preserved is the very essence of geometry. Thus one has projective transformations and projective geometry, affine

---

*Reproduced by permission from the Annals of the Association of American Geographers, vol. 52, no. 2 (1962), 167-175.

transformations and affine geometry, Euclidean transformations and Euclidean geometry, continuous transformations and
topology, etc.

Still other classifications are based on the appearance
of the meridians and parallels on the map, i. e., whether
these consist of circles, ellipses, quartics, etc.[2] Projections can also be classified according to the form of the equations; whether these are linear, algebraic, transcendental,
and so forth. Maurer, in his study of map projections,[3] attempts to partition 237 projections into classes and subclasses
based on combinations of these systems. Several of the problems of projection classification are discussed by Maurer,
and a most interesting but very involved Venn diagram is
presented showing the overlap and interrelations of the various classes. Tissot is another who recognized fine distinc-
tions and obtained an elaborate classification of map projections.[4] More recently, classifications have been presented
by Lee[5] and by Goussinsky.[6]

A parametric classification is proposed here. This
system has the advantage of being intermediate in difficulty
and yet including all possible map projections. In addition to
the overview afforded, the parametric classification suggests
simple graphic methods which have been found useful in teaching the subject of map projections. The classification is
adapted to an orderly development of the subject and also indicates classes of projections, which, to the author's knowledge, have never before been employed or explicitly suggested.
The system is not radically new and does not invalidate the
many alternate methods of classifying map projections. The
ideas are developed for a sphere, but this is not essential.

A PARAMETRIC CLASSIFICATION

One general notion of a transformation of a two-dimensional surface, such as the surface of a sphere, is given by
a pair of equations of the form:
$$u = f_1(\phi, \lambda)$$
$$v = f_2(\phi, \lambda),$$
where u and v are coordinates used to describe the location
of positions on the transformed surface, ϕ and λ are coordinates used to describe the location of positions on the original
surface, and f_1 and f_2 are any functions whatever. In the
theory of map projections it is usually assumed that f_1 and
f_2 are real, single-valued, continuous, and differentiable
functions of ϕ and λ in some domain and that the Jacobian

determinant, $\quad J = \dfrac{\partial u}{\partial \phi} \dfrac{\partial v}{\partial \lambda} - \dfrac{\partial v}{\partial \phi} \dfrac{\partial u}{\partial \lambda}$,

does not vanish.[7] The $\underline{u}$ and $\underline{v}$ are to be interpreted as independent coordinates on a plane surface, and ϕ and λ are to be interpreted as geographical coordinates on a sphere. In practice the equations for a map projection are not always given in explicit form. There also are a few map projections whose construction is relatively simple, using graphic scaling and plotting techniques, but for which equations have never appeared in the literature.

The parametric classification is based on the fact that the equations for the location of lines of latitude and of longitude on the map in some cases depend on only one of these quantities. For example, in the cylindrical projections, the lines of longitude depend on longitude alone, $x = f(\lambda)$, and the lines of latitude depend only on latitude, $y = f(\phi)$. Here it is immediately apparent that the parametric classification tacitly assumes the normal case for each projection. It is convenient to require that the origin of the $\underline{u}$, $\underline{v}$ system coincides with the respective origin of the parametric curves of the surface of the sphere. Hence, when the ϕ, λ parameterization is used, the $\underline{u}$, $\underline{v}$ coordinates are to be interpreted as rectangular coordinates $(\underline{x}, \underline{y})$ in the plane. When the spherical coordinates ρ, λ are employed, the $\underline{u}$, $\underline{v}$ coordinates are to be considered polar coordinates (r, θ) in the plane. In the ensuing discussion, rectangular coordinates are used when the map is centered on the intersection of the equator and the prime meridian; polar coordinates are used when the map is centered on the north pole. When the map is not centered on either of these two positions but at some arbitrary point, the origin of the system of parametric curves will be moved to this new position. The new values can be related to the earlier systems by equations given in standard cartographic texts. To consider oblique or transverse versions of the same projection as entirely different, projections when a spherical model is used, as many authors have done, is an unnecessary complication.

In addition to rectangular and polar coordinates, more obscure systems (bolique, parabolic elliptic) could be used. In fact, any system of coordinates in a plane (meeting rather simple requirements) can be considered a map projection. In terms of the classification to be presented this would have as a consequence that all map projections belong to category D. Mathematically, this is a more appropriate approach, of course.[8] The rationale for the procedure employed is perhaps best demonstrated by an example. The equations for the polar aspect of the stereographic projection are:

$$r = f(\rho) = 2R \tan (\rho/2)$$
$$\theta = f(\lambda) = \lambda.$$

The general oblique aspect in rectangular coordinates on the other hand requires the more complicated equations:

$$x = f(\phi, \lambda)$$
$$= 2R \frac{\cos \phi \sin (\lambda - \lambda_0)}{1 + \sin \phi_0 \sin \phi + \cos \phi_0 \cos \phi \cos (\lambda - \lambda_0)}$$
$$y = f(\phi, \lambda)$$
$$= 2R \frac{\cos \phi_0 \sin \phi - \sin \phi_0 \cos \phi \cos (\lambda - \lambda_0)}{1 + \sin \phi_0 \sin \phi + \cos \phi_0 \cos \phi \cos (\lambda - \lambda_0)}.$$

The criterion is clearly one of simplicity. Employing both polar and rectangular coordinates as is done here is clearly not necessary; at times it is awkward; in other instances the treatment is simplified.

Two (real) equations are required to specify the location of both curves of equal latitude and equal longitude on the map. Since each equation can be a function of two parameters, there are logically sixteen possible combinations of the general transformation u = $f_1 (\phi, \lambda)$, v = $f_2 (\phi, \lambda)$, eliminating parameters one after another. These special cases are:

$$\begin{array}{llll}
u = f_1(\phi, \lambda) & u = f_1(\lambda) & u = f_1(\phi) & u = f_1(C) \\
v = f_2(\phi, \lambda) & v = f_2(\phi, \lambda) & v = f_2(\phi, \lambda) & v = f_2(\phi, \lambda) \\
u = f_1(\phi, \lambda) & u = f_1(\lambda) & u = f_1(\phi) & u = f_1(C) \\
v = f_2(\lambda) & v = f_2(\lambda) & v = f_2(\lambda) & v = f_2(\lambda) \\
u = f_1(\phi, \lambda) & u = f_1(\lambda) & u = f_1(\phi) & u = f_1(C) \\
v = f_2(\phi) & v = f_2(\phi) & v = f_2(\phi) & v = f_2(\phi) \\
u = f_1(\phi, \lambda) & u = f_1(\lambda) & u = f_1(\phi) & u = f_1(C) \\
v = f_2(C) & v = f_2(C) & v = f_2(C) & v = f_2(C)
\end{array}$$

where C is a constant. The sixteen cases have been arranged in the form of a matrix which can be said to be interchange-symmetric. The symmetry results in projections which can be achieved by interchanging the roles of u and v; these need not be considered further. [9] Six additional cases can usually be eliminated from consideration. These include the last row and column which map the entire domain (sphere) into a line or point.

Elimination of the interchanges and the degenerate cases (for which J $\equiv$ 0) leaves four valid classes of map projections:

$$(A) \quad u = f_1(\phi, \lambda) \qquad (B) \quad u = f_1(\lambda)$$
$$v = f_2(\phi, \lambda) \qquad \qquad v = f_2(\phi, \lambda)$$
$$(C) \quad u = f_1(\phi, \lambda) \qquad (D) \quad u = f_1(\lambda)$$
$$v = f_2(\phi) \qquad \qquad v = f_2(\phi).$$

For the sake of brevity these have been labelled A, B, C, and D, respectively. Because of the present dual intrepretation of the u̲ and v̲ values as rectangular or polar coordinates, it is convenient̄ to treat two situations in each category, a total of eight:

$$(A) \quad x = f_1(\phi, \lambda) \qquad \theta = f_1(\rho, \lambda)$$
$$y = f_2(\phi, \lambda) \qquad r = f_2(\rho, \lambda)$$
$$(B) \quad x = f_1(\lambda) \qquad \theta = f_1(\lambda)$$
$$y = f_2(\phi, \lambda) \qquad r = f_2(\rho, \lambda)$$
$$(C) \quad x = f_1(\phi, \lambda) \qquad \theta = f_1(\rho, \lambda)$$
$$y = f_2(\phi) \qquad r = f_2(\rho)$$
$$(D) \quad x = f_1(\lambda) \qquad \theta = f_1(\lambda)$$
$$y = f_2(\phi) \qquad r = f_2(\rho).$$

The eight cases are illustrated schematically in Figure 1. It can be seen that the classification places a certain emphasis on the shapes of the meridians and parallels. All projections with straight meridians and parallels are not in category D, however. Collignon's projection, for example, belongs in category C.[10] The classification can be extended if desired by grouping together projections for which the second derivatives are greater than, equal to, or less than, zero, or by the addition of further conditions.

RELATION TO THE GEOMETRIC CLASSIFICATION

The relation of the parametric classification to the more common classification based on perspective models is not difficult. Category D of the classificatory scheme is clearly the simplest of the four. The cylindrical projections can be obtained by interpreting the u–coordinate as abscissa and the v–coordinate as ordinate in ā Cartesian system, x = $f(\lambda)$, ȳ = $f(\phi)$. The meridians and parallels are orthogonal straight lines. The conventional cylindrical projections are further restricted to the very special case x = $f(\lambda)$ = Rλ, which implies a right circular cylinder. Ēlliptic, parabolic, hyperbolic, and more general cylinders never seem to have been considered (with the possible exception of maps of the ellipsoid). If the right circular cylinder is taken as basic, then the spacing of the parallels is all that can be varied on

the projection. Symmetry
is usually taken about the
projection equator, though
this is not a mathematical
requirement in all cases.
The most important projections in this category are
Mercator's conformal, Lambert's equal-area cylindrical,
the equirectangular, and
Miller's cylindrical pro-
jection.

Conic projections
are another realization of
category D in polar coordi-
nates, with $\theta = f(\lambda) = C\lambda$, where C is a constant
restricted to the interval
$0 < C < 1$, implying a
right circular cone. These
projections have straight
lines as meridians and
arcs of concentric circles
as parallels. The maps
are pie or fan shaped.
The constant C is often
called the constant of the
cone; the vertex angle of
the fan-shaped map de-
pends on this constant.
Non-constant (one para-
metric) functions for the

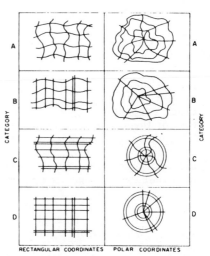

RECTANGULAR COORDINATES   POLAR COORDINATES

Fig. 1. Schematic illustration of map projections
in the classificatory system. The diagrams do not represent any specific projections but are indications of
the possible form of the lines of latitude and longitude
on the map. In category A both families of parametric lines may be variably spaced curves. In category B the meridians may be variably spaced straight
lines (parallel or radiating, depending on the coordinates employed). The parallels may be variably
spaced curves of highly variable curvature. Category
C is similar to category B except that the role of the
meridians and parallels are interchanged; the parallels
in polar coordinates are circles of course. The forms
of category D are familiar; the spacing illustrated is
more variable than that usually encountered, however.
Interruption, similar to that on conic projections, and
truncation have not been illustrated but also are possible. The diagrams all refer to the normal cases of
the projections.

spacing of the meridians, or the use of constants greater than
unity, are only rarely mentioned in the cartographic literature.
The center of the concentric circles which define the lines of
latitude may be the north pole (normal case), or this pole
may itself be one of the circular arcs--a truncated conic projection. The most frequently employed of the conic projections are Lambert's conformal and Albers' equal-area projections.

The centrally symmetric azimuthal projections also appear in category D, using polar coordinates, as the special
case $\theta = f(\lambda) = \lambda$. This is clearly a limiting position of
the conic projections with C = 1. A non-azimuthal projection
($\theta = f(\lambda) \neq \lambda$) has appeared in the Soviet literature. The

more important of the azimuthal projections are the gnomonic, stereographic, equidistant, equal-area, and orthographic.

Category C contains some of the so-called oval projections, the pseudoconic projections and several lesser known varieties. The oval projections with straight parallels and curved meridians (sinusoidal, Mollweide, Eckert) are of the form $x = f_1 (\phi , \lambda)$, $y = f_2 (\phi)$, and in virtually all cases encountered, the simpler situation $x = \lambda f (\phi)$. Certain of these can be shown to be polycylindrical developments. The pseudoconic projections (Bonne, Werner, Weichel) are of the form $\theta = f_1 (\rho , \lambda)$, $r = f_2 (\rho)$ with curved meridians and concentric circular arcs as parallels. Category C also includes the pseudoazimuthal projections, as recognized in the Soviet literature.[11]

Projections belonging to category B are not at all well known. This category does, however, contain azimuthal projections as the special case $\theta = \lambda$. Certain geographic uses of these projections have recently been investigated by the author.[12] The azimuthal projections used in practice have the simpler form of category D.

Category A includes the polyconic projections, the oval projections with curved parallels and generally the projections with curved meridians and parallels. These projections are often referred to as conventional projections or unclassified projections. A few of the other projections in this category are Lagrange's projection of the sphere within a circle, Hammer's projection, August's conformal projection within a two-cusped epicycloid, and the elliptic projections of Guyou and Adams. Strictly speaking, of course, all the other categories are special cases of category A.

GRAPHIC ANALYSIS

The classification presented has certain graphic implications. The equations for category A, the most involved possibility, can be rewritten as:

$$F_1 (\phi, \lambda, u) = 0, \quad or \quad F_2 (\phi, \lambda, v) = 0,$$

which can be interpreted as two separate surfaces in space. Each such surface can be represented diagrammatically by level curves or by a block diagram. This may appear somewhat involved, only one diagram being required to show the entire projection as a map. However, as an aid to analysis and understanding, particularly for students with minimal

mathematical training, the graphs are very useful. Four variables (u, v, ∅, λ) appear in the pair of equations used to
specify a map projection, hence a complete graphic representation would require a four-dimensional diagram. Nevertheless, by assuming one of the equations to be fixed, the effects of changes in the other equation can be examined. Observations regarding elementary properties of projections are
particularly easily deduced from the one-parameter graphs.
The block diagrams are less susceptible to rapid visual analysis, at least without practice.

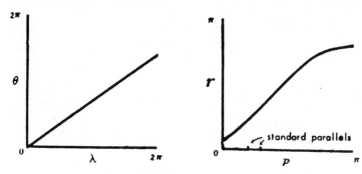

Fig. 2.   Graphs for Albers' equal-area projection.

         The accompanying figure (Fig. 2) shows the graphs cor-
responding to Albers' equal-area projection.   The truncated
form of this conic projection appears as an intercept of the
axis which is not at the origin.   Graphs for the sinusoidal
projection portray a slightly more difficult case (Fig. 3).
This pictorial representation should suffice to illustrate the
procedure for extending the graphic method to further projections.

         A graphic comparison of projections is easily derived
from the foregoing statements.   A polar or circular diagram
(Fig. 4) is commonly drawn to illustrate the differences between several azimuthal projections--a difference in the spacing of parallels.   Another method of illustrating the same relation is to plot spherical distances from the point of projection against map distances on a graph (Fig. 5).   This graph
shows the radius equation for the azimuthal projections in
question.   The graph can also easily be related to the perspective method of construction often used for azimuthal projections (Fig. 6).

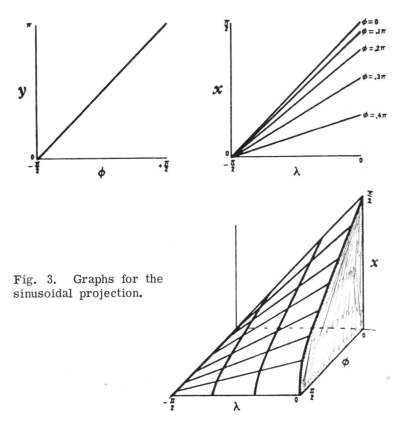

Fig. 3. Graphs for the
sinusoidal projection.

        In addition to simple visualization and comparison of
projections the graphs provide a rapid method of analyzing
certain properties of these projections. The discussion treats
only azimuthal projections of category D, but extensions of
the method are simple. The azimuthal equidistant projection
is perhaps the most basic, for the radius equation can be
represented as a straight line on the graph. If the diagram
is scaled in radians, this line is a forty-five degree line (of
slope + 1). As the name implies, all places are represented
on the map at their correct spherical distance from the center.
If the curve representing the radius equation of any other
centrally symmetric azimuthal projection crosses this line,
the intersection point will also lie at its true distance from
the center of the map. Similarly, whenever the radius equation of an azimuthal projection of category D intersects the
graph of the corresponding equation for the equal-area azimuthal projection twice, the projection in question has an area

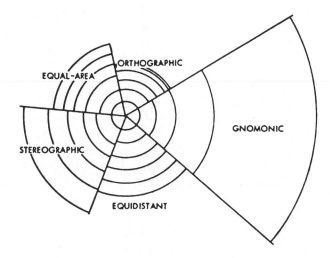

Fig. 4. Azimuthal projections--representation using circular diagram.

in some sector which is equal in area to the corresponding sector on the globe. Similar comments can be related to the lengths of the parallels and intersections with the graph of the orthographic projection. Projections with some of these properties have been sought from time to time. A change of scale on an azimuthal equidistant projection corresponds to a raising or lowering of the straight line on the graph, keeping the origin intersection fixed. This can also be seen from the equations as a constant change in slope. The standard parallel is where the curve representing the radius equation has a slope of +1. From this it is easy to demonstrate why the most used azimuthal projections can have only one standard parallel and why conic projections can have two standard parallels. The slightly more difficult concepts of isometric latitude and equivalent latitude also

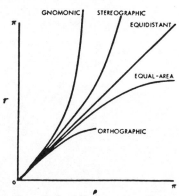

Fig. 5. Azimuthal projections --representation using rectangular graph.

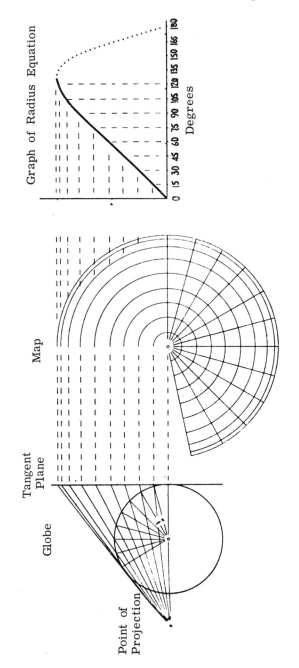

Figure 6. Relation of perspective development and graph of the radius equation for azimuthal projections.

can be elucidated by graphic methods.   The radial scale distortion on an arbitrary azimuthal projection of category D can
be estimated by noting the slope of the radius equation.
Curves which are concave downward in general expand the
central area of the map and diminish the peripheral areas.
The reverse is generally true of curves which are concave
upward.   This is correct for the radial scale of the map,
but for areal distortion it is true to only a limited extent due
to the spherical model of the earth.   The graphic analysis, of
course, should be undertaken only when the analytic considerations are understood and can be demonstrated.

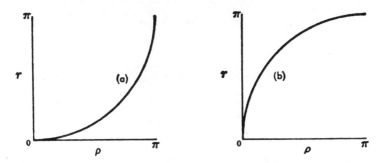

Figure 7.   Two "new" azimuthal projections, $r = f (\rho)$,
$\theta = \lambda$.   The curves are arcs of circles with equations:
(a) $r = (2\pi\rho - \rho^2)^{\frac{1}{2}}$,   (b) $r = \pi - (\pi^2 - \rho^2)^{\frac{1}{2}}$.
To obtain projections comparable to (a) and (b) but with the
radius equation given by an ellipse rather than a circle divide
the right side of the equations presented by the ratio of the
major axis to the minor axis.

To create composite projections, one need only join
projections where their graphs intersect.   A well-known (non-
azimuthal) composite is Goode's famous homolosine, combining the homolographic (Mollweide) and sinusoidal equal-area
projections.   Somewhat comparable is Wray's combination of
the azimuthal equidistant and the azimuthal equal area projection.   A composite map, with large scale near the center,
has recently been employed for the use of aviators in the vicinity of airports. [13]   Interruption of projections appears on
the graph as an interruption of the curve.

The graph can also be employed to invent new projections.   Any line drawn on the graph can be interpreted as a
transformation.   For example, arcs of circles drawn on the

Fig. 8. An azimuthal projection with radius equation r = $R\rho^{1/2}$, centered on New York City. The distortion and applications for this projection are given in Tobler (op. cit., 55, 91).

graph can be interpreted as a transformation. For example, arcs of circles drawn on the graph yield two "new" azimuthal projections (Fig. 7); the equations are obtained from a simple algebraic manipulation. As another example, the generating equations $r = R\rho$, $\theta = \lambda$, for the azimuthal equidistant projection can be generalized to create a large class of "new" projections, namely $r = R\rho^{q}$, $\theta = \lambda$, where the exponent q is an arbitrary positive element from the set of real numbers. In this formulation the azimuthal equidistant projection is the special case q = 1. As an illustration, a map centered on New York has been prepared using q = 1/2, a square-root azimuthal projection (Fig. 8). Further azimuthal projections can be developed by fitting a map to an arbitrary theoretical or empirical curve. Thus map projections are particularly easy to create by arbitrarily writing down equations which satisfy certain simple requirements.

Such a procedure may be interesting and occasionally fruitful, but is somewhat foolish as there are infinitely many; it is also necessary to demonstrate some property, relation, or use. Nehari appropriately remarks that the investigation of particular functions, though yielding much insight, is of necessity a piecemeal procedure. Much more fruitful are investigations akin to those of Bernhard Riemann which examine general existence conditions. [14] The classification presented here is not particularly well adapted to this latter purpose since it is not independent of the particular coordinates employed. The interest is certainly not in coordinates, but in the properties of the projections.

CONCLUSIONS

A recent book includes the following statement:

> The mathematical details of map projections are completely unknown to the average user, whether navigator, cartographer, or engineer. The reason is apparent from the reference books on this subject, which offer either a pictorial description of the main projections or else a lengthy development starting with the spheroidal earth. The former approach is too superficial to satisfy the intellectual curiosity of anyone with technical background, while the latter is extremely demanding because of its use of higher mathematics and its tedious developments in Fourier and power series. [15]

To this should be added that increased use of electronic computers and quantitative methods on the part of geographers in the future will necessitate a more detailed understanding of map projections than has been required in the past. In this regard the parametric classification seems more satisfactory for a working knowledge of map projections than several of the other classifications available in that it leads to a simple approach to the subject. This does not deny the validity of other approaches. The classification presented here also is not the most general classification possible. For example, Kao has recently suggested use of Cartan's method to derive map projections. [16] In this instance the mapping equations might be written in the form $\underline{x}' = f_i$ $(\underline{x}_1, \underline{x}_2, \underline{x}_3)$, $\underline{i} = 1, 2, 3$. Alternately, the topic can be studied using complex variables or vectors. Such generality has not been sought in the present discussion.

NOTES

1. The author wishes to express his appreciation to Drs.
   J. C. Sherman and W. R. Heath of the University of
   Washington for comments. The National Science
   Foundation, through its program of Graduate Fellow-
   ships, provided financial support for a portion of
   this study. The remarks of course remain the author's responsibility.

2. At one time the drawing of a projection graticule constituted a major problem. This led to a search for
   projections on which the meridians and parallels are
   curves of specific classes. The solutions now available are: all conformal projections with parametric
   curves as circles (with the straight line as a special
   case; solved by Lagrange) or conics (the circle being
   a special case; solved by Von Der Mühll); all equal-
   area projections with parametric curves as circles
   (solved by Grave) or conics (solved by Brown). See
   B. H. Brown, "Conformal and Equiareal World Maps, "
   American Mathematics Monthly, vol. 42 (1935), 212-
   223.

3. H. Maurer, "Ebene Kugelbilder, ein Linnesches System
   der Kartenentwürfe, " Petermanns Geographische Mitteilungen, Ergänzungsheft 221 (1935), 1-80.

4. M. A. Tissot. Memoire sur la representation des surfaces et les projections des cartes géographiques.
   Paris: Gautier-Villars, 1881.

5. L. P. Lee, "The Nomenclature and Classification of
   Map Projections, " Empire Survey Review, vol. 7
   (1944), 190-200.

6. B. Goussinsky, "On the Classification of Map Projections, " Empire Survey Review, vol. 11 (1951), 75-
   79.

7. The detailed conditions for an allowable mapping and
   definitions of surfaces, and so forth, in terms of
   equivalence classes have been omitted. The reader
   is referred to E. Kreyszig, Differential Geometry
   (Toronto: University of Toronto Press, 1959), 3-9,
   18-20, 72-79.

8. This can be achieved by defining a different set of parametric curves on the original surface for each projection. The coordinate systems are then the same
   for both surfaces and the mapping equations are
   $u' = u$, $v' = v$. This method is used by Kreyszig
   (ibid., 175); or E. P. Lane, Metric Differential
   Geometry of Curves and Surfaces (Chicago: Univer-

sity of Chicago Press, 1940), 188-189.

9. Brown (op. cit., 215) has given an example of an inter-
    change on which the parallels are rays from an ori-
    gin and the meridians are arcs of concentric circles.
    The distinction between sense-preserving and sense
    reversing projections also has been ignored. See
    W. Kaplan, Advanced Calculus (Reading: Addison-
    Wesley, 1952), 580-581.

10. See T. Craig. A Treatise on Projections. Washington,
    D. C.: Government Printing Office, 1882; 110, 127,
    128. A slightly different version of Collignon's pro-
    jection is described by Kreyszig (op. cit., 78).

11. A. V. Graur. Matematischeskaya Kartografiya. Lenin-
    grad: Leningrad University Press, 1956. Or D.
    Maling, "A Review of Some Russian Map Projections,"
    Empire Survey Review, vol. 15 (1960), 203-215, 255-
    266, 294-303.

12. W. R. Tobler. "Map Transformations of Geographic
    Space" (unpublished doctoral dissertation in geogra-
    phy, University of Washington, 1961). Available
    from University Microfilms, Ann Arbor, Michigan.

13. L. Y. Dameron, Jr., "Terminal Area Charts for Jet
    Aircraft," Military Engineer (May-June, 1960), 6.

14. Z. Nehari, Conformal Mapping (New York: McGraw-
    Hill, 1952), 173.

15. D. Levine, et al., Radargrammetry. New York: Mc-
    Graw-Hill, 1960; 55.

16. R. C. Kao, "Geometric Projections of the Sphere and
    the Spheroid," Canadian Geographer, vol. 5, no. 3,
    Autumn, 1961), 21, footnote 9.

VISUAL PERCEPTION AND MAP DESIGN*

Michael Wood

Introduction

The psychology of perception often brings to mind certain strange illusions of shape and colour. Although far from the core of the subject, this aspect of the science will now be used as a point of entry into it. To begin with, consider examples of one of the phenomena of visual perception, namely simultaneous contrast--i.e., how adjacent colours affect one another.

(1) The affect of contrast on brightness alone where a grey ring is light on a dark background and dark on a light background.
(2) The effect of contrast on hue, the appearance of hue being changed by its surroundings.

Other examples of this show how surrounding colour influences a central colour.

Having seen a few of these illustrations (which form part of the study of the visual perception of colour), one might say, "Our maps are seldom as simple as these and thus what value can be drawn from such studies?" The maps we draw are complex images and they contain many variable elements which must communicate certain information to the user. Can study of the above examples of colour contrast be of any benefit to the map designer? Can they help him to see his problems more clearly or even provide some answers?

There have been a number of experiments into the perception of map symbols and these have been reported in vari-

*Reprinted by permission from the Bulletin of the Society of University Cartographers, vol. 3, no. 1 (1968), 13-16.

ous journals over the past ten years. Names such as Williams, Jenks, Knos, Saunders and of course Professor Robinson of Wisconsin come to mind. Some research workers have taken a general approach while others have made more specific measurements of how and what people aee and have attempted to formulate laws to govern certain aspects of the design of symbols. For instance, we have seen analysed the judgment of the sizes of isolated graduated point symbols, also the grading of shaded tones into equal steps and, of course, the legibility of letters and figures. All these are very necessary, as it is on such basic research that new ideas and theories can be founded. So far, however, there are few specific guides and it is not unusual for the closing paragraphs of the experiment reports to contain the statement, "Cartographers should be aware of the special circumstances described."

Map Design

As in other fields, an approach to the design of the functioning object must be preceded by a clear statement of its intended uses and users. This is difficult. For example, has the formula been devised for the perfect chair? Not at all, and yet all one has to do with a chair is sit on it! How much more difficult, then, it is to define all the uses of a map. The problems which normally face those who draw maps are:

(a) a certain quantity of information must be shown
(b) a map of a certain size and
(c) with limited colours, often only one.

We soon discover that for most of our work, the results of existing research are still of little practical value and are difficult to relate to the map in hand. We may feel that the subtle modifications suggested to improve the judgment of proportional symbols will be annulled in the complex environment of the map. None of this is the fault of the workers, but merely of the present stage of investigations. Nevertheless it means that we must return to our empirical rules which, do not provide all the answers, but on which we can rely. Rules such as "boldly striped areas disturb the balance and attract too much attention," "the map should have complexity and interest but also possess unity," "do not juxtapose large areas of bright colour," or "dots are more stable than line patterns." At the same time, we must have a healthy respect for the conventional uses of colour and pattern

in maps--e. g. , blue sea, red/orange deserts, white snow and
ice.

Colour and Shape

However, to return again to perception psychology,
are there any other alleys to be explored or shortcuts to be
found? We have read that colour and pattern affect our basic
feelings. The former can have meanings and associations and
provide for harmony or discord. But what of the more tan-
gible aspects?

The eye sees colour and shape. Colour is seen in
several qualities, commonly known as:

Hue: the colour
Saturation: the dullness or richness of a hue
Brightness: the darkness or lightness of a hue

As was described at the outset of the paper, however, complex environments can cause false impressions of the real
colour. Consider some more examples and examine their
relevance to cartography:

The smaller the size of an object the duller will be
its colour, and dull greens and blues at small sizes
are difficult to distinguish.
Thematic map makers sometimes employ blue and
green dots for distributions. Yellow is very difficult
to see at small sizes. The "Spreading Effect" of
black lines makes other colours look darker.
This can be observed when red roads are cased by
black lines. In some maps, narrow orange roads
look darker than the wider orange roads, because of
black.
Identical grey areas, if influenced, one by black the
other by yellow, are given either a darkish or a yel-
lowish appearance.
White inclusions in the yellow areas make them weaker than areas of solid, continuous yellow.

The eye perceives shape only if there is adequate contrast with the background and the size of the object is sufficient. Hence size and contrast are important. Some shapes
are easier to detect than others. One of the main concerns
of the map reader is to see groups of associated objects within the map, as well as being able to pick out individual points

and names. This user requirement leads us into what is
known as Gestalt psychology, this being the German word for
"organization. " This theory states that we see things in
groups and various laws are as follows:
> Area: the smaller a closed region, the more it tends
> to be seen as a figure.
> Proximity: objects close together tend to be grouped.
> Closedness: areas with closed contours are seen
> sooner than those with open ones.
> Good continuity: that which makes fewest changes
> from straight or gently curving lines.

Some maps can be seen to comply with or contravene
these "laws" which may thus provide an approach towards a
set of guiding principles for map design.

Clarity, Contrast and Meaning

What is essential in the image to provide for the easy
detection of symbols. First of all clarity and contrast. We
can, however, have both clarity and contrast without comprehension. The second requirement, therefore, is "meaning, "
to reinforce the object, and we can aid this by drawing the
symbol in a familiar form. But even when we have contrast
and meaning there may still be confusion, as one area or
symbol may stand out at one moment, and another at the
next. This is called the "figure-ground" effect and is illustrated by the well-known diagram in which we may see a vase
in the foreground, or, alternatively, two faces in the foreground. This results when the ideas associated with the alternative shapes, inside and out, are either both clearly understood, or both vague. Hence if we had a map showing
two regions separated by a line only, the eye would have no
preference, but if one side could be recognised as the boundary of a familiar town, then this might take preference and
become figural. Generally, however, colours or patterns
are added to the areas to enhance visibility. This secondary
stimulus nevertheless, could make clear recognition more
difficult, as one side of the line could be dull, but familiar,
while the other is bright but irrelevant.

This figure-ground is one of the most significant phenomena to affect our reading of maps, and again, some examples can soon be found.

Theory of Visual Places

One has experienced the frustration of not being able

to pick out a pattern of lines, etc., from a map, and also
the satisfaction of achieving this goal. We must ask what it
is which aids good figural effect. The problem of perceiving
patterns or distribution is greatest when the map is visually
flat, and there is inadequate contrast of line thickness, tonal
gradations and name sizes. One appreciates this and generally tries to introduce the required contrast of colour or tone,
but only according to rules of experience. There is no theory
of perception, or clue in nature which can draw all these
rules together, like the law of gravity which is a constant
force acting upon a body.

Next to landscape paintings and photographs, there are
few graphic images which contain so much complex, overlapping and superimposed information as a map but at least
the landscape has depth. If a map has to hold much information, it cannot be flat or shallow, it must have depth. This
idea of having visual planes of depth or distance in maps is
not a new one. Psychologists, also, have studied depth perception, and have indicated clues which increase the illusion
of depth--e.g. the size of a familiar object decreasing in
size with distance. What has been lacking, however, is a
simple, logical idea to link all the clues together.

The American psychologist, G. G. Gibson, published
some ideas in 1950 which may provide this link. He analysed the normal field of view of the human eye, be it a
landscape or a room, and isolated various qualities which
give us clues to depth (apart from the binocular one.) These
he called "gradients," i.e., a change from large to small,
coarse to fine, etc. His gradients were texture, size, and
all the effects associated with aerial perspective, which is
the influence of haze on the colours and tones of a landscape.
For example the natural textures of grass, stones and brick
walls grow finer with viewing distance.

He was concerned with continuous gradient, but perhaps we can modify this to a series of separate receding
planes. In this way we can stack data according to importance, or effect, and introduce adequate contrast to make the
study of one of a series of superimposed distributions much
easier.

What are the rules? The foreground has coarsest texture, richest hues and darkest shadows, but, with increasing
distance, saturation falls off, and colours get lighter and
weaker, while brightness also falls off and shadows get duller.
Objects and lines become smaller and thinner.

Can we see any of these manifested in maps? If colours are strong they appear to be in the foreground, and image is flat. Clear separation is required. By subduing the background we can add more symbols. Crisp black and white circles, for instance, can be placed on a background which is of dull and impure hues, or the background can have paler tints, while the foreground has richer hues. A pale background with grey lines is surmounted by thick black distribution lines in the foreground.

These rules can be applied to black and white maps as well as those in full colour. The thickening of one set of lines to raise them above another is the most obvious example. If lines are too similar and texture too coarse the whole map is "too close" to the observer, and overpowering. Finer textures, thicker lines and better contrast improves this situation. This method is effective, even over dark images.

One could examine the thorny problem of the choice of shading tones under this theory of planes. If a purely mathematical basis is used for the choice of graded tones-- e.g., proportional spacing of parallel lines--it is not graphically effective. The more common solution is to associate darkness with importance, using various textures. Recall, however, the textural gradients, where nearness was represented by coarse and distance by fine grain. The top four darker steps of a graded series may seem to work, but, although the fifth has the correct percentage of ink a coarse pattern or grain may make it stand out. This helps to explain how "correct percentage-of-ink" steps may get out of place in the visual scale if texture is not considered.

Having studied examples one can now make the hypothesis that in the map, as in the landscape, the foreground could have bright, purely coloured objects, strong contrast and very dark, crisp shadow colours, thick lines, large objects and large and bold letters. The background has pale colours, dull shadow colours, poorer contrast, thinner lines, smaller symbols and small or light letters, and, between the two, a gradient of visual planes.

This is as far as one can advance with an inadequately tested theory. If may seem to be too simple an idea for the linking of all rules of map design, but perhaps it can help to clarify things in certain situations. It can be analysed and explained through the study of visual perception, but the secret or clues may well lie in the art of the landscape painter.

PRODUCTION OF PHOTOMAPS*

L. Van Zuylen

In nearly all countries of the world there is an increasing need for topographic maps.   In the more developed
countries which already have topographic coverage at medium
scales 1:50, 000 or 1:24, 000, there is a need for maps at
large scales (1:10, 000 or larger) and for practical applications such as re-allotment and cultural technical work, town
planning, regional planning and engineering work it is necessary that these should be very up to date.

In developing countries which often do not have a complete topographic cover of their territory on a medium scale,
the need exists for a multi-purpose base map on a scale
1:50, 000 or larger.   The first aim for such a map is to provide an inventory of the natural resources and to assist the
planning and execution of development projects.

The production of maps can be split up into three main
steps.   (1) The determination of coordinates for the geometric
base.   (2) The representation of the landscape in the map.
(3) The reproduction of the map.   The second step, the cartographic part of the job, which includes drawing or scribing,
field completion and generalisations, is very time consuming,
and in most cases it is only possible to make maps available
to the users a long time after the field completion.

It is necessary that map production should keep pace
with the rapid economic and technical developments in other
fields.   In this respect, cartographers have tried to accelerate their methods, for example with the introduction of plastic

*Reprinted by permission from the Cartographic Journal, vol.
6, no. 2 (1969), 92-102.   Paper presented at the Annual Symposium of the British Cartographic Society in 1969.

sheets, scribing on glass or on plastic, stripmask methods, modern techniques for text mounting, high-speed offset presses and, most recently, the introduction of pencil-followers, electronic coordinatographs, etc. All these techniques are applied in the production of line maps, i.e. maps in which the landscape is represented by lines, surface-colours and symbols.

Since the introduction of photogrammetry, especially aerial photogrammetry, the cartographer has had at his disposal an image of the terrain of quite another kind, namely a continuous tone photograph. Such an aerial photo makes it possible for the producer and the user to obtain a picture of the landscape in a very short time; a picture that in most cases will fulfill the desired requirements.

Production of Orthophotographs

Having an aerial photograph of an area as shown on Figure 1 it will be clear that on the negative the top T of the hill and the point F will never coincide as would be necessary for a map having orthogonal projection. If we use this photo on its own it is impossible to eliminate the "mistake" T^1F^1. It is of course clear that aerial photos of absolutely flat horizontal terrain do not suffer from this defect. So it is possible to use aerial photos of such terrain directly as a map provided these photos were taken with a camera at the exact height above the terrain, having a vertical optical axis and an absolutely flat horizontal negative plane.

Because it is not possible for the photographer to fulfil these requirements in practice it is always necessary to rectify such a photograph. That is, the aerial photo is adjusted to points determined by geodetic and/or photogrammetric methods. This adjustment is done in a rectifier and the result is a continuous tone image on photographic paper, or better on polyester film material. Such a rectified photo image has the geometric properties of a well controlled map and for absolutely flat horizontal terrain can replace a traditional line map.

It will be clear that for accidented terrain this method of rectification can not be used, and so stereophotogrammetry must be applied. If the hill of Figure 1 is photographed from two positions (as shown in Figure 2) then it is possible with stereoplotters using both aerial photos and with the aid of geodetically or photogrammetrically determined control points, to obtain a stereoscopic image of the photographed area. The photogrammetrist can now map this area by driving the floating mark of the stereoplotter along the objects shown in the stereoscopic model. The movements of this floating mark are realised by a scribing needle or pencil directly connected with the floating mark. The result is a line image of the mapped area (contours and planimetry).

The stereoplotting of a very dense area is a very time consuming job and the plotters are very costly. However, the photogrammetric method is still much faster than terrestrial

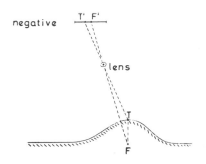

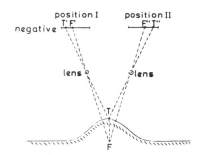

Figure 1. Relief displacement due to perspective projection. T and F, when projected to the aerial photo negative do not coincide (T^1 and F^1) as they would in the case of orthogonal projection.

Figure 2. The principle of stereoplotting.

methods. Since a photo-interpretation stage and subsequent fair drawing are necessary to transform the stereoscopic image into a line image, very often even this relatively rapid photogrammetric production method for line maps is not capable of satisfying the urgent demands of map users.

From the above it will be clear that with rectification it is possible to produce very quickly a rectified photo image of flat terrain but with the stereoplotting necessary for accidented terrain the production of a line map takes considerably more time. If it were possible now to break up an accidented terrain area into a number of flat areas at different heights above sea level it should be possible to apply the rectification method for these flat areas. However, it would be necessary to know the elevations of the terrain.

As early as 1931, at the time of the first developments in photogrammetry, Lacmann, and later Ferber had ideas about the application of this concept of rectification of different height zones.   They went as far as suggesting methods of obtaining a mathematically-adjusted photo image of the terrain with many of the positional properties of a traditional map. A general application however of these methods was not developed.   The idea of producing a photomap image of accidented terrain haunted photogrammetrists and in 1955 Russel Bean (U. S. A.) introduced a new instrument which he called an "orthophotoscope. "   However, it took several years before this development was appreciated, and in the meantime others developed similar instruments.   In 1959 the Russians published data about a so-called "slitrectifier" and in East and West Germany orthoprojectors were also constructed.   At the International Photogrammetric Congress in Lausanne in 1968 nearly all manufacturers of photogrammetric instruments demonstrated a similar instrument.   Instruments so far developed can be divided into two types, namely machines using image transfer with the use of cathode ray tubes and instruments applying optical projection.   Both systems have advantages and disadvantages, but here only the principles of the optical type instruments will be described to explain how orthophotos

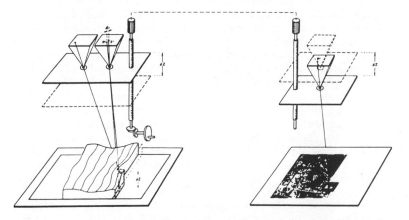

Figure 3.   Schematic diagram of the Orthoprojector.   On the left is the stereoplotter (e. g. C8 or Planimat) and on the right the Orthoprojector unit itself.   The Orthoprojector is housed in a darkroom, and linked by a coupling system to the stereoplotter.

are produced. Every point in the stereoimage created from the two aerial photographs in the stereoplotter can be reconstructed with the help of the floating mark. In such a plotter the floating mark must be positioned very accurately "upon the ground" giving the accurate intersection of the two construction rays.

If we now instead of locating each point by means of the floating mark, use a diaphragm with a very small slit under which is placed photographic material (film or paper) then the point can be recorded on this material by optical projection of the photo image. To be absolutely accurate, the slit width would need to be infinitesimally small as true orthogonal projection is only achieved for a point. In practice this is not feasible and in order to give an efficient solution for normal production a slit with a width of for instance 4 X 2mm is used. Then the point with its immediate surroundings will be reproduced on the photographic material. This principle is used in the Gigas-Zeiss Orthoprojector (Figure 3).

In the working situation for the production of orthophotos the Orthoprojector is coupled with the stereoplotter so that all movements of the right part of the stereoplotter are imitated by the Orthoprojector. In order that the whole of the area of the stereoscopic model created from the aerial photos can be reproduced, the slit has to be moved over the table of the Orthoprojector. It is driven by synchromotors in a series of parallel scans until the whole area is covered (Figure 4). Because the Orthoprojector and the stereoplotter are coupled the floating mark in the stereoplotter will move in the same way, and the operator of the stereoplotter must keep the floating mark "upon the ground" during this movement. So in fact now the Orthoprojector is the leader and the stereoplotter has to follow. After the scanning of the area to be mapped has been completed the photographic material can be developed, the result being a continuous tone image at correct scale and, as it is often called, differentially rectified.

Besides this continuous tone image, in the GZ-Orthoprojector and in many other instruments so called "droplines" can be produced (Figure 5). The wheel with which the operator keeps the floating mark "upon the ground" in the stereomodel, is coupled with a disc with a series of different openings. During the scanning movement of the floating mark a light ray bundle is projected via an optical system upon this

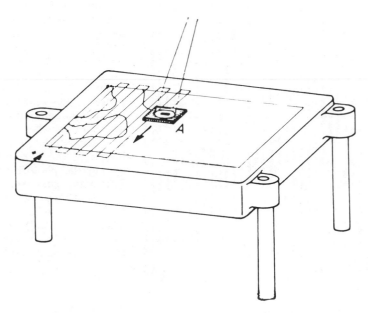

Figure 4.   Schematic diagram of the scanning system of the Orthoprojector.   The slit is contained in the platen A, and moves over the table in a series of scans as shown, exposing the photo-image onto film.

disc, and the opening in the disc which coincides at that moment is exposed to form an image on a second sheet of photographic material, placed on the projection table of the Orthoprojector.   The disc is so coupled with the handwheel of the operator that the type of the opening in the disc changes when the floating mark passes a certain height above sea level (for instance 75, 80, 85, 90m above mean sea level). So if the floating mark moves during a scanning trip between 75 and 80m above sea level than the same opening in the disc remains in the bundle of light rays and forms a line of that type on the film.   Such a dropped line image can be used to construct contours by connecting the ends of the dropped lines of the same type.

The accuracy of such contours and of course also of the continuous tone orthophoto depends very much on the experience of the photogrammetrist at the instrument, the slit width and the speed of movement of the slit.   Tests carried

out on the Orthoprojector by Visser at ITC[13], have shown that an orthophoto can produce the planimetry with a mean square error of about 0.2 mm in the scale of the orthophoto and the height with an accuracy of about 0.4⁰/oo of the flying height of the aeroplane during the photoflight. For many purposes this accuracy will be acceptable, especially when the advantage of the map being very up-to-date is realised.

Figure 5. Portion of a "dropline" plot showing part construction of contours

Production of Orthophotomaps

Orthophotos and rectified aerial photos have formed the base for the production of photomaps and line maps in the Netherlands, for South Korea, and will also be used for production of such maps in Saudi Arabia and also in Mauritius. These particular examples will now be examined in greater detail.

Netherlands

Because 70 per cent of the territory of the Netherlands is flat the producers of the Dutch topographic maps accepted the rectification method as early as 1930 as an efficient method of obtaining basic material for topographic maps at the scale 1:25,000.

In the beginning aerial photos were rectified on glass plates, and the line map was made by drawing pencil lines on plastic material (Astralon) by using this plastic as an overlay upon the glass diapositive. Working at a light table the draughtsman traced the required lines onto the plastic, thus transforming the photoimage into a line image. With this method the line image was built up in steps by using another diapositive plate for the next part of the map. Considerable problems arose in the case of long straight lines like railways which had to be drawn in three or more steps, with all the attendant disadvantages.

To overcome this difficulty another method for base map production was developed. A complete photomap was produced by rectifying the photos on "correctostat" (i.e. sensitive photographic paper with aluminium reinforcement), and mounting these stable opaque photos upon a large metal plate covered with paper. On this the pass points had been pricked with the coordinatograph to enable a correct mounting of the photos. This assembly of rectified photos was then photographed with the reproduction camera and reproduced on one sheet of correctostate. Upon this sheet the draughtsmen drew their lines for the base map with waterproof ink and after that the photographic image was bleached out, leaving only the line image. This could be used as a guide for the colour separation sheets for the production of coloured topographic maps.

This method was replaced when engraving (scribing) techniques were introduced about 1950. At first this meant a return to the old method of production using photo after photo, but now using scribing instead of drawing with pencil. This was compensated by the saving in production time by using the scribing method and the possibility of getting a much better quality guide for the colour separation sheets for the 1:25,000 scale map. Since it became possible to buy scribe coats on polyester base with a diazo-type emulsion the two methods used have been combined, and now the aerial photos are rectified upon continuous tone polyester film (Gevaert-Agfa N31P or N41P, depending on the gradation) and these diapositives are mounted upon a polyester film (Gevaert-Agfa N31P or N41P, depending on accurate mounting. The photos are cut very accurately from point to point and glued with rubber solution upon the base sheet. This assembly is exposed upon Stabilene no. 453047 (polyester base, yellow scribe coat, diazo emulsion). To get a sharp image the aerial photos are rectified as mirror reversed diapositives and mounted in mirror reversed position. Then contact of emulsion to emulsion is possible giving a right reading image on the scribe coat. For this exposure on Ozalid material the diapositives need to have a very soft tonal gradation. This production of

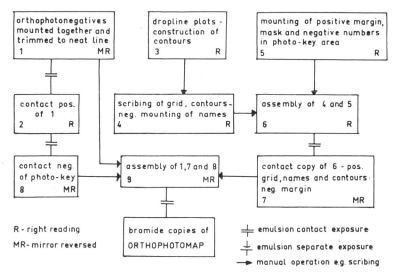

Figure 6. Flow diagram: the method followed in the construction of the Korean orthophotomap.

the continuous tone photo image on the scribe coat material enables the direct scribing of a line map. A second big advantage of this production method is the fact that rectified diapositives are available for every photomap production wanted. (Incidentally the same procedure can be followed with orthophoto diapositives.)

For reallotment technical work in particular engineers prefer to use a photomap instead of a line map. Thus it is possible to use the mounted photomap sheet and to reproduce this on the scale 1:5000 and 1:10, 000 for these users. They prefer this map image in continuous tone form because (a) it is available more quickly; (b) it gives the extra information that is not given on a line map such as boundaries between small agricultural parcels, more details in swampy areas, small wooden sheds, parts of built-up areas that are generalised on the map, etc. Because the line map is also an indispensable product for them they sometimes ask for a combination of the photomap and the line map. This combination is delivered as a mirror reversed diapositive on polyester film from which they can make Ozalid prints for the field engineers. They can then add to the base line map the extra information that is required and the photo-image makes possible the plotting of this field information directly.

Figure 7. Section of an orthophotomap of the "Korean type,"
with continuous tone photo image, white contours, names and
grid.

        The engineers of the rural reallotment technical ser-
vices even use these photomaps or photo line maps in their
discussions with the farmers, and they are very disappointed
when they learn that such a photomap is not available for
some areas because that particular area is too hilly for rectification.   In addition many people use photomaps for urban
area work, forest inventory, recreation, etc.

Photomaps for Developing Countries: South Korea

        South Korea being a very densely populated country,
conventional stereomapping at scale 1:25, 000 would be extremely time consuming, requiring many conventional stereo
instruments.   About 60, 000 man-instrument hours would be
necessary for the pencil plots only of a 30, 000 square kilo-
metres coastal area in South Korea.   This area must be developed according to the second five-year plan for Korea,

covering the period 1967-1972. Large projects for flood control, land reclamation and development have to be executed within this hilly coastal area. It was clear that the maps would not be available in time using conventional mapping methods. Thus a faster method was chosen: the production of orthophotomaps.

ITC purchased a Zeiss Orthoprojector GZ-1 to be coupled directly to the C8 Stereoplanigraph. This purchase was made possible by the plan for development support for South Korea by the Dutch government. According to this plan the Netherlands (ITC) will produce the orthophotos and drop lines and will advise South Korea on how to make orthophotomaps and line maps for their country. The measurement necessary for the production of pass points is done by the Koreans. ITC produces coordinates from triangulation and block adjustment and also the aforementioned orthophoto material. Aerial photography for the project area has been flown at scale 1:12,500 to enable the production of photomaps at the same scale. Figure 6 shows the flow diagram for the production method. The orthophoto negatives are combined and trimmed to the map neat line, and at the same time the drop line diapositives are mounted together to enable the construction of the contour lines, checked with photo detail from the photo diapositive.

On a clear base sheet the marginal data is struck up together with the negative numbers in the photo key area.

When the contours are constructed on the drop line diapositives they can be scribed on Stabilene no. 443127 (polyester base with yellow scribe coat) together with a grid (on the coordinatograph) and the names. The names are produced on a photosetter in the form of negative wax film, and are mounted in the negative contour scribe coat in open windows scribed out in their exact positions. Next a combination of the positive marginal information and the negative scribed contours etc. is made, and a contact copy of this gives a negative margin area together with positive contours and names.

In the meantime a negative of the photo key area is made, and the original orthophoto negative, the photo key negative and the positive/negative combination of contours and the marginal information can be combined. Prints of this assembly on bromide paper give the desired orthophotomap.

For good maintenance of proper connection between the negative and the constructed contours it is necessary to use the corner register marks. A better method for good registry involves the use of a punch. 14 In this case the negative and the contours with marginal information have to be mounted together and punched. The punch holes are made in the dark parts of the marginal area. The continuous tone negative must then have a clear margin around the neat line. By employing a punching machine with punches in fixed positions, use can be made of glass plates with fixed studs on to which the punched sheets can be placed. By locating the punch holes in asymmetric positions confusion with mirror reversed and right reading is not possible.

To produce a line map the same procedure as for the Dutch base maps was advised. From the orthophoto negatives a contact diapositive, mirror reversed, is produced and from this a guide on Stabilene with scribe coat and diazo coating (Stabilene no. 453047). With this technique of photomap production the result is an orthophotomap with complete border information, continuous tone photo detail with white names, contours and grid (Figure 7). Furthermore it is possible to start the line map production directly photo interpretation and or field completion deliver the first results. Good management of this opens up a fast production procedure. Because the orthophoto projector produces so much in such a short time it is possible to feed about 10-15 photo-interpreters and 10-15 draughtsmen and technicians for the production of photo and line maps.

Orthophotos and Map Revision

Another advantage in using this technique is its adaptability to an interesting and rapid revision method for base maps: a revision method using orthophotos.

If a whole area represented on a map sheet has undergone a total change, physical and cultural, there is a need for the compilation of an entirely new map. But if we assume that a map sheet of a dense area has to be revised and that many changes, large and small are needed all over the map sheet, we can again use orthophotos (or rectified photos for flat areas).

As the costs of aerial photograpny for topographic mapping are less than 10 per cent of the total costs, in

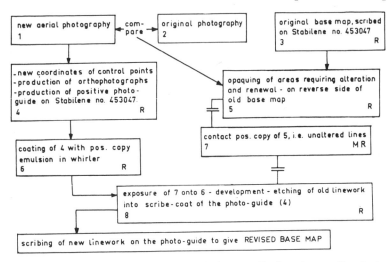

Figure 8.   Flow diagram: revision method using orthophotographs.

nearly all cases it will be more efficient to take new photographs when maps must be revised.   The control points of the preceding mapping could be used, at least in part, provided the new flight is navigated so that the old and the new strips cover each other.   Using an efficient block adjustment system a new photomap of the area concerned can be produced and the revision of the line map can be done according to the flow diagram shown (Figure 8).

On the old scribed base map the changed parts are removed and with a diapositive of the corrected old map sheet, all unchanged lines can be etched into the new photomap on Stabilene.   The new altered parts can then be scribed in direct contact with the old etched base map. [13]   This revision method is already successfully in use at the Topographic Service of the Netherlands, and Dutch experience in this field can now be used by our colleagues in Korea.

Saudi Arabia

The government of this very large country asked for a fast method for coverage of a part of their territory at the scale of 1:50,000.   Here there is a problem quite different from that of South Korea: a very sparsely populated country

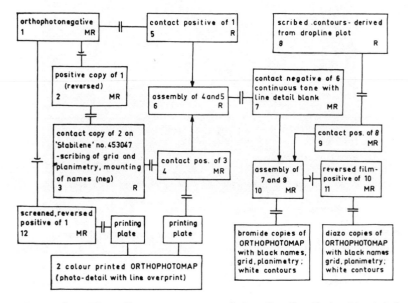

Figure 9.   Flow diagram: as used for the Saudi Arabia trial,
showing the production of bromide copies and two-colour
printed orthophotomaps.

with extensive desert areas, only a few towns and roads.
However, details like isolated houses and oases are so important that they must be recognised on the maps.   The area
to be covered is so large that in this case line map production is not the first goal to aim for, and perhaps for certain
areas a line map will never be necessary.

Thus orthophotomap production has also been chosen
for this area.   In order to establish a sound method before
production of the complete series is started some pilot projects have been executed or are underway.   In this case the
production of aerial photographs on a very small scale such
as 1:90, 000 for the triangulation and block adjustment procedure is envisaged.   As this scale is very small for photo
interpretation probably further aerial coverage at the scale
1:50, 000 will be necessary for the photo interpretation and
field completion.

At ITC a system for the production of a printed photomap with line annotations as an overprint has been developed

Figure 10.   Section of the Saudi Arabian orthophotomap.
Scale 1:50,000.   Annotations, text and grid have been added
to the photo-image in black, contours in white.

(Figure 9).   Here again the orthophotoprojector produces the
orthophoto negatives at map scale.   From these negatives a
mounting is made, and this assembly is exposed on continuous tone film with a mirror-reversed continuous tone diapositive as the result.   In the meantime a photo interpretation of
the area concerned is carried out.   The diapositive is exposed
again on the sensitive scribe coat material, (Stabilene 453047)
and interpreted annotations are engraved on this scribe coat.
The names are stuck up, again in negative, and the grid is
also scribed.   A contact diapositive from this scribe sheet
is combined with a continuous tone diapositive of the original
orthophoto negatives, the result being a continuous tone negative of photo detail with the scribed annotation being blank.
This film is further combined with the diapositive of the
scribed contours of the drop lines.

     This combination can be exposed on bromide paper.
The result then is continuous tone photo detail, black annotations and white contours (Figure 10).   An exposure of the
same sandwich on film produces a mirror-reversed diapositive which can be used for the production of Ozalid prints.
The printed photomap can be made by using a very fine screen
(70 lines per cm or more)[1, 5, 8, 11] for the diapositive of the
photo detail.   From this and the annotation diapositive printing plates are made and the photomap is printed in two colours.

Mauritius

This project concerns photomaps at a large scale. As a consequence of improved and newly proposed irrigation systems for areas producing sugar cane the need has arisen for reallotment. The execution of this means that cadastral maps must be available. The present land registration system has as the only entry--the name of the owner. Lots and their boundaries are only defined by a verbal description and their exact location is not clearly defined.

Pressure to renew the system is increased by the fact that the name of any particular owner may appear in the registers several times with different spelling, and the distinction between people having the same name is not always clear.

Figure 11.   Section of the Mauritius orthophotomap. "Cadastral" boundaries have been added to the photo image.

The large scale maps required for cadastral purposes could also serve many other needs.   It has been recommended that orthophotomaps be used as a basis for this mapping.   They will provide the general geometrically sound base to which additional information for special purposes can subsequently be added quite simply.

This additional information may consists of:--

(a)   property boundaries for a cadastral map (Figure 11);
(b)   contour lines for engineering purposes;
(c)   administrative data such as names, civil boundaries, etc.

A pilot scheme, using existing photography at the scale of 1:9000 has been undertaken by ITC.

In the Orthoprojector negatives of the photo detail and drop lines were produced at a scale of 1:3000 from the aerial photos. These negatives of the photo detail were combined, and contours constructed from the drop lines and scribed. The negatives and the scribed contours were then enlarged to the desired scale of 1:2500 with the copy camera.

The following results were required: (a) bromide copies with black grid and white contours and names; (b) diapositives mirror reversed with black grid, white contours, names and grid numbers; (c) guides of the photomap on Stabilene for the scribing of cadastral and topographic features. The object of the trial will be to test the feasibility of delimiting the boundaries of the properties on the photomap. Photomaps would thus become the official document for proof of property ownership. In Mauritius tests are to be made to establish how this works in practice. In addition the photomaps will be used for engineering purposes, and perhaps it will even be possible to have one photomap with the annotation of the property boundaries and the topographic features. Such an application could be one of the most important in the future.

Time and Costs

Summing up the time necessary for the production of a photomap of the South Korean type (50 km^2) the following figures result.

		hours	material
(a) mounting the orthophoto negatives and dropline positives	O	1	--
(b) mounting of border information + names	D	6	$5
(c) construction of contours	O	4	--
(d) scribing of contours + grid + negative names etc.	D	16	$6
	Pr (photo-setter)	3	$2
(e) assembly of border + contours	D	1/2	--
(f) contact copy of (e)	P	1/2	$5
(g) 2 contact prints on film	P	1	$5
(h) assembly of photo detail, border	O	1/2	--
(i) contact copy on bromide paper	P	1/2	$2

O = operator   Pr = printer
D = draughtsman   P = photographer

So the first bromide copy of a photomap of this kind costs

Operator	5 1/2 hours
Draughtsman	22 1/2 hours
Printer	3 hours
Photographer	2 hours
Material	$25

Each extra copy of this photomap costs

Photographer	1/2 hour
Material	$2

It is also interesting to note the time required for scribing the photomap on Stabilene. The following figures refer to scale 1:12,500. As a mean for normal dense terrain of the Dutch type it takes about 10 weeks to scribe 62.5 km^2 per week of 42.5 hours; or 1.25 km^2 per day. For terrain with a greater density we estimate a reduction in the ratio 10/14. So then about 0.90 km^2 is scribed per day. The landscape with the highest density can be scribed for 10/18 X 1.25 km^2 = 0.70 km^2 per day.

These figures are the result of long experience, and are based upon the fact that the draughtsman has at his disposal an interpreted aerial photograph of the area for scribing.

Future Developments

In conclusion some remarks may be added about possible new developments in the use of photomaps.

One of the most important is the development of a new type of film by Agfa-Gevaert, the so called Aquidensitenfilm; in English, "equal density" film. With this film it is possible to separate from an aerial photograph all elements of equal density. That is, a film separation can be made for a number of steps in the range of tonal values. Thus it is possible for example to isolate areas of forest together with other shadows of the same density. The other shadows, e.g. of buildings, can be removed by hand leaving the forest areas only. Similar separations can be made for light tones such as roads, sand, etc. This perhaps opens new possibilities for the production of "Pictomaps."[8] This type of map can be well applied in the representation of areas of few cultural details, swamp areas, desert landscapes etc. but it is not particularly successful when applied to densely built up areas. It is possible that the Äquidensitenfilm may extend the production possibilities of this type of map.

Another possibility for this new film may be the production of depth lines in a photomechanical manner. An aerial photograph of a coastal area taken in very calm weather gives much information of depths through analysis of the tones of the photograph. With this film it will be possible to determine depth-lines in the photographic dark room by using a grey wedge, exposure time, equal density film and the aerial photo negative.

As previously mentioned a general disadvantage of photomaps is the fact that some users may find interpretation difficult. [8, 9, 10, 11] Newly developed remote sensing techniques are some help in this respect. Recent research in the U.S.A. in the field of multiband spectral scanning enables distinction of up to 24 different colours. If this information can be programmed it may be possible to obtain automatic interpretation of photographs. A further advantage of such systems is that unlike conventional photography the quality of the imagery is not affected by weather conditions.

One final point may be made concerning the accuracy of orthophotographs. The accuracy of this kind of photo combined with contours constructed from drop lines is questioned by some users. Thus we find for example in Germany the production of the 1:5000 scale map (Grundkarte) in Nordrhein-Westfalen as a photomap from orthophotos, but the contours are plotted with a conventional stereoplotter.

The Russian photogrammetrist Drobyshev (SIP Congress 1968) at Lausanne proposed the following procedure. (1) plot the contour lines in the conventional way; (2) digitise this data and compute profiles to be followed by the scanning slit of the orthoprojector. In this way the orthophoto can perhaps be improved and even be acceptable for cultivated areas. However, the photomap has great possibilities for developing countries and in the coming decades these maps will be introduced more and more in many fields. They offer fast and efficient methods for topographic mapping and revision, and even for cadastral mapping new possibilities are to be expected.

ACKNOWLEDGMENT

The author wishes to thank J. Shearer, M.A., DIP. CART., staff member of the International Institute for Aerial Survey and Earth Sciences, for his valuable cooperation in the preparation of this paper.

REFERENCES

1. Beck, W. "Reproduktions und drucktechnische Nach-
   bildung und Umgestaltung von Orthophotos. " B. u. L.
   1 (1967), 3.
2. Brucklacher, W. A. "Rationalisierung der Kartenher-
   stellung durch Umstellung auf Photokarten. " Kartographische Nachrichten 4 (1967), 109.
3. Canadian Surveyor, vol. 22, no. 1 (March 1968). "Proceedings of the International Symposium on Photomaps
   and Orthophotomaps, " September 1967, Ottawa, Canada.
4. Drobyshev, F. V. "Differential Rectification of Aerial
   Photos in tl ꞉ U. S. S. R. " XI Int. Congress of Photogrammetry, Lausanne, July 1968.
5. Koeman, C. Photomap of Saudi Arabia, ITC publication
   A38.
6. Landen, David. "Photomaps for urban planning. " Phot.
   Eng. , January 1966.
7. Mullen, Roy R. "Orthophotography in the United States
   of America. " 12th Int. Congress of Surveyors, London, September 1968.
8. Pumpelly, Jack W. "Colour Separation and Printing
   Technique for Photomaps. " March 1966, Publ.
   U. S. G. S.
9. Radlinski, William A. "Orthophotomapping. " Conference
   of Commonwealth Survey Officers, Cambridge, England, 14th-22nd August 1967.
10. Radlinski, William A. "Orthophotomaps v. conventional
    maps. " September 1967, Publ. U. S. G. S.
11. Schweissthal, R. "Grundlagen, Bearbeitung und Her-
    stellung grossmasstäbiger Luftbildkarten. " 1967 No.
    34 Wissensch. Arbeiten der Techn. Hochschule Han-
    nover, Lehrstühle für Geodäsie, Photogrammetrie und
    Kartographie.
12. Sebert, L. M. "Photomaps for resource development
    in Canada. " Canadian Cartographer, vol. 5, no. 1
    (June 1968).
13. Visser, J. & van Zuylen, L. Orthophotos at the ITC.
    ITC publication A41/42.
14. Van Zuylen, L. & c/d Linden, J. A. "A punching ma-
    chine for accurate register in making coloured maps. "
    Tijdschrift voor Kadaster en Landmeetkunde (Nether-
    lands), October 1964.

3. MAP CLASSIFICATION AND USE

A NEW MAP FORM: NUMBERS*

William C. Aumen

Probably the first question that will cross the mind of anyone reading the title of this article will be: "Why does anyone need a new map form?" The very fact that one of the themes of this symposium is directed at maps of the future points out the need or the question would not have been raised at all. This paper then is an expression of my opinion (1) as to why there is this need for new map forms, and (2) that a new form already exists in the form of numbers which has certain implications and advantages.

Basically, I attribute much of the need for new map forms to the growing realization by both producers and consumers that they are dealing in an information process which completely transcends the charting (mapping) process. The dissemination of information can take many forms and the graphic form used by cartographers is only one of them. It is quite easy to point out the many problems associated with the use of the printed graphic as an information storage and retrieval method. To mention only a few there are: the problems of projecting the round earth on a flat surface; the limited space available on the map surface which forces displacement or deletion of some symbol features to make room for others; the quality control to maintain some semblance of accuracy; the physical storage and retrieval problem; and finally, the absolute requirement that the information be read and interpreted by a human being. It is this last requirement, that all map data from the graphic form must be read

*Reprinted by permission from International Yearbook of Cartography, vol. 10 (1970), 80-84. Published by the Bertelsmann Verlag/Kartographisches Institut Bertelsmann, Güttersloh.

by a human being, that has incurred the immediate conflict
with the application of electronic computers to problem solutions using map data. Thus arose the requirement for the
new map form of numbers. Acknowledging that needs exist
for many other new map forms, I will address my discussion
only to the numerical version and its uses, some of which
could well be the production of other new forms.

To begin with, a definition or description of a map in
number form--a numerical map--is in order. Basically, a
numerical map uses the number symbols to replace the special graphic and alphabetic symbols commonly used in cartography. This is not as revolutionary a practice as it might
seem at first because it is only necessary to examine the contour line symbol in detail to discover that the number symbol
is much more appropriate in many cases. What is the purpose of that line, usually printed in brown, on the topographic map? Simply, it indicates that the elevation of the ground
anywhere on that particular line has the same numerical value. This numerical value may be printed on the line somewhere or the value may be deduced from the value of some
other line. In either case, the line is a shorthand method of
recording repeated values of elevation which must be converted back to numbers to be useful in a quantitative sense. The
numerical version of the contour line records the repeated
elevations in "longhand" and no conversion is necessary for
quantitative use. The same logic and evaluation can be applied to the other location-type symbols on the graphic such
as streams, trails, roads, buildings, etc.

The descriptive aspects of a graphic map are somewhat more complicated in numerical map construction perhaps; however, the numerical map has a capability of storing
and furnishing to the user much more complete descriptions.
For example, from a numerical map not only could the location of a building be obtained, but also the physical description of the size and material of construction.

Toponymy in the numerical map is converted to numeric form and is then called "alphanumeric." It might seem
that this information is less accessible or legible in the numerical version than in the graphic, but if you remember the
electronic computer aspect of applying map data in this form,
then the problem disappears since all output from the computer for visual consumption is equally legible, be it an elevation value or a place name.

This is an appropriate place to delve deeper into this computer aspect of the numerical map. First, the electronic computer is essential to the production, storage, retrieval and use of the numerical map information. An electronic computer is used to process the source data into numerical form and it must be used to retrieve the data for further use. One of the uses of the data could well be the production of a graphic of some sort in the "automated cartography" procedure; however, by far the more important uses will be in the direct application of the numerical map data to the comprehensive computer solution of a much larger problem. In this use the map data will never leave its numerical form nor assume any shape which would suggest a map. Instead, it will be simply more information affecting the solution of a problem.

The ability to solve a complete problem on an electronic computer without the need for intermediate results is one of the very promising applications of numerical map data. I will illustrate this application by example later in this paper.

Obviously, the establishment of a "Numerical Map Library" as complete as I have implied is an extensive task with many side effects requiring policy changes and reorientation of the ideas and concepts of producer and user alike. The time element is also extensive and should be thought of in terms of tens of years to be realistic. Despite these problems a start has been made towards the establishment of a Numerical Map Library by the Army Map Service, U. S. A. Corps of Engineers [on 15 January 1969 the Army Map Service was integrated into the newly formed U. S. Army Topographic Command (Topocom)].

Current production of the terrain portion of numerical map data is being carried out by use of digitizing devices known as Digital Graphics Recorders (D. G. R. 's). The total system involving several of the devices is entitled the Digital Topographic Data Collection System (D. T. D. C. S.) and it is somewhat unique in its use of a small general purpose computer to control the flow of information from several (four) D. G. R. 's through a checking process to a final magnetic tape which can be transmitted to a central computing facility for further processing. This D. T. D. C. system requires a manual line-following operation to quantize the line trace and identify the line by elevation if it is a contour line or by some other label if it is another type of symbol such as drainage or highway. This whole process employs a graphic of some kind as source material. The digitizing of photography will be discussed later.

I will describe the production of the elevation data to illustrate the process and some of the problems involved. Once the graphic contour lines have been quantized and labeled by the D. T. D. C. S. , they are sent to a central computer facility for completion of the library data. This completion process involves the reintroduction of all of the elevation data omitted from the graphic because of the lack of space on the graphic. In other words, all the elevations between contour lines are interpolated by the computer process to produce a matrix of elevations at one one-hundredth of an inch (0. 01 inch) spacing. This resolution of 0. 01 inch is essentially the equivalent of the line weight on a graphic which is the intent of the numerical map form. The interpolation logic, itself, is quite difficult to formulate for a computer and the procedure used involves fitting planes to known elevations (from contours) and determining the elevations of the unknown points to put them on the planes. Although each point solution is trivial, the need to solve anywhere from four to five million points per map sheet makes the task quite formidable. As a result of this process, approximately six million elevations are recorded for each map sheet (nominal 20 X 30 inch size). Approximately two reels of magnetic tape are required to store these six million elevations. Adding cultural data to the records will more than double this storage.

As promised, I will discuss the possibilities of obtaining numerical map data directly from photography. Although there are many unsolved (and even unknown as yet) problems in this approach, the ultimate value of this method of obtaining numerical data is inestimable. Fortunately, the basic tools for such a process are already available in the form of the "automatic" stereocompilers, such as the Autometric Stereomat, the Bendix-Nistri AS-11, and the Bunker-Ramo UNAMACE, which scan photography and quantize the stereoimagery. The basic problems envisioned are ones of eliminating "noise" and identifying the quantized information. The value of the approach lies in the purity of the data collected which has not been subjected to the distortion of the cartographic process.

Since the production and storage of the binary bits required to create a Numerical Map Library quickly reaches astronomic proportions, it is mandatory that an evaluation of this map form from an economic standpoint be attempted. This leads to a discussion of applications both known and projected.

Let's start with a very common problem facing civil engineers or planners--that of earthwork computation. The problem arises in the transportation area in the form of economic highway, railway, and canal alignment; in all types of irrigation projects; and in dam construction. By use of a properly programmed electronic computer it is possible for an engineer to submit several alternative alignments to the computer and receive only the comparative evaluation of each as the output from the computer. Gone will be the cross-section layouts, the end-area and volume computations, and the mass diagram construction. These will be performed by the computer but never displayed since they are really intermediate values which are unnecessary in themself for an engineering decision. It is reasonable to expect an average-size modern computer to produce solutions to such alignment problems in a matter of minutes. The key point in the context of this paper is the availability of the terrain in numerical form which is immediately available to the computer in the course of its problem solution. The opportunity for experimentation with different alignments by the engineer is invaluable.

Consider the problem of establishing a communication network involving radio, television, or micro-wave transmitters and receivers. Terrain has a significant effect on the layout of such a system and anyone who has labored with a graphic to determine lines-of-sight will appreciate the ability of a computer to produce a graphic profile of a line in minutes or even better, simply inform the engineer that intervening terrain obstructs the line and one or both sites should be moved for optimum transmission. On this same topic, wouldn't it be nice to request the computer to print out the locations of all the points above a certain elevation within a particular area? This would certainly ease the problem of the original site selection. Again, this computer solution is possible only with the terrain (and cultural features) available in numeric form.

In the cases where a graphic is still the preferred form from which to assimilate the map information, it is possible to direct the computer to draw (or display) a customized map of one or several specific items. For example, it is

feasible to request the computer to draw the network in an
area showing only the all-weather roads. Perhaps the drainage is desired also and the computer could add this to the
road network in a matter of minutes. No longer need the
planner pore over a typical topographic map to extract only
the information he wants. The computer will do the extracting for him. As I implied earlier, it is not necessary to
produce such special graphics on a piece of paper. It is
quite feasible to display these graphics on cathode ray tubes
which are connected to the computer by some sort of electronic communication media such as microwave. Once the
display is used it is destroyed by turning off the receiver.
The data, itself, never left the central Numerical Map Library!

Obviously, the concept of map appearance must change
if these new display forms are to be accepted, but this leads
us back to an examination of some of our traditional mapping
procedures which are predicated on visual interpretation of the
graphic symbols. Color, for instance, is used to help the
user discriminate features on the graphic; however, if the
computer can discriminate these features in a different way
and only show that which is desired, the need for color is
drastically reduced or eliminated entirely.

In conclusion I wish to point out how this one new map
form of numbers touches on each of the themes originally established for this symposium. First, of course, the use of
electronic computers for comprehensive problem solution has
already forced the numerical map into being. This one new
form lends itself to an excellent prospect of timely map revision since it will remain essentially in one central location.
Production of small quantities of graphics is quite feasible
since the computer can scribe an up-to-date press plate in
a matter of minutes. This also allows frequent editions.
Generalization of map data is concommitant with customized
graphics as previously described. The map library problem
may grow larger because of the additional information which
can be stored in a Numerical Map Library; however, that is
what libraries are for--to store information--so if the problem is larger because of more information, it must follow
that the library is more useful. The mapping of developing
countries should be enhanced by the ability of computers to
do things so rapidly including the production of interim graphics if desired. The education of cartographers will have to
include more emphasis on electronic devices, including computers, as the coming "tools-of-the-trade" and the standardization of terms will have to include these new devices.

Since the primary aim of this paper is to stimulate thought, discussion, and controversy on the departure of map-making from its traditional course, any disagreements with my opinions, statements, or concepts are welcome.   Debate is one path leading to progress.

MODERN MAPS AND THEIR USES*

G. R. Crone

At present more forward thinking is probably being devoted to national and regional planning and to the economic
development of the emerging countries than to any other subject.   Such planning must be based on facts which, when collected, are usually presented as statistical tables or in other
indigestible forms.   It has now been shown that some types
of facts can be presented cartographically, that is, through
maps, as a clearer manner than by any other means.   In
fact, maps are now, more than ever, the primary tool of the
planner.

This is a tremendous challenge to the cartographer.
These new demands open up a whole new vista for him.   He
is still faced with his centuries-old task of representing the
surface features of the earth of interest to man in his daily
coming and going; but now he has to be able to show beneath
the surface of the earth or the seas, what man is doing wherever he is, his occupation, his earnings, his use of the land
and many other subjects.   Fortunately, the modern cartographer can call upon a greater variety of technological aids than
were at the disposal of his predecessors.

An idea of the tasks and methods of a national survey
of today can be obtained from a brief review of the history
and development of the Ordnance Survey Department, the
government agency responsible for the production of the official maps of Britain.   Many people, motorists, cyclists, and
walkers in particular, are familiar with the One-Inch Ordnance Survey maps (one inch to one mile, or 63, 360 inches),
and indeed it is still the most popular of the Department's

*Reproduced by permission from the Geographical Magazine
(London), vol. 36, no. 8 (1963), 449-457.

publications, hundreds of thousands of sheets being sold yearly.   This is the map which, for many years after the foundation of the Survey in 1791, was the basis of its output.   It
was originally designed for military purposes at a time when
Britain was threatened by invasion.   Hence it concentrated
upon representing the topographical features--mountains, hills,
valleys, rivers, lakes, woods, marshes, etc.--and the roads
and bridges, in particular their width, condition, whether they
were enclosed by hedges, and so forth; in fact, all the information of value to marching and fighting troops.   Because of
the good representation of the countryside, however, it was
often known, rather unfairly, as the "fox-hunters' map."
With the passage of time, changing conditions and improved
techniques, the one-inch map has gone through numerous
changes; the current series, the Seventh, the first to cover
the whole of Great Britain in a uniform style, is an ad-
mirably clear map which will stand comparison with any national series.

The industrial development of Britain, the advent of
canals and railways, of vast engineering construction schemes,
the growth of population and other social problems, created
a demand for maps on a larger scale.   The immediate cause
of the first addition was the demand for a map which would
show the holdings of land in Ireland, to facilitate the working
of land reform.   The scale selected for this was six inches
to the mile (1:10, 560).   So useful did this map prove that it
was decided to map Great Britain on this scale when the Irish
survey was completed.

Thereafter, there was much discussion on what other
scales should be adopted, while Parliament was unwilling to
vote the necessary funds; this controversy reached a point at
which the work of the Survey was actually suspended.   However, "the battle of the scales" was eventually decided and
the Survey was charged with production of map series on the
additional scales of twenty-five inches to the mile (1:2500)
and fifty inches (1:1250).   The six-inch scale is the largest
on which the whole country is covered; the others are confined to the more inhabited areas and the great centres of
population.   These large-scale maps, or plans, are much
used in connection with property transactions (the smallest
scale on which buildings, for example, are truly represented,
is the six-inch), civil engineering projects, public works and
similar undertakings.   Very largely at the request of geographers, though it has also a military value, another scale was
recently introduced, that of two and a half inches to the mile
(approximately 1:25, 000).

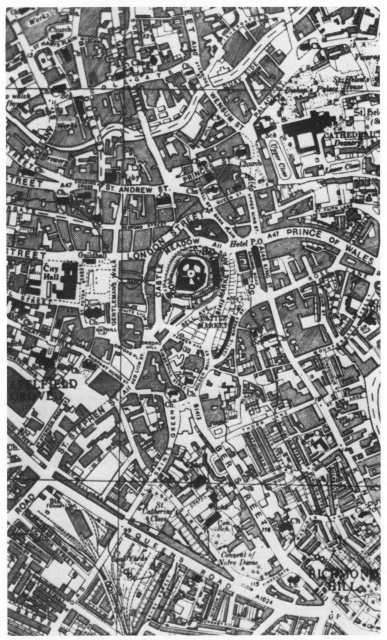

On the six inches to the mile map (1:10,650) [the scale is not true in this reproduction] detail is considerable, but only comparatively rarely are individual buildings shown separately.

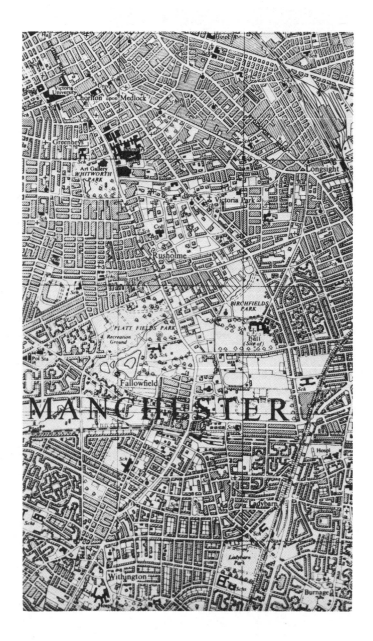

The two and a half inches to the mile map (about 1:25, 000) [scale not true in this reproduction], mainly for geographers and civil engineers, and also for military use.

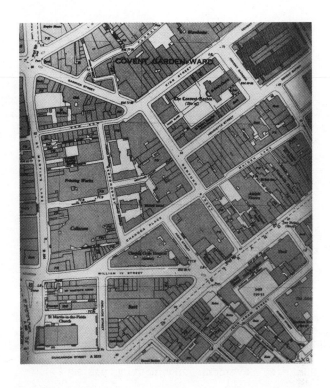

The 1:2500 or twenty-five inches to the mile map [scale not true in this reproduction] on which buildings are shown in detail. The editorial offices of The Geographical Magazine are at bench mark 61.77, in St Martin's Lane.

        But the greatest demand upon the Ordnance Survey is now made by the planning authorities, central and county, and cooperation with the Ministry of Housing and Local Government is particularly close. Under the Town and Country Planning Act of 1947, local authorities are required to submit a statement of their plans, revised at regular intervals, accompanied by maps, those for county boroughs and urban areas on the six-inch scale, and for counties on the one-inch scale. But the physical planners--surveyors, architects and engineers--also require the large-scale plans for their detailed calculations and drawings.

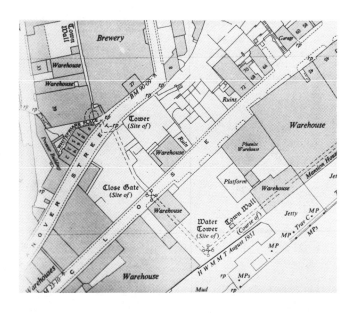

Part of Newcastle being considered for redevelopment. The
1:1250 map [scale not true in this reproduction] is of great
value for this work, for much detail can be shown, including
such things as pavements and mooring posts.

It is commonplace that the countryside is undergoing
rapid and continual change. Since the planners obviously require maps as accurate and correct as possible, perhaps the
greatest problem facing the Ordnance Survey, after the execution of the basic surveys, is that of revision. The base is
the 1:2500 plan and all smaller scales are now ultimately re-
ductions from this. A system of continuous revision is practised, which means that revisers are continually at work in
the areas of greatest change, while other areas are revised
periodically. There must still be a time lag before corrections and additions are incorporated in the published sheets,
and local authorities must then rely on their own services,
making available the new details to the Department. Even
so, with resources at present available, the new regular six-
inch series is unlikely to be complete within the next twenty
years. The task therefore before the Department is to establish priorities and to balance resources against the demand: from the Services, the national and local offices

(including such bodies as the National Coal Board), scientists
and the general public.

From the above summary, much condensed, it will be
seen that the ideal requirements for an effective and economical survey of a country are: (i) a firm decision on the basic
scale giving complete coverage; (ii) a programme to secure
completion within a reasonable time; (iii) a technique for revision; and (iv) adequate financial and technical resources.
These are difficult objectives for emerging countries, particularly in Africa, to secure, engaged as they are in the
task of establishing viable economies.   This task must begin
with an accurate assessment of the nature and distribution of
the natural resources--including soils, vegetation and water
power, in addition to mineral wealth--as well as the more
obvious facts of relief, the nature of the surface and the distribution of settlements, required to devise an effective system of communications.   Experience, sometimes bitter, has
proved that the first essential for national planning of this nature is an accurate and comprehensive base map.   All former
British territories possess Survey Departments inherited from
the earlier period, which have done good work on limited resources, but a national survey on this scale, apart from funds,
requires a numerous and highly skilled staff, possession of
the necessary "know-how," and costly specialized equipment,
if the work is to be completed within a reasonable time.

It is here that a second British mapping agency is
rendering important aid.   This is the Directorate of Overseas
(Geodetic and Topographical) Surveys, with headquarters at
Tolworth in Surrey.   The Directorate was established in 1946
with funds provided by Parliament for the purpose of providing
overseas territories with an adequate series of maps to permit the orderly development of land and mineral resources.

Far from finding its work terminating abruptly as the
territories gained independence, the Directorate has continued
to function and to extend its services in conjunction with the
new administrations, as a part of the Department of Technical Co-operation.   A considerable advantage of the present
arrangements is that, by pooling the requirements of several
countries in one central organization, economies in staffing
and equipment are secured together with the best technical
advice.   Facilities are also made available for the training
of staff.   These services are not now restricted to former
British territories.   Mapping projects are being carried out,
for example, for the republics of Guinea and Cameroon.

LEGEND

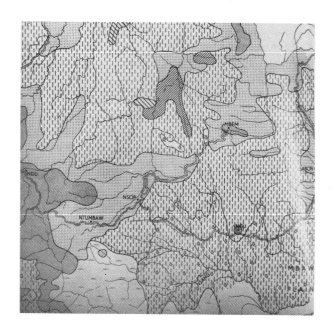

1 Dense cultivation
2 Scattered cultivation, with some grazing
3 Settlements in forest
  a) with obvious cultivation
  b) with little/no sign of cultivation

4 Grazed land (mainly grassland)
5 Ungrazed land (mainly grassland)
6 Forest and other woody vegetation
7 Swamp

A map of the Bamenda area in the hills of Southern Cameroon at 1:250,000 [scale not true in this reproduction], to show the vegetation and agricultural use of the land.

At the outset, it was estimated that the Directorate was faced with the task of mapping 1,500,000 square miles, approximately half the area of the United States. The original aim was to obtain complete coverage at the scale of 1. 125,000 (approximately two miles to one inch), half to be produced in ten years. This ambitious programme has not been achieved, partly because some of the existing survey material was found useless for this purpose, but also because this

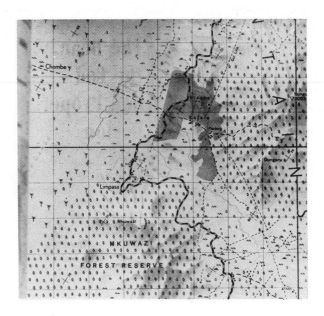

A hill-shaded map of Nyasaland. The hill-shading is done
from air photographs, giving a picture of the relief illuminated from the north-west. The scale is 1:50,000 or 1.27
inches to the mile [scale not true in this reproduction].

basic scale proved inadequate. A series of maps on the
scale of 1:50,000 (rather larger than one inch to a mile)
were called for. Among other things this involves a more
than four-fold increase in the number of map sheets.

The work of the Directorate of Overseas Surveys is
to provide in the first instance what are known as "provision-
al plots," outline maps with the network (parallels of latitude
and meridians of longitude), reference points, altitudes, etc.,
which form the basic framework of the map. The local Survey Departments often add boundaries, names, etc., and
check the work generally. In the interests of speed and
economy, much of the original data is obtained through the
use of air photographs, taken on carefully planned flights.

Nor is the work confined to topographical mapping; the
Directorate has sections concerned with land use and forestry

which make valuable contributions to agricultural development.
In certain special projects the Directorate works in cooperation with agencies of the United Nations organizations, e. g.
in the Kafue Basin development scheme, Northern Rhodesia
and land use problems in Southern Cameroon.   The total expenditure for all this varied work is about £1, 000, 000 a year,
but the contribution to the future exceeds this in value many
times.

     The story of the Directorate illustrates one of the
most practical and fruitful methods of rendering aid to the
developing countries.   Instead of being in a position rather
similar to that of the Ordnance Survey in 1791, their Survey
Departments have nearly two centuries of experience at their
disposal.

MAPS AND MEDICINE IN EAST AFRICA*

B. W. Langlands

The history of medical mapping in East Africa dates back almost a hundred years to the publication of James Christie's Cholera Epidemics in East Africa in 1876. Given the fact that East Africa was still in the process of becoming known to the outside world at this time, a book of this sort, containing information about the interior, as well as Zanzibar and the coast, was a remarkable achievement. Christie interviewed all the trading caravans reporting into Zanzibar and constructed a picture of the spread of cholera in the Lake Victoria area, the vicinities of Mounts Kenya and Kilimanjaro, and from Lake Tanganyika (Ujiji) and Nyasa. The book contains two maps which clearly represent the first attempt at medical mapping for a very long time to come. Christie's work may have provided the essential foundation for medical work in East Africa on problems of epidemiology and the adoption of medical mapping as a respectable procedure, but, in point of fact, it was probably seldom consulted in East Africa or anywhere else. It does, however, represent an early extension of the principles of epidemiology and geographic medicine (as laid down by such pioneers of the subject as Dr. John Snow, who in 1848 had developed his ideas of cholera propagation) into the field of tropical medicine. The sub-title of Christie's book is of interest, for it also indicates his concern to establish the geographic and cultural factors underlying a disease distribution--"An account of the several diffusions of the disease in that country from 1821-1872 with an outline of the Geography, Ethnology, and Trade Connections of the Regions through which the epidemics passed." It is fortunate that after being so little known this interesting book is about to be reprinted. [1]

---

*Reprinted by permission from Special Libraries Association, Geography and Map Division, Bulletin No. 78 (1969), 9-15.

One would not wish to suggest that the present enthusiasm for a geographical approach to medical problems is
directly dependent on the tradition established by Christie;
there has doubtless been an intervening period in which, at
an academic level at any rate, doctors were not map con-
scious.   As a geographer writing, however, in the late 1960's,
one is obliged to pay tribute to the impressive geographic research laboratory which is now firmly established at the leading, and for a long time the only, teaching hospital in East
Africa at the university level, Mulago Hospital, in Kampala.
A map consciousness exists here to a degree unparallelled
in my knowledge elsewhere in the world.   Geographic thinking prevails in many departments, particularly in pathology,
microbiology, preventive medicine and medicine.   Recently
the present incumbent of the chair of pathology took this subject as the theme of the inaugural lecture. [2]   To a geographer
the current practice in the medical school of recording the
distribution of diseases by sticking colored pins in base maps
is encouraging.   Likewise, the frequency with which publications from the Makerere Medical School are illustrated by
maps is also commendable; though sometimes the maps may
show little other than the location of Kampala, more normally
they are indicative of a keen consciousness of the importance
of distributions and of the necessity to use a map for illustration of a distributional problem.   In the light of the map consciousness among the medical practitioners in East Africa,
one may wonder what the geographer per se has to contribute.

The present firm establishment of geographic thought
among doctors in East Africa owes a good deal to the interest
and activity of Professor J. N. P. Davies, who, while occupying the chair of pathology from 1950 to 1961, was also Vice-
President of the International Institute of Geographical Pathology.   Much of his contribution lay in defining the difference
in the incidence of disease in Uganda, as compared with
Britain and America.   Secondly, one should recognize the
service of Dr. A. M. M. Wilson, Reader in Microbiology
from 1953 to 1962, who in 1958 or thereabouts established a
Committee for Geographic Medicine at Makerere.   This committee was relatively short-lived, for it was brought to a de-
liberate conclusion in 1963 on the basis that so many people
were already adopting geographical principles in their routine
work that there was no point in having a committee to encourage them to do so.   The committee had attained its prime
objective within five years; a map room had been established,
a collection of atlases and texts of the local geography was
brought together, and a supply of base maps was made available.

The role of the geographer on this committee was slight.   His
main function was seen to be that of advisor on map scales
and locator of obscure place names.   However, since the
geographer on this committee also had a bibliographic mania,
it fell to him to prepare a bibliography of the publications on
diseases in East Africa that had a locational significance. [3]
In all, over 1100 references were found for which a location
to the problem was evident.   For a surprisingly large number of these references the distributional significance was
made manifest by the presence of a map in the text.   The
citations were then listed on a district by district basis for
the whole of East Africa, with a fair amount of duplication
giving a total of 1, 335 entries.   This bibliography deals only
with publications to the end of 1963.   Since then there has
been a considerable out-pouring of papers in the field of geographical medicine, and the prospect of bringing it up to date
is forbidding.

The concern for maps in the study of disease and medicine in East Africa takes a variety of forms.   Priority of
place should probably be given to the medical entomologist,
for he had been using the map as a tool in his field work.
In many instances, working in poorly mapped areas, he had
to prepare his own base map.   Since many of East Africa's
diseases are insect-borne, such as malaria, trypanosomiasis
(sleeping sickness), oncherocerciasis (river-blindness), kala-
azar (leishmaniasis), the professional services of medical entomologists have for a long time been recognized.   In so far
as these persons become involved in studying the distribution
of their cases of the disease in relation to the vectors, one
must recognize the epidemiologist as a practicing field worker
for whom the map is an essential tool.   It is perhaps invidi-
ous to single out some such workers for particular mention.
Much work in sleeping sickness control falls clearly into this
category and was being adopted effectively as early as the
1920's and 1930's by such persons as Swynnerton[4] and Maclean[5] in Tanganyika, Morris[6] initially in Ghana (then the Gold
Coast) but latterly in Uganda, and Robertson in south Uganda. [7]
On malaria, field distributional studies had been undertaken by
D. B. Wilson[8] from 1934 to 1962, particularly in coastal Tanzania.   More recently, one may see the same approach adopted by a malaria control unit at Taveta[9] in studies on the Ken-
ya-Tanzania border.   Another insect-borne disease, the understanding of which called for field mapping exercises for both
disease incidence and the vector, is Kala-azar, a disease
found in the semi-arid areas of Kenya, and conveyed by sand-
flies, the special concern of Fendall and others in the 1950's.[10]

The success of epidemiologists with the problem of plague in central Kenya also depended on a detailed mapping of the infested settlements in Nyeri district by Dr. Isegear Roberts in the 1930's. [11] More recent field mapping has been undertaken for Buruli ulcer on the banks of the Nile in Bunyoro, where a house-by-house survey was undertaken. [12] Another interesting example of combined field-mapping has been undertaken by a geographer and a medical ecologist on the locational aspects of water-borne diseases and water use habits in East Africa. [13] These examples of geographic principles being adopted by medical entomologists and field epidemiologists may be placed first in that they represent an early and continuing use of maps for the elucidation of medical problems. The examples given are only a small sample of the whole field.

Secondly, and again it is probably secondly in course of time, one must recognize the interest of the district medical officer in the distribution of environmental phenomena in relation to the pattern of disease in his district. In the enormously busy occupation of running the medical services of an entire district, administering the hospital, to say nothing of having to conduct surgical operations and deal with hundreds of out-patients a week, some district medical officers have become experts on the geography of their district, and have set about mapping the distributions of rainfall and population, etc., against which they compare their maps of helminths, tropical ulcers, and such like. There is at least one article in a respectable geographical publication which was obtained by photographing the maps on a district medical officer's wall. Again, to single out only a few people does less than justice to this rare group of practicing geographers. Professor G. Nelson, now Professor of Helminthology at the London School of Hygiene and Tropical Medicine, was one such map-conscious D. M. O. of the West Nile district in northwest Uganda who worked on the patterns of disease distributions, mapped them in the early 1950's, and wondered if anyone would ever be interested in publishing this sort of work. [14] Some districts of East Africa have become particularly well mapped from the medical standpoint. The West Nile district of Uganda is one such, not only because of the work of Nelson, but also because of the interest in leprosy and cancer distributions as mapped by the Drs. Williams at the missionary hospital of Kuluva. [15] Another well-worked district for medical distributions is the Meru district of Kenya, owing to the work of Dr. Bell. [16]

A third manifestation of map-consciousness may be seen in the manner already referred to, plotting the home locations of all persons reporting to hospital, or the home location of all autopsies sent into the hospital. Mapping of this sort is particularly evident in the work of Professor Hutt and the pathologists working with him, and has led to advancements in the knowledge of cancer, heart diseases, and big spleen disease in Uganda.

Fourthly, an interesting role for maps may be seen in the now famous work of Dr. Burkitt (famous in the sense that a popular account of it has now appeared in Reader's Digest). Dr. Burkitt has worked on a cancerous lymphoma, which now commonly carries his name, Burkitt's tumor. Having plotted the distribution of this disease of the jaw in young children in Buganda, he then toured eastern and central Africa, plotting its incidence over the continent. He came to the conclusion that precise altitudinal, temperature, and rainfall parameters exist, restricting its occurrence to warm humid conditions. By comparing maps of the incidence of the disease with other geographical distributions, the lymphoma distribution was seen to be closely similar to that of intense malaria transmission, and similar to that of mosquitoes and tsetse-flies. From this a deduction was made that possibly the disease was related to these or similar insect vectors, carrying a cancer-producing virus or agent; in which case it would be the first evidence that some forms of human cancer were introduced by an arthropod-borne virus. The argument is somewhat speculative, but it does represent an application of geographic thinking and cartographic tools to a medical problem.[17] Similarly causal associations between some forms of cancer and fungus distributions or soil types may be postulated by comparative map analysis; though the danger is that these speculations may be disproved by detailed chemical analysis.[18]

Another way in which the medical profession has used maps has been in arriving at a better understanding of the distribution of ill-health, but without going to the extent of arguing for causal relationships. A good example may be seen in the use put to the geographer's mapping of food crops and subsistence agriculture[19] as a basis for a better understanding of such nutritional diseases as kwashiorkor and marasmus. In this respect medical science has benefited from the high quality of mapping that characterizes the Atlas of Uganda, a more valuable, though admittedly more recent, production than its counterparts from Tanzania and Kenya.

Most of these uses to which maps have been put by
the medical profession have depended on relatively simple
techniques of cartographic plotting of symbols showing the incidence of the diseases, and of lines showing the environmental parameters of conditions determining those distributions. In the last few years more refined statistical techniques have been developed to show patterns of disease and
the relationship of different types of disease to each other.
Two examples will serve to illustrate this point, one on the
geographic variations in the distribution of various helminthic
diseases, and the other on the relationship of various forms
of cancer to each other. Dr. H. Diesfeld of the Institut für
Tropenhygiene in Heidelberg has analyzed and mapped the distribution of five intestinal helminths--Ascaris, Taenia, Schis-
tosoma mansoni, and the larvae of hookworm and Strongyloides
--for forty-four hospitals throughout Kenya. By a statistical
correlation of absolute and relative frequency of each of these
with altitude, rainfall, temperature, population densities, and
cattle number, he has postulated the existence of ten distinct
helminthic regions, depending on the dominance of particular
helminths. Dr. Diesfeld's paper, which was presented at a
conference in preventive medicine on "Change and Disease in
East Africa, " in January 1968, was unfortunately not published
with the majority of papers of that conference. [20]   The exercise was one of considerable geographical importance and
represents a rare attempt at a systematic statistical analysis
based on the hospital records of an African country. The
failure to give wider publicity to the paper possibly reflects
a skepticism concerning the validity of the hospital statistics,
or a lesser concern for problems in geo-medicine in Nairobi,
where the journal is published, then in Kampala. Another
operation in the field of more detailed statistical mapping may
be seen in the work of Miss Paula Cook of the Medical Research Council, Statistical Research Unit of London, on cancer distribution. A geography graduate with training as a
medical statistician, she is mapping the incidence of cancer
of the stomach, esophagus, liver, penis, Kaposi's sarcoma
and Burkitt's tumor for the whole of East Africa as related
to such groupings as age, sex, and tribe.

A final manifestation of the value of maps to the medical profession may be seen in the planning of medical services. Theoretically the geographer should have a role to
play in the application of central-place theory and the analysis of "thresholds" for determining the location of hospital
and dispensary services. As yet, very little geographical
theory has been applied to the problems of development in

East Africa.   However, one may see at least one example of
the medical expert pointing to the need for such an approach.
In a most important work for the planning of medical facilities
Professor M. King, now Professor of Social Medicine at the
University of Zambia, but formerly a lecturer in microbiology at Makerere, has examined the extent of the supply area
for patients to Mityana Hospital (forty miles west of Kampala)
and of the relationship of the hospital to its surrounding dis-
pensaries.   This study, in a book of wide circulation in Africa,
Medical Care in Developing Countries, [21] provides a model for
such studies which could be done throughout East Africa, and
which could be undertaken by any settlement geographer.

There is no need for an apology for much of this review concentrating on work done in Uganda.   The fact is that
largely due to the presence there of a university medical
faculty of long standing a great deal more work on distributional aspects of medicine has been undertaken.   This work
exists in a wide range of medical journals which may not be
easily accessible to the geographer.   Fortunately, much of
this work has now been consolidated into one volume.   Under
the direction of Dr. S. A. Hall there has recently been compiled, and published, with the assistance of financial aid from
the World Health Organization, an Uganda Atlas of Disease
Distribution. [22]   This is unlike other atlases of disease distributions, such as that by Dr. M. Howe for Britain, largely
because the medical statistics are poorer and not collected
on a uniform basis.   The atlas contains as much information
as is available about the distribution of each disease prevalent in Uganda, and sets these distributions, wherever possible, against the relevant environmental and vector factors.
It contains fifty maps on a uniform scale, and is divided into
fifty sections, each written by the main authority in the field,
and each containing a valuable bibliography.

As a compendium of information about the variations
in the location of different diseases and the factors affecting
disease incidence, this atlas is of great importance to the
doctor.   It is also of considerable value in demonstrating the
importance of human disease as a factor of the environment
as a better approach to regional geography and to the bio-
geographer.   However, it also highlights a problem of fundamental importance; that it is that, where in a country like
Uganda, the medical profession is fully map-conscious, there
is very little place for the geographer other than as a cartographer.   There must be few examples of the geographer
in Africa, or anywhere else, contributing to the solution of

a medical problem, though there are some geographers, who
as specialist medical geographers, would see this as their
potential role.

REFERENCES/NOTES

1. Christie, J.   Cholera Epidemics in East Africa.   Lon-
    don: Macmillan, 1876; 508 p., 2 maps.   There is
    not a copy of this book in the Makerere Medical Li-
    brary, and the comments here upon it have been
    drawn from J. N. Davies, "James Christie and the
    Cholera Epidemics of East Africa," East African
    Medical Journal, vol. 36 (1959), 1-6.
2. Hutt, M. S. R.   "The Geographical Approach in Medical
    Research."   East African Geographical Review, vol.
    5 (1967), 1-8.
3. Langlands, B. W.   Bibliography of the distribution of
    disease in East Africa.   Kampala: 1965; 184p.
    (Makerere Library Publications, no. 3.)
4. Swynnerton, C. F. M., subsequently became a famous
    authority on tsetse flies, but as early as 1923 was
    mapping the location of sleeping sickness cases near
    Mwanza; see Bulletin of Entomological Research, vol.
    13 (1923), 317-372; Transactions of the Royal Society
    of Tropical Medicine and Hygiene, vol. 17 (1923),
    142-150.
5. Maclean, G., worked on the mapping of T. Rhodesiense
    in Ufipa; see Annals of Tropical Medicine and Para-
    sitology, vol. 20 (1926), 327-339.
6. Morris, K. R. S., formulated various theories on sleep-
    ing sickness outbreaks as a result of detailed mapping
    of epidemics in Ghana; see particularly "The Ecology
    of Epidemic Sleeping Sickness: I, The Significance
    of Location [and] II, The Effects of an Epidemic,"
    Bulletin of Entomological Research, vol. 42 (1951),
    427-443, and vol. 43 (1952), 375-396.   In Uganda
    he did more field work, but his work then also took
    on an historical role of determining where outbreaks
    had occurred in the past; this also proved eminently
    mappable; see numerous articles which appeared in
    Transactions of the Royal Society of Tropical Medi-
    cine and Hygiene between 1959 and 1962 (vols. 53-56).
7. Robertson, D. H. H., wrote sometimes with J. M. Baker
    on a T. Rhodesiense area in south Busoga in Uganda,
    Transactions of the Royal Society of Tropical Medi-
    cine, vol. 52 (1958), 337-348, and Bulletin of the

World Health Organisation, vol. 28 (1963), 627-643.
8. Wilson, D. B.; see his work on malaria surveys at
    Tanga which appeared in the Transactions of the
    Royal Society of Tropical Medicine and Hygiene be-
    tween 1936 and 1963 (vols. 29-56).
9. Various research projects involving field mapping have
    been undertaken by the East African Institute of Ma-
    laria and Vector-borne Disease, in Amani, Tanzania.
10. Fendall, N. R. E., has various articles on Kala-azar in
    the East African Medical Journal, from 1950-1953
    (vols. 27 to 30). A series of papers then appeared
    on the vectors and the mapping of environmental con-
    ditions in the Annals of Tropical Medicine and Para-
    sitology by a variety of authors in 1962 and 1963
    (vols. 56 and 57).
11. Roberts, J. I.; see various papers in the Journal of
    Hygiene, from 1935 to 1939 (vols. 36 to 39).
12. This work on Buruli ulcers is only beginning to be pub-
    lished; see article by R. H. Morrow and others in
    Lancet, 18 January 1969.
13. White, G., and Bradley, D. Drawer of Water. Chi-
    cago: University of Chicago Press, 1970.
14. Nelson, G. N.; see various articles in East African Med-
    ical Journal, 1955 to 1959 (vols. 32-36), and Trans-
    actions of the Royal Society of Tropical Medicine and
    Hygiene, 1958 (vol. 52).
15. Williams, E. H. and R. H.; see Leprosy Review 1955
    and 1964 (vols. 24 and 35), and East African Medical
    Journal, 1951 and 1966 (vols. 28 and 43).
16. Bell, S.; a series of nine articles appeared in the Jour-
    nal of Tropical Medicine and Hygiene, 1955 to 1956
    (vols. 58 and 59).
17. Burkitt, D. N., has produced a large number of articles
    on this problem, and it is therefore difficult to de-
    termine which best illustrates his argument. The
    article covering the widest area is probably "A Tu-
    mour Safari in East and Central Africa," (British
    Journal of Cancer, Vol. 16, 1962, p. 379-386). The
    geographical approach however, is apparent in many
    of his titles: "Observations on the Geography of
    Malignant Lymphoma," East African Medical Journal,
    vol. 38 (1961), 511-514; "Determining the Climatic
    Limitations of a Children's Cancer Common in Afri-
    ca," British Medical Journal (Oct. 1962), 1019-1023;
    "A Children's Cancer Dependent on Climatic Factors,"
    Nature, vol. 194 (1962), 232-234; "A Great Patholo-
    gical Frontier," Postgraduate Medical Journal, vol.

42 (1966), 543-547; (with D. Wright) "Geographical
and Tribal Distribution of the African Lymphoma in
Uganda," British Medical Journal (March 1966), 569-
573); and (with others) "Some Variations in Disease
Pattern in East and Central Africa," East African
Medical Journal, vol. 40 (1963), 1-6. In some re-
spects the most controversial implications are in
A. J. Haddow, "An Improved Map for the Study of
Burkitt's Lymphoma Syndrome in Africa," East Afri-
can Medical Journal, vol. 40 (1963), 429-432.

18. Robinson, J. B. D., and Clifford P., provide a salutary
reminder of the difficulty of supporting this sort of
theory in finding that chemical trace elements from
the soil via maize could not be regarded as being
correlated with carcinoma of the nasopharynx in Kenya (East African Medical Journal, vol. 45 (1968),
694-700).

19. McMaster, D. N. A Subsistence Crop Geography of
Uganda. Bude: Geographical Publications, 1962.
This is a work frequently referred to in nutritional
literature.

20. Diesfeld, H. J., "Intestinal Helminths, Their Association to Environmental Factors and Their Geographical Distribution in Kenya," is only available in
cyclostyled format without the graphs and maps. A
shortened version of this paper appeared (in German)
in Die Erde, vol. 100 (1969), 30-37. Part of this
work, together with relevant parts of a similar exercise for Uganda will be published under the auspices
of the German Research Council project, Kartenwerk,
under the editorship of Professor J. Schultze of the
Free University of Berlin. Most of the other papers
of geographical relevance from this conference are
printed in the East African Medical Journal, vol. 45
(May 1968).

21. King, M. Medical Care in Developing Countries. Nairobi: Oxford University Press, 1966. The book is
not paginated; the relevant section is on "The Organisation of Health Services," in Chapter 2. A map is
given, designated an out-patient "isocare" map, showing the frequency of hospital and dispensary visits.

22. Hall, S. A., and Langlands, B. W. Uganda Atlas of
Disease Distribution. Nairobi: East African Publishing House, 1969. (A limited preliminary edition has
been available as a publication of the Departments of
Preventive Medicine and Geography ("Occasional Paper No. 12"), Makerere University College, 1968;
187 p.

THE GLOBE*

William M. McKinney

In teaching geography, the instructor has recourse
to a number of aids. One of the most obvious and appropriate is the map. Another is the model, a category which includes the topographic relief model, the mechanical planetarium, and several other useful devices.

The map and the model may be combined in the terrestial globe, a sphere whose surface has been treated to
transform it into a representation of the earth. (A spherical
form is entirely satisfactory, since the actual deviations of
the earth from this geometrical shape are extremely slight.)
The common globe has the greatest utility of any visual aid
in geography. Most readers will be aware of its use, as a
highly accurate version of the map, to show locations, directions, etc., on the earth's surface. Far fewer will be aware
of the full potentials of the globe as a model of the earth in
space.

The Globe and Its Construction

One of the disadvantages of the globe is its greater
cost, when compared with a map of the same scale. This,
in turn, stems from the difficulty of constructing a globe.
Maps, like any material printed on a flat sheet, can be turned
out cheaply and in volume. The globe must represent the
earth upon a spherical surface, and this presents special
problems.

In the study of map projections one learns how difficult it is to represent the spherical earth upon a flat sheet

*Reprinted by permission from The Journal of Geography,
vol. 68, no. 7 (1969), 406-410.

of paper. In the construction of the globe, one is faced with
the same problem in reverse. Map projections are customarily devised for flat surfaces or for developable ones. (A developable surface is one, such as a cone or cylinder, which
can be cut and unrolled to form a flat plane.) If the sphere
were a developable surface, fewer problems would exist for
either the cartographer of the globe maker; we could easily
combine the realism and accuracy of the globe with the cheap
convenience of the map. Alas, the sphere is not developable,
and compromises must be made if one is to turn the globe
into the map or vice versa.

        The solution to this problem can be obtained by look-
ing out your window. In any small area the world appears
to be flat, as its curvature deviates from the horizontal by
only a few feet. A number of sections of the earth could be
printed upon paper, and each small piece could be stretched
sufficiently (when wetted) to fit the spherical shape. Therefore the outline of the earth is printed upon an interrupted
map, each section of which is termed a <u>gore</u>.

        If a gore is not more than 30° of longitude in width,
it can be conveniently pasted onto the base of the globe. This
base is customarily made of strong cardboard, which is light
and somewhat resistant to blows. A good stroke will still
damage the globe, which is why one company mounts its
globes on a base of resilient plastic which will even permit
the globe to be bounced as if it were a basketball. (I would
not recommend this stunt as a regular practice, as grit on
the floor can damage the surface of the globe!)

        In an age when the use of plastics has been subjected
to criticism, one might ask why globes are not made of durable metal. This has often been done, particularly for small
cheap globes. But steel is not as resilient to blows as we
would like it to be, and I rarely see such a globe (even a
"new" one in the store) which does not have at least one dent
in it. Getting the dents out of such globes can be as frustrating a task as trying to do the body and fender work on
your own car!

<u>Detail on the Globe</u>

        Globes, like maps, can be classified by the type of
detail that they have printed on the surface. The old-fashioned
classroom models were political globes, in which the governmental units of the world were rendered in bright colors.

Many globes sold for home use are of the same type; sometimes, to render an "arty" appearance, the seas are rendered in a contrasting black.   For the average man, who listens to the news broadcast and then wonders whether Rhodesia is in South America or south Africa, such globes can be practical and convenient.   But, for the varied conditions of classroom teaching, many other types of detail might be considered.

The most common alternative has been the physical-political globe, which is primarily a representation of relief features.   The usual method of portraying relief is by hypsometric tint in which different colors are employed to indicate different ranges of altitude.   Dark green is used for lowlands, which progressively changes to lighter green, yellow, and then brown.   The seas are customarily blue, with a lighter blue or white used for the continental shelves and other shallow waters.

Over this essentially physical base, political information can be printed in dark red or in black.   Despite the fact that the red lines are sometimes a little too prominent, these globes still give an essentially naturalistic appearance, as the shades of green, brown, and blue are associated with the landscape.

Yet, a closer look will show that these are not strictly realistic portraits of our planet.   Low lying lands are not always green to the eye especially not in the deserts, and the elevated surfaces of Greenland and Antarctica are not the dull brown of their hypsometric color key.   In a search for greater realism, perhaps inspired by the widely published color photographs of the earth from space, manufacturers are now offering globes which portray the colors of vegetation.   A few years ago, these were only offered in large globes constructed to special order, but now a number of smaller models are available to the educator and to the general public. The different classes of vegetation are shown in various shades of green, yellow, and brown, and the ice caps of the mountains and polar regions appear in white.

For greater realism, such globes can also show relief.   One method actually raises the surface of the globe to portray the mountains and valleys of the earth.   Another method obtains even more realistic results by employing the shaded relief principle.

Although more realistic than the usual physical-

political globe, these models still do not give an exact astronaut's picture of the earth.   The raised relief must be exaggerated to be visible to the globe use.   At no season does
the vegetation, in both hemispheres, present the appearance
of maximum growth depicted on the surface.   Finally, the
turbidities of the atmosphere and oceans are eliminated.   The
changing cloud cover, which obscures so much of the detail
in photos from space, is removed.   Some globes even give
detailed shaded relief of the ocean basins, which is almost
completely lost to the astronaut.   An even more ingenious
method is to portray the ocean surface with a round surface
of clear plastic, which permits one to peer through at the
raised relief of the ocean bottom below.   Globes can even be
made to reveal the secrets of the solid earth; one model for
earth science instruction has been divided into two parts at
the equator.   When the two halves are separated, they reveal
the pattern of the crust, mantle, outer core, and inner core.

Even if one prefers to work with a primarily political
globe, details of physical relief need not be overlooked.   The
simplest solution is to add raised relief to the surface, but
this tends to be lost in the patchwork of bright colors.   A
better method is to add shaded relief to a subdued political
color pattern.   One globe obtains this effect when a central
light is turned on, throwing a shadow pattern onto both the
continents and ocean bottoms.   Although more expensive than
simple globes of its size, it does offer a maximum of versatility in one model.

Astronomical Globes

Globes can be made to portray any distribution over
a spherical surface.   Despite the fact that the ancients knew
that the earth was round, some of the oldest globes did not
show the actual sphere of the earth but rather a purely imaginary sphere, that of the heavens.   This should not surprise
us, since the classical geographers had only a limited knowledge of the earth's surface and had to fill in the remainder
with hypothetical continents.   But the astronomers of that
time, living in low latitudes, could view most of the heavens
during the course of a year.

The celestial globe is a double fiction, as it presents
the theoretical heavenly sphere from an imaginary position,
that is, as it would appear to an observer far out in space
and looking at it from the outside.   We can create a concave
celestial globe and view it from the inside, but this requires

the large dome and expensive projection apparatus of the
planetarium.   Nevertheless, a planetarium is an excellent
device for teaching earth-sun relationships, and I would
recommend its use to anyone with access to such a facility.

There are many uses of celestial globes in the classroom, some of which relate to geography.   (For example,
Posidonius' attempt to measure the earth by measuring the
elevation of Canopus could be explained with such an aid.)
Yet, the most practical and readily understood device is the
mechanical planetarium, which is a system of globes: sun,
earth, moon, and perhaps an inferior planet.   These are
mounted and geared so that the earth may revolve about the
sun and the moon about the earth.   Since the earth's axis is
tilted with respect to its orbit, the differential illumination
during the seasons can be shown.   (Some models have an illuminated "sun" which throws a spotlight onto the earth,
heightening the realism.)   The revolution of the moon is also
of great use in explaining the monthly variations in the tides.

One deluxe model combines the celestial globe with
the mechanical planetarium, the latter being electically driven
and illuminated.   While recommended for general astronomy,
such miniature universes lose some of the detail needed for
thorough study of earth-space relationships.   For more definitive work, a large, properly mounted globe can also be used
as an astronomical instrument.

Mathematical Geography with a Terrestial Globe

For these demonstrations, it would be best to obtain
a large globe, at least sixteen inches in diameter.   One
could start with the study of measurement, as this is fundamental to the understanding of other phenomena.   A spherical
surface can be treated in two ways, with either linear or circular (sometimes called angular) measurement.   Linear measure is best handled with tapes stretched over the surface;
if they read in inches or centimeters, one can convert these
distances to miles by knowing the scale of the globe.   (Globes
are better than maps for introducing the concept of scale, as
they do not have the distortions of distances which plague
map projections.   Further, the scale of the globe can be
readily explained by comparing its easily visualized diameter
with the known diameter of the earth.)

The tautly stretched tape will describe a great circle
route, a good point of transition to the spherical geometry

which underlies circular measurement. The circuit of the equator or of a complete meridian circle will illustrate the number of degrees to a complete circumference. Relating these degrees to the linear distances will show the relationships between kilometers, statute miles, and nautical miles to circular measure. Some of these relationships will not be coincidental, but designed to correlate with circular measure.

Next one might examine the grid of meridians and parallels which are based upon circular measurement. Where two such lines cross, a single and unique point will be located by latitude and longitude. On a common classroom globe, 506 points will be located by intersections of these lines, which should be sufficient for a number of examples. Even greater flexibility can be achieved with the slated globe, which permits the instructor to draw his grid lines at will to show many more unique locations. This demonstration has the added advantage of showing that the 33 lines of the common globe are by no means the only ones which might be drawn upon the surface.

Terminator and Subsolar Point

The foregoing demonstrations have concentrated upon the measurement of the earth itself. When we remember that the earth is not an isolated entity in space, but a component of a solar system which revolves about a central source of light, we are ready to employ the globe for the next topic of mathematical geography illumination.

The earth is so far from the sun that, for practical purposes, the rays of light from the sun may be assumed to be parallel when they reach the planet. Under these conditions, one half of the sphere will be illuminated, one half will be in darkness, at any given time. The boundary between the two is a great circle which is called the terminator. (Older sources use the term "circle of illumination," but interest in our space program is popularizing the shorten term used by astronomers.)

In the center of the illuminated hemisphere is a location known as the subsolar point. A person at this place would observe the sun to be directly overhead, or at the zenith. On a rotating and revolving earth, the sub-solar point is continually changing. Its longitude changes 360° every twenty-four hours. Due to the inclination of the earth's axis, the latitude of the point changes 23 1/2° each season.

The position of the terminator, which is 90° away from the subsolar point, is likewise changing constantly. The results of these motions are the phenomena of day and night, variations in local and standard time, differing sun angles and lengths of day and night during the seasons, etc. Any experienced teacher knows how difficult it is to teach these principles to students on any level.

Illumination and the Globe

A solution to this problem is to employ a globe for the demonstrations of illumination. These can range from the simple to the complex. One of the easiest demonstrations uses an axially mounted globe with the standard 23 1/2° inclination. When this is bathed in the light from a spotlight and rotated, the phenomena of alternation of day and night can be shown. By varying the positions of the inclined axis and the spotlight, the conditions of illumination during the different seasons will be readily apparent.

More detailed information concerning illumination can be obtained by rectifying the globe. For this purpose a globe mounted within a cradle with a horizon ring is preferred. When the globe is shifted within the cradle so that the locality of the observer is at the very top, the globe is rectified. One can then study the relations between the parallels and the horizon ring and deduce much information concerning the paths of the sun and lengths of daylight during the seasons. Another fascinating demonstration is to place the rectified globe in direct sunlight, with its axis aligned with that of the earth, and see how the globe assumes the illumination of the earth at that moment. A valuable adjunct to these demonstrations is the analemma, the graph shaped like a figure eight and placed over the eastern Pacific. It shows how the location of the subsolar point changes from day to day during the course of the year.

The Globes of the Future

Although much can be done with our traditional globes and globe mountings, these are not the only possible resources at our disposal. Even the traditional horizon ring can be modified for the study of earth-space relationships. One manufacturer has a hinged horizon ring which can be rotated over

the earth to demonstrate the changing position of the circle
of illumination or the orbit of an artificial satellite.   Another
company has supplemented the axial mounting with accessories,
such as a "half circle arc, " which do some of the work of
the horizon ring without interfering with the view of the globe.

Another distributor provides globe users with a transparent "geometer, " a plastic cap which can be placed over
any section of the sphere for comparisons of areas and the
measurement of distances.   Although mainly intended for
classroom teachers and the general public, I have also seen
this device used as a research tool by a geophysicist inves-
tigating continental drift.   (He stated that it gave results
nearly as accurately as a computer, but more quickly and in
better visualized form.)   Continental drift can be demonstrated to a classroom by the equipment provided by another
company; an overhead projector flashes the continental outlines onto an inflatable globe which acts as a screen.

The space program is also providing new globes for
our use.   The Orbiter photographs of the moon have now
been transformed into a lunar globe of greater accuracy and
detail than any of its predecessors.   Future probes of Mars
may result in globes of that planet.   What accessories may
be combined with these models will depend upon the imagination of the designers and the users.   In any event, one must
stop thinking of the globe as a staid, dusty accessory of the
old-fashioned classroom.   So much can be done with a good
assortment of globes in the hands of a knowledgeable teacher
that one might literally say "the sky is the limit!"

Sources of Additional Information

It would be hard to give complete details of the experiments involving rectification and illumination, and of
many other potentialities of globes, within one article.   Thus,
if you are strongly interested in the subject of globe usage,
it would be well to examine some of the publications which
are listed here.

Books

Hubert A. Bauer.   Globes, Maps and Skyways.   New York:
      Macmillan, 1942.
Frank Debenham.   The Use of Geography.   London: English
      Universities Press, 1950; chapter 3.
David Greenhood.   Mapping.   Chicago: University of Chicago

Press, 1964; chapters 2, 3, 5, 6, 9.

Ruby M. Harris. The Rand McNally Handbook of Map and
    Globe Usage. Chicago: Rand McNally, 1959.

Lucia C. Harrison. Sun, Earth, Time and Man. Chicago:
    Rand McNally, 1960.

Robert Hues. Tractatus de Globis. London: Hakluyt Society
    Publications, 1st Series, vol. 79, 1889. (Reprinted
    by Burk Franklin, New York.)

William M. McKinney. "The Globe and Its Uses," in Meth-
    ods of Geographic Instruction, John W. Morris, ed.
    Waltham, Mass.: Blaisdell Pub. Co., 1968.

Erwin Raisz. General Cartography. New York: McGraw-
    Hill, 1948; chapter 28.

Arthur N. Strahler, Physical Geography. New York: John
    Wiley, 1969; chapters 2, 4, 23.

Zoe A. Thralls, The Teaching of Geography. New York:
    Appleton-Century-Crofts, 1958; chapter 2.

Booklets and Monographs

Cram's Outer Space and World Globe Handbook. Indianapolis:
    George F. Cram Co., 1962.

William M. McKinney. Geography Via Use of the Globe.
    ("Do It This Way" Series, No. 5.) Normal, Ill.:
    National Council for Geographic Education, 1965.

Successful Teaching with Globes. Chicago: Denoyer-Geppert
    Co., 1957.

Teaching Some Basic Concepts of Mathematical Geography.
    Chicago: Denoyer-Geppert Co., 1961.

Rand McNally Geosphere Globe. Chicago: Rand McNally,
    1965.

Articles

Melville B. Grosvenor. "A Globe for the Space Age," Na-
    tional Geographic Magazine, CXIX, 5 (May 1961),
    698-701.

Dorothy H. Davis. "The Project Globe--A Teaching Tool,"
    Journal of Geography, LXVI 8 (November 1967), 437-
    439.

Ary and Linda Lamme. "Utilizing the Earth's Grid," Journal
    of Geography, LXVI, 8 (November 1967), 425-427.

William M. McKinney. "Maps and Globes in Earth-Space
    Relationships," Journal of Geography, LXVI, 9 (De-
    cember 1967), 481, 488.

Erwin Raisz. "Globes," Geographic Approaches to Social
    Education. 19th Yearbook, National Council for the

Social Studies, 1948.
William T. Skilling. "Astronomical Geography Taught from
    the Globe," <u>Journal of Geography,</u> IX, 9 (May 1911),
    246-247.

HOW TO SELECT AN ATLAS*

Roy E. Porter

With the likelihood that there will be more atlases
purchased by libraries this year than for any other previous
single year, some suggestions on selecting an atlas may be
helpful. The newest census figures and the changes they
reflect in American life; the creation of many new nations
and the changes in the status of others; the shifting battle
lines of the "cold war"; discoveries in outer space; and other
recent changes in social, political, and economic patterns,
have made any pre-[1971] atlas almost as obsolete for practical usage as a 1920 road map. Those familiar, dog-eared
volumes from two, three, or five years ago--still relied
upon by many libraries--won't do any longer, except for historical reference.

For librarians this means that as far as atlases are
concerned, they should start over from scratch. To keep
up with the growing interest of the American public in world
affairs and the accompanying demand for accurate, up-to-date
reference material, many librarians will also need to build
larger atlas sections. An illustration of the potential demand is a Pictorial Atlas recently offered at a special pre-
publication price in a Time, Inc. mail-order campaign and
quickly sold well over 250,000 copies. At this writing, I
have no idea what the total mail-order sale will be, but when
250,000 copies of a $20 atlas can be sold sight unseen it is
a good indication of general public interest.

In selecting an atlas, the basic point to keep in mind
is the necessity of comparing one with another, point by

*Reprinted by permission from Library Journal, vol. 86, no.
19 (1961), 3747-3750. Published by R. R. Bowker (a Xerox
Company). Copyright 1961 the Xerox Corporation.

point, and evaluating each feature with the needs of your library in mind. If this suggestion sounds obvious, it can bear emphasis because it rarely is followed. This is understandable since only the trained reference specialist is apt to feel competent to evaluate the many complex elements of an atlas. Most librarians are forced either to take the reviewer's word at face value, with no consideration of their own specific needs, or to make a selection on the basis of too little background information.

Your best approach in selecting an atlas is to spread out two or three atlases on a desk and begin asking questions in terms of what is important to your particular library. If you want to achieve a degree of systematization, you can establish a point value scale of from 1 to 5 points, assigning each atlas an appropriate number of points for each "plus" feature you find. While you cannot reduce your decision to a mathematical formula, you can use this method as an important aid in organizing your thinking. Although I am speaking here mainly in terms of a major world atlas, the same technique will work equally well in comparing any type of atlas, despite the wide range in prices, approach, and purpose. Lower-priced atlases, incidentally, may vary far more in quality and adequacy than higher-priced ones. By carefully evaluating even the least expensive atlases, you can materially enhance the value returned per dollar invested. Furthermore, if you are purchasing a number of book-size atlases for circulation, which many librarians would find surprisingly profitable, your total investment may amount to as much as one or two big, expensive atlases.

Two generalizations can be made in evaluating an atlas. First, the most important consideration is the reputation and competence of the publisher, or the publisher and the map maker if they are not the same. There are certain technical considerations in maps and atlases which only an expert in cartography or demography is competent to judge. Your only guarantee of quality in these areas is the ability of the producer to do his job well. Second, the frequency and thoroughness with which a publisher revises a particular atlas are important. A conscientious publisher will keep charts, tables, and even minor maps completely up to date. This is not only a measure of the publisher's sense of pride and responsibility. It also makes it easier for you to determine when your edition has become out dated.

Now, back to those atlases you have scattered about

your desk.   First compare the map coverage by turning to
the map sections and counting: (1) the total number of map
pages; (2) the number of pages devoted to the United States,
the number for Africa, and for any other area you consider
particularly important; (3) the number of "specialty" maps
such as special projections, distribution of resources and
population, etc.   Maps are obviously the heart of an atlas,
and it is reasonable to begin by seeing how extensive a coverage you are getting.   Naturally you will want an atlas which
will keep you in step with current trends in world affairs;
an alert publisher expands the coverage of areas on which
events have focused attention and seem likely to continue to
do so.   Africa provides one quick and simple check on currency of information or timeliness of approach because of
the numerous new independent nations and boundary changes
which have recently occurred there.   No atlas, however, can
be as up-to-date as yesterday's newspaper or even last
month's Atlantic Monthly; the only fair judgment is, "Which
atlas is most up-to-date?"

Also important in evaluating an atlas is the emphasis
on political maps as opposed to physical maps.   School and
public libraries with particularly heavy student use must provide an atlas with comprehensive physical maps even though
this may, in some cases, mean buying two atlases to provide
adequate political and physical coverage.   A student should
be able not only to determine spatial relationships of one
place to another--often the prime concern of many map users
--but also to visualize something of the shape and structure
of the earth and its relationships to the climate, economy,
and inhabitants of the area which he is studying.   Next, turn
in each atlas to a map of a specific area, for example the
United States, and see which atlas gives you the greatest detail with the greatest legibility.   Which looks most attractive?
If you are comparing physical maps, which atlas portrays
terrain relief most accurately, graphically, and understand-
ably?   In both political and physical maps, are the color
shadings appealing and an aid to reading the maps, or a glar-
ing hodgepodge which confuses and misleads the eye?

Take a close look at the type on the maps.   Which
maps are easiest to read in terms of type size and method
of placement?   Are an adequate number of important place
names included?   Are there so many that the type has been
jammed together or reduced in size so that the names are too
difficult to locate and read?   Illegibility of type is often a
problem in larger atlases and is particularly common in small

atlases with substantially reduced page sizes. Some of these utilize maps from larger atlases which have not been designed for a smaller book format. On the other hand, some of the smaller atlases not only have maps specially created for greater legibility but are specifically designed to meet the needs of grade school students, high school and college students, or the general adult reader.

Compare the scales on maps of various areas. In some atlases the maps of India and China, for example, are on the same scale as the maps of Canada and the United States while regional maps are on a scale twice or four times that of an individual country within the region. In other atlases there is no consistency in scales whatever. The advantage of a degree of consistency is that it allows the reader to make comparisons of the relative sizes of different areas. No atlas, however, will be completely consistent throughout. In this respect the most thoroughly consistent atlases now on the market maintain readily comparable scales between all areas except continents, United States state maps and Canadian province maps, and polar regions and ocean areas. These exceptions are made in order to give these areas the particular emphasis which the map makers feel they deserve and which they believe will be most useful to the reader.

Now compare the indexes in the atlases. How much an index tells you and how easy it is to use are almost as important in determining the usefulness of an atlas as the maps themselves. As a first step, compare the explanations at the beginning of the indexes to get an idea of what one atlas provides that another does not. Most American atlases, in contrast to foreign ones, provide population figures, but some are kept more up-to-date than others. One good way to check both timeliness and comprehensiveness is to compare the entries and figures for cities in your own area or state. Comprehensiveness can also be judged simply by counting the entries from "A" through "Ab," for example, in each index.

Different publishers and different atlases by the same publisher may provide several special features, such as listing physical features in italic type or marking in some special way cities listed in the index but not shown on the maps. You might take a section of the indexes and compare the number of cities listed as not shown on maps with the number for which city-suburban area populations are given. One of the important considerations in this era of sprawling urbanization is the growing significance of metropolitan areas as compared to cities defined in terms of their corporate limits. Some atlases include far more of these special features than others.   Evaluate each of them on the basis of how important it is to you.

Now the third main element of an atlas: charts, tables, diagrams, specialty maps, and the other types of miscellaneous information which determine its versatility.   These can vary widely between otherwise comparable atlases.   Here you will find a great deal of specialized information which may be extremely valuable to you, particularly in answering for example, students' questions on agricultural products, industries, and other pertinent data for individual states.   Study each table and chart; ask, "How important is this to me?" If you use the "point system" suggested earlier, you may discover that one atlas will have twice as much useful material in this category as another.   Particularly in some of the big atlases, there is much tabular information which is more readily available than in any other source.   All of this miscellaneous information makes an atlas look complex and difficult to evaluate.   A systematic approach will banish most of the confusion.

Finally there are three aids to the reader which are highly important in any major atlas.   First, an explanation of the symbols used on the maps.   Second, an explanation of technical cartographic terms used on, or in describing the maps.   Third, a general explanation of the various map projections used in the atlas, supplemented by a specific note on each map stating the projection upon which it is based.   Maps, after all, are simply symbolic representations of the earth's surface; the reader may be seriously hampered if he is unable to interpret some of these symbols.   While all of this may sound like a rather tedious process to go through in evaluating an atlas, it can be surprisingly interesting and illuminating.   When you consider the proportion of your budget allotted to atlases, you will undoubtedly find that it is time well spent.

VALUE OF MAPS AS REFERENCE TOOLS*

Lawrence E. Spellman

Too many people, in and out of our profession, consider a map little more than a graphic representation, i. e., a picture which any relatively unskilled person can read and interpret just about as easily as he might a magazine or news article. This is folk wisdom, a popular notion not supported by facts. Experience over a number of years in the Army shows that the majority of young American males accepted for military service--draftees or enlistees, educated or not--have only the most nebulous idea of what a map is and what can and cannot be done with it. It is necessary to devote many precious hours during basic training to correct --at least partially--this almost complete lack of literal and figurative down-to-earth know-how. My years here at Princeton reaffirm this deficiency.

Why should this be? How can a nation which undoubtedly is the international leader in development and use of audio-visual aids produce so many individuals who are cartographic illiterates? I don't know the answer, but I believe there are certain facets of our American life-style which, taken in toto, contribute to this lamentable situation.

One of the reasons maps are not used more frequently and intelligently is that students are not taught how to use maps. Our schools devote little effort to instruction in actually reading a map. If Johnny or Joanie can point out the capital of Venezuela or trace the Danube's course or read

---

*Reprinted by permission from Special Libraries Association, Geography and Map Division, Bulletin No. 81 (1970), 24-28. "This account represents a compilation or amalgam of various viewpoints on the subject, rather than the author's original work."

off the height of Mount Everest correctly, they are fine students. Understanding the map's <u>overall meaning</u> and its impact is not a requirement as it is in most European schools.

Another consideration--road maps are too easily obtained in our nation to be taken seriously. We fill the glove compartments of our cars with them as rapidly as the oil companies grind them out. Is it any wonder our children grow up regarding them--and in fact, all maps--as insignificant items of transient value? Not so our European cousins. They pay cash for their road maps. It is an investment, and like all things costing coin of the realm they are carefully taken care of and regarded as items of genuine and continuing usefulness.

Another factor affecting the average citizen's outlook on maps is their production. Our commercial mapmakers, with but few exceptions, are years behind the state of the art in mass cartographic publishing. One has only to examine a few of the physical, political or transportation maps put out by such foreign firms as Bartholomew of Scotland, France's Michelin, Cartographia in Hungary or the Japanese Company Teikoku-Shoin to realize how much better they are from the standpoint of legibility, the esthetic use of color tinting, and the logically balanced approach taken to optimize information value of the map without creating visual clutter. They are, incidentally, less expensive to buy.

There are other factors, of course, but they all add up to reveal Johnny and Joanie as unschooled in map reading and interpretation; ignorant of the map's potential in learning, planning and research; reluctant to refer to and utilize maps, especially if other more familiar printed data is available; and--generally speaking--missing a bet when it comes to gathering, comparing and displaying the sort of information which maps uniquely embody.

Outside of some supersaturated computer software there is no more concentrated form of data presentation than the map. Consider an ordinary United States Geological Survey topographic map of a small portion of the United States. By the use of lines, color, shading, conventional signs and symbols it contains millions of bits of information. Unfortunately, this very compaction of data too often makes people shy away from maps. They consider map markings as some kind of secret language. The more symbols a map contains the less they like it.

Such an attitude is based on ignorance. There are
actually in use today throughout the world not more than one
to two hundred basic conventional map signs and symbols.
Many of these closely resemble the features they represent.
For example: blue for bodies of water, a dotted green grid
for an orchard, white areas streaked with blue to show gla-
ciers, brown for desert areas, geometric figures in black
mean man-made features. Additionally--and unlike the spoken
or written word today--map signs and symbols have been
pretty well internationalized, and we have what approximates
a cartographic Esperanto.

At the local level, however, the picture remains rather
murky. Too many librarians today regard maps as neither
fish nor fowl unless they are bound together in the familiar
time-honored book form. Problems of classification, cataloguing and filing are brought up constantly to discourage map
acquisition. Retrieval efforts are magnified and search time
is considered out of all proportion to effective library management because the "map collection" is ill-housed all too
frequently in a sort of library limbo where sheets are piled
--not filed--and then hopefully put out of mind and left to
gather dust. Of all the dire things that can happen to maps
it seems to me that disuse is the worst.

Admittedly, the picture drawn is simplistic. There
are some librarians who appreciate maps as original sources
of information; first-rate map libraries or collections do op-
erate in some parts of our country--but the reason we realize
this is because of their relative rarity. The bright side is
noteworthy primarily because of its stark contrast with the
whole picture.

This poses an intriguing dilemma. Never before in
our history have so many critical problems surfaced in the
man-environment system in such a brief period. We are
today enormously concerned with knotty issues like population
control, urban sprawl, commuter transportation, air and water pollution, vital resources conservations--issues affecting
every one of us--issues, incidentally, where appropriate and
timely map materials constitute a primary source of knowledge,
rich in scope and variety, indispensable to man if he is to
know his environment and manage it effectively. From es-
thetics to politics, from the making of studies to the setting
of priorities, new technology and emerging social patterns
demand a clarity in objectives which the map can assist significantly in achieving.

Where are we now? Where have we been? How did we get here from there? In what direction are we headed? These are questions which map users on the ground and upon the high seas have asked for centuries. Their requirement, of course, was one of physical orientation. Maps were indispensable to their needs. Without them they were lost.

This situation applies today, but more acutely in a sociological rather than a geographic sense. I am not saying we no longer need maps for navigation, rather we now require maps for purposes other than terrestrial location. We find it necessary to turn to maps because mere words and figures cannot provide the imagery required for clear and full understanding. The text-oriented researcher suffers information hangups which often may be solved by the skillful use of maps. This is where the map librarian enters the scene. He is the catalyst bringing together the specialized reference tool which is the map and the user of that map who, more often than not, is a specialist himself but not in the field of cartography or map reading.

The basic ingredient needed at this juncture is a lively imagination, and the map librarian finds himself wearing two hats--or two gloves. On one hand he attempts to find out to what extent the researcher can actually interpret map information, on the other he tries to determine what map or mix of maps will contribute most to a solution of the problem. This is not an easy task. The primary roadblock encountered in practically every map collection worthy of the name is cataloguing. Let's face it--no major collection is adequately catalogued. The grandaddy of them all, that of the Library of Congress (numbering three and four million flat sheet maps) is estimated as having catalogue cards for less than five percent of the total collection.

Thus, when it comes to map librarians and map library users we are equally disadvantaged. It is an invigorating challenge. I see some very interesting times ahead of us. From a technical standpoint, cartography is now entering into a sort of Golden Age, unparalleled since Dutch mapmakers turned out their super productions in the 17th century.

For one thing, the collection and recording of raw data from which maps are produced has been revolutionized in the past decade and promises to open up new areas yet undreamed of. We now employ airborne and satellite detection capabilities in locating and identifying earth types and resources via infrared, side-looking radar, scatterometer and passive microwave devices. The increased use of on-line communication links and computerized quality control measures makes accurate and up-to-date mapping information available to the cartographer in only a fraction of the time it used to take.

Our technology is reaching into outer space. Current lunar maps are now so accurate that it is claimed we know the moon better than certain parts of Antarctica, central Greenland or the bottom of the sea. Highly imaginative innovations in map content and composition are being researched and developed to take advantage of technological advances. One example is the United States Geological Survey's photo-revision mapping program now being conducted in selected metropolitan areas of the country.

This technique involves the use of high resolution aerial photos to detect, identify and record man-made changes on the terrain. Alterations in highways and built-up areas are transferred directly to the previous base map without time-consuming and expensive ground survey checks. The new information is overprinted upon the surface of the old map in a distinctive color tint not used previously by the Geological Survey. Result: an up-to-date and complete topographic map produced in a very short time with man-made changes instantly identifiable. The value of such maps in urban planning, population research and highway development is beyond estimate.

The Soviets have not been asleep in the cartographic arena either. Their space mapping efforts, including the first photos made of the moon's dark side, are of a very high order. Not so well publicized or appreciated, however, has been their concentration on terrestrial mapping, particularly as it applies to environmental engineering. One of the most fascinating Russian developments is noise factor measurement mapping. This technique, still in the trial stage, endeavors to produce maps which indicate the type, intensity and duration of man-made sound and vibration in an urban atmosphere. New York's mayor might be interested in this research program.

While map data collection procedures consume progressively less time and thematic map applications proliferate at an astounding rate, what about our technical capacity to produce and distribute the map themselves? Ironically enough, the war in Vietnam may be credited with bringing forth several unorthodox but apparently successful approaches to high speed map production. The expertise of military mapping agencies in Vietnam, if applied alertly by commercial publishers, should help significantly to reduce the time lag so prevalent in present map publishing. In addition, the advanced state of the art in reproduction promises to produce copies of antique maps just as legible as the original but at a tiny fraction of the cost.

The wave of the future in map libraries is growing bigger and rolling faster. We can expect more and more maps in an ever greater variety of context and format. Our present reference problems will increase proportionately and may even overwhelm us unless some obvious changes occur. Among these I would recommend the following:

(1) Teaching maps for maps sake in our schools, not merely as a skill adjunct to formal courses such as social studies.

(2) Re-educating other librarians to the fact that maps are intrinsically valuable reference tools and not all are found between the covers of books.

(3) Encouraging the establishment of graduate level map librarianship courses of study.

(4) Recruiting bright young people into map library work at both the professional and non-professional level.

In summation, we must become activists. Map librarianship is certainly in a transitional stage these days. Where that transition takes us is our problem. We must find the solution or somebody else will, and if we don't like their solution there is no one to blame but ourselves. Make no mistake--the value of maps as reference tools will wax or wane primarily because of the librarians who handle them.

USE AND APPRECIATION OF MAPS*

Walter G. Stoneman

One of the foremost problems facing your profession as map librarians is that of developing map appreciation and use, to increase the understanding and use of all forms of maps. The term "maps" includes charts, aerial photography, globes, atlases and special purpose maps.

There are a great many potential users of maps and surveys who would benefit greatly by using them, but who do not understand their value, how to use them nor how to get them. Untold millions of dollars and much potential efficiency are wasted each year because a lot of people who really need maps and surveys are not properly using the ones even now available. All of the maps that are made are really absolutely worthless unless someone uses them and benefits from their use.

We're not talking about high-pressure advertising. We're talking about legitimate education and dissemination of information. Governmental agencies especially seem to shy away from doing much on increasing map appreciation and use. And when they do do something, they usually put out something on how maps are made. To most map users, this is quite inconsequential as compared to the more obscure points of how they can use them to their benefit and where they can get them.

Now after a Government map is made, the taxpayer already has a significant investment in it (about $30,000 for

*Reprinted by permission from Special Libraries Association, Geography and Map Division, Bulletin No. 22 (1955), 7-10. This is a transcript of a talk given to the Washington Chapter of the Geography and Map Group, SLA, February 1955.

the standard 15-minute topographic quadrangle) but most of
the taxpayers don't even know about it.   It'll only cost about
1% more on this initial investment to print four times the
presently-used number of copies and to inform more of the
taxpayers of the map's existence.   In such a manner, for 1%
additional cost, the usage by the taxpayers of this map that
they've already paid for might be quadrupled.   This is one
angle of what I mean by saying that it is a real responsibility
of the Government and the library profession to do something
about increasing map appreciation and use.

        Most of you in speaking to potential users of maps or
to persons from whom you need support, tend to speak in
terms of the technical aspects of your work and its peculiar-
ities, not of its uses or benefits.   Let us turn this around
and consider something for which you are the user, not the
producer, for instance a car.   Are you greatly concerned
with the power presses that stamp out your car's body, and
with its piston displacement, bore and stroke, or are you
more interested in where you can get a car at a markdown
of $500 that runs 23 miles per gallon?   Or how would it ap-
peal to you to learn how to eliminate the need for a car completely by investing $300 in some new transportation develop-
ment?   Or consider a fountain pen.   You probably own one.
Yet how many of you know or care how it is made?   You are
more concerned with how it will write and how much it costs.
Keep these simple illustrations in mind when talking to the
public and potential users of maps.   In considering whether
to use maps, they're no different from you when you're considering a fountain pen or a car.

        Here is a list of only a few of the things that each of
you as individuals can do to increase map use and appreciation.   If you only follow up on one or two of these suggestions,
you'll be helping both your profession and the public.

        1.   Keep on hand a supply of local and national map
and aerial photographic indices and a supply of "give-away"
copies of the most useful and interesting maps of your vicinity.   Pass them out and advise on how to use them.
        2.   Write.   Write for. all sorts of publications, from
a Sunday School mimeographed newsletter to Fortune Magazine.   Don't write a lot of technical jargon--tell folks about
your product, about how useful maps are and about the many
ways in which they can be profitably used but aren't.

        3.   Talk.   Speak before local neighborhood groups,

professional meetings, or national conventions. Here again--
don't confuse them or put them to sleep with your technical
jargon. Tell them simply about some of the striking examples of the value of maps, about how their particular group
can use maps for work or for play, and about where they can
get them.

4. Tell your friends and neighbors some specific
ways in which they can use maps in their everyday living and
work. Then do a little informal instructing on map use and
interpretation. Some specific "target groups" and commonplace uses are suggested below.

5. Go to your local schools and encourage them to
use maps--including local, large-scale maps that you can
give them--in the teaching of their regular subjects. Take
off a little time to teach the teachers so that they can teach
others. Volunteer to give a talk on mapping and map use to
the local eighth grade or high school group. Local maps can
be used in the teaching of math, civics, geography, etc. You
can think of more ways than I can. (How many of your own
children can or do use maps?)

6. Encourage your local Boy Scout troops, 4-H Clubs,
etc. to use local maps. Give them a hand with some samples and a little advice on map use as related to their specific interests. For instance, plan and sketch out a hike for
them on the local topographic quadrangle and show them how
much they can interpret from it. They can enlarge their map-
reading ability by ground-checking your map to see if certain
features are really there.

7. Drop in on some of your local city or county officials. See if they have the local maps and know how to use
them. You'll be surprised how many don't even know what's
available for their own neighborhood. Always spread the
word about where to get maps.

8. Encourage local libraries to use a map collection
and help to get it. It doesn't have to be a big one. In fact,
I've just recently seen recommendations on how to effectively
use small collections which emphasize complete sets of indices and lists of map sources. For instance, one might
cheaply get a photo-index of local aerial photographic coverage (which within itself gives some detail). This plus a few
sample photographs, together with information on how and
where to order other local photographs of specific interest
to specific individuals, could be of great value to a commun-
ity or certain particular professional groups.

9. Spread the idea that you can often mail a sketch
on a map to very effectively convey a message in place of a
long letter. The map may be free or cost 10¢. The cost of
a typed letter usually runs from $1.50 up--more often up.
Oftentimes the narrative in a letter can't begin to put across
your ideas effectively as can a few lines on a map. How
many of you map librarians even do this yourselves?

10. Volunteer to post a local topographic map in various public places such as the courthouse, town hall and other
public bulletin boards. Always attach a note explaining where
more like it can be obtained. Also accompany it with an index showing map coverage of the surrounding county or state.

11. Compile and keep in mind a list of specific sen-
sational examples of the value of maps--such things as dis-
asters or great losses resulting from the lack of maps, estimates of great financial savings from the use of maps, and
examples of time and money saved in specific cases from the
use of maps or aerial photographs. Use these examples freely to illustrate your conversations in behalf of map use. Such
illustrations are a hundred times more effective than your abstract generalities. The American Congress of Surveying and
Map Committee on Map Use has compiled and distributed a
preliminary, 26-page collection of such material.

12. Remember that even if he wants some maps, the
layman is usually confused about where and how to get them,
except those from gas stations. Continually strive to simplify and clarify this for him in your professional capacity.
Those of you who work for the Federal Government should
keep in mind that the taxpayer who pays for your maps is
entitled to know that they exist and where to get them. Also,
continually tell all of your interested contacts about where
and how to get maps and aerial photographs. Do you know
exactly where to get the various types of maps and photographs that are available from the Federal Government and
how to order them easily?

13. Remember that about 98% of the people that you
contact will be more interested in how they can use maps in
connection with their own personal interests than they will be
in the technical aspects of how maps are made or in what a
hotshot librarian or geographer you are.

4. MAP BIBLIOGRAPHIES/ACQUISITIONS

U. S. GOVERNMENT MAPPING AGENCIES*

Catherine I. Bahn

From 1500 to 1800, thousands of different types of maps were made of the United States areas, mostly by European map makers. Scientific mapping based on triangulation and astronomical observation developed in the United States and territories after the Louisiana Purchase of 1803 when Thomas Jefferson negotiated a grant of money from Congress to explore the territory and to survey a route to the Pacific. Over the past century and a half, numerous mapping agencies of the United States Government have been set up to fill different needs, at first for the expansion and opening up of the territory; and later to satisfy military and civilian requirements. Representative government research activities and changes in the mapping agencies in recent years show they they "have come a long, long way."

These are some of the notes used in my class discussion (Maps and Charts) for the United States Department of Agriculture Graduate School which you may find of some interest. Unless otherwise noted the information presented in this article was obtained from press releases issued by the agencies; from phone calls to the technical liaison and information officers; and by direct calls to the agencies concerned. The 1968-1969 United States Government Organization Manual was consulted as were the notes on surveying and mapping from the recent issues of Military Engineer.

THE MILITARY AGENCIES

Department of the Army. The Army recently approved

---

*Reprinted by permission from Special Libraries Association, Geography and Map Division, Bulletin No. 75 (1969), 14-20.

a major reorganization of mapping and geodetic activities.
On January 15, 1969, the Army Topographic Command (TOPO-
COM) was established combining all the mapping functions
previously performed by the Directorate of Topography and
Military Engineering Office of the Chief of Engineers, with
those of the Army Map Service and the Engineer Topographic
Laboratories at Fort Belvoir, Virginia in the U. S. Topograph-
ic Command or TOPOCOM. The Commanding General of
TOPOCOM has been designated Topographer of the Army and
will act for the Chief of Engineers on topographic matters.

The U. S. Army Engineer Topographic Laboratories
(USAETL), located at Fort Belvoir, Virginia under TOPOCOM,
is the principal field activity of the Army for research and
development of equipment, procedures, and techniques applicable to the topographic sciences including mapping, geodesy
and military geographic information. USAETL was established
in 1960 under its former name, the U. S. Army Engineer
Geodesy, Intelligence and Mapping Research and Development
Agency (GIMRADA) which became USAETL in 1967.

Since World War II, Army research and development
activities in support of mapping and geodesy have been concentrated primarily upon combat mapping and survey systems
items and components for issue to Army tactical units and
these requirements are still vitally important. However, the
missile and satellite era, the stressing of Army world-wide
military mapping and geodetic responsibilities by the Department of Defense, and the marked advancements in the state-
of-the-art for future geodetic and mapping operations have
highlighted the urgent need for greatly increased emphasis
by the Army on global mapping and geodetic control for common use by all elements of the Armed Forces.

One of the USAETL developments of the past year of
special interest to mapping agencies was Project RAMP (Radar Mapping in Panama), an experimental progran using side-
looking radar to map areas which are under permanent cloud
cover and can't be mapped by aerial photography. The Dari-
en Province of the Republic of Panama was selected as a test
site because portions of this province have never been mapped
due to the perpetual cloud cover over the area. Radar mapping of Darien began in January 1967, using the Army radar
system developed by Westinghouse. In less than a month, by
February 10, data acquisition was completed of an area of
about 6600 square miles. The first map was published in
October 1968. The side-looking radar imagery was also used

to prepare basic geographical information: geology, drainage, surface configuration, state of the ground, and military and engineering characteristics of the area. The project has demonstrated the feasibility of radar as an all-weather mapping sensor, and the development of a radar mapping capability will be a major goal.

New automatic equipment which can produce a map from an aerial photograph in 24 hours was created by the engineer scientist at the Laboratories. The Universal Automatic Map Compilation Equipment (UNAMACE) has been successfully tested at the USAETL and Army Map Service site installations. It produces ground elevation information (contours) and completely corrected photographs (orthophotomaps) from a wide variety of photographic material of any scale or tilt and from any type of common system as a step in the map production process. This equipment, a combination compilation/comparator instrument represents a definite breakthrough in automatic mapping and improvement in the art of map compilation.

Another instrument to speed production of maps from aerial photographs is called an "Automatic Point Transfer Instrument" (APTI). It is designed to identify, mark, measure and record the coordinates of points on aerial negatives and diapositives despite possible differences in format, size, tilt, focal length, scale and image distortion. It will greatly shorten the time required to provide the photo measurements as a necessary step in the production of a final map from an aerial photograph.

SECOR is an acronym for Sequential Collation of Range. This USAETL experiment led to the design of an all-weather geodetic tool designed to improve man's knowledge of the size and shape of the earth. SECOR can precisely locate selected points on the earth's surface by trilateration. Range is measured from a signal transmitted to a satellite and returned. Several EGRS (Engineer Geodetic Research Satellite) satellites have been launched and support the Army Map Service worldwide geodetic satellite operation. The Lightweight Gyro Azimuth Surveying Instrument provides a North reference, similar to the needle in a magnetic compass, from which azimuth angles can be measured. This instrument is designed for artillery use in performing position surveys and weapon orientation.

Contour lines on map sheets can now be read auto-

matically and stored by a computer in a system that has been
made on the Automatic Contour Digitizer (ACD). Information
on the contours is stored in the, computer memory. The output of the equipment is on magnetic tape that can be used in
other computer systems to give users information on height
of terrain to be used in construction, aircraft operation, terrain slope studies, sonic boomstudies, missile guidance, or ·
the construction of radar and other transmittal towers. Another device is the Geodolite, perhaps the world's finest portable distance measuring instrument with precision capabilities
in long distance measuring. The original purpose was to
study the "index of refraction" of the atmosphere but the
laser device works as well in surveying work.

The Army Map Service under TOPOCOM is responsible for the production and supply of maps required by the
Department of the Army. During periods of hostilities, the
production is augmented by that of the military topographic
units working on coordinated programs under the direction
of the respective theater commanders. TOPOCOM has been
studying the use of laser beams emitted from high flying aircraft to determine exact elevations of objects on the ground
and the Laser Terrain Profile Recorder may be adapted for
making contoured maps.

The AMS will help the National Aeronautics and Space
Agency to make simulated man landings on the moon. The
area on which they "land" will be a simulated surface built
by the AMS scientists from a high fidelity lunar relief map
made from Orbiter IV and V photography provided by the
space agency. Technicians in the Relief Model Branch have
built the 22 x 14 foot hand carved model of the landing site
which astronaut trainees will see as they approach the target
area. The model is a part of a Lunar Module Simulator
(LMS) which has been installed at the Kennedy Space Center
to provide flight crew training and orientation on the Apollo
landing site. Through the use of the LMS, closed circuit
TV and other equipment, the astronauts will experience a
lunar landing approach without leaving Florida.

A new three sheet series of MARS planning charts is
being prepared for NASA for use in planning the Mariner
Mars 1969 Flyby. The charts will indicate appearance of
the planet including surface markings and the extent of the
polar caps during the flight period, August 1-15, 1969. Photography obtained by the Mariner IV spacecraft in 1965 which
gave a close up view of about 1 percent of the surface of

Mars will be used with earth based photography to form the charts. Sheets 1 and 2 at a scale of 1:12,500,000 on a Mercator Projection will show the planet as a globe, sheet 3 will contain two charts on the Polar Stereographic Projection, centered on the North and South Poles to show the extent of the polar caps.

There is continued experimentation with conversion systems in color separation procedures for map reproduction. An electronic color separation scanner has been procured which requires a skilled operator but has eliminated all of the tedious and time consuming efforts of skilled photography and dot etchers. It has an output of color corrected separations for four color process printing. The day may not be too far away when composite map copy may be prepared in full color, color separated, and reprinted in a short period of time and the Army Map Service plans to channel its efforts in this direction. (From "Trends in Map Reproduction," a paper presented to the 1968 convention of the American Congress on Surveying and Mapping and the American Society of Photogrammetry in Washington, D.C. in March 1968.)

In the Lunar and Planetary program, Army Map Service has been active in the Photogrammetry, Geodesy, Cartography, Technical Illustrations, Graphic Arts and Engineering Design Sections. Each Lunar Orbiter becomes a satellite of the moon and photographs the lunar surface upon commands issued from the earth by NASA. The images are recorded on photographic film and later developed within the satellite. The photographic images are electronically transmitted in small segments (framelets) to the various Deep Space Instrumentation Facilities. The electronically transmitted images are recorded on 35 mm film by the Ground Reconstruction Equipment and are reassembled and used by AMS in the mapping process.

The Corps of Engineers is responsible for the performance of surveys and production of topographic maps required by the Department of the Army. It directs the activities of several mapping organizations such as the Mississippi River Commission, the Lake Survey and the District Engineer Offices which perform survey and other activities.

Maps for military purposes are normally produced in the United States by the Army Map Service and overseas by military topographic units of the corps. They also make topographic maps of a few quadrangles not surveyed by the

Geological Survey, besides revising some of the older topographic maps of the Geological Survey.

The Corps of Engineers which handles much of the
civil mapping includes the Lake Survey which has recently
celebrated its 127th anniversary.   In general the Lake Survey provides accurate charts of the Great Lakes, the out-
flow rivers, Lake Champlain, the lakes and rivers of the
New York State Barge Canal System and the Minnesota Ontario Border Lakes.   They maintain the water level records
on the Great Lakes, and work on the hydraulics and hydrol-
ogy of the Great Lakes Basin.   As of 1966 it was designated
as the Great Lakes Research Center.   In 1967 field surveys
were conducted through the Great Lakes area to collect material to update nautical charts and to conduct oceanographic
research.

In addition to the Lake Survey in Detroit and the Mississippi River Commission centered in Vicksburg, Mississippi,
the Divisional Offices of the Engineers handle much of the
civilian watershed and recreational area surveys for the improvement of rivers, harbors and waterways for navigation
as well as for flood control and related purposes including
shore protection.   The District Engineer offices are in St.
Louis; Rock Island, Ill.; St. Paul, Minn.; Chicago; Pittsburgh;
Huntington, W. Va.; Louisville; Nashville; Kansas City; Oma-
ha; Galveston, Texas; and Cincinnati.

The Civil Defense Administration publishes studies in
cooperation with state agencies showing usable roads, hospitals, related centers, etc.

In recognition of the fact that most developing nations
need assistance in planning for the development of their water
and related land resources, the Corps of Engineers is now
utilizing its experience and knowledge in support of world-
wide development programs.   The Engineer Agency for Resources Inventories, established in 1963 is the newest of the
Corps of Engineers elements assisting in international development efforts.   Basic to the operation is a system of cooperative resources data collection, active field research, and the
blending of a variety of analytical and production abilities.
Typical of its inventories is a resource development project
in the Lower Mekong Basin in Vietnam; a Pilot and Demonstration Area in the Mekong Delta, another automatic data
processing system of land records in An Giang Province.   It
has published national inventories of national resources for

Venezuela, Panama, Honduras, Nicaragua, Costa Rica, El
Salvador, and a report on the U. S. Mexico Border Development Commission.

The Inter American Geodetic Survey has been conducting extensive collaborative mapping projects in Latin America.
The U. S. agencies actively participating in this cooperative
effort include the Army Map Service, the Air Force, the Navy,
the Coast and Geodetic Survey and the Agency for International Development. The collaborating countries include Columbia, Guatemala, El Salvador, Venezuela, Paraguay, Antilles,
Haiti, Brazil, Chile and Peru. By furnishing technical training and advice, providing equipment and assistance wherever
possible, IAGS works towards the goal of developing modern
self-sufficient mapping organizations in each collaborating
country. A feature of the agencies is the production of pictomaps, which is a simplified and rapid conversion of standard photomosaics into practical maps which may be easily
interpreted by the layman. Such maps are especially useful
in city planning and survey of natural resources. The city
plan of Masaya, Nicaragua, was the first pictomap reproduced
with IAGS assistance. At a scale of 1:5,000 it was published
by the Direccion General de Cartografia, Nicaragua in August
1967. Similar pictomaps have been made for cities in Costa
Rica and Colombia.

Department of the Navy. The Naval Oceanographic
Office (NAVOCEANO) is charged by law with producing and
maintaining complete nautical chart coverage for foreign
waters of the world for the United States Fleet, Merchant
Marine and other needs. Many of the river mouths and other
coastal areas covered are subject to heavy silting and continually changing depth. Frequent surveys and revisions and
reissues of such charts are required for safe navigation.
Since other nations had similar programs in publishing charts
of the United States coastal water, the Naval Oceanographic
Office and the Coast and Geodetic Survey in 1953 developed
agreements with other nations to grant rights to reproduce
and sell each other's original nautical charts in modified
facsimile form using rapid photolithographic reproduction
methods. Thus the mariner is provided with the most up-
to-date information in a timely manner. The modified facsimile reproduction has gone beyond its original intent and is
now an established international practice. Agreements for
this have been made between the United States and fifteen nations and negotiations for additional agreements are underway.

To increase and more widely distribute technical information dealing with hydrographic surveying and marine charting, the Naval Oceanographic Office in 1966 began a program to exchange senior cartographers with hydrographic offices of other nations. The first exchange was made with the Canadian Hydrographic Office in Ottawa. Later exchanges include Germany, Japan and Italy. Useful practical techniques should result from this cooperation.

Concerted effort and emphasis have been placed on the progressive development of highly automated systems and instrumentation aimed at more rapid collection, timely retrieval and evaluation, and dissemination of ocean sciences information. The motion picture "Mission Oceanography" tells of the discoveries and research by ocean scientists in the early 1800's and the Navy's involvement with the seas and oceanography. It illustrates the importance of oceanography and hydrography to the development of the United States as a maritime nation.

The South Pacific leg of the Oceanographer's Global Expedition, New Zealand to the continental shelf off Valparaiso, Chile, provided a continuous profile of the ocean bottom with the aid of electronic equipment aboard the ship including sonar and geophysical devices which plumb both the bottom and the rock beneath. The use of satellite navigation, together with precise depth soundings from a narrow beam echo sounder, gave an extremely high degree of accuracy. Various unreported rock areas, mountains (seamounts) and a 180 mile wide mountain range were located east from the Fiji and Samoan Islands toward South America.

NAVOCEANO has served as the prime agent of NASA for determining the technical feasibility of conducting scientific studies of the world ocean from manned spacecraft. NAVOCEANO operated in cooperation with the Bureau of Commercial Fisheries, Federal Water Pollution Control Administration, Geological Survey, National Academy of Engineering, Navy Space Systems Activity, Office of Naval Research, Smithsonian Institution, U.S. Army Cold Regions Research and Engineering Laboratory, U.S. Coast Guard, and Naval Air Systems Command. A hydrographic surveying and charting system, an integrated geophysical survey system and bottom topography survey system are being developed by the Directorate of Mapping, Charting and Geodesy as a research and development program.

Expanded use was made of the photogrammetric processes in the production, maintenance, and photo revision of
a variety of items. A total of 183 map manuscripts were
stereo compiled or revised for use in charting programs.
Efforts continued to implement utilization of color and infrared color photography and the use of precision stereoscopic
plotting information. Most interesting perhaps was the Surtsey Island survey. Surtsey, one of the world's youngest vol-
canic islands located about 20 miles south of Iceland, had a
violent birth on 14 November 1963. Although dormant today,
the island has an area of 2-1/2 square kilometers and its
highest point is 570 feet above mean sea level. A resurvey
conducted during the second week of July 1966 showed a magnetic anomaly over the island not evident during the 1963 survey. Oceanographic surveys in the Antarctic and the Arctic
areas were made for temperatures, salinities, nutrients,
plankton samples, etc. Stereo bottom photography has been
developed and used by the survey and research ships.

Automatic Digital Coordinatographic Systems produces
various types and kinds of plates including map projections,
shorelines, annotated overlays indicating positions of cities,
military grids for overprinting on Southeast Asia nautical
charts and a wide range of electronic navigational lattice systems. (From the NAVOCEANO Annual Report to the OCEAN-
OGRAPHER)

A new hydrographic chart of the Port of Corinto, the
most important harbor in Nicaragua has been published through
the cooperation of the United States Navy, the Army Inter-
American Geodetic Survey, and the Direccion General de
Cartografia (the government mapping agency of Nicaragua).
This chart of Corinto, the first to be issued since 1929, is
also the first hydrographic chart to be published from survey
data obtained under the Navy Harbor Survey Assistance Program (HARSAP), which is sponsored by Naval Oceanographic
Office. This program is to provide data for updating nautical
charts of harbors and approaches, and to assist other countries in the development of hydrographic surveying.

Department of the Air Force. Aeronautical Chart and
Information Center (8900 South Broadway, St. Louis, Missouri
63125) provides the Air Force and related aviation and space
agencies with aeronautical charts, air target materials, flight
information publications, geodetic missile data, astronautical
and geophysical charts and reference materials. A 16mm.,
color-sound motion picture, "Pathways in Aerospace," SFP

1216, which portrays ACIC's mission and function in 25
minutes of exciting detail, can be borrowed without charge
from the USAF Film Library Center, 8900 South Broadway,
St. Louis, Missouri 63125.

The lunar control (selenodetic) program began in 1960
with the acquisition of lunar photography from the Pic du
Midi observatory in the Pyrenees Mountains.   Over 80, 000
high quality lunar photographs showing a wide variety of phase
and libration angles have been obtained, and are used together with Orbiter IV photography for positioning studies and the
determination of relative heights through shadow measurements.   ACIC lunar observers use the facilities of Lowell
Observatory at Flagstaff, Arizona, to study the moon for
topographic details to be used in the Air Force Lunar Chart
Series.   The aerospace graphics and charts are available to
the public through the Government Printing Office and include
the Lunar Astronautical charts, (LAC's), the Lunar Reference
Mosaics, the Apollo Intermediate Charts, the Chart of the
Planet Mars, and the several Ranger charts of the moon
series.   The agency also supports NASA's Project Gemini
but the resulting charts are not available to the public in
general.

WORLD-WIDE MAPPING SURVEY*

Arthur J. Brandenberger

We all know that today, and even more so in the future, we have to solve some crucial problems such as:

> Increase the agricultural output in developing countries whose population amounts to 70 percent of the world's population.
> Accelerate the exploration and exploitation of natural resources as a measure to increase national wealth and to reduce poverty.
> Cope with the staggering population concentration in urban areas.
> Solve the problem of securing sufficient water and power supply.
> Provide adequate facilities to have available an efficient transportation and communication system.
> Cope with the problem of air and water pollution.

The solution of these problems requires intensive planning on a national as well as on an international level. On an international level, because financial and technical assistance to developing countries is becoming more and more indispensable, to create more stable economical and social conditions on a worldwide basis. The organization of the United Nations requests that the industrial countries contribute one percent of their Gross National Product to such assistance programs (the present contribution falls short of this figure and amounts to only about one-half of one percent).

---

*Reprinted by permission from Photogrammetric Engineering, April 1970, 355-359. Originally a talk delivered in 1969 to the annual convention of the American Society of Photogrammetry.

Here the question arises, where do we as surveyors
and map makers fit into this worldwide development program,
and what is our present role and what will be our future ob-
ligations.   This applies also to the photogrammetrists.   Already at the present time a large portion of the world's surveying and mapping tasks are solved by photogrammetry;
this will be even more so in the future.   For this reason, I
believe it is justified to discuss these problems as a photogrammetrist.

The solution of the problems listed above required, as
already mentioned, extensive planning.   Surveying and mapping
in general, and photogrammetry in particular, have to provide the necessary bases for such planning.   To satisfy this
requirement, it will evidently be necessary to make an inventory of the surveying and mapping status and potential in various countries and on a world-wide basis.   The Department of
Photogrammetry at Laval University is presently involved in
such a project which is sponsored by the National Research
Council of Canada.   Some specific data are presented herein
on the surveying and mapping activity for the four countries
of the world with the greatest populations, namely the USA,
the USSR, India and China.   The combined population of these
four countries at the present time amounts to about half of
the world's population.

The USA

The USA, with a population of [205] millions and an
area of 3.6 million square miles, (including Alaska), is the
country with the highest growth of urban population in the entire world.   Presently, 3/4 of the American population live
in urban areas resulting in an annual increase of urban land
of 0.05 percent of the country's entire area.   Only 9 percent
of the population is involved in agriculture distributed over
3.2 million farms.   The geodetic framework of the country
is well advanced.   About 70 percent of the main triangulation
network is completed (115,000 marked horizontal control
points).   For the main levelling network, the percentage is
about 80 percent (400,000 marked vertical control points).

There is full aerial photography coverage, particularly
at the scale 1:20,000 but also at smaller and larger scales.
As far as the mapping status is concerned, there is full map
coverage at the scales 1:1,100,000, 1:500,000 and 1:250,000.
There is partial map coverage at larger scales such as the
topographic map at the scale 1:24,000 which covers about 40

percent of the country.   Federal, state and local governments
occupied in the years 1966/68 a surveying and mapping personnel of about 16, 000 with annual expenditures in the order
of $300 millions US.   In 1966, the federal government had on
its pay-roll the following personnel in the field of surveying
and mapping (geodesy, photogrammetry, cartography, surveying and hydrography):

> Professional scientific and technical personnel (at
>   least half with a college degree):   3400 (1. 7 percent
>   of the total)
> Non professional scientific and technical personnel (tech-
>   nicians, etc.):   7600 (7. 1 percent of the total)

The average annual salary for the 150, 000 scientists
and engineers working for the federal government was $12, 300
in 1966, whereas the average annual 1966 salary for scientists and engineers working in surveying and mapping was
only $10, 300, i. e. $2000 less than the overall average.   This
is possibly due to the fact that quite a number of professionals
in surveying and mapping attended fewer college years or
have no complete college education when compared with other
professions.   It is interesting to note, however, that also on
the technician level, surveying and mapping was nearly as
much below the average annual salary ($6400 compared with
the overall average of $8300).   Only the professional scien-
tific and technical personnel in agricultural sciences, forestry
and micro-biology earned a lower average annual salary than
the surveyors and map makers in the federal government.
The other 40 groups of professional scientific and technical
personnel in the federal government earned average salaries
in 1966 in excess of those for the surveyors and map makers.

Much more difficult it is to evaluate the potential of
private surveying, photogrammetry and cartography offices
and companies.   According to estimations of various people,
between 60, 000 to 80, 000 persons are involved in the private
sector.   The overall annual turn-over of private surveying
and mapping enterprises for the years 1966/68, after sub-
traction of direct contract work for government agencies, is
estimated to be in the neighborhood of $400 millions.

Surveying and mapping is presently taught to various
extents at about 400 higher educational institutions.   At more
than 40 universities, photogrammetry is covered by one or
more special courses.   The annual influx of professional surveyors (including professional engineer-surveyors and photo-

grammetrists) appears to be in the neighborhood of 1200.

From the foregoing inventory, it follows that the United States presently spends about $700 millions per year for surveying and mapping.   This amount represents 0.087 percent of the Gross National Product, ($796 billions for 1967) or 0.31 percent of the total annual public expenditures (approximately $225 billions for 1967) or $3.60 per capita, or approximately $200 per sq. mi.   The ratio of the number of professional surveyors to the number surveying technologists and surveying technicians is larger than 1, and one person is employed in surveying and mapping out of 2700 inhabitants. The amount of $700 million annual expenditures for surveying and mapping represents a minor figure in the national economy; nevertheless, it is higher in comparison with some other professions, for instance, geology (excluding mining) or geography.

As far as photogrammetry is concerned, the available information and material allows only a first guess.   Evidently more than 10,000 full-time or part-time photogrammetrists of different levels are active in the United States.   The annual expenditures for photogrammetric operations is estimated to be in excess of $100 millions.

The USSR

The Soviet Union with a population of 234 millions (1966) has an area of 8.75 million sq. mi., which is about 1/6 of the entire land area of the earth.   A strong trend toward urbanization exists.   This is evident from the fact that the proportion of rural population has fallen from 82 percent in 1926 to 48 percent in 1964.   In 1966, the percentage of population in agriculture was 36 percent distributed over 36,500 collective farms (average area: 50 sq. mi.) and 12,200 state farms (average area: 190 sq. mi.).

The USSR is covered by a fairly homogeneous network of main triangulation (system of chains with distances between the chains varying from about 150 miles to 700 miles). Large portions of the country are covered by second-order triangulation and, in some areas, third- and fourth-order triangulation also does exist.   Vertical control (levelling of first order and of lower order) is of less density when compared with the USA.

Complete air photo coverage exists at scales between

1:35,000 and 1:70,000 (mostly Russar super-wide angle photography), and in urban areas photo coverage is at larger
scales. As far as map coverage is concerned, particularly
the scale 1:100,000 should be mentioned: topographic mapping
was completed in 1955. Map coverage at 1:50,000 scale has
been completed in some areas, and maps at the scales
1:25,000 and 1:10,000 exist in urban areas.

Several reports are available on the professional and
educational status of surveying and mapping in the Soviet
Union. Of particular interest is a report prepared by the
office of Mr. M.V.P. Yelgutin, Minister of Higher and Specialized Secondary Education. From the available information,
it can be concluded that the total surveying and mapping personnel in the USSR is approximately 100,000 (20,000 surveying engineers, 45,000 surveying technicians and 35,000 auxiliary personnel). The average annual salaries are (year 1966):
Survey engineer, (US) $2900; Survey technician, $2000; Auxiliary personnel, $1600. No private enterprise surveying and
mapping activity exists in the USSR.

Surveying and mapping is taught as a special discipline
at some large institutions of higher education, e.g. at the
Moscow University (Moscow Institute of Geodesy, Photogrammetry and Cartography), at the Leningrad Mining Institute
and at Novosibirsk Institute of Technology. Survey technicians
are trained at specialized secondary educational institutions.
In 1965/66, the total enrolment at both levels was:

> Surveying students at college and university level
> 7700 (0.19 percent of the total).
> Surveying students at technician level: 7300 (0.18
> percent of the total).

For 1965, the number of graduates in surveying and
mapping was: University level, 900 (0.22 percent of the
total); Technician level, 1100 (0.18 percent of the total).
In practice, presently a ratio of 1:2.3 exists between surveyors with a college degree and surveying technicians. It is
planned to modify this ratio to 1:3 by 1970. From the available information, it can be estimated that the Soviet Union
presently spends about US $280 millions per year for survey-
ing and mapping. This amount represents 0.106 percent of
the GNP ($264 billions for 1966), or 0.16 percent of the to-
tal annual public expenditures ($175 billions for 1966), or
$1.20 per capita, or approximately $36 per sq mi. Presently
one person is employed in surveying and mapping out of 4300
inhabitants.

As far as photogrammetry is concerned, one can assume that the photogrammetry potential of the Soviet Union personnel and expenditure wise amounts to about 10 to 20 percent of the national surveying and mapping potential.

India

India, with a population of 520 millions (1967) and an area of 1.19 million sq. mi., is mainly an agrarian country with only 18 percent of the population living in urban areas. In spite of this situation, the country faces some serious problems in the existing urban areas. Cities are overcrowded and population densities are staggering. For instance, areas in the city of Calcutta have population densities up to 650,000 persons per sq. mi. At least 40 percent of the country is covered by a fairly homogeneous network of main triangulation (system of chains with distances between the chains from about 150 miles to 400 miles). Prime vertical control is of a density somewhere between that of the USA and that of the USSR.

Air photo coverage is complete, mainly at the scales 1:30,000 or 1:60,000. Air photo coverage at the scale 1:10,000 is also in some urban areas. Mapping of the country is done almost entirely by the Survey of India at the scales 1:50,000 (topo maps), 1:25,000 (topo maps) and at larger scales. Also maps exist at smaller scales which are however often of older date. Apparently the new 1:50,000-scale topo map has been compiled for about 10 to 20 percent of the entire area of the country.

From the available information, it can be estimated that the personnel properly concerned with surveying and mapping is somewhat in excess of 25,000. The average annual salaries are (years 1966-68): Professional surveyor, (US) $700; Survey technician, $400; Auxiliary personnel, $300. Private enterprise surveying and mapping activity is negligible and includes only about 50 persons. Training in surveying and mapping is mainly done as in house training in the Survey of India. Also some universities offer surveying and mapping courses as part of the civil engineering program. Worthwhile mentioning is the Roorkee University with about 15 students majoring in photogrammetry.

Based on the available information, it can be estimated that India presently spends slightly more than US $10 millions per year for surveying and mapping. About 2/3 of the

country's surveying and mapping personnel as well as of the
expenditures are engaged by the Survey of India. The $10
millions represent 0.025 percent of the GNP (about $40 bil-
lion for the years 1966-68), or 0.11 percent of the total annual public expenditures (about $9 billion for the years 1966-
68), or $0.019 per capita, or approximately $8.50 per sq.
mi. Presently one person is employed in surveying and mapping out of about 20,000 inhabitants.

With regard to the photogrammetry potential of India,
only estimations can be made at this time: the number of
photogrammetrists is somewhat in excess of 500 and that the
annual expenditures for photogrammetric work exceeds $1
million.

China [Mainland]

China's population exceeds by far the population of any
other country of the world. With 760 million people distributed over an area of 4.49 million sq. mi., China's population
amounts to nearly 1/4 of the world's population. A major
portion of the population, i.e. about 80 percent, depends on
agriculture which is mainly concentrated in a relatively small
area of 425,000 sq. mi., representing only 11 percent of the
total area of the country.

According to GUCK, the Central Administration of Geodesy and Cartography of the Chinese People's Republic, it
was planned to complete the first-order triangulation by 1961.
Based on available information, it is impossible to verify
whether this goal has been reached. However, it can be
stated that a large portion of the country is covered by triangulation of various orders. Already before 1950, the office
of the Minister of Interior, Tsao-Mo, (at that time) reported
that the following numbers of points have been determined:
First-order, 930; Second-order, 8142; Third and Fourth-order,
62,357.

Comparable progress has been made as far as vertical
control is concerned. Already before 1950, 30,000 km. of
first-order and 56,000 km. of second-order levelling were
completed. Photo coverage exists for a major portion of the
country (a considerable amount of the photography is Russar
super-wide angle photography). Again according to GUCK,
topographic mapping at the scales 1:100,000 and 1:50,000 was
supposed to be completed by 1967. Not enough information
is available to verify whether this goal has been reached.

According to the program, mapping at scales 1:25,000 and larger in specific areas was supposed to start in 1967.

Based on available information, it can be estimated that the total surveying and mapping personnel in China is approximately 160,000 (20,000 surveying engineers, 60,000 surveying technicians and 80,000 auxiliary personnel). The average annual salaries are (1966): Surveying engineers, (US) $2000; Surveying technicians, $700; Auxiliary personnel, $550. No private enterprise surveying and mapping activity exists in China. Surveying and mapping is taught at a limited number of the 400 universities and colleges, such as at the Tonching University in Wuhan. The number of annual graduates in surveying engineering is presently about 2000. In practice, a ratio of 1:3:4 exists between surveyors with a college degree, surveying technicians and auxiliary personnel.

From the above information, it can be estimated that China presently spends about $150 million per year for surveying and mapping. This amounts to 0.20 percent of the GNP (about $76 billions for 1966), or 0.37 percent of the total annual public expenditures (approximately $40 billions for 1966), or $0.20 per capita, or $33 per sq. mi. Presently one person is employed in surveying and mapping out of approximately 5000 inhabitants.

Concerning photogrammetry, it is known that at least 20 survey airplanes, 20 first-order plotters and more than 200 Multiplex are in China. Furthermore, photogrammetric instruments of Chinese make are evidently manufactured. Considering this situation, it must be assumed that several thousand photogrammetrists are employed in China and that possibly an amount in excess of 19 percent of the overall surveying and mapping costs is spent for photogrammetric work.

Conclusions

If the four countries (USA, USSR, India and China) representing about half of the world's population are combined, the following average values for the annual expenditures for surveying and mapping are obtained (years 1966-68):

0.097 percent of the GNP
0.25 percent of the total public expenditures

$0. 67 per capita
$63 per sq. mi. or $25 per km.

The personnel involved in these operations is in the order of
410, 000 including at least 40, 000 photogrammetrists.   It is
obvious that for the entire world, somewhat different values
would result.   It is believed that analyses of the kind as presented in this paper are indispensable for planning purposes
on a national as well as on an international level, and it
seems evident that much more effort must be undertaken in
the future in performing such analyses.   The results will in
many cases be surprising and will show quite large differences
in the surveying potentials of various countries, as is evident
already in analyzing the four countries considered in this
paper.

References

National Science Foundation.   Review of Data on Science
     Resources.   NSF 68-16, Washington, D. C.
Joint Economic Committee, Congress of the United States.
     Soviet Economic Performance 1966-67, 90th Congress,
     2nd Session.   Materials prepared for the Sub-Committee
     on Foreign Economic Policy.   Washington, D. C.:   U. S.
     Government Printing Office, May 1968.
Brandenberger, A. J.   "Economical Considerations in Pho-
     togrammetric Surveying and Mapping, Planning."   In-
     vited Paper, Commission IV, International Congress of
     Photogrammetry, Lausanne, 1968.

NOTES ON THE ANTIQUARIAN MAP TRADE*

Louis Cohen

Dealing with old maps, which Argosy Book Store has been doing for over forty years, has been a pure delight. Among the beneficiaries of this activity we must mention Argosy, as well as historical societies, libraries, government archives, collectors, geographic societies, cartographers and research workers.

Aside from their scholarly uses as historical documents, we at Argosy found old maps to be endlessly fascinating to the layman and collector alike, and uniquely beautiful objects as well. Many are printed on the finest of rag papers, hand colored with lovely old pigments and embellished with beautifully engraved illustrations of ships, monsters and elaborately costumed figures. Cherubs with puffed out cheeks indicate the direction of the winds from each corner of many an early map. The points of the compass first appeared as a four petal rose, which increased later to 8, 16 and 32 petals as knowledge of the compass improved. Forests, mountains, villages represented by houses, Indians and occasionally cannibals busily engaged in their culinary art, are some of the features delineating land maps, while spouting whales, sea serpents and galleons inhabit the seas. In later seventeenth and eighteenth century maps, heavily ornamented cartouches show coats of arms of the nobility, and the products and natives of the country.

In the abundance of maps produced from the fifteenth through the eighteenth century, art and romance vied for honors. Ptolemy, Ortelius, Hondius, Speed, Mercator and Blaeu were indeed all magical names. Precise accuracies and

*Reprinted by permission from Special Libraries Association Geography and Map Division, Bulletin No. 64 (1966), 2-4.

delightful inaccuracies abound in their works.   Greenland is
shown as a peninsula of Asia in a Ptolemy map, 1507.   An
elongated Mediterranean Sea remained uncorrected until De
Lisle's map in 1700!   Nikolaas Visscher's map ca. 1720 has
minutely accurate delineation along the Atlantic seaboard and
wild conjecture in the interior.   It is amusing to see the St.
Lawrence River originate in the Rocky Mountains and flow
into the Atlantic Ocean.   The 1719 Senex map of America features "Great Lake of Thoya" between Missouri and the Pacific, draining into the latter.   Moses Pitt's map of the world
(London 1680) shows the primary mountain ranges running
east to west!

Mid-eighteenth-century maps show our Northwest and
Alaska as a blank, "Terra incognita." Ortelius in 1570 correctly shows California as a peninsula.   Despite this, it appears as an island in maps over a hundred years after this
date.   On some maps California is shown in the Arctic region (a distinction even Texas couldn't claim).   Pre-sixteenth-
century maps had quaint primitive effects produced by the
woodcut process, later abandoned for the refined copperplate
technique.

Many old maps of America are enlivened with interesting detail picturing U.S. mail and pony express routes, early
land grants, Indian paths and villages, unknown or unexplored
territory, trails of travelers and explorers (Frémont, Kearny,
Stansbury, Lewis and Clark, Long); Civil War battle plans,
canals and railroads merely proposed or actually built, evolution of new counties, Indian villages, abandoned mines,
early turnpikes, Indian battles and covered wagon trails.
Other early American maps show areas now vanished, such
as lost counties, extinct towns and transitory territorial
boundaries.   Then of course there are the not too early maps
of America that reflect the imperfect state of geographic
knowledge, the result of myth frequently, or explorers' fabri-
cations.

All this fascinating content was evident to us at Argosy decades ago, and since it dovetailed as well with the
books we were handling, we decided to make old maps one
of our specialties.   We purchased several large aggregates
of maps over the years, one of the largest being the entire
stock of the now defunct Robert Fridenberg Company which
yielded several thousand maps.   All auctions were regularly
attended, foreign and American dealers' catalogs were regularly scanned, and answers to our advertisements seeking

maps followed up.   The scouts knowing of our interest would
offer us items they came across in their peregrinations.
Despite our activity the general interest in maps in the 1920's
and 30's remained rather dormant, and consequently we were
able to amass a stock second to none.

In building up this specialty we have broken up many
atlases with little compunction, on the theory that their sacri-
fice as books was amply recompensed by the many uses and
specific needs for the individual maps by far flung historical
societies, libraries and collectors.   A Peruvian museum or
society for example, might want a particular seventeenth-
century map of Peru desperately, but would have no interest
in the atlas in which it appeared.   Specific maps are very
meaningful to local collectors and institutions throughout the
world, and it is in the fulfillment of these many needs that
atlases are dismantled.

As members of the bibliophilic fraternity, we of course
note exceptions, and they are numerous.   We do sell atlases
as complete volumes when they are either rare or important,
and have sold many complete atlases over the years (that we
wish we now possessed) such as:

> Munster, Sebastian.   Cosmographia 1550
> Ortelius, Abraham.   Theatrum Orbis 1584
> de Bry, Theodore.   Grands et petit voyages 1590-
> Wytfliet, Cornelius.   Descriptionis Ptolemaicae...
>   (1597)
> Mercator, Gerardus.   Atlas Minor (1607)
> Jansson, Jan.   Atlas Minor 1651
> Cellarius, Andreas.   Harmonia Microcosmica... 1661
> de Goos, Pieter.   Sea Atlas 1670
> Speed, John.   Theatre of Empire of Great Britain
>   1676
> Visscher, C. J.   Atlas Minor (1684)
> Coronelli, V. M.   Atlante Veneto 1695-7 (published
>   1707)
> Vandermaelen, P. M. G.   Atlas Universel... 6 vols.
>   1827

We often have mixed feelings in buying atlases, wel-
coming and even favoring the atlas that lacks some plates,
as it settles the sometimes difficult and responsible decision
of break-up.   It is a sad fact, however, that during the last
hundred years and before, some of the rarest atlases were
dismembered, a practice attested to by prize examples of the

cartographer's art in the archives of our leading institutions.
Most collections of rare maps, of necessity, were derived
from atlas volumes.   The number of maps published separately
were few indeed.

The interest in and demand for old maps have spiralled
in recent years and so have the prices.   The ever increasing
scarcity of old atlases due to their break-up or acquisition by
libraries and collectors will certainly insure present price
levels.   The likelihood is that present 'high' prices may appear low in the not distant future.

BIBLIOGRAPHIES AS TOOLS FOR MAP
ACQUISITION AND COMPILATION*

Roman Drazniowsky

The human being, anxious to safeguard and improve
his existence, always tries to obtain knowledge of everything
which tends to serve or endanger his life. And for this reason, he surveys his surroundings, the surface of the earth,
the layers of the atmosphere he can reach and the solid
ground. He studies vegetation, land use, geology, minerals,
precipitation, population distribution, diseases and many other vital phenomena. The best way to show the location and
distribution of these phenomena is by representing them on a
map. The value of the map as a means of storage of spatial
information, as a graphical solution to problems and as an
experimental tool in geography, geomorphology and related
fields, was recognized long ago by researchers, educators
and planners. However, the real "map explosion" started
after the Second World War. The reason for such an increase in the publication of maps was the broader application
and need for maps in many fields other than the military,
which was previously preeminent. Also, the development of
automation in printing and duplicating techniques has influenced
the rapid growth of map production.

With the "map explosion" a critical problem has arisen.
How can the proper map for a specific purpose be found in
the avalanche of printed material? Usually, a bibliography is
the best source to consult; providing of course that there is
one in existence. The science of cartography being so extensive, the compilation of a single bibliography on the entire

*Reprinted by permission from The Canadian Cartographer
[formerly The Cartographer], vol. 3, no. 2 (1966), 138-144.
Published by B. V. Gutsell, Department of Geography, York
University, Toronto.

subject is impossible.   The whole subject area can be divided
in the following manner for bibliographic purposes:

> Maps, atlases and globes
> General cartography, covering the nature of cartography
>   and its history and methods
> Bibliographical aids and gazetteers.

Each of the above-mentioned divisions can be subdivided
chronologically and according to geographical or political regions and by subjects.

Maps, Atlases and Globes

The current comprehensive bibliography for maps, atlases and globes is Bibliographique Cartographique Internationale. [1]   Each volume has an author and subject index and
is arranged according to major geographical divisions beginning with the world and then continents which are subdivided
by individual countries in alphabetical order.   In the same
category belongs the Referativnyi Zhurnal--Geografiya. [2]   In
addition to map and atlas entries of worldwide coverage, there
is also a section on general cartography.   As a unique feature,
this publication includes a bibliography of thematic maps which
accompany articles which are cited.   As a supplement to the
aforementioned bibliographies, individual governments, commercial map dealers, cartographic establishments and major
map collections publish catalogs, annual reports or lists of
maps, atlases, globes and gazetteers.   These publications do
not always offer worldwide coverage, but are of value as regional bibliographies.   The following publications are examples.

Publications of the Geological Survey, 1879-1961. [3]
Coverage is limited to the United States, individual states and
U. S. possessions.   For up-to-date additions, a monthly supplement, New Publications, is also compiled by the U. S. Geological Survey.   Catalog of Nautical Charts and Publications, [4]
covers all oceans and seas.   Although the charts are primarily for navigational purposes, in some instances they also
show the relief of small islands; very often, these are the
only maps available for such islands.

Catalog of Nautical Charts, Tide Tables, Coast Pilots,
Current Tables, and Tidal Current Charts, [5] provides information on material limited to the United States waters.   A very
helpful bibliographical source for new maps and atlases is

Catalog of Copyright Entries, Maps and Atlases.[6] Similar
publications are prepared by other governments. For example: Index of Publications of the Geological Survey of Canada,
1845-1958.[7] The coverage again is strictly regional and the
index is confined to Canada. The same agency also compiles
an Accessions List[8] which in some issues gives world-wide
coverage. Entries begin with maps of Canada, followed by
world maps and conclude with countries arranged in alphabetical order.

The Annual Report of the Ordnance Survey of Great
Britain describes the map coverage and mapping progress of
the United Kingdom. The D.O.S. Map Additions List[10] is of
particular value; references to the new and revised editions
of maps of the British Possessions are given. Authoritative
information and indexes for topographical maps of France and
her former possessions in Africa are included in Exposé des
Travaux, Année 1963.[11] For the German-speaking area in
Europe, the most important bibliographical sources for maps
are Berichte zur Deutschen Landeskunde[12] and Deutsche Bibliographie, Beilage: Karten.[13]

Additional information of bibliographical value is supplied by the major map collections in lists of their publications and acquisitions. Notable among these publications are:
Current Geographical Publications,[14] Selected New Acquisitions,[15] New Acquisitions,[16] and New Geographical Literature
and Maps,[17] the latter having an exceptionally good section
titled "New Atlases and Maps: Additions to the Map Room."
The entries are arranged geographically beginning with the
world, followed by continents, then subdivided by countries.
Commercial map publishers issue sales and advertising catalogs which form a special group of cartobibliographies. Very
often they are overlooked or discarded as nonessential, but
they provide important information on newly-published maps,
atlases, gazetteers, travel guides, globes and transparencies.
Some outstanding catalogs are: Bartholomew Maps,[18] De
Agostini,[19] Denoyer-Geppert,[20] Kümmerly & Frey,[21] Philips
Educational Catalogue,[22] Reise u. Verkehrs Katalog,[23] Stanford Map Bulletin,[24] and Zumstein Katalog.[25]

The increased production of world, regional and thematic atlases created a need for a separate bibliography. In
addition to the famous List of Geographical Atlases in the Library of Congress[26] there are the following recent publications: National and Regional Atlases,[27] Geographical Atlases,[28]
Catalog of Foreign Atlases in the Library of the Academy of

Sciences of U.S.S.R. 1940-1963, [29] and Catalogo de Atlas
Archivo de Planos. [30]   Also, a section devoted to atlases is
included in Guide to Reference Books. [31]   Globes form a
separate branch of cartography; therefore, a special bibliography dealing with this subject is desired.   Unfortunately, at
the present time, there is little work done on world-wide
coverage and only a few publications of regional importance
can be cited.   The description of globes by E. L. Stevenson
in Terrestrial and Celestial Globes[32] is a basic source.   Also, a more recent publication, Der Globen in Wandel der
Zeit, [33] is a significant aid.

The following works are of regional value: Catalogo
dei Globi Antiche Conservati in Italia, [34] Altere Erd-und Himmelsgloben in Beyern, [35] Die Ersten Forschungsergebnisse
der Globus Inventarisierung in der Deutschen Demokratischen
Republik. [36]   The periodical Der Globusfreund[37] is a helpful
supplement for research on this subject.

General Cartography

Although the map bibliography published in Geographisches Jahrbuch[38] is not up-to-date, it is still a salient contribution to this field.   The more recent publication Die Kartographie 1943-1954[39] may be considered a supplement or
continuation of Geographisches Jahrbuch.   Also, a very helpful contribution, A Guide to Historical Cartography[40] has been
prepared by Walter W. Ristow and Clara E. LeGear.

The most useful sources of current bibliographical information and information on recent developments in cartography are included in cartographical and geographical periodicals such as Bibliotheca Cartographica, [41] a comprehensive
bibliography of cartographic literature; The Cartographer[42]
an informative journal reporting on technical developments
and promoting the exchange of ideas in the field of cartography; The Cartographic Journal[43] which presents news and
articles on all aspects of cartography; International Jahrbuch
für Kartographie[44] which contains articles on development,
new methods and new techniques in cartography; Kartographische Nachrichten, [45] a quarterly publication providing a selected map bibliography as well as information about cartographic progress; Osterreichische Zeitschrift für Vermessungswesen, [46] which presents articles on general cartography,
geodesy and photogrammetry; Surveying and Mapping, [47] a
quarterly journal offering articles on all aspects of cartography and in each issue, a short bibliography citing recent maps

and mapping literature.   For a more complete list of periodicals, the International List of Geographic Serials[48] is
highly recommended.

Bibliographical Aids

Apart from the previously mentioned map bibliographies
and periodicals there is an unorganized wealth of information
on cartography in general reference and guide books.   A
prominent contribution in this category still belongs to J. K.
Wright's Aids to Geographical Research;[49] it includes a separate section on maps and cartography, as well as a bibliography of atlases.   Geographisches Taschenbuch[50] has references to maps and general cartography.   There is also very
general information in the Guide to Reference Books[31] in
which atlases and gazetteers are cited but a section on cartography is, unfortunately, omitted.   The complete separation
of geology from geography in this latter work is a generally
hampering division in that it necessitates checking the map
bibliography in several places in the same book.

For map compilation, gazetteers are important and
are basic reference material for geographical features and
place names.   In addition to some private institutions dealing with place names, their history and changes, some governments have created special agencies which are solely responsible for official publications of place names.   In the United
States, for example, the Board on Geographic Names is publishing a series of gazetteers[51] for individual countries and
major geographic areas throughout the world.   It is most
disconcerting that there is no official gazetteer of the United
States at this writing.   As a substitute, the Rand McNally
Commercial Atlas and Marketing Guide,[52] published annually,
is available.   It contains names of populated places in the
United States but does not have the geographical coordinates.

In closing, I should like to strongly suggest that map
publishers include all necessary bibliographical data in the
map legend, and that government agencies, as well as private companies, should offer adequate information on published
material for bibliographical purposes.   If these two suggestions were faithfully executed, many of the most debilitating
and distressing problems in this field would be solved.   Generally, the difficulties in compiling map and atlas bibliographies are related directly to the unique nature of the map,
which demands a completely different handling and approach
than books.

SELECTED BIBLIOGRAPHY

1. Bibliographie Cartographique Internationale. Comité
    Nationale de Géographie; International Geographic
    Union. Paris. Annual.
2. Referativnyi Zhurnal--Geografiya. Akademiya Nauk
    SSSR. Institut Nauchnoi Informatsii. Moscow.
    Monthly.
3. Publications of the Geological Survey 1879-1961; and
    New Publications of the Geological Survey, monthly.
    U. S. Department of the Interior, Geological Survey.
    Washington, D. C.: Government Printing Office,
    1964; 457 p.
4. Catalog of Nautical Charts and Publications. 2d ed.
    U. S. Navy Hydrographic Office, Washington, D. C.,
    1963. (Name changed to U. S. Naval Oceanographic
    Office.)
5. Catalog of Nautical Charts, Tide Tables, Coast Pilots,
    Current Tables, Tidal Current Charts. Washington,
    D. C.: U. S. Department of Commerce, Coast and
    Geodetic Survey, 1964; 41 p.
6. Maps and Atlases. Catalog of Copyright Entries: Third
    Series. Copyright Office--The Library of Congress,
    Washington, D. C.
7. Index of Publications of the Geological Survey of Canada
    (1845-1958). Johnston, A. G. Geological Survey of
    Canada, Department of Mines and Technical Surveys,
    Ottawa, 1963; 378 p.
    Index of Publications of the Geological Survey of Cana-
    da (1959-1964). Rice, H. M. A. Ottawa: Geological
    Survey of Canada, Department of Mines and Tech-
    nical Surveys, 1965; 163 p.
8. Accessions List. Ottawa: Geographical Branch, De-
    partment of Mines and Technical Surveys. Irregular.
9. The Ordnance Survey Annual Report. Ordnance Survey,
    Chessington, Surrey. Annual.
10. D. O. S. Map Additions List. Directorate of Overseas
    Surveys, Tolworth, Surbiton. Monthly.
11. Exposé des Travaux Année 1963. Ministère des Travaux
    publics et des Transports. Paris: Institut Géo-
    graphique National, 1965; 340 p. and 44 pl.
12. Berichte zur Deutschen Landeskunde. Bad Godesberg:
    Bundesanstalt für Landeskunde und Raumforschung.
    Irregular.
13. Deutsche Bibliographie. Beilage: Karten. Im Amat-
    lichen Auftrage des Bundesministeriums des Innern

und Hessischen Kulturministers herausgegeben und bearbeitet von der Deutschen Bibliothek, Frankfurt am Mein. Weekly.

14. Current Geographical Publications. Addition to the research catalogue of the American Geographical Society, New York. Monthly, except July & August.

15. Selected New Acquisitions in the University of Kansas Map Library. University of Kansas Libraries, Lawrence. Monthly.

16. New Acquisitions. Map Library. University of Illinois Libraries, Urbana. Bi-monthly.

17. New Geographical Literature and Maps. London: Royal Geographical Society. Bi-annual.

18. Bartholonew Maps. Edinburgh: John Bartholomew & Son Ltd. Annual.

19. Catalogo Listino Cartografico. Novara: Istituto Geografico de Agostini. Annual.

20. Denoyer-Geppert Maps, Globes, Charts, Atlases, Models, Transparencies. Chicago: Denoyer-Geppert Co. Annual.

21. Gesamtkatalog. Bern: Kümmerly & Frey. Irregular.

22. Philips' Educational Catalogue. London: George Philip and Son Ltd. Irregular.

23. RV-Katalog. Stuttgart: Reise und Verkehrsverlag. Monthly supplements.

24. International Map Bulletin. London: Edward Stanford Ltd. Annual.

25. Zumstein Katalog mit Register. Grosse Ausgabe. Munich: Zumstein Landkartenhaus, 1966.

26. A List of Geographical Atlases in the Library of Congress. 1909-1920. Phillips, P. L. 4 vols.
A List of Geographical Atlases in the Library of Congress. With bibliographical notes (a continuation of four volumes by Philip Lee Phillips). LeGear, Clara Egli, vol. 5, 1958; vol. 6, 1963. Library of Congress, Washington, D. C.

27. National and Regional Atlases. Sources, bibliography, articles. Drecka, Jolanta and Tuszyńska-Rekawek, Halina, under the direction of Stanislaw Leszozycki. Polish Academy of Sciences. Institute of Geography. Dokumentacja No. 1, Warsaw, 1964; 155 p.

28. Geographical Atlases. Churkin, V. G. Zapiski Geograficheskogo Obshchestva SSSR. vol. 21. Novaya seriya. Moscow: Akademiya Nauk SSSR., 1961; 116 p.

29. Catalogue of Foreign Geographical Atlases of the Library of the Academy of Sciences of the U.S.S.R. Melni-

kova, T. N. and Stanchul, T. A. Luppov, S. P. (Editor). Moscow: "Nauka," 1965; 164 p.

30. Catalogo de Atlas Archivo de Planos. Madrid: Servicio Geografico del Ejercito, 1962; 420 p.

31. Guide to Reference Books. Winchell, Constance M. Chicago: American Library Association, many editions.

32. Terrestrial and Celestial Globes. Their history and construction including a consideration of their value as aids in the study of geography and astronomy. Stevenson, Edward Luther. Publication of the Hispanic Society of America No. 86. New Haven: Yale University Press, 1921; vol. 1, 218 p.; vol. 2, 291 p.

33. Der Globus im Wandel der Zeit. Eine Geschichte der Globen. Muris, Oswald. Berlin: Columbus Verlag-Paul Oestergaard K. G., 1961; 288 p.

34. Catalogo dei globi antichi conservati in Italia. Fasc. 1, I globi Blaviani. Deschki, Leo S. (Editor). Florence: Istituto e Museo di Storia della Scienza Biblioteca, 1957; 54 p.

35. Altere Erd und Himmelsgloben in Bayern. Fauser, Alois. Im Auftrag der Bayerischen Staatsbibliothek Herausgegeben von Alois Fauser unter Mitarbeit von Traudl Seifert. Stuttgart: Schuler Verlagsgesellschaft, 1964; 184 p.

36. Die ersten Forschungsergebnisse der Globusinventarisierung in der Deutschen Demokratischen Republik. (Eine Beitrag zur Internationalen Weltinventarisieurung durch UNESCO). Grötzsch, H.

37. Der Globusfreund. Vienna: Coronelli-Weltbund der Globusfreunde. Irregular.

38. Fortschritte der Kartographie (1930-36). Haack, Hermann. In Geographisches Jahrbuch, Bd. 51, 1936; p. 230-312. Geographisches Jahrbuch, Bd. 52, 1937; p. 3-74.

39. Die Kartographie. Eine Bibliographische Übersicht. Kosack, Hans-Peter, and Meine, Karl-Heinz. Kartographische Schriftenreihe, Bd. 4. Lahr/Schwarzwald: Astra Verlag, 1955; 216 p.

40. A Guide to Historical Cartography; A Selected List of References on the History of Maps and Map Making. 2d ed., rev. Ristow, Walter W. and LeGear, Clara E. Library of Congress Map Division. Reference Department, Washington, D. C., 1960; 22 p.

41. Bibliotheca Cartographica. Bibliography of cartographic literature. Bad Godesberg: Institut für Landeskunde (and) Deutsche Gesellschaft für Kartographie. Two nos. a year.

42. The Cartographer. The Ontario Institute of Chartered
        Cartographers, c/o The Editor, Department of Ge-
        ography, York University, Toronto 12, Canada. Two
        nos. a year.
43. The Cartographic Journal. The British Cartographic
        Society. (Journal subscriptions: 2 Calder Court,
        Gringer Hill, Maidenhead, Berks, England.) Two
        nos. a year.
44. International Jahrbuch für Kartographie. Herausgege-
        ben von Eduard Imhof. Gütersloh: C. Bertelsmann
        Verlag. Annually.
45. Kartographische Nachrichten. Herausgegeben von der
        Deutschen Gesellschaft für Kartographie, Bielefeld.
        Quarterly.
46. Österreichische Zeitschrift für Vermessungswesen.
        Herausgegeben von Österreichischen Verein für Ver-
        messungswesen, Vienna. Offizielles Organ des
        Bundesamtes für Eich-und Vermessungswesen der
        Österreichischen Kommision für die Internationale
        Erdmessung und der Österreichischen Gesellschaft
        für Photogrammetrie. Bi-monthly.
47. Surveying and Mapping. American Congress on Survey-
        ing and Mapping, Washington, D. C. Quarterly.
48. International List of Geographical Serials. Harris,
        Chauncy D. and Fellman, Jerome D. University of
        Chicago, Dept. of Geography. Research Paper No.
        63, Chicago, 1960; 194 p.
        Annotated World List of Selected Current Geographical
        Serials in English. 2d ed. Harris, Chauncy D.
        University of Chicago, Dept. of Geography. Research
        Paper No. 96. Chicago, 1964; 32 p.
49. Aids to Geographical Research: Bibliographies, Peri-
        odicals, Atlases, Gazetteers and other Reference
        Books. 2d ed. Wright, John Kirkland and Platt,
        Elizabeth T. American Geographical Society Re-
        search Series No. 22. New York: For the Society
        by the Columbia University Press, 1947; 331 p.
50. Geographisches Taschenbuch und Jahrweiser für Landes-
        kunde. Meynen, E. In Zusammenarbeit mit dem
        Zentralverband der Deutschen Geographen unter mit-
        wirkung von Angehörigen des Instituts für Landes-
        kunde in der Bundesanstalt für Landeskunde und
        Raumforschung. Wiesbaden: Franz Steiner Verlag.
        Annual.
51. Official Standard Names Approved by the United States
        Board on Geographic Names. Office of Geography,
        Dept. of the Interior, Washington, D. C.

52. Commercial Atlas and Marketing Guide. Chicago:
        Rand McNally & Co.   Revised annually.

MAP ACQUISITION, ARRANGEMENT AND DESCRIPTION AT THE NATIONAL ARCHIVES*

Ralph Ehrenberg

The map librarian and the archivist who specializes in maps have many things in common: both are concerned with items of a similar physical form; both have similar problems in the housing and preservation of their holdings; and both require some specialized training in geography and cartography.

Although librarians and archivists have similar interests and problems, their holdings differ in one important aspect--their origin! A library map collection contains items of a discrete nature. Each map is generally an individual item, separate from others and "with a significance of its own, independent of its relation to others" (T. R. Schellenberg, Modern Archives Principles and Techniques, Chicago: University of Chicago Press, 1956; p. 20). The Cartographic Branch of the National Archives, on the other hand, houses maps which have been "produced or accumulated in direct connection with the functional activities of some government agency; and much of their significance depends on their organic relation to the agency and to each other" (Ibid., p. 17). This difference in map origin necessitates a different professional approach by the librarian and the archivist in the acquisition, arrangement and description of maps.

Acquisition

Unlike a library, which as a "collecting agency" obtains its material from diverse sources through gifts and purchases, an archives is a "receiving agency," established

*Reprinted by permission from Special Libraries Association Geography and Map Division, Bulletin No. 68 (1967), 10-13.

for the purpose of preserving material produced by the body it serves. As such an agency, the National Archives has established certain procedures to facilitate the acquisition of public records. The Federal Records Act of 1950 requires that each Federal agency establish a records management program, and authorizes the Archivist of the United States to determine which records have sufficient value to warrant their continued preservation. A second law, Public Law 85-50, passed in 1957, requires the transfer to the National Archives of any noncurrent records of any Federal Agency that are more than fifty years old, and that are determined by the Archivist to have sufficient historical and evidential value.

In order to assist record managers in carrying out these laws, the Cartographic Branch has prepared a schedule describing which maps are of a record character and which are not. In general, two kinds of maps are considered to have enduring value (The National Archives, Circular Letter No. 48-2, Nov. 28, 1947). The first are maps which have not been printed or otherwise reproduced in numbers. Manuscript maps form the bulk of this class. In addition, printed or processed maps which have been annotated for record purposes or which bear manuscript signatures to indicate official approval are also considered of record character. The Cartographic Branch contains some 800,000 manuscript and annotated maps which probably make it the single largest manuscript map collection in the Western Hemisphere. Examples include:

> Manuscript and annotated maps of Indian Reservations, tribal lands, and townsites prepared by the Bureau of Indian Affairs,
> Manuscript and annotated maps of military campaigns and engagements prepared by the Corps of Army Engineers,
> Manuscript quadrangle sheets compiled by the Geological Survey,
> Manuscript rights-of-way maps showing the official routes of land grand railroads as submitted to and approved by the Secretary of the Interior.

A second class of maps which have been defined as being of record character are printed or processed maps issued by Federal agencies. The holdings of the Cartographic Branch include a record set of maps from each map-producing agency. A record set consists of one copy of each edition or

variant of each printed or processed map.   These are normally transferred to the National Archives semi-annually.
Many sets are unfortunately incomplete, but those of the major mapping agencies are complete or nearly so.   Examples
of record sets in the custody of the National Archives include:

> General Land Office record set of the individual pub-
>   lic-land states,
> The published quadrangles of the Geological Survey,
> Post Office record set of maps of individual states or
>   groups of states showing means and frequency of
>   transportation of United States mail,
> Forest Service record set of its maps showing the in-
>   dividual national forests.

Arrangement

        A map collection, from a geographer's point of view,
should be arranged or classified regionally and cross-refer-
enced by subject.   Archival map arrangement, on the other
hand, is based upon the principle of provenance or the maintaining of records in the organic units in which they are accumulated or created by an agency.   Mr. W. L. G. Joerg,
the first Chief of the Cartographic Branch, and a pioneer in
applying archival principles to maps, put it this way: "The
regional principle, at least as a primary principle of classification and arrangement, is not appropriate for an archival
map collection.   To have applied the regional principle would
have merged together maps derived from different agencies
and would have broken down the agency of derivation structure.   As a corollary, it would have cut across the threads
connecting the maps with their related textual records"
(W. L. G. Joerg, "Archival Maps As Illustrated by Those in
the National Archives," The American Archivist, IV (April
1941), 190).

        After maps have been received from an agency they
are placed in the stack areas by record group in keeping with
the principle of provenance.   "A record group consists, as
a rule, of the documentation produced by an administrative
unit at the bureau level of the Government."   (The National
Archives, Staff Information Paper No. 18, June, 1951.)
Record groups are subdivided into smaller units called subgroups and series.   A typical subgroup contains the records
of a specific office, often a division, within an agency.   Records that can not be assigned to a specific office are arranged

as "General Cartographic Records." Within subgroups the records in the Branch are arranged into series of homogeneous units. The following is an example of map arrangement by the record group concept:

Record Group 48, Records of the Office of the Secretary of the Interior.

      Subgroup a.   General Cartographic Records.
          Series 1.   Maps relating to southern and western
             U.S.
          Series 2.   Maps relating to states and territories.
          Series 3.   City maps.
          Series 4.   Maps of mineral lands.
          . . .
          Series 25. Maps of project areas.

      Subgroup b.   Office of Explorations and Survey of the
             War Department - Pacific Railroad Survey.
          Series 26. General Survey and Exploration Records.
          Series 27. Routes near the 47th and 49th Parallels.
          Series 28. Routes near the 41st Parallel.
          . . .
          Series 34. Published maps.

      Subgroup c.   Pacific Wagon Roads Office.

In the subgroups and series maps are arranged, if practicable, as they were arranged in the agency. Therefore, some of the records are arranged according to a numbering system, some by subject, and some by area. For instance, the 26,000 maps of the Headquarters Map File, Office of the Chief of Engineers, are arranged according to an alphabetical regional classification scheme beginning with the North Atlantic states and moving southward and westward to the Pacific Coast. Each map is numbered within this scheme and for each there is an index slip. An example of maps arranged according to a number representing the tube in which it was formerly kept, and a map file serial number. The map number will frequently be found on correspondence or other textual documents in the Department of the Interior to which the maps relate.

Occasionally records are accessioned which do not have any apparent system of arrangement. An Archivist will then have to study and arrange them in the most practicable manner for easy servicing. The maps of RG 98, Records of U.S. Army Commands, were of this nature. They have been

arranged into subgroups and series by geographic area--each
command representing a separate series, and within the series
by chronological order.

Description

The total number of maps in the Branch is about
1, 600, 000.   They are distributed among 131 different record
groups which are under various degrees of control.   When
records are transferred to the National Archives, the agency
of origin is required to furnish all related finding aids that
will facilitate searching the records.   The finding aids to the
maps received in the Branch vary with the record groups and
include card catalogs, descriptive lists, and index maps.   For
example, with the Headquarters Map File, Office of the Corps
of Engineers, the Branch received index cards cross-refer-
enced by author, subject and area; the field notes from the
Bureau of Land Management were accompanied by index maps;
and the Coast and Geodetic Charts were indexed in published
catalogs.

Unfortunately, many of the map files of the Government have either inadequate finding aids or none at all.   In
such cases appropriate aids have been prepared.   A Descriptive Entry Card designed specifically for cartographic records
has been found to be very useful and effective in facilitating
the description of maps.

In addition to the finding aids prepared for use in the
search room of the Cartographic Branch, the staff has also
prepared several inventories, special lists, and catalogs of
records by record groups.   These are processed and distributed to interested searchers and organizations.   The preliminary inventory is the most general approach to any description.   It is prepared as soon as possible after a record
group is received without waiting to screen out disposable material or to perfect the arrangement of the records.   It is
compiled both as a finding aid to assist the staff in reference
service and as a means of establishing administrative control
over the records.   The special list goes beyond the general
description contained in a preliminary inventory and describes
records in terms of individual record items.   A third type of
publication is a subject guide or catalog which includes various items from different record groups.

Staff members are currently in the process of compiling a Guide to all cartographic records in the Branch.   It

will in a general way perform the same function for the Cartographic Branch that a standardized central card catalog performs for a map library, although control will be over subgroup and series rather than individual items.

MAPS, CHARTS AND COPYRIGHT*

Abraham L. Kaminstein

Copyright protection of maps in the United States began before the adoption of the Constitution. A resolution of
the Colonial Congress in 1783 recommended that the colonies
grant copyright to authors or publishers of "new books."
Twelve of the original 13 colonies enacted copyright laws and
these dealt mainly with books. Some of the laws covered
"books and pamphlets" (New Jersey, Pennsylvania, Virginia,
New York and South Carolina), some referred to "books or
writings" (Maryland) and others dealt with "books, treatises
or other literary works (productions)" (Massachusetts, New
Hampshire and Rhode Island). Only Connecticut, Georgia and
North Carolina specifically included "maps or charts."

The Constitution in Article I, Section 8, did not
enumerate the kinds of works to be protected; in stating the
purpose of promoting "the progress of Science and useful
Arts," it referred generally to "Writings and Discoveries."

Shortly after the convening of the First Congress in
March 1789, private and general copyright bills were introduced. On April 15, 1789, two petitions were presented, one
of them by John Churchman requesting the exclusive right of
vending "spheres, hemispheres, maps, charts and tables" on
the principles of magnetic variation, which would permit the
determination of longitude if latitude were known. The committee considering the request recommended that a law be
passed to give Churchman rights in the publication of "these
several inventions." More important, the House of Repre-

*Reprinted by permission from Special Libraries, vol. 51,
no. 5 (1960), 241-243. Copyright by Special Libraries Association. Originally a paper presented in 1959 at the 50th
SLA Convention.

sentatives, in considering this report, ordered that a bill be
brought in to make general provision for copyrights and patents.   A committee was appointed, and a first draft submitted
on June 23, 1789.   Another private bill sought to protect The
American Geography by Jedidiah Morse of which "two sheet
maps of the Southern and North States ... had been surrepti-
tiously copied."

        The House passed a bill; the Senate adopted it but
changed its title from "Maps Charts Books and other Writings"
to "Maps, Charts, and Books."   This apparent intention to
narrow the scope of the bill indicates that maps probably
would not have been covered by the first federal law if they
had not been specifically mentioned.   It has even been argued
that, since a literal reading of the word "Writings" in the
Constitution does not necessarily include maps, their inclusion
in the law of May 31, 1790, still left open the question of
whether they came within the constitutional provision.   This
seems a very forced argument, especially since many of
those in the First Congress also served in the Constitutional
Convention.

        The 1790 law required the deposit of a map, if already
printed.   For the future a printed copy of the title of a map
was to be deposited before publication in the clerk's office of
the district court; within two months, the author or owner
was to publish a copy of the record made in the district
court in a newspaper for four weeks.   Within six months
after publication, copies of the map were to be delivered to
the Secretary of State.   The term was 14 years, with the
privilege of renewal for another 14 years.   Early map makers
took advantage of the new law, and Reading Howell made some
of the earliest entries in the district court in Philadelphia.
The third entry in that court for An Explanation of the Magnetic Atlas was made by the John Churchman mentioned above.
The first entry in the Boston court was for The American
Geography and Geography Made Easy by Jedidiah Morse.

Requirements of Present Law

        A review of the changes in copyright law from 1790 to
the enactment of what is in essence the present law, in 1909,
would be interesting and instructive, but I leave that task to
the historian and proceed to consider the present requirements.   Today titles are no longer filed in advance of publication, but it is crucial that when a map is first published,
it bear the statutory copyright notice.   If the notice is not

carried on the first publication, the opportunity of securing
copyright is lost.

The statute provides a long and short form of notice.
The long form consists of: 1) the word, Copyright, the abbreviation Copr. or the symbol © ; 2) the name of the proprietor of the copyright; and 3) the year date of publication.
The shorter form permits the use of the symbol © and the
initials of the proprietor, provided his full name appears
elsewhere on the map. The committee considering the 1909
law had before it bills that did not require a year date in
any notice. In its final report, the committee commented:

> Serious objections were made to the elimination of
> the date. It was said that the public would have
> no means of ascertaining whether the copyright had
> expired and that the public was entitled to that
> knowledge.
> Your committee felt that in case of books or
> printed publications including dramatic and musical
> works, the year in which copyright began should be
> stated in the notice, and we have provided for the
> insertion of the date in the notice in all such works.
> Your committee did not feel that it was necessary
> to have the date printed on works of art, etc. Art-
> ists have always objected to the copyright notice
> which they were obliged to put on the pictures, be-
> cause it was considered a disfigurement, and we
> have retained substantially the provision of the orig-
> inal bill regarding the notice in such cases....

While the arguments as to the omission of the year
date were couched in terms of disfigurement of paintings,
photographs and similar works, the statute as adopted required the year date only for a "printed literary, musical,
or dramatic work." Under this language, the notice for maps
need not include the year date. Where a particular map also
includes text matter for which protection is claimed or where
the map is reprinted from a book which used the full form of
notice, it is the better part of caution to include the year date.
It is also worth emphasizing that, while the year date is not
needed for protection in the United States, the Universal Copyright Convention, which enables Americans to secure protection abroad, does call for its inclusion.

The usual notice might read, "Copyright by John Draftsman" or " © John Draftsman 1959." It is important that the

copyright notice follow the strict statutory form. The name
of the proprietor should include at least the first initial and
last name of an individual and in the case of a firm or corporation, the full legal name. Statutory copyright in a published map begins upon first publication with notice and not
upon registration. After first publication, two copies of the
map, an application on Form F and a fee of $4 should be
submitted to the Register of Copyrights, Washington 25, D. C.
The law specifies that the copies shall be of the "best edition, " and if at the time an application is submitted, the map
has been published in two different forms, e. g. , gores and
globes, the best form, in this case the globes, should be submitted.

Minor changes in a map when a new edition is issued
do not require a new registration, but counsel should be consulted in determining when the changes are sufficient to warrant a new application. Maps issued in two or more sizes
do not require separate registration; only copies of the largest
size should be submitted. The term of copyright is 28 years,
and an additional 28 years may be secured if the party entitled to do so files a renewal application in the Copyright Office during the final year of the first term. The courts have
accepted most of the different forms in which maps may ap-
pear--sheets, globes, relief maps, etc. This general acceptance does not mean that courts have found all maps in each
category copyrightable. Only "original" maps showing some
creative effort are copyrightable, but this does not require
something startlingly original or completely new. Most maps
are a combination of the old and new.

A map that is copied, even though reprinted from an
old manuscript, is not original. Nor would a court protect
a map created by placing existing maps of two contiguous
counties together--a merely mechanical operation. The courts
have been liberal in supporting "original" work done by authors but they have been a little stricter in the map field.
The general rules applied in other fields of copyright are
also germane here. Thus, courts do not protect ideas or
methods under copyright, and they have refused to protect
systems of marking maps.

General Considerations

The problems of the librarian in dealing with copyrighted works are complicated and difficult. The librarian
who is unable to answer some of these perplexing questions

may take some consolation from the fact that lawyers experience the same difficulty.   The librarian should refer complicated legal questions to a qualified attorney.

There are a few, very few, general guideposts.   If no copyright has been claimed in a map and the map has been published without a copyright notice, it may be copied. Even here, there is a conceivable risk since the copy may be an unauthorized one reprinted without notice.   If a map was published more than 56 years ago, whether or not it bore notice, it is in the public domain in the United States. If it was published more than 28 years ago, the Copyright Office catalogs may be consulted or a search requested of the Copyright Office, to determine whether the work has been renewed.   Unless there is such a renewal on record, and many original map copyrights are not renewed, the work may be copied.

Beyond this, copyrighted maps may be copied only within the limits of the doctrine of "fair use."   There is no statutory guide as to what amounts to "fair use."   The cases deal with very specific situations, and it is difficult and dangerous to try to formulate general rules.   There have been continuing efforts to write some general ground rules in other fields.   Special Libraries Association is cooperating in the attempt to arrive at reasonable criteria, but I am not sure that these efforts include the map area.

On July 1, 1959, the present statute had been in effect 50 years.   Much of it has stood the test of time and is still appropriate, but there have been technological changes that vitally affect the industries using copyrighted material; there are new uses and changes in marketing.   Inevitably, a good portion of the law merits study in order to determine whether changes are necessary.   Four years ago, Congress authorized the Copyright Office to undertake a program of studies looking toward general revision.   Some 19 studies have now been issued, and a few more are in various stages of preparation.   Some of the studies, e.g., those on history of copyright law revision, notice, uses of the copyright notice and fair use may be of particular interest to map librarians.   I mention them because at some point Congress will consider these studies, the necessity of revising the law and how it should be done.   There is therefore an opportunity for cartographers, map publishers and librarians to consider the question of revision, to make comments on the studies and to make known to the Copyright Office and even-

tually to the Congress their position on those segments of
the law that affect them.

PUBLISHED SOURCES OF INFORMATION ABOUT MAPS AND ATLASES*

Richard W. Stephenson

Published information about maps and atlases may be divided into five categories:

1. Geographical journals which regularly carry lists and reviews of maps and atlases,
2. Cartographic accession lists,
3. National bibliographies containing map and atlas citations,
4. Catalogs and lists of publishers and dealers, and
5. Catalogs and lists of second hand dealers.

Geographical Journals

Geographical journals are a primary source of information about currently produced cartographic works. Many geographical journals include reviews of outstanding atlases, but only a few contain citations and reviews of individual maps. The bibliography describes 28 journals which have been found to be particularly valuable for acquisitions purposes. Basically, it is a revision of John Wolter's "The Current Bibliography of Cartography: An Annotated Selection of Serials," published in the [SLA] Geography and Map Division Bulletin (Dec 1964).

When discussing serials of special importance to the map acquisitions librarian, one should begin with the great international effort, the Bibliographie Cartographique Interna-

*Reprinted by permission from Special Libraries, vol. 61, no. 2 (1970), 87-98, 110-112. Copyright by Special Libraries Association. Originally a paper presented in 1969 at the 60th Conference of the SLA.

tionale, prepared by the Comité Nationale Française de Géographie and the International Geographical Union. Published annually, this is the most comprehensive list of maps presently being produced. The value of this list as an acquisitions tool, however, is somewhat diminished by the lag in time between the date of information and the date of publication of the bibliography. For instance, the latest volume, published in 1968, describes maps and atlases issued in 1966.

The German semiannual serial, Berichte zur deutschen Landeskunde, presents annually (in its Heft 2) an extensive list of maps of Germany, Austria, Switzerland, and Liechtenstein. A new and significant periodical is the British Cartographic Society's Cartographic Journal which contains a list of "Recent Maps." This fine serial also includes valuable reviews, notes, and articles about maps. The International Hydrographic Bulletin, published monthly in Monaco, should not escape the attention of acquisitions librarians, for here is found a very useful "List of New Charts and New Editions of Charts." By using this list it is a rather easy matter for the librarian to be aware of the current production of hydrographic charts.

The American Congress on Surveying and Mapping's quarterly journal, Surveying and Mapping, has a very useful "Map Information" section containing data about large-scale maps and charts produced by government agencies. Another regular feature of this magazine is the section, "Distinctive Recent Maps," which contains descriptions of interesting general and topical maps from all parts of the world. Last, but certainly not least, is the [SLA] Geography and Map Division Bulletin which includes notes concerning maps, an occasional review of an outstanding atlas, and an extensive list of "New Maps" by Charles W. Buffum of the Library of Congress.

Cartographic Accession Lists

Current accession lists produced by colleagues in other libraries provide valuable information on current maps, and serve as a useful check on the quality of your own acquisitions program. In the bibliography I have cited 17 accession lists which I have found to be very helpful. A list of New Acquisitions of the Map and Geography Library, University of Illinois, is issued bimonthly by Robert White. This is a fine accession list of one of the leading university map collections in the United States. The Map Library Acquisitions Bulletin, issued at irregular intervals, records the maps acquired by Rand McNally and Company. This is a very useful publication, and to my knowledge the only accession list prepared by a commercial publisher. <u>Current Geographical Publications</u>, published ten times a year, contains "Additions to the Research Catalogue of the American Geographical Society." Section 3 of each issue is a list (prepared by Dr. Roman Drazniowsky) of newly acquired maps.

In England, the semiannual publication, <u>New Geographical Literature and Maps</u>, cites the accessions of the Royal Geographical Society Library. <u>Selected Map and Book Accessions,</u> issued monthly, lists receipts of the Map Section, Bodleian Library, Oxford University. In Canada, the Departmental Map Library of the Department of Energy, Mines and Resources began in 1968 to issue a quarterly, <u>Selected List of Maps, Atlases, and Gazetteers</u>, which is worthy of note.

It may perhaps be appropriate to mention here that one of the anticipated products of the map automation project undergoing development and tests in the Library of Congress will be a current list of accessions, as well as author-subject-shelf list book catalogs. Initially, the maps recorded in these publications will be limited to those in the English language. Ultimately, the accession list and catalogs may be expanded to include all current map accessions of the Library of Congress.

National Bibliographies

National bibliographies are no strangers to the acquisitions librarian who orders books as well as maps. It is quite possible, however, that librarians dealing solely with maps and atlases may be completely unaware of the potential value of certain of these bibliographies. Many countries throughout the world produce a bibliography of materials published within their borders. Most of the works described are books, but some include useful descriptions of maps and atlases. Recently I surveyed the national bibliographies currently received by the Library of Congress and found that 24 of them regularly describe at least a few cartographic works. Thirteen are the products of nations of Western Europe, five are from Eastern Europe, two from Australasia, and one each from Africa, Asia, Latin America, and North America. The List of National Bibliographies describes the bibliographies in detail. I would like especially to mention the bibliographies of Austria, East Germany, New Zealand, Poland, Switzerland,

Turkey, France, West Germany, and Australia. The last
three (France, West Germany and Australia) are noteworthy
because each publishes special supplementary lists of maps.
The others include separate sections or chapters listing substantial numbers of maps in their regular issues. Information provided by national bibliographies is particularly useful
because they are generally current and accurate, and--in
most instances--provide the map librarian with the ever elu-
sive price.

SELECTED GEOGRAPHICAL JOURNALS
Containing Lists and/or Reviews of Current Maps and Atlases

Australian Geographer. (Geographical Society of New South
        Wales, Sydney) Sydney v. 1- (1928-) Irreg. Selected
        atlases are reviewed. [51]*

Berichte zur deutschen Landeskunde. (Zentralarchiv für
        Landeskunde von Deutschland. Institut für Landeskunde)
        Bad Godesberg. v. 1-4 (1941-1945); v. 5- (1948-).
        2 nos. in each vol. Semiannual. Maps are listed in
        section entitled "Kartenneuerscheinungen" published in
        Heft 2. [508]

Bibliographie cartographique internationale. (Comité nationale
        française de géographie; International Geographical Un-
        ion) Paris. (1936-) Annual. Comprehensive inter-
        national list of maps. [342]

Boletin de información. (Servicio Geográfico del Ejercito)
        Madrid. v. 1- (1968-) Lists new maps published by
        the Servicio Geográfico del Ejercito.

Bollettino della associazione italiana di cartografia. (Asso-
        ciazione italiana di cartografia) Firenze. v. 1- (1964-).
        3 times a year. Selected maps are described in section
        entitled "Segnalazioni Cartografiche."

Bulletin du comité française de cartographie. (Comité

*Bracketed numbers refer to entries in Harris, Chauncy D.
and Fellman, Jerome D. International List of Geographical
Serials. Chicago: University of Chicago, 1960; 194p. (University of Chicago, Dept. of Geography, Research Paper no.
63.)

français de cartographie)   Paris.   v. 1- (1958-   )   Irregular.   Atlases, maps and mapping programs are described in reviews and articles.   Fasc. no. 37 (July-August 1968) is entirely devoted to "Rapport cartographique national-France, pour les travaux exécutés de 1964 à 1968."

Bulletin of the Society of University Cartographers.   (Society of University Cartographers)   Liverpool.   v. 1- (1966-   ). Semiannual.   Includes articles about mapping and reviews of selected atlases.

Canadian Cartographer.   Bernard B. Gutsell, ed.   Toronto. v. 1- (1964-   ).   Semiannual.   Formerly The Cartographer, 1964-67.   Maps and atlases are described in articles, notes, and reviews.

Cartographic Journal.   (British Cartographic Society)   Glasgow, Scotland.   v. 1- (1964-   ).   Semiannual.   Includes a list of "Recent Maps" as well as reviews, notes, and articles about maps.

Cartography.   (Australian Institute of Cartographers)   Canberra.   v. 1- (1954-   ).   Semiannual.   Includes reviews and articles about maps.

Geografisch Tijdschrift.   (Koninklijk Nederlands Aardrijkskundig Genootschap).   Amsterdam.   Nieuwe Reeks. v. 1- (1967-   )   Irregular.   "Kartografische Sectie" includes articles about maps, reviews of atlases, and a list of "Neiuwe Kaartbladen" of The Netherlands.

Geographical Journal.   (Royal Geographical Society, London) London.   v. 1- (1893-   ) Quarterly.   Selected maps and atlases are reviewed.   [1445]

Geography and Map Division Bulletin.   (Geography and Map Division, Special Libraries Association)   N. Y.   v. 1- (1950-   ) Quarterly.   "New Maps" are listed by Charles W. Buffum of the Library of Congress.   Atlases are occasionally reviewed.   [1596]

Globen.   (Generalstabens Litografiska Anstalt)   Stockholm. v. 1- (1922-   ) Quarterly.   Maps, atlases and globes are described.   [1151]

International Hydrographic Bulletin.   Supplement to the Inter-

national Hydrographic Review. (International Hydro-
graphic Bureau) Monaco. v.1- (1928-   ) Monthly.
Includes a "List of New Charts and New Editions of
Charts."

International Map of the World on the Millionth Scale. (United
Nations, Department of Economic and Social Affairs)
N. Y. v.1- (1955-   ). Annual. Includes an "Index
Map showing the Status of Publication of the IMW
Sheets," a "Table of Published Sheets," and an "Alpha-
betical Index" of published sheets.

Irish Geography. (Geographical Society of Ireland) Dublin.
v.1- (1944-   ) Annual. Maps relating to Ireland are
reviewed. [316]

Journal of Geography. (National Council for Geographic Education) Chicago. v.1- (1902-   ) Monthly except Je,
Jl, Ag. Occasional review of an atlas. [1568]

Kartographische Nachrichten. (Deutsche Gesellschaft für
Kartographie e.V.) Gütersloh. (1951-   ) Issued 6
times a year. Includes map articles and reviews.
[653]

Kulturgeografi. Tidsskrift for befolkninsgeografi, bebyggelses-
geografi, erhvervsgeografi, politisk geografi, regional-
planlaegning, anvendt geografi. København. v.1-
(1949-   ) Issued 5 times a year. Each issue includes
a section entitled "Kort, atlas og litteratur." [307]

Military Engineer. (Society of American Military Engineers)
Washington, D.C. v.1- (1920-   ). Issued 6 times a
year. New maps are described in the section, "Geodesy,
Mapping, Oceanography," published in each issue.

Nachrichten aus dem Karten- und Vermessungswesen. (Insti-
tuts für angewandte Geodäsie) Frankfurt, a.M., Germany. Reihe I, Deutsche Beitrage und Informationen.
v.1- (1951-   ) Irreg. Maps are listed in section titled
"Kartenarchiv und Bücherei."

Petermanns geographische Mitteilungen. (VEB Hermann Haack,
Geographisch-Kartographische Anstalt) Gotha. v.1-91,
no. 3 (1855-1945); 92- (1948-   ) Quarterly. Atlases
are reviewed in section entitled "Kartographie." [708]

Professional Geographer. (Association of American Geographers. Journal) Washington, D.C. v. 1-8 (1943-1948);
ns v. 1- (1949- ·) Issued 6 times a year. New maps
are sometimes noted and an occasional atlas is reviewed.
[1588]

Surveying and Mapping. (American Congress on Surveying
and Mapping) Washington, D.C. v. 1- (1941-) Quarterly. Includes a "Map Information" section describing
large scale maps and charts by government agencies.
Another section describes "Distinctive Recent Maps."
Atlases are sometimes reviewed in the section "Books
in Review."

Universo. (Italy. Istituto geografico militare) Firenze.
v. 1- (1920-) Issued 6 times a year. Each issue
includes a section entitled "Rubrica Cartografica" which
lists new maps by the Istituto geografico militare.
[928]

World Cartography. (United Nations, Department of Economic
and Social Affairs) New York. v. 1- (1951-) Irreg.
(8 v. published through 1967) Includes reports of current cartographic activities in various countries.

Zeitschrift für den Erdkundeunterricht. (German Democratic
Republic. Ministerium für Volksbildung) Berlin v. 1-
(1949-) Monthly. Atlases are occasionally reviewed.
[777]

SELECTED MAP AND ATLAS
Accession Lists

Australia

Mitchell Library
Macquarie St.
Sydney, N. S. W.
    The Public Library of New South Wales; Maps Received
in the Mitchell Library.   Quarterly.

Brazil

Mapoteca
Ministério das Relações Exteriores
Rio de Janeiro

   Bibliografia cartográfica.   Monthly, with annual cumulations.

Canada

Department of Energy, Mines and Resources
Departmental Map Library
Ottawa 4, Ontario
       A Selected List of Maps, Atlases, and Gazetteers.
1968-.   Quarterly.   Cover title: Acquisitions.

University of British Columbia Library
Map Division
Vancouver, British Columbia
       List of Maps Added to the Library.   Bimonthly.

University of Toronto Library
Map Library
Toronto, Ontario
       Selected Acquisitions.   Bimonthly.

Ethiopia

Economic Commission for Africa
Map Documentation and Reference Centre
P. O. Box 3001
Addis Ababa
       Catalogue of Maps and Charts Received by the Centre.
Sep 1966.   (4 supplements published in 1967)

Great Britain

Oxford University
Bodleian Library
Map Section
Oxford, England
       Selected Map and Book Accessions.   Monthly.

British Museum
London WC 1
England
       Catalogue of Printed Maps in the British Museum.   Ac-
cessions.   London.   Irreg.

Map Research and Library Group
The Survey Production Centre, R. E.
Block "A"

Hook Rise South
Tolworth, Surbiton
Surrey, England
    Directorate of Military Survey, Ministry of Defence,
Selected Accessions List of the Map Library.   (serial)

Royal Geographical Society
Kensington Gore
London, SW 7
England
    New Geographical Literature and Maps.   Semiannual.

Mexico

Instituto Panamericano de Geografia e Historia
Biblioteca "Jose Toribio Medina,"
Mexico, D.F.
    Lista de adquisiciones.   Bimonthly.

United States

American Geographical Society
Broadway at 156th St.
New York, N.Y. 10032
    Current Geographical Publications.   Additions to the Research Catalogue of the American Geographical Society.   Issued 10 times a year.   Maps are listed in Section 3 of each issue.

DoD Nautical Chart Library
Maritime Safety Division
U.S. Naval Oceanographic Office
Washington, D.C. 20390
    Accession List of Domestic and Foreign Charts, Cumulative List.   Monthly.

Library of Congress
Processing Department
Exchange and Gift Division
Washington, D.C. 20540
    Monthly Checklist of State Publications.   Monthly.   Includes descriptions of maps issued by state authorities which are received by the Library of Congress.

University of Illinois
Map and Geography Library
Urbana, Illinois 61803
    New Acquisitions.   Bimonthly.

University of Kansas Libraries
Kenneth Spencer Research Library
Map Library
Lawrence, Kansas 66044
    New Books; Selected New Acquisitions in the University
of Kansas Libraries. Map Library [accession list] 1969-.
Irreg.

Rand McNally & Company
Geographic Research Department
Attn: Map Library
P. O. Box 7600
Chicago, Illinois 60680
    Map Library Acquisitions Bulletin; A List of Atlases,
Maps and Books Received by the Map Library.   Irreg.

                    NATIONAL BIBLIOGRAPHIES
              Containing References to Maps and Atlases

Australia

        *Australian National Bibliography, Jan 1961- . Can-
berra, National Lib. of Australia, 1961- . Monthly. Maps
and atlases were described in monthly issues of the Australian National Bibliography through Dec 1967.   In 1968, a
separate listing of maps was initiated.   Entitled Australian
Maps, the first issue covered Jan-Sep 1968, and the second,
Oct-Dec.   Future issues will be published quarterly with annual cumulations. [AA369]†

Austria

        *Öesterreichische Bibliographie: Verzeichnis der öster-
reichischen Neuerscheinungen.   Bearb. von der österreich-
ischen Nationalbibliothek.   Wien, 1946- . v. 2- . Semimonthly.   Cartographic works are described in Section 16,
"Karten, Atlanten."   Includes prices. [AA372]

---

*Asterisks identify bibliographies which are especially valuable
for obtaining information about maps and atlases.
†Bracketed numbers refer to Winchell, Constance M.   Guide
to Reference Books.   8th ed.   Chicago: Amer. Library As-
soc., 1967; 741p.   See p. 30-65 for citations to national and
trade bibliographies

Belgium

Bibliographie de belgique, 1. partie: Liste mensuelle des publications belges ou relatives à la Belgique, acquises par la Bibliothèque Royale. v. 1- . année, 1875- . Bruxelles, Bibliothèque Royale, 1875- . v. 1- . Monthly. Occasional cartographic item listed in Section 91, "Géographie, Aardrijkskunde." Includes prices. [AA378]

Brazil

Rio de Janeiro. Biblioteca Nacional. Boletim bibliográfico. Rio de Janeiro, 1951- . Semiannual. See Section 912, "Mapas." Includes prices. [AA387]

Bulgaria

Bulgarski knigopis: mesechen bibliografski biuletin za depoziranite v Instituta Knigi i Novi Periodichni Izdaniia. Sofia, 1897- . Monthly. In Cyrillic. Maps and atlases are cited in some issues. See separate section entitled "Kartografski Izdaniia." [AA391]

Canada

Canadiana, 1950- . Ottawa, Nat. Lib of Canada, 1951- . Monthly, with annual cumulations. Maps and atlases are occasionally listed in Section I, Class 912. Includes prices. [AA402]

Denmark

Det danske Bogmarked [København, Den danske Forlaeggerforening]. Weekly, with annual cumulations. Arrangement of all publications in weekly list, including maps, is alphabetical by author and title. Annual cumulation, Dansk Bogfortegnelse: Arskatalog (København, G. E. C. Gads), includes separate list of maps. See Section 40. 1, "Kort og Atlas." Includes prices.

Finland

Suomen Kirjakauppalehti. Finsk bokhandelstidning. [Helsinki: Suomen Kustannusyhdistys ja Kirjakauppias liitto] 1907- . Semiannual. Publications, including maps, are listed by author and title in single alphabet. Abbreviated citations appear in classified list at end of each issue. For

cartographic works in classified list, see Section 4, "Geography, Travel, Ethnology. " Includes prices.

France

Bibliographie de la France: journal général de l'impri-
merie et de la librairie. Paris, Cercle de la Librairie,
1811- . v. 1- . Weekly. "Atlas, cartes et plans" are
described in Supplement E issued at irregular intervals.
Prices are not included. [AA473]

Germany, East

*Deutsche Nationalbibliographie und Bibliographie des im
Ausland erschienenen deutschsprachigen Schrifttums. Reihe
A, Reihe B. Leipzig, Verlag für Buch- und Bibliothekswesen,
1931- . Issued in two parts; Reihe A, Neuerscheinungen
des Buchhandels, weekly; Reihe B, Neuerscheinungen ausser-
halb des Buchhandels, semimonthly. Each part contains map
and atlas citations. See Section 16 in each, titled "Karten,
Atlanten. " Commercially published maps are listed in Reihe
A and officially published maps in Reihe B. Includes prices.
[AA483]

Germany, West

*Deutsche Bibliographie: wöchentliches Verzeichnis.
Frankfurt a. M. , Buchhändler-Vereinigung GmbH, 1947- .
Weekly. A few atlases are described weekly in Section 16,
"Kartenwerke. " Cross references are given for atlases filed
elsewhere in bibliography. Maps are cited in Supplement C
published quarterly. Includes prices. [AA487]

Great Britain

British National Bibliography. 1950- . London, Council of the British Nat. Bibliography, British Museum. 1950-
Weekly, with quarterly cumulations and annual volume. This
list describes items deposited for copyright. Works are arranged according to the Dewey Decimal Classification. Cartographic works are listed in Section 912, "Atlases & Maps."
Includes prices. [AA507]

Hungary

Magyar nemzeti bibliográfia: bibliographia hungarica.
Kiadja az Országos Széchényi Könyvtar. 1 füzet, január-

március 1946-   . Budapest, 1946-   . Semimonthly. Maps
and atlases are listed in Section 912, "Térképek." Includes
prices. [AA540]

Italy

Bibliografia nazionale italiana: nuova serie del bollettino delle pubblicazioni italiane ricevute per diritto di
stampa. Gennaio, 1958-   . Firenze, 1958-   . Anno 1-   .
Monthly. See Section 912, "Atlanti-Carte Geografiche." Includes prices. [AA565]

New Zealand

*New Zealand National Bibliography. [Wellington] Na-
tional Library of New Zealand, Feb 1967-   . Monthly. See
Section II, "Maps." Includes prices.

Norway

Norsk Bokhandlertidende. v. 1-   . Oslo, Grøndahl,
1880-   . Weekly, with annual cumulations. Arrangement
of all publications in weekly list, including maps, is alphabetical by author and title. Maps are not collected together
in one section. A separate list of maps titled "Karter" appears in the annual cumulation, Norsk Bokfortegnelse ...
Arskatalog. Includes prices. [AA625]

Poland

Przewodnik Bibliograficzny: Urzedowy Wykaz Druków
Wydanych w Rzeczypospolitej Polskiej ... R. 2 (14), no.1/3-.
Warszawa, Biblioteka Narodowa, 1946-   . Weekly. See
Section XIIIa, "Mapy. Plany." Includes prices. [AA645]

South Africa

SANB: Suid-Afrikaanse Nasionale Bibliografie. South
African National Bibliography, 1959-   . Pretoria, State Lib.,
1960-   . Quarterly, with annual cumulations. See Section
912, "Atlases and Maps /Atlase en Landkaarte." Includes
prices. [AA681]

Spain

Boletin del depósito legal de obras impresas. Madrid,
Dirección General de Archivos y Bibliotecas, 1958-   .

Monthly. Atlases are included in Section 91, "Geografia. Viajes." Includes prices.

Spain

El libro español: revista mensual ... t.1, num.1- . Enero, 1958- . Madrid, Inst. Nacional del Libro Español, 1958- . Issued in 2 parts. Part 1, monthly; Part 2, semimonthly. The first part consists of articles about the Spanish book trade. The second part, entitled El Libro Español. II. Repertorio Bibliográfico Quincenal contains citations to new books. Atlases are sometimes listed in Part two, Section 9, "Geografia e Historia." The Instituto Nacional del Libro Español also reprints part two semimonthly under the title Libros Nuevos. Includes prices. [AA707]

Sweden

Svenska Bokförläggareföreningens och Svenska Bokhandlareföreningens Officiella Organ. Stockholm, Svensk Bokhandel, 1952- . Weekly, with monthly, quarterly, seminnual, and annual cumulations. Arrangement of all publications in weekly list, including maps, is alphabetical by author and title. Maps are not collected together in one section. The annual cumulation entitled Svensk Bokförteckning ... Arskatalog, includes descriptions of maps in the general author-title list as well as separately in Section Ny, "Kartor." Includes prices. [AA713]

Switzerland

*Das schweizer Buch: Bibliographisches Bulletin der schweizerischen Landesbibliothek. Le livre suisse ... Il libro svizzero. v.1- ; 11 März 1901- . Bern-Bümpliz, Benteli, 1901- . v.1- . Beginning with v.43 (1943) issued in two series: Série A, semimonthly, listing publications in the book trade; Série B, bimonthly, listing publications outside the book trade, e.g., theses, institutional publications, etc. Section "16. Karten, Atlanten-Cartes, Atlas" included in both series. Includes prices. [AA723]

Turkey

*Türkiye Biblioğrafyasi ... 1934- . Istanbul, Milli Egitim Basimevi, 1935- . Quarterly. Maps ("Haritalar") are listed following Section 910, "Coğrafya, Turizm." Includes prices. [AA725]

Yugoslavia

   Bibliografija Jugoslavije: Knjige, Brosure i Muzikalije,
Jan 1950- . Beograd, Bibliografski Inst. FNRJ, 1950- .
Semimonthly. See Section 912, "Mape. Kartografija." Prices
are not included. [AA738]

SECOND HAND DEALERS

        Some map librarians not only engage in the acquisition
of currently produced maps and atlases, but are also actively
involved in acquiring out-of-print cartographic works to fill
existing gaps in their collections. Although this can be a
very time-consuming and frustrating task, it also may be a
very rewarding experience; especially when you are finally
blessed with success and manage to acquire a long sought
after item at a modest price. The search for out-of-print
maps requires a thorough knowledge of the strengths and weak-
nesses of your collection. Furthermore, it is desirable for
the acquisitions librarian to maintain an accurate file of specific items needed.

        The search for desiderata requires an almost total
dependence on sales or auction catalogs. Rarely does a
seller seek out the acquisitions librarian and offer him the
specific item needed for the collections. A list of some 50
dealers who regularly list second hand maps and atlases in
their catalogs is presented. A few, such as Argosy Book
Stores, L. S. Straight, and Kenneth Nebenzahl, specialize in
the sale of maps; most, however, are general out-of-print
book dealers or auction dealers. The following is a selected
list of dealers in out-of-print maps and atlases. Each of the
firms listed issue catalogs which include descriptions of maps
and /or atlases.

Austria

Christian M. Nebehay
Annagasse 18
Vienna I

Canada

William P. Wolfe
222 rue de l'Hopital
Montreal 1

Denmark

Boghallens Antikvariat
Raadhuspladsen 37
Copenhagen V

Rosenkilde and Bagger
3, Kron-Prinsens-Gade
Copenhagen K

France

Département Etranger Hachette
Service "R"
3, rue Christine
75-Paris 6e

Librairie Thomas-Scheler
19, rue de Tournon
Paris 6e

Louis Loeb-Larocque
36, rue le Peletier
Paris 9e

Germany, East

Karl Markert
Robert-Schumann Str. 12
Leipzig C1

Norddeutsches Antiquariat
    Rostock
Kröpelinerstr. 14; Postfach 30
DDR-25 Rostock

Germany, West

Buchhandlung Weidlich
Savignystr. 59
Frankfurt

F. A. Brockhaus
Räpplenstr. 20
Stuttgart 1

H. Th. Wenner
Grossestr. 69
Postfach 1507
4500 Osnabrück

Interart-Buchversand Klaus
    Renner
Tangastr. 22
München 59

Karl u. Faber (Auction deal-
    er)
Karolinenplatz 5a
8 München 2

Kubon & Sagner
Hess-str. 39
München 13

Ludwig Rohrscheid GmbH
Am Hof 28
53 Bonn

Lüder H. Niemeyer
Simrockstr. 34
Postfach 493
5320 Bad Godesberg/Rhein

Margit Melnikow
8399 Neuburg am Inn

Great Britain

Bertram Rota Ltd.
4, 5 & 6 Savile Row
London, W 1

Christie, Manson & Woods
    (Auction dealer)
8 King St., St. James's
London, SW 1

E. M. Lawson & Co.
The Priory, Maney
Sutton, Coldfield

Francis Edwards Ltd.
83, Marylebone High St.
London, W 1

Frank Hammond
67 Birmingham Rd.
Sutton, Coldfield
Warwickshire

Henry Stevens, Son & Stiles

4 Upper Church Lane
Farnham, Surrey

Marlborough Rare Books
35 Old Bond St.
London, W 1

Peter Barrie
380 Birmingham Rd.
Wylde Green
Sutton, Coldfield

Sotheby & Co. (Auction dealer)
34 and 35 New Bond St.
London, W 1

Stanley Crowe
5, Bloomsbury St.
London, WC 1

Greece

Les Amis du Livre
7, Valaoritis St.
Athens 134

Jamaica

P. Alan Gert
Box 83
Kingston 10
Jamaica, West Indies

Netherlands

Antiquariaat Broekema
Titiaanstraat 28
Amsterdam

C. P. J. van der Peet
33-35 N. Spiegelstraat
Amsterdam

E. J. Brill
Leiden

Martinus Nijhoff

Lange Voorhout 9-11
The Hague

N. Israel
Keizersgracht 539
Amsterdam C

Norway

Damms Antikvariat
Tollbodgaten 25
Oslo

Lunge Larsen
1340 Bekkestua
Øygardveien 16 c

Sweden

Thulins Antikvariat AB
Humlegardsgatan 15
Stockholm

United States

Alfred W. Paine
Wolfpits Rd.
Bethel, Conn.   06801

Argosy Book Stores
116 E. 59th St.
New York, N. Y.   10022

Charles Hamilton Galleries
   (Auction dealer)
25 E. 53rd St.
New York, N. Y.   10022

Elizabeth F. Dunlap
6063 Westminster Pl.
St. Louis, Mo.   63112

H. P. Kraus
16 E. 46th St.
New York, N. Y.   10017

John C. Daub

604 Wood St.
Pittsburgh, Penna.   15222

John P. Coll
2944 Pine Ave.
Berkeley, Calif.   94705

Kenneth Nebenzahl, Inc.
333 N. Michigan Ave.
Chicago, Ill.   60601

L. S. Straight
157 E. 28th St.
New York, N. Y.   10016

The Lamp
William G. Mayer
1100 Rico Rd.
Monroeville, Penna.   15146

The Old Print Shop
Kenneth M. Newman
150 Lexington Ave.
New York, N. Y.   10016

Parke-Bernet Galleries, Inc.
   (Auction dealer)
980 Madison Ave.
New York, N. Y.   10021

Richard T. Anderson Books
101 Northfield Dr.
North Syracuse, N. Y.   13212

Rouse's Bookhouse
Route 2
Eaton Rapids, Mich.   48827

Samuel T. Freeman & Co.
   (Auction dealer)
1808 Chestnut St.
Philadelphia, Penna.   19103

Swann Galleries, Inc. (Auction dealer)
117 E. 24th St.
New York, N. Y.   10010

PUBLISHERS' CATALOGS

On the list of Map Publishers and Sellers, there are
names and addresses of 173 commercial firms and government agencies who are known to have issued a sales catalog
or list of publications in the last two or three years.   Publishers' catalogs are an essential tool of the acquisitions
specialist because they provide him with up-to-date sales information.   The librarian of a small library, however, may
find it more convenient to deal with one vendor in acquiring
maps.   The use of one vendor simplifies ordering, bookkeep-
ing, and payment procedures.   Two map vendors who handle
a wide assortment of maps of all scales, subjects and areas
are Reise- und Verkehrsverlag in Stuttgart, and Zumstein's
Landkartenhaus in Munich.   Both of these West German firms
publish excellent sales catalogs.   Reise- und Verkehsverlag
produces the extraordinary looseleaf R-V Katalog which is
regularly updated and expanded by supplements.   R-V also issues periodically Kartenbriefs; these are designed to inform
the patron of new map publications available for sale.   Annually, the firm publishes a useful Kleine RV-Katalog summarizing the current maps available from the firm.

In 1968 Zumstein's Landkartenhaus published an excellent detailed sales catalog and has supplemented it periodically with lists of new materials. Although their catalog is not as large as that produced by R-V, it appears to be quite comprehensive in coverage. Names and addresses of mapmaking authorities are always difficult to obtain. Of special note is a 15 page list published in 1968 by the Departmental Map Library, Department of Energy, Mines and Resources, Ottawa. This List of Map Sources records some 250 addresses of mapping agencies.

MAP PUBLISHERS AND SELLERS
(each of the following agencies or firms produces a current catalog or list of its publications)

Argentina

Instituto Nacional de Geologia
    y Mineria
Departamento de Geografia
Buenos Aires

Australia

Division of National Mapping
Derwent House
22-34 University Ave.
Canberra City, A.C.T. 2601

Department of Lands
Bridge Street
Sydney, New South Wales

Austria

Bundesamt für Eich-u.
    Vermessungswesen in Wien
    (Landesaufnahme)
Krotenthalergasse 3
1080 Vienna VIII

Editio Totius Mundi
Gussenbauergasse 5/9
A-1090 Vienna

Freytag-Berndt u. Artaria K. G.

Schottenfeldgasse 62
A1071 Wien

Belgium

Editions-Uitgaven Girault Gilbert
rue du Congres 13; Congresstraat
Bruxelles 1

Institut Géographique Militaire
13, Abbaye de la Cambre
Bruxelles 5

Brazil

Instituto Brasileiro de Geografia,
Rio de Janeiro

British Honduras

Survey and Lands Office
Belize

Cameroun

Institut Géographique National-Paris
Annexe au Cameroun
Yaoundé

Canada

Canadian Hydrographic Service
Chart Distribution Office
615 Booth St.
Ottawa 4, Ontario

Department of Energy, Mines
    and Resources
Map Distribution Office
615 Booth St.
Ottawa 4, Ontario

Department of Forestry and
    Rural Development
Information and Technical
    Services Division
Ottawa, Ontario

Department of Highways,
    Ontario
Keele St. and Highway 401
Downsview, Ontario

Department of Lands and
    Forests
Lands and Surveys Branch
Surveys Section
Parliament Buildings
Toronto 5, Ontario

Department of Lands, Forests,
    and Water Resources
Lands Service, Geographic
    Division
Parliament Buildings
Victoria, British Columbia

Department of Mineral Re-
    sources
Government Administration
    Building
Regina, Saskatchewan

Department of Mines and
    Minerals
Technical Division

Agriculture Building
9718 107th St.
Edmonton, Alberta

Department of Mines and
    Natural Resources
Surveys Branch
Room 816 Norquay Building
Winnipeg 1, Manitoba

Department of Natural Re-
    sources
Province of Quebec
Quebec

Dominion Map Limited (Map
    seller)
626 Howe St.
Vancouver 1, British Colum-
    bia

Geological Survey of Canada
Department of Energy, Mines
    and Resources
Ottawa 4, Ontario

Mundy Map Company
4696 W. 5th Ave.
Vancouver, British Columbia

Oil and Gas Conservation
    Board
603 Sixth Ave., S.W.
Calgary, Alberta

Ontario Department of Mines
Parliament Buildings
Toronto 2, Ontario

Department of Natural Re-
    sources
Surveys Branch
2340 Albert St.
Regina, Saskatchewan

Chile

Instituto Geográfico Militar
Santiago

Congo

Institut Géographique National-
   Paris
Centre de Brazzaville
Brazzaville, Congo Republic

Cyprus

Government Printing Office
Nicosia

Denmark

Geodaetisk Institut
Rigsdaggsgarden 7
Kφbenhavn K.

Ethiopia

Mapping and Audio Visual Sec-
   tions
Education Department
Ministry of Education and Fine
   Arts
Asmara

United Nations Economic
   Commission for Africa
Map Documentation and Refer-
   ence Centre
P. O. Box 3001
Addis Ababa

Fiji Islands

Department of Lands, Mines
   & Surveys
Suva, Fiji Islands

Finland

Merenkulkuhallituksen
Merikarttaosasto
Helsinki

France

Hatier
59, blvd. Raspail
Paris 6e

Institut Géographique National
107, rue la Böetie
Paris 8e

Librairie Blondel La Rougery
7, rue Saint-Lazare
Paris 9e

Michelin
97, blvd. Pereire
75 Paris 17e

Service de l'Information
   Aéronautique
2, rue Victor-Hugo
92 Issy-les-Moulineaux

Service de la carte géologique
   de la France
62 blvd. Saint-Michel
Paris 6e

Service Hydrographique de la
   Marine
13, rue de l'Université
Paris 7e

Germany, East

Deutsches Buch-Export und-
   Import GmbH
Leninstr. 16; Postfach 160
   (Map seller)
701 Leipzig

VEB Herman Haack
Geographisch-Kartographische
   Anstalt
Justus-Perthes-Str. 3-9
58 Gotha

VEB Landkartenverlag
Neue Grünstr. 17
102 Berlin

Germany, West

Bayerisches Landesvermes-
    sungsamt
Alexandrastr. 4
München

Bibliographisches Institut
6800 Mannheim

Bollmann-Bildkarten-Verlag
    KG
Richterstr. 5
Braunschweig

Bundesanstalt für Boden-
    forschung und des Nieder-
    sächsischen Landesamtes
    für Bodenforschung
Postfach 54
Hannover-Buchholz

Deutsche Kreiskarten Verlag-
    sanstalt Rudolf Ernst
Hans-Bartels-Str. 2
8 München 9

Deutsches Hydrographisches
    Institut
Bernhard-Nocht-Str. 78
Postfach 220
2000 Hamburg 4

Dr. Götze & Co. (Map seller)
Hermannstr. 7
2 Hamburg 1

Falk-Verlag
Burchardstr. 8
2 Hamburg 1

Flemmings Verlag Kartogr.
    Institut

Leinpfad 75
2 Hamburg 39

Georg Lingenbrink
Libri-Haus
Hamburg 36
(Map seller)

Georg Westermann Verlag
Braunschweig

H. Hugendubel
Salvatorplatz 2
München 1
(Map seller)

Hessisches Landesvermes-
    sungsamt
Schaperstr. 16
62 Wiesbaden

Institut fur Angewandte
    Geodäsie
Kennedyallee 151
6 Frankfurt am Main

JRO-Verlag
Landsbergerstr. 191
8000 München 12

Justus Perthes Geographische
    Verlagsanstalt
Donnersbergrine 14
Postfach 849
Darmstadt

Kartographisches Institut Ber-
    telsmann
Gütersloh

Kiepert KG
Hardenbergstr. 4-5
1 Berlin 12 (Charlottenburg)

Landesvermessungsamt Baden-
    Würtemberg
Buchsenstr. 54
7 Stuttgart 1

Landesvermessungsamt Nordrhein-Westfalen
Muffendorfestr. 19-21
532 Bad Godesberg

Landesvermessungsamt Rhein-
land- Pfalz
Postfach 1428
5400 Koblenz, Hochhaus

Landesvermessungsamt
Schleswig-Holstein
Mecklenburgerstr. 12-16
2300 Kiel-Wik

Niedersächsisches Landes-
verwaltungsamt-Landes-
vermessung
Warmbüchkenkamp 2
3 Hannover

Otto Harrassowitz
Wiesbaden
(Atlas seller)

Paul List Verlag KG
Goethestr. 43
8 München 15

Ravenstein Geographische
Verlagsanstalt u. Druckerei
GmbH
Wielandstr. 31/35
6 Frankfurt/Main

Reise-und Verkehrsverlag
Honigwiesenstr. 25
Postfach 80-083
7 Stuttgart-Vaihingen
(Map publisher and seller)

Vermessungsamt Hamburg
Wexstr. 7
2 Hamburg 36

Wilhelm Stollfus Verlag
Dechenstr. 7/11

Postfach 287
53 Bonn
(Map publisher and seller)

Zumstein's Landkartenhaus
Liebherrstr. 5
8 München 22
(Map publisher and seller)

Ghana

Survey of Ghana
P. O. Box 191
Accra

Great Britain

Blackwell's
Broad St.
Oxford
(Atlas seller)

Collet's Holdings Limited
Denington Estate
Wellingborough, Northants
(Map seller; specializes in
USSR & Eastern Europe)

Directorate of Overseas Sur-
veys
Kingston Rd.
Tolworth
Surbiton, Surrey

Ed. J. Burrow & Co., Ltd.
Imperial House
Cheltenham

Edward Stanford Ltd.
12-14 Long Acre
London WC 2
(Map publisher and seller)

Foldex Ltd.
45, Mitchell St.
London, EC 1

Geographers' Map Company
    Ltd.
Vestry Road
Sevenoaks, Kent

Geographia Ltd.
114 Fleet St.
London, EC 4

George Gill and Sons Ltd.
67/68 Chandos Pl.
London, WC 2

George Philip and Son Ltd.
Victoria Rd.
London, NW 10

Greater London Council
The County Hall
London, SE 1

Hydrographer of the Navy
Hydrographic Department
Ministry of Defense
Taunton, Somerset

Imray, Laurie, Norie and
    Wilson
Wych House, Saint Ives
Huntingdon

John Bartholomew & Son, Ltd.
12 Duncan St.
Edinburgh 9, Scotland

Ordnance Survey
Leatherhead Rd.
Chessington, Surrey

W. & A. K. Johnston &
    G. W. Bacon Ltd.
Edina Works
Easter Rd.
Edinburgh 7, Scotland

W. Heffer & Sons Ltd.
Petty Cury

Cambridge
(Sells new and out-of-print
    atlases)

Guatemala

Instituto Geográfico Nacional
Avenida Las Américas 5-76
Zona 13
Guatemala, C. A.

Guyana

Cartographic Section
Lands Division
Victoria Law Courts
Georgetown

Geological Survey
P. O. Box 789
Georgetown

Hong Kong

Government Publications Centre
Star Ferry Concourse
Hong Kong

Hungary

Kartográfiai   Vállalat
Budapest

India

All India Educational Supply
    Co.
Shri Ram Building
Jawahar Nagar
Delhi 7
(Map seller)

Clifton & Company Ltd. (Map
    seller)
Hitkari Building No. 1
Des Bandhu Gupta Road
Karol Bagh, New Delhi 5

Iran

Sahab Geographic & Drafting
    Institute
P. O. Box 236
Tehran

Italy

Istituto Geografico de Agostini
Novara

Istituto Geografico Militare
Viale Filippo Strozzi, 14
Firenze

Istituto Idrografico della Mar-
    ina
Genova

Litografia Artistica Carto-
    grafica
Via del Romito 11-13 r.
Firenze

Servizio Geologico d'Italia
Via S. Susanna, 13
Rome

Touring Club Italiano
Corso Italia, 10
Milano

Japan

Geological Survey of Japan
Tokyo

Japan Geographical Survey In-
    stitute
1000-7-chome, Kami-Meguro
Meguro-ku, Tokyo-to

Naigai Trading Company, Ltd.
P. O. Box 38
Akasaka
Tokyo

(Sells official government
    maps)

Maruzen Company, Ltd. (Map
    seller)
6-Tori 2-chome
Nihonbashi, Chuo-ku
Tokyo

Kenya

Survey of Kenya
P. O. Box 30046
Nairobi

Laos

Service Geographique National
Vientiane

Lebanon

Directorate of Geographic Af-
    fairs
Ministry of National Defense
Grand Serail, Beirut

Netherlands

Centrum voor Landbouwpub-
    likaties en Landbouwdocu-
    mentatie
Generaal Foulkesweg 1a
Wageningen

Meulenhoff & Co. n.v. (Map
    seller)
Beulingstraat 2-4; Postbus 197
Amsterdam-C

Rijkswaterstaat
Directie Algemene Dienst
Boorlaan 2
's-Gravenhage

Theatrum Orbis Terrarum
Ltd.

O. Z. Voorburgwal 85
Amsterdam

Topografische Dienst
Westvest 9
Delft

New Zealand

Department of Lands and Survey
P. O. Box 8003
Wellington

Nicaragua

Dirección General de Cartografia
Managua

Nigeria

Federal Ministry of Works
and Surveys
Survey Division
P. M. B. 12596
Lagos

Norway

Norges Geografiske Oppmaling
St. Olavs gt. 32
Oslo

Norges Geologiske Undersøkelse
Leiv Eirikssons vei 39
Trondheim

Norsk Polarinstitutt
Oslo

Peru

Dirección de Hidrografia y
Foros
Ministerio de Marina

Sáenz Peña 590
La Punta, Calláo

Poland

Instytut Geologiczny
Rakowiecka 4
Warszawa

Państwowe Przedsiebiorstwo
Wydawnictw Kartograficznych
Ulica Solic 18/20
Warszawa

Portugal

Instituto Geográfico e Cadastral
Praça da Estrela
Lisboa 2

Serviços Geológicos
Rua da Academia das Ciências, 19
Lisboa

Rhodesia

Department of the Surveyor
General
Electra House
Jameson Ave.
Salisbury

South Africa

The Government Printer
Bosman St.
Pretoria

Spain

Aguilar
Apartado núm. 1 F. D.
Madrid

Servico de Publicaciones
Ministerio de Obras Publicas
Madrid 3

Sweden

Generalstabens Litografiska
    Anstalts Förlag
Vasagatan 16
Stockholm 1

Rikets Allmänna Kartverk
Hässelby torg 20, Hässelby
    gård
Stockholm

Sjokartebyran
Stockholm 27

Svenska Reproduktions AB
Fack 162
10 Vällingby 1

Switzerland

Kümmerly & Frey Editions
    Geographiques
Halberstr. 6-10
3001 Bern

Tanzania

Survey Division
P.O. Box 9201
Dar es Salaam

Uganda

Department of Lands and
    Surveys
15, Obote Avenue
P.O. Box 7061
Kampala

U.S.S.R.

Vsesoiuznoe Ob'edinenie

Mezhdunarodnaia Kniga
Moskva, G-200

U.S.A.

American Map Company, Inc.
3 W. 61st St.
New York, N.Y. 10023

Benefic Press
1900 N. Narragansett Ave.
Chicago, Ill. 60639
(Formerly Weber Costello)

Carson Map Company
Watertown, S.D. 57201

Champion Map Corporation
P.O. Box 17435
Charlotte, N.C. 28211

Denoyer-Geppert Co.
5235 Ravenswood Ave.
Chicago, Ill. 60640

George F. Cram Company,
    Inc.
730 E. Washington St.
Indianapolis, Ind. 46206

Hacker Art Books
54 W. 57th St.
New York, N.Y. 10019
(Distributor of facsimile at-
    lases published by Theatrum
    Orbis Terrarum, Amster-
    dam, Netherlands)

Hammond, Inc.
Maplewood, N.J. 07040

Hearne Brothers
First National Building
Detroit, Mich. 48226

Historic Urban Plans
P.O. Box 276
Ithaca, N.Y. 14850

Kistler Graphics, Inc.
4000 Dahlia
Denver, Colo.   80216

Lake Survey District
Corps of Engineers
630 Federal Building
Detroit, Mich.   48226

Maryland Geological Survey
Latrobe Hall
The Johns Hopkins University
Baltimore, Md.   21218

National Geographic Society
Washington, D. C.   20036

New York State Department
  of Transportation
Map Information Unit, State
  Campus
1220 Washington Ave.
Albany, N. Y.   12226

A. J. Nystrom & Co.
3333 Elston Ave.
Chicago, Ill.   60618

Office Planning Coordination
Map Distribution
488 Broadway
Albany, N. Y.   12207

Orbis Terrarum Booksellers
606 Metropolitan Ave.
Brooklyn, N. Y.   11211
(Seller of Russian language
  maps and atlases)

Rand McNally & Co.
P. O. Box 7600
Chicago, Ill.   60680

Superintendent of Documents
Government Printing Office
Washington, D. C.   20402

Telberg Book Corp.
P. O. Box 545
Sag Harbor, N. Y.   11963
(Map seller)

Thomas Bros. Maps
550 Jackson St.
San Francisco, Calif.

U. S. Aeronautical Chart and
  Information Center
Second and Arsenal Sts.
St. Louis, Mo.   63118

U. S. Army Topographic Com-
  mand
Corps of Engineers
Washington, D. C.   20315
(Formerly Army Map Service)

U. S. Department of Commerce
Bureau of the Census
Washington, D. C.   20233

U. S. Department of Commerce
Environmental Science Ser-
  vices Administration
Coast and Geodetic Survey
Rockville, Md.   20852

U. S. Geological Survey
Map Information Office
Washington, D. C.   20242

U. S. Naval Oceanographic
  Office
Washington, D. C.   20390

West Virginia Geological Sur-
  vey
P. O. Box 879
Morgantown, W. Va.

Zambia

Geological Survey Department
Ministry of Mines and

Co-operatives
P. O. Box RW. 135
Ridgeway
Lusaka

Survey Department
Ministry of Lands & Mines
P. O. Box RW. 397
Lusaka

AN ANNOTATED SELECTION OF SERIALS
IN CARTOGRAPHY*

John A. Wolter

The acquisition of maps, atlases, and related cartographical materials is recognized as a major problem area
in the field of map librarianship.   There have been a few
monographs and several periodical articles which deal with
the subject published since World War II.   An extensive
search of the literature pertinent to the topic at hand has
failed to turn up any really descriptively annotated articles.
Most of the current writing seems to be concerned with
merely mentioning the publications and not really describing
their possible usefulness to the harassed map librarian who
must somehow provide his patrons with a good selection of
maps of all types.

The following selection is by no means all inclusive.
I have included those serials which contain, as a regular
feature, lists or reviews of currently published maps and
atlases, serials which review or list maps at periodic intervals in addition to their main subject interest, and serial
lists and bibliographies of maps, atlases and related materials of wide or international scope which may not be quite so
timely in their coverage.   Also included are publications
which deal with the current status and bibliographic history
of the International Millionth Map of the World.   The reader
will no doubt discover some important omissions.   I have included only those publications which were available to me for
personal examination.   For this reason, perhaps a supplementary list can be published at some later date.

AMERICAN Congress on Surveying and Mapping.   Washington,

*Reprinted by permission from Special Libraries Association,
Geography and Map Division, <u>Bulletin</u> No. 58 (1964), 9-13.

D. C.   Surveying and Mapping.   1+ (1941+)   Quarterly.
Contains a section on map information which lists
U. S. G. S. topographical maps on all scales, public land survey plats, maps and charts produced by other government
agencies, and state and county highway maps.   Each issue
has an article dealing with distinctive recent maps.   Current.
Indexed.

BERICHTE zur deutschen Landeskunde.   (Zentralarchiv für
Landeskunde von Deutschland.   Institut für Landeskunde).
Bad Godesberg.   v 1-4 (1941-1945); v 5+ (1948+).   2 nos.
in each vol.   Semiannual.
The second volume of the yearly issue contains a bibliographical section entitled "Kartenneuerscheinungen. "   Arranged by area with Germany as the first entry followed by
Switzerland, Liechtenstein, and Austria.   Includes maps of
all types.   General headings and synopsis by area in the
yearly index lead to entry.   Usually one year behind publication.

BIBLIOGRAPHIE cartographique internationale.   (Comité Nationale de Geographie; International Geographic Union).   Paris.
(1936+)   Annual.
Lists by area the new maps which have appeared since
the previous issue.   Includes national topographic maps and
other maps of all types, world, regional, and topical atlases,
and globes.   The entries are consecutively numbered.   Indexed alphabetically by author and by country, by editor and
publisher, and by subject.   The editor and publisher index
underlines official mapping agencies.   Usually two or three
years behind publication, but nevertheless, an exhaustive
work.

BIBLIOTHECA Cartographica.   Bibliographie des kartographischen Schrifttums; Bibliography of Cartographic Literature;
Bibliographie de la Littérature Cartographique.   (Institut für
Landeskunde and Deutsche Gesellschaft für Kartographie).   Bad
Godesberg.   1+ (1957+)   Semiannual.
The table of contents and chapter headings are in German, English, and French.   A classified list including bibliography, history, congresses and meetings, and other information on all phases of map making and use.   Includes sections on atlases and globes.   There is an alphabetical list of
periodicals checked, a list of abbreviations and an index.   The
information is the most current internationally of all of the
works mentioned.

_____. Sonderheft 1. International Bibliography of the
"Carte Internationale du Monde au Millioneme" (International
Map of the World on the Millionth Scale). August, 1962.
        An historical bibliography of the IMW containing many
references to papers and reports. Arranged by subject in
chronological order. A selected bibliography of IMW/ICAO
maps. Lists of published maps which conform to IMW specification, and 12 valuable index maps of the published maps
are included.

_____. Sonderheft 2. IMW/CIM 1:1,000,000 MAP exhi-
bition. August, 1962.
        A catalogue of the exhibit containing published and
manuscript maps arranged by topic and by publishing country.
References are made to early papers and reports dealing with
the IMW.

CANADA. Department of Mines and Technical Surveys. Geographical Branch. Ottawa. Accessions List. 1+ (1948+)
Monthly.
        In two parts; Part I. Books, Pamphlets, Periodicals.
Part II. A selected list of Maps, Atlases and Gazetteers
received in the Map Research Unit. Arranged in Part II by
World, subdivided by country Canada and by province. Maps
of all types. (Part II is evidently superseded by the following entry.)

CANADA. Department of Mines and Technical Surveys. Geographical Branch. Ottawa. Selected Accessions: New Maps.
1+ (1963+) Bimonthly.
        Begins with entries for Canada including all types maps
and charts, then world and country coverage. (Evidently
supersedes Part II. of previous entry.)

CANADA. Department of Mines and Technical Surveys. Geographical Branch. Ottawa. Bibliographical Series. 1+
(1950+) Irregular.
        This bilingual bibliography is divided into two parts.
The first section contains books, periodical articles, and
theses which deal exclusively with Canadian geography. The
second section lists maps and charts of all types. Arrangement is classified under area headings and arranged by
province and by subject. Certain issues have dealt exclusively with maps. Check the list of publications on the back
cover.

CANADA. Department of Mines and Technical Surveys.

Geographical Branch.   Ottawa.   Geographical Bulletin.   1+
(1951+)   Irregular, about 2 a year.
　　　The section entitled "Map Notes" describes selected
recent maps of Canada published by official national and
provincial government departments.

CARTOGRAPHY.   (Australian Institute of Cartographers)
Melbourne.   1+ (1954+)   Semiannual.
　　　Articles on all phases of cartography and mapping.
Each issue has an article entitled "Contemporary Cartography."
Also has abstracts of cartographic articles which include many
map references.   Usually about a year behind in publication.

CARTOGRAPHIC Journal.   (British Cartographic Society.)
Chessington, Surrey.   1+ (1964+)   Semiannual.
　　　The first issue of this journal contains articles on
several topics of interest to cartographers and map librarians.
Also includes news and reviews.   Section entitled "Recent
Maps" contains references to maps added to the Bodleian Library during the previous six months.   Lists maps of all
types arranged as follows: first, small scale Ordnance Survey maps followed by world, continent, and individual country
maps.   Also includes atlases and map catalogues.   Section
on "Recent Literature," contains articles on all phases of
cartography.

CURRENT Geographical Publications: Additions to the Re-
search Catalogue of the American Geographical Society.
(American Geographical Society of New York).   New York,
New York.   1+ (1938+)   10 times a year.
　　　Maps are listed in the regional sections.   They are
also listed separately in the cumulative annual indexes.

FRANCE.   Centre National de la Recherche Scientifique.
Centre de Documentation Cartographique et Geographique.
Paris.   Memoires et Documents.   1+ (1949+)   Irregular.
　　　Each issue 1-4, (1949-1954), contained a section "C"
entitled "Documentation Bibliographique," including lists of
maps of certain countries available in the Centre and also a
list of maps in books and serials received at the Centre.

GEOGRAPHISCHES Taschenbuch; Jahrweiser zur deutschen
Landeskunde.   (E. Meynen, Zentralverband der deutschen
Geographen and Bundesanstalt für Landeskunde und Raum-
forschung.   Bad Godesberg).   Wiesbaden.   1+ (1949+) Bi-
ennial.
　　　The 1962/63 volume contains a table of contents in

both English and German. The section of Cartographical and
Topographical Services, Publishers, and Distributors is of
great value. There is a cumulative subject index for all volumes which lists maps and atlases of all types.

GLOBEN. (Generalstabens Litografiska Anstalt). Stockholm.
1+ (1922+) Quarterly.
    Each issue contains a list of published maps of Sweden
of all types. The last issue each year is entirely devoted to
a cumulative listing of maps of all types published by the
author.

ILLINOIS. University. Map and Geography Library. Cham-
paign-Urbana. New acquisitions. (1958+) 6 times a year.
Mimeographed.
    The acquisition list of the most active American uni-
versity map and geography library. In three sections: maps,
books (including atlases), and serials. Classified and alphabetical listing. No cumulation and no index.

INSTITUT für Augewandte Geodäsie. Nachrichten aus dem
Karten- und Vermessungswesen. Reihe I: Deutsche Beiträge
und Informationen. Frankfurt A.M. 1+ (1951+) Irregular.
    The section entitled "Kartenarchiv und Bibliothek, "
lists maps and atlases acquired by the library of the Institute.
Listed by subject and area. Indexed.

INTERNATIONAL Map of the World on the Millionth Scale.
United Nations Department of Economic and Social Affairs.
New York. (ST/ECA/Ser.D/1.) 1+ (1955+) Yearly.
    The first section deals with international cartograph-
ical meetings and important material concerning the IMW.
The second section contains an index map of current IMW
coverage, a classified list of maps with complete bibliographical information and an alphabetical list of the maps published.
A list of sheets in preparation and a list of the national publishing agencies completes the work.

KARTOGRAPHISCHE Nachrichten. (Deutsche Gesellschaft
für Kartographie e.v.) Bielefeld. 1+ (1951+) Quarterly.
    Articles on national mapping activities, cartography,
and lists of newly published maps. News and reviews of
maps, atlases, guidebooks and geographical works. Indexed.

THE MILITARY Engineer. (The Society of Military Engineers.) Washington, D.C. 1+ (1920+) 6 times a year.
    The section "Surveys and Maps" contains information

on new mapping activities by government agencies, both U.S.
and foreign.   Lists new United States Geological Survey topographic maps and new county highway maps.   (Reprints available from the Army Map Service for AMS depository libraries.)
Cumulative annual index under subject heading, "Surveys and
Maps."

NEDERLANDSCH Aardrijkskundig Genootschap, Amsterdam.
Amsterdam.   Tijdschrift.   1-7 (1876-1883); s2 v1+ (1884+)
Quarterly.
     The section entitled "Kartografie" contains articles on
cartography and mapping, reviews of books, atlases and related materials, and a list of the newly published Dutch federal "Topografische Dienst" topographic maps in various
scales.   Indexed.   These sections are now numbered consecutively within the parent work.

PETERMANNS geographische Mitteilungen.   Gotha.   1-91,
no. 3 (1885-1945); 92+ (1948+)   Quarterly.
     After 1934 reference must be made to the index lo-
cated on the verso of the back cover.   The section "Kartographie" contains articles and reviews which deal with books
on cartographical subjects, atlases, and individual maps.

PROFESSIONAL Geographer.   (Association of American geographers.   Journal.)   Washington, D.C.   1-8 (1943-1948);
nsv1+ (1949+)   6 nos. a year.
     Most issues since 1961 contain reference in a standard
format to some recent maps of importance.   This section is
not well developed as yet, but it has potential.   Maps indexed
under heading "New Maps," in annual index.

REGIO Basiliensis; Hefte für juranische und oberrheinische
Landeskunde.   (Geographisch-ethnologische Gesellschaft in
Basel.)   1+ (1959+).   Quarterly.
     In addition to geographical articles contains "Karten
bibliographie" for stated periods for the Basel region.   Lists
Swiss, French, and German maps of all types.   Indexed.

ROYAL Geographical Society.   London.   New Geographical
Literature and Maps, ns 1+ (1951+)   Semiannual.
     Lists the additions to the society's collection of maps
and atlases in addition to general geographical bibliographical
information.   Arranged by area and alphabetically under area
by country.   Indexed.

SCOTTISH Geographical Magazine.   (Royal Scottish Geographi-

cal Society.)   Edinburgh.   1+ (1885+)   3 nos. a year.
      Reviews, in the "Book Review" section, recent atlases
and maps of all types which deal with Scotland.   There is a
good deal of general information on cartographic subjects in
all issues.   Maps are indexed under the heading "Cartography,"
in the yearly subject index.

SPECIAL Libraries Association.   Geography and Map Division.
Washington, D.C.   Bulletin.   1+ (1950+)   Quarterly.
      The official organ of the Geography and Map Division
of the Special Libraries Association.   Lists new maps, books,
and atlases.   Contains reviews and articles on maps, map
making, and map bibliography, and other cartographical and
geographical information.   Cumulative indexes cover no. 1-
50.   1950-1962.

UNITED STATES Copyright Office.   Washington, D.C.   Catalog of Copyright Entries.   Third series.   Part 6:   Maps and
Atlases.   1+ (1947+)   Semiannual.   (Preceded by the Catalog
of Copyright Entries: Pamphlet Section, which included maps.)
      Lists domestic and foreign maps, atlases, and other
cartographic works registered in Class F, together with similar works currently registered in other classes.   Arrangement
is alphabetical by copyright claimant.   Contains current registrations, renewal registrations, area list (important), and a
publishers directory.   The best source for current U.S. commercial cartography.

UNITED STATES Department of the Interior.   Washington,
D.C.   Publications of the Geological Survey.   1+ (1953+)
Monthly.
      Lists the topographic quadrangles on all published
scales, special maps, base maps, reprints, resurveyed maps,
mineral investigation maps, and many other publications.   The
five year cumulations include a finding list for states, areas,
and subjects.   The only limitation is the length of time between cumulations.   Index sheets and order forms are useful
supplements to the list.

UNITED STATES Library of Congress.   Washington, D.C.
Quarterly Journal of Acquisitions.   1 (1943+)   Quarterly.
      One issue a year contains an article on recent impor-
tant acquisitions in the Map Division and information on division activities.   Some issues have contained bibliographical
essays on the historical cartography of the United States.   Indexed.

UNITED STATES Library of Congress. Exchange and Gift
Division. Washington, D. C. Monthly checklist of state publications. 1+ (1910+) Monthly.
   Arranged by state and alphabetically by agency within
the state government. Maps are listed under the publishing
agency. Indexed annually with references to maps under state,
county and city entries. Current with some entries for previous year.

UNIVERSO. (Italy. Istituto Geografico Militare.) Florence
1+ (1920+) Bimonthly.
   Contains section "Rubrica Cartografica" which lists
new cartographical publications. Lists and reviews of maps
and map series of the IGM. Indexed.

WORLD cartography. (United Nations Department of Social
Affairs.) New York, New York. (ST/SOA/Ser. 1/1.) 1+
(1951+) Irregular.
   Each issue is devoted to some specific phase of mapping activity. Topographic mapping in selected countries is
described. Also contains technical notes and studies, reports on activities in various countries, and an occasional
subject bibliography. International in scope. No cumulations
and no index.

5. MAP PROCESSING AND CATALOGING

A COMPUTERIZED APPROACH TO
INCREASED MAP LIBRARY UTILITY*

Kate Donkin and Michael Goodchild

A library catalog is essentially an information retrieval system enabling a book to be located from a knowledge of some characteristic of the book, notably its title, publisher or author. This is conventionally achieved by filing cards according to each of these characteristics. Thus, a library with author, title and subject catalogs would have three copies of each card sorted alphabetically by author, subject and title.

A further means of locating books is conventionally available. The books may be placed on the shelves in a particular logical order. In both the Dewey and Library of Congress systems, some degree of subject sorting is achieved by shelf location. Librarians argue that a subject shelf sorting is preferable to any other as it gives very great savings in user time and energy, grouping together on the shelves books related in subject matter. An author and title are usually unique to a book. Though at times a book may have to be classified by more than one author, or more than one alias, it is a sample matter to enter the book in the appropriate number of places in an author catalog.

A subject catalog is less simple, however. Any book is a collection of facts and ideas, and a complete information retrieval system must allow for the classifying of the facts and ideas into the appropriate subject areas beyond the conventional single subject classification. The problem of finding

*Reprinted by permission from The Canadian Cartographer (Formerly The Cartographer), vol. 4, no. 1 (1967), 39-45. Published by B. V. Gutsell, Department of Geography, York University, Toronto.

a single subject heading for a book is responsible for bottle-necks in library cataloging departments with different cata-logers disagreeing regarding the appropriate subject heading. But progress is being made: key word abstracting projects being used in legal and medical libraries are equivalent to multiple subject heading classification. The number of key words abstracted must be a compromise. The larger the number of words abstracted the closer a complete information retrieval system is approached, and the greater is the amount of material which must be sifted in a search for key words. The cost of setting up such a system is high, and the time for a typical search is long. Furthermore, a search for a word will often produce so much output that little may be gained by the user of the system. Consequently, the number of key words must be limited.

With only a few subject headings or key words being entered in a catalog for any book, a certain level of educa-tion is being assumed on the part of the searcher. Level of education initially affects the grouping of facts and ideas un-der subject headings, and also influences knowing where to look in a subject catalog. For example, consider the word "topographic" as applied to maps. A trained geographer is well acquainted with the meaning of the word "topographic," and a single subject classification is all that is necessary for the vast number of topographic maps in libraries. But to a non-geographer, the term conveys little idea of the informa-tion to be found on a map; a multiple subject classification with entries for contours, roads and even windmills would be necessary.

The problem of differential knowledge may be over-come, however, by an initial step before the catalogs are con-sulted. This step might take one of three forms:

1. A consultation with library staff
2. A book entitled "How to use the subject catalog"
3. A book of synonyms, such as the blue-green pages of a telephone book.

As the number of subject headings and other cataloged char-acteristics increases, new means of information retrieval are needed. A computerized sorting system can lead to catalogs in book form in seconds, starting with one set of punched cards in any order. For large collections, the entire collec-tion can be searched in seconds for a certain title or subject using magnetic tape. Once collection searching becomes a

computer operation, other peripheral activities readily follow.
Interlibrary searches may be made with considerable time
savings by linking data banks.   Ordering of materials and
interlibrary borrowing may be speeded and simplified.

The McMaster University Map Library is not cataloged.
This situation led to a search for the best method of cataloging possible within our present technology.   Some systems
have been proposed (Murphy, 1963; Thomas, 1963; Donohue,
1964; Hagan, 1964; Stallings, 1966) but only in one case were
any useful proposals made.   Stallings proposed a system which
draws heavily on the Library of Congress book classification
system to develop a subject catalog for maps.   We believe
that this system is unsatisfactory and that the proposed list
of map characteristics is inadequate.   The following proposals
are made in the hope that they will stimulate interest and a
greater interchange of ideas, and that they will lead towards
a system of general applicability.   The system described is
currently being put into operation at McMaster University.

Classification of a map is designed to fill a standard
IBM data card, which can carry 80 characters of information,
either numerical or alphabetical.   The 80 characters are
divided among 13 fields as follows:

Data Array on 80-Column Card

Field	Card Columns	Characteristic
1	1-20	Title
2	21-27	Publisher's code
3	28-32	Latitude of lower right corner
4	33-38	Longitude
5	39-46	Scale / 10.0
6	47-52	Library location
7	53	Type code, e.g. wall map
8	54-59	Political division
9	60-62	Date produced
10	63-74	Three subject codes
11	75	Language
12	76	Projection
13	77-80	Spare user codes

Each characteristic, or each field, is a means of access to
a map.   Thus, a user requiring a map of a certain subject
in a certain area, say goats in Ungava, can either consult

the subject catalog under goats (field 10) or the political catalog under Ungava (field 8). Each of these catalogs consists of lists of maps printed from punched cards sorted by one characteristic. Only one set of cards has to be punched; the catalogs are produced on a computer using a program written by M. Goodchild. Figure 1 shows a set of maps coded according to the card layout pattern, and Figures 2 and 3 show maps after sorting for political division and scale. The advantage of using a computer rather than a card sorter is illustrated in Figure 2. In the case of political division, and with several other fields, the information on the card is in code form. By using a code file, illustrated in Figure 4, the names can be replaced before printing, making the output more readable.

The program was written in Fortran IV, and is suitable for use in any computing centre possessing a Fortran compiler. The program requires a verbal specification of the field to be sorted, the particular file of maps to be examined, a code file if necessary, and will produce a list sorted for any of the 13 fields, in the case of field 1 sorting alphabetically. By allocating codes in a particular fashion, maps with related characteristics can be placed in logical proximity in the catalogs. Canada is allocated the political code 200000, and all subdivisions of Canada begin with a 2 with, for example, 240000 indicating Ontario and all subdivisions of Ontario having the same two first digits. In the political division catalog, the list appears in this order. If

```
ACHRAY                   31F13 4545   7730     633 10310 513000938
ASIA PHYSIOG PROV                           200000 5040427000009455300
ATLANTIC OCEAN                 4000   2000  200000 50102        939
AUSTRALIA STRATEGIC            4000  15400   80000 50410 81000094355055504
AUSTRALIA VEGETATION                         50000 50209 810000956
BALFOUR TSP                                   2534 10307 24000095613011201
BARI                        38 4000   1721    2500 30507 5170009344101
BATTLEFORD                 267 5230  10815    3801 20604 25200091523075504
MANITOBA SOUTH                 4900   9200   10137 20501 251000952550461096110
BELGIUM PAFT FRANCE         19 5100    300    4000 30703 534000917640665016601
BEVERLEY TSP SOUTH P                            10 103003241100
BROWNFIELD DIST ALB        572B 5215 11000     633 20208 253000957
BURLINGTON                30M5C 4315   7545    250 10304 249400960
CALI                       NA18        7200  10000 40504 34200094225045100    5
CAMBRIDGE DIST FTPATH                          250 30203 51100093658095600 6502
CANADA EAST COAST              3663   6300   22176 10103 210000245811
CENTRAL AMER ISLANDS           600   6200   57001 40102 33000094459006104
CHERRY POINT ALBERTA      84D5W 5600  11900    1267 10109 2530009515100220700
COLUMBIA RIVER BASIN       MS38 5132  11713     316 20406 26000095551105104 5504
ELGIN AND KEITH             29 5700    325     633 20501 51300093456004104 5108
EMO LAND USE VANCOUVER416MI 4911 12252         250 50302 2600009665601
EMO NIGHTPOP TORONTO 40BM12 4331   7929        2500 50304 24000096610454010
ENGLAND SOUTH               11 5030     50   25344 30107 51100093451075808 6601
GASPE N NEW BRUNSWICK       14 4706   6100   500000 5010132110009447302
GEOG FACTORS OF RECREATION                  760320 402022100000960530023025701
HAMILTON MARKET                4300   7900    6336 50201224110095051096406 7306
HANNA KINDERSLEY          72NW 5000  10800   50000 20705       9645600
```

Figure 1.   Print-out of information sorted by title.

SØRTED FIELD	TITLE AND CØDE		LAT	LØNG	SCALE LIB	LØCN	TYP	PØLIT	DATE	SUBJECT CØDES			LG	PJ	SPR
000000000C000C000C000000000000	ATLANTIC ØCEAN		40.00	20.00	2000000	50102	•	-0	1939	-0	-0	-0	•	•	-0
0000C00CCCC00000000000000C0000	HANNA KINCERSLEY	72NW	50.00	108.00	500000	20705	•	-0	1964	5600	-0	-0	•	•	-0
0000C000C00000000C000000000000	SANBØRN INSURANCE	6	-0.00	-0.00	600	50405	•	-0	1950	5600	-0	-0	•	•	-0
0000000000000C000000000000000C00	MAP FILE ENDS		-0.00	-0.00	-00	-0	•	-0	1 -0	-0	-0	-0	•	•	-0
UNITED STATES ØF AMERICA	GEØG FACTØRS ØF RECREATIØN		-0.00	-0.00	7603200	40202	2	100000	1960	5300	2302	5701	•	•	-0
ALABAMA	PHENIX CITY	N11612	32.40	84.00	250000	40204	•	134000	1955	5107	5804	-0	•	•	-0
ALABAMA	SCØTTSBURG		34.30	86.00	125000	40206	•	134000	1892	5107	2501	-0	•	•	-0
MARITIMES	CANADA EAST CØAST		36.63	63.00	221760	10103	•	210000	1924	5811	-0	-0	•	•	-0
NEW BRUNSWICK	GASPE N NEW BRUNSWICK	14	47.06	61.00	5000000	50101	3	211000	1944	7302	-0	-0	•	•	-0
PRINCE EDWARD ISLAND	TIGHNISH	21116	46.45	64.00	63360	10807	•	213000	1945	5109	-0	-0	•	•	-0
ØNTARIØ	BALFØUR TSP		-0.00	-0.00	25340	10307	•	240000	1956	1301	1201	-0	•	•	-0
ØNTARIØ	EMØ NIGHTPØP TØRØNTØ	40BM12	43.31	79.29	25000	50304	•	240000	1966	1045	4010	-0	•	•	-0
NIAGARA REGIØN	NIAGARA PENINSULA		42.00	79.00	126720	10307	•	241000	1940	1208	1303	-0	•	•	-0
WENTWØRTH CØUNTY	BEVERLEY TSP SØUTH P		-0.00	-0.00	100	10300	3	241100	1 -0	-0	-0	-0	•	•	-0
WENTWØRTH CØUNTY	HAMILTØN MARKET		43.00	79.00	63360	50201	2	241100	1950	5109	6406	7306	•	•	-0
MIDDLESEX CØUNTY ØNTARIØ	MIDDLESEX CØUNTY		-0.00	-0.00	36680	10309	•	242400	1931	2105	-0	-0	•	•	-0
ESSEX CØUNTY ØNTARIØ	PELEE	40G10	41.40	82.30	50000	10308	•	242600	1962	5600	-0	-0	•	•	-0
LAKE ØNTARIØ REGIØN	LAKE ØNTARIØ	68	43.00	76.00	4000000	50207	•	248000	1923	5201	5510	-0	•	•	-0
HALTØN CØUNTY ØNTARIØ	BURLINGTØN	30M5C	43.15	75.45	2500	10304	•	249400	1960	-0	-0	-0	•	•	-0
MANITØBA	MANITØBA SØUTH		49.00	92.00	101370	20501	•	251000	1952	5504	6109	6110	•	•	-0
SASKATCHEWAN	BATTLEFØRD	267	52.30	108.15	38010	20604	•	252000	1915	2307	5504	-0	•	•	-0
ALBERTA	BRØWNFIELD DIST ALB	572B	52.15	110.00	6330	20208	•	253000	1957	-0	-0	-0	•	•	-0
ALBERTA	CHERRY PØINT ALBERTA	84D5W	56.00	119.00	12670	10109	•	253000	1951	5100	2207	0	•	•	-0
BRITISH CØLUMBIA	CØLUMBIA RIVER BASIN	MS38	51.32	117.13	3160	20406	•	260000	1955	5110	5104	5504	•	•	-0
BRITISH CØLUMBIA	EMØ LAND USE VANCØUVER	416MI	49.11	122.52	2500	50302	•	260000	1966	5601	-0	-0	•	•	-0
BRITISH CØLUMBIA	LARDEAU W KØØTENAY	1147	50.00	117.00	253440	20304	•	260000	1903	1205	-0	-0	•	•	-0
BRITISH CØLUMBIA	MT REVELSTØKE NAT PARK		51.00	117.40	50000	20301	•	260000	1927	2504	5504	5505	•	•	-0
BRITISH CØLUMBIA	PINCHER CREEK	14	49.00	114.00	380160	20107	•	260000	1916	6109	6110	-0	•	•	-0
YUKØN TERRITØRY	KATHLEEN LAKE	115A11E	60.30	137.00	50000	20806	•	271000	1950	5107	-0	-0	•	•	-0
YUKØN TERRITØRY	PEEL RIVER	2078	64.00	127.00	1000000	50107	•	271000	1964	5900	2206	2504	•	•	-0
CENTRAL AMERICA	CENTRAL AMER ISLANDS		6.00	62.00	570010	40102	•	330000	1944	5900	6104	-0	•	•	-0
CØLØMBIA	CALI	NA18	-0.00	72.00	100000	40504	•	342000	1942	2504	5100	-0	5	•	-0
ARGENTINA	SANTA CLARA BUEN VIS	4809	31.48	61.12	50000	40603	•	371000	1949	5100	2204	-0	•	•	-0
AFRICA	LIBREVILLE	NA32	-0.00	12.00	1000000	50304	•	400000	1935	5106	2507	2505	•	•	-0
EURØPE AND MIDDLE EAST	PHYSIØGRAPHIC EURØPE		46.00	34.00	9000000	30104	2	500000	1923	5300	-0	-0	•	•	-0
EURØPE AND MIDDLE EAST	RAINFALL EUR MEAN AV		30.00	50.00	5000000	30101	1	500000	1920	3101	-0	-0	•	•	-0
ENGLAND	CAMBRIDGE DIST FTPATH		-0.00	-0.00	2500	30203	•	511000	1936	5809	5600	6502	•	•	-0
ENGLAND	ENGLAND SØUTH	11	50.30	0.50	253440	30107	•	511000	1934	5107	5808	6601	•	•	-0
WALES	SWANSEA	153	51.30	3.40	63360	30201	•	512000	1960	5108	-0	-0	•	•	-0
SCØTLAND	ACHRAY	31F13	45.45	77.30	6330	10310	•	513000	1938	-0	-0	-0	•	•	-0
SCØTLAND	ELGIN AND KEITH	29	57.00	3.25	6330	20501	•	513000	1934	5600	4104	5108	•	•	-0
EIRE	BARI	38	40.00	17.21	25000	30507	•	517000	1934	4101	-0	-0	•	•	-0
IBERIAN PENINSULA	MALLØRCA	NE382	38.00	6.20	506880	30304	•	520000	1940	5101	2507	-0	•	•	-0
BELGIUM	BELGIUM PART FRANCE	19	51.00	3.00	40000	30703	•	534000	1917	6406	6501	6601	•	•	-0
WEST GERMANY	LANDAU AC ISAR	149	48.15	13.20	100000	30403	•	535000	1937	4102	5100	-0	•	•	-0
BALKAN STATES	LARISA	77	37.30	1.00	1000000	30502	•	540000	1944	5106	6104	-0	•	•	-0
BALKAN STATES	TIGHINA	R56	40.00	29.00	250000	30601	•	540000	1945	5101	4001	-0	•	•	-0
SCANDINAVIA	SCANDINAVIA	A2	58.00	30.00	2000000	30301	•	550000	1944	5101	5102	4101	•	•	-0
RUSSIA	WEST SIBERIA ARCHANGEL		75.00	45.00	4000000	50502	•	600000	1965	5811	6104	-0	•	•	-0
RUSSIA	WEST SIBERIA		52.00	88.00	2500000	50501	•	600000	1955	6104	6603	6401	•	•	-0
ASIA	ASIA PHYSIØG PRØV		-0.00	-0.00	2000000	50404	2	700000	1945	5300	-0	-0	•	•	-0
ASIA	KØYANG	652711	-37.40	127.00	50000	50206	•	700000	1954	5102	-0	-0	•	•	-0
ASIA	NAHA	NG52	24.00	132.00	1000000	50408	•	700000	1944	5106	5101	2407	•	•	-0
AUSTRALIA	AUSTRALIA STRATEGIC		40.00	154.00	800000	50410	•	810000	1943	5505	5504	-0	•	•	-0
AUSTRALIA	AUSTRALIA VEGETATIØN		-0.00	-0.00	500000	50209	•	810000	1956	-0	-0	-0	•	•	-0

Figure 2. Print-out of information sorted by political division.

SORTED FIELD	TITLE AND CODE		LAT	LONG	SCALE	LIM	LOCN	TYP	POLIT	DATE	SUBJECT CODES			LG	PJ	SPR
-00/1	MAP FILE ENDS		-0.00	-0.00	-00		-0	•	-0	1 -0	-0	-0	-0	•	•	-0
100/1	BEVERLEY TSP SOUTH P		-0.00	-0.00	100		10300	3	241100	1 -0	-0	-0	-0	•	•	-0
600/1	SANBORN INSURANCE	6	-0.00	-0.00	600		50405	•	-0	1950	5600	-0	-0	•	•	-0
2500/1	BURLINGTON	30M5C	43.15	75.45	2500		10304	•	249400	1960	-0	-0	-0	•	•	-0
2500/1	CAMBRIDGE DIST FTPATH		-0.00	-0.00	2500		30203	•	511000	1936	5809	5600	6502	•	•	-0
2500/1	EMO LAND USE VANCOUVER	416MI	49.11	122.52	2500		50302	•	260000	1966	5601	-0	-0	•	•	-0
3160/1	COLUMBIA RIVER BASIN	MS38	51.32	117.13	3160		20406	•	260000	1955	5110	5104	5504	•	•	-0
6330/1	ACHRAY	31F13	45.45	77.30	6330		10310	•	513000	1938	-0	-0	-0	•	•	-0
6330/1	BROWNFIELD DIST ALB	572B	52.15	110.00	6330		20208	•	253000	1957	-0	-0	-0	•	•	-0
6330/1	ELGIN AND KEITH	29	57.00	3.25	6330		20501	•	513000	1934	5600	4104	5108	•	•	-0
12670/1	CHERRY POINT ALBERTA	84D5W	56.00	119.00	12670		10109	•	253000	1951	5100	2207	0	•	•	-0
25000/1	BARI	38	40.00	17.21	25000		30507	•	517000	1934	4101	-0	-0	•	•	-0
25000/1	EMO NIGHTPOP TORONTO	40BM12	43.31	79.29	25000		50304	•	240000	1966	1045	4010	-0	•	•	-0
25340/1	BALFOUR TSP		-0.00	-0.00	25340		10307	•	240000	1956	1301	1201	-0	•	•	-0
36680/1	MIDDLESEX COUNTY		-0.00	-0.00	36680		10309	•	242400	1931	2105	-0	-0	•	•	-0
38010/1	BATTLEFORD	267	52.30	108.15	38010		20604	•	252000	1915	2307	5504	-0	•	•	-0
40000/1	BELGIUM PAFT FRANCE	19	51.00	3.00	40000		30703	•	534000	1917	6406	6501	6601	•	•	-0
50000/1	KATHLEEN LAKE	115A11E	60.30	137.00	50000		20806	•	271000	1950	5107	-0	-0	•	•	-0
50000/1	KOYANG	652711	-37.40	127.00	50000		50206	•	700000	1954	5102	-0	-0	•	•	-0
50000/1	MT REVELSTOKE NAT PARK		51.00	117.40	50000		20301	•	260000	1927	2504	5504	5505	•	•	-0
50000/1	PELEE	40G10	41.40	82.30	50000		10308	•	242600	1962	5600	-0	-0	•	•	-0
50000/1	SANTA CLARA BUEN VIS	4809	31.48	61.12	50000		40603	•	371000	1949	5100	2204	-0	•	•	-0
63360/1	HAMILTON MARKET		43.00	79.00	63360		50201	2	241100	1950	5109	6406	7306	•	•	-0
63360/1	SWANSEA	153	51.30	3.40	63360		30201	•	512000	1960	5108	-0	-0	•	•	-0
63360/1	TIGHNISH	21116	46.45	64.00	63360		10807	•	213000	1945	5109	-0	-0	•	•	-0
100000/1	CALI	NA18	-0.00	72.00	100000		40504	•	342000	1942	2504	5100	-0	5	•	-0
100000/1	LANDAU AD ISAR	149	48.15	13.20	100000		30403	•	535000	1937	4102	5100	-0	•	•	-0
101370/1	MANITOBA SOUTH		49.00	92.00	101370		20501	•	251000	1952	5504	6109	6110	•	•	-0
125000/1	SCOTTSBURG		34.30	86.00	125000		40206	•	134000	1892	5107	2501	-0	•	•	-0
126720/1	NIAGARA PENINSULA		42.00	79.00	126720		10307	•	241000	1940	1208	1303	-0	•	•	-0
221760/1	CANADA EAST COAST		36.63	63.00	221760		10103	•	210000	1924	5811	-0	-0	•	•	-0
250000/1	PHENIX CITY	NI1612	32.40	84.00	250000		40204	•	134000	1955	5107	5804	-0	•	•	-0
250000/1	TIGHINA	R56	40.00	29.00	250000		30601	•	540000	1945	5101	4001	-0	•	•	-0
253440/1	ENGLAND SOUTH	11	50.30	0.50	253440		30107	•	511000	1934	5107	5808	6601	•	•	-0
253440/1	LARDEAU W KOOTENAY	1147	50.00	117.00	253440		20304	•	260000	1903	1205	-0	-0	•	•	-0
380160/1	PINCHER CREEK	14	49.00	114.00	380160		20107	•	260000	1916	6109	6110	-0	•	•	-0
500000/1	AUSTRALIA VEGETATION		-0.00	-0.00	500000		50209	•	810000	1956	-0	-0	-0	•	•	-0
500000/1	HANNA KINDERSLEY	72NW	50.00	108.00	500000		20705	•	-0	1964	5600	-0	-0	•	•	-0
506880/1	MALLORCA	NE382	38.00	6.20	506880		30304	•	520000	1940	5101	2507	-0	•	•	-0
570010/1	CENTRAL AMER ISLANDS		6.00	62.00	570010		40102	•	330000	1944	5900	6104	-0	•	•	-0
800000/1	AUSTRALIA STRATEGIC		40.00	154.00	800000		50410	•	810000	1943	5505	5504	-0	•	•	-0
1000000/1	LARISA	Z7	37.30	1.00	1000000		30502	•	540000	1944	5106	6104	-0	•	•	-0
1000000/1	LIBREVILLE	NA32	-0.00	12.00	1000000		50304	•	400000	1935	5106	2507	2505	•	•	-0
1000000/1	NAHA	NG52	24.00	132.00	1000000		50408	•	700000	1944	5106	5101	2407	•	•	-0
1000000/1	PEEL RIVER	2078	64.00	127.00	1000000		50107	•	271000	1964	5900	2206	2504	•	•	-0
2000000/1	ASIA PHYSIOG PROV		-0.00	-0.00	2000000		50404	2	700000	1945	5300	-0	-0	•	•	-0
2000000/1	ATLANTIC OCEAN		40.00	20.00	2000000		50102	•	-0	1939	-0	-0	-0	•	•	-0
2000000/1	SCANDINAVIA	A2	58.00	30.00	2000000		30301	•	550000	1944	5101	5102	4101	•	•	-0
2500000/1	WEST SIBERIA		52.00	88.00	2500000		50501	•	600000	1955	6104	6603	6401	•	•	-0
4000000/1	LAKE ONTARIO	68	43.00	76.00	4000000		50207	•	248000	1923	5201	5510	-0	•	•	-0
4000000/1	WEST SIBERIA ARCHANGEL		75.00	45.00	4000000		50502	•	600000	1965	5811	6104	-0	•	•	-0
5000000/1	GASPE N NEW BRUNSWICK	14	47.06	61.00	5000000		50101	3	211000	1944	7302	-0	-0	•	•	-0
5000000/1	RAINFALL EUR MEAN AV		30.00	50.00	5000000		30101	1	500000	1920	3101	-0	-0	•	•	-0
7603200/1	GEOG FACTORS OF RECREATION		-0.00	-0.00	7603200		40202	2	100000	1960	5300	2302	5701	•	•	-0
9000000/1	PHYSIOGRAPHIC EUROPE		46.00	34.00	9000000		30104	2	500000	1923	5300	-0	-0	•	•	-0

Figure 3. Print-out of information sorted by scale.

the searching for a map is by magnetic tape rather than catalog, a call to 241100 would produce a list of the maps coded
241100, then 241000, then 240000 and finally 200000.   The
sample of code file in Figure 4 is allocated in this manner;
there is no consistent areal unit for a particular digit.

       The subject codes are allocated similarly.   The first
three digits are arbitrary, for example, 2340 is urban land
use.   Successive degrees of detail in the subject are given
increasing values in the final digit with 2341 denoting urban
land use divided into major categories such as retail and
residential, and 2343 indicating
urban land use with retail establishments differentiated.
The type code is used to indicate the form of the map; 1
means a wall map and 2 means
a raised relief map, etc.   The
language code signifies the language in which the map was published.   The projection code is
used for maps with notable or
unusual projections.   Spare
user codes are indicators of
interest to a particular researcher, or of relevance to a particular course; they are not applicable to more than one library.   The date of a map is
taken to be the date at which
the information given was collected.   At McMaster University, the coding of non-topo-
graphic maps is being done first.
Topographic sheets constitute
the majority of the collection
but pose the smallest retrieval
problem.   Listings of the codes
so far allocated, and Fortran

```
192000ALASKA
200000CANADA
210000MARITIMES
211000NEW BRUNSWICK
212000NOVA SCOTIA
213000PRINCE EDWARD ISLAND
220000NEWFOUNDLAND
221000NEWFOUNDLAND        ISLAND
222000LABRADOR
230000PROVINCE OF QUEBEC
240000ONTARIO
241000NIAGARA REGION
241100WENTWORTH COUNTY
241200LINCOLN COUNTY  ONTARIO
241300WELLAND COUNTY  ONTARIO
241400HALDIMAND COUNTY ONTARIO
241500BRANT COUNTY  ONTARIO
242000LAKE ERIE REGION
242100OXFORD COUNTY  ONTARIO
242200NORFOLK COUNTY  ONTARIO
242300ELGIN COUNTY ONTARIO
242400MIDDLESEX COUNTY ONTARIO
242500KENT COUNTY ONTARIO
242600ESSEX COUNTY ONTARIO
242700LAMBTON COUNTY ONTARIO
243000LAKEHEAD AND NW ONTARIO
243100THUNDER BAY DISTRICT
243200RAINY RIVER DISTRICT
243300KENORA DISTRICT ONTARIO
243400PATRICIA PORTION  KENORA
244000UPPER GRAND RIVER REGION
```

Figure 4.   Print-out of
Codes for Political Divi-
sions.   (Part)

listings of the sorting program may be obtained from the
authors.

REFERENCES

Donohue, J. C.   Proceedings of the American Documentation
       Institute, 1964; 137-140.

Hagan, C. B.   An Information Retrieval System for Maps,
     UCLA Map Library, 1964.
Murphy, M.   Special Libraries, vol. 54, no. 9 (1963), 563-
     567.
Stallings, D. L.   S. L. A. Bulletin, Geography and Map Divi-
     sion, 1966; 5.
Thomas, K. A.   S. L. A. Bulletin No. 54, Geography and Map
     Division, 1963; 8-12.

THE NEED FOR MAP CATALOGING

Roman Drazniowsky

Not long ago it was believed, among some librarians, that map cataloging was not necessary. Cataloging was simply a waste of time. To those professionals a simple alphabetical filing of maps, by geographic or political regions, was satisfactory enough. Soon after, the demands placed on map collections showed the shortcomings of such an approach. Unfortunately, all discrepancies created by such a system could not be improved overnight and as a reault, at the present time, there are many uncataloged map collections, or perhaps it would be better to say, there are very few cataloged map collections.

At this point, it would seem appropriate to ask the question, "Is map cataloging really necessary?" I would not dare to ask this question regarding book cataloging. Of course, map cataloging is just as necessary as book cataloging--in order to make use of, to the full extent, the wealth of information provided by maps. It is a well-known fact that cataloging is one of the most difficult tasks in any library operation; it is more so for map cataloging, because, unlike the systems developed for book cataloging, there is a lack of any accepted map cataloging rules.

This problem is not limited only to maps. At the present time there is no adequate classification for geographical material in general. Dr. Arch Gerlach, in his article, "Geography and Map Cataloging and Classification in Libraries,"[1] stressed these problems quite well:

*Reprinted by permission from Special Libraries, vol. 61, no. 5 (1970), 236-237. Copyright by Special Libraries Association. Originally a paper presented in 1969 at the SLA 60th Annual Conference.

The basic difficulty appears to be that librarians
have had too little contact with modern geography
to recognize works in this field when they see
them, and to little understanding of maps to give
them the attention they deserve as sources of information.

Major libraries have hesitated to introduce radical
changes, despite the fact that they recognize the need for
such changes, because of the great number of already cataloged material that is scattered throughout their collections,
and because of the high cost of recataloging projects. As a
result, individual map collections were forced to develop or
modify map cataloging methods according to their needs.

The problems of map cataloging could be divided into
two groups. First, the shortage of properly trained personnel, which could be easily overcome by training them in
library schools. However, the second group of problems is
rather complicated. To solve them satisfactorily it is necessary to understand the nature of the map and to deal with
these non-book materials accordingly. It is advisable, therefore, to develop the ideal map cataloging rules or to modify
existing ones which could be acceptable to all map collections.
At the present time, the American Library Association rules[2]
and the Library of Congress rules for entry are based on the
supposition that maps should be cataloged as books are cataloged. The main entry for books is author, title. The primary interest in a book is the subject. For maps, however,
the author or title has little significance. No one asks for a
Bartholomew map. The area is of primary importance in
map cataloging. In fact, the earliest map catalog printed in
America by Harvard University--in 1831--was arranged by
area. And, since 1885, the catalogs of the British Museum
followed an area arrangement. The subject, in most cases,
is of secondary importance and is always related to the area.
If a subject is not related to the area, then there is no need
for a map.

Since the area entry is of primary importance in map
cataloging it must be clearly defined. The problem is not
as easy to clarify as it first appears. For example, the
shifting of long-established geographical regions, due to political changes, as in Central Europe or Eastern Europe,
Near East or Middle East. The boundary between Asia and
Europe. What type of boundary--cultural, political? It is
difficult to mention geographical. Even more complicated

are those with undecided territorial changes.   I can mention, at this point, the Polish-German territorial problems.   How should such territories be cataloged?   The constant name changes are also creating problems, not only to catalogers but also to map-makers, who complain constantly.

Perhaps, further research into automation for map cataloging may be the answer in solving these problems.

NOTES

1.   Special Libraries, vol. 52, no. 5 (May-June 1961), 248-251.
2.   "A map, series or set of maps, an atlas, a relief model, or a globe is entered under the person or corporate body that is primarily responsible for its informational content." --Description of Main Entry in Anglo-American Cataloging Rules.   Chicago: ALA, 1967; 272.

AUTOMATING THE ILLINOIS STATE UNIVERSITY
MAP LIBRARY*

William W. Easton

In the fall of 1964 I started my job as map librarian
at Illinois State University. We were all new--the map room,
the secretary, and I. In fact the map cases were still being
delivered and assembled. Approximately 19,000 maps were
waiting to be sorted, classified, and cataloged. The maps
were scattered over the campus. Some were located in
drawers in the Geography Department, some in the library
stacks, and others stored in boxes. My secretary and I
moved the maps by hand truck from the Geography Department across the campus to new quarters in the basement of
a recently-completed annex to Milner Library. The map
room is 29 x 60 feet and is windowless, but well lighted.
There are 63 map cases which contain 375 drawers. After
moving the 19,000 maps into the Map Room, our next project was to unfold, iron, trim, and mend a disorganized
assortment of material.

Prior to our taking over the map collection it had been
supervised by a series of Geography graduate students and no
coherent control system had been established. The majority
of the maps had not been cataloged. During the past two
years, our map collection has grown from 19,000 to over
75,000 and is increasing at the rate of over 15,000 a year.
We started out as a depository for one agency and now receive material from 85 additional sources either on a depository or permanent mailing list status. Our major suppliers
of maps are the U.S. Army Map Service, the U.S. Geological

*Reprinted by permission from Special Libraries Association,
Geography and Map Division, Bulletin No. 67 (1967), 3-9.
The author thanks Richard P. Palmer of the Milner Library
Staff (Ill. State Univ.) for his help.

Survey, and the U.S. Coast and Geodetic Survey. Since our
collection has been growing so rapidly, we have endeavored
to construct an efficient and functional cataloging system.
After careful consideration, we decided to adopt the Library
of Congress "G" schedule. This schedule provides tables of
uniform subdivision for geographic areas by their regions,
political divisions, and cities--as well as for each area on
a subject basis. It also gives an outlined breakdown for
Atlases and Maps.

The numbers in the schedule assigned to Maps are
3160 to 9980. Classification starts with celestial globes and
maps and then world maps with subdivisions following for
hemispheres, continents, countries, regions, and states and
other political subdivisions. Following land areas, the ocean
areas are listed. These are subdivided into large regions
such as North Atlantic and South Atlantic, with further subdivisions into island groups. Unlocalized maps, such as theoretical, imaginary, and unidentified maps are grouped in the
classification after ocean areas.

The LC "G" schedule provides a detailed breakdown of
area classification which is specific enough for our use in
the preparation of the code work sheets, for our automated
classification system. Following the pattern established in
the outline, it starts with the most general: celestial globes,
terrestrial globes, universe, celestial maps, and so on.
Next are listed parts of the world by hemisphere and zone.
Following these, we have classification by continent and by
country.

Each area, large or small, is assigned a block not
exceeding five consecutive four-digit numbers. For example,
Nova Scotia is assigned 3420-3424. Likewise New York
(State) is assigned 3800-3804. We employ these 4-digit code
numbers for our main entry. Each of the five four-digit numbers has a special significance which is determined by the
concluding digit. The basic pattern for the area subdivisions
which are represented by these 4-digit numbers, is provided
in the LC Tables of Subdivisions for Atlases and Maps. The
concluding digits have the following meanings as shown on this
table: 0 indicates a general map: 1, a map that presents a
subject; 2, a regional map; 3, a major political division and
4, cities and towns. In other words 3800 is a general map
of New York State, and 3803 would cover a major political
subdivision, in this case a county, in New York State. If
one has a map of a specific city, such as Rochester, New

York, the code is 3804. R6. It should be mentioned that only
cities and towns in the United States and Canada are treated
in this manner. Cities and towns of all other countries are
grouped under country, and not under the political subdivision
in which they are located. It should also be mentioned that
while the LC uses a letter and a number to indicate specific
counties and cities and towns, such as the R6 for Rochester,
we have found it necessary to establish a more detailed coding than this. We have, therefore, used the Two-Place Cutter Table--or, perhaps I should say--we have been trying to
use the Two-Place Cutter Table but have not found it entirely
satisfactory. This is no reflection on the Cutter Table as it
was not designed for the use we are putting it to. In the LC
"G" schedule, the subdivision of Atlases and Maps by subject,
is accomplished by using the letters A through S to indicate
seventeen major subject subdivisions. O and I are omitted
from this alphabetical list. F represents Political Geography,
P is used for Transportation and Communication, and J stands
for Agriculture. These seventeen letter subdivisions are
further divided by number. For example, A stands for Special Category Atlases and Maps, while A1 is used for Outline
and Base Maps, and A4 is reserved for Photomaps.

In working out our automation project, we found it
necessary to devise not only a more detailed code for cities
and towns, but also our own codes and abbreviations for map
publishers and authors, since the LC "G" schedule is not detailed enough for our purposes. We also had to set up our
own codes for map projections, map language, and map color.
For these, we used codes that are compatible with those used
for authors and publishers. To handle sub-areas we chose
to use C. A. Cutter's Two-Figure Author Table. It has been
necessary to expand on this, and we have come up with some
rather extensive code sheets. We have considered the possibility of using the three-figure Cutter-Sanborn table. Another
possibility is IBM Manual, C20-8073, Numerical Code for
States, Counties, and Cities. We have also thought about
setting up a system based on the index of a large atlas. If
we employed such an index, we would assign codes ahead of
time. At this time, no final decision has been reached.

In our map library, the L. C. "G" schedule, modified
with area as the main entry, is coupled with the use of IBM
data processing cards for the coding-cataloging and eventual
publication of a print-out book catalog of maps. As far as I
know, in the fall of 1964, the Army Map Service Library in
Washington and the UCLA Map Library in Los Angeles were

the only two institutions, or agencies, in the United States
that had done anything relative to the automation of their map
collections. The Army Map Service uses Remington Rand
90-column cards. The cataloging system they use is their
own. UCLA is set up for the Library of Congress "G" schedule and IBM cards. I learned by personal communication with
S. D. Stevens that the Santa Cruz Branch of the University
of California has their entire collection cataloged and entered
on the Form for Key Punch Operator. Their system is based
on the one originated by UCLA. At that time their collection
contained only 537 maps.

Our endeavors to automate our map collection are being
aided by the Illinois State University Computer Center which
has an IBM 1620 containing 60, 000 positions of core storage;
four 1311 disk storage drives, each containing two million
positions of numerical storage; a 1443 model 2 on-line printer; an on-line card reader and card punch; an on-line paper
tape reader; floating point hardware; automatic multiply-
divide; and indirect addressing. This gives us, a total of
eight million numerical storage positions. In addition, the
Computer Center at the University of Kentucky has offered
to help us with the project.

After considerable experimentation on our own and
consultation with the chairman of the Geography Department,
various geography professors, the director of the library, and
the computer people, we decided on three cards using approximately 220 columns, since modified. The pertinent information is taken from all the maps in our collection and placed
on code work sheets. We designed our code work sheet by
first drawing a proposed layout for library punch cards. This
gives the name of the item, whether it is to be coded or not,
and the size of the field or the number of columns to be used
per item. From this we came up with the first in our series
of code work sheets. Also developed was the Multiple Layout
Form which shows how and where the information will appear
on the three punch cards.

After coding about 193 maps we discovered that multiple subject headings were going to be a problem. For instance we had an Economic Chart of the Northern Hemisphere
put out by the Aeronautical Chart and Information Center.
The Library of Congress has a subject subdivision entitled
Economic Geography, but they also make separate subject subdivisions for (1) mines and mineral resources, (2) agriculture, (3) forests and forestry, (4) fish and fisheries,

(5) manufacturing and processing, and (6) commerce and trade. As each of these subjects appears on the economic chart in question, we have a subject code of six items: H1L3J1J5M1Q1. H1 being Mines and Mineral Resources, General; L3 is for Fish and Fisheries, Exploitation of Fisheries; J1 stands for Agriculture, General; J5 for Agriculture, Mineral Resources; M1 means Manufacturing and Processing, General; and Q1 represents Commerce and Trade, General and Trade Routes. This is bad enough on the map but is much worse for a machine since it can decipher only one code at a time. Further, there is the problem of converting the code back to words. At this point we came to the conclusion that it was time to put the atlases and maps portion of the LC "G" schedule into machine memory. We decided to make separate code sheets for each subject, where we had a multiple subject heading. This was accomplished by adding a letter to the accession number, thereby keeping our holdings straight and allowing the machine to get to each subject heading. Examples are as follows: 000185; which is the accession number for H1; 000185A, the accession number for L3; 000185B used with J1, etc. We also did away with the area heading since it is synonymous with the L.C. classification code. We decided that color could, and should, be coded. As a result of the foregoing decisions, we were able, at least for a while, to reduce our data processing cards from three to two. It was decided to have a cover sheet for series. To keep our accessioning straight we planned to use the accession number with the letter "S" added to it for the series cover sheet. For each individual sheet in the series we added the letter "Z." The cover sheet would take into consideration such things as change of series number by listing all series numbers. It was also decided to use a dash to indicate changes in date, edition, and language. For size changes, the maximum size for both height and width would be used.

Having made such extensive revisions in our map code, we found it necessary to call back all sheets sent to the coding room and revise them. First the new proposed layout for map library punched cards was drawn up (Illustration 1). Next came a new code work sheet. The multiple layout form also had to be revised. The computer center thought it advisable to incorporate information to the key punch operator, on our code work sheet, as to where the material appears on the punched card. After coding about 750 maps, we discovered that we did not have enough columns for Sub Area, Sheet Number, and International Numbers entries. As a result it

1. -- Proposed Layout for Map Library Punched Cards

Name	Code	Size of Field
Accession Number	no	7
Card Number	no	1
L. C. Classification Code	no (yes)	5
Sub-area	yes	4
Subject	yes	3
Publisher	yes	2
Scale	no	6
Date	no	4 *1
Sheet Number	no	4
Series Number	no	9
Series Name	no	24
Color	yes	1
Projection	yes	2
Author	yes	2
Edition	no	3 *1
Number of Sheets	no	3
Title	no	26
Size (CM) (H x W)	no	7
Relief (contour)	no	6
Language	yes	3 *1
International Numbers	no	20
Insets	no	2
Copy Number	no	2
Number of Code Sheets (series only)	no	2

*1 Indicates multiple information on source map.

was necessary to put over-flow information on a third card.
We were back with three cards again. We designed a new
multiple layout form. At that time we came up with our present
work sheet (Illustration 2). The computer center put out their
Suggested Instruction for Key Punching Map Library Punch Cards.
We have made no further changes and have approximately
5000 maps coded now. We feel well pleased with our present code work sheet.

From the completed code work sheets the information
is being punched into data processing cards. We are considering placing the information on either paper tapes, magnetic
tapes, disk storage or some other type of media, and we may

SAMPLE

2

Z = Sheet in a series
000764 = Map in order of
accession

ILLINOIS STATE UNIVERSITY
MAP LIBRARY CODE WORKSHEET

ACCESSION NUMBER

Z 000764

G = Maps
3730 = Maine
2 = Region

CARD NUMBER 1

L. C. CLASSIFICATION CODE (9) (13 ALPHA)   G 3732

SUBJECT (CODED) (18 RZ)   *C1 = Physical Sciences, Topographic*

PUBLISHER (CODED) (21 RZ)   *24 = U.S. Geological Survey*

SCALE (23 R)   *25 = 1:125,000*

DATE (29)   *961 = 1961*

SERIES NUMBER (MAX. 9 CHAR.) (37)   *1301*   *44°07'30"*
44°00'00"

.SERIES NAME (MAX. 24 CHAR.) (46)   *7.5 MINUTE ← 7'30"*

COLOR (CODED) (70)   *1 = 3a Color*

PROJECTION (CODED) (71 RZ)   *13 = Polyconic*

AUTHOR (CODED) (73 RZ)   *24 = U.S. Geological Survey*

EDITION (75)   *2 = 2nd*

NUMBER OF SHEETS (78 RZ)   *75*

CARD NUMBER 2 (8)

TITLE (MAX. 26 CHAR.) (9)   *FRYEBURG, MAINE—N.H.*

SIZE (CM) (H X W) (35)   *58 X 42 (In Centimeters)*

RELIEF (CONTOUR) (42)   *20 FT (Contour Interval)*

LANGUAGE (CODED) (48 RZ 50 - OR BLANK)   *1 = English*

INSETS (71 RZ)   *1*

COPY NUMBER (73 RZ)   *2*

NUMBER OF CODE SHEETS (SERIES ONLY) (75 76 RZ) *90*   *SEE KEYPUNCH*
INSTRUCTIONS

CARD NUMBER 3 (8)

SHEET NUMBER (15 R)   *36 N*

G 3732
F99
C1
USGS
25
1961
Sheet 36 N

INTERNATIONAL NUMBERS (MAX. 25 CHAR.) (41) *N4900 – W 7052.5 / 7.5*

SUB-AREA (CODED) (70 RZ)   *F99 = Fryeberg*

N44°00' – W 70°52'30" – 7.5 Minute Quadrangle
Found On Lower Right Hand   F003
Corner of Map

Is placed on lower left hand corner of map

put it on more than one of these. We believe that most map libraries throughout the United States and Canada have many of the same maps that we have in our collection. Therefore the storage media could be sent to any other institution that wished to use the information stored by us, thus economizing on the work involved in coding-cataloging. This could be a tremendous saving of money, time, and labor to all other map libraries.

It is our plan to turn out a pilot program print-out book catalog using the first 3000 maps. Ultimately we plan to produce a print-out book catalog of all maps. At present we have code-in and code-out, so our pages are quite unreadable to anyone but us. Soon we will be turning out pages that can be read by everyone. We hope to achieve upper and lower case entries, and an ultimate format that will be most useful and acceptable to map librarians. Copies of our print-out book catalog will be sent to all interested colleagues in various departments of our university and to interested map librarians in the United States and Canada for their information and comments.

Some map libraries using our storage media might also wish to make book catalogs, as is now being done by the University of Toronto for their book collection. They have an author-title catalog and a subject catalog. Other map libraries might choose to turn out a data processing card catalog such as Yale University Medical Library, while in a transition stage, is currently doing for medical literature. Their data processing cards are printed out in 3" x 5" cards and may be put in a regular catalog drawer. Our storage media may be used as the basis for any of these applications.

Our print-out book catalog of maps will come out annually, or semi-annually, with monthly supplements. It will approach each map from various points of view as is now done by a divided card catalog using author, title, and subject. We shall use all or some of the following: area, subarea, subject, and publisher. During our research on this automation project, we wrote letters to 355 map librarians in the United States and Canada. We told them what we are doing, what we plan to do, and asked them for their comments or opinions. Most of the librarians contacted responded favorably to our endeavors, and many asked to be kept informed of our progress.

Needless to say, the reaction has confirmed our belief

that there is a substantial need for automated cataloging of
maps immediately, and that there will be an increasing need
for machine cataloging in the future.   Since we are convinced
of the value of our project to other map libraries and librarians, we are seeking to acquire a grant to continue and extend
our work.   We hope to produce our basic catalog information
in a form which will be most useful to other librarians--eith-
er data processing cards, machine produced 3" x 5" cards,
print-out book catalog, paper tapes, magnetic tapes, disk
storage, other media records, or some combination thereof.
We trust that our printed book catalog will be compatible
enough to most map libraries that it will save thousands of
hours of cataloging time and thousands of dollars of library
funds for our fellow map librarians.   We believe our goal is
an important one, and while we have not yet attained it, we
are far closer than we were two years ago, and we are now
confident of reaching it.

A COMPARISON OF MAP CATALOGING SYSTEMS*

Mary Ellin Fink

Whether one's goal is to find the "best" method of
cataloging maps, or merely to find the method that works
best for any given library, the first step is to examine the
available systems and to compare and evaluate their features.
Since the published descriptions of map cataloging systems
use different vocabularies and vary considerably in scope and
purpose, comparison is a tedious and uncertain task. If a
great deal of attention is not given to the descriptive comparison of systems, however, the usefulness of any comparative evaluation will suffer. This article describes certain
features of eleven well-known map cataloging systems in such
a way that they can more easily be compared and evaluated.
These features are: 1) the items found on the catalog card,
2) the way each item is used, and 3) the choice of main
entry.

The Cataloging Systems

The eleven cataloging systems described here are the
following: 1) the system used in the Library of Congress,
as described by Phillips in 1921; 2) the system represented
in the Library of Congress's Rules for Descriptive Cataloging
in the Library of Congress in 1949, which is really just another stage in the evolution of the first system but different
enough to be counted separately; 3) the system used in the
American Geographical Society, as described in the Society's
1952 Manual; 4) the system recommended by Crone in 1936
and based on practice in the Royal Geographical Society's map
collection; 5) the system recommended by Brown in 1940 and
based on practice in the William L. Clements Library's map

*Reprinted by permission from Special Libraries Association,
Geography and Map Division, Bulletin No. 50 (1962), 6-11.

collection; 6) the system used by the Army Map Service Library in the 1940's, as described by Murphy in 1945 and by the Army Map Service in 1951; 7) the system set forth in the Boggs-Lewis manual of 1945; 8) the system used in the Directorate of Military Survey in Britain's War Office, as described by Parsons in their 1946 Manual; 9) the system used by the U. S. Office of Strategic Services during the Second World War, as described in an article by Wilson in 1948 (and in the department's earlier manual, not consulted); 10) the new system used by the Army Map Service Library, as described by AMS in 1951, and 11) the system advocated by the Special Libraries Association in 1953, including the use of the LC Rules for notes, as suggested in the Committee's report.

Seven map collections in all are represented in the above list. All except the Clements Library, which had something less than 45,000 maps at the time it was described, were large enough to have the size of the collections described as fractions or multiples of a million. Two of the libraries (RGS and DMS) are English, and the rest, American. All of the systems use catalog cards, one or more for each map, filed in alphabetical or other order. The eleven cataloging systems will be referred to here by the date and author of the publication in which they are described. They are arranged at the head of the columns in Table I in approximate order of their appearance on the historical scene.

Items on the Catalog Cards

Out of a possible sixty or more items of information appearing on the cards used in these eleven systems, twenty-two items were selected for comparison, largely on the basis of popularity. Table I shows these items arranged from most-used at the top to least-used at the bottom. Omitted from the table are: 1) classification numbers in code, except when the whole catalog card is in code (AMS's new system), 2) items in the tracing of other headings used, 3) items used for local identification or clerical records (accessions number, data catalogued, price, immediate source, number of copies), and 4) about thirty other items mentioned by fewer than four sources (e.g., format, coordinates, type of boundaries, place of printing or engraving). The intention was to include only items used for strict cataloging purposes, that is, for description and identification of a library's map holdings.

Table I

Use of Items Included on Map Catalog Cards in Eleven Cataloging Systems*

	Phillips '21	LC Rules '49	AGS '52	Crone '36	Brown '40	AMS '51, old system & Murphy '45	Boggs & Lewis '45	Parsons '46	Wilson '48	AMS '51, new syst.	SLA '53
Area or Geog. feature	$\bar{H}$	$\bar{H}$	Ⓗ	$(\bar{H})$	$\bar{H}$	BHH	ⒷN_2	$\bar{B}$	$\bar{B}$	$\bar{B}\bar{B}$	Ⓗ
Author	Ⓑ	Ⓑ	$\bar{B}$	$(\bar{B})$	Ⓑ	B$\bar{H}$	B$\bar{H}$	B	B	$\bar{B}\bar{B}$	B
Subject	$\bar{H}$	$\bar{H}$	$\bar{H}$	N_2	$\bar{H}$	$\bar{H}$HN	HN$_2$	$\bar{B}N_2$	B		B$\bar{H}$
Title	B	B	B	B	$\bar{B}$	B	B	B	B	B	B
Scale	B	B	B	B	N_2	BH	B	B	B	B	B
Publisher	B	B	B	B	B	$\bar{B}$	B	B	N_2	N_2	B
Date of publication	BH	B	B	B	B	BH	B	B	B	B	B
Notes; Misc. description	$N_{1,2}$	$N_{1,2}$	$N_{1,2}$		$N_{1,2}$	B	$N_{1,2}$	$N_{1,2}$	$N_{1,2}$		$N_{1,2}$
Edition	N_1	N_1		N_1		·	N_1	N_1	N_1	N_1	N_1
Series note or Pubr's no.		N_1		N_1		H	N_1	N_1	N_1	N_1	N_1
Projection		N_2		N_2	N_2		N_1	N_2	B	B	N_2
Size	B	B	B	B	B		B				B
Place of publication	B	B	B	B	B		B				B
Date of situation			H			B	H	B	N_2	B	B
Type of reproduction		N_2			N_2	N_2	N_2		B	N_2	N_2
Prime meridian		N_1		N_2	N_2		N_1	N_1			N_1
Inset note	N_1	N_1			N_1		N_2	N_1			N_2
Number of sheets		B			N_1		B	N_1	N_1		B
Delineator, engraver, etc.	N_2	N_2	N_2		N_1		N_2				N_2
Portrayal of relief		N_2		N_2			N_2	B		B	N_2
Colors used; whether col.		N_1		N_2			N_1		B		B
Language		N_2		N_2			N_2		B	B	N_2

* Items included as part of the body are indicated by B; as a required note, N_1; as an optional note, N_2; as part of a heading, H. A bar over the letter ($\bar{B}$, $\bar{H}$) indicates that the card is filed by that item. Circles indicate main entry; dotted circles indicate that either item may be used as a main entry. Two or more letters in the same cell indicate that the item appears one way on one card and another on a second or third card.

The following more or less arbitrary decisions were made regarding the inclusion of various items: 1) where the system includes both a long and short form, the long form was used; 2) where the system permits a choice, as "scale or size," both are counted; 3) where one of a pair is recorded on the card only if different from the other, as "publisher if different from author," both are counted; 4) where one is preferred but the other accepted, the first is counted as part of the body and the second as an optional note (N2).

Definitions of "author" varied so widely that it seemed artificial to compare the systems on this point. According to Brown, Boggs and Lewis, and AGS rules, author and publisher are separate entities, though the author may be the surveyor, compiler, engraver or copyright holder. But Parsons does not distinguish between author and publisher at all! Furthermore, the old AMS rules lump "compiler or publisher" together as one category, at the same time providing for recording of the "responsible agency" (also called the "authority"), and the "source." Under the new AMS rules, only "authority" and "secondary authority" are recorded--no publisher or source--which indicates that AMS, like Parsons, now fails to distinguish between publisher and author. Crone and SLA advise giving the publisher if different from author. Wilson advises giving the author (undefined) if possible but "in the absence of authorship information, Publisher serves as a weaker means of determining responsibility." Even when allowance is made for differences in terminology, for the cooperative nature of most mapmaking, and for changes in the nature of map authorship since 1800, the lack of consensus among cataloging systems on this point could hardly be more striking. Although there was some disparity in the various definitions of "date of the situation" and "series note or publisher's number," there was not nearly as much as for "author." The remaining items seemed to be defined in fairly comparable terms, as far as it was possible to judge from the literature consulted.

How the Items Are Used on the Cards

No matter how different the systems might be from each other in some respects, there seem to be only four basic ways in which they used any given item of information: 1) to put it on all cards for all maps, 2) to put it on all cards for all maps only if the information is different from that expected, 3) to put it on all cards for some maps, or 4) to put it on some cards for some or all maps. If used in the first way, the item is called part of the body; the second or third way, notes; and the fourth, part of a heading. This corresponds fairly closely to common usage among librarians. The exact definitions used in constructing Table I are given below.

Body (B): Information put on every card for every map if at all possible. Usually, if the information

is not available, a substitute item is used, or lack
of the information is specifically stated.

Required note (N1): Information noted only if different from that expected. If nothing is noted, a
definite inference may be made, as when lack of a
note on the number of sheets indicates that the map
is complete on one sheet.

Optional note (N2): Information noted only if important,
as for example when only rare or interesting projections are mentioned. Lack of this sort of note
has a less definite meaning.

Heading (H): Second or third item in an added heading
for most maps.

Entry (B̄ or H̄): First item by which card is filed,
and consequently the name of a type of entry (e.g.,
author entry, subject entry).

Main entry (B̄ or H̄): First item by which the main
entry is filed.

The difference between the two types of notes is important. It was necessary to distinguish them in order to make
a meaningful comparison between conventional and form-card
systems. The Required Note (N1) may include less important
information, but the function it fills is the same as that for
an item from the body. The information it conveys by its
absence is no less definite than if it had been written out in
full. The Optional Note (N2) is probably closer to the common meaning of the term note, and implies the use of more
skilled judgment by the cataloger.

Only important headings are included in the table. No
item, with the exception of subject, was counted as part of
a heading unless the writer explicitly stated that it was part
of a heading for most maps. The rule was relaxed for subject headings because most systems do not assign subject
heading to over half of all maps catalogued. It was felt that
if the rule were enforced, subject heading would not be fairly
represented. No such exception was made for other items.
It must be kept in mind that if an item does not appear in
Table I as a heading, this does not mean that it is never
used as one. Most or all systems of cataloging permit entries to be made for any unusual or important item, at the
discretion of the cataloger. To record all possible entries
would have made the table unnecessarily full.

There are a few sources of error in Table I which
should be pointed out. First, information for the Office of

Strategic Services' map cataloging system (Wilson '48) is less accurate than it might be, because the OSS cataloging manual, probably the best source of information, was not available. Second, headings for the OSS and several other systems are very probably underreported. This is partly because some of the writers were not very specific about 'items used in headings. Perhaps they felt that the exact headings used were not an integral part of the system, but depended on the needs of the individual library.

Choice of Main Entry

Several criteria were used for deciding which systems probably used a bona fide main entry, and, among those which did, which item it was filed by. Phillips' author card is called the main entry solely because the cross-reference cards lead to it. He does not use the words "main entry" or "main card" and gives no information about tracings. In the system Crone describes, either area or author may be used as the main entry, depending upon the age of the maps in the collection. Author entry is more appropriate for old maps and area entry is more appropriate for new maps. Four systems (Parsons, Wilson, AMS old and new) are not credited here with a main entry because they apparently do not utilize tracings (a sine qua non of the main entry, according to the American Library Association). In all of the other systems, either area or author is specifically designated as "main card" or "main entry." We have to assume, because there is no way of checking, that each writer uses this phrase in the same correct sense.

Discussion

Certain historical trends seem to exist in map cataloging, if one may judge by the information in Table I. There is more emphasis recently on the date of the situation, the edition, the series, and the projection, and less on the place of publication, the size of the map, and individuals other than the author who are involved in the map's production ("delineator, engraver, etc."). Area is more often used recently as main entry, when main entry is used at all. But these apparent developments may be only artefacts. Four of the six most recently-developed cataloging systems belong to agencies specializing in military maps and using printed form-cards (Parsons, Wilson, AMS old and new), and their characteristics may be due only to the nature of their holdings, or the administrative organization of the government agency concerned. Probably they all owe a great deal to the Williams system of cataloging maps, first made publicly available in 1930.

Table I shows that the systems are in very close agreement on the first seven items. Not only do all the systems include all of these seven items on their cards, but with few exceptions they include them in the same way. Author, title and date of publication are always part of the body, and so is scale, with one exception. All but three systems regularly make author entries; the same with subject. All of the systems regularly make area entries, in which area may be either an added heading or an item in the body. These comments are enough to demonstrate the usefulness of a detailed and systematic comparison. Some questions which may profitably be investigated by means of descriptive comparison concern cataloging time (Wilson has made an interesting start here), cataloging systems used in foreign libraries, the meaning, importance and function of "main entry," order of items in the main entry, and the systems best adapted for large and for small libraries.

REFERENCES

American Geographical Society. Manual for the Classification and Cataloging of Maps in the Society's Collection, by Ena L. Yonge and Mary Elizabeth Hartzell. 2d ed., rev. AGS Mimeographed and Offset Publication No. 4. New York: AGS, 1952.

Boggs, S. Whittemore and Dorothy C. Lewis. The Classification and Cataloging of Maps and Atlases. New York: Special Libraries Association, 1945.

Brown, Lloyd A. Notes on the Care and Cataloguing of Old Maps. Windham, Conn.: Hawthorn House, 1940.

Crone, Gerald Roe. "The Cataloguing and Arrangement of Maps." Library Association Record 38, (1936), 98-104.

GEOGRAPHY AND MAP CATALOGING AND
CLASSIFICATION IN LIBRARIES*

Dr. Arch C. Gerlach

In 1952 the International Geographical Union established
a Commission on the Classification of Geographical Books and
Maps in Libraries. One member was named from each of
five countries (Brazil, France, Germany, Italy and the United
States). The chairman is Professor André Libault of France,
and the United States member is the author of this article.
Following the death of the Brazilian member, Dr. B. Winid
of the Polish Academy of Sciences was added to the Commission, which also has corresponding members in several countries. The primary purpose of this Commission was to study
classification systems for geographical and cartographical collections with a view toward recommending improvements and
possibly even developing an ideal system for those materials.
Because of the Commission's narrow scope, it has had only
partial success in achieving recognition for geography as a
discipline or identification of its works as such in the collections of large libraries.

The basic difficulty appears to be that librarians have
had too little contact with modern geography to recognize
works in this field when they see them, and too little understanding of maps to give them the attention they deserve as
sources of information. It seems futile, therefore, to perfect further the classification schemes for geographical and
cartographical materials until something is done to stop the
routing of maps into storage bins and the cataloging of works
prepared by eminent geographers, primarily for use by

*Reprinted by permission from Special Libraries, vol. 52,
no. 5 (1961), 248-251. Copyright by Special Libraries Association. A revision of a paper presented in 1960 at the 19th
International Geographical Congress.

317

geographers, as anthropology, economics, geology, history, political science, sociology or some other subject with which the cataloger associates them. We must take into account the broader aspects of descriptive and subject cataloging that are short circuiting geographical and cartographical publications.

Classification Considerations

The function of classifying a particular item in a collection involves only the assignment of a notation or call number to designate its logical filing position within a group of related materials. The notation may be numerals, letters or a combination of numerals and letters. It is the basic philosophy of the classification system, however, which determines how different groups of materials will be arranged in relation to each other and what types of subdivisions may be made within the groups. For example, one system might group materials by subject, then subdivide them by areas. Another might group materials by areas, then subdivide them by subjects. Or, to take a more limited example, one might classify works on military geography adjacent to political geography in one system and to physical geography in another. But what becomes of the work on military geography when the librarian identifies it as military science? It is classified as military science and separated from geography.

Unfortunately for geographical and cartographical research in libraries, the widest used classification systems do not treat geography as an independent discipline or facilitate the grouping of geographical materials together. Members of the International Geographical Union's Commission on Classification realize that long established and widely used classification systems for large general libraries, such as the Dewey Decimal or Library of Congress systems, are frozen into existing patterns by the tremendous mass of material already classified. Geographers and cartographers may, however, work toward the establishment of alternative schedules for use in special geography and map libraries.

Such an alternative arrangement has been provided in connection with the 16th edition of the Dewey Decimal Classification, which was published in the United States in 1958 and is supplemented or expanded from time to time by issues of Decimal Classification Additions, Notes, and Decisions. The 16th edition of the Dewey Decimal Classification has incorporated a number of geographical topics proposed by Dr.

Meynen, but the basic arrangement subdivides subjects into
local or geographical areas by affixing to the number for the
subject the digits 09 followed by the number of the country,
state, city and so on. The editors realize that many subjects
are treated according to various regions of the earth that cannot be identified by the 940-999 sequence and have recognized
some of these in the 16th edition through form division 091--
zones and physical regions. They are considering the possibility of a regional subdivision scheme similar to that used
by the British National Bibliography: continents, islands,
mountains, plains, coasts, oceans, lakes, rivers, forests,
grasslands, deserts and so on.

       More important, however, is the recognition that ge-
ographers would like to have all, or nearly all material of a
geographical nature kept together in one part of the Dewey
Decimal Classification. To enable such an arrangement in
special libraries there is provided in the March 1960 issue
of Decimal Classification Additions, Notes, and Decisions,
an expansion of 910.1 for topical geography. Libraries wishing to keep works on all fields of geography together may
divide 910.1 like 000-899; for example, economic geography
910.133 or physical geography 910.155 14. If desired, area
subdivisions may be added after a zero, as between 940 and
999; for example, economic geography of the United States,
910.133 073 or physical geography of the United States,
910.155 140 73.

       If similar alternative schedules for geographical and
cartographical publications can be inserted into other classification systems, real progress will be made toward organizing branch libraries and specialized card catalogs for research in those fields. Working out more detailed plans of
classification without taking into account the training and judgment of catalogers may, however, be about as ineffective as
plotting the precise distribution pattern for irrigation water
over field A and leaving the cataloger in control of the master
valve through which the water may be channeled into fields B,
C, D or X. The basic problem is how to gain recognition
for geographical and cartographical works together rather than
how to classify the small percentage so identified by subject
catalogers.

Cataloging Considerations

       The principles and techniques of cataloging as presented
in the Rules for Descriptive Cataloging in the Library of

Congress (page 7) state: "The objectives of descriptive cataloging are: 1) to state the significant features of an item
with the purpose of distinguishing it from other items and
describing its scope, contents and bibliographie relation to
other items; and 2) to present these data in an entry which
can be integrated with entries for other items in the catalog
and which will respond best to the interest of most users of
the catalog.... The descriptive elements are given in the
entry in the order that will best meet the needs of users of
the catalog and will facilitate the integration of the entry in
a catalog with entries for other items."

Careful analysis of this statement reveals three areas
of interpretation that cause difficulty for geographers. First,
most users of library catalogs are not geographers, so when
the cataloger scatters geographical works among a wide variety of other disciplines to which they do bear some overlapping relationship, he can conscientiously maintain that the
entry "will best respond to the interests of most users of the
catalog." Second, whenever there is a conflict between the
requirement for presentation of data in an entry "that will
best meet the needs of users" and the requirement for an entry which "can be integrated in a catalog with entries for
other items," the latter principle is given priority. The catalog is the thing! Entries cannot be modified to fit different
disciplines. They must conform to the standards that will
expedite their integration into the catalog. Third, the subject
cataloger analyses the content of items cataloged. This requires some knowledge of the subject fields as well as the
principles and techniques of cataloging. Practically no catalogers have formal training in geography at the college or
university level. How, then, can catalogers recognize and
identify geographical works? They can't. A multitude of
doctoral dissertations in geography and monographs or books
written by past-presidents of the Association of American
Geographers may be found cataloged in subject fields quite
foreign to the authors.

To prevent the continuation of such a situation, the
International Geographical Union's Commission on Classification should prepare a semi-popular, descriptive summary of
modern geography for distribution to library schools. The
resultant document could be distributed to library school administrators with a covering letter urging that it be made
required reading for all students working toward degrees in
library science.

Another report should be compiled and distributed to library associations and the principal libraries in each country, explaining and justifying in detail the need for alternate rules of entry for specialized collections, classed card catalogs and libraries wishing to keep works on all fields of geography together, subdivided by subject and area or area and subject.

Problems of Maps

Alternate rules of entry are even more essential for maps and atlases than for books, because readers in those fields characteristically approach the catalog or map files to find materials by area and subject. The American Library Association and the Library of Congress rules for entry are based on the supposition that maps should be cataloged like books. The main entry for books is author-title. More than 95 per cent of map reference requests require searching by area-subject entries. A survey of 360 map libraries in the United States, made by a committee of the SLA Geography and Map Division in 1953, revealed that 74 per cent of the requests were by area, 24 per cent by subject and a few scattered ones were by title, publisher, scale or date.

Clearly the objective of a catalog is to identify each item in a collection but for whom? The author-title entry for books is a useful approach for catalogers and acquisitions personnel but not for map reference use, so alternate rules of entry must be provided for control over map reference collections. A map lies in character between a book and a picture and combines some features of both. The main entry for cataloging maps should begin with geographical area, followed by subject, date, size or scale, publisher or authority, and notes on edition, series, number of sheets and classification number. The main entry heading should be one that can be applied to every kind of map and one that is useful in the information it provides.

The earliest map catalog printed in America (Harvard University, 1831) was arranged by area, with map titles listed alphabetically under areas. The printed map catalogs of the British Museum have followed an area arrangement since 1885. A concerted effort to convince library administrators that special provisions can be made for servicing special form and subject materials without disrupting the general collections and catalogs seems both essential and fully justified.

Future Objectives

The scope and objectives of the International Geographical Union's Commission on Classification should be broadened
to deal with a wide variety of problems such as: 1) gaining
recognition in libraries for geography as a discipline; 2) promoting more use of geographical and cartographical publications; 3) development of better bibliographic tools; 4) preparation of effective exhibits to strengthen public recognition of
work in these fields; 5) improvement of research and publication standards; and 6) monitoring the cataloging and classification of geographic and cartographic publications in libraries.
The Commission could inspect at frequent intervals the cataloging and classification of new acquisitions in selected major
libraries and protest promptly and vigorously all improper
identification of geographical and cartographical works. This
monitoring function might even be extended to solicit the pro-
tests of authors and publishers when their works are improper-
ly cataloged in other fields.

To meet the requirements of rapidly growing geography
and map libraries throughout the world, two basic objectives
must be achieved: 1) librarians should be better acquainted
with modern geography; and 2) alternate schedules of classification for geographical and cartographical works, like the
one for the new 16th edition of the Dewey Decimal Classification, should be created and put into use. In short, detailed
classification of geographical and cartographical works is futile unless library philosophies and procedures can be broadened to recognize and provide for the selection, organization,
evaluation and utilization of such works to serve specialists
in those fields.

U. S. ARMY TOPOGRAPHIC COMMAND LIBRARY PREPARES TO AUTOMATE*

Mary Murphy

National and international conferences of librarians, information scientists, cartographers, hydrographers, geodesists and geographers are devoting more and more time to the problems of how to make the rapidly expanding quantities of information in the fields of geography, geodesy, and cartography more readily available. Many recent discussions have been devoted specifically to maps, both to the use of computers in the production of maps and to the handling of them in libraries or map collections. The British Cartographic Society (1), the Soviet All-Union Conference on Automation and Mechanization of Cartography (2), the Ninth International Hydrographic Conference (3), and the International Cartographic Association (4)--to name only a few--have published papers in the last few years on various aspects of automation and maps.

In the United States there is, of course, a great deal of activity and interest in automation of map libraries. In Nov 1968, a conference on Automation in Federal Map Libraries was held at the Library of Congress. Of most probable interest is the progress being made on the Automation Project in LC's Geography and Map Division where the Marc II format is being adapted to catalog single maps. The U. S. Army Topographic Command has been working for several years on preparations to automate its library. Various phases of the program have reached different stages of development. This report is a brief review of the procedures

*Reprinted by permission from Special Libraries, vol. 61, no. 4 (1970), 180-189. Copyright by Special Libraries Association. Originally presented in 1969 at a workshop of the SLA 60th Annual Conference.

we are following and the kinds of problems we have encountered in laying the foundations for automation.   The Army
Map Service (now TOPOCOM) Library was developed through
the years from a relatively small collection of maps to an
organization with a staff of about 150, a collection of more
than 1 1/2 million maps, one million pieces of film (reproduction material or "repromat" sometimes referred to as
manuscript), 120, 000 books and periodicals, and about 30, 000
documents.

The library was structured along classical lines based
primarily on the types of material handled.   There were four
distinct libraries: the Map Library itself, Repromat Library,
Book Library, and Document Library--each with its own system.   Although the four libraries were under a common administration, and although acquisition and interlibrary loan functions involved all types of material, there was very little
interface among the four collections.

Each "library" had its own cataloging system.   The
Map Library which used EAM equipment) had developed a
punched card system based on the Williams System (5, 6) (designed in 1929 for the War Department General Staff Map Collection which in 1942 became the Army Map Service Library).
The Williams System originally used a 4" X 6" card with
printed headings (Fig. 1).   A master card was typed and then
run through a duplicating machine using different colored card
stocks to produce cards for the various files: Geographic
Area, Subject, Scale, Date, Special Number, Authority,
Source, M. I. D. No., Obsolete Number, and Daily Record.
When the files were converted to Remington Rand 90-column
punched cards in 1945, the same basic system was followed,
but some of the written information such as geographic area
and authority were converted to numeric or alphanumeric
codes.   The 30 subject numbers (often referred to as the Williams Classification) that Williams had used only in the call
number for filing maps were now used without the written
headings.   Other elements such as date and scale were already numeric (7-10).

The Repromat Library is a file of reproduction materials (facsimiles of map sheets on stable base materials).
For each map sheet the repromat material consists of a set
of "pulls" or photographic films, one for each color that appears on the map.   The printing plates are made from these
pulls.   The files are arranged by series and sheet numbers.
The records were originally on 90-column punched cards but

are now on magnetic tape. From this tape a semi-annual
tabulation of repromat material and monthly supplements are
prepared. The information shown for each sheet of repromat
material includes the series and sheet number, agency, the
number and kinds of film, date and edition. In addition to
the tape there is a file of 5" X 8" cards which serve as a
manual index to the files and as a circulation record (Fig.
2). The Book Library followed traditional cataloging rules,
using LC classification and subject headings with some modifications.

The Document Library has developed an entirely separate system using a 3" X 5" form card (Fig. 3). The subject heading numbers were taken from the Intelligence Subject
Code (11). This is a six-digit code made up of a single-
digit for chapter number, a two-digit number for major subject class and a three-digit subject subdivision within each
class. The seven chapters are: Politics; Social and Cultural Forces; Science and Technology; Commerce, Industry,
and Finance; Transportation and Communications; Commodities
and Weapons; and Armed Forces. A Duplimat master is prepared by the cataloger and reproduced on pre-printed card
stock, eight cards to a sheet. The cards are cut apart and
are filed in separate files by AMS number, geographic area
and subject, source or originator, report number, title (if
distinctive), and security classification.

The four libraries were physically separated from each
other and also separate from the Interlibrary Loan Section in
the Services Branch. Each had its own receiving procedures,
its own catalogers and card files, its own charge-out system,
its own reference personnel, and issued its own accessions
list. The Army Map Service Library had official responsibility for topographic maps and related data for DoD. The
relationship of the related data to the maps had not been
emphasized. Although the whole field of topographic mapping
covers a wide range of related subjects, nevertheless in the
whole field of knowledge, it is a rather specific sphere. All
the information in the AMS Library was more or less directly
related to that sphere.

We had learned through experience that, although a
user sometimes wanted a specific kind of material (such as
a map or a technical report), more often his requirement was
for all the information--graphic or textual--available on a geographic area or a particular subject. Yet in order to get information or materials on one subject, a researcher had to go

	Outline of Title			
Country	Authority		Old File No.	
Filed as	Date	Scale 1:	Negative	Store Room
Exact Title				
Shows				
Source			Received	No.
M.I.D. No.			Sheets Copies Total Sheets	
Remarks			Date of Survey	
			Compiler or Publisher	

Fig. 1.   Williams System Card (4" X 6")

REPROMAT CONTROL RECORD						
SERIES	SHEET NO		NAME			
SCALE	COUNTRY		EDITION		DATE	
SETS RECEIVED	DATE	NEG	POS	OTHER	SOURCE	
REMARKS						

DATE OUT	P O NUMBER	UNIT	INITIALS	DATE IN	INITIALS

Fig. 2.   Repromat Control Record (5" X 8")

to the Book Library, Document Library, Map Library, and
Interlibrary Loan Section.

In addition to the inconvenience to the users, such
compartmentalization fostered specialization of the library

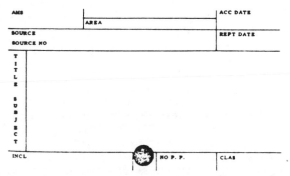

Fig. 3.   Document Catalog Card (3" X 5")

staff and inhibited flexibility.   It was difficult, if not impossible, to transfer personnel from one library branch to another.   Not only was super-specialization developed on the job, for example, map catalogers, book catalogers, and document catalogers were familiar with entirely different systems and procedures, but there were several different Civil Service Series Classifications represented on the Library Division Staff.   Librarians, Intelligence Specialists, and Translators were not interchangeable.   In place of one rather extensive career ladder, there were several rather limited ladders--all mutually exclusive.

Who Doesn't Have a Complex Problem? Or Its Solution?

As the library grew larger and more complex, the problems also increased.   The time and attention of the library administrators were turned toward solving these problems.   They felt that a more efficient organization could be developed if the library were reorganized on functional lines, with all related activities coordinated and if a single system were developed that could be applied to maps, books, and documents.   The application of automation to library operations had been developed by this time to a point that indicated it might be a help in developing a unified system.   Early in 1965, several library committees were appointed--each one representing several branches of the library, different points of view, and a total of 70-80 man-years of professional experience.   Functions, procedures, materials, and files of all elements of the library were analyzed in detail with a dual

purpose: 1) to recommend an improved organizational structure, and 2) to determine whether a single automated system
could be developed that might provide the answers to many
of the perplexing questions that were becoming more urgent
every day.

In February 1966, one series of meetings culminated
in the preparation of a combined subject code and alphabetical
index based on the headings then in use for cataloging maps,
books, and documents.   By March, basic agreement had been
reached on rules for establishing authorities.   In April, a
tentative data sheet was ready for testing.   By May, tentative
plans had been drawn up for automation and reorganization of
the Library Division.   In June 1966, a contract was awarded
to North American Aviation Corporation, now North American
Rockwell (NAR), to analyze all mapping, charting, and geodetic activities of the Department of the Army and to design
a total ADP system to be coordinated with other ADP systems
of the Department of Defense.

Representatives of NAR studied all phases of our library operations.   They frequently sat in on library committee meetings concerned with data elements, card formats,
etc. and acted in an advisory capacity.   The library committee would indicate what characteristics were absolutely essential to carry out our mission and functions.   The contractor
would indicate what additional features could be provided and
which desirable but not essential features could be added
easily to the system, and which would be too cumbersome or
too expensive to be practical at the present time.

To implement a single system in which format or type
of material would be subordinate to content, the whole concept and structure of the library had to be changed.   The
trend in DoD and, indeed, in the government as a whole,
had been toward specialization.   No one organization could
hope to keep up with the rapidly increasing masses of information in more than a relatively narrow field.   This trend
toward specialization has led to a need for subject specialists
in the library field, and to the establishment of information
centers in place of or in addition to traditional libraries.

The Civil Service Commission series for professional
librarians makes no provision for automation.   Computer
specialists and programmers as well as systems analysts are
in an ADP series; but any library developing ADP operations
needs qualified personnel versed in a combination of library

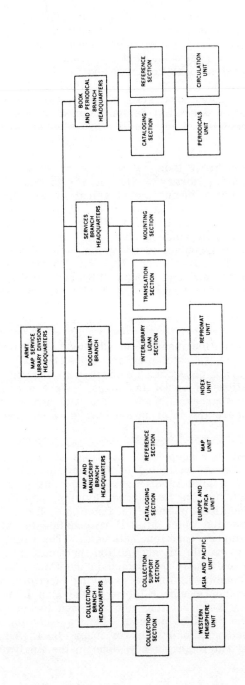

Fig. 4.   U. S.   Army Map Service Library.   Organization Chart (before May 1968)

science, information science, and ADP. In addition, the special librarian also needs some subject matter knowledge.
Fortunately the Civil Service Commission has created the
Technical Information Specialist Series, which bridges the
gap between the professional librarian and the subject specialist on the one hand and the ADP specialist on the other.
Converting all the professional staff of our library to the
Technical Information Specialist Series seemed to offer a
solution to the problems of inflexibility and stunted career
ladders.

The question arose then: If there were no more librarians, would there be a library? The answer to that is Yes
and No. No--if library means the classical library that had
been the only kind of library in the past. Yes--if library is
considered as a broad term to cover all types of collections
of information. Actually some people, such as Mr. Skelton
of the British Museum, object to using the term library at
all in connection with maps. They feel that library implies
a collection of books, and that a map "library" should be
called a map collection. Certainly at TOPOCOM the emphasis is not on books. Emphasis is on maps and related data.
The related data can be in the form of books, but it may also
be in the form of journal articles, documents, photographs,
and any other information media. In addition, the traditional
library functions such as cataloging and classification are
changing. We are not concerned so much with accurate bibliographic descriptions of books and maps. We are concerned
with analyzing any sources of map-related data and making
available to our users the information that is of specific interest to them.

The changes in concepts and functions of the Army
Map Service Library are reflected in its reorganization which
actually took place in May 1968 (Figs. 4-5). The name has
been changed to Information Resources Division, and the structure, with one exception, is based on function. The exception
is the Repromat Section which is still responsible for all functions connected with reproduction materials. The Collection
Branch continues to handle all acquisition functions, but the
receiving function previously performed in the Collection
Branch has been combined with the receiving functions from
the Book Library, the Document Library, the Map Library,
and the Interlibrary Loan Section, and assigned to the Data
Records Unit in the Services Section. Separate cataloging
systems are continuing temporarily for maps, books, and
documents, but all cataloging is now done in the Analysis

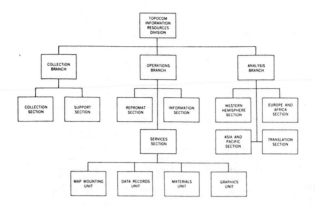

Fig. 5.   U.S. Army Topographic Command, Information
Resources Division.   Organization Chart (after May 1968)

Branch, and all the cards for unclassified maps, books, and
periodicals are now in one room.

A single loan record has replaced the three circulation forms previously in use, and all circulation, filing, and
shelving are the responsibility of one element in the Services
Section.   All reference services have been combined with the
interlibrary loan function and are handled by the Information
Section.   The changes that have already taken place and the
service projected for the future are illustrated in Figs. 6-8.
Key personnel from the Library or Information Resources
Division have been working with the contractor for several
years on the details of the new system.   Specific codes had
to be considered and in many cases developed for each data
element.

In designing a data sheet to be used in providing input
to the new system, it was first necessary to decide what data
fields were needed and to define each field.   In examining the
cataloging systems for maps, books, and documents, we found
amazingly few data elements that were unique to only one type
of material.   There were some differences in essential elements especially between maps and texts.   There were also
some differences in terminology for the same concept.   For
example, the "author entry" on a book card was equivalent
to the "authority" on a map card and the "source" on a
document.   Subject headings, geographic areas, and authorities

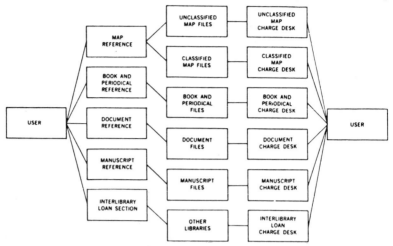

Fig. 6.   User Contact with AMS Library

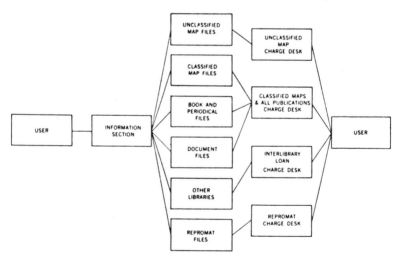

Fig. 7.   User Contact with TOPOCOM/IRD Today

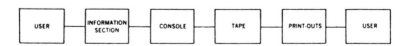

Fig. 8.   User Contact with TOPOCOM/IRD in the Future

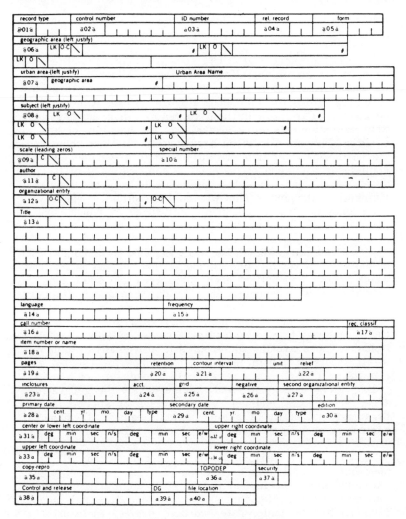

Fig. 9.   Catalog Data Sheet

or organizational entities are three of the major data fields
that required coordination and coding. Subject headings and
geographic areas have been developed as two parts of a common thesaurus with a common program which is now on magnetic tape. A print-out can be produced in either an alphabetical or hierarchical arrangement. In the alphabetical
print-out each heading is followed by its broader term, nar-

rower terms and related terms if any. Definitions or scope
notes are included in many cases.

The present TOPOCOM code for map authorities will
be used for all organizational entities. Rules for establishing authorities (12) have been written, but will be expanded
to include rules for individual authors, whose names will not
be coded. Far more difficult to resolve than the question of
what data elements were needed was the problem of how the
various elements should be arranged on the data sheet and in
the card files. At first we attempted to group the elements
common to all types of material at the beginning of the data
sheet, and to put the fields applicable to only one type of
material at the end. This proved impractical. There was
a tendency at first to be unduly influenced by punch card formats and their limitations.

Eventually, the fields were grouped by a combination
of criteria: first the importance of the field to TOPOCOM,
which resulted in putting geographic area and subject as the
primary fields. Secondly, data fields were grouped according to whether they are applicable to groups of material or
to individual items. The upper portion of the data sheet that
finally evolved (Fig. 9) contains what we call the master data
fields. These are the elements that are generally common
to all sheets of a map series, all volumes of a series of
reports, all issues of a periodical, all editions of a monograph, etc. The master data elements are the geographic
area, urban area, subject, scale, series or special number,
organizational entity or author, title, language, frequency,
control number, and form (Data Fields 1-17).

The lower part of the data sheet and card will be for
specific information on each item, that is, each map sheet,
individual book, periodical issue, etc. Item information will
include such data elements as ID (for identification) number,
item number or name, date, edition, paging, inclosures, geographic coordinates, security and control, type of reproduction, number of copies, file location, etc. (Data Fields 18-
40). The control and ID number will appear on each piece
of material. The control number will apply to all parts of a
series. The control and ID number together will provide a
unique identification of each item in the collection.

In addition to specific data elements and their arrangement on the card, it was necessary to decide what kinds of
card files, accessions list, query responses, and other possible

outputs would be needed.   A 5" X 8" card to be computer
generated was designed.   The appropriate heading for each
file will be added at the top of the card.   The same format
can be used for text; for example, an issue of a periodical.
In most instances whereinformation is coded, the code is
given on the card in parentheses and is followed by the heading in clear text.   In some files only master information will
be shown; in others each individual item will be described.
The codes used in these samples are not necessarily authen-
tic.

The design logic and flow charts for computer operations are available in the TOPOCOM Library.   These charts
include Area-Subject Cards, Control-ID, Organizational En-
tity-Author, Urban Area, Scale, Special Number, and Title.
Specific queries will probably be answered from the card files.
For general queries, the requester will be able to ask for
either master or item information arranged in a variety of
ways.   If the number of responses to any query is greater
than a specific number, this will be indicated so the query
can be modified.   If the number is not too high, the records
will be printed out in a predetermined format.   North American Rockwell's contract was renewed to October 1969.   At
that time a detailed report (13) was submitted defining and
describing all data elements, inputs, outputs, files, logic,
and conversion tables for the new system, and recommending
a pilot test using a 10% sample of the holdings in order to
evaluate the design of the system and confirm it as operational or modify it before converting the entire Topographic Command Collection.

Conclusions

1.   A thorough detailed analysis of every procedure
in the present system including the reason for every action,
its present importance and probable continued importance is
essential in order to make an efficient evaluation of the system and to determine whether automation is desirable.   If the
decision is made to automate, the analysis will help to achieve
an effective automated system.   If the decision is not to automate, the analysis may suggest improvements in the manual
system.
2.   The mission and functions of the library should
be considered.   If the present procedures are satisfying the
requirements, there may be no advantage to automating.   Factors to be considered are the degree to which the present
system is satisfying the requirements; the additional accom-

plishments, if any, to be achieved by automation; the extent
to which these added benefits would justify the extra costs inherent in automating; and whether a computer is already available for library use.

3.   Cooperation between librarians and systems analysts familiar with "hardward" and "software" will probably
produce a better system than one designed by a computer
specialist who is not familiar with the library--or a librarian
who is not familiar with computers.
4.   As much flexibility as can be built into a system
without making the costs prohibitive should be provided to
take care of the changes that will almost inevitably have to
be made when the system is in operation and to prepare for
future developments.

5.   Procedures, codes, input forms, programs, etc.
should be tested as they are developed.   Sample outputs should
be prepared, preferably by the personnel who will be operating
the system.   All library elements concerned, especially cataloging and reference personnel, should have an opportunity to
evaluate the outputs and add the benefit of their knowledge and
experience to the development of the system.
6.   As a new system is developed it should be completely documented.   Decisions should be recorded and dated
as they are made.   Terms should be defined.   Specific instructions should be written for both the cataloger and the
computer.   An alphabetical index to any non-alphabetical data
code makes it easier to use and may reveal duplications.

7.   Designing an automated library system and putting
it into operation is likely to take more time, money, and
personnel than anticipated.   When such a system is developed,
it is usually a long-range project, and if it is worth doing,
it is worth doing well enough to achieve the best system possible.

LITERATURE CITED

1.   Proceedings of the Symposium of the British Cartograph-
       ic Society.   University College of Swansea, 17-19
       September 1965.   Cartographic Journal, vol. 3 no. 1,
       (June 1966), 9-13.
2.   All-Union Conference on Automation and Mechanization
       in Cartography.   Geodesy and Aerophotography [Engl.
       ed.], no. 4 (1967), 244-256.   (April 1968)

3. Moitoret, Capt. V. A. and Johnson, Norman E. "Au-
    tomation of Hydrographic Source Data." International
    Hydrographic Review, vol. 45, no. 1, (January 1968),
    7-20.
4. International Cartographic Association. Meeting of Com-
    mission III. Surveying and Mapping, vol. 38, no. 3,
    (September 1968), 493-4.
5. *Terrell, Lt. Col. J. P. The Williams System of Classi-
    fiction, Cataloging, Indexing, Filing, and Care of
    Maps as Adopted for the General Staff Map Collection.
    2d ed. Washington, D. C. , 1930; 26p.
6. Murphy, Mary. "The Army Map Service Library--Map
    Cataloging." Special Libraries, vol. 36, no. 5,
    (May-June 1945), 157-59.
7. *U. S. Army Map Service Library. Guide to the Williams
    System Map and Engineer Plan Subject Classification
    and Cataloging in Use at Map Library, The Army
    Map Service. Rev. (Washington, D. C.): February
    1952; 49p. (mimeo.)
8. *Guide to the AMS Library Map Subject Classification
    System. Rev. January 1960; 65p.
9. *U. S. Army Map Service. Library Division. Guide to
    the Map Accessions List. Washington, D. C. , 1964;
    18p.
10. *U. S. Army Map Service. Library Division. Automa-
    tion of a Map Library Pt. I, September 1966; Pt. II,
    November 1967.
11. United States Intelligence Board. Committee on Docu-
    mentation. Intelligence Subject Code and Area Clas-
    sification Code. 4th ed. March 1967.
12. *U. S. Army Topographic Command. Information Re-
    sources Division. Rules for Establishing Authorities.
    Rev. August 1968; 22p.
13. North American Rockwell Information Systems Company.
    Topographic Data Library System (DACA 71-69-C-
    0106) 15 October 1969, Washington, D. C.

*Unpublished papers available in the TOPOCOM Library.

AUTOMATION AND MAP LIBRARIES*

Albert E. Palmerlee

Over the last few years more and more emphasis has been placed on the field of information storage and retrieval and the benefits that may be derived from the new automated techniques. Several ideas have been proposed for the automation of map libraries. Most of them, however, either do not provide enough flexibility to cover the full range of map retrieval problems or do not take full advantage of the capabilities for information storage and retrieval that are inherent in modern computers. I have attempted in this paper to outline a type of program that will satisfy the needs of most map libraries, from those supporting detailed geological research to collections in historical cartography. The goals of this program were:

a. A data base designed to permit retrieval of citations for all maps required by any researcher, with a minimum of extraneous items.
b. Automated preparation of catalogs of the holdings of participating libraries.
c. Automated preparation of detailed cartobibliographies and union lists of maps based on any of the basic map characteristics.
d. Easy standardization for simplicity in cooperative cataloging.
e. Input sheets designed so that only minimal training would be required for personnel doing the cataloging.
f. Minimal time required for preparation of an entry.

No attempt has been made to discuss the automation of

*Reprinted by permission from Special Libraries Association, Geography and Map Division, Bulletin No. 69 (1967), 6-16.

physical retrieval through the use of microreproduction techniques.

The Cataloging Record

Coordinate indexing permits the greatest flexibility for automated retrieval of bibliographic citations, and, if carefully designed, can also serve to produce detailed carto-bibliographies in varied formats. To apply this theory to the search for maps, the indexing coordinates that will serve as retrieval parameters must be established. Basically these may be grouped into three categories:

> The bibliographic citation, for identification of the map,
> The subject classification, for contents of the map,
> The union listing, for organizations holding the map.

Using the input sheets shown in figures 1 through 3 we will examine each of these specific areas in detail. These sheets have been designed as general purpose entry forms. Figure 4 shows a more specialized form arranged for use on a typewriter; some of the indexing fields have been omitted. Each record would be assigned a unique record or accession number which would identify it in the data base. Numbers would be assigned serially, and entered in columns 1-8 of each card for that record. If several institutions were to use the program cooperative, numbers could either be assigned in blocks to each installation, or assigned by the central facility handling the master data base.

It is impossible to provide an adequate description of any map on a single card. A record is, therefore, made up of a series of punched cards. Each different item of information is assigned to a specific card (identified by the card number in col. 9-10), or, for short fields, to specific columns on a card. Thus the card number serves as a tag to identify the information punched into it. Some fields cannot even be satisfactorily limited to one card; the addition of a secondary sequencing number in column 11 permits up to nine cards to be used for a given field. For example, the title of a map might require several cards. On the attached cataloging sheet (Fig. 1), the title has been assigned card number ∅2;* three cards have been printed on the sheet, but more could be added if necessary.

---

*Throughout this paper ∅ will be used to represent the number zero; O the letter O.

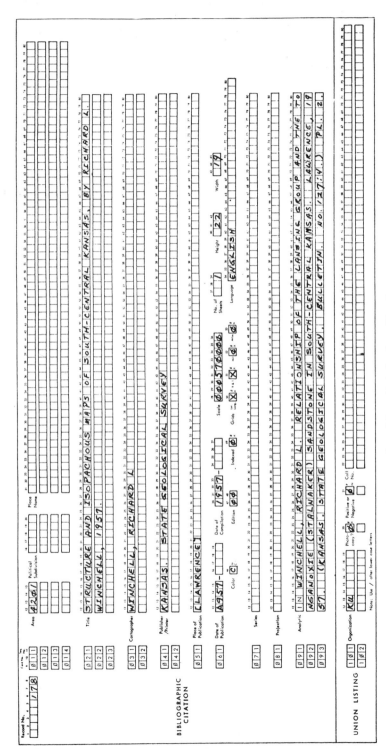

Figure 1. Map Cataloging Sheet.

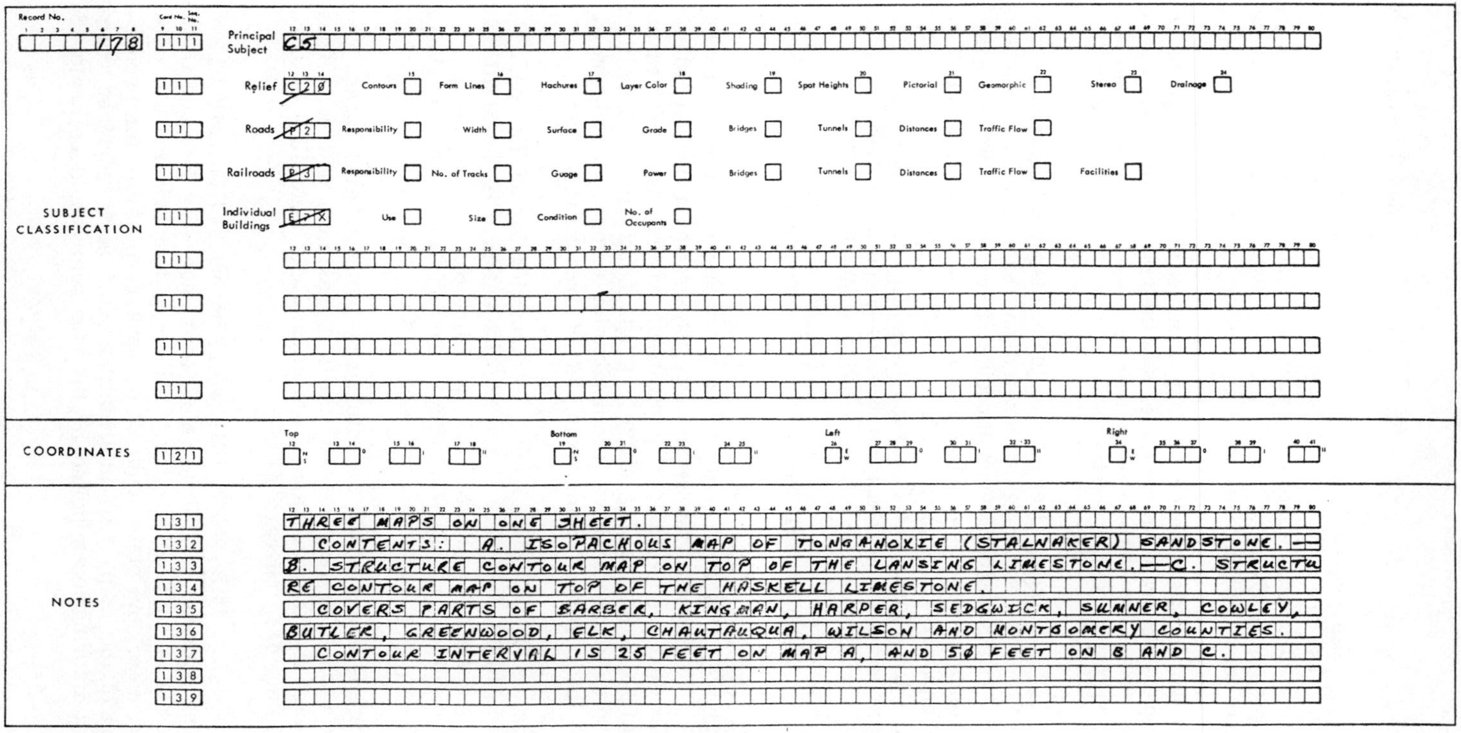

Record No. 178 | Card No. Seq. No. 111 | Principal Subject C5

SUBJECT CLASSIFICATION

11 Relief C2Ø Contours Form Lines Hachures Layer Color Shading Spot Heights Pictorial Geomorphic Stereo Drainage

11 Roads P2 Responsibility Width Surface Grade Bridges Tunnels Distances Traffic Flow

11 Railroads P3 Responsibility No. of Tracks Gauge Power Bridges Tunnels Distances Traffic Flow Facilities

11 Individual Buildings E7X Use Size Condition No. of Occupants

11

11

11

11

COORDINATES 121 Top N S ° ′ ″ Bottom N S ° ′ ″ Left E W ° ′ ″ Right E W ° ′ ″

NOTES

131 THREE MAPS ON ONE SHEET.

132 CONTENTS: A. ISOPACHOUS MAP OF TONGANOXIE (STALNAKER) SANDSTONE.—

133 B. STRUCTURE CONTOUR MAP ON TOP OF THE LANSING LIMESTONE.—C. STRUCTU

134 RE CONTOUR MAP ON TOP OF THE HASKELL LIMESTONE.

135 COVERS PARTS OF BARBER, KINGMAN, HARPER, SEDGWICK, SUMNER, COWLEY,

136 BUTLER, GREENWOOD, ELK, CHAUTAUQUA, WILSON AND MONTGOMERY COUNTIES.

137 CONTOUR INTERVAL IS 25 FEET ON MAP A, AND 5Ø FEET ON B AND C.

138

139

Figure 2. Map Cataloging Sheet.

Although each field is printed on the input sheets, only those that are required to describe a given map would be used. If a map were not issued as part of a series, for example, card Ø7 would not be used. These cataloging sheets have been designed to take information in fairly free format, and at the same time to be largely self explanatory. A person with a basic understanding of maps should be able to prepare accurate entries with a minimum of training.

The Bibliographic Citation

1. <u>Area.</u> Because of the undisputed importance of area in the cataloging of maps it has been placed as the first item in the record, even though it more truly identified the contents of the map. The general area would be entered in columns 12-15 using the area classification scheme for maps from the Library of Congress <u>Classification, Class G.</u> For example, a general map of Kansas would have 42ØØ entered, while a map of the city of Wichita would have 42Ø4.

The political subdivisions of countries, being limited in number, and generally listed in <u>Class G,</u> will be entered following the Cutter number pattern in columns 16-20. For example, Douglas County, Kansas, would be entered as 42Ø3 D7. Regional divisions and city names would be entered in plain text in the remaining positions on the card. Cities and regional areas falling within a single county or other political subdivision would have the subdivision entered in addition to the local name. Some examples of area entries are:

57ØØ		General map of Europe
4861		Subject map of Costa Rica
42Ø2	FLINT HILLS	Flint Hills of Kansas
42Ø4 D7	LAWRENCE	City of Lawrence, Douglas Co., Kansas.

Multiple areas would be entered by using several cards, one for each area represented, up to a maximum of nine. Thus, a map of Nicaragua and Costa Rica would have 485Ø on card Ø11 and 486Ø on card Ø12.

2. <u>Title.</u> The title would be entered on card Ø2 along with any additional information normally included in the body of a cataloging entry. This would include the full edition note, and statements of persons responsible for production of the map. All information would be transcribed verbatim; information supplied by the cataloger would be enclosed

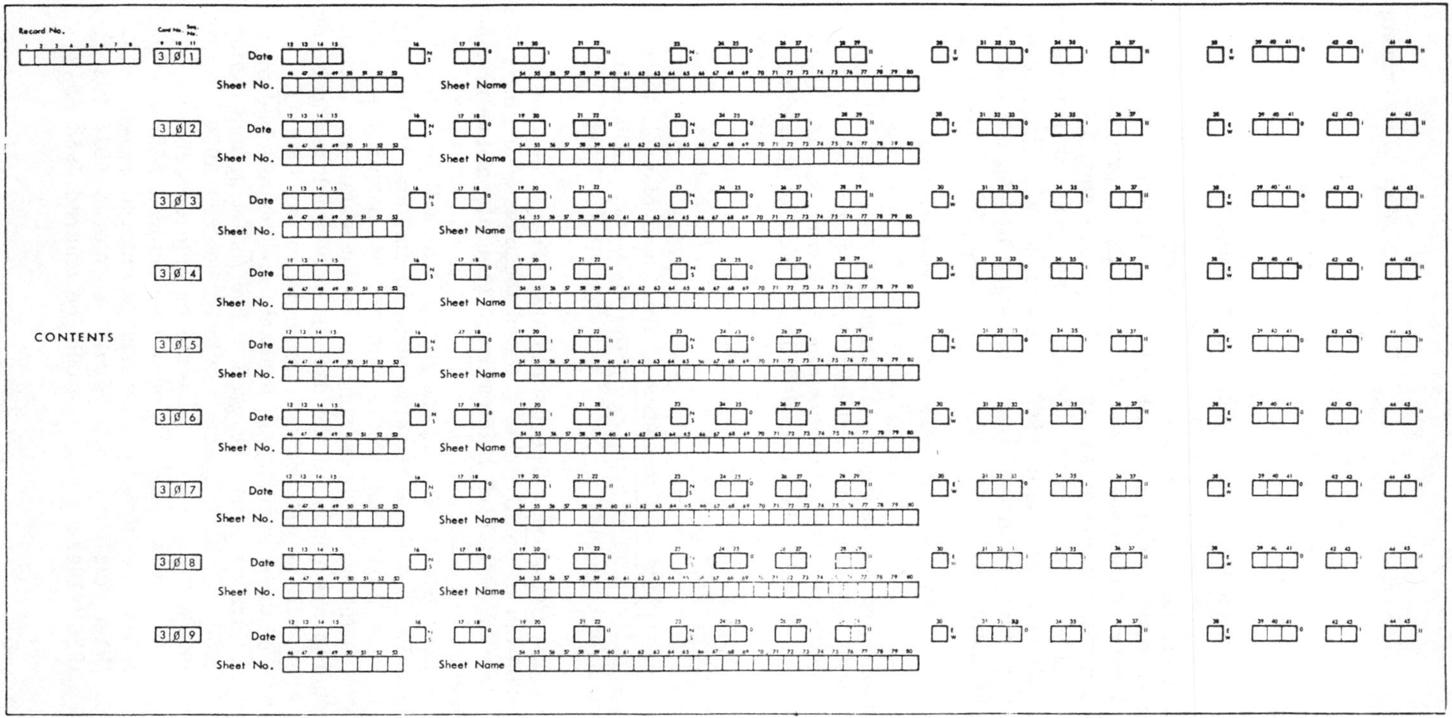

Figure 3. Map Cataloging Sheet

in brackets. The use of brackets would be, of course, dependent on having these characters on the print chain of the
computer being used.

        3. Cartographer. This field would be used to re-
trieve by the names of persons, and is not strictly limited
to cartographers. The entry would be made in the traditional
inverted order, with personal dates when known. The entry
would serve as a tracing and not normally be printed as part
of a record; any statement about the person should be included
in the title entry or in the notes. If an authority main entry
were desired, this field might be combined with that for pub-
lisher/printer, with the first card designated as the authority
for the main entry.

        4. Publisher/Printer. The names of firms and insti-
tutions associated with the production of the map would be entered on card Ø4, using the standard library rules of entry.
The entry appearing on card Ø41 would be included in the imprint; any other would be considered as tracings and appear in
the print out only when included in the body of the entry or in
notes. It would be quite possible to have the computer automatically cross reference or standardize the forms of entries
for commercial firms.

        5. Place of Publication. The place of publication
will be entered as it appears on the map, or, if supplied,
enclosed in brackets.

        6. Collation. The collation as treated here is an
accumulation of small fields grouped together on a single card:
        a. Date of Publication. The date of publication
is entered in columns 12-15. For maps on various sheets issued over a period of time the initial date will be entered in
columns 12-15 and the terminal date in columns 16-19. To
simplify the positioning of the date and yet permit the flexibility of notation for dates supplied by the cataloger, several
procedures are used. If the date is to be enclosed in brackets, an A will be entered in column 12 rather than a1. If
the date is to be enclosed in brackets and be followed by a
question mark, a J will be used. The following are examples:

        1958   would be entered A958
        1958?   would be entered J958
        195-   would be entered A95-
        195-?   would be entered J95-
        1914 -1921   would be entered A914 1921
        1936?-1942   would be entered J936 A942

These dates will be printed in the body of the entry.

      b. <u>Date of Compilation.</u> The date of compilation is here used to represent the effective date for the information on the map. For example, a 1956 reprint of a map compiled in 1921 would be listed as published in 1956, with a date compilation of 1921. As this date will not be printed in the body of the entry, brackets to indicate information supplied are not required.

      c. <u>Scale.</u> Scale will always be entered as the denominator of a representative fraction, right justified in the nine positions allowed in columns 28-36. A scale of 1:1, 140, 000, for example, would be entered ØØ114ØØØØ.

      d. <u>Number of Sheets.</u> The number of sheets is entered in columns 37-39. This serves for either of the standard notations "36 maps" or "map in 4 sheets." Single sheet maps will have ØØ1 entered, but it will not be printed in the entry.

      e. <u>Size.</u> The height and width of the map will be entered in columns 40-42 and 43-45 respectively. Although in the examples for this article I have used measurements in inches, either inches or centimeters could be used. For maps issued on more than one sheet the maximum dimensions of the map after it is assembled will be used. For sets of maps, the maximum height and maximum width occurring on individual sheets in the set will be used.

      f. <u>Color.</u> Either a <u>U</u> or a <u>C</u> will be entered in column 46 to indicate an uncolored (monochrome) or a colored map respectively.

      g. <u>Edition.</u> The number of the edition, when given on the map, will be entered in columns 47-48. This entry will be used only for machine searches, and not be printed. The full edition statement should be included in the body of the entry.

      h. <u>Indexing and Grids.</u> If a map is indexed, an <u>X</u> will be entered in column 49. The index may either be on the map itself or in a separate pamphlet; if in a pamphlet, a description should be entered in the cataloger's notes. In columns 50-53 <u>X</u>'s will be entered to indicate the types of grids shown on the map. The present format lists four kinds of grids: latitude and longitude, range and township, military and atlas grids.

      i. <u>Language.</u> The language of the map will be entered in the remaining columns of the collation card. If several languages are used, all will be entered, separated by commas. Should the map itself and the marginal information

Map Cataloging Sheet.

00000217 *Record number*

011   B010   *Area*

021   Viet Nam, Cambodia, Laos and Thailand. Wellman Chamberlin, Chief Car *Title*
022   tographer; Athos D. Grazzini, Associate Chief Cartographer. Washing
023   on

031   Chamberlin, Wellman   *Cartographer*
032   Grazzini, Athos D
041   National Geographic Society   *Publisher*

051   Washington   *Place of Pub.*

061   Date of Publication `1 9 6 7 -` (12 13 14 15 16 17 18 19)

Date of Compilation `1 9 6 7 -` (20 21 22 23 24 25 26 27)

Scale `Ø Ø 1 9 Ø Ø 8 Ø` (28 29 30 31 32 33 34 35 36)

No. of Sheets `Ø Ø 1` (37 38 39)

Height `Ø 3 9` (40 41 42)

Width `Ø 3 1` (43 44 45)

Color `C` u c (46)

Edition `Ø Ø` (47 48)

Indexed `X` B/x (49)

Grids Lat./Long. `X` B/x (50)

`Ø` B/x (51)

`Ø` B/x Mil (52)

`X` B/x Atlas (53)

Language `E N G L I S H .` (54 55 56 57 58 59 60 61 62 63 64 65 66 67 68 69 70 71 72 73 74 75 76 77 78 79 80)

071		*Series*
081	Modified conic projection	*Projection*
101	DLC Photo-copy? [20] Ø s/x Positive or Negative [21] Ø p/N Call No. G8010 1067.N3	
111		*Subjects*
112	omitted	
113		
114		
131	Issued with the National Geographic Magazine, v. 131, no. 2, Feb. 19	*Notes*
132	67.	
133	Insets: A. Continuation of Thailand.--B. [Location map]	
134	---- -----Index ... with 9,669 names. [Washington, 1967]	
135	35 p. col. map. 26 cm.	
136		
137		
138		
139		

Figure 4

be in different languages, both will be listed, with appropriate explanation made in the notes.

7. Series. The series note will be entered on card ∅71. As there is no authority entry, the term its cannot be used. Maps issued in more than one series will have additional series cards, starting with card ∅72.

8. Projection. The projection, when given, will be entered on card ∅81, in the form that it appears on the map. Should it be desirable to supply projection information, it will be enclosed in brackets.

9. Analytic. For maps issued as parts of larger publications, an analytic note will be made on card ∅9. This will be the full citation under which the larger work is cataloged:

IN SAPPER, KARL. MITTELAMERIKANISCHE REISEN UND STUDIEN AUS DEM JAHRES 1888 BIS 19∅∅. BRAUNSCHWEIG, 19∅2. P. 26.

The Union Listing

Each library holding a copy of the map being cataloged would be listed on a separate card 1∅, with the abbreviation for the library, photocopy notation, and, when desired, the call number assigned by the institution. A virgule will be used after lower case letters occurring in the library symbols. For example, MiU would be entered MI/U. Once the cataloging record is established, the list of holding institutions can be updated by the submission of an additional card 1∅ for each library acquiring the map.

Subject Classification

The subject classification system described here is not more than an outline of one way in which the problem might be approached. Multiple subjects are the rule, rather than the exception in maps, and any automated system must be designed to cover all subject possibilities. Also, map libraries have many different view points that may require different depths of subject indexing. For example, a library with its principle interest in geology would want very detailed indexing of this one subject, with minor emphasis placed on housing and population data.

In the system outlined here each subject would be entered on a separate card. The leading positions, columns 12-14, would contain the subject classification from the Library of Congress <u>Classification, Class G.</u> For example, the portrayal of relief on a map would be indicated by <u>C2</u>, geology by <u>C5</u>. A more detailed breakout of the subjects can then be made using the remaining positions on the card. On the enclosed cataloging sheet 2, ten methods of showing relief are listed. The cataloger only needs to mark with an <u>X</u> those that apply to the map. The same is true for road, railroad and building information. The cataloging sheets for a geological library would have a similar breakout by geological subjects and periods. Instructions would be included in the computer program to have these markings interpreted. <u>X</u>'s in columns 15 and 19 of the card for relief, for example, would result in the note "Relief shown by contours and shading." Positions for contour interval could be designated.

Card 111 would be reserved for the "principal subject," the one by which the map would be known. For example, a road map would have "roads" as its principal subject, a geological map, geology. The remaining subject cards would then be used for secondary subjects, as roads and terrain information on a geologic map. As a special subject field, the corner coordinates for the map might be indexed. This would permit the retrieval for a broad area, such as Western Kansas, by coordinates, locating all detailed maps of small areas falling within that portion of the state. A ten-card field has been left at the end of sheet 2 for any notes the cataloger feels should be made. For set maps, a detailed contents listing may be prepared using sheet 3, but would not be required. The use of coordinates here would permit the computer to designate the exact sheets within a large topographic set that should be retrieved for a detailed area.

Program Output

Three principal print outs would be available from this data base. The one of greatest interest to each participating organization would be a catalog of the institution's collections, generally prepared as a book catalog. The entries could, however, be printed on catalog cards. Figure 5 provides a sample of a book catalog entry. The arrangement in which the information is printed would be completely flexible, and up to the individual institution concerned. The computer would select all documents with the particular institution's

abbreviation on card 1Ø, and then print these entries in the
order specified by the institution (by area, subject, etc.).
Entries would be numbered automatically, and call numbers
included. Special indices could be prepared based on specific
subject fields or cartographers.

Each institution might also be furnished a complete
union list of all maps within its particular field of interest.
A state library, for instance, might receive a list of all maps
covering the state held by the participating libraries. Cartobibliographies, the third type of output, would actually be a
specialized form of the union listing. These could be assembled on demand based on any indexing field or combination of
fields, as, for example:

> Maps showing Missouri mineral resources (area and
> subject),
> The Maps of Henry s. Tanner (cartographer), or
> XIX Century Maps of the South Pacific (area and date).

The notation of holding institutions would normally be included.
These might be prepared for any specific research project.

Cooperative Cataloging

Although this type of automated cataloging program
could be undertaken by a single library, its potential is only
realized when it is operated cooperatively by a number of institutions. Each would submit cataloging sheets, or the finished punched cards, to a central facility designated to maintain the master data base. Each month a complete list of
new acquisitions by all libraries would be furnished to all
participating organizations. Some of the cooperating institutions would not require the depth of cataloging afforded by
the full catalog sheets. Simplified code sheets like that in
figure 4 could be prepared showing only those items of interest to that particular institution. The record number
would be filled in at the top, and the succeeding entries would
be entered on specific lines. The card numbers at the left
correspond to the card numbers on the full cataloging sheets.
The lines are just long enough to permit an elite typewriter
to include the maximum numbers of characters permitted on
a single card; typewriter margins could be set accordingly.

When one of the participating libraries added new maps
to its collections that were already included in the master data
base, it would only need to submit a series of card 1Ø's list-

ing the record numbers of the entries in the master data
base.   The entries would automatically be included in the
next edition, or supplement to, the institution's catalog.   For
a specialized library requiring a more detailed subject classification than had originally been made when the catalog entry
was first submitted, a revised subject card would also be submitted along with the union list card.

An institution with its own computer facility would be
able to receive the complete data base in digital form
(punched cards or magnetic tape) for local use, relieving it
of dependence on a central facility for production of its own
records, and yet providing it with the benefits of cooperative
cataloging.   As the conversion between different digital storage media is not difficult, punched paper tape might be used
for initial preparation of catalog entries by some institutions
when this would better fit in with other automation plans.   A
successful program would require a great deal of effort by
the participating organizations to satisfy all needs.   But the
type of approach described here provides the flexibility that
would be the key to new horizons in map cataloging.

VIET NAM, CAMBODIA, LAOS AND THAILAND. WELLMAN CHAMBERLIN,
CHIEF CARTOGRAPHER: ATHOS D. GRASSINI, ASSOCIATE CHIEF CARTOGRAPHER.
WASHINGTON, NATIONAL GEOGRAPHIC SOCIETY, 1967
  SCALE 1:1,900,800. COLORED. 39" x 31". INDEXED.
GEOGRAPHIC, ATLAS GRIDS.
  MODIFIED CONIC PROJECTION.
  ISSUED WITH THE NATIONAL GEOGRAPHIC MAGAZINE, V. 131, NO. 2,
FEB. 1967.
  INSETS: A. CONTINUATION OF THAILAND. --B. LOCATION MAP
---- ----INDEX ... WITH 9,669 NAMES. WASHINGTON, 1967.
  35 P. COL. MAP. 26 CM.

Figure 5

SOME PROBLEMS IN CLASSIFYING
AND CATALOGUING MAPS*

Joan Winearls

There are probably as many individual map cataloguing
and classification systems in the world as there are map libraries and I think that the time has come to do something
about this. Surely we are wasting an enormous amount of
time laboriously working out our own area lists, our own classifications, and our own card styles. What is needed is a
detailed map cataloguing and classification system which we
could all implement; we would then all save a considerable
amount of time, effort, and money. What I would like to do
now is to suggest some of the problems in devising such a
system.

The card you see here represents one of the hundreds
of systems I mentioned earlier--that of the Map Library at
the University of Toronto! Nevertheless it is probably a
fairly typical card, in that it generally satisfies the requirements for recording the information about a map. There are
places for a call number, for an area name, subject, scale,
date, title, author, physical details (no. of sheets, col.,

```
3513        ALGOMA, Ont. (Dist.)  ADMINISTRATIVE.
A4F7            1:253,440.  1960
253
1960            Parts of the districts of Algoma and
            Sudbury.  Toronto, Ontario Dept. of Lands
            & Forests, Lands & Surveys Brahch.
            (Map 32a)
                1 sheet.  Col.  46 X 40in.

                roads; railways; townships; provincial
            parks & forests; mining divisions; land
            grants; power; survey grid.
```

*Reprinted by permission from Proceedings of the First Na-
tional Conference on Canadian Map Libraries, Ottawa, 1967;
27-32.

size), and some description.   Moreover it is a unit card or
main card; that is, an exact duplicate of this card, with
added entries where necessary, will appear in all card files.

Classification

First of all then the classification represented by the
call number (1).   What is a classification system and what
is a good one for maps?

1.   Basically a classification system is a method of
physically locating the map in the collection and because it
is a systematic organization of some kind of knowledge, it
allows browsing.
2.   For maps the main connotation represented by the
first and/or succeeding lines must outline the exact area of
the map.   There should also be notations for subject, date,
and possibly scale and authority.   The inclusion of the last
two items depends largely on the size of the collection.
3.   The particular classification must also be worked
out in some detail before it is used and kept up to date in a
thorough fashion.   Otherwise, individual expansions of a basic,
common classification system will result in what is in fact a
multitude of systems.

Heading or Entry

For an alphabetically arranged catalogue the heading
or entry is of course essential.   It is now generally accepted
that the main entry for maps must be under area and not author.   I say generally because the new Anglo-American Cataloguing Rules (2) which were published this year still maintain that the main entry for maps should be author.   This
code represents many years of work by committees of leading cataloguers from Britain, the United States, and Canada.
That they should still recommend main entry by author when
probably no map library in the world is now or has been for
20 years using this system is either a travesty of our profession or an indication of our disorganization.

In addition to area entry, what else should go into the
heading?   Naturally there has been much difference of opinion
over this.   The Final Report of the Committee on Map Cataloguing, Geography and Map Division of the Special Libraries
Association (3), recommended area-date-scale.   Thomas
Smith's system (4) at the University of Kansas called for
area-subject-scale.   The American Geographical Society's

system (5) is area-subject, arranged chronologically.   Mine
is yet another one--area-subject-scale-date.

At least, an area-subject entry appears essential.   My
choice then has been to follow this with scale and date.   Both
are useful as entry and filing mechanisms and I put scale
first because date is meaningless with topographic series.
With subject maps, date is always considered of greater importance than scale.   However, in practice, once the user
has found his way to Canada - Population, for instance, he
has narrowed his choice down to few enough cards that he
can locate the date he is interested in with relative ease.
But scale-date or date-scale the order does not matter that
much.

Area Name

There are two problems here; first, do we want a
direct or indirect designation, and secondly, how do we establish the actual name?   Do we use the direct name such as
Algoma or an indirect name, such as Canada-Ontario-Algoma.
The indirect method takes up much room and is certainly
harder to establish.   When, for instance can you leave out
intervening steps?   Do you say Canada-Ontario-L. Huron-
Georgian Bay or Canada-Ontario-Georgian Bay.   At the same
time the indirect method is a verbalization of the classification and is not really practical if you are going to supply a
classed catalogue or shelf list for your users.

The actual establishment of the area names is perhaps
the main problem and much work is needed here.   There are
some reasonably good sources and lists of names: Gazetteer
of Canada; U.S. Board on Geographic Names, Gazetteers (a
world-wide collection); Columbia Lippincott Gazetteer of the
World; Times Index-gazetteer of the World (6-9).   These help
us to make decisions on spelling.   There is however no official gazetteer for the United States.   Nor is the United States
covered in the series of the United States Board on Geographic Names.   And as a majority of countries in the world also
lack official gazetteers we have no alternates to the American
series.

The other large gap in established procedure is in the
rules for the qualification of the area name.   The new Anglo-
American Cataloguing Rules (2) include some specifications
but these are not detailed enough for a map library.   (a) To
what extent must we identify a name?   If we have an entry

for Mulmur Twp. in Ontario should we say Mulmur Twp.,
Dufferin Co., Ont. or just Mulmur Twp., Ontario. (b) Do
we indicate the form of the area in brackets as in this ex-
ample--(Dist.) or should it be contained in the name as Algoma District, Ontario. (c) And then there is the very large
problem of older names. The recommendation in the book,
Subject Headings (7), is that we should use the latest name
for an area if the boundaries have remained substantially the
same, with cross-references from the older names. Should
we then reject names like Upper Canada, Lower Canada, and
York or should we, as map librarians, give some consideration to the problem from the particular point of view of maps.
This is certainly a problem for the collection that is trying
to provide one catalogue covering both early and current maps.

Subject

The subject presents another topic of concern.

1. There is no complete or proper list of map subjects and one must be compiled. The LC list of Subject
Headings, 7th ed. (11) is lacking in some concepts and has
awkward terms for others. The map librarian, therefore,
to establish terms must also use geographical dictionaries,
as well as some of the small lists compiled by other map
libraries.

2. But what sort of subject headings do we want?
Broad concepts or very specific headings which would require more work to establish. Should a map of the locations
of marinas in Ontario have the heading "marinas," or should
it have a general term, "navigation." Subdivision is also a
problem if you have this sort of heading, as the space is
limited. The tremendous increase in subject maps in the
last decade is putting more and more pressure on us and
we should seek a consensus before the situation gets out of
hand.

Body of the Card

The details of format on the rest of the card are relatively unimportant to me. I prefer to follow standard library
procedure (Anglo-American Cataloguing Rules) as much as possible here because I believe that users are trained to read
cards like this and they can therefore get much more out of
them. The physical detail, for instance, can go where the
collation is located as it is the same type of information.
The notes can be detailed or non-existent. I myself do not

particularly like a box card but I can see some of its virtues.
It is certainly almost impossible to use on a 3 X 5 card and
a 5 X 8 card may or may not be the answer. The important
thing is that we should have at least a basic card style. This
would then leave the archivist free to have extensive notes for
his early maps and the current map librarian free to have
notes or not as he wishes.

Classed vs. Alphabetical Catalogue

Probably the most important question of all, though,
is that of the type of catalogue. Do we want a classed or an
alphabetical catalogue? That is, should the card file be arranged by the number or by the heading. Many map libraries
are in fact using a classified catalogue or shelflist and many
other map libraries have recently been finding it unsatisfactory. Generally speaking as far as book libraries are concerned the classified catalogue is better known in Europe
than it is in North America.

Classed Catalogue

What does it require? And what are its virtues?

1. To a certain extent area lends itself to a hierarchical classification. It is very useful to find all maps of
Canada together in one section of the file or all maps of Ontario.

2. Moreover there is an automatic progression in the
mind from the greater to the lesser area, i.e., North Amer-
ica--Canada--Ontario--Ottawa.

3. Other groupings, however, cannot be termed hierarchical and are chosen arbitrarily. Is there for instance
any logical way to break down Africa or the United States?
Do you move from east to south to west or vice versa.
Should you have a few large sections such as north, central,
and south and then move to individual countries or states, or
should you have 5 to 6 groupings? There are probably several equally satisfactory methods for grouping maps of these
areas.

4. Moreover, when we come to the smaller units
such as counties or cities it seems preferable to group these
alphabetically.

5. How does the user approach this? (a) A full alphabetical index is of course essential. (b) A map of the
world is required visually outlining the classification system.

For example, here is one used by the United States Army
Map Service.   This shows up to three levels: continents--
grouping of nations--and individual countries.   A larger one
would be needed for Canada to show the breakdown to province level at least.   (c) A subject index (or catalogue) and
possibly an author index must also be provided.   (d) A copy
of the classification should also be available to give the user
some sense of the breakdown.

The Alphabetical Catalogue

1.   The merit of the alphabetical catalogue is that it
requires one step in the search instead of the two required
by the classed catalogue.   Moreover, there are many requests that are satisfied by going directly to the area name
that the user has in mind.
2.   In this catalogue, the entry now shoulders the
main responsibility for guiding the user.   Here the area name
assumes the greatest importance and the necessity of specific
rules for establishing it becomes obvious.   The whole question of direct or indirect entry becomes momentous, to say
nothing of the position and merit of the other three elements
in the heading.

Filing rules must be carefully worked out and explained
to the user.   And cross-references are essential.   For instance, if the 1:63, 360 Department of Highway maps of Ontario are entered under Ontario as a series then references
must be made from the name of each county.

What Can Be Said For and Against These Two Systems?

1.   In both methods maps will still be buried in topographic series, subject series, and broader connotations.
Only the computer can really remedy a situation such as this.
2.   But with facilities for rapid and cheap reproduction of cards we can seriously consider using both approaches.
One could then have four files: one by the classification (with
the map and the classification code to hand); one by area
first (the area should be the direct name in this instance);
one by subject; one by author.

In using both the classified and alphabetical approaches,
we would substantially increase the access to the catalogue
for the users.   It would at the same time serve as a compromise for map librarians that now strongly recommend one
or the other.   These in my opinion are some of the main

problems that must be worked out before we can hope for a
system complete enough for widespread adoption. If we could
arrive at some agreement on the broad issues of map cataloguing and classification and if we were then able to compile complete lists of rules for area names and map subjects
and a complete classification system then Canadian map libraries can make a major contribution in the field. Because,
in Canada, map libraries are in an embryonic state we have
a unique opportunity to organize ourselves before it is too
late.

REFERENCES

1.   This classification number is part of my own Canadian
      expansion of U. S. Library of Congress, Subject Cata-
      loguing Division, Classification Class 'G', 3rd ed.
      Washington, 1954; 30-183.
2.   American Library Association. Anglo-American Cata-
      loguing Rules, North American text. Chicago:
      A. L. A. , 1967.
3.   Special Libraries Association, Geography and Map Divi-
      sion, Committee on Map Cataloguing. Final Report
      ... SLA G&M Div. Bull. , 13:19-24, 1953. Reprinted
      in Bulletin, 24:3-16 April 1956.
4.   Smith, T. R. The Map Collection in a General Library:
      A Manual for Classification and Processing Proce-
      dures. Lawrence: University of Kansas, 1961.
5.   American Geographical Society. Cataloguing and Filing
      Rules for Maps and Atlases in the Society's Collec-
      tion. New York, 1964.
6.   Gazetteer of Canada. Ottawa: Queen's Printer, 1952-   ,
      Vol. 1.
7.   U. S. Board on Geographic Names. Gazetteers. Wash-
      ington, 1955- .
8.   Columbia Lippincott Gazetteer of the World. New York:
      Columbia University Press [1962].
9.   The Times (London). Index-Gazetteer of the World.
      London: Times Publishing Co. , 1965.
10. Haykin, David J. Subject Headings: A Practical Guide.
      Washington, D. C. : U. S. Gov. Printing Office, 1951.
11. U. S. Library of Congress. List of Subject Headings.
      7th ed. Washington, 1966.

6. MAP STORAGE AND PRESERVATION

CONSERVATION AND CIRCULATION IN MAP LIBRARIES*

Patricia Greechie Alonso

As extremely clumsy as they are eminently useful, maps require special attitudes and operations for maintaining them in good condition as well as for promoting their use. Such operations receive exact and comprehensive description in the classic reference on physical techniques for map handling: <u>Maps, Their Care, Repair, and Preservation in Libraries</u> by Clara Egli LeGear (Washington, D.C., Library of Congress Map Division, rev. ed. 1956). This paper therefore considers the choice of such techniques and concentrates on attitudes and policies in map conservation and circulation. Deterioration of the collection may occur at any stage of processing, consultation, or storage and retrieval; therefore, each member of the staff should be consciously concerned with this pervasive problem. The chief map librarian, entrusted with the dual responsibilities of serving consultants and preserving maps, must constantly guide the staff in proper maintenance. The head of acquisitions should select maps for durability and wearability as well as for content. Cataloguers should look out for rare and irreplaceable material, in order to effect as soon as possible special treatment in storage and handling. Map room assistants have the delicate task of policing users who may not be familiar with special map handling techniques.

Maps in books and atlases present problems typical of illustrations in general, to be treated with standard conservation procedures. The map librarian also faces the difficulties of diverse forms peculiar to areal representation, such as globes, three-dimensional models, relief maps that cannot be folded, rolled maps, wall maps, large sheet maps, desk maps,

*Reprinted by permission from Special Libraries Association, Geography and Map Division, <u>Bulletin</u> No. 74 (1968), 15-18.

and maps with special overlays or coverings. These forms
are usually not standard in size, strength, folded size, or
durability, and lack the hard attached covers that protect
books. Stacking or moving sheet maps raises the dangers of
fraying, ripping, tearing, and wrinkling, as the map room
assistant files the maps in drawers, or as the consultant
turns the map for better viewing. However, no other graphic-
literary form communicates so much data so clearly, perma-
nently, and concisely; let us realize the value of maps and
consider now the ways best to keep them.

The best possible protection for a map is a back
mounting, but the process is quite expensive, as are good
backing linen and gauze. Few libraries can afford to mount
all their maps. The protection of the future may possibly
be lamination after de-acidifying, but this form needs further
developing and the test of time. For now, the economically
feasible way to reinforce maps is with adhesive cloth strips
placed along folds, edges, and cracks, and under areas of
strain. This alternative also saves margins often trimmed
in mounting, therefore improving the conservation of histor-
ically interesting details such as extra wide margins or
decorative frames or notations by users. Both mounting and
taping can conveniently be done in the library by relatively
unskilled workers, although the rarer maps may demand professional mounting. Repairs are usually made with modern
transparent library tape or adhesive tape. Even repaired
tears cause trouble, because the slightest rough edge of tape
catches as the maps are stacked for storage or removed for
use. Tape may also discolor or dry the area it covers.
Therefore, mending must be regarded as a very poor second
to mounting the whole map or replacing it.

Maps do not lend themselves to microcopying unless
very expensive machines are available to provide full size
and very clear reproductions for use. Such economy must
be practiced in producing maps with the smallest possible
type faces and lightest line weights and subtle color mixes
on the original map that reduction or reproduction often results in illegible squiggles on the copy, instead of carbon-
copy accuracy. Full size optical projections on a screen are
readable, but very difficult to consult for specific details. If
one tries to measure or trace a projected map copy, one
usually trips visually over one's own fingers. This last comment applies to the common machines available to read microfilm or microfiche today. In the development stage are cathode ray tubes (like television screen) over which the viewer

can trace or read small detail.   Photographing black and white
maps without reduction or with enlargement is quite satisfactory, but color photography remains too expensive at this
time to make photographing colored maps feasible for general
purposes, although publishers produce some fine color reproductions based on photographs.   Reprography is limited at
this time by the size that the machines can handle.   Usually
it is not advisable to fold the average sheet map many times
to fit standard office copying machine sizes.

Folds weaken maps and predispose to tearing, so it
is good practice to store maps as flat as possible.   Office
file cabinets that receive the material vertically serve for
storage of desk maps, but are detrimental to larger formats
that must be creased to fit.   Vertical files consisting of
large panels on which maps are hung do prevent folds but
require staples or clamps or hooks and eyes to hold the maps
up.   This kind of case also takes up more floor space than
alternate choices.   It is more fitted to browsing than to consultation, because the user has no flat surface on which to
write, trace or copy.   Roller shelves and horizontal drawers
are best suited to map storage.   The top of the case may be
used for work space.   All but the largest maps fit unfolded
into the bigger drawers on the market today.   To protect
from dust and to permit easier sorting of many maps in a
drawer, heavy paper folders are generally used.   They can
be labeled to distinguish maps of different areas or different
topics in the same drawer.   These folders also absorb the
wear caused by sliding maps in and out, prime source of
wrinkles and rips.   Some map libraries use folders only
doubled over; others use envelope styles.   Wall maps on
rollers present peculiar storage difficulties, because if left
rolled for any considerable length of time, they deteriorate
badly.   To avoid this, they may be removed from the roller
and cut up to drawer size; or they may be chemically treated,
an expensive process, and left rolled on special rods and
covered with custom-made cloth protectors.

No matter what kind of case is used, maps profit from
the same air-conditioned storage rooms that are best for other library material.   Per collection unit, maps require even
more floor space than other library holdings.   Handling even
small numbers of awkward, flapping, large maps requires
much maneuvering room, ample consultation space, and copi-
ous storage spots (as well as considerable strength and a certain swinging skill on the part of the handler).   Maps demand
ample consultation space also because often the only map

available on the studied topic is in a foreign language which
must therefore be used with the help of foreign language glos-
saries, special indexes, or translation manuals; handling
these reference materials on the high counter of many map
consultation rooms, with the table-sized maps sliding beneath
the reference books and one's magnifying glass rumpling
pages and getting lost in the process of looking up terms,
challenges the user not to harm the materials and the librarian to suggest optimum handling techniques without obstructing
study. The librarian must seek to provide adequate shelves
and table space in the consultation area to facilitate reference,
for consultants may be able to make do with limited space,
but the maps will suffer. Map libraries are usually reference
libraries that do not circulate their materials for use outside
the building. However, they often honor requests for interlibrary loans. Transportation by messenger is the best method, but if the mails must be used, rigid packing in stout
tubes serves best. Big, bulky maps in boxes often suffer
creasing and sometimes cracking through the outer covering.

Because maps offer special acquisitions problems,
even a map printed in quantity and for sale may be considered
difficult to replace and therefore not for loaning. The map
librarian must exercise particular tact in refusing to loan
materials which, were they books printed in the same year
and in the same way the maps in question were, would be
suitable for loaning. The copying equipment considered above
allows limited loaning of black and white photocopies, but
photocopies of colored maps are generally not available.
When loans are made, the standard multiple-unit request
form of the Interlibrary Loan Committee of the Association
of College and Reference Libraries provides a file copy that
records the item, borrowers, and time limit, if any. The
American Geographical Society Map Department has their own
mimeographed loan agreement, of which one copy goes out
with the item and the other is filed under date loaned. There
are few enough loans so that a separate file by item is not
needed. Columbia University Geology Map Library uses
standard patron-completed charge cards, treated for maps as
for books.

Verification of map requests is often difficult because
cartobibliographic control is not yet complete, or rather,
adequate, as "complete" is too grandiose a term for such an
interminable task. Even the best in international cartobibliography, Bibliographie Cartographique International, lags
years behind the publication dates of the maps included. The

sender of interlibrary loan requests for maps does well just
to select the nearest map library from the Special Libraries
Association Directory, <u>Map Collections in the United States
and Canada</u> (New York, 1954).   If the library selected does
not have the required item, usually it can suggest another
possible source and verify the reference for the sender.
Since map collections are difficult to search, misplaced maps
are even more of a disaster in a map library than misplaced
books in a book collection.   Instead of checking the call numbers on the spines of books, the map librarian and assistants
must search maps in piles in folders in drawers.   Because
of this exaggerated trouble arising from sloppy filing, map
libraries optimally employ full-time and well-trained assistants to "shelve" maps who are better qualified than the average part-time, non-professional library helpers.

(These observations on conservation and circulation
are based on readings in the general area of library conservation and circulation practices and on visits to the British
Museum Map Room, the Museum of the City of Barcelona,
and various New York City map collections and primarily,
on experience working as assistant to the Map Curator in the
American Geographical Society Map Department.)

MAP LIBRARIES--SPACE AND EQUIPMENT

Catherine I. Bahn

The Geography and Map Division is sharing in the Special Libraries Association program to prepare a set of professional standards for space and equipment. As a result of the work of the Division's Committee on Standards, we are submitting this report on space and equipment for Geography and Map Libraries. The work of the Committee in general was based on a preliminary study of the literature on both map and other library standards, current research and development on documentation and on plans for libraries such as the Army Map Service, the National Archives, the American Geographical Society, Dartmouth College's Baker Library, the Library of Congress, Rand McNally & Co., General Drafting Company, the University of Illinois' Map Library and their Geological Library, the District of Columbia's Public Library and many others. In addition, the Committee studied various equipment and supply catalogs, consulted competent authorities and visited other libraries prior to preparing a preliminary report.

First and foremost, we agreed that the librarian should be consulted when a new library is planned or when a change is made in the location of the Map and Geography Library. If the librarian is not a specialist in geography, cartography or maps, such a specialist (preferably one familiar with library operations) should be consulted. Planning a new or renovating an old map library should start with a program statement covering objectives, activities and requirements. This provides a basis for using general standards or evolving specific ones to fit the special circumstances of the library concerned. There are differences in the types of reference books and maps used in college, university, public, private

*Reprinted by permission from Special Libraries Association, Geography and Map Division, Bulletin No. 46 (1961), 3-17.

(industry) and government agency libraries and in the amounts
and kinds of services rendered.

The map library need not be restricted to library activities if the policy of the supporting agency permits such
activities as group instruction, tours or visits.   Arrangements
for these should be made in advance.   Some libraries which
handle security classified materials could not permit the entrance of unauthorized personnel or a non-library use of the
area.   The multi-purpose room facilities in some larger libraries might be utilized for map or geography lectures,
meetings or conferences, generally to be held after regular
working hours.   A detailed plan involving these and related
factors will help to insure the full and efficient use of available space.   The physical facilities of the library are a symbol of service within the environment and should represent
functional efficiency and beauty.   Consultation with an architect is a necessity to achieve this.   Parking space for the
staff and public is rapidly becoming an item of primary importance.

A map library, which should be an integral department within the parent organization, should be as close as
possible to supporting operations, both to facilitate maximum
use by readers and to expedite work of the library staff.
There should be ample space and equipment to arrange materials properly and to provide for the comfort of employees.
The physical facilities of the map library should, for maximum economy and effectiveness, conform wherever possible
to equipment throughout the general library or organization.
Sections frequently used by readers, such as the reading
areas, bookcases, lending desk, catalogs, information resources, etc., should be located in logical functional relationship to each other and to locations for receiving, cataloging
and physical processing of materials.   One large room may
be preferable to several small rooms.   When desired, divisions may be made by arrangement of file cases, book
shelves or other equipment.   Map rooms should be located
on the first or ground floor and adjacent to the map files.
This location is essential because the weight, and resultant
stress load of the map cases, requires special strengthening
of building supports if map cases are placed on an upper
floor. (See Figure 1).   The reading room should be part of
or adjacent to the map files for ease in transporting the
wanted maps and atlases to readers.   Because of the bulk of
special materials such as maps, atlases, plastic models and
globes, it is highly desirable to provide a separate reading

Figure 1. This represents filled cases about 4' x 3' in size with 2"-deep drawers. For larger or smaller flat file cases, refer to various catalogs for weights and heights as well as sizes and project. For average of 100 maps/drawer divide weight by 2. The resultant weight per square foot should be checked with the building inspector prior to height determination.

No. of Maps	No. of 2" Drawers	Weight in lbs. per 5-drawer section-case	Wt. of Maps-lbs.	Top and Base wt.	Total wt.	Area in sq. ft.	Height	Weight / square ft.
200	1		68	83				
1,000	5(1-sect.)	245	340	83	668	12	2'	55 lbs.
2,000	10(2-sect.)	490	680	83	1,253	12	3 1/3'	107 lbs.
3,000	15(3-sect.)	735	1,020	83	1,838	12	4 2/3'	158 lbs.
4,000	20(4-sect.)	980	1,360	83	2,483	12	6'	207 lbs.
5,000	25(5-sect.)	1,225	1,700	83	3,008	12	7 1/3'	264 lbs.
6,000	30(6-sect.)	1,470	2,040	83	3,593	12	8 2/3'	310 lbs.

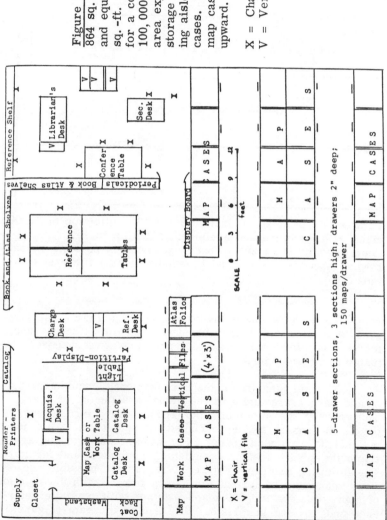

Figure 2. Map Room.
864 sq. ft. of furniture
and equipment in a 2016-
sq.-ft. room (48' x 42')
for a collection of
100,000 maps. Work
area expandable into
storage area by narrow-
ing aisles between map
cases. Storage area
map cases expandable
upward.

X = Chair
V = Vertical Files

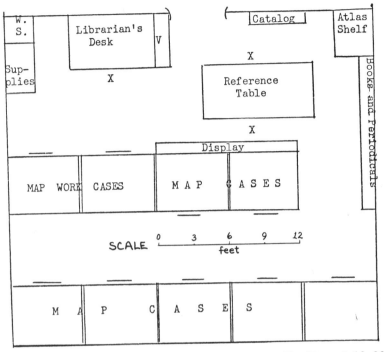

Figure 3. An adequate installation for a collection of 10,000 maps with furniture and equipment sized as in Figure 2. Room size is 20' x 20'. Space expansion is possible by narrowing map case aisles and by extending map file cases upward.

room. For the small or average size map library one large area is preferred. It may be subdivided for reference use, for storage, for working and for administrative purposes, by furniture or equipment.

Careful planning of the arrangement of equipment should be a prerequisite to the actual assignment of space. To arrive at the minimum floor space needed for storage, double the square footage occupied by equipment. This does not include expansion space. For reading and working areas, triple the square footage occupied by equipment and furniture. The following diagram (Figure 2) represents possible use of floor space and equipment for a map library with a collection of approximately 100,000 maps together with requisite reference and working materials. The second diagram (Figure 3) shows an adequate installation for a collection of 10,000 maps. Three large, five-drawer sections will hold a maximum of 3000 maps and provide work space on the top to handle maps for processing or examination. Libraries with historical or single-map collections may have only 500 to 1,000 maps within that space. Adjustments in weight and space should be made for the specific map case sizes and heights used in a particular library. An additional three sections should be maintained for supplies and for maps in an incomplete stage of processing.

Map collections range from the small (fewer than 5000 maps) through the medium (100,000 to 500,000) to the very large with a million or more maps. Space allotments will vary from a corner of a library proper to a separate building or wing. The smaller collections may include only a few cases adjacent to the bookshelves, making use of reference materials in the regular reading rooms. The medium sized collections usually have special reading rooms, which in many instances include the map cases, reference materials and other equipment as part of the area. (Refer to Figure 2.) Many of the map libraries are now crowded into limited space with narrow aisles and overloaded map cases piled four to six high, which makes for inefficient filing and retrieval of maps. The growth in the map and geography libraries has been phenomenal with collections doubling in size every 20 years. The rate of expansion should be planned in accordance with the probable growth of the parent organization itself.

A map library should include--in addition to map filing equipment--roller shelves for large atlases, shelves for reference books, a magazine rack, vertical files for pamphlets, documents, indexes and clippings, and card catalogs or other information retrieval devices. Globes and relief models effectively displayed are decorative items as well as reference tools. Exhibition cases, display boards, or swinging panels may be used likewise for maps or books. A glass-topped, illuminated tracing table and a drafting table may be useful for libraries supporting map making or cartographic course activities. Duplicating and microreading equipment may be advantageous if the map library is large. Readers should be free to use the facilities of the map library but in general, access to the map files should be limited to authorized staff members. The location of reference materials and service points should be well marked with legible signs, as should the specific map case areas.

Modular planning is possible for established medium
or large libraries only if the size of the collections is known.
Their measurement by the cu-book formula may be supplemented by the area required for storage of a set number of
maps as shown in Figure 2.   Arrangements should be made
for the purchase of coordinated equipment and furniture from
companies such as Art Metal, Inc., Sjöstrom, Cole Steel
Equipment and the Library Bureau of Remington Rand (see
page 377). Because actual use of maps may be a noisy procedure, sound absorbing floors and ceilings are advisable in
the reading room and the work areas.   This should be taken
care of through the services of the library architect.   A rubber or vinyl tile floor covering has proved suitable for the
Library of Congress, as has a cork type material used on
the ceilings.

Air conditioning is strongly recommended for the
preservation of maps, atlases, books, printed materials and
globes as well as for the comfort of staff and readers.   Experts recommend that books be kept in a place where the
temperature is between 65° and 75° F. with the humidity between 30 and 50 percent.   Filtered air will also save much
cleaning of materials as a large part of the dirt is removed
from the air before it is circulated in the area.   While outside lighting makes for a pleasant atmosphere in a reading
room, care must be taken to avoid the glare of direct sunlight.   Because of the small print used on many maps and
the lack of clarity of many of the older maps, supplementary
artificial lighting is needed to eliminate glare and shadows.
Indirect, incandescent lighting producing uniform illumination
of 30 to 50 foot-candles (depending on reflecting, balance and
color) is recommended.   Professional advice would be required for each situation to insure the correct amount of
light.

If the work flow diagram (Figure 4) is applied to the
two map room diagrams (Figures 2 and 3), the work may be
identified within the specific areas.   The librarian should
have an office, or an area affording some degree of privacy,
since administrative duties require conferences, interviews
and telephone conversations.   There must be a general service desk from which reader activities can be supervised.
Each staff member must have a desk in his own working
area.   Although some libraries allot only 40 square feet per
person for book cataloging, a more realistic floor space allotment for the map library is from 65 to 100 square feet.
This may include a desk and a table, possibly to be shared.

A separate work room or screened area which includes a
place to process the map materials is desirable.   Supply
cabinets, coat racks, a sink and a drinking fountain are
also needed.

        Card catalogs, graphic indexes and general and spe-
cial reference work should be located between the reading
room and the work area for accessibility by the staff as well
as the readers.   Use of equipment or furniture as partitions
simplifies placing of the various operations in proper relation
to one another.   The service area where circulation and reference activities are conducted should be near the library entrance and adjacent to the reading tables.   Some of the map
libraries use special equipment for viewing microprints,
microfilm and microcards.   In some cases, the parent library may make such equipment available for use by the map
library.   Information and retrieval systems based on automation have not been widely adopted in the map field.   A
clear concept of requirements before consultation with manufacturers regarding equipment of this kind is essential.   The
Special Libraries Association publication Scientific and Technical Libraries--Their Organization and Management, 2nd
ed., 1972 includes information on this subject (pp. 31-35).
Security classified maps and documents must be stored in
safes or vaults in accordance with regulations.   Safes must
have adequate locks, fireproofing and weight.   A vaulted area
simplifies the work of storing these materials.   Cole Steel
Equipment Co., Mosler and Shaw-Walker are specialists for
files of this type (see pp. 376-377).

        The size and bulky nature of maps and atlases make
it especially desirable in the map library to have the storage
area adjacent to both the reading room and the processing
unit for economical movement of materials.   Standardized
equipment and supplies should be used for uniformity and in-
tra-library cooperation and exchange.   Catalog cards and
card cases, as well as book shelving, are examples.   Thomas'
Register of Manufacturers is useful for a listing of dealers,
as are local telephone directories.   Sections for shelving may
be of standard type--either wood or metal.   The shelves
should be adjustable to permit non-standard spacing for special reference materials.   Shelf width should be 9 to 12
inches.   On the average, 7 ordinary books or 5 bound periodical volumes occupy one foot of shelf space.   This "cu-
book" formula (a standard unit representing the averaged
sized volume) indicates that one hundred "cu-books" will go
into a section measuring 36" x 7'6" x 9".   Special wide

Figure 4.   Work Flow Chart.

Administrative

Policy, Correspondence, Personnel

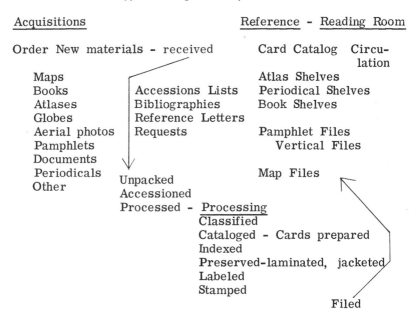

Acquisitions   Reference - Reading Room

Order New materials - received   Card Catalog   Circu-
                                                     lation
   Maps   Atlas Shelves
   Books   Accessions Lists   Periodical Shelves
   Atlases   Bibliographies   Book Shelves
   Globes   Reference Letters
   Aerial photos   Requests   Pamphlet Files
   Pamphlets   Vertical Files
   Documents
   Periodicals   Unpacked   Map Files
   Other   Accessioned
                      Processed - Processing
                                   Classified
                                   Cataloged - Cards prepared
                                   Indexed
                                   Preserved-laminated, jacketed
                                   Labeled
                                   Stamped
                                              Filed

There is a direct flow of materials from acquisitions
to processing files for reference use to circulation.

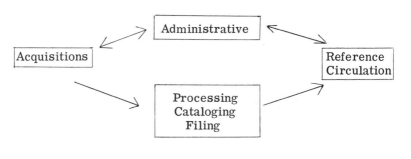

shelving or built-in wooden cabinets may be used for oversize atlases and folios.   Roller shelves, such as those used
in the Library of Congress' Map Reading Room, provide excellent protection for frequently-used large atlases, reference

catalogs and indexes.   The selection of suitable filing equipment is very important.   A librarian needs to consider the
amount and nature of the material to be filed, the wall and
floor space available, the accessibility of items in the files,
the objectives of the collection, servicing the collection, future expansion, relative costs and availability of equipment.

Mrs. Clara E. Le Gear, Head of the Reference and
Bibliography Section of the Map Division in the Library of
Congress states in Maps, Their Care, Repair and Preserva-
tion in Libraries that:

"Maps have certain characteristics that make special storage equipment imperative.   It is when their
requirements are ignored that maps are found to be
troublesome 'stepchildren.'   Properly housed and
thoughtfully handled, maps become exceedingly useful
tools....
"Map files may be wood or steel, horizontal or
vertical, built-in or sectional.   The choice of wooden
or steel cases will probably be governed by library
policy.   Horizontal files are more generally used than
vertical files.   Map cases in the middle of a room
should not exceed center height.   Cases over six feet
high are somewhat less accessible than those below
eye level.   Where storage space is at a premium,
sectional horizontal files may be stacked to a height
of six feet or more....
"If a map collection is housed in the reading room
of a library, counter high horizontal or vertical files
may hold the entire collection.   As the collection
grows, it may be expedient to keep only the most active material readily accessible.   The less frequently
used items may be stored in the more distant stacks
....
"Special equipment for the storage of maps should
be selected with the utmost care.   The comparable
features of each type should be considered with reference to durability, capacity, accessibility, and costs.
"Horizontal filing cases, both wood and steel,
were in use long before vertical map files were introduced.   It is generally agreed that shallow drawers
have stood the test of adequate storage protection.
Material is easily accessible and can be removed and
refiled with a minimum expenditure of effort.   For
greatest efficiency, the inside drawer measurements
should not exceed 2-1/2 inches in height, 44 inches

in width and 30 inches in depth. If the drawers are
higher, the weight of the maps becomes so great as
to impede the removal of the bottom maps, even to
the extent of damaging them. If they are wider and
deeper, the maps may be too large for one person to
handle without damaging them. Maps of varying sizes
may be inter-filed without harm beyond the ever-pres-
ent danger of careless handling.

"Horizontal storage may be provided in two types
of cases, that is, 5-drawer sectional map cases and
cabinets with thin strong shelves and roll fronts or
doors....

"Each manufacturer has some individual variations
in his equipment. Some feature a dust cover fastened
at the back to keep the maps from riding out and
hooked at the front to insure protection. Others feature metal hoods at the back of the drawers to keep
the maps in and hinged metal flaps or compressors
at the front to keep them from curling. Other special
features include drawer dividers, safety stops, fric-
tion control to prevent slamming, etc. Of primary
importance, of course, is the durability and substantial construction of the map cases in relation to
drawer sizes. "

Horizontal files are more generally used than vertical
files for maps and blueprints larger than 14 x 17 inches.
Economy and flexibility in filing maps and charts may be increased in large collections by the use of three or four sizes
of file drawers. The units should be sectional so that they
may be increased (generally upward) where expansion is
necessary. These files are available in sizes varying from
an overall width of 25 to 75 inches and a depth of 19 to 47
inches, with drawer depth of 1 to 4 inches. It should be
possible to select the cases that will best fit in the assigned
space as well as cases best suited to contain the collection
from such manufacturers as All Steel Equipment, Mayline,
Art Steel Co., Inc., Cole Steel Equipment Co., Hamilton
Manufacturing Co. The Estey Corporation and the General
Fireproofing Co. manufacture map storage equipment on a
custom basis only for libraries who desire specially designed
files. Mrs. Le Gear also states:

"Vertical files are a comparatively recent development, and seem to have been used first at the University of Illinois Library. P. L. Windsor described 'A
New Vertical File for Maps, ' in the Library Journal,

vol. 35, 1910, p. 509, which was constructed according to an original design and was then believed to be a new application of vertical filing. Art Metal Incorporated manufactures vertical 'planfiles' in five sizes for maps up to 37 x 50 inches and 28 to 58 inches. A planfile 30 inches deep has 15 pockets with four red rope folders in each pocket, and is said to have a capacity of 3000 maps in active use, and between 5000 and 6000 in storage.

"Vertical file cases meet the requirements of quick accessibility, of maximum storage space, and minimum aisle space. When the floor space is used up, they cannot be stacked one on the other. It is claimed by the manufacturer that one 30-inch deep vertical file holds as many maps as 30 horizontal drawers, that is, six 5-drawer units. Vertical files work well when they are moderately full, and when the maps are of fairly uniform size....

"Vertical files, preferably legal size, in either wood or steel, make suitable filing equipment for small maps and aerial photographs as well as for larger maps folded to pocket or letter size.

"The Globe Wernicke Company of Cincinnati, Ohio, manufactures 'Cello-Clip' map and plan files. These are cabinets in which sheets are suspended from rods by means of 'Cello-clips' two of which are fastened to the top of each sheet. The drafting rooms of a number of engineering firms are equipped with them. Such a filing system may be practicable for the storage of vinyl plastic relief models which are quite light in weight.

"Several American libraries store their maps in dustproof buckram-covered boxes resembling large pamphlet boxes. They are made of plywood or heavy cardboard and are so constructed that the front of the box is double; the inner part of the front drops and the outer hinged part rests upon the top of the box when open. This provides easy access to the maps and facilitates filing.... They can be made in a library bindery or commercially by a box manufacturer.

"Portfolios made of two hinged pieces of binder's board may serve to store a small collection of maps. For protection from dust, paper or buckram flaps should be pasted or glued along three open sides of the bottom board. Tapes fastened at the middle of each side will keep the material from sliding out when a portfolio is moved. The width and depth of available

folio shelves may have to govern the sizes of the portfolios. Extraordinary care is necessary to keep maps
well within the covers of portfolios to prevent broken
edges and bent corners. "

Rolled maps may be stored in cabinets, laid on shelves,
placed in pigeonhole racks, as the Plan Hold roll files, or
held upright by a sloping rack spaced with dowels. Scrolls
should be protected by a cloth guard and placed in a cylinder
or stored in deep drawers. Dust covers of cloth or a transparent polyethelene or vinyl material should be placed over
globes to protect them from dust. Relief models that will
fit in the standard map file drawers can be protected in that
manner. Clothesline and clips may be attached to one edge
of vinylite plastic models and hung from rods. Some libraries are experimenting with hanging racks with horizontal bars
and clips on a cardboard device with special attachments for
such materials.

ADDRESSES FOR SUPPLIERS
of standard and special types of files and shelving

All-Steel Equipment, Inc.
245 John Street
Aurora, Illinois

Angle Steel, Inc.
Plainwell, Michigan

Art Metal Incorporated
Jamestown, New York

Art Steel Company, Inc.
170 West 233rd Street
New York 63, New York

C. S. Brown & Co.
7535 Hillcrest Drive
Wauwatosa 13, Wisconsin

Charles Bruning Co., Inc.
1800 Central Road
Mount Prospect, Illinois

Cole Steel Equipment Co.
415 Madison Avenue
New York 17, New York

Estey Corporation
One Catherine Street
Red Bank, New Jersey

The General Fireproofing Co.
413 Dennick Avenue
Youngstown 1, Ohio

The Globe-Wernicke Co.
5009 Carthage Avenue
Cincinnati 12, Ohio

Hamilton Manufacturing Co.
1935 Evans Street
Two Rivers, Wisconsin

Lyon Metal Products Co.
1933 Montgomery Street
Aurora, Illinois

Mayline Company, Inc.
619 North Commerce St.
Sheboygan, Wisconsin

The Mosler Safe Company
320 Fifth Avenue
New York, New York

Shaw-Walker Co.
1950 Townsend Street
Muskegon, Michigan

Plan Hold Corporation
5206 Chakemco Street
South Gate, California

John E. Sjöstrom Co., Inc.
1717 North 10th Street
Philadelphia 22, Pennsylvania

Remington Rand (Library
  Bureau)
315 Fourth Avenue
New York 10, New York

Stacor Equipment Co.
335 Emmet Street
Newark, New Jersey

Furniture in the library should be sturdy, comfortable and attractive in design. It is recommended that table space allotted to each reader measure at least 10 square feet. A variety of types of seating should be studied. Some libraries require stools and high sloping tables, or straight chairs at reader's tables. Chairs should be short-seated for comfort and to avoid the impediment of circulation to the feet. Staff desks should be the standard office or library size, 60 x 36 inches, with supplementary working tables the same size. Typewriter desks are advisable for catalogers, acquisitions personnel, reference assistants and secretaries. Adequate shelving on top of cases or in bookstands adjacent to desks should be provided for reference materials. A conference table and chairs may be useful in the administrative offices if the size of the library and type of clientele warrant it. Generally carrells are not useful, nor are lounge chairs. A stand for the unabridged dictionary with space below for frequently used reference books, a rack for displaying new books and a rack for periodicals are needed. Some manufacturers of library furniture are Art Metal Incorporated, Cole Steel Equipment Co., Remington Rand (Library Bureau) and John E. Sjöstrom Co., Inc.

Wide, flat-topped trucks with dividing shelves are essential in handling maps. Generally they are made the desired width to clear doorways and hold the maps. Book trucks are unsatisfactory for map use. Wooden map file cases with the drawers removed may be fastened together and, with wheels added, serve as holders for roughly sorted maps prior to filing. The service area where circulation and reference activities are to be conducted should be near the library entrance and adjacent to reading tables. Map file cases, two sections high, or an arrangement of open roller-type shelving for atlases which are counter height, may be

used for the circulation desk. Standard reference materials
such as general atlases, gazetteers, and regularly used index
catalogs should be within this area. Bulletin boards, display
cases, shelf display frames and window display facilities may
be used to publicize the library collections and services.
John E. Sjöstrom Co., Inc. sells table and wall display units
for exhibits.

Card catalogs, special bibliographies or cartobibliographies and graphic index catalogs should be within the
service area. The card catalog itself could be the regulation
drawer sets as recommended by regular library supply centers such as the Remington Rand Library Bureau. Folders
to preserve the maps in horizontal files can be made from
rope manila paper, press board, jute tag or red rope paper.
Some agencies use the kraft paper that is in the new map
case drawers, but the acid reaction of the paper discolors
the maps. Folder paper should have a pH factor exceeding
4. 5. Rope manila paper weighing 160 pounds per 100 sheets
or a heavier 175-200 pound jute tag comes in rolls 48" wide
and may be purchased from:

The Riegel Paper Corporation   Hollingsworth & Vose Co.
260 Madison Avenue   112 Washington Street
New York 16, New York   East Walpole, Massachusetts

St. Regis Paper Co.
150 East 42nd Street
New York 17, New York

Supplies of manila envelopes are needed for map ad-
denda such as gazetteers, brochures or texts accompanying
certain maps. Manila folders, notebooks or binders, mailing
tubes, a trimming board, boxes, cord, wrapping paper, labels, mending and acetate tapes may be obtained from the
following library or stationery suppliers:

Demco Library Supplies   Gaylord Brothers, Inc.
Box 1488   P. O. Drawer 61
Madison 1, Wisconsin   Syracuse 1, New York

Minnesota Mining & Manufacturing Co.
900 Bush Avenue
St. Paul 6, Minnesota

Other useful supplies which may be obtained locally include
bowls for paste and water, brushes, sponges, lintless cloth

for map backing, bone folders, squegees, scissors, magnifying glasses, sharp knives, razor blades and holders, paper
weights, staplers, wax paper, rubber stamps, stamping
machines, waste baskets and trash bins. Special map equipment such as steel straight edges, T-squares, lettering guides
and pens, electric erasers, dividers, scale indicators and
map tacks may be purchased from drafting supply companies
such as the Mayline Co., Inc., the Charles Bruning Co.,
Inc., Jeuffel & Esser Co., 303 Adams St., Hoboken, N.J.,
and Moore Push Pin Co., 113-125 Berkley Street (Wayne
Junction), Philadelphia, Pennsylvania. Laminate materials
and equipment for the preservation of maps may be obtained
from Gaylord, Demco, General Binding, Ditto, Inc., 6800 N.
McCormick Road, Chicago 45, Illinois and American Photocopy Equipment Co., 2100 Dempster Street, Evanston, Illinois.

Typewriters should be the regular library typewriters,
and if needed, non-Roman characters and diacritical marks.
Large capital letters are useful for signs or labels. Specially designed cabinets are required for microfilm, regular
film and lantern slides or transparencies. Provision should
be made for humidity control. The Recordak Corporation,
415 Madison Avenue, New York 17, N.Y. makes such a
cabinet. The Technicon Company, Saw Mill River Road,
Chauncey, New York, designs special equipment for slides.
A variety of record keeping equipment for periodicals and
serials is manufactured by the Art Metal, Demco and Remington Rand Library Bureau as well as Acme Visible Records,
Inc., 8900 West Allview Drive, Drozet, Virginia and Wheel-
dex & Simpla Products, Inc., 425 Park Avenue, South, New
York 16, New York.

Few libraries have microfilm cameras in their organizations but many do keep microfilm or microcopy records. Microfilm reading machines have become standard
equipment in many libraries. Listed below are some machines that are now in use, with names of their manufacturers.

Dea-Graph Readers. Distributed by Dea-Graph Equipment Ltd., 1577 West Georgia St., Vancouver 5,
B.C., Canada; manufactured by the Tokyo Micro-
photo Works Limited, 38 Chiyodocho Nakanoku,
Tokyo. Charles Bruning Co., Inc. is U.S. agent.
Documat Microfilm Reader-Printer. Documat, Inc.,
75 E. 55th St., New York, N.Y. 10022

Draftsman. Distributed by Microdealers, Inc., 1560
    Trapelo Rd., Waltham 54, Mass.; manufactured by
    Schwayders Bros., Denver.
Filmac-Reader-Printer. Minnesota Mining & Manu-
    facturing Co., 900 Bush Ave., St. Paul 6, Minn.
Flofilm Readers. Photostat Corp., P.O. Box 1970-T,
    Rochester 3, N.Y.
Microfilm Filmstrip Slide Viewer and Micro Scanner.
    Taylor Merchant Corp., 48 W. 48th St., New York,
    N.Y. 10036. Also have Task Master--10X, a
    pocket size reader-scanner.
Micro-Master Lens Viewer Scanner. Keuffel & Esser
    Co., 303 Adams St., Hoboken, N.J.
Recordak Readers and Projectors. Recordak Corpora-
    tion, 415 Madison Ave., New York, N.Y. 10017.
Thermo-Fax Reader Printers. Minnesota Mining and
    Manufacturing Co., 900 Bush Avenue, St. Paul 6,
    Minn.
Webco. Western Blue Print Co., 909 Grand St.,
    Kansas City, Mo.

The above is by no means a complete listing of dealers or
manufacturers. Only one foreign manufacturer was mentioned,
but there are many in both European and Asiatic countries.

Duplicating equipment for card-size items to document-
size materials generally starts with manual typing on a standard typewriter, electromatic machine, vari-typer, etc. Care
must be exercised in the selection of the typewriter and kind
of type used, to provide foreign language markings for the
kind of copy to be made. Master copies may be used in the
following types of reproduction.

1.   Stenciling and hectographing

Copy-rite. Wolbert Duplicator & Supply Co., 1201
    Cortland St., Chicago 14, Ill.
Ditto. Ditto, Inc., 6800 N. McCormick Rd., Chicago
    45, Ill.
Mimeograph. A. B. Dick Company, Dept. TR-50,
    5700 West Touhy Ave., Chicago 31, Ill.
Rex-o-graph. Rex-o-graph, Inc., 7840 West Hicks St.,
    Milwaukee 14, Wis.
Rocket. Standard Duplicating Machines Corp., 1935
    Parkway, Everett 49, Mass.

2.   Photocopy and contact prints, Offset duplicators

Apeco-Unimatic-Auto-Stat.   American Photocopy Equip-
    ment Company, 2100 Dempster St., Evanston, Ill.
Card to Card Printer and Developer.   Tecnifax Cor-
    poration, 200 Appleton St., Holyoke, Mass.
Copyflex.   Charles Bruning Co., Inc., 1800 Central
    Rd., Mount Prospect, Ill.
Dea-Graph Printers.   Dea-Graph Equipment Ltd., 1577
    West Georgia St., Vancouver 5, B.C., Canada.
    Charles Bruning Co., Inc.
Dietzgen.   Eugene Dietzgen Co., 2424 N. Sheffield Ave.,
    Chicago 24, Ill.
Documat Microfilm Printers.   Documat, Inc., 75 E.
    55th St., New York, N.Y. 10022
Kecofax Projector-Printer.   Keuffel & Esser Co., 303
    Adams St., Hoboken, N.J.
Ozamatic.   Ozalid, Division of General Aniline & Film
    Corp., Ozalid Rd., Johnson City, N.Y.
Peerless Rotary Printer and Dri-Stat.   Peerless Photo
    Products, Inc., Shoreham, L.I., N.Y.
Photostat Viewprint Processor.   Photostat Corp., 1001
    Jefferson Rd., P.O. Box 1970-T, Rochester 3,
    N.Y.
Thermo-Fax.   Minnesota Mining and Manufacturing
    Microfilm Products Division, 900 Bush Ave., St.
    Paul 6, Minn.
Xerox Copyflo.   Xerox Corporation, Rochester 3, N.Y.

3.   Special copyright camera--copying bound volumes.

Apeco-Panel-Lite.   American Photocopy Equipment Co.,
    2100 Dempster St., Evanston, Ill.
Contoura.   F. G. Ludwig Associates, 302 Coulter Ave.,
    Old Saybrook, Conn.
Cormac Book Printer.   Cormac Photocopy Corp., 80
    Fifth Ave., New York, N.Y. 10011

    Coding systems for bibliographic references may be
recorded on key punch cards by hand or machine and the information retrieved by a sorting needle.   Equipment for
these systems is produced by:

E-Z Sort.   E-Z Sort Systems, Ltd., 45 Second St.,
    San Francisco, Calif.
Keysort.   Royal McBee Corp., 700 Westchester Ave.,
    Port Chester, N.Y.
Needlesort.   Arizona Tool & Die Co., 31 E. Rillito
    St., Tucson, Ariz.

Map Librarianship

Unisort. Burroughs Corp., Todd Company Division,
University and Thomas Sts., Rochester 3, N.Y.

Systems for data processing, mechanical coding and
sorting of cards, electronic brains, photographic film devices,
and minicard systems have been developed by various companies. There is considerable experimentation in this line
and the librarian should follow the current research and development for trends prior to a final selection for use in the
library. These are some of the companies:

> Bendix Aviation Company, Fisher Building, Detroit.
> Computer, punched card and tabular couplers, mag-
> netic tape unit, multi-code paper tape readers.
> International Business Machines Corporation, 590 Madi-
> son Ave., New York, 10022. IBN card punch
> sorter, collator, printer.
> Remington Rand, Inc., 23rd St. & Fourth Ave., New
> York, 10010. Tabulating cards, automatic punch,
> electronic sorter, alphabetical tabulator, collating
> reproducer, collator, computer, tape to card con-
> verter.

The space in which the library operates should be efficiently planned with the arrangement in line with the overall functions of the organization. The increase in the use of
the library together with the amount of material in its collection should determine the expansion space for the housing of
both standard library items and "fugitive" materials such as
maps, pictures, aerial photographs, films, etc. Standard
library furniture is advised and special types of equipment
should be mechanized as needed for the use of both staff and
the users of the library. Scientific research and developments in documentation have been accelerating at a fantastic
pace. The Office of Science Information Service of the National Science Foundation publishes reports on such activities
and describes specific projects in the United States and foreign countries. The projects are grouped under the categories of information requirements and uses, information
storage and retrieval, mechanical translation, equipment and
potentially related research. In general these and other special materials programs reflect a growing concern with the
need to develop accurate information systems and the requisite
devices for reading, storing, searching, and retrieval of information.

CITATIONS

ACRL Committee. "Standards for Junior College Libraries." College and Research Libraries, vol. 21, no. 3 (May 1960), 200-206.

Brown, Lloyd Arnold. Notes on the Care and Cataloging of Old Maps. Windham, Conn.: Hawthorne House, 1940.

Bureau of Government, University of Wisconsin Extension. Contemporary Library Planning, Fourth Institute, 1952 and The Public Library Building, Fifth Institute--1953 (typed).

Carnovsky, L. "Standards for Special Libraries; Possibilities and Limitations." Library Quarterly, vol. 29 (July 1959), 168-173.

Casey, Robert S. and James W. Perry, Madeline M. Berry, Allen Kent. Punched Cards--Their Applications to Science and Industry. 2d ed. New York. Reinhold Publishing Corporation, 1958.

Collison, Robert Lewis. The Treatment of Special Material in Libraries. 2d ed. London: Aslib, 1957.

ACRL Committee. "Standards for College Libraries." College and Research Libraries, vol. 20 (July 1959), 274-80.

Dean, Crowell O. [Mrs.] "Planning the New Library: A. E. Staley Manufacturing Co." Special Libraries, vol. 50, no. 4 (Apr. 1959), 166-170.

Devlin, Thomas J. and W. T. King. "Technical Correspondence: Control and Retrieval Through Microfilm and Punch Card Technique." Special Libraries, vol. 51, no. 8 (Oct. 1960), 421-432.

Faden, B. R. "Information Retrieval on Automatic Data Processing Equipment." Special Libraries, vol. 50, no. 4 (Apr. 1959), 162-165.

Fisher, Eva Lou. A Checklist for the Organization, Operation and Evaluation of a Company Library. New York: Special Libraries Association, 1961.

Goodman, Marie Cleckner. Map Collections in the United States and Canada: A Directory. New York: Special Libraries Association, Geography and Map Division, Map Resources Committee, 1954.

International Federation for Documentation (FID). Manual on Document Reproduction and Selection. The Hague: TNO, Nov. 1953 (FID Pub. No. 264, Vol. A).

Kiersky, Loretta J. Bibliography on Reproduction of Documentary Information 1955-1960. New York: Special Libraries Association [Reprint for the 10th Annual Meeting and Convention, National Microfilm Association,

Chicago, Ill. April 4, 5, 6, 1961].

Le Gear, Clara Egli. Maps: Their Care, Repair and
    Preservation in Libraries. Rev. ed. Washington,
    D.C.: Library of Congress, Map Division, 1956.

McCrum, Blanche Prichard. An Estimate of Standards for
    a College Library. Rev. ed. Lexington, Va.: Journal-
    ism Laboratory Press, Washington-Lee University, 1937.

The National Microfilm Association. The National Micro
    News. No. 45, Apr. 1960. 1960 supplement to the
    Guide to Microreproduction Equipment. Annapolis.

National Science Foundation, Office of Science Information
    Service. Current Research and Development in Scien-
    tific Documentation. No. 7 (NSF 60-65), Washington,
    D.C.: U.S. Govt. Print. Off., 1960.

Parker, F. M. "Engineering Drawing Processing System."
    Special Libraries, vol. 51, no. 8 (Oct. 1960), 429-432.

Price, Milburne. Information Processing Equipment. New
    York: Reinhold Pub. Corp., 1955.

Roneo Limited. Planning the Library. London, 1950.

Sharp, Harold S. "Planning the New Library." Special
    Libraries, vol. 51, no. 8 (Oct. 1960), 444-448.

Strauss, Lucille J. Scientific and Technical Libraries:
    Their Organization and Administration. 2nd ed. New
    York: Wiley, 1972.

White, Herbert S. "Application of Machines to Library Tech-
    niques." Special Libraries, vol. 51, no. 9 (Nov. 1960),
    p. 492.

RESTORATION AND PRESERVATION OF MAPS*

Robert I. Boak

It is probable that many maps now in use in libraries
have suffered some type of damage or possibly they will in
the future.   In order that we may deal effectively with this
damage, it would be best if we classify it as (1) chemical
damage and (2) mechanical damage.   For the moment, we
shall consider the older maps which possibly have been dam-
aged by one of the above or possibly by a combination of
both.   The sure signs of chemical attack in paper, whether
the paper be a map or another type of document, are discoloration and brittleness, both signs probably varying in
degree from one item to the next.   This visual evidence of
deterioration should alert the librarian that steps should be
taken to arrest this condition.   Fortunately, due to the efforts of the National Archives and Mr. William Barrow, we
have learned the cause of chemical attack and how to combat
it.

The acids in paper, which are the prime cause of deterioration, are there as residual substances left over from
the manufacturing process or possibly the acids have been
picked up from contaminated air.   Regardless of the source,
the acids should and can be neutralized, thereby eliminating
chemical activity as a source of deterioration.   The method
most frequently used was developed by the National Archives,
this being a one-step process in which the paper is completely immersed in a magnesium bicarbonate solution and
left in the solution until the saturation point is reached.   The
above solution is slightly alkaline in nature and consequently
it is an effective means of deacidifying (neutralizing) the
paper.   When dried, the paper will retain a quantity of the
magnesium which acts as a buffer to combat attack by acids
in the future.

*Reprinted by permission from Special Libraries Association,
Geography and Map Division, Bulletin No. 81 (1970), 21-23.

There are other means of deacidifying paper, one of
them being a two-step combination of solutions. This is also
an effective process but it is more time consuming than the
methods mentioned above. In selected cases, paper may be
dusted with magnesium powder or exposed to an alkaline gas.
Unfortunately neither of these is as effective as the aqueous
solutions. The deacidification process may be carried out in
most photographic or binding departments with a minimum of
equipment but before doing so, the librarian should take all
precautions to determine if the ink is fast and whether the
paper will support its own weight when wet. Mechanical
damage is evidenced by the usual rips, folds, tears, and
missing portions. We might include in this classification
surface soil and previous repairs of one kind or another.

The basic rule to follow when making repairs is not
to do anything which cannot be undone. In keeping with this
rule, when dealing with rips, tears, etc., the reinforcing material should be affixed to the paper with a bonding medium
which is readily soluble in water or a non toxic solvent.
When choosing the mending material, consideration should be
given to the nature of the printing and coloring, if any, on
the surface of the map and whether it will be affected adversely by the mending material. Consideration should also
be given to the possibility of distortion of the paper if a
water-base adhesive is used. Mending materials which are
generally acceptable would include the glassine tapes, tissues
which are applied with water soluble adhesives and tissues
which are applied with solvent activated adhesives. The same
solvent used to activate the adhesive may be depended upon to
remove the mending material if necessary. The temptation
to use the pressure sensitive tapes should be resisted, even
those which are said to be permanent and stainless.

The lamination process may be used if an entire map
is to be repaired and strengthened. Again, the materials
used should be readily soluble and this is the case when the
acetate/tissue type is used. It is possible to incorporate in
the lamination process various types of reinforcing materials
such as Nylon, fibreglas, and cloths of natural fibres. It is
not advisable to use the Mylar/Polyethylene or other heat-
sealable types of plastics for archival maps or documents.
These types are fine for items which may be easily replaced
and which may need protection when used in the field.

Surface soil may be removed from maps by means of
a soft rubber eraser or in some cases the commercial

cleaners which are available. In some stubborn cases, very fine sand-paper may be used. If it is necessary to remove old repairs, a variety of methods may be tried. Those paper and cloth tapes which have been applied with a water-soluble adhesive possibly will peel off when a dull knife is used. If this fails then the patch may be dampened with water. If possible, the entire document should be immersed to prevent staining. The pressure sensitive cellulose tapes present more of a problem, especially if the paper is very soft. Sometimes the older tapes will simply peel off but in most cases they must be removed by the use of a solvent such as xylene or trichloroethylene.

Old wall maps present special problems because of their size, weight, and the fact they are usually coated with shellac. In most cases, the paper is quite discolored and brittle. There may also be rips and tears near the wooden rods and possibly the paper has become separated from the muslin. It is also probable that the muslin has become torn and is very weak. The general overall condition of the map would determine what course of action would be followed to restore and preserve the map. Those in the very worst condition would be stripped from the cloth backing material and re-mounted on a wood-grain hardboard. This type of rigid mounting is recommended because it would be futile to re-mount the map on cloth as the map undoubtedly would continue to crack and fragments would be lost if the paper were allowed to bend.

Consideration should also be given to the possibility of removing the darkened shellac from the map. If it were determined that this could be done without damaging the map, the shellac would be dissolved. After re-mounting, the map could be re-coated with a modern acrylic lacquer or a sheet of Mylar or acetate placed over the face. Those wall maps which have suffered a small amount of damage probably could be left on the cloth backing. If needed, the cloth could be repaired or reinforced with a modern fabric or maybe the map could be mounted on hardboard. If the map were not mounted on hardboard, provisions should be made to store the maps in the special racks which will accommodate them vertically in an unrolled manner. The utmost care should be taken when handling the large maps to see that the paper is not fractured by sharp creasing. New maps which have not suffered damage should if possible be stored flat in map drawers. If this is not possible then they may be rolled but never folded. Those maps and charts which may be used in the field may be laminated with one of the several types of plastic films which will strengthen and protect them.

It is possible that the map librarian will have items which present special problems. In cases such as these, help and advice may be obtained from the State librarian, Federal agencies such as the National Archives and the Library of Congress, or the several private firms which specialize in the restoration and preservation of archival material. All of the above are anxious to be of service to you.

EQUIPMENT FOR MAP LIBRARIES*

Mary Galneder

The selection and arrangement of equipment for the map library are among the most important decisions the librarian must make. Suitable equipment results in a collection in which the maps are easily accessible and yet given adequate protection from dust, sunlight, dampness, careless handling, or chemical deterioration. Unsuitable equipment, however, has given rise to the reputation of maps as "troublesome 'step-children'" in libraries.[1] This paper examines the question of equipment for current, research-oriented map collections; archival map materials are not considered as they require special handling and are often in the care of a rare book librarian.

Few map librarians are given an opportunity to design their own rooms; if a new area is set aside for the map collection, it will have built-in features (for example, full-length windows or support pillars) which must be considered in the arrangement of equipment. The physical condition of the area is the first consideration. Maps require large horizontal areas, occupy much space and exert a very heavy floor loading. A basement or ground floor location is often desirable or the floor should be inspected to determine that it can support the weight of filled map cases.

The room should have temperature and humidity control. It is estimated that temperatures between 60° and 75° F with relative humidities between 50 and 60% are best for the conservation of library materials. In addition, the room should be well-ventilated; the air should be filtered to

*Reprinted by permission from Special Libraries, vol. 61, no. 6 (1970), 271-274. Copyright by Special Libraries Association. Originally presented in 1969 at the SLA 60th Annual Convention.

eliminate contaminants which may introduce grime, abrasion
and chemical deterioration. 2 These conditions should exist
in a newer building with a central air conditioning system;
otherwise the librarian should try to obtain room-size air
conditioners and humidifiers.

Map Storage Equipment

After the location of the map room has been determined, the choice of filing equipment is a primary decision
for the map librarian. Various considerations need to be
analyzed, and they will influence the purchasing decision--
among them, the size and growth rate of the collection, frequency of use, current and future space available, and cost.
Once the style of filing equipment has been decided, it can
be estimated how many cases will be needed to house the
maps on hand and to accommodate future growth. It may
be necessary to match previously purchased equipment, but
if older equipment is unsuitable it may be possible to set it
aside for storage of little used maps. If the appearance of
the library is important, cases on hand may be repainted to
match newly ordered ones so that differences in color and
style are minimized.

Most map librarians agree that horizontal cases, with
shallow drawers, are most efficient for the storage of maps.
They combine adequate protection with relatively easy access.
The type most commonly used is produced as drafting room
equipment; these are five-drawer units with separate tops and
bases. These units are available in either steel or wood.
They are available with various features, such as canvas dust
covers, hoods at the back of the drawers and compressors
or wires at the front to hold the maps in place, dividers,
ball bearing rollers, or safety stops. Specific features vary
with the manufacturer. Some features may not be available
in the less expensive cases. The most substantial and durable cases possible should be purchased as they will be more
satisfactory for a longer period. A comparison between the
costs of steel or wood cases shows a cost of approximately
$460 for a steel unit consisting of two five-drawer units (in-
side drawer dimension, 45-1/2 X 35 X 2 inches) with top
and flush base and a similar wood unit (inside drawer size,
42-3/8 X 32 X 2 inches) priced at about $330. 3 Except for
the lower cost, wood cases are far less satisfactory than
steel. They are adversely affected by humidity changes;
their fiberboard drawer bottoms sag when heavily loaded; and
their drawers do not run on ball bearings nor do they have
safety stops.

The dimensions of drawers in horizontal map filing units vary according to the manufacturer, but they may be broadly grouped as small, medium, large, and oversize. In these ranges one manufacturer produces cases with drawers designed to hold map sheets in the following sizes: 36 X 24 inches, 42 X 30 inches, 48 X 36 inches, and 72 X 42 inches.[4] Drawer sizes in the cases of other manufacturers will vary slightly but also correspond to these general ranges. The medium size drawer, for 42 X 30 inch map sheets, is the most practical. It will store the majority of maps without folding and yet will not have a lot of wasted space. If it is possible to alternate the size of the map cases, those with larger drawers may be useful for housing large maps (such as navigation charts) or they may be divided to house double stacks of uniform size set maps (for example, the U.S. Geological Survey's topographic quadrangles).

A drawer height of 2 inches (or no more than 2-1/2 inches) is recommended. When maps are stacked higher, it is difficult to withdraw those at the bottom. Within the drawers, additional protection from dust is given to the maps by storing them in paper folders. These folders also expedite finding maps through labels showing contents. The folders also serve to keep maps covering the same area or sets of maps in one place. For preservation of the maps, folders should be made of non-acid paper with a pH factor of 4.5 or higher.[5] Open edges of the folders may face the back or the front of the drawers. Access is easier if the open edge is at the front so the map desired can be seen before it is removed; the drawback, however, is the temptation to remove and to refile maps without taking the folder from the drawer--thus it is easy to wrinkle or tear the maps. When the open edge of the folder is at the back of the drawer, it is necessary to remove the entire folder before maps may be consulted.

Space Estimates

The number of cases needed to house a collection of maps and their arrangement depends on the size of the room. Approximately 200 maps in folders can be stored in one horizontal drawer, and cases may be stacked as high as the floor will support--and the librarian finds convenient. [Figure 1 of previous article--page 366] shows the weight per square foot of filled cases. It was originally published in a report, "Map Libraries--Space and Equipment," prepared by the Committee on Standards of SLA's Geography and Map Division

under the chairmanship of Catherine Bahn. [6]   Much valuable
information for anyone who is planning a map library or considering the ordering of new equipment is contained in the
report mentioned plus the section on filing equipment in Maps:
Their Care, Repair, and Preservation in Libraries, by Clara
LeGear, [7] and "Map and Atlas Cases" by J. Douglas Hill. [8]
If space for expansion of the library will be limited after the
initial allotment is made, it is advisable to stack the cases
only two five-drawer units high.   This provides a convenient
work surface.   If more cases are needed later, they may be
added on top.

Other Types of Storage

        Although vertical cases are a newer way of handling
maps, they are generally less satisfactory than horizontal
cases.   In vertical filing units, the maps are filed in folders
or clamped together in binders suspended from racks at the
sides.   These racks may swing forward to provide easier
access.   Approximately half as much floor space is required
to house 3,000 maps in vertical units as in horizontal units
but the storage space cannot be expanded upward, the tops
are not usable for work space, and the units are more expensive. [9]

        Other methods of filing maps are not considered as
satisfactory when easy access is a factor.   Two such methods
are storage in portfolios or buckram covered boxes.   While
these protect the maps from dust more completely than horizontal drawers, the extra time involved in handling the maps
makes such storage uneconomical except for archival collections where the long term conservation need outweighs ready
accessibility. [10]   Special storage facilities are needed for
globes and plastic relief models.   Globes which are not left
standing around the map room as display materials may be
stored in standard supply cabinets with adjustable shelves.
Cloth or plastic covers may be obtained for further protection
from dust.

        Two types of storage are usable for plastic relief
models.   In the first, which works primarily where they may
be stored in a relatively private area, one or two holes are
punched in one of the sides and the model is suspended from
a hook or wire.   Another method is to store the relief
models in cabinets, approximately 40 inches wide X 28 inches
deep X 40 inches high.   Shelves about four inches apart will
each hold about 12 maps.   Additional shelves could be added

to provide narrower spaces but if too many are used, storage capacity is quite restricted. As long as reasonable care is taken in removing and replacing the models, this method is satisfactory for the storage of models in current use.

Other Considerations

Another important consideration in equipping a map room is the provision of adequate space to consult the maps. Between 10 and 16 sq. ft. of space per reader is recommended by LeGear[11] and Bahn.[12] Vertical files (either letter or legal size), should be located in the map library for storage of map texts, indexes, maps which are kept folded (such as expendable road maps), aerial photographs, and catalogs. If the use of the map collection warrants, a drafting table and a light table are useful items for readers, as is the maintaining of an empty drawer or two in which maps in use over several days can be stored temporarily.

Depending on the size of the collection a map truck may be a helpful addition. These are the same style as conventional book trucks; in fact, a book truck with a large flat board on top is an adequate substitute. If a truck is also to be used for sorting or other processing of maps, it must be ordered specially. The top surface should be flat, approximately 2-1/2 X 5 feet, and about waist high. There should be two or three shelves for sorting or storing maps. The shelves should be far enough apart to enable the maps to be inserted or taken out easily. At least two wheels should have ball bearing swivel casters for easier maneuvering.

Standard library shelves should be part of the map room to hold reference materials and atlases in book form. Oversize shelves, about seven inches apart, or atlas stands should be provided for material which must be shelved flat. While not exactly part of a map library's equipment, space to display maps should be available. Displays, which ordinarily attract many viewers, call attention to the existence of the map collection and the types of maps in it. Last, but not least, an extremely useful item in the map room-- if it can be arranged--is a sink in the work area or nearby.

REFERENCES

1. LeGear, Clara Egli. Maps: Their Care, Repair, and Preservation in Libraries. Ref. ed. Washington,

D. C.:   Library of Congress, Map Division, 1956;
75p. (p. 42).

2.   Cunha, George D. M.   Conservation of Library Materials: A Manual and Bibliography on the Care, Repair and Restoration of Library Materials.   Metuchen,
N. J.:   Scarecrow Press, 1967; 405p. (p. 80-83).

3.   Drafting Furniture List Prices, November 1, 1969.
Two Rivers, Wisc.:   Hamilton Manufacturing Co.,
8p. (p. 2-3).

4.   Hamilton Drafting Room Furniture.   Two Rivers, Wisc.:
Hamilton Manufacturing Co., 1968; 40p. (p. 34-35).

5.   Ref. 1, p. 10.

6.   This article is reprinted in this chapter.

7.   Ref. 1, p. 42-49.

8.   Hill, J. Douglas.   "Map and Atlas Cases."   Library
Trends, vol. 13, no. 4 (April 1965), 481-87.

9.   Ref. 8, p. 484.

10.   Ref. 8, p. 485.

11.   Ref. 1, p. 51.

12.   Ref. 6, p. 10.

MAPS: THEIR DETERIORATION AND PRESERVATION*

Richard Daniel Smith

Map papers are made from cotton fiber or chemical wood pulps or a mixture of these fibers, depending upon their intended use. The important properties of map papers include finish, printing quality, dimensional stability (to avoid poor register), good folding properties, and in some cases (for example, road maps) high opacity. Frequently, map papers are manufactured specifically for high wet strength, water repellency, mildew resistance, luminescence, abrasion resistance, or other properties required for a particular use. Paper used for maps weighs about the same per unit area as paper used to manufacture books. In general, however, map papers are more durable and have greater dimensional stability than book papers. Both types of paper are composed primarily of paper fibers which in turn are mostly cellulose. Hence, cellulose, the fundamental material in paper, is the structural element upon which to focus this discussion about the useful life of paper. Chemically speaking, cellulose is the same regardless of source. Consequently, existing knowledge about book papers can be applied to examine the potential future for map papers.

Cellulose is a relatively stable chemical and it is resistant to most forms of deterioration. The causes of aging in paper, which is composed primarily of industrial cellulose, include the effects of (1) acid-catalyzed hydrolysis, (2) oxidative reactions, (3) photochemical attack, (4) biological attack, and (5) the effects of use on cellulose. The work of many investigators has demonstrated unequivocally that the principal cause of book stock loss in American

*Reprinted by permission from Special Libraries, vol. 63, no. 2 (1972), 59-68. Copyright by Special Libraries Association. Originally presented in 1971 by SLA 62nd Annual Conference.

Table 1. Expected Life of Paper in Years from Date of Publication*

Study No.	Origin of Books Studied	Books Published Between	No. of Books Tested	Expected Life in Years (with 95% Confidence Limits) Until	
				Leaves are too weak to re-bind	Leaves break when turned
1	Lawrence Univ. Library, Appleton, Wisc.	1923-1964	20	58±28	107±43
	The Newberry Library, Chicago, Ill.	1923-1964	20	54±20	95±31
	The Research Libraries, New York Public Library, New York, N.Y.	1923-1964	20	34±9	64±17
2	The Newberry Library, Chicago, Ill.	1900-1966	231†	55±9	88±13
	The Newberry Library, Chicago, Ill.	1900-1966	231†	56±9	98±13
	The Newberry Library, Chicago, Ill.	1900-1966	231†	62±12	99±17
3	Discards from Libraries in the Richmond, Va. area	1900-1949	500	55±7	90±11

*See Smith[4] (p. 37-46, 215-20) for methodology, discussion, and sources of data. The data for study no. 1 was published in early 1972 as Restaurator, Supplement no. 2, "A Comparison of Paper in Identical Copies of Books from the Lawrence University, The Newberry, and The New York Public Libraries."

†Three leaves were tested in each of the 231 books. The first figure reports the expected life for leaves at the one third point, the second for leaves at the middle, and the third for leaves in the final signature of the book.

libraries is the acid-catalyzed hydrolysis of the cellulose in paper fibers. [1]

Condition of Library Book Collections

The size of the problem which libraries face is summarized in Table 1 for 20th century publications.   Table 1 indicates, based upon folding endurance data on paper in books from four different library collections, that most books published between 1900 and 1966 will be so weak by the time these books are 60 years old that they cannot be bound by the conventional library binding methods.   The paper in these same books will probably become so embrittled by the time they are one hundred years old that their leaves will break if they are turned.   Librarians can evaluate the validity of these statistical predictions on the basis of their professional experience.   For example, the leaves of books published during the 1870's and 1880's regularly break when they are turned.   Library binders are finding it difficult today to rebind the books published during World War I.   Hence, Table 1 merely documents the fact that research libraries are falling surprisingly short of their goal to retain books for whatever period they are needed by patrons.

It is rather depressing to report that these findings and more were anticipated 50 years ago by Sudborough and Mehta. [2] (Their article as well as the articles of Chapman[3] are recommended because they contain information on the deterioration of book collections that is not reported elsewhere.) In 1920, research techniques differed greatly and much of the experimental methodology we take for granted had not even been imagined.   Nonetheless, Sudborough and Mehta were able to verify that retention of folding endurance was the most sensitive physical test available to evaluate aging rates. They also verified that acid attack was the chief cause of deterioration over prolonged periods of time.   The causal relationship of acidity to deterioration was demonstrated by soaking badly deteriorated acidic papers in water and then drying the extract into new paper.   Accelerated heat aging studies (at $60°C$ for 30 days plus 30 days at $80°C$ with moisture maintained) demonstrated that acid-treated papers deteriorated more rapidly than their untreated counterparts.

Effect of Storage Conditions

Sudborough and Mehta as well as Chapman also investigated the condition of identical copies of various titles in library collections located in different climates. The comparative data indicated that although detrimental quantities of acidic materials were introduced into paper during manufacture, even larger quantities developed in paper during library storage as a consequence of natural aging processes. The combination of relative humidity and temperature was found to be a critical factor in the life of many books. Copies of books from libraries located in the cool Himalayan foothills were found to be in excellent condition while identical copies of these same books from libraries on the hot Indian plains were completely embrittled. The book stock of libraries which had been on the hot plains and then was moved to the cool foothills was in an intermediate condition, a finding which demonstrates the merit in air-conditioning existing collections. A persuasive argument for low relative humidity storage was established when Sudborough and Mehta found that books stored in Madras (hot and humid) were more deteriorated than books stored in Calcutta (hot with wet and dry seasons).

The effect of storage conditions (relative humidity and temperature) on the expected life of paper is given by Table 2. An expected life factor of 1.00 was assigned for an average annual relative humidity of 50% and temperature of 77° F. Then expected life factors were computed for other combinations of relative humidity and temperature on the basis of published data. The results indicate that air-conditioning should be considered as one choice when libraries desire to stretch the useful life of their collections. For example, the 34 year period from date of publication to non-rebindability, shown for books from The New York Public Library in Table 1, would change to 126 years (3.71 X 34) if the books were stored at 68° F and 30% relative humidity rather than at 77° F and 50% relative humidity.

Table 2 explains one reason why so many books published during the 15th, 16th, and 17th centuries still exist. It suggests that their future life will be shorter than their life to date. Libraries were not heated until relatively recent times. The average annual relative humidity and temperature inside library book stacks probably were similar to the humidity and temperature outside the library. In Europe, the relative humidity averages about 70%. The average temperature varies from about 50° F in the north to 59° F in the south. Thus, from Table 2, we can estimate (assuming that the practice of heating book stacks commenced about 1900) that present-day storage conditions in American libraries may have caused incunabula to age more during the last 70 years than they aged during the previous 400 years.

Table 2.   Expected Life Factors for Paper at
Various Relative Humidities and
Temperatures*

Average Annual Storage Temperature	Average Annual Storage Relative Humidity					
	70%	50%	40%	30%	20%	10%
95° F	0.14	0.19	0.23	0.30	0.41	0.68
86° F	0.32	0.43	0.52	0.67	0.93	1.53
77° F	0.74	1.00	1.22	1.56	2.17	3.57
68° F	1.76	2.38	2.90	3.71	5.16	8.49
59° F	4.30	5.81	7.08	9.05	12.6	20.7
50° F	11.1	15.0	18.3	23.4	32.6	53.5

*See Smith[4] (p. 54-57) for additional discussion and expected life factors.

The standard recommendation for relative humidity in libraries has become 50%, probably because paper has optimal physical strength around 50% R.H.   This recommendation makes sense if one believes that books should have maximum durability today rather than as long a life as possible. The effect of relative humidity on maximum durability now and expected life is shown in Figure 1.

Figure 1 indicates that although paper is more durable at 50% relative humidity than it is at lower relative humidities, its permanence or expected life is greater when it is stored at lower relative humidities.   In other words, conventional storage recommendations favor the present-day user, but they are detrimental to the interests of future patrons because they accelerate paper deterioration.   Although paper does lose some of its physical strength at lower relative humidities, there is a side range of relative humidity wherein paper remains more than strong enough for library purposes.[5]   In time, as depicted by Figure 1, paper stored at lower relative humidities (e.g., 20% to 30% R.H.) will come to be much stronger than paper stored at 50% relative

humidity. [6]   Unfortunately, maintaining a book collection
through air-conditioning is expensive.   The air-conditioning
plant (for cooling and dehumidification) to keep a 1,000,000

Figure 1.   Effect of Relative Humidity on the
            Useful Life of Books.

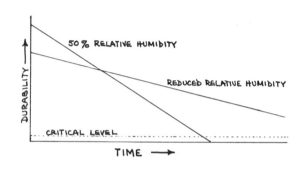

volume book stack at an annual average temperature of 68° F
and 30% relative humidity instead of 77° F and 50% relative
humidity might increase building costs by $250,000 or $0.25
per volume.   The cost of maintaining and operating the facility might run $100,000 annually or $0.10 per volume per
year.

         The accepted method for slowing the rate at which
acidic papers deteriorate is deacidification, but accepted deacidification treatments use aqueous solutions which are harmful to whole books.   Aqueous deacidification methods are slow
and expensive.   They require dismantling the books and treat-
ing each leaf separately.   Librarians know these treatments
are effective in prolonging book life but they also recognize
that aqueous deacidification is out of the question because of
its cost.   Many books will not be available to patrons in the
future because libraries cannot afford to spend $50.00 to
$80.00 per book to deacidify and rebind them.   For this rea-
son, a new, low cost method of deacidifying paper and books
has been developed and it is reported upon in "The Nonaqueous Deacidification of Paper and Books."[4, 7]

Deacidification Treatments

         Our understanding of the mechanisms of paper deteri-
oration suggests that the deterioration of map papers is

analogous to the deterioration of book papers. However, no empirical data exist upon which librarians may argue for the preservation of map collections. Therefore, the remaining objectives of this study are (1) to characterize the probable condition of map collections and (2) to estimate how map life could be extended by a deacidification treatment. Essentially, the purpose of deacidification treatments is to reduce the probability that the cellulose in paper fibers will be attacked by acids. Deacidification treatments do not extend the life of paper indefinitely. They are believed to extend the potential life of many book papers two to three or more times.

Most present-day deacidification treatments introduce more than a sufficient quantity of an alkaline chemical to neutralize the acidic components of paper. The excess is deposited to protect against the future development of an acidic condition. These deposits typically produce a water extract pH for the treated papers ranging from 8.0 to 10.5. Many deacidification treatments have been proposed but the treatments generally accepted by conservators fall into two groups: aqueous and nonaqueous treatments.

Aqueous deacidification processes typically consist of soaking paper in or spraying paper with a saturated solution made up of water as the solvent and a calcium or magnesium bicarbonate, carbonate, or hydroxide as the deacidification agent. Frequently, a substantial quantity of carbon dioxide is dissolved into the water because the carbon dioxide forms bicarbonates with the calcium or magnesium and increases their solubility. The background required by inexperienced librarians who wish to practice aqueous deacidification is presented by Smith[4] (p. 65-70, 124-5, 226-32).

Nonaqueous deacidification processes consist of impregnating paper and books with a nonaqueous solution containing an organic solvent and an alkaline deacidification agent. Organic solvents are used because they wet paper more rapidly than water, have less swelling or distorting effect on paper, and are easier to dry from paper than water. The solvent selected dissolves the deacidification agent and carries it throughout the article during treatment. The quantity of deacidification agent dissolved in the solution is selected (1) to neutralize the existing acidity and (2) to deposit an excess of alkaline buffering residue in the treated paper and books. This residue provides long-term protection against acid attack. The solution may be applied by immersion, spraying, brushing or other techniques provided the

Table 3. Some Properties of Selected U.S.G.S. Maps

Date Printed	Years Since Map Was Printed	pH*	Fiber Content†		No. of M.I.T. Double Folds at 1.0 kg Tension‡
1971	0	6.30	Rag Bleached kraft softwood Bleached kraft hardwood	27% 42% 31%	152.3
1968	3	6.00	Not tested		313.3
1962	9	6.05	Rag Bleached sulfite softwood Bleached kraft softwood Bleached kraft hardwood	58% trace 42% trace	139.8
1957	14	6.00	Not tested		66.6
1953	18	6.00	Rag Bleached kraft softwood Bleached kraft hardwood	66% 31% 3%	363.9
1948	23	5.50	Not tested		168.5
1944	27	6.00	Not tested		89.1
1937	34	5.95	Rag Bleached sulfite softwood Bleached kraft softwood	71% 14% trace	145.5
1932	39	5.70	Not tested		28.3
1927	44	5.20	Rag Bleached sulfite softwood	50% 50%	13.9
1924	47	5.50	Not tested		61.4
1918	53	5.35	Rag Bleached sulfite softwood Bleached kraft hardwood	29% 64% 7%	1.6

*See[8], T509su-68, "Hydrogen Ion Concentration (pH) of Paper Extracts--Cold Extraction Method," 1968, for test method.

†See[8], T401m-60, "Fiber Analysis of Paper and Paperboard," 1960, for test method.

‡ See[8], T423m-50, "Folding Endurance of Paper (M. I. T. Folding Endurance)," 1950, for test method. The portions of U. S. G. S. maps tested were chosen randomly and conditioned at 73° F, in 95%, 11% and 50% relative humidities for 24 hours respectively prior to testing. Values reported are the antilogarithms of the means of the logarithms of the folding endurance data for the test specimens.

---

solution impregnates the article being treated. The solvent may be removed by any drying method that deposits the de-acidification agent throughout the treated article.

Properties of U. S. Geological Survey Maps

        Twelve maps, ranging from 0 to 53 years of age,
were donated by the U. S. Geological Survey (U. S. G. S.) for
the experimental work conducted in this study. Some properties of the paper in these maps are presented in Table 3.
The pH, fiber content, and folding endurance data suggest
that these U. S. G. S. maps had excellent durability at the time
of manufacture and would be expected to have a useful life
substantially longer than that of the book papers discussed
previously. This latter possibility was investigated by using
a standard least squares statistical method[4] (p. 39-40, 215-
20) to regress the present-day folding endurance of the map
papers on their age (taken as the number of years since
printing). The results of the analysis, presented in Figure
2, suggest that paper from the average U. S. G. S. map will
break halfway through the first fold at 1. 0 kg tension 97. 2
years after the map was printed. The 95% confidence limits
for this estimate are ±7. 0 years. In other words, these results imply that the condition of paper in the average U. S. -
G. S. map will be equivalent to the "leaves break when turned"
category of Table 1 about 100 years after the map is printed.
The assumptions underlying this interpretation include the belief that the end point for loss of folding endurance on aging
is similar at both 1. 0 kg tension and 0. 5 kg tension. (If a
0. 5 kg tension had been used, it is believed that the expected
life prediction would have been greater than 97. 2 years but
probably less than the upper 95% confidence limit of 104. 2
years.) In any event, the prediction of 97. 2±7. 0 years for
useful life is remarkably similar to the expected length of
time that would be required for books to deteriorate to the
point where their leaves would break when they are turned.

        A lifetime for U. S. G. S. maps of 100 years probably
is sufficient for almost all normal uses of these maps. Research libraries, however, also aim to serve indefinitely as
libraries of record and their librarians may be interested in
examining the possibilities for stretching out the useful life
of map collections. The factors given in Table 2 can be
used to evaluate the benefit that relative humidity and temperature control might bring to map libraries. For example,
storage at 30% relative humidity and 68° F theoretically could
increase the useful life of the average U. S. G. S. map paper
3. 71 times, that is, from 97. 2 years to 361 years.

Effects of Deacidification Treatments

     Although treatment costs have not been established for production scale operations, experience to date indicates that

Figure 2.   Folding Endurance of U. S. Geological Survey Maps

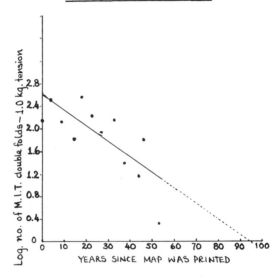

nonaqueous deacidification treatments offer a less expensive method than air-conditioning does for extending the useful life of maps. Without knowledge of their properties, six of the twelve U. S. G. S. maps used in this study were selected to evaluate the potential benefit of deacidification to the life of maps. Four of these six maps were used to compare the merit of aqueous and nonaqueous deacidification treatments developed by this author. The other two maps were used to investigate the effect of the water, naturally present in paper, on a nonaqueous spray treatment.

     The maps selected for use in the comparison of treatment study were cut in half again and again until 16 equal-sized rectangular pieces were produced. Four of these pieces, chosen at random, were treated by each of the methods described in Table 4. The M. I. T. folding endurance test specimens were cut in the machine direction (grain direction) of the map. Only eight test specimens could be cut from each of the four randomly selected pieces. These eight test specimens were placed one after another as they were cut into one of four groups. One of these groups of eight test specimens was randomly selected for control purposes, that is, it was not aged. Each of the other three randomly selected groups was aged for five, or ten, or fifteen days at 105° C. After aging, the five, ten, and fifteen day test specimens were treated at relative humidities of 95%, 11% and 50% for 24 hours respectively to reduce dried-in stains and produce a consistent moisture content. [9]

The M. I. T. folding endurance data were analyzed by a statistical method analogous to the method previously described by the author[4] (p. 110, 112). In essence, a computation was made to determine the time required for the treated and untreated specimens to deteriorate to the point where they would break halfway through the first fold. Then, measures of treatment value were obtained by dividing the expected life-time of the treated papers by the

Table 4. Comparison Study— The Deacidification Treatments

Treat-ment	Treatment Solution	Treatment Method	
		Immersion Time (minutes)	Spray
1	Standard; no treatment	0	—
2	Saturated solution of magnesium bicarbonate in cold Canada Dry soda water, air dried	20	—
3	7% Magnesium methoxide in methanol-trichlorotrifluoroethane (1-3 parts by volume) air dried (maps were conditioned at 50% R.H. before treatment)	8	—
4	Same as Treatment 3	—	Both sides until wetted thoroughly

· ·

Table 5. Comparison Study— The Value of Treatment Indices*

Date Printed	Years Since Printed	Treatment No.†			
		1	2	3	4
1971	0	1.00	0.99	1.19	1.20
1953	18	1.00	1.08	1.21	1.59
1937	34	1.00	2.55	4.01	3.18
1918	53	1.00‡	2.49‡	1.58‡	1.27‡

* The value of treatment indices is computed using M.I.T. folding endurance retention data obtained in an accelerated aging study. Folding endurance specimens cut in machine direction of paper. Folding endurance data analyzed essentially as described by Smith[4] (p.110, 112).

† See Table 4 for a description of the treatments.

‡ Tension of M.I.T. Folding Endurance Tester set at 0.5 kg tension because the paper in the U.S.G.S. map was greatly deteriorated. All other value of treatment indices are based upon folding endurance data obtained at 1.0 kg tension.

expected life-time of the respective untreated standards.
These standardized measures are presented in Table 5 as
value of treatment indices.

Table 5 indicates that nonaqueous spray and immersion
deacidification treatments using magnesium methoxide as the
deacidification agent produce results equal or superior to
those obtained by an aqueous process using magnesium bicarbonate.   The results also indicate that near-neutral papers
(e.g., the 1971 map) have greater resistance to accelerated
heat aging than the more acidic papers do (e.g., the 1937
map).   A partial explanation for the variations between the
value of treatment indices of the nonaqueous deacidified papers may be that only 32 M.I.T. folding endurance specimens
were available per treatment to evaluate the effect of deacidification.   Nonetheless, the effect of deacidification, from the
statistical standpoint, was strong.   The one-tailed Student's
t statistics comparing the slopes of the untreated to treated
regression lines were sig-
nificant at the 5% level
for all but the 1971 map.
However, it is possible
that the effect of deacidification would become
significant for the paper
in the 1971 map because
the paper probably will
become more acidic as
a consequence of the
acidic reaction products
which develop in paper
during natural aging.

Table 6. Variation in Relative Humidity Study —The Deacidification Treatments

Treatment	Treatment Solution	Relative Humidity of Paper When Sprayed
1	Standard; no treatment	—
2	7% Magnesium methoxide in methanol-tri-chlorotrifluoroethane (1–3 parts), air dried	11%
3	Same as Treatment 2	50%
4	Same as Treatment 2	95%

. .

Table 7. Variation in Relative Humidity— The Value of Treatment Indices*

Date Printed	No. of Years Since Printing	Treatment No. (See Table 6)			
		1	2	3	4
1962	9	1.00	2.33	1.79	2.21
1927	44	1.00	1.28	2.25	1.57

* The value of treatment indices is computed using
M.I.T. folding endurance retention data obtained in
an accelerated aging study. Folding endurance specimens cut in machine direction of paper. Folding endurance retention data analyzed essentially as described by Smith[4]   (p.110, 112).

The two maps se-
lected to evaluate the effect of water naturally
present in paper on non-
aqueous deacidification
treatments were cut into
16 rectangular sections
as described above.
These sections were ran-
domly divided into four
groups and one of the
four treatments described
in Table 6 was applied to
each group.   The amount

of water taken up by the maps during the different relative humidity treatments was not determined. The preparatory procedure was first exposure for 24 hours at 95% relative humidity, second exposure for 24 hours at 11% relative humidity, and third exposure for 24 hours at 50% relative humidity. After exposure, the samples were maintained at the respective relative humidities until they were sprayed with the non-aqueous deacidification solution. Then, the samples were air-dried and the M. I. T. folding endurance specimens were cut. After aging, the five, ten and fifteen day test specimens were treated again at relative humidities of 95%, 11% and 50% for 24 hours to reduce dried-in strains and produce a consistent moisture content.

The value of treatment indices presented in Table 7 imply that the water naturally contained by air-dry paper is not a critical factor when single sheets of paper are deacidified. This implication is supported by a statistical analysis (based on Student's t statistics for the slopes of the regression lines) which indicates that the effect of all the deacidification treatments was significant at the 1% level. Although these findings indicate that librarians may ignore the practice of drying maps before deacidifying them by a nonaqueous spray process using magnesium methoxide, the data are insufficient to establish the relative humidity at which optimum results may be obtained.

Certain properties of the 1937 and the 1962 maps were investigated after aging at 105°C for fifteen days. The cold extraction pH value and buffering capacity values presented in Table 8 were obtained using a one gram sample of paper taken from the M. I. T. folding endurance specimens after they were tested. Both the pH determination and buffering capacity titration were carried out on the same sample extract. The function of buffering capacity is to evaluate the degree of protection that the deacidification treatments produce when an alkaline residue is deposited. The pH values are not satisfactory for this purpose because they only indicate the balance between the hydrogen and hydroxyl ions. The buffering capacity (reported in milliequivalents--X 100-- of acid or alkali required to change the pH of a 70 milliliter extract of one gram of paper by one pH unit at a pH of 7) measures the ability of a paper to resist changes in pH. In other words, the pH value is a measure of the current acid-alkali relationship within a paper while the buffering capacity evaluates the ability of a paper to maintain this relationship. Hence, the results may be interpreted as indicating (1) that

Table 8. Some Properties of the 1937 and 1962 U.S.G.S. Maps After Heat Aging

Year Printed	Treatment No. (See Tables 4, 6)	Properties After Aging at 105° C for 15 Days		
		pH*	Folding Endurance†	Buffering Capacity‡
1962	1	6.00	49.9	0.4
	2	10.50	84.2	7.0
	3	10.48	84.7	10.8
	4	10.50	79.5	7.3
1937	1	5.80	12.5	0.3
	2	8.08	56.5	1.0
	3	10.42	73.2	5.7
	4	10.50	58.8	6.4

* See (8), T509su-68, "Hydrogen Ion Concentration (pH) of Paper Extracts—Cold Extraction Method," 1968, for test method.

† See (8), T423m-50, "Folding Endurance of Paper (M.I.T. Folding Endurance)," 1950, for description of test procedure. Values reported here are the antilogarithms of the means of the logarithms of the test specimens after aging.

‡ Buffering capacity is reported as the quantity of acid or alkali (in milliequivalents × 100) required to change the pH of a 70 milliliter extract of one gram of paper by one pH unit at a pH of 7.

both the aqueous and non-aqueous treatments are effective in deacidifying paper, and (2) that the nonaqueous treatments provide much more protection against the development of harmful acidity in the future.

Acknowledgments

This investigation was made possible through assistance from and facilities made available by the Graduate Library School of The University of Chicago, Chicago, Illinois; the Chicago Paper Testing Laboratory, Chicago, Illinois; the Graphic Conservation Department of R. R. Donnelley and Sons Co., Chicago, Illinois; and The Institute of Paper Chemistry, Appleton, Wisconsin. The author is also grateful to the U.S. Geological Survey, Washington, D.C., for selecting and donating the maps studied in this investigation.

REFERENCES

1. See the following references: (a) Permanence by J. Byrne and J. Weiner, Appleton, Wis.: Institute of Paper Chemistry, 1964; and Permanence, Supplement No. 1, by J. Weiner and V. Pollack, Appleton, Wis.: Institute of Paper Chemistry, 1970, for an annotated bibliography of the literature. (b) Deterioration and Preservation of Library Materials, ed. by Howard W. Winger and Richard Daniel Smith, Chicago: University of Chicago Press, 1970, for discussions of the scholarly needs for preservation, the physical nature of the materials to be preserved, the means and care required in manufacture and storage and handling to

achieve permanence, the effects of different manufacturing techniques, programs for conservation and restoration, and personnel needs and requirements. (c)
V. W. Clapp, "The Story of Permanent/Durable Book-
Paper, 1115-1970," Scholarly Publishing, 2 (January
1971), 107-124; 2 (April 1971), 230-45; and 2 (July
1971), 353-67, for a nontechnical review of the problem and efforts to solve it.

2. Sudborough, J. J., and Mehta, M. M. "The Perishing
of Paper in Indian Libraries." Journal of Indian Institute of Science, 3 (August 1920), 119-226.

3. Chapman, J. A. "An Enquiry into the Causes of the
Perishing of Paper." Calcutta Review, n. s., (July
1919), 301-7. "The Perishing of Paper, II." Calcutta Review, n. s. (July 1920), 233-46. "The Imperial Library, Past and Future." Calcutta Review,
3d ser., 3 (March 1922), 447-57.

4. Smith, R. D. "The Nonaqueous Deacidification of Paper
and Books." Unpublished Ph. D. dissertation. Graduate Library School, The University of Chicago, December 1970. (The abstract of this dissertation was
published in American Archivist, 34:(January 1971),
75-76; and Tappi, 54 (May 1971), 787-88.)

5. See W. Gallay, "Cellulose-Water Relationships." In:
Pulp and Paper Science and Technology, vol. 1, Pulp,
ed. by C. E. Libby, New York: McGraw-Hill, 1962;
p. 444, for a graph of burst, tensile, tear, and folding endurance properties of paper over the range of
20 to 80% relative humidity.

6. Some conservators, noting that leather, parchment, and
vellum as well as other bindings are dimensionally
sensitive to fluctuations in relative humidity, have expressed concern about detrimental side effects from
storage at lower relative humidities. The potential
benefits probably are analogous to those described
above for paper. Obviously, since bindings are thicker and less able than paper is to adjust for dimensional change, appropriate attention must be given to
allow for strain release within the binding. The proper
practice is to effect relative humidity changes gradually, at a rate slow enough that the moisture content
of the book changes uniformly. It may also be necessary to include conditioning treatments for purposes of
insuring that bindings composed of leather, parchment,
and vellum remain soft and pliable.

7. The author initially described his Chicago Process in
"Guidelines for Preservation," Special Libraries, 59

(May-June 1968), 346-52.   His article, "New Approaches to Preservation, " containing additional information, appeared in the Library Quarterly, 40
(January 1970), 139-71; and in Reference 1(b), p. 139-
-71.   Two U. S. patent applications covering novel aspects (deacidification is one aspect) of the Chicago
Process have been allowed and will issue as patents
in 1972.

8.   Technical Association of the Pulp and Paper Association.
TAPPI Standards and Suggested Methods.   New York:
Technical Association of the Pulp and Paper Industry,
various dates.

9.   Some brownish component of the brown contour line on
certain maps was soluble in water.   A sufficient
quantity of this component was transported during
wetting and drying to cause staining.   Such staining
also occurred on the specimens of Treatment 1 as a
consequence of the 95% relative humidity treatment.
(It is believed this type of staining could be eliminated
under controlled drying conditions.)   No effect was
observed with the other printing inks on the maps.

DEVELOPING THE MAP COLLECTION IN
SMALLER LIBRARIES*

John G. Fetros

The problems involved in developing map collections
of smaller libraries are not unknown nor are they new, as
witness the March 15, 1950, issue of Library Journal which
devotes itself entirely to maps in the library. In his article,
"Public Libraries Must Have Maps, " in this issue, Gerald
McDonald notes that maps in public libraries had not been in
the past a significant feature of library collections. However, he also states: "Without a good basic collection of
maps a library forfeits a vital resource in reference and
research; it loses a key to the better understanding of many
of the books it circulates. "[1] Yet, as the Library Journal
editorial accompanying the articles notes, maps are treated
as "second class citizens" by librarians who give them cursory processing and consign them to inaccessible corners of
the library. Maps are considered by librarians to be "costly, difficult to process, and a nuisance to handle. "

In the period since 1950 little has changed. The very
useful booklet by Jessie Watkins, Selected Bibliography on
Maps in Libraries (Syracuse University Libraries, 1967),
provides references to articles of a non-technical nature on
map acquisition, classification, cataloguing, storage, and use,
yet few of the references would seem to be specifically applicable to the problems of the public library. The problem
is also neglected in the Minimum Standards for Public Library
Systems, 1966 (American Library Association, 1967). In
discussing materials for public library systems, maps are
not mentioned as a special category. Thus, the problems of
building a map collection in a public library remain even

*Reprinted by permission from Special Libraries Association,
Geography and Map Division, Bulletin No. 85 (1971), 24-28.

though in the articles in the Library Journal of March 15,
1950 there were indicated means whereby the problems might
be alleviated.

E. B. Espenshade in his article in the 1950 Library
Journal, "No One Source for Acquiring Maps," noted that the
major problems were a lack of well established bibliographic
aids, the multitude of sources of maps, and the fugitive and
documentary nature of maps. As a solution to the lack of
bibliographic aids Gerald McDonald in his article suggested
a solution by stating:

> If the Library Journal should undertake to appraise
> new maps as it now does new books, recordings
> and informational films, its contribution would great-
> ly help to remedy the situation. Keeping in mind
> the problem of the average public, it could offer
> them the help they now need in developing collec-
> tions of maps. 2

The Bulletin of the Geography and Map Division of the
Special Libraries Association does provide a partial solution
to this problem for the public library by listing and reviewing both maps and also books of interest to a map collection
such as atlases and books on cartography or map makers.
Yet the emphasis in the Bulletin is on materials for the
larger library or the specialized map library and it is unlikely that a librarian in the smaller public library with little map experience would be able to sort from the material
in the Bulletin those aspects of interest to his users.

In discussing the problems of maps in public libraries
it should not be thought that the solution exists in restricting
the collection to atlases. Gerald McDonald's article notes
that while atlases are basic tools they have limitations in size,
subject matter, and the finer points of cartographic expression. Therefore, they cannot be relied on exclusively, nor
can they take the place of separate sheets, folded maps, or
unbound sets in a complete and relevant map collection.
Recognizing the problems of map collecting in the smaller
library, libraries can easily devise a plan to ensure that this
category of material will be provided for in their collections.

Once again, it should be recognized that the problems
of a smaller library differ from those of a university library
or a specialized map library. Ena Yonge makes this point in
her article, "These Maps Are Essential," by stating that "a

large collection of maps is not advised for the small library
but that is simply saying that each one must be carefully
chosen. "3   To choose carefully, it is necessary for the library to plan carefully and to develop written procedures different from those used for books.   Among the elements the
library should consider in developing the collection plan are:

1. <u>Scope</u>. What areas will the collection cover--city,
    county, economic or metropolitan area, state, adja-
    cent states, country, adjacent foreign countries,
    countries with economic connections, etc.
2. <u>Formats.</u> A collection is dependent on the uses the
    map formats will be put to and the extent the library
    will be able to maintain up-to-date formats for that
    purpose. For instance, the library should consider
    if it should collect any navigational, air, or photo
    maps if it does not have the money, staff, or facili-
    ties to maintain a current up-to-date collection.
3. <u>Circulation policy</u>. Whether maps are to be cir-
    culated or whether the collection will be strictly
    reference creates differences in processing of maps
    and also in staffing a department to service the maps.
4. <u>Cataloging.</u> Will there be separate cataloguing or
    will there by any cataloging at all?
5. <u>Historical</u>. Which areas of the map collection will
    be developed as a permanent historical collection and
    which will be discarded when new maps arrive?
6. <u>Foreign languages.</u> Should maps and material in
    foreign languages be collected?

Another useful set of factors to consider in developing
the plan and in acquiring maps is a list of six questions noted
in a catalogue on <u>Business and Reference Maps, Atlases,</u>
<u>Guides</u> published by Rand McNally.   These six questions are:

1. For what purpose are you going to use the map?
2. What area do you want your map to include?
3. How large a map do you want?
4. What specific data do you want shown on the map?
5. Do you need an index?
6. Do you want a colored or black and white map?

These factors may be used to prepare an outline for a purchasing plan and to assist in tailoring a map collection to
the needs of a particular public library.

In discussing sources of maps, the smaller library is

still faced with difficulties.   The opposing purposes of college
and specialized libraries and public libraries has to be considered.   Lists useful for map acquisition in large and specialized libraries are likely to be too inclusive to be useful
to a librarian in a public library who often is not assigned
full time to maps and consequently is not able to evaluate the
list in relation to the needs of the public library.   Too many
names and addresses of map publishers and map sources are
confusing.   Since the needs of the public library are smaller,
a more selective list of sources will be useful.   In the area
of United States government maps this would imply that most
needs of smaller libraries should be satisfied by the maps or
the types of maps noted in the price lists.   Price List 53,
"Maps, Engineering, Surveying," Price List 70, "Census
Publications," and Price List 81, "Charts and Posters," all
include a selection of maps.   In addition, Price List 53
notes sources of nautical, aeronautical, topographic and other
government maps not sold by the Superintendent of Documents.
For state publications in the map field which would be useful
in smaller libraries, State Libraries should be contacted to
see if similar lists have been prepared.

    In the field of privately published maps the alternatives
available to the public library become greater.   The ads and
articles in the March 15, 1950, Library Journal, are still
useful in indicating map publishers and the types of material
they produce.   In this area logic will sometimes indicate how
the particular library can build up a list of sources to suit
its own needs.   Automobile clubs and oil companies are the
most obvious sources of maps for the smaller library, especially since these maps will usually be distributed at no
charge.   Libraries should contact the headquarters of auto
clubs and oil companies operating in their area for assistance
in collecting from these sources.   In addition, the small library should consider tourist bureaus and chambers of commerce as sources.   And while there are few stores specializing in the sale of maps, any city of fair size will have some
listings in the yellow pages of the telephone book which should
be considered.   For the library located near a city in which
there are stores dealing principally in maps, visits will be
very useful.   The advantage is, however, not merely the
chance to visit the map store to see the maps before buying.
Another advantage is that a dealer will usually stock what
people want.   Therefore by looking at the types of maps the
dealer stocks the librarian can get an idea of the sort of
maps a general public will want for frequent use.   Then, too,
by inspecting the maps, the librarian will become acquainted

with the publishers of maps. And, even if the store does not
carry a full line of maps of all publishers, it is likely to
have some maps from many and for those which seem to be
of quality the publishers can be queried for their full catalogues and price lists.

Just as useful, perhaps, is the simplification the existence of map stores brings about in the ordering of inexpensive maps. When it becomes difficult or not feasible to
order inexpensive maps from a variety of publishers it becomes useful to order from a single retail store even if library discounts do not prevail. The libraries in a larger
city, while often being many times too large to be too useful
in providing guidelines to a smaller public library, might
also be considered by librarians in building collections. Many
times the larger library by its arrangement of material might
emphasize some aspect of maps that the smaller library could
utilize. For instance, some large map libraries include
tourist guide books in the map department for their value in
including street maps of cities, especially foreign cities.
Other large map libraries clip newspapers and periodicals
for maps and this too could be a way for the smaller library
to quickly and easily build its collection of map material.
Finally the most useful source for smaller libraries in building collections is perhaps the library's own staff. With the
proliferation of traveling, staff members should be encouraged
to save maps they pick up and use on their vacations and to
offer them to the library for possible addition to the collection.

In developing a listing of sources for maps of greater
usefulness to smaller collections, three tools should be especially noted:

The Reference Guide for Travellers, J. A. Neal, compiler and editor (Bowker, 1969; $17.50), besides listing trav-
el books with detailed annotations, lists under each country
and state a selection of "Official Travel Publications." This
indicates the main United States address for those foreign
countries with tourist offices here and the address of the
tourist promotion office of each state. Lists of free brochures,
pamphlets and maps are noted. As a guide for initial selection of map material and a source of addresses to use later,
this is invaluable. It might be noted here that tourist pamphlets are an important part of any complete map collection
since many times they will include detailed maps of cities or
areas that are unobtainable in other ways.

The Europa Yearbook, 2 volumes (Europa Pubs. Ltd., annual; $47.50), lists under the category "Tourism" for each country the headquarters of the country's tourist bureau and also the cities in the world in which there are branch offices. Cities in the United States with a bureau are noted and a library could utilize this in seeking map material from the closest tourist bureau of the country.

The Worldwide Chamber of Commerce Directory (Johnson Publishing Company, Box 455, Loveland, Colorado 80537, annual; $4.00), is useful for building a mailing list for maps and other tourist information on cities to fill gaps in the collection.   Among the data included in the listings are the foreign embassies and foreign chambers of commerce in the United States and the foreign chambers of commerce outside the United States.

In conclusion, attention might be given to a comparative review of "World Atlases for General Reference," which appeared in Choice for July-August 1969, p. 625-630.   This is useful both in selecting new world atlases and in helping to understand the value and disadvantages of the atlases that might already be in the collection.   The discussion of the factors making a good atlas would seem to be particularly valuable, especially for librarians who do not deal with maps on a full time basis.

NOTES

1. McDonald, Gerald D., "Public Libraries Must Have Maps,"
    Library Journal, March 15, 1950, p. 453.
2. Ibid., p. 455.
3. Yonge, Ena L., "These Maps Are Essential," Library
    Journal, March 15, 1950, p. 440.
Interested readers may want to know about the article by
    Charles E. Current on "The Acquisition of Maps for
    School (and Other Small) Libraries," which appeared
    in the Wilson Library Bulletin, vol. 45, no. 6 (February 1971).

EDUCATION AND TRAINING IN MAP LIBRARIANSHIP*

C. B. Hagen

Talking about education and training in map librarianship is almost like talking about the one-tenth of the iceberg
that stands above the water because there are vast underlying issues that must be touched upon.   Maps, as well as
most other special materials, have for a long time been the
step-children of traditional libraries and librarians who have
developed through the years an almost unconscious, but nevertheless real, system of castes or class levels in terms of
"respectability" and "desirability" of library materials.   For
centuries, and until some 50 years ago, the only printed material that was considered proper in the library was the
familiar book.   Today the aristocrats of the library still
seem to be the collections of art, rare books, first editions
and literature, followed in a descending order by standard
books, periodicals, technical reports, and newspapers.   Materials such as maps, recordings, or films are at the bottom
of the ladder in terms of development policies, budget and
space allocations, personnel support, and the like.   This attitude is not only American; it also permeates other countries,
perhaps to an even greater degree.   The actual case which
follows tells the story better than statements or figures.   A
team of American librarians conducted a long survey of libraries in a South American country.   In one case they found
that the librarian of a university library was spending most
of the yearly budget for the acquisition of rare books and expensive bindings and first editions despite the fact that the
most essential tools of reference, technical periodicals, and
research and textbooks were lacking.   For that librarian,
this policy was the natural course, the best way to give great
prestige and respectability to his library.

*Reprinted by permission from Special Libraries Association,
Geography and Map Division, Bulletin No. 77 (1969), 3-7.

The present revolution in media and communications
is a significant indication of things to come. For this reason I consider the term "librarian" (from liber = book) an
outmoded misnomer, because I firmly believe the "librarian"
of today and tomorrow must be a person entrusted by civilization with the task of acquiring, preserving, and making
available to the public the human knowledge recorded on any
permanent and usable medium. We can apply the famous
statement by Marshall McLuhan, "The medium is the mas-
sage," to what I have been discussing so far. In other words,
more than the context, it is the medium, in this particular
case the physical appearance, value and age of the medium,
that counts. This is an attitude that has seeped almost unconsciously into most library systems and librarians.

This attitude is partially responsible for irreparable
damages caused to our cultural heritage. As officer of two
major organizations dealing with special materials, * I have
visited many collections and I have seen many sad and frustrating situations. Even in large universities I have consistently seen collections of maps or collections of fragile phono-
graph records piled up in basements and attics, subject to
rodents and thieves, suffering from extremes of heat and humidity, and often stored in the original boxes or rolls in
which they were brought or donated to the institution. Such
collections are deprived of the most basic rules of care,
maintenance, security and development policies. It is generally argued that such situations are due to lack of funds.
This is often quite true. It is a fact that libraries are in
most cases under-staffed and have to struggle with inadequate
budgets. But on the other hand the attitudes I have mentioned
can be clearly observed in the fact that the cuts, economies
and postponements always affect the collections of special materials which seem afflicted with a perennial case of second
or even third-class citizenship in most library systems. This
is most serious because in so doing librarians are ignoring
the immense revolution that is taking place in the communications media and the rapid emergence of the new materials.
It is serious too because in their eagerness to cling to a
medium, the printed word in the form of the familiar and respectable book, librarians are often too eager to relinquish to
other inexpert hands the custody of the new materials. Thus,

---

*The author was in 1969 president of the Western Association
of Map Libraries and vice president of the Association for
Recorded Sound Collections.

instead of providing such materials with the protection of the admirable procedures and methods developed by American librarianship through the years, librarians have eagerly abandoned them as being undesirable, unbelonging "things." Thus maps are generally given to geography departments, recordings to music departments, films or video tapes to theater arts departments, etc. The results can be disastrous and in many visits I have seen some very distressing situations. In many cases such collections become almost the personal domain of a certain professor or department and thus are jealously guarded against "outside users." In other cases, the materials are deprived of the most elementary measures of preservation and security, and are at the disposition of almost any faculty or student of a department who happens to have a key and who can use them on a self-help basis without any control whatsoever.

The discussion thus far may seem to be rather unrelated to the subject of education in map librarianship, but, if so, it is because I have been concentrating on the nine-tenths of the iceberg that lies below the water, without which a full understanding of the educational problems in map librarianship cannot be fully grasped.

Coming now to more specific matters, anyone familiar with special materials will agree that the collecting, acquisition, technical processing, reference services, and the like affecting special materials are as complex or perhaps even more so than in the world of books. However, the reading of the curricula offered by schools of libraries throughout the country consistently reveals the fact that in most places the entire subject of special materials is crowded into one optional course offered to a handful of students, generally for a couple of hours a week for one quarter or semester. This generally means that the entire world of map librarianship is crowded into perhaps three or four hours of discussion. As all special materials are grouped in a single package, no specialized instructors can be provided. The general pattern is to have this course taught by a junior instructor or by one with a casual interest in some of the special materials to be discussed. Comparing this with what happens in the realm of racial matters, it would be the same as if the entire world of the Negroes, Mexican-Americans, Orientals, and American Indians would be treated in a single course taught by an instructor who had some Spanish in high school, spent a couple of weeks in Mexico City, and had a "nice" liberal attitude towards minorities. Imagine such an instructor trying to teach

the entire and complex range of the Mexican-American or
Negro cultures. It is no wonder that racial minorities feel
insulted when the college administrations try to compromise
by offering them such token courses. The same comparison
can be applied to the case of special materials. Some of the
appalling inadequacies of the instruction offered in various
schools even reaches us at the UCLA Map Library. We often
receive interlibrary loan requests for old books or bibliographies that have been superseded or have been out-of-print
for many years. Almost always the requests can be traced
to some library student or newly appointed map librarian
who was trying to follow the outlines he was given in his
course on special materials. Some of the materials and bibliographies recommended might have been appropriate some
twenty or thirty years ago, but not any longer. Another instance of the neglect given to maps in library schools could
be seen in the federally sponsored Institute on Map Librarianship held at UCLA in the summer of 1968. My intention as
principal instructor was to teach the course at an advanced
seminar level. However, after the first day we had to lower
the level almost to that of an introductory course. The students, all professional librarians, were eager and most enthusiastic, but most had never been exposed in their schools
to even introductory lessons on map librarianship.

There are some signs indicating that a few schools
may begin to realize the need to teach at least the fundamentals of map librarianship. For some schools planning a
more in-depth curricula in this field, a caution that immediately comes to mind is that two basic elements must first
be considered: they are the size of the map library and the
local facilities of map production, the latter indispensable for
frequent field visits. It may be argued that most map librarians will go on to organize small collections in public or
college libraries. However, I think, even if this is the case,
the students need during their course of studies to be continually exposed to all of the problems and work situations
encountered in a large map library. I am basing this firm
belief on my experience of several years in this field. I believe that any institution planning to undertake a specialized
course of studies in map librarianship should consider having
a map library of at least one-quarter million maps and should
be located in an area having several map-producing agencies
or companies. A parallel can be found in almost any profession, such as medicine. General librarians, like the general practitioner in medicine, may secure an adequate training in most schools. Highly trained specialists, however,

must come from a medical school associated with a large
research-oriented clinical hospital. A case in point is a
large western university which has a department of geography
with heavy emphasis on applied cartography and mapmaking.
Unfortunately, neither the department nor the library has
even given enough emphasis to the map library which is relatively small (about 100,000 maps) and not well-maintained
due to perennial problems of lack of budget and personnel.
A very interesting course offered is Map Intelligence for
which the students must prepare a term paper called "Cartobibliography." This paper is basically a study and evaluation of the mapping agencies, map coverage, reliability of
the various cartographic materials, etc., for a given country.
The professor is extremely knowledgeable, and the students
are eager and capable. The papers, however, on close examination leave much to be desired and are often frankly inadequate and obsolete, a direct reflection on the collection
and materials available for the project. Comparing this to
medicine would be like asking a medical student to do highly
specialized research on a certain disease or a clinical case
at a medical school with rather moderate research facilities.
The handicaps, perhaps, are even greater for map librarians,
because in this field there is presently no mechanism of
unionized catalogues, interlibrary loans, microfilm, and
microcards similar to those already in full operation in the
biomedical or physical sciences.

Faced with the almost total absence of organized
courses in map librarianship, the question obviously is --
What can be done at the present to provide training for prospective map librarians? None of the alternatives given below provides a satisfactory answer but at least they represent a start. One answer is, of course, summer institutes
similar to the one held at UCLA in 1968. A major problem
is the difference and degree of backgrounds and the almost
complete lack of previous experience and exposure to cartographic materials on the part of most students. This makes
the teaching task quite difficult as it forces the instructor to
lower the levels, leaving the few more experienced students
in a rather uncomfortable position.

Another solution is a series of internships. The UCLA
Map Library has had a number of interns, varying in time
from a week to six months and coming from California, Canada, and Chile. I understand that other large map libraries
have also accepted occasional interns. In such cases personal attention can be given to the person and a program of

supervised tasks, duties, and readings can be assigned to
each intern to fit his particular needs and length of stay.
The problem for the host library, however, is considerable
and often made critical by lack of space and personnel. As
an example, one intern staying at the UCLA Map Library for
six months represented for us an expenditure of several hundred hours of labor (teaching, discussions, preparation of
assignments, supervision) which in turn represents a few
thousand dollars, a sort of "invisible expense" for which the
host library could seldom if ever expect a compensation.
The Summer Project of the Library of Congress is sometimes referred to as an internship. However, this is quite
misleading as its value in terms of education in map librarianship is questionable. Basically the program is a swap of
duplicate maps no longer needed by the Library of Congress
for free student labor sent by the cooperating libraries. The
students are mostly assigned to routine clerical jobs, generally filing and sorting maps, but except for a couple of
visits to mapping agencies no organized course of studies
covering the multiple aspects of map librarianship could possibly be afforded by the Library of Congress. On the one
hand, this would overload their reduced staff and, on the
other, it would greatly diminish the work output of the students, labor badly needed by the Library of Congress to process the immense backlog accumulated during the year.

Finally, a most interesting phenomenon in the field of
map librarianship is the emergence of two strong associations,
the Association of Canadian Map Libraries and the Western
Association of Map Libraries. They were created only a few
years ago to provide closer ties between map libraries of two
geographic areas, Canada and the Western United States,
whose basic features in common are vast distances. Very
soon however, both organizations assumed an active educational role in the form of periodic meeting-workshops. The
second annual conference of the Association of Canadian Map
Libraries, held in June of 1968 in Edmonton, Alberta, featured three days of exciting technical talks and professional
papers. The Western Association of Map Libraries meets
twice a year in the San Francisco Bay area. Each meeting
lasts for one day, and is crammed with technical talks and
workshops. There are, of course, the problems of people
who cannot attend, and necessarily the talks must be short
and concise; but at least these associations provide one of
the most promising starts in an experiment of partial education in the field of map librarianship. I also believe these
associations can exercise some amount of pressure to show

university administrations the need for establishing courses
in map librarianship, recognize the importance of these materials and their rightful place in modern libraries, and also
establish some minimum standards of space, personnel, budget, and equipment applied to map libraries.   Speaking as an
officer of the Western Association of Map Libraries and the
Association for Recorded Sound Collections, I would like to
conclude by saying that I believe the most gigantic problem
we face is to convince the library schools and library administrations of the importance of such materials, to acquire
for them first-class citizenship, and establish once and for
all their rightful place in the modern academic and scholarly
environment.   I know well that we belong with a new era and
the new media revolution.   We have little to lose and much
to gain.

DESIGN FOR A NATIONAL COLLECTION*

Theodor E. Layng

I see rising amidst government complexes, in all the
great capitals of the world, huge globular structures of stainless steel and glass, looking from above like one of Homan's
celestial spheres; and these are called national map collections or research centres. (Mark you, and thank God for
purity, none of them are called national map libraries.)
This is stretching the imagination a bit--I question whether
from above they will look like a Homan production, but give
and take a few specifications here and there is this merely
the stuff of dreams, or is it a practical and present desider-
atum, or shall it ever be that cartographical collections and
research centres should take their place now or in the future, as autonomous institutions alongside other national repositories. Have they indeed the potential or the dynamics
so to do?

Since this is by way of a valedictory address to the
association I beg some latitude in prefacing my remarks.
First I confess I was a little chagrined while pondering this
paper to realize how few in number are the guidelines or
principles I can offer at this point as worthful to my profession, as compared with the many in the past I have found
illusory. But the few I have in mind to present have been
fortified with the years. These I will define. In fact I in-
tend to use this occasion to do a little plain speaking which
I rather hope will ruffle the philistines wherever and who-
ever they may be.

No one will appreciate more than this audience how
much it has meant to me to have the privilege of discussing

*Reprinted by permission from Association of Canadian Map
Libraries, Proceedings of the 6th Annual Conference, 1972;
7-13.

these present matters ad infinitum with the keepers of maps
in many countries.   How enjoyable and how stimulating it has
all been!   But sadly I must report that I have never met a
true keeper of the maps who was happy with the state of his
particular bailiwick, or was he able to extract much comfort
in projecting the shape of things to come.   It would be pre-
sumptuous from my vantage point to make specific references
to the state of map collections in countries other than Canada.
Sufficient to say that I can not positively identify one which I
believe measures up to the true potential of a national map
collection.   I should like to underscore the last statement for
the benefit of those Canadians with colonial complexes who
have upon occasion sought to upset the integrity of the embryonic national map collection of Canada because it does not
conform in every way to the structuring of similar institutions
in other countries.   The maturity and holdings of Old World
institutions will always be a wonder and delight to scholars
everywhere.   In so many cases however their natural growth
has been stilted by subordinate structuring and design.   I believe we must from our own experience adopt the strictest
criteria before accepting any part of a pattern which may
still be in existence simply because a point of no return has
long since been reached.   (For my own part, and for those
of my peers whose careers will have spanned the third quarter
of a century which was to have been ours--Canada's--I say
gentlemen, it is later than you think.)

        I am not concerned here with practices and procedures.
These are and should be the variables in any organization.
Every junior staff member should have the privilege of ques-
tioning them.   This is surely the way of distributing shares
in an organization, and one way of keeping it healthy.   In
fact it is basic to the design of the institution I envisage that
it be not contained within fixed boundaries, but face on all
sides a free frontier; that whatever techniques are employed
they shall not be pressured indefinitely to present a facade
of efficiency but that they shall be servants of concepts de-
manding frequent revision and change.   Moreover I would give
the largest concepts, the master plan, the furthest objective
only a little longer life: they too must be considered expendable if an institution reaching maturity is still to maintain
the dynamics of youth.   I demand only one fixed quantity, a
hard magnetic core at the centre of things that will bring together and keep together a nation's cartographical treasures,
and all the lore relating thereto.

        I know it is a bit naive in this day and age in the

process of planning to consider the mere role of people.   I
still believe however that they are, and will remain, pecu-
liarly enough, at the heart of the matter.   It is people for
instance--and not data processing--who will hold our institutions in trust from one generation to another.   It is people
in fact who bestow the mantle of an institution upon the dull
precincts of a repository.   I think it is especially encumbent
upon the planner to consider the role of people in the custodial sciences.   I desire that my institution will offer the
complete professional fulfillment to the people who work
there.   Therefore it is essential that they are surrounded,
not by just a fraction but by all the tools of their profession,
that in the performance of their various functions they are
experiencing the rich rewards of a chosen intellectual pur-
suit.   These are the people who serve best.   These are the
people who with easy competence will engender the relaxed
atmosphere so necessary for research and writing.

I think there will be in the next few years--in fact
I think there had better be--much talked about national repositories and their relationships, one with another.   Is
there for instance a place for a national repository which
houses only one medium of information: or have we already
laid the foundations for overall custodial palaces where several institutions will be embalmed, reverting as it were to
mere repository status for purposes of physical control only,
while intellectual control is superimposed by top level authority, extracting knowledge, I suppose simultaneously, via
subject matter from all available media.   Without question
these custodial palaces smack of the future--the kinds of fu-
turity explored so frequently for us on television and in science fiction, and all the automatic data processing boys will
dwell happily in their halls forever after, and perhaps they
will be able to make the rest of us happy.

How many, and broad, and deep must be our considerations before we accept carte-blanche this type of planning.
Will the planners be trapped in terms of status quo instead
of potential when they assess the place of individual repositories in their scheme of things?   Can any combination of
large repositories, each responsible for assembling together
one medium of information, and which inevitably will grow
and grow out of all present proportions, be brought together,
and kept together in harmony to form a macro institution?
Are the natural growth elements inherent for instance in a
cartographical collection likely to be stilted, or maimed, or
in other ways, bear the brunt of subordination if it is but a

small part of a huge complex? Something to be gained, something to be lost, and who will predict the net profit and loss?
What sort of philosopher-custodian will lay down guidelines
with sufficient flexibility to satisfy all the specialized custodial sciences now in existence? Who will identify and develop the nuclei of new custodial sciences?

Automation will of course render valuable assistance
in the future as we have heard ad nauseam. I have noticed,
particularly in the younger men and women in our profession,
a beautiful optimism as they talk of the multi millions of this
and that of the products of the future which will accrue to
their custody. They apparently trust implicity in the progress
of technology to aid and abet them in keeping physical and intellectual control of the nation's litter. They have every
right in their thinking: confidence of youth today in facing
tomorrow's problems is absolutely essential for a well-ordered
future. Mine is only a footnote: before knowledge is cap-
suled and disseminated in effective and full meaningful array
there must be a most thorough screening of the broadest possible assemblage of material. High selectivity requires research and more research. There are no shortcuts at the
intake end of data processing. In other words there is a
tremendous amount of homework to be done. I think that independent development of the specialized custodial sciences
in autonomous and distinctively designed institutions is the
surest guarantee of producing the high calibre of professional
capacity needed to get the job done. To which I add a wist-
ful hope that through the clouds or sunshine of the new world
of technology--whichever it is to be--our custodians will not
confuse physical control and quantity with intellectual control
and quality.

Whatever happens I hope governments have the per-
spicacity to realize that they should pay particular attention
to the future of the smaller national repositories such as a
national map collections. I think that these institutions may
well be the oases of the future--think centres for a world
just slightly out of balance. They should be considered something more than workshops. People will have more leisure
time in future and why not accent for them a leisurely enjoyment of intellectual pursuits?

There are many ways of measuring the number of
people needed to staff a national map collection. But why
bother? I notice several devices amongst old notes of mine
which now only serve to depress me. For instance at one

time I devised a very pat formula indeed. There were to be
twenty-five staff members for the first million maps, and so
many added for each subsequent million. As I remember my
mechanics were based on the size and staffing of map collections in other countries, which was rather witless of me because of course there are no institutions in the world so un-
derstaffed as map collections. Moreover the formula which
other keepers of maps use or have thrust upon them is no
concern of mine. I am concerned with effectively developing
the potential of a national institution and the people needed
to do that job. I now have a staff of twenty-five less two,
and my holdings have not yet reached the half-million mark,
and I have the very distinct impression that I could double
the staff and still be found wanting. Recently, an eminent
economist chided me with the fact that we were not absorbing enough university graduates in our types of institutions.
He had no trouble at all in persuading me--now all he has
to do is persuade government and administration. In all
seriousness I am distressed at the number of unemployed
graduates, and some of the meaningless jobs which others
are given to do. How much better to absorb them where
they are needed in government and where they can make a
real contribution to the nation's wealth. I offer a national
map collection as a particularly good training ground for
graduates in a variety of the social sciences. People are
needed who have a comprehensive knowledge of history and
geography, who can readily adapt themselves to archival sciences, and have rather avant-garde views on library science,
to serve adequately the diversity of disciplines requiring
maps.

     Through the years in the developed countries some
fascinating games must have been played in the field of the
custodial sciences, in which incidentally The Keeper of the
Maps seems to have been perennially behind the eight-ball.
In retrospect little else of the pattern of play is discernible
since evidently everyone played according to their own rules
if any, and, from the results, I believe without any referee
and sometimes of course one of the players would grab the
ball and go home. That was the name of the game. In
1450 or so, the librarians who wielded the most authority,
forgetting their Latin roots, declared that a library was actually a place where all objects of study were assembled;
and since in many cases a library was the only haven in
sight, through expediency the definition was found by many
to be acceptable, custodians, especially keepers of maps,
must give every credit to librarians for having preserved

many cartographical gems, and in a very good state, since usually they were placed in a back room out of harm's way and forgotten about.

It has not been easy, and never will be easy, to lay down the lines of demarcation between different custodial sciences--to render unto Caesar.... It has remained a perennial problem in many countries much more mature in these matters than Canada. Everywhere there seems to be confusion in sorting out the relationship between library science and the newer specialized custodial sciences. Librarianship is the oldest, the most entrenched, and possibly the most authoritarian of all custodial sciences, but isn't it time the younger sciences weaned themselves completely from mother librarian? Even though she is loath to let them go, modern society demands that she do so. That libraries mostly on the basis of expediency, have in many instances become the repositories of a hotch-potch of records, does not change the true image of a librarian or the functions of a library. The essence and meaning of library science is books and nothing else. Miles of book shelves may contain a multifarious range of subject matters, but who will suggest that this fact imputes some special omnipotence to libraries which allows them to maintain intellectual control over their holdings. The breadth of library science is measured in terms of physical control only. The breadth and depth of the specialized custodial sciences are measured in terms of both physical and intellectual control; accessioning, classification, cataloguing and such functions are not in any way peculiar to librarians. Is a librarian qualified to analyze the map content of an atlas in relation to our cartographical heritage or legacy, or a single archival map? Is there for instance any part of a librarian's training which can substitute for a comprehensive knowledge of history and geography in the cataloguing unit of a map collection? The 1450 definition of a library ought to be held to be valid today only in undeveloped countries, small communities and universities. By which you will gather that my design has no place for any designs the National Library may have on the National Map Collection.

However indiscriminately records may have been distributed in the past, all custodians must now act in concert, and each one within his competency to set the record straight; otherwise the massive build-up of millions of multifarious records must present to all an awesome prospect for the future. We must forget those decisions made in the past on the basis of tradition or expediency, or merely on some

punctilious whim.   The lines must be drawn in certain knowledge of what distinguishes such classes as archivists, librarians, keepers of maps, and the custodians of various kinds of
econography.   Each science must be given sufficient dimension
that it may be characterized by a total comprehension of its
particular field of interest, and the range of its custodianship
should reflect its complete identity.

Last year before this group I think I laid down the
first commandment of the Keeper of the Maps: "thou shalt
covet thy neighbours' atlases, his maps and charts, and his
plans, and his related cartographical, geographical and historical material, of whatever vintage and source." I forgot
to mention however, and this is important, because I find
even in this day and age that some custodians would still
distribute the nation's cartographical records on the basis of
whether they are printed or manuscript, archival or current,
and some librarians will even covet an atlas because super-
ficially it looks like a book.   I think therefore, we should
add to the commandment the words, "in any form whatsoever"; and perhaps "books with maps." Seriously, there is
no class of material that goes into repositories which is any
easier to identify than cartographical material; and if we are
looking for rational and simple ways of dividing the nation's
pot-pourri into collections for permanent retention would you
not agree that the National Map Collection of Canada is a
model?   As far as I know it is the only structurally complete map collection in the world.   If ever an occasion arises
when its integrity is in jeopardy I hope the Association will
let its voice be heard loud and clear.

I should mention before I proceed with the next block
in my design that I am bespeaking my own personal thoughts
today; none of my remarks in any way should be construed
as official.   You have gotten my message I hope of what material should be placed in a national map collection.   Now
these are the tools (to use again that lovely phrase of the
late Peter Skelton) of a diversity of disciplines.   I think it
would not be too designing of me to suggest that at some
point in the future some government activities now carried
on close to the map production end of things might very well
become functions of the National Map Collection.   I am thinking of the highly specialized research work that goes into
such projects as the Atlas of Canada, and of single thematic
maps that do not fit into the great national series.   It seems
to me that here are the tools that geographers use in assembling mapping data of the variety where field work is not

an essential part of their research.   Perhaps too, toponymic
studies could be carried on most effectively in the National
Map Collection.   Later I should like to hear your views on
these matters.

I think you would also be interested to hear that feasibility studies are now in progress to determine whether or not
the National Map Collection should take over the resources
and management of one or more of other government map collections.   These collections would of course be left where
they are to serve the needs of the departments that house
them.   The idea is to avoid duplication wherever possible,
to give more strength and greater dimensions to the functions
of the map keepers, and provide the latter with better career
opportunities.   All of which of course means that we are continually exploring the potential of a National Map Collection,
and one day, who knows, we may see rising ... etc.

Before I close I would like to pay my tribute to the
parent body of the National Map Collection, the Public Archives of Canada, in this her centennial year.   I was very
proud not long ago to hear from this platform very sincere
and glowing tributes to the Archives from eminent archivists
from several countries.   The Archives has carried through a
great experience in custodial science, having successfully
spawned five great national repositories.   If in the future the
National Map Collection is not to have its own dome there
can be no better place for it than the Public Archives.   I
have spoken of the need for autonomy in building up an institution.   A wise succession of Dominion Archivists has seen
to it that the divisions of the Archives were allowed to develop their own principles and procedures, and in this way
have contributed as much as any institution in the world to
the custodial sciences.   If the National Map Collection reaches
the proportions I envisage it will be because it was lucky
enough to have been born in the Public Archives of Canada.

THE RISE OF MAP LIBRARIES IN AMERICA DURING THE NINETEENTH CENTURY*

Lynn S. Mullins

Easily accessible map collections are one of the vital information needs of our time. Maps are tools of our geographical knowledge, and may assist in the solution of myriad problems related to our physical, political, and cultural environment. The systematic amassing of maps, and storing and arranging them for use is essentially a twentieth century phenomenon, and today there are literally hundreds of organizations in America with active map libraries. The Geography and Map Division of the Library of Congress, the American Geographical Society, and various other governmental, public, university, and commercial libraries are mentioned as types of map collecting agencies in the nation today. In the nineteenth century there were a variety of environmental needs which gave rise to the development of map libraries. Three of our major libraries which made significant contributions in the field are Harvard University, the American Geographical Society and the Library of Congress. The activities of these institutions help to illustrate various objectives of map collecting.

The main reasons for map collecting probably fall into three categories: (1) educational, e. g., collecting maps so as to learn the basic geographical facts about the regions of the earth and its place in the larger celestial systems; (2) utilitarian, or "compilation," e. g., collecting maps so as to be able to compile new ones as the old ones become outdated; (3) scholarly, e. g., collecting maps so as to understand better the many aspects of the discipline of geography.

---

*Reprinted by permission from Special Libraries Association, Geography and Map Division, Bulletin No. 63 (1966), 2-11. A longer documented version is on file in the American Geographical Society and the Library of Congress.

Map collecting for these reasons seems to require some sort of organization to support them, for instance a school, a government surveying bureau, or a body of geographers. However, before men collected maps as part of organized groups, they had an interest in particular maps and in the particular geographical knowledge that was represented in maps. This interest may not always have meant the immediate collecting of maps, but it is important to note as a preliminary stage in the overall development of map collecting.

This interest in geographical knowledge on the part of the American people, newly settled in a thin slice of a vast country-to-be, is not surprising. Their land was new to them, and constant military involvements forced familiarity upon them. George Washington, as General of the Continental Army, was aware of the importance of knowing the land upon which fighting was to take place. In 1777 he urged Congress to authorize him to establish a mapping corps. Washington himself was a map collector and his library contained a special section of maps and charts including forty maps, six atlases, and five navigational charts. His work as a surveyor is well known and he drew at least twenty-five maps, and annotated many others. Thomas Jefferson had an interest in the military importance of maps, and as governor of Virginia during the Revolutionary War collected and interpreted information about the British and American forces, and put it down on maps. In 1812, the nation was again involved in war, and felt the need for adequate maps, and this gave impetus to the mapping of the major waterways of the country. Maps were of importance after both the Revolutionary War and the War of 1812 in settling the peace and determining new boundaries. Harvard's famous Ebeling map collection was consulted by the government and used in settling the Northeastern Boundary dispute with Great Britain. In addition to the military and political interest in particular maps, much interest in maps stemmed from commercial factors. Colonial merchants, who made their living largely from the ocean, were particularly interested in the geography of the American sea coast. Benjamin Franklin, versatile American of many interests, drew up maps of the Gulf Stream. Writing about Franklin's interest in the navigation of the Gulf Stream, Lawrence Martin, onetime Chief of the Division of Maps of the Library of Congress, says:

> He seems to, as is too often forgotten, to have
> been not only the first person to recognize and
> make clear to European as well as American navi-

gators the uses of the Gulf Stream, but also one of
the first to deduce its existence, the first to verify
it by observation and report, and the first to publish it upon a map, which he did upon the basis of
a rough sketch by Captain Folger, a Nantucket ship
master. [1]

During the third decade of the nineteenth century merchants looked further than their own coast line.   Industries,
such as whaling, were growing rapidly, and they promoted
exploration of other than American waters.   Charts of the
seas resulted from these exploring expeditions, and these
were sought by the merchants.   Countless other persons, who
fall into no particular category, were interested in looking
at maps of the newly acquired territories of the nation.   Following the rapid national expansion and acquisition of new territory, came explorers, surveyors, and mappers.   Thomas
Jefferson, as President, did much to spur interest in this
country's expansion by encouraging and supporting its exploration.   Jefferson was somewhat of a geographer, with a personal library containing almost two hundred volumes on the
geography of America alone.   His father had been a cartographer in Virginia, and Thomas Jefferson himself had done surveying and cartographic work.   Notably, as part of this activity, he had been involved in the division of the Old Northwest Territory into new states.

Thus, good reasons existed for Americans to be interested in maps.   Where could they find these maps and
charts of waters and land that were of concern to them?
There was no central agency that served as a depository for
newly compiled maps, and maps were scattered among different government bureaus.   Citizens could, however, go to
the libraries of various societies and find a recent atlas; or
to one of the libraries of the several universities in the East
to consult a new geography textbook that might have recent
maps.   Local booksellers were unlikely to have new maps,
but society and university libraries were places of map reference.

In Philadelphia the American Philosophical Society
existed as an intellectual discussion center where scholarly
papers on many scientific subjects were presented.   Geographical topics were but one of the many subjects discussed
there.   In that period, however, it must be remembered
that men were not generally specialists, and had interests
in many fields.   Certainly all could not be Franklins or

Jeffersons, but many came close to these ideals. Early proceedings of the Society indicate that books relating to the
geography of the United States were acquired for the library.
The Library Company of Philadelphia had several members
who were geographically oriented. Benjamin Franklin, of
course, but also the surveyor Nicholas Skull, and Thomas
Godfrey the inventor of a mariner's quadrant were members.
If a scholar wanted up-to-date geographical treatises and maps
of America, however, he could not have found much recent
material in the Library Company's holdings. The Academy
of Arts and Sciences of Boston was another center where map
consultants might go. Members of this Academy included
Nathaniel Bowditch, Dr. Holyoke, and other persons interested
in navigation, weather observation, and general geographical
topics.

The university library was also a source of reference.
Most of the American universities had included geography
courses as a part of their curriculum during the eighteenth
century, and their libraries contained geography textbooks,
globes, maps and atlases. If a quest was not specifically
for the most recent compiled maps of new American territory, it could probably be satisfied at any of the university
libraries. One of the three major map collecting agencies
of the nineteenth century was Harvard University. In 1818
Harvard received the Ebeling collection which made it the
largest map library in America at the time and for most of
the century, towering above all other university and society
collections. The Ebeling collection of 10,000 maps and charts,
and 3200 books on America was purchased for the University
by Col. Israel Thorndike of Boston, for $6500.

Christoph Daniel Ebeling was a professor of Greek and
history in Hamburg who was much interested in American history. To facilitate his study he bought a collection of maps
and books from Dr. Brandes, a professor at Hanover. This
formed the nucleus of his collection. In addition Dr. Ebeling
spent some time in this country and made purchases of books
and maps to augment his collection of Americana. Ebeling
worked for forty years on his major opus Erdbeschreibung
und Geschichte von Amerika (1793-1816), and at his death in
1817 had completed seven volumes. The maps and atlases in
the collection, dating from the sixteenth century, were principally of America. Many of the maps had been cut out of
books, and then systematically arranged in geographical and
chronological order.

Prior to this major acquisition, the largest in the library's history since the fire of 1764, Harvard had had no map collection to speak of. The library did have many geographies, atlases and globes, which had primarily been used in connection with courses in geography. In the early history of the study of geography in America globes were at least, if not more so, as useful as maps. Globes enabled the user to obtain a picture of the entire surface of the earth, and were ideal for a study of geography which was mainly concerned with general descriptions and theoretical observations on the planet. Globes were frequently donated to the library in pairs, terrestrial and celestial, and were always welcome gifts. By the time of the Ebeling acquisition, however, the nature of college geography had shifted away from the abstract and towards the minute detailed descriptions of the divisions of the earth. Jared Sparks, as a spokesman for the new geographical approach, wrote that the commercial man should know "every sea, bay, harbor, and navigable river," as well as the soil, climate, and commodities of foreign countries if he is to avoid losses in men and money.

Thus one might say that the scholars at Harvard were ripe for the advantages of a collection of detailed maps on assorted scales at the time of the Ebeling acquisition. Of importance, however, is the fact that the Ebeling collection was not primarily made up of current minutely-descriptive maps, but included rare and historical maps produced by cartographers of three centuries. In 1831 Harvard's Library, under the direction of Benjamin Peirce, printed a catalogue of its entire holdings, with the map collection taking up a separate volume entitled Catalogue of Maps and Charts in the Library of Harvard University. By this time the Ebeling collection had been increased somewhat by further gifts, notably the David Warden collection of 1200 volumes and many maps which were the gift of Samuel A. Eliot in 1823. However, the map collection was still primarily Ebeling. The collection appears to have been neglected for several decades after the printing of the catalogue, and no aggressive map acquisition policies were followed.

These were not years of neglect in the map collecting activities for the rest of the country. Two new and distinct movements were visible by the middle of the nineteenth century. One stemmed from the increasingly widespread surveys and map compilations made by government bureaus and agencies, and the other from the interaction between the growing discipline of geography and developing commercial,

financial, and journalistic factors. Specifically the first was
the movement towards a central governmental depository
agency for all government-compiled maps, and the other was
the rooting of a geographical society in which the collecting
of maps was one of the charter-stated purposes. Each of
these movements was a major landmark in the overall picture of developing map collections.

Perhaps the first spokesman for a federal geographical
and map department was Lieutenant Edward B. Hunt of the
Office of Engineers of the U. S. Army. At a meeting of the
American Association for the Advancement of Science held in
Cleveland in 1853 he presented a paper on the need for establishing a specifically geographical library. Such a proposal was prompted by the fact that he had had much difficulty in his research work on coastal geography. The necessary reference sources were scattered throughout the country,
and he was never sure that he had not omitted anything of
prime importance. He noted that all existing map collections
were incomplete, mentioning the fact that Harvard had an excellent collection of old maps, but was deficient in the maps
resulting from the surveys which took place between 1800 and
1850. No collection, he said, had enough material for any
extensive investigations in the geographical aspects of history,
science, commerce, and foreign affairs. Hunt wanted Congress to establish a complete geographical collection, and
emphasized its benefits to the many government departments
that did surveying and allied research work--the State Department, Engineer and Topographical Engineering Bureaus,
Coast Survey, National Observatory, and others. He spoke
of its value to Congress as an illustrative aid to its legisla-
tive work with up-to-date answers to its questions on different localities. After establishing this need, he tidily outlined
his proposal:

> Among the materials thus to be collected the fol-
> lowing classes may be mentioned: 1. A first-
> class terrestrial globe. 2. All material illustrat-
> ing the early and recent geography of the United
> States, both its seacoast and interior, including
> traced copies of all valuable maps and charts in
> manuscript, and not published. The materials for
> illustrating the past and present geography of each
> State, county, township, and city should be gathered
> by purchase, correspondence, and tracing. 3. All
> maps and charts on the remainder of America.
> 4. The admiralty or sea-coast charts of all the

European and other foreign states, and the detailed
topographical surveys of their interiors, where such
have been made. 5. The most approved maps published from private resources, whether as atlases,
nautical charts, or naval maps, including publications on physical geography, guide-books, railroad-
maps, and city hand-books. 6. A complete collection of all the narratives of voyages of discovery
and exploration, especially those undertaken by the
English and French governments. 7. Geographical,
geodetic, and nautical almanacs and treatises, with
all the requisite bibliographical aids to the amplest
geographical investigation. 2

    If Hunt were not alone in his plea, and we have rea-
son to believe he was not, we can see the enormous progress
that had been made by surveyors and researchers in the
government bureaus in the first half of the nineteenth century.
The country was stretching out to the Mississippi Basin, and
beyond that to the Pacific Ocean. The newly acquired land
was explored, surveyed, and mapped. New waters were
being charted, and mountains probed for natural breaks and
gaps. Maps and charts were being turned out by all of these
tapping and probing agencies, and some of the country's researchers were becoming concerned by the lack of a key to
available materials. After Hunt's paper was read, a committee was appointed to inform Congress of this proposal. Members of the committee included Hunt, A. Guyot, distinguished
geographer, Lt. Maury, superintendent of the National Observatory, Prof. Bache, superintendent of the Coast Survey, and
Lt. Davis, superintendent of the Nautical Almanac. The committee drew up a memorial based on the Hunt proposal, urging the importance of such a department in the Library of
Congress. They mentioned that just as the Ebeling collection
was used for important negotiations on the Northeastern
Boundary question, this proposed collection would be used to
settle other political questions. They even outlined the ap-
propriation figures necessary to purchase such a collection
--$30,000, and discussed the necessary qualifications of the
superintendent of such a collection. On March 30, 1854, the
proposal was presented to the Senate, and then it was referred to the Committee on the Library, where it remained.

    The next step in the proposal of a government deposi-
tory came from a different source. In 1856 Johann Georg
Kohl (1808-1878), a learned German geographer and important
figure in American map collecting, presented a plan for a

national cartographical depot before the Smithsonian Institution. He emphasized that maps were unique historical documents, and should be preserved as such. Primarily his concern was with the old maps of America drawn by explorers, navigators, and travelers showing the changing geographical knowledge behind the cartography. Kohl suggested that the government collect a series of dated maps covering identical routes, rivers, and regions at different periods of time. Less detailed in plan than Hunt's proposal, Kohl's achieved no more positive results. It is important to note that Kohl, a foreigner doing research for the U.S. Coast Survey, came to a conclusion similar to Hunt's about the scattering of maps among different bureaus. They both felt that if these maps were not collected by one agency, they would gradually disappear and be lost to future researchers. Kohl's collection of 474 maps (handmade copies and facsimiles) relating to the discovery and progress of America eventually found its way to the Library of Congress.

Eighteen years after Hunt's proposal geographers were still making the same plea for a central map depository in the government. Daniel Gilman, Yale geographer, wrote in the Bulletin of the American Geographical Society:

> The extreme difficulty of ascertaining what there is in the various departments of the general government is only surpassed by the difficulty of knowing how to get at it.... [There should be pointed out] the importance of having established in Washington, or elsewhere, as a department of the general government, a bureau of maps and charts and geographical memoirs, where all these vast accumulations may be stored, classified and rendered accessible like the books in the Library of Congress, or the books and models in the Patent Office, so that persons who have the right may make inquiry respecting them. [3]

Eventually, of course, the Library of Congress was to acquire a Map and Charts division in 1897. The pleas of Hunt, Kohl, Gilman, and others may not have contributed much to the immediate achieving of their goal, but are certainly important as representative of the nineteenth century movement towards the establishment of such a division.

The second important event of the mid-nineteenth century was the organization in New York of the first geo-

graphical society in America.   This was the American Geographical and Statistical Society, an organization of individuals
with an interest in geography.   Before this time geographically interested persons could only attend meetings of the more
general scientific societies where they might hear occasional
geographical lectures, and thumb through the atlases in the
libraries.   This new society, with its primary geographical
orientation, was to have the first specialized map and geographical literature collection in the country.   The Society's
1851 charter states, "The American Geographical and Statistical Society of New York is instituted for the collection and
diffusion of geographical and statistical information."

    New York in the 1850's was very much a maritime
city, and many of the Society's members had some maritime
connection.   There were numerous merchants, a shipping mag-
nate, a hydrographer, a former Secretary of the Navy, and
persons associated with the promotion of nautical engineering
works listed as members.   Geography with its description of
the seas and shores was of practical concern to such men,
and the revised charter of 1871 emphatically states that the
Society should have information "at all times accessible for
public uses in a great maritime and commercial city."   Other
members were engineers affiliated with projects such as conversion of the land around the reservoir in New York into
Central Park.   Many, though not directly involved themselves,
shared the country's concern selecting the best railroad routes
to the West, and eagerly sought maps of the Far West.
Quite a few of the Society's members were journalists and
publishers interested in news from all over the world.   News
from little-known regions of the Arctic and of Africa was of
vital interest, and details of the latest explorations in these
exotic places were sought.   The clergy were also represented
in this group, and of practical concern to them was the spreading of the gospel to these foreign parts.   Some of the more
scholarly interests were represented by well-known historians
who sought data on the geography and history of America.

    Banding together, these men formed a group which
sponsored expeditions, lectures, discussions, publications and,
of course, a library and map collection.   The impetus behind
the formation of the Society was the tremendous expansion
and opening up of new areas both within and without the country, and concomitant strides in the development of the newly
opened areas.   New York, as the largest and most cosmo-
politan city in the country, had shown by the 1850's that it
had enough people with geographical interests to form such a
society.

The Society's map collection began with gifts of maps
and charts from its members, and grew very slowly by further donations, small purchases, and exchange of the Society's
Bulletin with other organizations.   It was to take nearly fifty
years for it to come close to where Harvard's map collection
was in 1818, for it was never to acquire such a huge and assembled collection as Ebeling's.   The Society had attempted
in the early 1850's to purchase the collection of copies of
early maps of America that Kohl was putting together in his
work for the Coast Survey, but the State Department had already made arrangements to purchase it.   Kohl, however,
did maintain correspondence with the Society, and sent maps
from Germany for the collections.   The Society's library and
map collection by the 1870's included collections of voyages,
gazetteers, a connected series of atlases from Ortelius in
1573 to the nineteenth century, transactions of various learned
societies, and "works on the history of navigation not to be
found in any other public library in the country. "

The third quarter of the nineteenth century showed a
growing concern for systematic map collecting, and a movement toward a national depository.   Further it showed the
rise and early development of the first specialized geographical literature and map collection in the country.   Since the
time of Ebeling, there had been little map activity in Cambridge.   From time to time a few voices had spoken out
about Harvard's serious deficiency in modern maps.   It was
not until 1877, when Justin Winsor became Librarian, that
the map collection was to be reactivated.   Winsor gave the
existing collection much attention, believing it to be one of
the two special departments of the library needing more attention than the staff could afford to give.   He was impressed
with the holdings of Harvard, but espoused definite need for
indexing, labelling, re-cataloging, and re-arranging of shelves.
His annual reports emphasize his plans for improving the collection, and of progress in that direction.

Winsor secured the valuable Kohl collection of early
maps from the War Department, where they had lain unused
for twenty-five years, and prepared a catalogue of it that
was published by Harvard.   Earlier Congress had appropri-
ated $6000 for the preparation of a catalogue, but this had
never been done.   At the time that Kohl went back to Germany he had deposited his collection of facsimiles of American maps with the State Department, where it remained practically unused until the Civil War, when it was placed in the
custody of the War Department.   Winsor had wide acquaintance

with scholars who knew of the collection, and appreciated its importance, but who were frustrated in the use of the collection by want of a key to it. Winsor made arrangements with the librarian of the War Department to prepare a key, using the resources of Harvard's map collection to assist in the preparation.

Current map publications of the United States and of foreign governments were aggressively collected by Harvard during these renaissance years, and by the turn of the century there were about 20,000 loose sheets and 900 volumes of bound maps and atlases in their holdings. In this paper Harvard, the American Geographical Society, and somewhat indirectly, the Library of Congress have been singled out as representative examples of the state of map collecting in America during the nineteenth century. That there were, by the third quarter of the century, many other libraries with sizable map collections was shown by a survey made by William Lane of Harvard's library in 1892. Some statistics indicating the size of these collections in that year are as follows:

U.S. Geological Survey	20,000 maps
U.S. Coast and Geodetic Survey	12,000 charts; 300 atlases
Hydrographic Office	12,000 foreign charts
Directory Library of Boston	7000 volumes of directories and gazetteers
Franklin Institute of Philadelphia	3000 maps
Appalachian Mountain Club	900 maps
Weather Bureau	600 meteorological charts
State Historical Society of Wisconsin	1500 maps

In addition, the Library of Congress opened its Map Division in 1897 with a total of 40,000 maps.

The different reasons for map collecting (educational, compilational, and scholarly) merged together to give rise during the nineteenth century to the map libraries of universities, societies and government bureaus. Much of interest could be written concerning the details and history of the acquisitions and arrangement of these individual collections, details which are beyond the scope of this paper. Only the high points of the trends of the century have been touched upon. It is hoped that the material presented can serve as background data for an understanding of these collections that were to expand so extraordinarily during the twentieth century.

REFERENCES

1. U.S. Library of Congress. Division of Maps. "An Account of the Activities and the More Important Accessions of the Division of Maps during the Fiscal Year Ending June 30, 1935," by Lawrence Martin. Washington, 1936; 17p.

2. E. B. Hunt. "Project of a Geographical Department of the Library of Congress." (American Association for the Advancement of Science, Proceedings, 7th Meeting, Cleveland, July 1853, pub. 1856, pp. 171-175.)

3. Daniel C. Gilman. "The Last Ten Years of Geographical Work in This Country." (Journal of the American Geographical Society in New York, vol. 3, 1872, pp. 111-115.)

WHAT IS A MAP LIBRARY*

I. Mumford

Maps are, and have been prepared for a variety of
reasons: national or private prestige; defence; offence; colonial and military government; economic control; physical
planning; education; commercial enterprise; artistic pleasure;
and so on. Every year a great number of new maps and
new editions of existing maps and compilations of all sorts
issue from the presses of the national civil and military
mapping agencies and a host of commercial publishers. Imhof estimated these at 30, 000 sheets a year, but this is probably an underestimate. As all maps are out of date the moment they are printed, and topicality demands at least an
appearance of up-to-dateness, there is little doubt that the
world wide flood of maps will continue, even after the completion of basic cover for vast areas of the world which are
not at present mapped, to make them adequate for current
needs.

It is unlikely that any organisation does or even could
get copies of all the maps published every year, owing to the
very considerable difficulties of ensuring supply from a host
of producers whose products are often regarded as confiden-
tial or ephemeral or of only local interest. On the other
hand, there is probably no good reason for attempting such
a gargantuan task even on grounds of national interest, especially if the financial implications have to be considered.
Even at a national level, a map library must have a purpose,
and for smaller collections this becomes even more important. What I suspect is that the purpose of map libraries is
obscured by tradition in many cases, undefined in real terms
in most cases, ineffective in large measure, and as such

*Reprinted by permission from Cartographic Journal, vol. 3,
no. 1 (1966), 9-11. Published by The British Cartographic
Society.

wasteful of money and resources.

To be effective, a map library must have the maps to fulfil its purpose, the means of acquiring, arranging and storing them, and a cataloguing system and professional management which ensures the availability of maps pertinent to the real requirements of potential users.

Specialist Map Libraries

It is reasonable to expect the purpose of a map library to be explicit and related to some degree of specialisation in the scope of the holdings. The corollary of this is that the nature of the specialisation in various map libraries should be known so that potential users can benefit from it. Let us consider the typical situations in which collections of maps accrue in relation to the academic discipline of geography, whether taught in a large school or an university department. The geography as taught will have a regional and a thematic emphasis. Even world and continental maps can raise a problem as soon as the overall uniform scale is considered. The world at 1:1,000,000 requires several hundred sheets, and smaller areas at larger but still relatively small scales require equally numerous sheets. When one gets down to the detailed regional study meriting consideration of topographic and large-scale maps, the number of maps involved becomes a severe problem. Therefore as the degree of detailed geographical interest increases, so the area of detailed map interest must be more and more limited, to make a manageable collection.

Most departments of geography teach 'British Isles.' The total map coverage of Great Britain currently published by the Ordnance Survey at all scales is about one hundred thousand different sheets. For many investigations with an historical approach, older editions will be required, and even at a rough average of four versions of each map the size of the problem of holding 'complete' map cover of even this small country becomes apparent. Areas of interest must be defined so that a proper balance is achieved between all maps at all scales of some areas of the country, and all maps at small scales of the whole of Great Britain. On this basis a student should at least be made aware of the full range of mapping in some area or areas. For most map libraries associated with the teaching of geography, a few counties covered at the six-inch scale would be the limit of holding if associated with other scales, with say the whole country

(England, Scotland or Wales) at 2 1/2-inch scale, and the
whole of Great Britain at one-inch and smaller scales. For
foreign countries the scales of interest would probably be
1:25,000 instead of six-inch, and 1:100,000 instead of 2 1/2-
inch for areas of comparable size. Regional thematic and
special mapping would of course be additional to the topographic cover.

Map Management

Apart from the collection of maps for their geographic
content there is the question of maps as maps. The approach
to cartography in many schools is based on the myth that to
understand maps you have to be able to draw them. The
stultifying result of hours spent drawing scale bars is often
a complete lack of any understanding of maps as expressions
of cartographic progress and as being worthy of 'bibliographic'
research. The selection and acquisition of items for their
cartographic interest is far from easy, since the essentially
graphic impact of a map is difficult to describe in the brief
words of a publisher's list or a bibliography. To be successful on any ambitious scale it probably requires a very well-
informed map librarian.

If what has been said so far can be taken as a guide
to the limitation of collection in the interest of purpose, I
believe that many associated with map collections will already
be reaching for the pulp sack. The thought that ought to stop
them clearing out dusty presses of long-untouched maps by
obscure producers in distant lands, which have arrived largely by chance disposals, is the question of information. How
many maps are stacked away unused and largely unusable,
because they are not understood as cartographic products and
therefore ill-catalogued or indexed? In how many other cases
are the particular maps which are available used again and
again for teaching, student work and research simply because
they are there, irrespective of their present cartographic
relevance? How much unnecessary fieldwork has been executed by students and research workers to provide a base
map for field studies because information on the real mapping
situation was lacking? Information is the key, and there is
no easy way of acquiring it, nor of marshalling it once acquired. Even large map libraries which receive the bulk of
their acquisitions as the result of formal deposit arrangements
can easily delude themselves into thinking that the maps received are sufficient evidence of the success of the arrangement and that completeness is automatic. Only a detailed

study, which is rarely possible, of the production, publication and stocking methods of map producers would reveal how many producers have 'topped up' map stocks with new editions placed at the bottom of the stack, or coded production and revision dates in the interests of stock management. Even today when map publishers are much more open with their publication information, especially on the maps themselves, it is possible to be misled in ordering maps on the basis of commercial agencies' map catalogues and lists which are vague on some relevant points.

Map Librarianship

There is no profession of map librarianship with a formal training and an academic discipline. Map libraries have usually formed part of the general library, and even where they are established as separate administrative units they have often been the preserve of librarians with a 'book-ish' approach to cataloguing and management. There is vir-tually no literature on map libraries which can be used in training of map library staff or the determination of map li-brary policy. In the bigger map libraries continuity of staff with great acquired on-the-job experience may have been largely satisfactory in the past, but in the newer map li-braries there can only be a pragmatic and personal approach which can be quite wasteful of resources.

Geography as a field of knowledge in the library has got into a very confused state, and although the recent I. G. U. Final Report of the Commission on the Classification of Geo-graphical Books and Maps in Libraries makes a bold effort, its recommendations on maps are very complex. Their ap-plication in a map library is made more difficult by the lack of an adequate literature in English on maps as compendia of geographical knowledge written in a special and largely sym-bolic language.

The few systems of map classification and cataloguing which are currently practised have mainly been developed in the specific circumstances of individual very large map li-braries, each with its own peculiar inertia. None of these systems can be applied successfully without an apt training "on the job" by experienced, albeit largely self-taught, peo-ple. What is almost entirely lacking is any formal body of information about maps, which would be as effective as say Gibbons' stamp catalogue is for philatelists. The size of the problem can be seen when I suggest that the German Army

wartime series of <u>Planheft</u> surveys of mapping, for all their
excellence, now fall as far short of present needs of knowing
about maps as Hinks's succinct descriptions in <u>Maps and Sur-</u>
<u>vey</u> did in comparison with the <u>Planhefte</u>.

   The reason I stress these problems of map librarianship is not to create an aura of mystery about my own particular field of activity, but rather to point to the need for
a proper appreciation of the aims and methods of map librarianship.   The danger is that a tradition of curatorship coupled
with narrow scholarship will result in an ability to produce
from the files what is asked for, but rarely to unlock the
real treasure of the great national surveys by detailed advice
based on a broad evaluation of mapping as a whole.   Eminent
scholarship has been applied to maps and charts of what one
may rudely term the decorative period.   Compared with this,
the published research in English on the great national surveys is practically non-existent; even our own Ordnance Survey maps have only been tentatively summarised in recent
years by Harley, while Skelton has delved to reveal some of
the story of the early products of the Survey.   There is not
even a <u>catalogue raisonné</u> of Ordnance Survey Maps.   Small
wonder that map librarians appear mysterious in the service
they offer.   And how easy for the enquirer to ask for what
he knows of, and get it, rather than pose a question that results in a real contribution to the advancement of research
in which maps, if they can be found and properly assessed,
are important sources.

   In this age of the information explosion, information
retrieval is throwing up problems all around even as computers are developed to deal with some of them.   When trying to construct a system of families of facts about maps
capable of being fed into a computer store, one realises how
often one can be misled into thinking that the person requesting a map has the slightest idea what he really wants it for.
If the question is stated correctly and in map terms, there
is probably a single map or small group of maps out of the
millions which exist which will contribute to a correct solution.   If time outweighs expense, a computerised system of
data retrieval may be the answer; otherwise a group of intensely experienced specialists in map research can reach a
close solution in time, where a single-handed map curator
may be overwhelmed by an <u>embarras de choix.</u>

   In considering "purpose" it is necessary to differentiate
two situations: the established map collection and the newly-

created one. In an established collection, managerial questions of staff and accommodation may point to the need to
reduce the size of the collection by weeding, and disposal of
items outside the decided "purpose." While this action may
be necessary, care must be taken not to disperse items which
form part of a whole, whether the whole is a series or a-
rises from historical reasons. Many map libraries contain
significant collections of material which were brought together for a "purpose," and the fact that this "purpose" may
have become obscured by the passage of time and changes of
staff should not be taken as complete justification for the
wholesale dispersal of material that is marginal to the present "purpose." Just as with modern mapping it is necessary
to understand such concepts as "series" and "editions," so
in some map libraries one must understand the evolution of
cataloguing and filing systems used in the past, in order both
to exploit the present holdings properly and to trim those
holdings satisfactorily to the "purpose." If large or older
libraries decide to dispose of significant collections of map
material, every care should be taken to ensure that some
other map library or libraries derive the maximum benefit
from the original collection.

Disposal is usually carried out under pressures which
do not seem to allow for careful consideration, and all too
often the pulp merchants and general book dealers reap a sad
harvest. But this is in fact not the main problem of disposal. With a more or less continual accumulation of dupli-
cates covering a great variety of scales and areas, listing
the items for disposal is usually out of the question, and
even sorting to meet the assumed interests of recipients requires time and relatively skilled labour. Where the volume
of disposals is very large and involves multiple copies and
different editions, a single heap of disposals becomes unman-
ageable and it is desirable to organise the accumulation into
categories by area or type. But even when this is done the
major problem remains of knowing what other map libraries
are interested in receiving, and particularly what they are
not interested in. A few state their requirements all too
specifically, but most say they will take anything, which
leads me to suspect that they do not know what they want
because they do not have an explicit "purpose" nor the expertise to implement it. Granted that it is impossible to
forecast in any constructive way what is likely to be available, it would be possible to make disposals more effective
if we knew something more about the real needs and interests
of the various map libraries. As far as I am aware nobody

knows what institutional map libraries there are in this country, let alone their scope, organisation and effectiveness.
Therefore, in asking "What Is a Map Library?" and offering
some thoughts on what I think it should be, I am also moved
to try and answer the question a little more practically by
finding out how the other map libraries in Great Britain function.

I have drawn up a questionnaire which could provide
the means for someone to prepare a survey, at present entirely lacking, of the country's map library resources. This
could lead to a more effective definition of purpose in individual map libraries as a whole. It could also result in
a much more positive sort of disposal by those who have
maps to give away.

THE EMERGENCE OF MAPS IN LIBRARIES*

Walter W. Ristow

One of the philosophical satisfactions of middle age, "
says Time magazine, "is not being young."1 Agreed. But
there are also some positive compensations when one has out-
distanced youth. The pleasure, for example, of reviewing,
in historical perspective, the development and growth of a
cause, activity, or profession. Bear with me, then, while
I re-run the reel on map librarianship. Three decades ago,
young and enthusiastic, I was employed as a map librarian.
Of maps I knew little, of librarianship somewhat less. The
profession then had few seasoned practitioners, and pertinent
literature was meager and dispersed. Some eight years and
one war later, map libraries had increased slightly in number, and one map librarian had been tempered by experience.
With self-education as the primary objective, the literature
relating to maps in libraries was comprehensively reviewed
and analyzed in 1946. Karl Brown, then editor of Library
Journal, thought the bibliography and analysis merited publishing. 2

In the decade after World War II, the profession came
of age. It was thus possible to report, in the October 1955
Library Trends, "that the foundations of map librarianship
[had] been greatly strengthened during the past ten years,
largely as a result of the energetic and enthusiastic work of
a small group of specialists."3 Warmed by the sweet wine
of accomplishment, we predicted, optimistically, that "continued cooperative action should result in further progress
toward standardization of processes, techniques, and equipment and in the compilation of additional reference tools and
aids." Progress there has certainly been during the twelve

*Reprinted by permission from Special Libraries, vol. 58,
no. 6 (1967), 400-419. Copyright by Special Libraries Association.

years most recently gone. Many of the proud hopes and objectives of 1955 are, however, largely unrealized. Two factors have, I think, contributed most significantly to the slowdown. First, the Army Map Service depository program, such a powerful stimulus to action in the postwar decade, has had no counterpart in the years here under review. Lacking such a compellant, most library administrators have continued to give low priority to map library problems. Their policies have all too often been influenced by the problems maps pose as nonbook-format materials.

The Manpower Drain

An even greater deterrent has been the heavy manpower drain from the profession's "small group of specialists." By various types of attrition map librarianship has lost, within the past ten or fifteen years, some forty or fifty of its most experienced, knowledgeable, and dedicated professionals. By retirement have gone Mary M. Bryan (Harvard), Hanna Fantova (Princeton), Amy Hepburn (Columbia), Clara E. Le-Gear (Library of Congress), Paul Lee (General Drafting Company), Dorothy C. Lewis (Department of State), Esther Ann Manion (National Geographic Society), Lois Mulkearn (Darlington Library), Helen White (Free Library of Philadelphia), and Ena Yonge (American Geographical Society). Several in this distinguished group had more than four decades of map library experience, and their combined service exceeds three hundred years.

Among those whom death has claimed are S. W. Boggs, Lloyd Brown, Arthur Carlson, Ruth Crawford, Jacques Frazin, and Carl Mapes. Former map librarians who have transferred their allegiance and talents to other disciplines or activities account for a further brain drain. Individuals in this category (some of whom continue a secondary interest in map librarianship) are Burton W. Adkinson, Catherine Bahn, Christian Brun, Maud D. Cole, George Dalphin, Ernest Dewald, Elsa Freeman, Herman Friis, Marie C. Goodman, Frank Jones, Robert Lovett, Richard E. Murphy, Albert Palmerlee, Joseph Rogers, Marvin Sears, John A. Wolter, and Bill M. Woods.

The loss of more than 10 per cent of its active workers, including many of the profession's most vigorous and productive leaders, has unquestionably been a crippling blow to map librarianship. There is promise, however, that the patient will recover. Youthful, intelligent, well-trained, and

enthusiastic map librarians have already moved into many of
the vacated ranks. Others with equally good qualifications
will soon join them. Supported by a small cadre of veterans,
the emergent generation of map librarians will, I am confident, lift the profession to new heights of service and pro-
ductivity. There are indications that the updraft has already
begun. A representative few of the new generation of map
librarians are Mrs. Thomas Anderson (Columbia University),
David Carrington (Interior Department, Office of Geography),
William Easton (Illinois State Normal University), Mary Galneder (University of Wisconsin), Carlos Hagen (University of
California at Los Angeles), A. Philip Munta (National Archives), Frank Nicoletti (Army Map Service), Jeremiah Post
(Free Library of Philadelphia), and Frank E. Trout (Harvard).

A number of institutions have established separate map
rooms or departments since 1955, and some have employed
full-time map librarians. Map libraries previously in being
have expanded their holdings by as much as 40 or 50 per
cent. There are now perhaps some fifty collections in the
United States with 100,000 or more sheets, and fifteen or
twenty of them have over 200,000 maps. Unfortunately,
these figures cannot be documented, for no census of map
collections has been taken since 1954. Updating Map Collections in the United States and Canada (Special Libraries Association, 1954) is one of several essential compilation tasks
that urgently await doing. A few of the larger United States
collections are included in Emil Meynen's "Important map collections," published in the 1964/66 edition of Orbis Geograph-
icus (Wiesbaden, 1964).

Notwithstanding the growth in number and size of university and public library map collections, there is still a
heavy imbalance between their holdings and those of the principal federal map libraries. The National Archives' Cartographic Records Branch, with 1,600,000, Army Map Service,
with two million (including multiple copies), and the Library
of Congress' Geography and Map Division, with three million
map sheets, are from five to ten times larger than the top-
ranking nonfederal map collections.

Map Library Surveys

There are several general map library surveys, as
well as articles describing specific collections, in recent professional literature. In the former category is Lynn S. Mullins' historic study on "The rise of map libraries in America

during the nineteenth century. "[4]   Major attention is focused
on the American Geographical Society and Harvard University
map libraries, which were the principal nongovernmental collections toward the end of the century.   Although a separate
Division of Maps and Charts was not established in the Library of Congress until 1897, by that date the Library's
cartographic holdings already numbered forty thousand pieces.
American libraries with significant holdings of historical
maps, among them the Library of Congress, John Carter
Brown Library (Brown University), James Ford Bell Collection (University of Minnesota), Lilly Library (Indiana University), Newberry Library (Chicago), and Yale University Map
Library, are mentioned in the Chronicle section of Imago
Mundi, no. 17, 1963. [5]

Described in articles, published in Special Libraries
Association's Geography and Map Division Bulletin in recent
years, have been the map collections of New York Public
Library, [6] Harvard, [7] University of Oregon, [8] Los Angeles
Public Library, [9] University of California (Berkeley), [10] University of California (Los Angeles), [11] and the Birmingham
Public Library. [12]   The American Geographical Society's map
collection was featured in the March 1955 Professional Geographer, [13] and Dartmouth's "tons of maps" were the subject
of a story in the Dartmouth Alumni Magazine. [14]   Bill Woods'
recommendations for University of Illinois' Chicago Undergraduate Division Map Library were published in Illinois Libraries, in March 1957. [15]   An article describing Cornell
University's map collection, initially published in Cornell
Alumni News, was reprinted in the April-June 1957 issue of
Surveying and Mapping. [16]   The map collection in Columbia
University's Geology Library, and some of its interesting historical maps, was the subject of three articles in the November 1958 number of Columbia Library Column. [17]   Esther Ann
Manion reported on her more than forty years of experience
in the National Geographic Society Library, in the George
Washington University Magazine. [18]   "Cartomania in the Louisiana State Library" is the title under which Edith Atkinson discussed activities in the SLU map library. [19]

The New York Public Library Map Division, confined
within inadequate walls for more than a quarter of a century,
was transferred, on March 1, 1963, to more spacious and
accessible rooms on the main floor of the Library's main
building.   Gerard L. Alexander, chief of the Map Division
for some ten years, continues in that position.   There are
approximately 280, 000 maps and 5, 600 atlases in the NYPL

Map Division.   In January 1960 the Map Collection of the
United Nations moved to an attractive well-lighted room in
the new Dag Hammarskjold Library. [20]   The collection, which
is under the supervision of Nathaniel Abelson, has about
seventy thousand maps and 350 atlases.   Access is limited
primarily to members of the UN Secretariat, the delegations,
the press, and various accredited groups or institutions.

The Winsor Memorial Map Room, Harvard College
Library, was one of the earliest established in the United
States.   For some years the Map Room has not maintained
the excellent reputation it enjoyed when Justin Winsor reigned
at Harvard Library.   From September 1962 to February 1964,
R. A. Skelton, superintendent of the Map Room, British
Museum, surveyed the map collection, while in residence at
Harvard.   Pursuant to Mr. Skelton's recommendations, Har-
vard Library is presently seeking to reestablish its former
map library leadership.   Toward this end Dr. Frank E.
Trout was appointed curator of the Winsor Memorial Map
Room in 1966.   Dr. A. Philip Muntz has, since 1961, been
chief of the Cartographic Records Branch, National Archives.
Herman Friis, former assistant chief and chief of the Branch,
is now senior specialist in Cartographic Records and chief of
the Polar Archives Branch.   The Cartographic Records
Branch has issued several additional guides to its collections
within the past decade. [21]

Units of the Library of Congress Map Division have
had several relocations in the past five years, all within the
Library's Annex Building.   In 1965, in recognition of the
Division's longtime responsibilities for recommending geographical publications and handling reference inquiries in this
area, it was redesignated the Geography and Map Division.
When the Library's James Madison Memorial Building is
completed, within five or six years, the Geography and Map
Division is expected to occupy enlarged quarters in the new
building.   The descriptive booklet on The Services and Collections of the Map Division, published in 1951, is unfortunately no longer in print.   Because it was not possible to
undertake a complete revision, an abbreviated brochure has
been prepared. [22]

Procurement continues to be a difficult and unresolved
problem for map libraries.   This is largely because an estimated 80 per cent of all maps are published by official federal, state, or local agencies.   Within the United States
government alone, some twenty separate agencies publish

maps.   Add to this, mapping agencies in all foreign countries, official map publishers in each of the fifty states, and innumerable county and municipal agencies that issue maps, and you have some slight understanding of the problem.   Few maps are listed in national bibliographies, and catalogs of official mapping agencies are numerous, generally uncoordinated, and not easily obtained.

Cartographic Production

There are no reliable statistics on the world's cartographic production.   Annual estimates range from 60 to 100 thousand sheets, including new and revised editions.   If issues of large and medium-scale official maps of all countries were included, even the latter figure might prove to be low. Among the undesirable consequences of government cartographic publishing are the security restrictions placed upon many maps.   Some of the best and most detailed maps are consequently not available to nonmilitary users and researchers. In recent years, annual additions to the Library of Congress collections, of newly published maps, have averaged around fifty thousand sheets.   Because the Library's procurement sources are extensive and comprehensive, this figure may represent as much as 75 per cent of the world's unrestricted cartographic production.   Some forty thousand retrospective, or noncurrent, maps are also added to the Library's map collection each year.   Included are some maps from which security restrictions have been removed.   Annual cartographic accessions of American university and public libraries range from a few maps to around fifteen thousand sheets.   Map libraries in the 150 to 250 thousand sheet category add ten to fifteen thousand maps per year.

The Bibliographie Cartographique Internationale is still the most comprehensive international list of cartographic publications. [23]   It represents, however, but a small percentage of the total output.   The 1966 edition, recording maps published in 1964 for example, includes under three thousand titles.   Including editions of set and series maps, this may represent as many as twenty to twenty-five thousand sheets. Collaborators in twenty-one countries, including the Library of Congress Geography and Map Division, assist in compiling Bibliographie Cartographique Internationale.   The utility of the BCI is increased by its list of publishers' catalogs, author index, and index of editors and printers, all arranged by countries.   Franz Grenacher summarized, in 1958, the BCI's contributions and accomplishments for its first two

decades. [24]   He also made some calculations on the world's
map output.   In 1964, Mlle. Myriem Fonçin, one of BCI's
editors, and former head of the Map and Chart Division,
Bibliothéque Nationale, traced the origin, history, development, and scope of this international map list. [25]

    Published monographs and articles offer some guidance
in map procurement.   William Hannah compiled, a decade or
so ago, lists of foreign mapping agencies. [26] World Cartography, an annual serial publication of the United Nations, has
informative and helpful data. [27] In Volume 5, 1955, there
was, for example, a "Preliminary survey of world topographic mapping," which was supplemented by a list of official
documents and technical publications of various countries.
An article entitled "Review of sources of information of surveying and mapping techniques in resource surveys," in
World Cartography, volume 6 (1958), included a list of mapping agencies in ninety-five countries.   Separate articles
about official maps and mapping in Finland, Sweden, and the
U. S. S. R. were published in volume 7, 1962.   World Cartography also includes, at periodic intervals, a world index
map showing progress on the International Map of the World
on the millionth scale.

    New Geographical Literature and Maps, published
semi-annually by the Royal Geographical Society, London,
lists all atlases and maps (excluding sheets of surveys) received in the RGS Map Room.   It is an excellent general
list.   Edward Stanford, Ltd., London, publishes annually an
International Map Bulletin which includes maps and atlases
published in various countries. [28]   The last issue examined,
no. 18, June 1965, contains a "List of Maps and Atlases
Published by many Official Overseas Surveys."

    The National Resources Unit, Department of Economic
Affairs, Pan American Union published, in 1964 and 1965,
"annotated indexes of serial photographic coverage and mapping to topography and natural resources" for all Latin American countries, except Cuba.   Each volume includes descriptive text, as well as index maps.   Information about all official United States maps and mapping agencies is available
from the Map Information Office, Geological Survey, U. S.
Department of the Interior, Washington, D. C.   Several MIO
leaflets are available on request to that office. [29]   Price List
53, of the Superintendent of Documents, U. S. Government
Printing Office, published periodically, describes United
States official map publications that are available from the

Superintendent of Documents.   A sampling of official U.S.
government maps was described by Dorothy Bartlett in the
January 1963 issue of Special Libraries. [30]

In a recent number of College and Research Libraries,
Clifton Brock noted that 55 per cent of U.S. government publications are produced outside the Government Printing Office. [31]   The percentage is probably even greater for maps,
for the major federal mapping agencies (e. g., Geological Survey, Coast and Geodetic Survey, Army Map Service, Aeronautical Chart and Information Center, Naval Oceanographic
Office) publish and distribute their own maps.   Sales catalogs
of mapping agencies are listed in the Monthly Catalog of
United States Government Publications (U.S. Government
Printing Office).   Some few official state maps are recorded
in issues of the Monthly Checklist of State Publications. [32]
Procuring state, county, and local official maps, however,
continues to be a major headache.   There are no easy paths
out of this jungle.   Of some slight assistance is an article
published in Surveying and Mapping a decade ago. [33]   It includes a list of state, county, and municipal agencies with
which the U.S. Geological Survey had (as of that date) cooperative agreements for topographic mapping, and a list of
the chairmen of state mapping advisory committees.

The most comprehensive listing of United States private and commercial map publications is contained in Maps
and Atlases, Part 6 of the Catalog of Copyright Entries. [34]
This semiannual serial has been published, in its present
form, since 1947.   Like the BCI, there is an unavoidable lag
in listings.   Volume 19, number 2, which lists maps and atlases registered for copyright in the last six months of 1965,
is the most recent issue (as of February 1967).   Titles are
arranged alphabetically by author, but there is also a supplementary listing by geographical area.   A particularly useful acquisition aid is the Publishers Directory, with latest
addresses, which is included in each issue of the Catalog.
A change in organization of the Catalog was reported by Buffum in 1959. [35]

Selected lists of new maps are regularly described,
by practicing map librarians, in issues of various serial publications.   Selections by Roman Drazniowsky (American Geographical Society) appear in Current Geographical Publications, [36] and Charles W. Buffum's (Library of Congress) compilations are published in the SLA Geography and Map Division
Bulletin. [37]   Numbers of the Handbook of Latin American

Studies published in odd-numbered years have geographical
references, including maps. [38] The latter are selected and
described by James D. Hill (Library of Congress). Some
twenty or twenty-five "Distinctive Recent Maps" are described
by Walter W. Ristow (Library of Congress) in Surveying and
Mapping, the quarterly journal of the American Congress on
Surveying and Mapping. [39] Helpful information relating to
map publications and acquisitions will also be found in the
annual acquisitions report of the Library of Congress Geography and Map Division, published in the Quarterly Journal of
the Library of Congress. The reports were in the August
issue from 1946 to 1961, the September issue in 1962 and
1963, and in the October issue in 1964. Since 1965 the Geography and Map Division report has been in the July Quarterly Journal.

Surplus Map Distribution

Although distribution of surplus maps has been appre-
ciably reduced in recent years, the Army Map Service depository program remains active, and deserves mention here.
For many map libraries the AMS is still the principal source
for medium- and small-scale foreign map series. Several
references are concerned with the Army Map Service and
its programs. A booklet published in 1960 was "prepared to
assist in the orientation and training of AMS personnel and
for the information of visitors and others interested in the
activities of the Army Map Service. It tells the story of
this mapping organization, describes its mission, and explains how it operates. In simple language, it broadly describes the various phases of map making." [40] The effectiveness of the AMS depository program to 1960 was evaluated by Marvin Sears as part of the requirement for a master
of library science degree. [41] In 1964 AMS initiated a Newsletter for depository members. Number 1, dated April 3,
1964, restated the distribution procedures, i.e., "The elapsed
time between shipments of maps, sometimes as much as one
year, is directly attributable to the procedures we must follow in administering the depository program. Maps supplied
to the depositories are not surplus, but maps especially selected. When a new map or publication is produced by the
Army Map Service, it is considered for inclusion in the depository distribution. If the map or publication is approved
for release, we must then program the actual distribution
into our production schedule."

Distribution is only made if there are 250 copies in

excess of military needs.   The administrators of the program have also "determined that a single distribution each
year to depository members is the frequency most compatible with ... present operational requirements." Five News-
letters have been issued, the latest dated September 19, 1966.
A revised list of depositories, distributed with that issue, includes 189 institutions.   College and university libraries pre-
dominate, with a total of 157.   Only twenty public libraries
participate in the program.

        Less formalized than the AMS program is the distri-
bution of surplus--duplicate maps and atlases by the Library
of Congress Geography and Map Division.   Faced with the
problem of processing a backlog of more than a million obsolete and surplus maps, transferred from other federal collections and agencies, the Geography and Map Division initiated, in the summer of 1950, a cooperative project.   Representatives of various geography departments and libraries
assisted Library of Congress personnel in sorting the large
backlog.   In exchange for their services cooperating partici-
pants selected duplicate maps for their sponsoring institutions.
The special project has been continued in the Geography and
Map Division each summer since 1950.   In 1951, and all subsequent years, the Library employed temporary processing
assistants in addition to those sponsored by other institutions.
More than two hundred graduate students and librarians,
representing sixty different institutions in thirty states and
provinces of Canada, have participated in Library of Congress special projects during the past seventeen years.   The
initial backlog has been supplemented by subsequent transfers
from federal map libraries.   Cooperating institutions have
received more than one million duplicate maps in exchange
for the services of their representatives.   The Library of
Congress permanent collections have been enriched by some
800,000 sheets of noncurrent, or retrospective, maps in the
same period.   The Library's Geography and Map Division
sponsored the eighteenth successive Special Map Processing
Project in the summer of 1967.

        Under provisions of Title II-C of the Higher Education
Act of 1965, the Commissioner of Education (HEW) is authorized "to transfer funds to the Librarian of Congress for the
purpose of ... acquiring, so far as possible, all library materials currently published throughout the world which are of
value to scholarship."[42]   Because Congressional appropria-
tions in fiscal years 1966 and 1967 were substantially below
the amounts authorized in the Act, the Title II acquisition

and cataloging programs have not yet been fully developed. Although excellent progress has been made, budgetary limitations, anticipated for fiscal year 1968, will further delay full development. The Association of Research Libraries, through its Shared Cataloging Committee, and the Library of Congress have, therefore, agreed that "periodicals and non-book-format materials," such as maps, will "not be covered at the beginning of the program." In view of the importance of maps as research materials in many disciplines and subject fields, map librarians regard the decision with concern and strongly hope that it will be reversed.

Map processing involves a broad range of physical and technical operations. They include such unskilled and semi-skilled tasks as sorting, arranging, indexing, and filing maps, as well as highly skilled cataloging and classification procedures. One map may require as many as ten individual handlings from the time it is accessioned until it is filed in its proper place in the collection.

Map Cataloging and Classification

As in the immediate postwar years, considerable thought, effort, time, and discussion were directed, during the past decade, toward map cataloging and classification problems. There is, however, little progress to report with respect to agreement on existing rules and codes, or on prospects for standardized and cooperative programs for cataloging and classifying maps. The hard core of professional map librarians continued, for a time, the attack on the Library of Congress--ALA Rules for Descriptive Cataloging (1949), as applied to maps. The arguments, formulated by a committee of SLA's Geography and Map Division, were summarized in reports published in 1948 and 1953.[43] Although the committee's attention was focused principally upon the RDC, its strongest shafts were directed at the use of author main entry (instead of area) in cataloging maps. Because of its uncompromising position on this issue, the committee concluded (in the preliminary report) that "constructive comment on individual rules for map cataloging is not possible because of some of the basic principles assumed." The members hoped that "the whole question of selection and arrangement of descriptive data on the printed cards [would] remain open, until the form of heading for maps is settled to the satisfaction of map users." The final report of the committee (1953) recommended "to the Library of Congress [a number of] suggestions for consideration at such time as the map

cataloging rules are reviewed. " The basic suggestion, as in
the preliminary report, was to replace author main entry
with an area-date-subject heading.

So preoccupied with the importance of area main heading was the Committee on Map Cataloging that little attention
was given to the collective body of rules in RDC, or to the
specific rules for maps. Only minor criticisms of the rules
relating to maps have, in fact, been received by the editors
of Rules for Descriptive Cataloging, since it was published.
The descriptive rules for maps, in the recently published
Anglo-American Cataloging Rules, 44 therefore, vary little
from those contained in Rules for Descriptive Cataloging.
Designed as they were for the general library, neither the
RDC nor the new Anglo-American Cataloging Rules adequately
meets the needs of the specialized map collection. The professional librarian, engaged in cataloging materials in various formats, will no doubt find in the "Maps, atlases, etc. "
chapter, guidance for handling occasional cartographic items.
Map catalogers in large map libraries, few of whom have
professional library school training, are more often confused
than aided by the rules assembled in the "Maps" chapter.
The latter have neither the technical background nor patience
to extract from the other chapters in the volume the guidance
they need. The final report of the Map Cataloging Committee recognized this in noting that "the Library of Congress
rules for cataloging maps have merely made concessions to
those vital characteristics of maps which differ from the
characteristics of books. "43 The same limitation (if it can
be so regarded) applies to the Anglo-American Cataloging
Rules. Namely, that they do not include a complete and
unified code of rules for cataloging maps. Such a code is,
nonetheless, urgently needed and must be compiled soon if
map cataloging is to achieve some degree of standardization.

Because of its long-established leadership in standardized and cooperative cataloging, its recently expanded activities in these areas, under provisions of Title II-C of the
Higher Education Act, and the preeminence of its cartographic collections, 45 the Library of Congress would be in the
best position to take the initiative in promoting standardized
and cooperative cataloging of maps. Throughout the seventy
years that have passed since a separate cartographic division
was established, maps have unfortunately, for various reasons, not received formal cataloging treatment. Perhaps
fewer than 2 per cent of the single maps (i. e., excluding
sheets of multiple-sheet map and chart series) are, therefore,

under catalog card control.   The remainder (some 1.5 million sheets), identified only with brief filing and retrieval
slips, are filed in an area-subject-date arrangement.

Although there are no major breakthroughs to report
for map cataloging and classification, a number of articles
and publications have enriched the literature in these fields.
Progress and development through the years was summarized
and evaluated in two papers.   In "Map Cataloging: Inventory
and Prospect, " prepared just before he assumed administrative responsibility for SLA Headquarters, Bill Woods reviewed the history of map processing theories and practices.46
The weight of evidence was enlisted principally to support
the area main entry concept for cataloging maps.   Mr. Woods
quoted extensively from the two reports of the SLA Cataloging Committee.   In looking to "the future" he listed several
problems, introduced but not considered by the committee,
which "merit further study. "   In his final paragraph he emphasized that "recognition of differences between maps and
books and the need for separate rules for the cataloging of
maps is long overdue. "

For a University of Michigan library science course,
Mary Ellin Fink made an exploratory study in 1962 of "The
Structure of Map Retrieval Systems. "47   The survey covered
eight map collections in the vicinity of Ann Arbor, Michigan.
Mrs. Fink observed that "it is hard to understand the great
variety of arrangements and classifications in map libraries
on the basis of experience with books. "   In another study
Mrs. Fink compared eleven cataloging systems of major map
collections in the United States and Great Britain. 48   A table
shows "use of items included on map catalog cards. "   The
value of this study is somewhat minimized because several
of the systems described and analyzed are no longer in use.

The viewpoint of librarians working with archival, historical, and manuscript maps is expressed in several interesting papers.   As a preliminary to establishing a cartographic department in the Illinois State Archives, Emma
Scheffler made a comparative study of various systems employed in cataloging and classifying maps. 49   All systems
she concluded "are designed a) to make it possible to locate
material with ease and with a minimum expenditure of time,
and b) to bring together in the map file all related material. "
Bordin and Warner believe that "manuscript maps should be
treated similarly [to printed maps].   Each map has its own
card which should include the following information: area

mapped, maker ..., date, scale, size, and number and subject of insets if any.   These cards will be filed first under
place name and then in chronological order. "50

Arguments supporting author main entry for maps are
presented by John B. White, Library and Archives Director,
Nebraska State Library. 51 "For an historical library, " he
states, "it is important to establish responsibility for the map.
Thus the identification of the 'author,' or cartographer, the
individual or the institution, government agency or publisher
responsible for the map, is an important responsibility of the
cataloger." He points out that "it is often the case that maps
do not show a well-defined, generally recognized, place-
name area.   Maps of the trans-Mississippi west illustrate
this difficulty with using area for the main entry." White
further believes that "with a card catalog, the user is not
handicapped in any way by the cataloger's choice of main entry.... There also appears to be confusion between the cataloging of maps and their arrangement.   Arrangement by
area," he insists, "can be achieved regardless of the choice
for main entry."   White concludes that "in short, the analogy
between map and book cataloging is sufficiently useful to
make the so-called author approach to maps preferable for
such libraries as the Nebraska State Historical Society."

Several map libraries have published new or revised
manuals relating to their collections.   Cataloguing and filing
rules for maps in the [American Geographical] Society's collections, 52 published in 1964, is a revision of a manual previously issued by the Society in 1947 and 1952.   The collection, which includes "more than 300,000 maps and more than
4,000 atlases," is cataloged "by area-subject classification,
chronologically arranged."   Prof. Thomas R. Smith, Kansas
University, is the author of The Map Collection in a General
Library; A Manual for Classification and Processing Procedures. 53   Although based on experience in the Kansas
University Map Library, "it is expected that the classification schemes and processing procedures detailed here will
be applicable to comparable situations in other libraries and
collections."   In a paper published several years earlier
Smith indicated that the Kansas University objectives, procedures, and schedule were to a) encompass the variety of
maps in the collection, b) be within the capabilities of inexperienced personnel, and c) arrange the maps in a logical
and simple arrangement, and with an efficient utilization of
storage space and equipment. 54

In response to numerous requests from depository members, the Army Map Service distributed, in 1965, a description of a cataloging and filing system which would be applicable to the average depository map library. [55] The instructions suggest "that a preprinted card with a check-list format is the best suited for the system [described]." A sample check card is appended to the instructions. Also recommended is "that your basic file system be oriented to geographical area." A "Glossary of Selected Mapping Terms" is a useful appendix to "A Simplified Map Collection System."

Most United States libraries that classify their maps use the Library of Congress' Classification, Class G. [56] The third edition (1954) of Class G has unfortunately been out of print for several years. In 1963, Charles Buffum reported a number of additions and changes in the atlas and map portions of the G schedule. [57] A reprinting, including additions and supplementary changes to January 1966, was published in February 1967. [58] Copies may be ordered from the Superintendent of Documents. The G schedule for maps and atlases, in common with all classifications, has its limitations and deficiencies. With the benefit of hindsight, there would be obvious advantages if the same notation sequence were used for both maps and atlases. In an areal classification it is inconsistent, for example, to classify an atlas of Denmark under G2055, and a map of the same country under G6920. The inadequacy of the G schedule in providing for various cartographic formats has also been criticized. Some map librarians, too, would still argue the relative merits of geographical and alphabetical classifications.

An extensive study of geography and map classifications has been conducted over the past fifteen years by the International Geographical Union's Commission on the Classification of Geographical Books in Libraries. The Committee's findings and recommendations have been summarized in several official reports. [59] The final report (1964) includes Emil Meynen's paper "On the classification of geographical books and maps and the application of the Universal Decimal Classification (UDC) in the field of geography." Among those who have published informal summaries of the Commission's work are Gerlach, [60] Libault, [61] and Wallis. [62] Among the positive results of the Commission's work are the inclusion of an alternate schedule for geography in the sixteenth edition of the Dewey Decimal Classification, and approval, in principle, to develop an alternate geography schedule within the Library of Congress Classification. At the Rio de Janeiro

International Geographical Congress (1956), Dr. Gerlach, the
US member on the Commission, presented a paper on "An
adaptation of the Library of Congress Classification for use
in geography and map libraries."[63] A useful list of geography and map classification schemes was compiled by Catherine
J. Bahn, for SLA's Classification Committee.[64] Publication
dates range from 1930 to 1960. The Title II-C program and
automation offer the best hopes for standardized and cooperative map cataloging. Individual maps, as previously noted,
are not yet being acquired in the Title II-C program supported
under provisions of the Higher Education Act of 1965.

Automation in Map Librarianship

The automation outlook is, happily, more promising.
Map collections, principally those within the federal government, were among the pioneers in library automation. The
Army Map Service has had a punch card catalog for maps
for more than eighteen years, and AMS acquired a Univac I
electronic computer over fifteen years ago. Other federal
map and areal photographic collections also have a number
of years experience in this field. Several map and chart libraries within the Department of Defense have automation
studies in progress. In March 1967 it was reported that the
Nautical Chart Library, Naval Oceanographic Office, was the
first DoD map library to be operational with computerized
catalog controls. The Library of Congress is presently involved in a program which is expected to achieve computerized controls of its central bibliographic record within the
next decade. Although maps, as nonbook (there's that ugly
word again) materials, are not included in the present study,
personnel in the Library's Geography and Map Division are
studying computer capabilities for cartographic collections.

A few individual map librarians have interested themselves in library automation over the past several years.
Not until 1966, however, did SLA's Geography and Map Division establish a Committee on Automation in Map Libraries.
A preliminary statement of objectives, and the names of committee members were published in the September 1966 Bulletin.[65] The Committee's first report, including "Selected
General References on Library Automation," appeared in Bulletin, no. 66, December 1966. Scheduled for publication in
the March 1967 issue was a list of "References on Automation of Cartographic Collections." Included in the latter are
several that describe proposed systems for automated map
libraries. Two or three other papers, outlining plans for

automated controls of map libraries, are in process and
scheduled for early publication.

The Army Map Service distributed, in September 1966,
a leaflet entitled "Automation of a Map Library." The introduction states that "the opinions are dynamic and are offered
as food for thought. They are not advanced as official policy
[of the AMS] or attitude, hence must not be considered as
such." Automation is defined, in the leaflet, as "the use of
electronic equipment, alone or in concert with film devices,
for mechanical processing of mass data." Before adopting
automation it is recommended that a feasibility study be made
"to insure that your manual system is the best possible within the limits of your resources." Further thoughts on "Automation of a Map Library" are scheduled for discussion in
subsequent issues of the AMS Depository Newsletter.

Several proposals for automated map library systems
that have been described in professional journals were developed for collections varying in size from 50 to 300 thousand maps. It is questionable whether automation is economically practical for collections of this size, particularly
for those in the lower range. Funding organizations are reluctant to give financial support for systems based on such
small collections. It is inevitable, therefore, that the Library of Congress, with its large and diverse cartographic
collection, and the recognized competence and experience of
its specialists in the Geography and Map Division, must assume the initiative and leadership in standardizing and automating map cataloging.

The almost limitless capabilities of the computer in
processing and controlling information will require reorientation of our viewpoints and abandonment of some pet ideas and
beliefs. The "area main heading" concept is almost certain
to be one of the first casualties. Information systems specialists point out that "the maintenance to the artificial distinction between a main entry and added entries may not be
necessary with electronic equipment nor may there be any
need to restrict the number of author entries used with any
single work, because the capacity and flexibility of the system will permit the use of all authors' names for their
work."66 Don Swanson similarly states that "the whole idea
of a 'main entry' or of deciding what a work is 'mainly a-
bout' expresses a sort of 'pigeonhole philosophy,' in which it
is attempted to enshrine each item of the collection in a
unique niche. This philosophy, I think, deserves abandon-

ment. "67   Wesley Simonton gives specific consideration to
maps (among other materials) in seeking to answer the question, "The computerized book catalog: possible, feasible,
desirable?"   "For maps, " he says, "it is frequently asserted
that area or subject is a more important entry than the author entry.... To an extent, but not completely, the 'added
entries' solves the problems raised in these and other situations. "68

Storage Equipment

There are few new developments to report with reference to storage equipment for maps and atlases.   United
States map libraries, with very few exceptions, store maps
in horizontal drawer metal cases.   Although there is as yet
no agreement, by map libraries or equipment manufacturers,
on sizes, the trend is toward drawers two inches deep, with
inside dimensions approximately 43 by 32 inches.   This size
will accommodate maps up to 40 by 30 inches in size.
Larger maps are folded, or cut into sections to this maximum size.   Maps no larger than 40 by 30 inches are conveniently examined at library tables.

In 1961 the Special Libraries Association's Committee
on Standards prepared a comprehensive report on various
types of library equipment.   The section relating to map libraries, prepared by Catherine I. Bahn, was published in
the Geography and Map Division Bulletin69 [reprinted in Chapter 6 of the present work].   It "was based on a preliminary
study of the literature on both map and other library standards, current research and development on documentation and
on plans for libraries such as the Army Map Service, the
National Archives, the American Geographical Society, Dartmouth College's Baker Library, the Library of Congress, "
and other map libraries.   The report includes a list of manufacturers of steel map filing equipment.

In a paper prepared for Library Trends, J. Douglas
Hill reports that "most map librarians now agree that [hori-
zontal drawers] offer the best combination of protection, accessibility and easy of expansion.   There is also unanimous
agreement that cases should be of steel for durability; that
drawers should be no more than two inches deep ... ; that
they should have a 'lock-out' feature to hold them in the open
position while contents are being handled; and that they should
be equipped with fabric 'dust covers' that hook at the front of
the drawer, not only for protection from dust but to prevent

maps from catching or rubbing on the underside of the drawer
above or being pushed out at the back, and to minimize sliding by exerting some downward pressure."[70] Mr. Hill's
paper also considers equipment for storing atlases, globes,
plastic relief models, and maps rolled on rods. Special Libraries Association published in 1963 a monograph entitled
Special Libraries: How to Plan and Equip Them, a project
of its New York Chapter. The section on "Map Filing Equipment" was prepared by Paul B. Lee.[71] "My own experience,"
he writes, "is entirely with horizontal files, and for a library that has maps of widely assorted sizes and shapes, I
believe this type of file is more generally useful."

Because they are the common format for classroom
teaching, maps mounted on cloth and attached to rods present a filing and storage problem in virtually every elementary and secondary school, as well as in colleges and universities. Many practical and ingenious methods and equipment have accordingly been devised to cope with the rolled
map storage problem. Collier,[72] Doerr,[73] and Roepke,[74]
are among those who have advanced solutions within the past
decade. The future relocation of the Library of Congress
Geography and Map Division to the projected new James
Madison Memorial Building offers an unexcelled opportunity
and challenge for planning and installing the most efficient
and effective layout and equipment for storing, processing,
and servicing all library cartographic formats. When the
James Madison Memorial Building is completed, some five
or six years hence, the collections of the Geography and Map
Division will total an estimated 3.5 million maps, thirty-two
thousand atlases, as well as various other cartographic formats such as relief models, globes, and rolled maps. Included will be one of the world's largest and most valuable
collections of rare historical maps and atlases. Map librarians throughout the world will await with interest the Library
of Congress' resolution of this problem.

Map Preservation

Mounting on cloth, with a flour-water adhesive, was
the standard method of map preservation for some four
centuries. Maps that were hung on walls as decorations,
or for teaching purposes, were generally also coated with
varnish. While the latter treatment may have protected maps
from dirt, dust, and moisture, it also contributed to their
deterioration, as varnish darkens and becomes brittle as it
ages. The life expectancy of many maps has, therefore,

been curtailed by the varnish treatment. In recent decades
laminating maps between sheets of plastic film (with or without cloth reinforcement) has been increasingly employed to
protect them against physical and chemical deterioration.
The National Archives developed techniques for laminating
maps some thirty years ago, utilizing a flatbed hydraulic
press. A Barrows Laminator (with roller press) was installed in the Library of Congress in 1951. Some twenty-
two thousand map sheets have been laminated each year since
that date. The Army Map Service has also had a Barrows
Laminator for over fifteen years. [75] Similar units, capable
of handling large-size map sheets, have been installed in
several other American institutions as well as in the British
Museum. Other types of laminating presses, adaptable for
map mounting, are also on the market.

Experience over the past two or three decades has
established laminating as a major procedure for preserving
maps. [76] While results are generally satisfactory, a critical
review of the procedures might be made with the possibility
of achieving even better results. If a film with greater tear
resistance were used in the Barrows Laminator, it might be
possible to omit the cloth reinforcement on many maps.
Further studies and experiments on the Barrows' recommendations for deacidifying paper might be made with reference to
developing equipment (bath or spray) for reducing time and
labor in deacidifying large map sheets. It is possible that
deacidifying, without lamination, might be adequate treatment
for sheets of some large- and medium-scale map sets, which
are printed on physically strong (but chemically vulnerable)
paper.

The 1956 revised edition of Clara E. LeGear's Maps,
Their Care, Repair and Preservation in Libraries, is still
the only publication in this field that deals specifically with
maps. [77] It is, unfortunately, no longer in print, although
microfilm reproductions may be ordered from the Library of
Congress Photoduplication Service. Because of Mrs. Le-
Gear's retirement, and the many new technical developments
during the past decade, no revision of the publication is
planned. Largely because of the studies and researches of
the W. J. Barrow Research Laboratory, supported principally
by the Council on Library Resources, a large body of new
data and information relating to the deterioration and preservation of paper is now available. Few of the studies are concerned specifically with maps but, because most cartographic
publications are printed on paper, the findings and recommen-

dations are applicable. Only a few references relating to the
work of the Barrow Laboratory are cited here.[78] Others can
be found through the catalogs of most research libraries.

The greatest preservation problem, for map librarians,
as well as others in the library profession, is posed by maps
and books published within the last century, and especially
from about 1870 to 1920. The heavily glazed pulp papers,
used for color lithographic printing in the last decades of
the nineteenth century, are particularly subject to chemical
deterioration. Some publications of this period (including
maps) have become so brittle and fragile that they are beyond preservation. Thousands of volumes, in this state of
deterioration, have been discarded by libraries, after the contents were transferred to microfilm.

Many of the illustrated atlases of United States counties, published between 1865 and 1890, were printed on such
impermanent paper, often in editions of not over three thousand copies. The preservation of historical cartographic
records of this type should be a major concern of map librarians. Because of the importance of color on maps, and
distortions in scale and size that are common in photorepro-
ductions, microfilms are not satisfactory substitutes for
printed maps and atlases. To insure the permanent preservation of the county atlases (and other atlases) published in
the last quarter of the nineteenth century, it may be necessary to disassemble each volume, deacidify the individual
pages, laminate each sheet with a tough plastic film, and
assemble and rebind them between new covers. This will
admittedly be a costly procedure, but it may be a necessary
one if we hope to preserve a reasonable number of copies
of these historical documents.

The physical and economic problems which these older
publications present emphasize the importance of printing today's publications on permanent/durable paper. This is in
fact one of W. J. Barrow's most persistent recommendations,
and his reports on permanence/durability of the book provide
excellent guidance. While librarians wholeheartedly support
the use of permanent paper, particularly for publications ear-
marked for library collections, publishers are deterred because of possible increased production costs. In the cartographic field, the best paper used by U.S. official mapping
agencies today has a life expectancy between thirty-five and
fifty years. At a Federal Map Users Conference, in 1964,
Walter W. Ristow called attention to this problem.

> Map papers [used] in recent years are supposedly
> very strong. They are designed to withstand the
> rigors of field operations, military maneuvers, and
> Geological Survey work.... In some recent tests
> of modern map papers [William J. Barrow] has
> found that they have a high acidity content and will
> be subject to a high rate of deterioration over a
> period of years. So, on behalf of the libraries of
> the country, I would toss out to you the possibility
> that the Survey, particularly in its library deposi-
> tory program, print quadrangle sheets on a more
> resistant paper. [79]

Because the interest of the majority of map users is in current maps, with no concern as their state of preservation
some forty or fifty years hence, there is little likelihood that
this suggestion will be acted upon.

Several recent general articles on preservation are of
map library interest. Regarding substitution of microfilms
for originals, John Allen observes that "at its best, microfilm is no more lasting than good paper and is subject to
comparable ills and damage. If it is to endure, similar conditions for storage must be provided in terms of temperature,
humidity, and atmosphere."[80] Lee Grove, reviewing the
"old old story" of paper deterioration, believes the problem
began "when the spread of literacy enlarged the market for
cheap reading matter, and faster presses operating at a lower unit cost were developed."[81] On the same subject Richard
Smith estimated that 90 per cent of the books published from
1900 to 1949 will be unusable for general library purposes
within thirty-five years if protective measures are not taken.[82]
"The most practical solution," in the opinion of a committee
of the Association of Research Libraries, "is a federally supported central agency that will assure the physical preservation, for as long as possible, of at least one example of
every deteriorating record, and that will make copies of
these records readily available to any library when required."[83] In the cartographic field, the Library of Congress
Geography and Map Division, within budgetary limits, has
served as such a "central agency" over a period of years.

The average map librarian, as well as many of his
specialized and unspecialized professional colleagues, is completely snowed under by the mass of published data relating
to library preservation problems. They read, with considerable relief and hope, therefore, the announcement (in the

spring 1966 issue of Library Resources and Technical Services) that the Council on Library Resources had made a grant, in the fall of 1965, to the ALA Library Technology Program to plan a three-volume manual covering the preservation and restoration of books and other library materials. In the latter category are maps, which with prints, microforms, recordings, films, slides, clay tablets, and papyrus, will be the subject of the third volume of the projected manual. According to the announcement, "the planning of the outline and text will probably take a year, and various specialists will be invited to contribute chapters." Map librarians can probably not, therefore, expect to see copies of volume 3 in less than three or four years.

New Cartographic Literature

The literature relating to maps, map makers, and map making has been greatly augmented over the last ten or twelve years. The Cartographic Research Guide project, planned by SLA's Geography and Map Division to provide a systematic approach to general and specialized cartographic literature was, regretfully, abandoned. Members of the Guide Committee found it impossible to carry the project to completion with only volunteer help. When attempts to secure foundation support to complete and edit the Guide were unsuccessful, the project was, reluctantly, terminated. One section of the projected Guide was published in preliminary form, in the Geography and Map Division Bulletin. [84] A preliminary draft of Part IV, The Cartographic Library and the Map Librarian, was issued in a limited number of mimeographed copies in 1957. [85]

Happily, Bibliotheca Cartographica, an international serial cartobibliography launched in 1957, is effectively serving as an index to current cartographic literature. Sponsored jointly by the German Cartographical Society and the Bundesanstalt für Landeskunde und Raumforschung (Bad Godesberg, Germany), Bibliotheca Cartographica is published, semi-annually, by the latter organization. Collaborators in some thirty-six countries (including LC's Geography and Map Division) supply entries for BC. In 1960 the editor, Karl-Heinz Meine, reported on the plan and organization of Bibliotheca Cartographica. [86] The table of contents, in each issue, is printed in German, French, English, and Russian. References are arranged in classified order, according to the alternate Dewey classification for geography. Monographs and articles in serials are indexed in Bibliotheca.

The Bibliography of Cartography, a comprehensive analytical card file on the literature of cartography, has been maintained in the Library of Congress Geography and Map Division for almost seven decades. Microfilm reels of the Bibliography, including supplements (some twenty-five reels to date), may be ordered from the Library's Photoduplication Service. Prices will be quoted on request. Selected references on cartographical subjects are listed in various geographical and cartographical serials. Geographical serials, including those that are no longer active as well as currently published works, have been indexed by Harris and Fellmann.[87] There is, unfortunately, no comparable guide to serials in the fields of cartography and surveying. K. A. Salisčev, one of the U.S.S.R.'s distinguished cartographers, however, surveyed the world's leading cartographic serials in a recent issue of Petermann's Mitteilungen.[88]

The principal cartographic reference and referral centers are within the federal government. Inquiries relating to current map and chart publications are handled by the Geological Survey's Map Information Office. "The primary purpose of the Map Information Office," as explained by its director, J. O. Kilmartin, "is not actually to sell or distribute maps, aerial photographs, or geodetic controls lists, but only to disseminate information on what is available, where it can be located, and how to order it."[89] The Cartographic Records Branch, National Archives, has custody of the official records, including those concerned with surveying and mapping, of all federal mapping agencies. Original manuscript maps of many of the early surveys of the west are among the records in the custody of the Cartographic Records Branch. Guides to a number of record groups have been published by the Branch. (See reference no. 21.)

The Library of Congress' Geography and Map Division, with its comprehensive and extensive collections of maps and atlases, continues to serve as the principal United States reference center for historical and current cartographical information. Because there is catalog card control for less than 2 per cent of the single maps (i.e., excluding sheets of multi-sheet set maps and chart series), the Division's potential for service is severely restricted. Cartobibliographies and map lists, compiled by various staff members, provide indexes to specialized segments of the collection. Among the more notable recent compilations are volumes 5 and 6 of A List of Geographical Atlases.[90] Volume 7, currently in compilation by Mrs. LeGear, will describe atlases

of the western hemisphere acquired since 1920. It will probably be published in late 1968 or 1969.   Specialized cartobibliographies, compiled in the Geography and Map Division
in recent years, list marketing maps, [91] maps of Antarctica, [92]
Civil War maps, [93] treasure maps and charts, [94] and maps of
explorer's routes. [95]   Bibliographies listing references relating
to specialized types of maps have also been compiled. [96]. A
list of currently available publications may be requested from
the Geography and Map Division, Library of Congress.

The Use of Atlases

        Atlases are standard tools in general reference collec-
tions as well as in map libraries.   In addition to the List of
Geographical Atlases in the Library of Congress, there are a
number of other guides and indexes that facilitate the use of
atlases, as well as reviews of special groups of atlases and
individual works.   Only a sampling of these publications can
be noted here.   Whyte's Atlas Guide, published in 1962, is
described as "a subject index to the atlases used in most public libraries, secondary schools and colleges. "[97]   It indexes
twenty English language atlases, most of them published in
the United States, ranging in date from 1946 to 1960.   Bowker published, in 1966, General World Atlases in Print,
which offers a number of "checkpoints ... to prospective pur-
chasers as a measure of assistance in choosing an atlas to
meet their individual requirements. "[98]   It was "compiled
primarily to provide average American users with a practical
guide in the choice of a general world atlas. "

        In a review article, published in 1962, Ena Yonge,
evaluated sixty-eight general world and subject atlases. [99]
The same reviewer also summarized briefly some one hundred regional atlases. [100]   Various aspects of modern and
historical atlases were covered in a series of papers published in the May 1960 issue of the Geographical Magazine.
In the lead article Balchin observes that "it is quite astonish-
ing to see how many kinds and sizes of atlases can now be
bought or consulted. "[101]   He places atlases in four classes,
i. e., general world, special world, general regional, and
special regional.

        Indexes to a number of American map collections have
been published during the past several years by the G. K.
Hall Company of Boston.   By photographic offset reproduction,
Hall has produced book catalogs of unpublished, and generally
inaccessible, geographical and cartographical card indexes.

Among Hall indexes already published (or soon available) are
the Research Catalog of the American Geographical Society,
the AGS's Index to maps in books and periodicals, Catalog of
the U. S. Geological Survey Library, Index to the printed maps
in the Mariner's Museum, and Index to the printed maps of
Bancroft Library, University of California, Berkeley. Because of their high cost, Hall reprint catalogs are beyond the
budgets of all but the larger research libraries.

Reference service on early maps and the history of
cartography has been greatly aided by new and revised mono-
graphic and serial publications. Of particular note is the
English translation, with revisions, of Bagrow's Geschichte
der Kartographie, originally published in 1951. 102 Revised
additions have also been published of well-known works by
Crone, 103 Skelton, 104 and Greenhood. 105 Several excellent
summaries and lists of early maps have been published for
regions of the United States. William P. Cumming's Southeast in Early Maps is a cartobibliographical study of the
southern Atlantic region in the colonial period. Originally
published in 1958, a revised edition was issued in 1962. 106
Mapping the Transmississippi West, is a comprehensive cartobibliographical survey of western United States between
1540 and 1884. 107

Serials on Cartography

Imago Mundi, an annual international serial, continues
to be the principal publication medium for scholarly papers on
the history of cartography. It also includes book reviews,
bibliographies listing recently published books and articles,
and a chronicle section which reports, by country, developments in the field of cartographical history. Leo Bagrow,
who founded Imago Mundi and edited the first thirteen issues,
died in 1957. Since 1962 the journal has been edited by
Dr. C. Koeman, and published by N. Israel, of Amsterdam.
Imago Mundi, no. 19, was published in 1966. A relatively
new serial, Map Collector's Series, is focused on the ever-
growing fraternity of private map collectors. 108 It is edited
by R. V. Tooley, author of numerous works on the history
of maps and map makers. Dealers in out-of-print maps, in
various countries, lend support to the Map Collector's Series.
Through 1966, twenty-five issues were published, an average
of four or more each year. The history of globes is the subject field of Der Globusfreund, a semi-annual serial. 109 It
was founded, and edited until 1962, by the late Dr. Robert
Haardt.

A particularly noteworthy contribution to early cartobibliography is the catalog of mappemondes dating from 1200
to 1500. [110] It was compiled by the Commission on Early
Maps of the International Geographical Union, Marcel Destombes, Commission chairman, edited the compilation. The
study of the history of cartography has been greatly facilitated by the large number of facsimile maps and atlases that
have been published in recent years. A list of cartobibliographic reproductions still in print was compiled, in 1960,
by the Library of Congress, and reissued in expanded format
in 1966. [111] The accelerated activity in cartographic facsimile publishing has been the subject of several articles. [112]

Exhibiting Maps

Maps are colorful and eye-catching exhibit pieces, and
cartographic displays are effective in promoting the use and
enjoyment of maps. Planning and arranging good exhibits
call for imagination, familiarity with the map collection, desirable display space and equipment, and an abundance of
time. It is the rare map library that meets all these conditions. Exhibits all too often, therefore, get low priority in
cartographic reference service. The literature, however,
does record a fair number of map exhibits in recent years.
International congresses and conferences invite displays of
official and commercial cartographic works of different countries. At the Pacific Science Congress, Honolulu, Hawaii
(August 21 to September 6, 1961), the National Archives displayed maps illustrating the "U.S. Scientific Exploration of
the Pacific Basin, 1783-1899."[113] The United States exhibit
of thematic maps, at the Stockholm (1961) International Geographical Congress, was described by Tuttle in the Professional Geographer. [114] The same journal carried Biggs' account of the cartographic exhibit at the Seventh General Assembly of the Pan American Institute of Geography and History (Buenos Aires, August 1-15, 1961). [115]

Exhibits of historical maps have been featured at various American libraries. John Carter Brown Library's exhibit on "Early Maps and Their Uses" was opened on May
17, 1963, with an address by Alexander O. Vietor, Map
Curator, Yale University Library. Princeton University displayed groups of early maps which were described by Mrs.
Fantova in the Princeton University Library Quarterly. [116]
Before his departure from Peabody Institute (Baltimore), in
1966, Frank Jones arranged a series of cartographic displays,
among them "Baltimore Mapmakers," "Roads Through History:

Road Maps from Rome to Today, " and "Outer Space in Ancient Maps. " A leaflet entitled "Notes on an Exhibit of Maps of the Pacific Northwest from the Collection of Edward W. Allen, " published by the Washington State Historical Society in 1963, records a cartographic display sponsored by the Society. The Birmingham Public Library published a catalog, in 1965, of "An Exhibit Depicting Cartographically the History of the Evolution of the Old Southeast in That Crucial Thirty Years, 1790-1820. " The maps displayed were from the Rucker Agee Collection, which was presented to the Public Library, in 1964, by Mr. Rucker Agee, a resident of Birmingham.

Employment in Map Librarianship

Employment prospects in map librarianship today are exceedingly favorable. In part because of retirements, but more especially because a number of colleges and universities have established separate map rooms or departments, the current demand for map librarians greatly exceeds the supply. This is reflected in salaries which are being offered. Current map librarian vacancies are posted at from $7500 to $10,000, as compared with $6500 to $7500 several years ago. Institutions that can afford to pay at or near the top of the scale will certainly attract the best trained and most experienced of the new generation of map librarians. Those still limited to salaries below $7500 must be satisfied with a lower level of competence.

There is little prospect that the supply of trained and experienced map librarians will meet present and anticipated future demands for some time. A few library schools give minimum encouragement to students who indicate an interest in map libraries by permitting them to carry out independent investigations or research in this field. No library school at present, however, offers a specific program for training map librarians. The University of Illinois Library School, which for a number of years had such a program, recently discontinued it. In March 1966, Drexel Institute Graduate School of Library Science sponsored a Map Library Workshop, at the Free Library of Philadelphia. It was directed by Bill Woods, former map librarian and recently resigned Executive Director of SLA. Mr. Woods was assisted by Ena Yonge, Map Curator Emeritus of the American Geographical Society, and Dorothy W. Bartlett, head of the Reference and Bibliography Section of LC's Geography and Map Division. The Drexel Workshop was reported briefly in the June 1966 issue of SLA's Geography and Map Division Bulletin (page 16), and in the September 1966 Cahiers de Geographie de Quebec (pages 336-337).

The literature on map library education has profited, in recent months, by two authoritative studies. Bill Woods' paper, entitled "Map Librarianship," was published in the Summer 1966 issue of Journal of Education for Librarianship. Walter W. Ristow's "Education for Map Librarianship," which summarizes results of a survey of accredited library schools, is scheduled for publication in a forthcoming number of Library Journal.

Developments Abroad

This summary has been concerned primarily with map libraries and map librarianship in the United States. The developments in this specialized branch of librarianship have been no less interesting and dramatic in Europe. Because of space limitations, it is not possible, however, to report the latter in this paper. We should perhaps note, however, that several major foreign map collections have also lost, by retirement, distinguished and experienced curators. Mlle. Myriem Fonçin, long-time head of the Map and Chart Department of France's Bibliothèque National, retired in 1964, G. R. Crone, librarian and head of the Map Room, Royal Geographical Society, London, retired at the end of 1966, and R. A. Skelton retired as superintendent of the Map Room, British Museum, on March 31, 1967.

The growing significance of map libraries in Great Britain is evident from reports of a meeting, in London, in May 1966, "to consider the proposal to form a Map Curator's group." Also, in September 1965 the newly organized British Cartographic Society held a symposium, at Swansea, Wales, on map libraries. Three papers presented at the symposium were published in the September 1966 Cartographic Journal.[117] We cannot conclude this cursory look at European map librarianship without calling attention to Cornelis Koeman's authoritative directory of Dutch map collections.[118] Mr. Koeman observes that "the scientific study of the history of cartography has in the past been seriously hampered by our limited knowledge of the source material and its whereabouts. The present work is designed to remedy in part this situation."

In summation we reemphasize that the future is bright

for map libraries and map librarians. Progress may be
slow in the next year or two, because of a temporary shortage of experienced leaders. Internal and external pressures
that are certain to build up, because of increased numbers
of separate map rooms and departments, growth in cartographic holdings in new and long-established collections, the
imperative need for standardization of map cataloging and
classification procedures, inclusion of maps in the Title II
program, and the inevitable mechanization of map cataloging,
will definitely accelerate the emergence of maps in libraries
within the next decade.

REFERENCES

1.   Cover story, issue of July 29, 1966.
2.   Ristow, Walter W. "Maps in Libraries." Library
     Journal, v. 71, Sept. 1, 1946: 1101-1107.
3.   _____. "What about Maps?" Library Trends, v. 4,
     Oct. 1955: 123-139.
4.   Mullins, Lynn S. "The Rise of Map Libraries in Amer-
     ica during the Nineteenth Century." In Special Li-
     braries Association Geography and Map Division Bul-
     letin, no. 63, Mar. 1966: 2-11.
5.   Ristow, Walter W. "Historical Cartography in the
     United States, 1959-1963." Imago Mundi, no. XVII,
     1963: 106-113.
6.   Alexander, Gerard L. "Some Notes Toward a History
     of the New York Public Library Map Room for the
     Years 1923-1941." In Special Libraries Association,
     Geography and Map Division Bulletin, no. 35, Feb.
     1959: 4-7.
7.   Bryan, Mary M. "The Harvard College Library Map
     Collection." In Special Libraries Association Geogra-
     phy and Map Division Bulletin, no. 36, April, 1959:
     4-12.
8.   Thatcher, E. P. "The Map Library Collection of the
     University of Oregon." In Special Libraries Asso-
     ciation Geography and Map Division Bulletin, no. 43,
     Feb. 1961: 20-21.
9.   Mueller, Anne. "The Map Collection of the Los Angeles
     Public Library." In Special Libraries Association
     Geography and Map Division Bulletin, no. 43, Feb.
     1961: 17-19.
10. Dowd, Sheila. "Map Collection of the University of
     California at Berkeley." In Special Libraries Asso-
     ciation Geography and Map Division Bulletin, no. 43,
     Feb. 1961: 13-16.

11. Johnson, Ralph. "The UCLA Map Collections." In
    Special Libraries Association Geography and Map
    Division Bulletin, no. 43, Feb. 1961: 15-16; and
    Hagen, Carlos B. "The UCLA Map Library." In
    Special Libraries Association Geography and Map Divi-
    sion Bulletin, no. 51, Mar. 1963: 18.
12. Drazniowsky, Roman. "New Public Library Map Collec-
    tion." In Special Libraries Association Geography
    and Map Division Bulletin, no. 59, Mar. 1965: 21.
13. Yonge, Ena. "The Map Department of the American
    Geographical Society." The Professional Geographer,
    v. 7, Mar. 1955: 2-5.
14. Jordan, Clifford L. "Tons of Maps." Dartmouth Alum-
    ni Magazine, v. 49, Dec. 1956: 20-23.
15. Woods, Bill M. "Recommendations for a Map Collec-
    tion at the Chicago Undergraduate Division, Univer-
    sity of Illinois." Illinois Libraries (Urbana), v. 39,
    Mar. 1957: 74-78.
16. Berthelsen, Barbara P. "Library has Maps of All
    Places." Surveying and Mapping, v. 17, April-June,
    1957: 187-188. Reprinted from Cornell Alumni
    News, Mar. 15, 1957.
17. Fairbridge, Rhodes W. "We Read Maps," 14-21; Pratt,
    Dallas. "From Sea-Serpents to Science," 3-7; Vie-
    tor, Alexander O. "The Cassini Planisphere of 1696,"
    8-13.
18. Manion, Esther Ann. "The National Geographic Society
    Library." The George Washington University Maga-
    zine (Washington, D. C.), v. 2, Fall, 1965: 28-31.
19. Atkinson, Edith. "Cartomania in the Louisiana State Li-
    brary." In Louisiana Library Association Bulletin,
    v. 29, Fall, 1966: 92-93.
20. Abelson, Nathaniel O. "Atlas Shrugged." [UN] Secre-
    tariat News, v. 14, Jan. 29, 1960: 4-5.

21. "Cartographic Records of the Panama Canal," by James
    B. Rhoads, 1956; "Cartographic Records of the Bu-
    reau of the Census," by Charlotte Ashby and James
    B. Rhoads, 1958; "List of Cartographic Records of
    the General Land Office," by Laura E. Kelsay, 1964;
    "Cartographic Records of the American Expeditionary
    Forces 1917-21," by Franklin W. Burch, 1966.
22. U.S. Library of Congress. "The Geography and Map
    Division of the Library of Congress." Washington,
    1966, 2 p.
23. Fonçin, M. et al., editors. Bibliographie Cartographique
    International, 1964. Paris, Armand Colin, 1966.

24. Grenacher, Franz. Die "Bibliographie Cartographique Internationale," In Petermann's Geographische Mitteilungen, v. 102, no. 2, 1958: 143-146.

25. Fonçin, Myriem. "Bibliographie Cartographique." Bulletin des Bibliothèques de France (Paris), v. 9, Feb. 1964: 39-42.

26. Hannah, William. "Foreign Topographic Mapping Agencies and Their Sales and Information Offices." Surveying and Mapping, v. 16, April-June, 1956: 212-216; Oct.-Dec. 1956: 506-508; v. 17, April-June, 1957: 200-201.

27. United Nations. "World Cartography." Annual. New York, United Nations."

28. Stanford, Edward, "Ltd. International Map Bulletin." Annual. London, Stanford.

29. For example, a) Types of maps published by Government agencies; b) Maps of the United States; c) Sources of lake and river charts.

30. Bartlett, Dorothy W. "New Government Maps for Everyone: A Select List." Special Libraries, v. 54, Jan. 1963: 24-28.

31. Brock, Clifton. "The Quiet Crisis in Government Publishing." College and Research Libraries, v. 26, Nov. 1965: 477-489, 531.

32. U. S. Library of Congress. Processing Department, Exchange and Gift Division. Monthly Checklist of State Publications. Washington, D. C.

33. "State, County, and Municipal Agencies for Planning and Integration of Mapping Activities." Surveying and Mapping, v. 17, Oct.-Dec. 1957: 427-429.

34. U. S. Library of Congress. Copyright Office. Catalog of Copyright Entries: Third Series. Part 6. Maps and Atlases. Washington, D. C.

35. Buffum, Charles W. "New Organization of Catalog of Copyright Entries." In Special Libraries Association Geography and Map Division Bulletin, no. 38, Dec. 1959: 9.

36. American Geographical Society. "Current Geographical Publications," Nordis Felland, edit. Ten issues per year. New York, American Geographical Society.

37. Special Libraries Association. Geography and Map Division Bulletin. Frank J. Anderson, edit. Quarterly. Spartanburg, South Carolina.

38. U. S. Library of Congress. Hispanic Foundation. Handbook of Latin American Studies. Annual. Gainesville, University of Florida Press.

39. American Congress on Surveying and Mapping. "Sur-
     veying and Mapping." Julius L. Speert, edit. Quar-
     terly. Washington, D. C.
40. U. S. Army Map Service; Its Mission, History and Or-
     ganization. Washington, 1960. 41 p.

41. Sears, Marvin. "Effectiveness of the Army Map Ser-
     vice Depository Program and Methods for Promoting
     Map Use." Washington, 1960. 46 p. Unpublished
     master's thesis. Washington, D. C. Catholic Uni-
     versity of America. Microfilm available.
42. U. S. Congress. Public Law 89-329, 89th Congress,
     H. R. 9567, Nov. 8, 1965. Sec. 231, p. 10.
43. Special Libraries Association. Geography and Map
     Division, Committee on Map Cataloging. Prelimin-
     ary Report. Appended to Geography and Map Divi-
     sion Bulletin, no. 3, Dec. 1948. Final report. Ap-
     pended to Bulletin, no. 13, Oct. 1953: 19-24.
44. American Library Association. Anglo-American Catalog-
     ing Rules. Chicago, 1967.
45. With more than three million map sheets and 28,000 at-
     lases in its custody, the Library's Geography and
     Map Division is the world's largest and most com-
     prehensive cartographic collection. Within the United
     States its holdings are ten times as great as the next
     largest nonfederal map libraries.
46. Woods, Bill. "Map Cataloging: Inventory and Prospect."
     Library Resources and Technical Services, v. 3,
     Fall, 1959: 257-273.
47. Fink, Mary Ellin. "The Structure of Map Retrieval
     Studies." Typescript. University of Michigan De-
     partment of Library Science. Revised August 1962.
48. _____. "A Comparison of Map Cataloging Systems."
     In Special Libraries Association Geography and Map
     Division Bulletin, no. 50, Dec. 1962: 6-12.
49. Scheffler, Emma M. "Maps in the Illinois State Ar-
     chives." Illinois Libraries, v. 44, June 1962: 418-
     426.
50. Bordin, Ruth B., and Warner, Robert M. "Manuscript
     Map Cataloging." In their The Modern Manuscript
     Library. New York, 1966: 65.

51. White, John B. "Further Comment on Map Cataloging."
     Library Resources and Technical Services, v. 6,
     Winter, 1962: 78.
52. American Geographical Society. "Cataloguing and Filing
     Rules for Maps and Atlases in the Society's Collec-

tion." [By] Roman Drazniowsky, map curator. New
York, 1964. 42 p.

53 Smith, Thomas R. "The Map Collection in a General
Library: A Manual for Classification and Processing
Procedures." Lawrence, Kansas, University of
Kansas, Feb. 1961. Ditto reproduction, 126 p.

54. Smith, Thomas R. "Map Classification and Arrangement at the University of Kansas Library." In Special Libraries Association Geography and Map Division Bulletin, no. 22, Dec. 1955: 11-17.

55. U. S. Army Map Service. Department of Technical Services. Library Division. "A Simplified Map Collection System." [Washington, D. C.] [1964] 8 p.
and appendix.

56. U. S. Library of Congress, Subject Cataloging Division,
Classification, Class G. Geography, Anthropology,
Folklore, Manners and Customs, Recreation. 3rd
ed. Washington, D. C., Government Printing Office,
1954.

57. Buffum, Charles W. "Additions and Changes in the
L. C. Atlas and Map Classification." In Special
Libraries Association Geography and Map Division
Bulletin, no. 53, Sept. 1963: 13-15.

58. U. S. Library of Congress. Processing Department.
Classification, Class G. Geography, etc. Washington, D. C. 3rd edit. 1954, reprinted 1966. Includes "Additions and Changes to January 1966."

59. International Geographical Union. Commission on the
Classification of Books and Maps in Libraries. A)
Proposal for a revision of the group U. D. C. 91
Geography. IGU 9th General Assembly and 18th In-
ternational Geographical Congress. Rio de Janeiro,
Aug. 9-18, 1956. B) Rapport [of the Commission].
17th International Geographical Congress. Rio de
Janeiro, Aug. 9-18, 1956. Includes an essay, on
objectives, by Andre Libault, the Commission's
Chairman, a paper by G. R. Crone on "Existing
Classification Systems," and a report by the U. S. A.
Member, Arch C. Gerlach. C) Final report on the
classification of geographical books and maps. 11th
General Assembly and 20th International Geographical
Congress. London, July-Aug. 1964.

60. Gerlach, Arch C. "Geography and Map Cataloging and
Classification in Libraries." Special Libraries, v.
52, May-June, 1961: 248-251.

61. Libault, Andre. "Classification of Maps and Geograph-

ical Publications. " UNESCO Bulletin for Libraries,
v. 9, May-June, 1955: 93-95.

62. Wallis, Helen. "Report on the Library Classification
of Books and Maps. " The Cartographic Journal,
v. 2, June, 1965: 14-15.

63. Gerlach, Arch C. "An Adaptation of the Library of
Congress Classification for Use in Geography and
Map Libraries. " Mimeog. , 32 p. Washington,
D. C. "Reproduced by the National Academy of
Sciences. " 1956.

64. Bahn, Catherine I. "SLA Loan Collection of Special
Classification Schemes and Subject Heading Lists
[Map and Geography extract]. " In Special Libraries
Association Geography and Map Division Bulletin, no.
41, Oct. 1960: 9-15.

65. Special Libraries Association. Geography and Map
Division, "Committee on Automation in Map Libraries. "
In Special Libraries Association Geography and Map
Division Bulletin, no. 65, Sept. 1966: 4.

66. Gull, C. D. "How Will Electronic Information Systems
Affect Cataloging Rules?" Library Resources and
Technical Services, v. 5, Spring, 1961, p. 138.

67. Swanson, Don. "Library Goals and the Role of Automation. " Special Libraries, v. 53, Oct. 1962, p.
467.

68. Simonton, Wesley. "The Computerized Book Catalog;
Possible, Feasible, Desirable?" Library Resources
and Technical Services, v. 8, Fall, 1964, p. 401.

69. Bahn, Catherine I. "Map Libraries--Space and Equipment. " In Special Libraries Association Geography
and Map Division Bulletin, no. 46, Dec. 1961: 3-
17.

70. Hill, J. Douglas. Library Trends, v. 14, April, 1965:
481-487.

71. Lee, Paul B. "Map Filing Equipment. " In Special Libraries Association Monograph no. 2. Special Libraries: How to Plan and Equip Them. New York,
Special Libraries Association, 1963, p. 43-45.

72. Collier, J. E. "Storing Map Collections. " The Professional Geographer, v. 12, July, 1960: 31-32.

73. Doerr, Arthur H. "Map Collections: Another Approach. "
The Professional Geographer, v. 12, May, 1960: 33-
34.

74. Roepke, Howard G. "Care and Development of a Wall-
Map Collection. " The Professional Geographer, v.
10, May, 1958: 11-15.

75.   U.S. Army Map Service. "Preservation of Maps by
        Lamination." Army Map Service Bulletin, no. 37.
        Washington, June 1961.
76.   Wilson, William K., and Forshee, B.W. "Preserva-
        tion of Documents by Lamination." Washington,
        National Bureau of Standards, 1959.
77.   LeGear, Clara E. "Maps, Their Care, Repair, and
        Preservation in Libraries." Washington, Library
        of Congress, 1956.
78.   Barrow, William J. "The Barrow Method of Restoring
        Deteriorated Documents." Richmond, Va., 1965.
        _____. "Deacidification and Lamination of Deteriorated
        Documents, 1938-1963." American Archivist, v. 28,
        April 1965: 285-290.
        Clapp, Verner W. "Permanent/Durable Book Papers."
        In American Library Association Bulletin, v. 57,
        Oct. 1963: 847-852.
        History of the Barrow Lab, or, the Thirty Years that
        Revolutionized Paper." Publisher's Weekly, v. 189,
        April 4, 1966: 72-80.
79.   U.S. Geological Survey. Federal Map Users Conference
        on National Topographical Program. Washington,
        D.C. Oct. 5-6, 1964. Proceedings, p. 69.
80.   Allen, John. "Reproduction vs. Preservation." Libra-
        ry Journal, v. 91, Nov. 1, 1966, p. 5319.

81.   Grove, Lee E. "Paper Deterioration--An Old Old
        Story." College and Research Libraries, v. 25,
        Sept. 1964, p. 366.
82.   Smith, Richard D. "Paper Deacidification: A Prelim-
        inary Report." The Library Quarterly, v. 36, Oct.
        1966, p. 273.
83.   Williams, Gordon R. "The Preservation of Deteriorat-
        ing Books." Part II: Recommendations for a Solution."
        Library Journal, v. 91, Jan. 15, 1966, p. 189-194.
84.   Ristow, Walter W. "Cartographic Research Guide:
        Weather and Climate Maps." In Special Libraries
        Association Geography and Map Division Bulletin,
        no. 42, December. 1960: 24-34.
85.   _____, edit. Cartographic Research Guide, Part IV,
        "The Cartographic Library and the Map Librarian."
        [Washington, D.C.], 1957. 55 p. mimeog.
86.   Meine, Karl-Heinz. "Recording the Literature of Car-
        tography." In Special Libraries Association Geography
        and Map Division Bulletin, no. 42, Dec. 1960: 12-23.
87.   Harris, Chauncy D., and Fellmann, Jerome D. "In-
        ternational List of Geographical Serials." Chicago,
        University of Chicago, Department of Geography, 1960.

88. Sališčev, K. A. "Die kartographischen Zeitschriften
     der Erde." Petermanns Geographische Mitteilungen,
     v. 110, no. 2, 1966: 147-149.
89. Kilmartin, Jerome O. "The Function of a National
     Map Information Office." In Special Libraries As-
     sociation Geography and Map Division Bulletin, no.
     48, April, 1962: 5-7.
90. U. S. Library of Congress. "A List of Geographical
     Atlases in the Library of Congress." Compiled by
     Clara E. LeGear. Washington, U. S. Government
     Printing Office. Vol. 5, 1958. Lists world atlases
     added to the collections between 1920 and 1955. Vol.
     6, 1963. Atlases of Europe, Africa and Asia added
     between 1920 and 1960.

91. Marketing Maps of the United States. Compiled by
     Walter W. Ristow. Washington, 3rd. edit., rev.
     1958.
92. Selected Maps and Charts of Antarctica. Compiled
     by Richard W. Stephenson. Washington, 1959.
93. Civil War Maps. Compiled by Richard W. Stephen-
     son. Washington, 1961.
94. A Descriptive List of Treasure Maps and Charts.
     Compiled by Richard S. Ladd. Washington, 1964.
95. Maps Showing Explorer's Routes, Trails, and Early
     Roads in the United States. Compiled by Richard
     S. Ladd. Washington, 1962.
96. A) Aviation Cartography, a Historic-Bibliographic
     Study of Aeronautical Charts. Rev. 1960, reprinted
     1962. B) Guide to Historical Cartography. Reprinted
     1962. C) Three-Dimensional Maps. 2nd ed., rev.
     1964.
97. Whyte, Fredrica H. Whyte's Atlas Guide. New York,
     Scarecrow Press, 1962.
98. Walsh, S. Padraig, comp. General World Atlases in
     Print, a Comparative Analysis. New York, Bowker,
     1966.
99. Yonge, Ena. "World and Thematic Atlases: A Sum-
     mary Review." Geographical Review, v. 52, Oct.
     1962: 585-596.
100. _____. "Regional Atlases: A Summary Review."
     Geographical Review, v. 52, July, 1962: 407-432.

101. Balchin, W. G. V. "Atlases Today." Geographical
     Magazine, v. 32, May 1960: 554-563.
102. Bagrow, Leo. History of Cartography. Revised and
     enlarged by R. A. Skelton. Cambridge, Harvard

University Press, 1964.

103. Crone, Gerald R. <u>Maps and Their Makers, An Introduction to the History of Cartography.</u> London,
1966.

104. Skelton, R. A. <u>Decorative Printed Maps of the 15th
to the 18th Centuries.</u> London, 1966.

105. Greenhood, David. <u>Mapping</u> (original title, <u>Down to
Earth, Mapping for Everyone</u>). University of Chicago Press, 1964.

106. Cumming, William P. <u>Southeast in Early Maps.</u>
Chapel Hill, University of North Carolina Press,
1962.

107. Wheat, Carl I. <u>Mapping the Transmississippi West.</u>
San Francisco, Institute of Historical Cartography,
1957-1963. 5 vols. (vol. 5 in two parts).

108. Map Collectors' Circle. Map Collector's Series.
London. 1963- .

109. Coronelli Weltbund der Globusfreunde. <u>Der Globusfreund.</u> Wien, Austria, 1952- .

110. Destombes, Marcel, edit. <u>Mappemondes A. D. 1200-
1500.</u> Amsterdam, N. Israel.

111. U. S. Library of Congress Geography and Map Division.
<u>Facsimiles of Rare Historical Maps.</u> Compiled by
Walter W. Ristow. Washington, 1966.

112. Koeman, C. "An Increase in Facsimile Reprints. "
Imago Mundi, no. 18, 1964: 87.
Parsons, E. J. S. "Atlases in Facsimile." <u>The
Cartographic Journal,</u> v. 2, June 1965: 39-42.
Wallis, Helen. "Landmarks in Atlas Cartography. "
<u>The Cartographic Journal,</u> v. 2, June 1965: 42-44.
Ristow, Walter W. "New Maps from Old, Trends in
Cartographic Facsimile Publishing. " Scheduled for
publication in July 1967 issue of <u>Quarterly Journal
of the Library of Congress.</u>

113. U. S. National Archives. <u>U. S. Scientific Exploration of
the Pacific Basin, 1783-1899.</u> Its publication no.
62-2. Washington, 1961. 26 p.

114. Tuttle, Jerry. "The United States Thematic Map Exhibit at the IGU in Stockholm. " <u>Professional Geographer,</u> v. 13, April, 1961: 42-44.

115. Biggs, Arthur P. "Cartographic and Geographic Con-
sultations and Exhibits at the Seventh General Assembly PAIGH. " <u>Professional Geographer,</u> v. 14,
Jan. 1962: 67-69.

116. Fantova, Johanna. "Map Exhibitions [Alaska, the 49th
State, Early Maps of Russia, Maps of Revolutionary

America]. " Princeton University Library Quarterly, v. 20, 1959: 194-196.
117. Mumford, I. "What is a Map Library, " p. 9-11.
Wallis, Helen. "The Role of a National Map Library, " p. 11-14.
Maling, D. H. "Some Thoughts about Miniaturization of Map Library Contents, " p. 14-15.
118. Koeman, Cornelis. Collection of Maps and Atlases in the Netherlands, Their History and Present State. Leiden, Brill, 1961.

DEVELOPING THE UNIVERSITY MAP LIBRARY*

D. S. Rugg

One of the important by-products of World War II is
the great increase in map coverage throughout the world.
With the aid of aerial photography entire countries or regions
were mapped and the area of large-scale coverage almost
doubled. More maps became available than had ever before
existed. However, libraries were not prepared to handle this
new type of acquisition. Little was known about procedures
of producing, classifying, and storing maps, and the use of
maps as research tools was neglected by reference libraries.
This was especially true of university libraries which began
to receive large numbers of maps, especially those acquired
under the Army Map Service Depository Program. Each university handled the problem in a different way, depending on
funds and personnel available. Even today, thousands of
maps remain unopened in university storerooms when American involvement in international politics has served to maintain interest in global geography.

Literature on the organization and development of map
libraries contains certain gaps. [1] Much has been written on
individual aspects of procurement, classification, cataloging,
and handling, but certain broad aspects of establishment and
operation of a map library have been neglected. It is the
purpose of this paper to outline some of the responsibilities
of a university map curator and to set forth some principles
of organization and operation which can be followed by any
map library. [2] Special emphasis will be placed on the development of an acquisition program, perhaps the most serious gap in map libraries today, even those which have solved
the problems of filing the holdings. The writer feels that
any college or university can develop an adequate collection

---

*Reprinted by permission from The Journal of Geography,
vol. 66, no. 3 (1967), 119-129.

of 10,000 to 50,000 maps provided it is supplemented by good
sources for procurement and reference purposes. Some of
the procedures stated below will illustrate this principle.
Mention will also be made of techniques for promoting the
use of maps since their potentialities are basic reference
and research aids have been realized only to a very limited
extent. As Lloyd Brown has stated "... good or bad, accurate or inaccurate, maps of a given period tell a story
such as few written documents can tell."[3]

Responsibilities of the Map Curator

Each institution should designate a map curator to assume the responsibility of map care. Every university will
not necessarily have a trained man for this position. However, a graduate student in geography or geology often can
fill this job on a full-time or part-time basis, depending on
funds available. Students in these two disciplines are ac-
customed to handling maps and are familiar with world areas
and map characteristics. In some cases, they could work
under the direction of a departmental staff member who may
have had previous experience with map library procedures
in other universities where maps are significant tools for
graduate work. In many universities, the position of map
curator is one of the regular assistantships offered by the
geography department in arrangement with the library. Direction therefore comes from both the department and the library; the former provides the specialized direction relating
to maps as tools while the latter supplies the framework for
procurement, cataloging, and use of maps within the overall
university system. The important thing, however, is that
some person be designated as map curator so that the responsibility is fixed.

The map curator's primary responsibility is the establishment or improvement of the map library. If no map
library exists, the curator's task for the first two years will
involve planning of the library itself and securing administrative support. Because of the recent availability of maps as
research tools, separate map libraries are found only in a
minority of institutions, and there is little provision for maps
in most university budgets. The map curator must frequently
start from scratch and the first two years are critical in
terms of acquiring support for a permanent branch library.
Support does not follow merely because a curator has been
designated, and he will have to sell the importance of this
tool to college officials so that funds and equipment are

provided.   These expenditures will be greatest in the early
years since map cases will generally be lacking and large
numbers of depository maps may remain in unopened cartons.
This is particularly true of the thousands of maps distributed
to universities under the Map Depository Program of the
Army Map Service. 4   This organization has set up certain
requirements for participation in the program; primary
among these are the establishment of facilities and personnel
necessary to care properly for the maps and make them accessible.

        Along with the planning responsibilities, the curator
will be occupied with the three main tasks of operation--
organization and processing, procurement, and reference service.   Often he will have to do this alone, although the help
of a student assistant a few hours per week may be possible,
depending on funds available.   The accessioning, classifying,
and cataloging of maps is a tremendous task, especially in
the first year or two, if depository maps have not yet been
incorporated into the collection.   This will necessitate establishment of a systematic organizational pattern for housing
the maps by areas and topics.   Later on, after the map collection is housed, an active procurement program can be
initiated and the reference value of maps as teaching and research tools can be promoted throughout the university.

Planning

        An important principle with respect to a map library
program is long-term planning.   In spite of the temporary
nature of the curator as an individual, this library should
be considered as a permanent unit in the general library
system.   The desire to make immediate use of available map
material before space and filing cases are available may
easily result in a decentralized and disorganized collection of
little value to anyone.   Planning in advance will help meet
map needs for the future, and will save much time, labor,
and money in map library operation.   A plan, well thought
out and carefully presented to university authorities, will
have a better chance of being accepted.   Once the acceptance
of a map library is secured, each additional step in planning
procedure will be likely to receive support.   Initial planning
for the map library will generally include the provision of
room space and filing cases.   The ideal library will have two
or more adjacent rooms.   The primary room should be large
enough for the cases plus the tables on which maps can be
spread flat for study.   The walls can be covered with plaster

board on which map exhibits and reference aids can be arranged. Other rooms would be used for processing operations to include storage, sorting, cataloging, and mounting.

Maps are most efficiently filed in steel cases composed of shallow horizontal drawers.[5] Permanent growth of the library is facilitated by selection of standard sizes of interchangeable five-drawer sections manufactured by a reputable concern; in this way, the possibilities of maintaining uniformity of storage over a long period is facilitated. A cost estimate per section of $175-$200, exclusive of discount, is reasonable. Utilizing a rough figure of 100-150 maps per drawer, an estimate of initial and annual requirements can be made. Drawers with a dust cover or combination of metal hood and hinged "compressors" are preferable in order that maps may be held flat and preservation encouraged. Drawer sizes of 43" X 32" X 2.5" are adequate for most maps, although a few extra large cases are advisable for certain requirements, such as hydrographic charts. The arrangement of cases will be governed by individual situations; basement locations permit higher tiers than upper floors do. Working space can be provided by utilizing case tops of adjacent tiers. Initial planning should also include folders for the purpose of subdividing the collection. Folders should be of non-acid paper or pressboard (pH 7 or higher) to prevent discoloration or deterioration of contents; a two-inch gusset is recommended, especially for heavier maps. In the absence of funds, folders or separators can be provided by ordinary wrapping paper.

There should be separate provision for the map library within the overall library budget. The curator should plan for the long-run growth of his special library. Three main items will be personnel, equipment, and acquisitions. Personnel items will be stable except for cases where groups of students might be used for a short period on a rush basis to index and file large series of maps such as those from the Army Map Service.[6] Equipment expenditures will be highest first for cases and folders but will level off later under a program an annual expansion. Finally, acquisitions will be systematically handled as a portion of the long-term procurement program which is discussed below. The curator will do well from the beginning to maintain a manual of procedures utilized in the map library. Such a manual is especially necessary to provide continuity since the position of map curator is generally held by a graduate student only during a limited stay at the university.

Organization and Processing

          Much has been written on the various systems of map
classification and cataloging.   No attempt will be made to
treat this subject in any detail here.   The system used for
the organization and classification of maps in the university
should be the one best suited to the facilities and personnel
available.   An important principle of organization which can
be applied in most cases is centralization.   The maps should
preferably be located in a central map library, accessible to
all parts of the university.   Main exceptions to central location would be specialized maps used largely in one department.   Provided personnel is available, a card catalog for
maps should be developed for research use in conjunction
with the normal university card catalog. [7]   Maps not housed
in the map library would be listed here as well.

          Most universities, however, lack personnel for under-
taking the complete cataloging of map collection.   The writer
feels it is unnecessary to store maps until facilities are
available for cataloging, but the maps may be made available
without a card catalog.   A catalog is actually less essential
for map reference than it is for books.   People generally do
not know specifically which map they want but only have an
idea concerning the area and subject.   So a system is generally necessary to permit the viewing of numbers of maps
in order to make a selection.   A system of maps separated
by large manila folders into areas and subordinate topics has
this advantage.   It also permits quick organization of a large
uncatalogued map collection.   The main disadvantage resulting from the lack of a catalog file is that a specific request
for a map would require checking in the collection.   However, if the subdivision is well carried out, such information
is quickly determined.

          The system of subdivision by folders starts with areas
of the world and these in turn are subdivided by topics. [8]
The number of divisions will be governed by the number of
maps available.   Areas will normally start with the world
and hemispheres and proceed to continents, portions of continents, states, areas within states, counties, and cities. [9]
Topical subdivisions may include physical, political, and economic divisions for any area if only a few maps are present,
or may be broadened to include geology, soils, climate, agriculture, industry, transportation, etc.   The flexibility of
the system is one of its greatest advantages.   In cases where
certain folders such as agriculture become over-loaded, a

time division can be made so that pre-World War II maps
are filed separately from those dating from the postwar period.

The folder system described above permits a widespread selection of pertinent maps by the user.   Several
folders on the desired subject can be brought to the reference
room, a system that is utilized in the Map Division of the
Library of Congress.   Such a system, of course, lacks catalog control of individual items but facilitates greater use of
maps in the absence of cataloging facilities.   A system of
"titling" the maps may serve as a substitute for cataloging
provided personnel is available.   In this case, duplicate
copies of a brief typed slip are prepared bearing the publisher, title, subject, scale, and date of the map; one copy
is pasted on the back of the map and the other copy is filed
in an area-subject sequence.

In addition to the special-subject maps organized
areally and topically, the map library includes functional
series of maps.   Topographic, nautical, and aeronautical
maps and charts cover certain areas but being of uniform
type should be kept together and used as a series.   This is
facilitated by the fact that index sheets accompany each of
these series; merely ticking off in color those sheets held
and their dates gives instant access to any sheet while at
the same time providing what is really a catalog.   Since
functional sets include the greater portion of all items in a
map library, the actual cataloging task is not generally so
great as one might suppose. 10 Furthermore, it is possible
to purchase, at a reasonable price, catalog cards from the
Library of Congress covering maps published by Army Map
Service and distributed to depository libraries.

Still another point on organization is drawer location
and allotment.   The areas and functional series should be
located in a fairly logical pattern with respect to adjacent
areas and amount to use.   Thus Europe and Asia should be
fairly close together rather than widely separated.   The
greatest demand will be for maps of the United States, especially political, historical, economic, and topographic
sheets.   Europe would probably rank next.   So these map
cases should be located in the most accessible portion of the
map library.   Empty drawers should be left throughout the
collection for expansion, with the greatest space in those
areas of maximum demand and production.   All map drawers
with their respective folders would be cited in a master list

to include both general and functional holdings. Procedures
for processing and handling of maps are closely related to
the organization of the collection. Several excellent sources
treat these procedures including preliminary and secondary
processing in addition to mounting and reconditioning of map
items. 11 Stamping and accessioning of maps are important
processes which should be carried out regularly, even though
classification and filing may be delayed, because such information is necessary for recording library growth and in establishing budgetary procurement plans.

Procurement Program

The map curator will necessarily have much of his
time taken up by organization of the collection and service
operations. However, all libraries must have an active procurement program, and it is important to initiate this early.
The first step is to acquire a knowledge of the major sources
of map materials. Map producing agencies vary considerably
but generally fall into one of three categories--governmental,
institutional, and commercial. 12 A card file on map agencies must be developed to include names and addresses of
the agencies, types of maps published, and information as
to the availability of catalogs. There is no one source for
acquiring maps, and a variety of bibliographic aids must be
consulted. 13 The fugitive nature of many maps is also a
problem, i. e., small restricted editions. In most countries,
more than eighty percent of all maps are issued by governmental agencies, so official sources are basic. Commercial
maps are largely restricted to atlases and road and wall
maps, while maps published by institutes are infrequent.
Very few books or articles have been written on the subject
of map intelligence. 14 Journals which regularly include map
information are Surveying and Mapping, The Military Engineer, The Cartographic Journal (British), Geographical Review, and Economic Geography. 15 The Current Geographic
Publications of the American Geographic Society, Bulletin of
the Geography and Map Division of the Special Libraries Association, and Petermanns Geographische Mitteilungen (German) include excellent summaries of new sources and items.
World Cartography, a United Nations publication, is helpful
on the activities of official map agencies. Certain government maps are listed in Price List 53 entitled "Maps" published by the U. S. Government Printing Office. 16 General
guides to U. S. maps are provided by W. R. Tobler's Maps
of the United States (Seattle, Washington, 1959) and an article
by Bartlett. 17 The catalog of Copyright Entries (Third Series,

Part 6) of the Library of Congress is a source for commercial maps copyrighted in the United States. Other map acquisitions by the Library of Congress are evaluated at intervals in the Quarterly Journal of this agency. Detailed catalogs and other procurement aids are available from Stanford
Map Company (London) and Reise- und Verkehrsverlag (Stuttgart). 18

The next step in the procurement program is establishing contact with the various agencies and building up current
information on maps published. Preprinted form cards can
be easily sent out to the agencies throughout the world requesting latest map catalogs, indexes, and price lists. It
is the acquisition of these catalogs that forms the foundation
to the map procurement program. Selective ordering on a
long-term basis from these catalogs makes it possible to develop map coverage for various areas of the world in a systematic fashion. 19

Once the information on map sources is relatively
complete, the actual procurement can begin. The curator
will be interested in extending coverage of two principle types
--(1) basic reference series ranging from atlases to topographic sheets and (2) special-subject maps. Owing to greater expense involved in basic reference coverage at detailed
scales, the goal of the procurement program will be decreasing intensity of coverage by scale. 20 At the smallest scale
(i. e., the last detail), world coverage is provided by various large atlases. The leading examples are the Times Atlas
(British), Atlante Internazionale (Italian), and the Atlas Mira
(Russian). 21 The Goode's World Atlas, published by Rand
McNally, includes both general reference and special-subject
maps. In these atlases, continental areas or portions thereof are represented at scales from 1:2,000,000 to 1:10,000,000.
In the same general category are national or regional atlases
and specialized map series which cover only parts of the
world but are sufficiently important to warrant procurement
consideration. 22 Such an example is the series of maps at
1:5,000,000 published by the American Geographical Society
and covering the major continents. At larger scales, nearly
worldwide map coverage is provided by series at 1:1,000,000
--either the "International Map of the World" or the "World
Aeronautical Charts. "23

At scales larger than 1:1,000,000 the problem of map
coverage owing to nonuniformity of series and great expense
involved in purchasing and housing the maps. In the United

States, complete coverage is provided by the series at
1:250,000 published by the U.S. Geological Survey. However,
in Europe and many other areas the fragmentation of political areas makes it necessary to order selectively from the
catalogs that have been acquired as a first step in the procurement program. The curator might order a number of
the general maps which portray political and economic aspects
of the country at scales of 1:250,000 to 1:1,000,000. In this
way coverage would be extended systematically beyond the atlases and world map series mentioned above. At the more
detailed topographic scales (i.e., 1:100,000 and larger), selective ordering of certain sample sheets becomes necessary.
In this way, the expense of acquiring and housing large numbers of rarely used maps is avoided but at the same time
sample sheets are available to familiarize prospective users
with the series. If the sample sheets represent different
physical or economic areas of the country, they are even
more effective in serving as a reference tool. The user can
then request those additional sheets which he needs. This
type of selective ordering can be extended to various countries on a long-term basis and illustrates a basic principle
stated earlier--a small adequate map collection can be maintained by any university or college. Priorities also can be
established for various world areas based on existing coverage through the Army Map Service series and on the specialized regional and local interests of the university.

        Procurement of the second type of coverage mentioned
above--special-subject maps--is more selective. Again the
map sources compiled in the early stages of the program
will be invaluable. The goal should be rather complete eventual coverage of various U.S. maps for terrain, climate,
soils, geology, agriculture, industry, transportation, etc. In
some cases these maps may be detailed enough to involve
series, e.g., road maps. However, for foreign areas the
situation may involve selection (European countries) or purchase of all maps (underdeveloped areas). The program for
long-term procurement of these special subject maps should
be combined with that for basic reference coverage mentioned
above. For example, procurement during the first year might
concentrate on French maps and U.S. road maps, the second
year on Japanese maps and U.S. hydrographic charts, etc.

        In addition to the direct purchase of maps from agen-
cies, other means of acquisition exist. Depository programs
are especially good as this permits automatic receipt of certain series publications, e.g., topographic quadrangles of the

Geological Survey and excess foreign maps published by the
Army Map Service of the Defense Department. Maps can
often be procured as gifts or at reduced rates for educational
institutions, especially state, county, and city maps published
by road, planning, engineering, and postal agencies. [24] The
Map Division of the Library of Congress has surplus duplicate
maps which can often be acquired through exchange for other
maps or comparable service (e.g., summer work program
for university students). If surplus maps are available, exchanges with agencies or other universities can be arranged.
Copies of research maps done at the university should be
obtained and filed in the map library and cards may be prepared for outstanding maps accompanying books. The procurement of wall maps is a separate problem but the curator
can usually provide assistance to university departments in
ordering these as lecture aids.

An expanding map library should take cognizance of
the teaching and demonstration value of globes and plastic
maps. [25] Two outstanding examples of general-purpose globes
are those distributed by the National and American Geographical Societies. A recent product of Replogle Globes, Inc. is
the Time-Life globe with special light adapter to add relief
features to the normal political boundaries. The unique embossed 12-inch globe of Geo-Physical Maps, Inc. (Rand Mc-
Nally) is a replica of the larger six-foot globe which has
been called the most elaborate ever constructed. Plastic
embossed maps are also available. Most important, perhaps,
are the Raised Relief Maps produced by A. J. Mystrom &
Company and U.S. map sheets at 1:250,000 and 1:1,000,000
prepared by the Army Map Service of the Department of Defense.

Aerial photographs are often filed in the map library
because of their similarity to maps and the ways in which
they complement them as reference material. Procurement
of these photos is facilitated by the use of an index map--
"Status of Aerial Photography of the United States" (published
by the U.S. Geological Survey)--which shows the agency responsible for coverage of particular areas. A map library
generally concentrates on the purchase of photos for the local
and state area. Detailed photo indexes for county areas in
most states are available and can be utilized to pinpoint exact photo numbers for ordering purposes.

The procedure for ordering maps will vary depending
on the relationship between the map library and the general

library. The information for orders will necessarily come
from the map curator since he possesses the catalogs and
other procurement aids. The actual orders, however, generally should go out from the ordering division of the general library where the expenditure or procurement fund is
controlled. Form orders can be printed which include space
for addresses and details of maps; general instructions of the
form would include a request that maps be sent flat and un-
mounted (unless specified otherwise) to the map library and
that a bill in duplicate be forwarded. Reminders concerning
more recent catalogs and educational discounts might also be
included. Such a system works satisfactorily in most cases.
The primary exception is where prepayment is required as in
the use of the Government Printing Office. Such cases require the determination of exact costs which can be ascertained from proper price lists.

Reference Service

        The service provided by the map library in meeting
needs of the university will help to promote early recognition
by the institution of the importance of maps as a reference
and research facility. The curator will have to serve as a
specialized reference librarian able to recommend maps to
different users. Such maps may be held in the collection or
can be ordered. He will find it necessary to keep abreast
of map sources and publications. This information, in part,
will derive from the procurement program discussed above.
Woods illustrates how a small map library with adequate
source information can provide reference service even without a large collection of maps on hand. [26] Ideas may be obtained as well by writing to or visiting other map libraries.
The Special Libraries Association has a panel of experienced
consultants which, for a nominal fee, will help set up or improve map libraries.

        The map library can do much to facilitate the teach-
ing and research goals of the university or college. Maps
held in the collection especially suitable for illustrating
courses in different fields can be pulled and a list circulated
to the departments involved. Such assistance is particularly
helpful to area-study programs. A similar list might be
prepared for available maps or map series which appear to
represent research aids. Examples of such teaching or research maps might include the following: oil and gas investigations for the geologist; representation of pre-war ethnic
groups in Europe for the historian; maps illustrating interna-

tional relations for the political scientist; changing population patterns in the United States for the sociologist; and levels of economic development for the economist.

Certain specialized reference aids should be a part of every map library. The most important of these aids include the Columbia Lippincott Gazetteer of the World, Webster's Geographical Dictionary, and gazetteers published for individual countries by the Board on Geographic Names of the Department of Interior. Gazetteers are a part of the Army Map Service Depository Program and include names for the series acquired. A useful reference volume is A Glossary of Geophysical Terms edited by L. Dudley Stamp.

A system of regular hours is certainly a first step in expanding the use of maps in the university. If the curator has an assistant, their respective hours can be staggered so as to permit greater accessibility. At other hours, the map library should remain closed, since the practice of leaving it unattended with self-service sign-out sheets will result in loss of the most widely used maps. It also results in considerable disorganization as users paw through various folders without any real idea of where to find what they are seeking. In any collection where there is no card catalog, the precise area and topical organization by folders must be preserved if the maps are to be easily located. Maps can be checked out for two-week periods, utilizing map tubes as containers to preserve the item and to prevent folding.

Promotion of the map library should go hand-in-hand with service, especially since few students or faculty members may be aware of the reference facility. Signs can be posted in prominent places giving the location and hours of operation. After the collection is organized, an "open house" might be held to permit faculty to visit and become acquainted with it. The curator may want to hold conferences with department heads so the needs of the faculty could be incorporated into the procurement program. The college newspaper or library bulletin can be utilized for notes regarding maps of interest or acquisition lists can be circulated. A mimeographed form can be prepared giving pertinent facts of the map library including information about types of maps available, an outline of the classification system, and a statement concerning the program for expansion. Finally, exhibits are one of the best ways of promoting interest in maps and the map library. Some typical exhibits might include "Recreation Maps," "Current Events Locale," "Historical Map Examples," and others. [27]

FOOTNOTES

*Note: The author wishes to express his appreciation to
        Professor Edward B. Espenshade, Jr. (Evanston,
        Illinois) and to Dr. Arch Gerlach (Washington, D. C.)
        for helpful comments on the original draft of this
        paper.

1.   An excellent evaluation of literature on map libraries
     is Ristow, Walter W., "What about Maps?" Library
     Trends, III (October 1955), 123-139. For material
     on the general subject of map library development,
     see Ferrar, A. M., "Management of Map Collections
     and Libraries in University Geography Department,"
     Library Association Record, LXIV (May 1962), 161-
     165. One entire issue (March 15, 1950) of the Li-
     brary Journal devoted to maps is now out of print.
     The Bulletin published by the Geographic and Map
     Division of the Special Libraries Association is also
     helpful.

2.   The author wishes to express his indebtedness to Dr.
     Edward B. Espenshade, Jr., Professor of Geography
     at Northwestern University. Many of the principles
     and ideas expressed in this article were developed
     by Dr. Espenshade in the Map Library of the Uni-
     versity of Chicago and later incorporated by the
     writer when he served as Map Curator at Northwest-
     ern University.

3.   Brown, Lloyd, "Problems of Maps," Library Trends,
     XIII (October 1964), 212-225.

4.   The Army Map Service was created in 1942 to satisfy
     the heavy demand for maps by U. S. agencies during
     the war. Some 30,000 different maps were prepared
     in the 1942-45 period and the agency has continued
     its work in the postwar period. In 1946 surplus
     stocks of AMS Maps were made available to some
     200 universities and colleges. See AMS Depository
     Manual.

5.   For information on map library equipment, including
     cases, see "Map Libraries--Space and Equipment"
     Bulletin of the Geography and Map Division, Special
     Libraries Association, XLVI (February 1961), 3-17.
     Wooden cases are less suitable than steel ones owing
     to lower capacity and to changes in size from hu-
     midity fluctuations. Vertical file cases, although
     having large capacities, are not as accessible as
     horizontal file cases; they are more suitable for the

rarely used functional map series. Additional details on cases are provided in Hall, J. Douglas, "Maps and Atlas Cases," Library Trends, XIII (April 1965), 481-487.

6. Progress on map library projects may be facilitated by use of students employed under the federal Work-Study Program.

7. See the following sources: (1) White, R. C., "Ideal Arrangement for Maps in a Library," Special Libraries. L (April 1959), 154-161. (2) Woods, B. M., "Map Cataloging: Inventory and Prospect," Library Resources and Technical Service, III (Fall 1959), 257-73. (3) Anderson, Ottilia C., "No Best Method to Catalog Maps," Library Journal, LXXV (March 15, 1950), 450-452.

8. This system is similar to those utilized at the Map Libraries of Northwestern University and the University of Wisconsin. All are similar to an area-subject breakdown which was developed in the Office of Strategic Services during World War II. This system, which emphasizes classification and cataloging on preprinted cards for greater speed, is described by L. Wilson in the Annals of the Association of American Geographers (March 1948), 6-37.

9. An example of such a breakdown in Europe might be Europe, Northwestern Europe, Belgium, Flanders (a region of Belgium), and Ghent (a city in Flanders). The areal divisions may be clarified by outline maps utilized for references. Political divisions and cities may also be filed alphabetically.

10. Underscored by the author.

11. Le Gear, Clara, Maps, Their Care, Repair, and Preservation in Libraries (Washington, D.C.: Library of Congress, 1949). This source is not out of print.

12. Espenshade, Edward B., Jr., "A Guide to Map Sources for Use in Building a College Map Library," College and Research Libraries, IX (January 1948), 46.

13. One international source is the Bibliographie Cartographique Internationale published by the French National Committee of Geography and the International Geographical Union through the auspices of UNESCO.

14. Although considerably out of date, a useful summary of federal map-producing agencies is Walter Thiele's book, Official Map Publications (Chicago: American Library Association, 1938). This work includes a discussion of the nature of the mapping activities by

the different government agencies and the types of
map materials that are produced. No similar book
exists for foreign agencies although Foreign Maps by
E. C. Olson and A. Whitmarsh (Harper, 1944) provides some helpful historic information. A recent
study of West German agencies is D. S. Rugg,
"Postwar Progress in Cartography in the Federal
Republic of Germany, " The Cartographic Journal,
December 1965.

15. Serial aids for map procurement are given in Felland,
Nordis, "Periodical Aids to Map Acquisition, " Li-
brary Journal, LXXV (March 15, 1950), 438, 488.
See also Espenshade, op. cit. 52-53.

16. See also Bowman, Nellie M., "Publications, Maps, and
Charts sold by U. S. Government Agencies other than
the Superintendent of Documents, " Special Libraries,
XLIV (February 1953) 53-65. Data on map services
and programs in the United States are available from
the Map Information Office of the U. S. Geological
Survey. See Kilmartin, J. V., "The Map Information Office, " College and Research Libraries, XVII
(March 1950), 132-134. A useful summary of U. S.
mapping progress is given in an unpublished paper
by Gerald Fitzgerald, "The National Mapping Pro-
gram--A Review of Progress, " Geological Survey,
1956.

17. Bartlett, Dorothy W., "New Government Maps for
Everyone: A Select List, " Special Libraries, LIV
(January 1963), 25-28.

18. Contact with Reise- und Verkehrsverlag facilitates procurement in many ways. This firm maintains stocks
of maps from all over the world. Offers can be
made from a detailed "Katalog" (including indexes)
and more current "Kartenbriefe" and "Sonderver-
zeichnisse. "

19. See Yonge, Ena L., "These Maps are Essential, " Library Journal, LXXV (March 15, 1950), 440, 446.

20. Espenshade, Edward B., Jr., "Maps for the College
Library, " College and Research Libraries, VIII
(April 1947), 1-6.

21. Ristow, Walter W., "World Atlases, " Library Journal,
LXXXVII (April 15, 1962), 1553-1554.

22. See Yonge, Ena L., "National Atlases: A Summary, "
Geographical Review, XLVII (October 1957), 570-
578, and Leszczycki, S., Drecke, J., and Tuszynska-
Rekawek, H., National and Regional Atlases (Warsaw:

Polish Academy of Sciences, Institute of Geography, 1964).

23. Meynen, E., "International Bibliography of the Carte Internationale du monde au millionieme," Bibliotheca Cartographica, Sonderheft I (Bad Godesberg, West Germany: Bundesanstalt für Landeskunde and Raumforschung 1962).

24. Procurement of items from the numerous agencies involved is most simply facilitated by the use of formletter post cards.

25. Bahn, Catherine I., "Plastic Maps and Globes," Journal of Geography, LXIX (January 1960), 41-43.

26. Woods, Bill M., "Map Information Reference Service," Special Libraries, XLV (March 1954), 103-106.

27. Ristow, Walter W., "Cartographic Exhibits," Surveying and Mapping, XIV (January-March 1954), 18-25.

LOCATION AND ADMINISTRATION OF A MAP AND ATLAS COLLECTION*

Mai Treude

Academic librarians have always been interested in whether special collections should be centrally located in the library or attached to specific academic departments as departmental libraries. Centralized collections are associated with minimal duplication of materials and are preferred by administrators. Faculty and advanced students, however, prefer decentralized departmental libraries. [1] Of equal interest is the matter of under which administrative jurisdictions special collections belong. The question of whether special collections should be administered by central administration (library director), reference department, department of special collections, division of departmental libraries, etc., remains to be debated. The following is a discussion of the theories of location and administration of a special collection: the map collection. The University of Minnesota map collection presents a classic example of map library growth and development, and offers one ample opportunity to critically analyze each stage of growth. The stages to be discussed are:

> Stage I: A collection of all non-book materials: maps, posters, records, United Nations documents, microfilms. Remote location, neither centralized nor decentralized. Administered by the Reference Department of the Library.
>
> Stage II: A collection of maps, atlases, aerial photographs, geography books and periodicals. Decentralized departmental library housed in the building with the geography department. Administered by the head of Departmental Libraries.

---

*Reprinted by permission from Special Library Association, Geography and Map Division, Bulletin No. 89 (1972), 32-40.

Stage III: A collection of maps, atlases, aerial photographs, books concerning cartography, carto-bibliographies, cartographic serials. Centrally located
and administered by the head of the Reference Services Department.

The statistical and chronological breakdown is presented in
Tables 1 and 2.

Discussion of Stage I

One finds that a fairly large map collection existed in
the realm of the University Library in the 1950's (see Table
1). The collection was housed in a "Map Room," located in
Johnston Hall (situated next to what was then the main library), and serviced by Reference Department personnel.
The room provided housing for maps, aerial photographs,
United Nations documents, microfilm, a collection of posters,
and a spoken word collection. The Geography Department
was located in another building a short distance across the
campus mall. Maps housed together with other non-book
materials may not necessarily be considered poor policy if
effectively administered. However, besides the problem of
crowded conditions, a definite drawback exists in that the librarian in charge is overly torn between various materials,
allowing little time for the development of the map collection.
The division of the librarian's attention between varying responsibilities does not allow for effective specialization in
the area of map librarianship.

Neither is the remoteness of the map collection advantageous. Ideally, a library collection should not be located in a basement corner of a building (other than the library) where one would least expect it. Occasionally it may
be unavoidable for emergency measures, and this, of course,
is understandable. But one should strive to remove the collection from such a situation.

In the Johnston Hall location, serious inquiries into
the role of the map collection were made in 1961-62. A
survey "... was initiated in order to determine who uses
the map collection, how they became aware of it, how it is
being used, what it is being used for, and how it can be
strengthened and made more useful."[2] The survey indicated
that the use of the collection by students far outranked use
by faculty and others. It also indicated that the Map Room
functioned primarily for the purpose of assignment related use.

Table 1. The Map Collection: Its Size, Location, Administration*

	1956/57	1961/62	1968/69	1969/70
Maps	40,000	80,333	150,915	160,357
Location	Johnston Hall	Johnston/Soc. Sci.	Social Science	Wilson Library
Administration	Reference Dept.- 1959	Special Collections 1959-1962	Dept. Lib. 1962-1968	Reference Services Dept.
Collection	Non-book: maps, posters, records, U.N. documents, air photos, microfilms.		Maps, air photos, geography books, atlases	Maps, air photos, cartog. books & serials, atlases
Staff	1 full, 1 pt.	1 full, 1 pt.	1½ full, 1 pt.	1½ full, 1½ pt.
Total space, sq.ft.	--	--	2776	6747
Reader space	--	--	18	52
Map cases (5-drawer sect.)	--	--	87	153

*From: Annual Reports, Univ. of Minn. Map Library (various years).

Table 2. Enrollment and Faculty Size in the Dept. of Geography, University of Minnesota†

	1956/57	1961/62	1968/69	1969/70
Geography enrollment	2308	3570	6832	7306
Geography faculty	5	10	16	16
Enrollment, cartography & map interp.	57	127	227	202
Enrollment in human & natural/physical resources	1242	1986	3861	4235

†From: Association of American Geographers, Directory of College Geography of the United States.

Since over half of the patrons had learned of the map collection's existence from faculty, it is probable that the bulk of the use was prompted by requirements of the Geography Department. The location of the collection may not have had significant influence on the student user as long as the visit was prompted by assignment. Unfortunately, no one can estimate how many potential patrons, who would have used the collection for other purposes had it been more accessible, were lost.

The total use of the collection, however, must have been significant enough to encourage attempts to enlarge the collection and obtain support from the library administration. One must keep in mind that the efforts of the various consecutive librarians in charge of the collection figured greatly in its enlargement through the solicitation of free materials. Many map libraries can trace part of their growth to persistent begging of free materials to supplement their depository collections and meager acquisitions funds.

Discussion of Stage II

The second important stage of change affecting the map collection occurred in the fall of 1962. The collection moved a considerable distance away from the main library to the area of latest campus expansion, the opposite bank of the Mississippi River. The new "Map Library" (the geographers called it the "Geography and Map Library") was housed with the Geography Department in the Social Sciences Building. Administratively, the Map Library obtained the status of a departmental library, joining some twelve other such libraries. Thus, it belonged in the library system, but worked closely with the Geography Department. Needless to say, the Department of Geography became the main influence in the development of the collection and the type and amount of use. As is natural to any departmental library, a vigorous acquisition of book materials to support the department's interests was pursued.

Along with a growing geography book collection, there were the maps, atlases and aerial photographs. Many map series were received on depository and others were selected and acquired. The map collection was well organized and accessibility was adequate. The atlases were unfortunately scattered in both the main library and the Map Library, even though an effort was made to gather them in the latter location. Most of the currently ordered atlases were sent to the

Map Library. Curiously, though, the newly acquired atlases
and books were only charged to the Map Library from the
main collection, and thus no catalog cards were ever received.
This practice was in contrast to other departmental libraries
that received books cataloged with their departmental symbols
as well as with the sets of cards. Compounding the problem,
the library had received an uncataloged collection of geography books from the department, and no attempt had been
made by the main library to catalog these books and officially incorporate them into the library's holdings.

Selection was done by the map librarian as well as
geography faculty and members of the Acquisitions Department of the central Library. This method of acquisitions
was not the most efficient, resulting in duplications, the purchase of unnecessary titles, and generally reflecting a lack
of knowledge of priorities (no blame on the map librarians!).
The map collection, as part of a departmental library, was
ideally located. It was only a few steps "down the hall"
from the offices of the Geography faculty and graduate students. The way it was situated and set up, the library was
used largely by Geography graduate and undergraduate ma-
jors. There was actually little room for others.

In order to gain more insight into the function of the
Map Library in this location, another use survey was taken
in 1968. The results were amazingly similar to those of the
1961 survey. The primary user was still the student doing
course related work. Even the volume of use had not increased, contrary to one's expectations because of the better
facilities and greater variety of materials. The faculty use
was also similar to the previous survey, although there was
quite a drop in the use made by "others." To a large extent the Map Library seems to have functioned as a laboratory for assigned work. Map assignments usually refer to a
specific set or category of materials; no matter how significant, such use tends to neglect the bulk of the collection.
The location of the collection in relation to the main library
denotes remoteness from the main center of information.
The departmental library may suggest a sense of "private"
library, and could thus serve as a psychological barrier to
the occasional user.

One can apply the "origin of the trip to library" theory
to the aforementioned case in weighing the pros and cons of
centralized versus decentralized location. [3] A departmental
library is justified if the majority of users originate from

the building housing the collection and the department. The
justification is strengthened if a highly specialized departmental collection is of a nature requiring particular knowledge of its use and is not of general interest to the majority of people in the institution. Attaching the map and atlas
collection to the Geography Department denotes special training for the use of these materials and deemphasizes use by
non-geographers. Yet, most people use maps and atlases in
varying degrees of sophistication at some points in their
lives. Perhaps the geographers will remain the elite of map
users, but why not educate the rest of the people and begin
this task by looking critically at where the maps are located? Librarians are anxious to serve and educate. They
should keep in mind the goal of providing service and information to the widest audience possible.

     In applying the "origin of the trip to library" idea to
the departmental map library in this case, one should look
at figures such as total geography enrollment, number of
graduate students in geography, and the size of the faculty.
In comparing a total geography enrollment of 6000 to a full
time faculty of 10-20, with approximately 60 graduate students,
it seems that only 60-80 users could possibly originate from
the same building. In that case, should one insist on having
a departmental collection? A figure so small hardly supports
the idea of a decentralized collection in this particular instance.

     The University of Minnesota map collection in the de-
centralized stage no doubt served the Geography Department
well, and meant to do the same for the rest of the academic
population. If it failed in anyway, one could blame its location, as well as the lack of administrative support. One
should question if a faculty's pressure on the library administration is serving the interests of other groups as well. Is
it beneficial to combine maps and geography books, but not
the atlases, in one collection? Quite a number of geography
libraries in this country do not maintain complete holdings of
the library's atlases in their collections. Since atlases and
maps complement each other it should be more useful to the
patron to find both in one location. Whereas the geography
books, so strongly overlapping other disciplines in social
sciences, could be housed with the rest of the books in a
general collection.

     The fact that the Map Library and its librarian re-
ported directly to the head of all departmental libraries seems

to have had little direct influence on its function and growth.
The map librarian's own efforts, interests and stamina are
probably most important. The department to which the collection is attached seems more influential than the library
administration. The latter, of course, can play a highly
supportive role (funds) in a decentralized situation if interest
warrants. In the case of the Minnesota Map Library, it
never had a chance to develop into an ideally functioning departmental library. As time went on, there were hints that
when the Map Library moved again, it would not continue as
a departmental library.

Discussion of Stage III

        The third stage important in the Map Library develop-
ment began when it moved to the new O. Meredith Wilson
Library in the fall of 1968. The Wilson Library contains
the humanities and social sciences collections and serves as
the headquarters for the University system of libraries.
Space for the Map Library was allocated in the sub-basement
of the building along with several other special collections.
The map collection gained more than adequate space with
room for expansion. At last centrally located, the Map Library had a chance to begin service as an information center
alongside the rest of the library's resources. Together with
the change in location, the collection came under the administration of the Department of Reference Services. The latter
consists of seven independently functioning and separately
staffed reference divisions. Thus there is now a Map Division.

        The change from the status of a departmental library
to a reference service unit called for a reevaluation of the
purpose of the map collection. The collection's redefined
purpose was to function as a source of information represented in cartographic form; the collection of books not defined as atlases was to be kept at a minimum. The previously held books of geography were thus transferred to the
Wilson Library main stacks. The Map Division's book collection consists of atlases, cartographic serials, and books
on historical cartography and related topics. The entire
University atlas collection is now concentrated in this one
location. Small reference collections of atlases exist, of
course, in other locations. In addition to the holdings mentioned, the Map Division also houses a collection of aerial
photographs of Minnesota.

With the more concentrated collection and accessible
location, one envisioned and hoped for a wider intensity of
use by a varying clientele. Nevertheless, the working relationship with the Geography Department as specialized clientele remained strong. In fact, it has even been intensified
through the effective communication that has taken place in
the geography library committee meetings and is continued
on informal levels. Another form of cooperation is the required Map Division orientation for new Geography graduate
students. A certain amount of discussion also takes place
in cases of unusual or costly acquisitions. Recommendations
about possible acquisition items are made to the librarian by
the Geography faculty, but the librarian has complete responsibility for selecting and acquiring materials.

As the process of reevaluating the function of the Map
Division continued, one came to see it as an integral part of
the central library system. Such an entity should obviously
function within the library framework in agreement with its
rules. In order to fit into the Reference Department, it
should be able to offer reference services at all times, meaning that the materials should be in the library, and not out
in the field. Some concern should also be given to the permanence (preservation) of the collection. These ideas were
considered and discussed with the members of the Geography
Department and others, and after weighing various possibilities the decision was made to turn the collection into a non-
circulating library. The new circulation policy went into effect in the fall of 1971 and probably constituted a controversial step in the field of map librarianship. The foregoing
may describe an operation that is too rigid, but one can rest
assured that the result is not what Hagen fears, "... an overall condition of stagnation and atrophy within the map collection."[4] In fact, the overall condition is far from "stagnation"! There is every indication that volume of use has increased. And exceptions are made for those patrons who
must use the maps outside the library for purposes such as
copying, lectures, displays, or for other reasons when use in
the library is difficult or impossible.

A 1970 survey indicated that the map use had doubled
from that of 1968. However, it also pointed out that the
primary user was still the student. But happily, the use by
"others" had also doubled. Since three different surveys
have indicated a dominating use by students, one might conclude that the student will use the collection for course assigned work regardless of where the collection is located

(within reasonable distance). One would expect, though, that a large and expensively maintained collection has a greater aim than catering to students who are forced to make use of it. Therefore, the increase in "other" patrons is a welcome sign. In addition to an increase in map use, a marked change in the pattern of use has been noticed. It has changed from the "self-service" type of use, peculiar to a departmental library because of familiarity with the collection, to complete guidance from the staff. The number of first-time and infrequent users is high when judged by the fact that almost all patrons ask for help in finding information and materials. Hopefully, the latter is not a reflection of a badly organized collection. A Map Division layout chart is located near the card catalog to help patrons in orienting themselves. However, some initiation into the secrets of the organization, and the mysteries of Library of Congress classification of maps, seems essential before most patrons can function independently.

The staff functions are well defined in relation to the patrons. The staff is oriented towards offering reference service; helping the patrons has high priority among many other activities. It is essential that the staff, including the student help, be trained to help the patrons, know the collection, and know location of materials. The map-related reference work most often goes far beyond the location of information from obvious sources. The staff must also offer informal instruction on map use and interpretation, locate publication sources, etc.

CONCLUSION

It would be proper to review the role of administration and location in the day-to-day functioning of a map library. After a brief discussion of the map library in three stages of development, one has observed that: the central administration has little effect on the daily activities of the map library, but its attitude in regard to the importance of the collection unavoidably sets the course for the development of the collection. This may best be reflected in the size of the acquisitions budget, equipment provisions, plans for the future, staffing, receptiveness to faculty and student needs, etc. An administrative decision could also be instrumental in changing the content of the library, thus influencing its function and clientele. Administration figures strongly in future plans for the library. Therefore, it is necessary to

establish effective lines of communication between the map
librarian and the administration, in which all intentions on
both sides are made explicit.   Any plans, when building or moving, must be made with an open mind and an eye
to the future.   Occasional reevaluation of the function of the
map library is necessary in order to provide effective service.   If the function is too narrowly defined, unfortunate
planning errors may result affecting service in the future.[5]

  If one were faced with the choice between a decentralized or centralized location, one should look at the collection on hand as well as know what are future possibilities
and needs for its growth.   One should ask what and who will
set the directions of growth.   Is the present status of the
collection a basic teaching unit with little interest or necessity to develop it?   If so, the decentralized location may be
satisfactory, especially if the collection is closely attached
to the geography department.   If the collection already consists of world-wide coverage and is of considerable size,
due to various depository programs and aggressive acquisitions, any possibility of a centralized location should be
probed if it does not already exist.   One should also take
into consideration what programs or studies of international
scope are or will be offered in the academic curriculum.
Regional studies like Latin American, African, Asian, etc.,
studies could be very important aside from the study of geography.   Ordinarily the new regional studies are supported
with energetic acquisitions of book materials in these fields.
Should not a library support these studies in non-book materials as well?   A large academic library, especially,
should be able to provide information in non-book form,
preferably housed in a central location.

  The map library in a centralized location is desirable
from the service point of view and for accessibility to the
widest possible clientele.   This preference is expressed by
C. Hagen, among others, when he describes the situation at
the U. C. L. A. Map Library: "... although the Map Library
is an administrative part of the campus-wide library system,
its obscure location within a departmental area has adversely
affected its accessibility to a campus-wide clientele, ... "[6]
Serious research, especially in the social sciences, is deeply
hindered by decentralization.   Research requires a multipli-
city of trips to departmental libraries in scattered locations
--unless the departmental collections are duplicated in the
central library.   A geography book collection in a departmental situation could be effective to a degree if immensely

large, and even then it could not possibly support the varied
research interests of most faculty and graduate students.
"Above all, we must approach our collection fully aware of
the new methods and tools of the present day researcher."[7]
Thus sound the cautioning words of one Canadian map librarian, as she indicates that the concept of the map library and
the approach to its use are obsolete. Perhaps these words
emphasize more than anything the need to look for a varying
clientele for the map library. A centralized collection, especially, should be able to support new teaching methods and
research interests in many disciplines.

If the choice of location and administration is beyond
the map librarian's control, the primary purpose of the librarian remains: developing and maintaining the present collection, organizing it for efficient use, and disseminating information from this resource to as wide an audience as possible. One should keep in mind the whole library function in
a campus-wide setting.

NOTES

1. Jeffrey Raffael and Robert Shishko. "Centralization vs.
    Decentralization: A Location Analysis Approach for
    Librarians," Special Libraries, vol. 63, no. 3 (March
    1972), 135.
2. John A. Wolter. "A Survey of the Use of the University
    of Minnesota Map Room Collection of Maps, Atlases,
    and Aerial Photographs." Plan B paper for M. A. de-
    gree in Library Science, Minneapolis, University of
    Minnesota, 1963.
3. Raffael, op. cit., 142.
4. C. B. Hagen. The Establishment of a University Map
    Library. A Report to the University Library, Univer-
    sity of California at Santa Cruz. Los Angeles,
    U. C. L. A. Map Library, Dec. 1965. (mimeographed)
    p. 2.
5. For example, the plans for the present University of
    Minnesota Map Division placed the circulation and ser-
    vice area at the rear of the room, near a back door
    for the purpose of shortening the distance between the
    Geography Department and the Map Division. Since
    using this door proved to be impractical, an awkward
    situation exists in which patrons have to search for
    the service desk in the back corner of the room.
6. C. B. Hagen, "A Survey of the Usage of a Large Map

Library," S. L. A., Geography and Map Division, Bulletin No. 80 (June 1970), 27.

7. Donkin, "Are Map Libraries Obsolete?" Association of Canadian Map Libraries. Fourth Annual Conference, June 1970, Proceedings, p. 62.

MAP LIBRARIANSHIP*

Robert C. White

The topic, map librarianship, is a large order, indeed. This discussion is limited to: (1) the responsibilities of the map librarian, (2) his qualifications, and (3) his day-to-day duties. The discussion is aimed at the general problems of the smaller map libraries. You may be surprised that the University of Illinois Map Library is in the category of a "smaller map library" with its collection of 250,000 maps and nearly 100,000 aerial photographs. But I prefer to judge size more from the point of view of the staff to serve the collection rather than the number of items in the collection. There are one professional, one clerical, and three part-time student positions. This staff, however, also services a collection of 14,000 geography books and the library is open for 56 hours a week. Thus our problems, so far as maps are concerned, are the same in kind and in magnitude as other small map libraries, except for those who are starting new collections.

The first responsibility of a map librarian is to build his collection. This requires knowing present needs and anticipating future needs. Know your users and anticipate their wants. Your library's overall acquisition policy will affect your building. A research library will acquire more intensely than a small university of college library. A public library will place greater emphasis on its own region, unless it has a special subject interest. To build your collection you need to know what the acquisition tools are; you must have them at hand; and above all you must use them. The tools include the map publishers' catalogs--governmental

*Reprinted by permission from Special Libraries, vol. 61, no. 5 (1970), 233-235. Copyright by Special Libraries Association. Originally presented in 1969 at the SLA 60th Annual Conference.

and private--map dealers' catalogs and sales lists, cartobibliographies, acquisitions lists, and periodicals.

Building a good collection is not enough. It must be
organized. By organization I mean classification, cataloging,
and physical arrangement. There are a number of classification schemes available to be used as they are or which can
be modified without too much difficulty. Of course you can
devise your own. I advise caution in modifying an existing
scheme or in devising your own--bear in mind the story of
book classification. Two very important considerations in
selecting or devising a classification scheme are:

Will it be kept up to date?
Will it meet the needs of a much enlarged collection?

Cataloging accomplishes what classification fails to do, and
this largely through subject and added entry cards. Unfortunately the complete cataloging of a map collection is a
rarity. There can be, however, at least brief cataloging--
at least one card for each map or map set or series. Such
a card bearing the class number, authority, title, imprint,
and scale will provide good control of the collection. This
sort of control should be within the capability of any small-
or medium-sized library.

The map librarian is responsible for the use of the
collection. He determines which maps will circulate, if
any, and to whom; what the loan period will be; and whether
they will be available on interlibrary loan. Some libraries
circulate virtually all maps freely; others permit no circulation whatsoever. A basic philosophy of American librarianship, as you know, is to make the book as freely available
to the public as reasonably as it can be done. As a consequence there has been a great deal of freedom in making the
book stacks open to the public. Can this same freedom be
allowed with the map collection? I do not think so, unless
the map librarian has no responsibility for preservation.
The risk of damage or loss of maps is very high when the
map files are open to the public. When you restrict access
to the map files, you place a greater burden on yourself, because you then take on greater responsibility in selection of
maps for use.

Maps that circulate need a protecting cover. Tubes,
in which many maps are shipped by the publishers, are very
suitable for this purpose. Maps that are torn need repair.

Maps can be protected by laminating and mounting. This requires a decision of selection because there is hardly a library that can afford to mount all maps. All librarians have a responsibility for assisting users in the selection of material, of course. But I think that the map librarian has to go beyond this service of selection-assistance to a greater extent perhaps than almost any other type of librarian. He must be able to assist the user in reading and interpreting maps. Many of the people who come to him for a map, need and should get this kind of help. Another important service of the map librarian is the determination of geographic location. By and large, most of the reference questions directed to him will be of this nature. So he needs all the tools at hand to perform this service--gazetteers, postal and shipping guides, map indexes, and so forth.

There are thousands of book stores in the United States where one can go and purchase a book, and if the book is not on the shelf the store will order it. But there are extremely few stores where you can go and purchase a map, or even get any help in purchasing one. For this reason the map librarian has a responsibility to help people buy maps: what to buy and where to buy it. Because he should have a file of publishers' and dealers' catalogs, it should be very easy to render this kind of assistance.

To perform these responsibilities what qualifications should the map librarian have? I would like to mention first three very general, but fundamental, qualifications that any public service librarian should have. I use the word "public" here in the sense of the particular kind of public you serve and not necessarily the general public; and I think that almost without exception all map librarians are public service librarians. The qualifications are dedication, personality (that is, a personality that makes for easy rapport with your public), and understanding. I think that most of you will find that a large proportion of the people who come to you for maps not only know very little about a map but also do not even know how to ask for a map. The map librarian must understand them, be patient with them, and be sympathetic with them.

Looking back for a moment, what were the qualifications of our first librarians? Let me quote from Walter Ristow's article "Map Librarianship" in Library Journal (Oct 1967):

The First Generation of American map librarians
was, of necessity, self-trained. Those few individuals who filled positions as map curators prior
to World War I, moreover entered the profession
largely by chance rather than design. They came
from a variety of noncartographic backgrounds, and
none had prior training in library science or geography. Cast adrift in a confusion of maps, they
struggled and learned as they sought to establish
order and control over the collection.

We can hardly say that they had ideal qualifications. The
map librarian should have a first degree and an advanced degree, the latter being in library science. His library science degree should include formal instruction in map librarianship, a type of which is almost impossible to obtain.

The first degree should be with a major in geography.
Why in geography? It is because the geographer deals with
aerial distribution of people, of plants, of animals, of climates, of transportation systems, of settlements, of industrial sites, of chain stores--and I could go on and on. Aerial distribution is very effectively presented graphically by
the map; and that is why the geographer considers the map
as a fundamental tool of his profession. Because of this he
makes a cartography course one of the requirements for a
major in geography. Besides a major in geography the map
librarian should have had courses in geology and history, and
he should have competence in two foreign languages.

My last point for discussion is the day-to-day duties
of the map librarian. If a collection is to be kept up-to-
date there must be constant searching of periodicals, catalogs, price lists, acquisitions lists and so forth for new
maps to be acquired. Another daily task--and it requires
considerable time--is helping in selecting the right maps and
atlases for the users of your collection. If you have an air
photo collection, you will be concerned with identifying and
selecting the photo or photos that cover the desired area.
Map users will ask you questions about maps you select for
them that will require you to do some map reading or even
map interpretation. The training and supervision of help is
a continuing task. Processing of maps is a constant task--
unwrapping, arranging, stamping, classifying, cataloging, indexing, and the placing of call numbers on maps. A common
duty is the answering of reference questions, and the most
common questions are about geographic locations--some of

which are simple to answer but others are difficult. The
more difficult, the more intriguing but the more time consuming. And lastly, weeding. It is difficult to fit weeding
into the day-to-day routine, but if you can, so much the better.

BIBLIOGRAPHY

CHAPTER 1

American Congress on Surveying and Mapping. "History of Surveying in U. S. " Surveying and Mapping, vol. 18, no. 2 (1958), 179-226.

Bagrow, Leo. History of Cartography. Rev. & enl. by R. A. Skelton. Cambridge, Mass.: Harvard University Press, 1964; 312p.

Bricker, Charles. Landmarks of Mapmaking: An Illustrated Survey of Maps and Mapmakers. Maps chosen and displayed by R. V. Tooley, text written by Charles Bricker, preface by Gerald Roe Crone. Amsterdam: Elsevier, 1968; 276p.

Brown, Lloyd A. Map Making; The Art That Became a Science. Boston: Little, Brown, 1960; 217p.

Coronelli-Weltbund der Globusfreunde. Der Globusfreund (a periodical). Vienna: Published by the Coronelli-Weltbund der Globusfreunde, 1952- .

Crone, Gerald R. Maps and Their Makers; An Introduction to the History of Cartography. 4th rev. ed. London: Hutchinson University, 1968; 184p.

Fauser, Alois. Die Welt in Händen. Kurze Kulturgeschichte des Globus. Stuttgart: Schuler Verlagsgesellschaft, 1967; 184p.

Fite, Emerson D. and Archibald Freeman. A Book of Old Maps, Delineating American History from the Earliest Days Down to the Close of the Revolutionary War. Cambridge, Mass.: Harvard University Press, 1922; xv, 299p.

Goldenberg, Leonid A.   Russian Maps and Atlases As His-
    torical Sources. (Cartographica, Monograph 3.) 1971;
    76p. Published by B. V. Gutsell, Dept. of Geography,
    York Univ. Toronto, Canada.

Harvey, Jon. "A Short History of Air Survey." Society of
    Univ. Cartographers, Bulletin, vol. 6, no. 2 (1972),
    32-35.

Heyden, Reverend Francis J. "Maps As the Heritage of
    Mankind." Surveying and Mapping, vol. 23, no. 4
    (1963), 539-546.

Imago Mundi. "A Review of Early Cartography." Stock-
    holm, 1935. Index: 1-10, The Hague: Mouton and
    Co., 1935-1954.

Lister, Raymond. How to Identify Old Maps and Globes with
    a List of Cartographers, Engravers, Publishers and
    Printers Concerned with Printed Maps and Globes from
    c. 1500 to c. 1850. Hamden, Conn.: Archon Books,
    1965; 256p.

Lister, Raymond. Antique Maps and Their Cartographers.
    Hamden, Conn.: Archon Books, 1970; 128p.

Marsh, Susan. "Maps, the Oldest Visual Aid and Primary
    Source Material." The Journal of Geography, vol. 66,
    no. 3 (1967), 130-132.

Muris, Oswald and Gert Saarmann. Der Globus im Wandel
    der Zeit: Eine Geschichte der Globen. Berlin: Colum-
    bus Verlag Paul Oestergaad KG, 1961; 288p.

Nordenskiöld, Adolf Erik. Facsimile-Atlas to the Early His-
    tory of Cartography with Reproductions of the Most Im-
    portant Maps Printed in the XV and XVI Centuries.
    Trans. from the Swedish Original by Johan Adolf Eke-
    löf and Clements R. Markham. Stockholm: P. A.
    Norstedt & Son, 1889; 141p., 51 pl. (Available as a
    reprint from Kraus Reprint Co., New York, 1962.)

Nordenskiöld, Adolf Erik. Periplus; An Essay on the Early
    History of Charts and Sailing Directions. Stockholm:
    P. A. Norstedt & Son, 1897; 208p. (Available as a
    reprint from B. Franklin, New York, 1969.)

Ristow, Walter W. Aviation Cartography: A Historic-Bibliographic Study of Aeronautical Charts. Washington, D.C.: Library of Congress, 1960; 245p.

Sanceau, Elaine. "Portugal's Contribution to Global Geography." The Journal of Geography, vol. 69, no. 3 (1970), 147-156.

Skelton, R. A. Maps--A Historical Survey of Their Study and Collecting. (The Kenneth Nebenzahl, Jr. Lectures in the History of Cartography at Newberry Library.) Chicago: University of Chicago Press, 1972; xvii, 138p.

Stevenson, Edward L. Terrestrial and Celestial Globes: Their History and Construction Including a Consideration of Their Value As Aides in the Study of Geography and Astronomy. 2 vols. New Haven, Conn.: Published for the Hispanic Society of America by the Yale University Press, 1921.

Thrower, Norman J. H. Maps and Man: An Examination of Cartography in Relation to Culture and Civilization. Englewood Cliffs, N.J.: Prentice-Hall, 1972; 184p.

Tooley, Ronald Vere. Maps and Map-Makers. 4th ed. New York: Crown, 1960; xii, 140p.

Verner, Coolie. "The Identification of Variants in the Study of Early Printed Maps." Imago Mundi, no. 19 (1965), 100-105.

Wheat, Carl I. Mapping the Transmississippi West, 1540-1861. 5 vols. San Francisco: Institute of Historical Cartography, 1957-1963.

CHAPTER 2

Best, Thomas D. "35mm Slides of Topographic Maps: Pitfalls and Prospects." The Professional Geographer, vol. 17, no. 3 (1965), 20-24.

Dainville, François de. "From the Depths to the Heights." Surveying and Mapping, vol. 30, no. 3 (1970), 389-403. (Trans. by Prof. A. Robinson.)

Dean, William G. "The Structure of Regional Atlases: An
    Essay on Communication. " The Canadian Cartographer,
    vol. 7, no. 1 (1970), 48-60.

De Lucie, Alan. "The Effect of Shaded Relief on Map In-
    formation Accessibility. " The Cartographic Journal,
    vol. 9, no. 1 (1972), 14-18.

Fielstra, Gerritt E. "Photoreproduction of Maps: Practical?"
    Library Journal, vol. 75, no. 6 (1950), 464-465.

Ehrenberg, Ralph. "Reproducing Maps in Libraries and Ar-
    chives: The Custodian's Point-of-View. " Special Li-
    braries, vol. 64, no. 1 (1973), 18, 20-24.

Greenhood, David. Mapping. Chicago: University of Chi-
    cago Press, 1964; xiii, 289p. (Phoenix Science Series.)

Kingsbury, Robert C. "Creative Cartography: An Introduc-
    tion to Effection Thematic Map Design. " Indiana Uni-
    versity, Dept. of Geography, 1969; 44p.

La Hood, Charles G. , Jr. "Reproducing Maps in Libraries:
    The Photographer's Point-of-View. " Special Libraries,
    vol. 64, no. 1 (1973), 19, 25-28.

Lawrence, G. R. P. Cartographic Methods. London:
    Methuen & Co. , 1971; 162p.

Makowski, Andrzej. "Aesthetic and Utilitarian Aspects of
    Colour in Cartography. " Internationales Jahrbuch für
    Kartographie, vol. 7, (1967), 62-85.

Maling, Derek H. "Some Thoughts about Miniaturisation of
    Maps Library Contents. " The Cartographic Journal,
    vol. 3, no. 1 (1966), 14-17.

Monkhouse, Francis J. and Henry R. Wilkinson. Maps and
    Diagrams, Their Compilation and Construction. New
    York: Barnes and Noble, 1967; 432p.

Mumford, Ian. "Lithography, Photography and Photozincogra-
    phy in English Map Production Before 1870. " The Car-
    tographic Journal, vol. 9, no. 1 (1972), 30-36.

Raisz, Erwin J. General Cartography. 2d ed. New York:
    McGraw-Hill, 1948; 354p.

Robinson, Arthur H. Elements of Cartography. 3d ed. New
York: John Wiley & Sons, 1969; 415p.

Scott, L. "Early Experience in the Photomapping Technique."
The Cartographic Journal, vol. 6, no. 2 (1969), 108-
113.

Skelton, Raleigh A. "Colour in Mapmaking." The Geographical Magazine, vol. 32 (1960), 544-555.

Steward, John Q. "The Use and Abuse of Map Projections."
The Geographical Review, vol. 33, no. 4 (1943), 589-
604.

Tobler, Waldo R. "Geographic Area and Map Projections."
The Geographical Review, vol. 53, no. 1 (1963), 59-78.

CHAPTER 3

Aune, Quintin A. "The Geologic Map: Preparation, Interpretation and Uses." Div. of Mines, Mineral Information Service, California, vol. 13, no. 8 (1960), 1-8.

Bartz, B. S. "Maps in the Classroom." The Journal of
Geography, vol. 69, no. 1 (1970), 18-24.

Clissold, Peter. "The Seaman's Chart." The Geographical
Magazine, vol. 33, no. 9 (1961), 496-504

Davies, W. K. D. "Reflection on Spacial Perception: Mental or Ignorance Maps?" Swansea Geographer, vol. 8
(1970), 5-10.

Dickinson, G. C. Maps and Air Photographs. London:
Edward Arnold, 1869; 286p.

Dury, G. H. Map Interpretation. 2d ed. London: Pitman
& Sons, 1960; 209p.

Gilbert, Perry R. "The Numerical Map." The Military Engineer, vol. 60, no. 395 (1968), 194-196.

Godstein, M. "Computer Mapping: A Tool for Urban Planners." Cleveland: Battelle Memorial Institute, Urban
Studies Center, 1969; 30p.

Gould, P. R. On Mental Maps. Michigan Inter-University
    Community of Mathematical Geographers, 1966; 53p.
    (Discussion Papers No. 9.)

Graham, Harry. Reading Topographic Maps. Toronto: Holt,
    Rinehard & Winston, 1968; 120p.

Gritzner, Charles F. "Sources of Map Information." The
    Journal of Geography, vol. 69, no. 3 (1970), 141-146.

Hanle, Adolf. "A Discussion on the Treatment of Thematic
    Maps Using as an Example: 'Meyer's Large Physical
    Atlas of the World'." Society of University Cartogra-
    phers, Bulletin, vol. 6, no. 2 (1972), 19-24.

Harrison, Richard E. "Atlases Revisited." Saturday Re-
    view, March 1962, 37-40.

Hill, R. T. "Maps for Television Use." The Journal of
    Geography, vol. 61, no. 5 (1962), 204-208.

Hopps, H. C. "Computerized Mapping of Disease and En-
    vironmental Data." S. L. A., Geography and Map Divi-
    sion, Bulletin No. 78 (1969), 24-30.

Jusatz, Helmut J. "Medical Mapping As a Contribution to
    Human Ecology." S. L. A., Geography and Map Divi-
    sion, Bulletin No. 78 (1969), 19-23.

Koeman, C. "The Principle of Communication in Cartogra-
    phy." Internationales Jahrbuch für Kartographie, Bd.
    11 (1971), 169-176.

Küchler, A. W. "Some Uses of Vegetation Maps." Ecology,
    vol. 34, no. 3 (1953), 629-636.

Laferriere, Andre J. "Importance of Mapping in a Modern
    Society." Surveying and Mapping, vol. 31, no. 4
    (1971), 581-586.

Leszczycki, S. "Some Remarks about National Atlases."
    Przeglad Geograficzny, vol. 32, no. 1 (1960), 3-19.

McGregor, D. R. "Geographical Globes." The Cartographic
    Journal, vol. 3, no. 1 (1966), 7-9.

Meine, Karl-Heinz. "Aviation Cartography." The Cartographic Journal, vol. 3, no. 3 (1966), 31-40.

Mene, A. H.   Reading Topographical Maps.   London: University of London Press, 1960; 84p.

Milgram, S.   "A Psychological Map of New York City."
American Scientist, vol. 60, no. 2 (1972), 194-200.

Nicolaisen, W. F. H.   "Mental Maps."   The Cartographic
Journal, vol. 5, no. 1 (1968), 72.

Preston, J. E.   "Toward a Future Understanding of the Regional Concept: The Map As an Analytical Device."
Association of American Geographers, Annals, vol. 42
(1952), 195-222.

Ristow, Walter W.   "Journalistic Cartography."   Surveying
and Mapping, vol. 17, no. 4 (1957), 369-390.

Ristow, Walter W.   "A Half-Century of Oil-Company Road
Maps."   Surveying and Mapping, vol. 24, no. 4 (1964),
617-637.

Ristow, Walter W.   "U. S. Fire Insurance Maps, 1852-1968."
Surveying and Mapping, vol. 30, no. 1 (1970), 19-41.

Ristow, Walter W.   "Cartographic Research Guide--Weather
and Climate Maps."   S. L. A., Geography and Map Division, Bulletin No. 42 (1960), 24-35.

Salishchev, K. A.   "The Topographic and Soil Maps of the
U. S."   Soviet Geography: Review and Translation, vol.
3, no. 4 (1962), 65-71.

Sherman, John C.   "Current Map Resources and Existing
Needs for the Blind."   Surveying and Mapping, vol. 24,
no. 4 (1964), 611-616.

Steward, H. J.   "The Error Factor and the Depiction of Settlements on Maps."   S. L. A., Geography and Map Division, Bulletin No. 82 (1970), 2-12.

Thackwell, D. E. O.   "The Importance of Cartography to
Modern States."   The Cartographic Journal, vol. 6,
no. 1 (1969), 7- .

Thompson, Morris M. and George H. Rosenfield.   "On Map

Accuracy Specifications." Surveying and Mapping, vol. 1 (1971), 57-64.

Troxel, B. W. "Maps Used in Mineral Investigations." California Div. of Mines, Mineral Information Service, vol. 13, no 2 (1960), 1-13.

Vietor, A. O. "Faculty, Students Must Have Maps." Library Journal, vol. 75, no. 6 (1950), 456-458.

White, Robert C. "The Oil Company Road Maps Revisited." S. L. A., Geography and Map Division, Bulletin No. 79 (1970), 7-9.

Wright, J. K. "Map Makers are Human: Comments on the Subjective in Maps." The Geographical Review, vol. 32 (1942), 527-544.

CHAPTER 4

Akademiia Nauk SSSR. Institut Nauchnoi Informatsii, Moscow. Referativnyi Zhurnal-Geografiia. (Monthly.)

Alexander, Gerard L. Guide to Atlases: World, Regional, National, Thematic; An International Listing of Atlases Published since 1950. Metuchen, N.J.: Scarecrow Press, 1971; xi, 671p.

American Geographical Society, Map Department. Index to Maps in Books and Periodicals. 10 vols. Boston: G. K. Hall, 1968. First Supplement, 1971.

Andregg, C. H. "The Need for National Survey and Map Information Office." Surveying and Mapping, vol. 28, no. 4 (1968), 643-647.

Association of American Geographers. Sources of Information and Materials: Maps and Aerial Photographs. Washington, D. C.: High School Geography Project; Supported by the National Science Foundation, 1970; 159p.

Balchin, W. G. "Atlases Today." The Geographical Magazine, vol. 32, no. 11 (1960), 554-563.

Bartlett, Dorothy W. "A National Cartographic Information Center." Surveying and Mapping, vol. 31, no. 3 (1971), 446-448.

Bartlett, Dorothy W. "New Government Maps for Everyone; A Select List." Special Libraries, vol. 54, no. 1 (1963), 24-28.

Bennett, Charles F. "Notes on Latin American Cartography and Geography." S. L. A., Geography and Map Division, Bulletin No. 74 (1968), 7-14.

British Museum. Catalog of Printed Maps, Charts and Plans. 15 vols. London, 1967.

Department of Energy, Mines and Resources (Canada). "List of Map Sources." Ottawa: Departmental Map Library, 1972; 31p.

Deutsche Gesellschaft für Kartographie. Kartographische Nachrichten. (A periodical.) Gütersloh, 1951- .

Fetros, John G. "State and Local Atlases; Some Observation on Collection Building." Western Association of Map Libraries, Information Bulletin, vol. 3, no. 2 (1972), 2-17.

Hoen, Philip. "Major Cartobibliographies of the West." Western Association of Map Libraries. Information Bulletin, vol. 2, no. 2 (1971), 8-13.

Horn, Werner, comp. & ed. Acta Cartographica. 12 vols., 1967-1971. Amsterdam: Theatrum Orbis Terrarum, 1972; 82p. (includes contents and index).

Institut für Landeskunde. Bibliotheca Cartographica; Bibliography of Cartographic Literature. Bad Godesberg: Institut für Landeskunde [and] Deutsche Gesellschaft für Kartographie. 2 nos. a year.

International Geographical Union. Bibliographie Cartographique Internationale. Comité Nationale Française de Geographie. (An annual.) 1936- . (Name of issuing body varies.)

Koeman, C., comp. & ed. Atlantes Neerlandici. 5 vols. Amsterdam: Theatrum Orbis Terrarum, 1967-1971.

Koerner, Alberta G. "Acquisition Philosophy and Cataloging
    Priorities for University Map Libraries." Special Li-
    braries, vol. 63, no. 11 (1972), 511-516.

Kosack, Hans-Peter and Karl-Heinz Meine. Eine Biblio-
    graphische Übersicht. Kartographische Schriftenreihe,
    Bd. 4. Lahr/Schwarzwald: Astra Verlag, 1955; 216p.

Lock, Muriel C. B. Modern Maps and Atlases; An Outline
    Guide to Twentieth Century Production. Hamden, Conn.:
    Archon Books, 1969; 619p.

Map Collector's Circle. Map Collector's Series. London:
    Map Collector's Circle, 1963- .

Overstreet, William B.   "The National Cartographic Infor-
    mation Center." S. L. A., Geography and Map Division,
    Bulletin No. 86 (1971), 9-10.

Paylore, Patricia. "Eye in the Sky." S. L. A., Geography
    and Map Division, Bulletin No. 80 (1970), 2-15.

Special Libraries Association. Geography and Map Division.
    "Bibliographies on Map and Mapping." The Bulletin
    No. 51 (1963), 19-21.

Stephenson, Richard W. "Atlases of the Western Hemisphere:
    A Summary Survey." The Geographical Review, vol.
    62, no. 1 (1972), 92-119.

Stephenson, Richard W. and Mary Galneder. "Anglo-Ameri-
    can State and Provincial Thematic Atlases: A Survey
    and Bibliography." Canadian Cartographer, vol. 6, no.
    1 (1969), 15-45.

Thompson, M. M. "Mapping the Surface of the Earth."
    Natural History, vol. 73, no. 8 (1964), 30-37.

U. S. Copyright Office. Catalog of Copyright Entries, 3rd
    ser. Part 6. Maps and Atlases. vol. 1- . Wash-
    ington, D. C., 1947- .

U. S. Library of Congress. A List of Geographical Atlases
    in the Library of Congress with Bibliographical Notes,
    comp. under the direction of P. Lee Phillips. Wash-
    ington, D. C.: vols. 1-4, 1909-1920; compiled by
    Clara E. LeGear: vol. 5, 1958; vol. 6, 1963.

U. S. Library of Congress. Geography and Map Division.
The Bibliography of Cartography. Boston: G. K. Hall,
1973.

Wicher, John F. "Originality, Cartography and Copyright."
New York University Law Review, vol. 38 (1963), 280-
300.

Wise, Donald A. "Sources of Cartographic Acquisition in the
Library of Congress." S. L. A., Geography and Map
Division, Bulletin No. 86 (1971), 11-15.

Witkege, Francis L. "The National Topographic Map Series."
Surveying and Mapping, vol. 25, no. 4 (1965), 567-572.

Woodward, David and Arthur Robinson. "Notes on a 'Genea-
logical Chart' of some American Commercial Map and
Atlas Producers." S. L. A., Geography and Map Division, Bulletin No. 79 (1970), 2-6.

Yonge, Ena L. "Regional Atlases; A Summary Review."
The Geographical Review, vol. 52, no. 3 (1962), 407-
432.

Yonge, Ena L. "World and Thematical Atlases." The Geographical Review, vol. 52, no. 4 (1962), 585-596.

CHAPTER 5

Alonso, Patricia A. G. "Feasibility Study on Computer-
Produced Map Catalogue." The Australian Library
Journal, July 1972, 245-252.

American Geographical Society. Cataloging and Filing Rules
for Maps and Atlases in the Society's Collection. Rev.
& exp. ed., by Roman Drazniowsky. New York:
American Geographical Society, 1969; 92p. (Mimeographed and offset Publication No. 4.)

Anderson, O. C. "No Best Method to Catalog Maps." Library Journal, vol. 75, no. 6 (1950), 450-452.

Boggs, Samuel W. and Dorothy C. Lewis. The Classification and Cataloging of Maps and Atlases. New York:
Special Library Association, 1945; 175p.

Bordin, Ruth B. and Robert M. Warner. "Manuscript Map
    Cataloging." New York: The Modern Manuscript Li-
    brary, 1966; 6p.

Carrington, D. K. and E. U. Mangen. Data Preparation
    Manual for the Conversion of Map Cataloging Records
    to Machine Readable Form. Washington, D. C. : Li-
    brary of Congress, 1971; 317p.

Hagen, C. B. "An Information Retrieval System for Maps."
    UNESCO Library Bulletin, vol. 20, no. 1 (1966), 30-35.

Hagen, C. B. "Maps, Copyright and Fair Use." S. L. A.,
    Geography and Map Division, Bulletin No. 66 (1966),
    4-11.

Harmon, G. H. "The Computer-Microfilm Relationship."
    Special Libraries, vol. 62, no. 7/8 (1971), 279-282.

Heim, Luceil D. "Classifying and Cataloging a Geographic
    Collection." S. L. A., Geography and Map Division,
    Bulletin No. 41 (1960), 16-32.

Hinckley, Thomas K. "Dewey Decimal Classification for
    United States Air Force Academy Map Collection."
    S. L. A., Geography and Map Division, Bulletin No. 82
    (1970), 13-20.

Hopps, Howard C. "Computerized Mapping of Disease and
    Environmental Data." S. L. A., Geography and Map
    Division, Bulletin No. 78 (1969), 24-30.

McLaughlin, Pat. "Federal Map Libraries and the Develop-
    ment of Automation Standards." S. L. A., Geography
    and Map Division, Bulletin No. 86 (1971), 21-23.

Murphy, Mary. "Will Automation Work for Maps?" Special
    Libraries, vol. 54, no. 9 (1963), 563-567.

Phillips, Brian. "Simon Fraser University Computer Pro-
    duced Map Catalogue." Journal of Library Automation
    vol. 2, no. 3 (1969), 105-115.

Stallings, David L. "A Look at Automated Cartographic Re-
    trieval." S. L. A., Geography and Map Division, Bul-
    letin No. 64 (1966), 5-11.

Stallings, David L. "Automated Map Reference Retrieval."
    Master of arts thesis, University of Washington, Seat-
    tle, 1966; 71p.

Thomas, Kenneth A. "The San Juan Island Project: Cata-
    loging Maps by Mechanized Techniques." S. L. A.,
    Geography and Map Division, Bulletin No. 54 (1963),
    8-12.

U.S. Library of Congress. Classification Class G: Geogra-
    phy. 3rd ed. with Supplement. Washington, D. C.,
    1966.

White, J. B. "Further Comment on Map Cataloging." Li-
    brary Resources and Technical Services, vol. 6, no. 1
    (1962), 78.

Wilkins, Eleanore E. "Coordinating the Map and Book Col-
    lection." Special Libraries, vol. 54, no. 4 (1963),
    226-227.

Woods, Bill M. "Map Cataloging: Inventory and Prospect."
    Library Resources and Technical Services, vol. 3, no.
    4 (1959), 257-273.

CHAPTER 6

Abrams, E. F. Map Coating Concepts Studies. Final Tech-
    nical Report prepared for U. S. Army Engineer Topo-
    graphic Lab., Topographic Engineering Div., Fort Bel-
    voir, Va., 1968; 77p.

Avedon, Don M. "Microfilm Permanence and Archival
    Quality." Special Libraries, vol. 63, no. 12 (1972),
    586-588.

Barrow, William J. "Deacidification and Lamination of De-
    teriorated Documents, 1938-1963." American Archivist,
    vol. 28 (April 1965), 285-290.

Brown, L. A. "The Problems of Maps." Library Trends,
    vol. 13, no. 2 (1964), 215-225.

Capps, Marie T. "Preservation and Maintenance of Maps."

Special Libraries, vol. 63, no. 10 (1972), 457-462.

Chatham, Ronald L. and Jay B. Vanderford. "The Wall Map Storage Problem: A Solution." *The Journal of Geography*, vol. 68, no. 2 (1969), 93-95.

Collier, J. E. "Storing Map Collections." *Professional Geographer*, vol. 12, no. 4 (1960), 31-33.

Cunha, George Daniel Martin. *Library and Archives Conservation: The Boston Athenaeum's 1971 Seminar on the Application of Chemical and Physical Methods to the Conservation of Library and Archival Materials.* Boston: The Library of the Boston Athenaeum, 1972; 255p.

Cunha, George Martin and Dorothy Grant Cunha. *Conservation of Library Materials: A Manual and Bibliography on the Care, Repair and Restoration of Library Materials.* 2d ed., 2 vols. Metuchen, N. J.: Scarecrow Press, 1971-1972.

Easton, William W. "Repair and Preservation of Map Materials." *Special Libraries*, vol. 61, no. 4 (1970), 199-200.

Hill, J. D. "Maps and Atlas Cases." *Library Trends*, vol. 13, no. 4 (1965), 481-487.

King, Antoinette. "Conservation of Drawings and Prints." *Special Libraries*, vol. 63, no. 3 (1972), 116-120.

Layng, T. E. "Care and Preservation of Maps." *Proceedings of the First National Conference on Canadian Map Libraries*, Ottawa, 1967; 35-41.

Lee, Paul B. "Map Filing Equipment." In *Special Libraries: How to Plan and Equip Them.* (Special Libraries Association, Monograph No. 2.) New York: S. L. A., 1963; 43-45.

Lewis, Willard P. "The Care of Maps and Atlases in the Library." *Library Journal*, vol. 55, no. 11 (1930), 494-496.

Mitra, D. K. "Maps in Libraries, Their Storage and Preservation." *Herald of Library Science*, vol. 7, no. 1 (1968), 27-32.

Roepke, H. G. "Care and Development of a Wall-Map Collection." Professional Geographer, vol. 10, no. 3 (1958), 11-15.

Royal Geographical Society. "Storage and Conservation of Maps" (Bibliography). The Geographical Journal, vol. 121, no. 2 (1955), 182-189.

Sajor, Ladd Z. "Preservation Microfilming, Why, What, When, Who, How." Special Libraries, vol. 63, no. 4 (1972), 195-201.

CHAPTER 7

Alexander, Gerard L. "Some Notes toward a History of the New York Public Library Map Room for the Years, 1923-1941." S. L. A., Geography and Map Division, Bulletin No. 35 (1959), 4-7.

Bergen, John V. "Map Library in Western Illinois University Geography Department: Purpose, Progress, Problems, Prospects." S. L. A., Geography and Map Division, Bulletin No. 80 (1970), 17-26.

Bergen, John V. "Geographers, Maps and Campus Map Collections." The Professional Geographer, vol. 24, no. 4 (1972), 310-316.

Brown, Lloyd A. "The Problem of Maps." Library Trends, vol. 13 (1964), 215-225.

Bryan, Mary M. "The Harvard College Library Map Collection." S. L. A., Geography and Map Division, Bulletin No. 36 (1959), 4-12.

Ciome, G. R. "The Map Room of the Royal Geographical Society." Geographical Journal, vol. 126, no. 1 (1960), 12-17.

Dowa, Sheila T. "Map Collection of the University of California at Berkeley." S. L. A., Geography and Map Division, Bulletin No. 43 (1961), 13-14.

Fetros, John G. "How to Win Administrative Support for a

Map Collection." Western Association of Map Libraries. Information Bulletin, vol. 2, no. 2 (1971), 14-20.

Ferrar, A. M. "The Management of Map Collections and Libraries in University Geography Departments." Library Association Record, vol. 64 (1962), 161-165.

Fortney, Mary. "Relocation of Map Collection at Northwestern." S. L. A., Geography and Map Division, Bulletin No. 84 (1971), 40-42.

Gerlach, A. "The Map Division, Library of Congress." Geographical Journal, vol. 126, no. 2 (1960), 244.

Goodman, Marie C. "Map Collections in the United States and Canada." Surveying and Mapping, vol. 15, no. 1 (1955), 31-35.

Hagen, C. B. "The Establishment of a University Map Library." Western Association of Map Libraries, Information Bulletin, vol. 3, no. 1 (1971), 2-15.

Hagen, C. B. "A Survey of the Usage of a Large Map Library." S. L. A., Geography and Map Division, Bulletin No. 80 (1970), 27-31.

Johnson, Ralph. "U. C. L. A. Map Collections." S. L. A., Geography and Map Division, Bulletin No. 43 (1961), 15-16.

Karpinski, L. C. "Cartographical Collections in America." Imago Mundi, vol. 1 (1935), 62-64.

Koerner, Alberta G. "Map Collections in Ann Arbor." S. L. A., Geography and Map Division, Bulletin No. 79 (1970), 31-34.

Koerner, Alberta G. "Floor Plans; The New Map Room of the University of Michigan Library." S. L. A., Geography and Map Division, Bulletin No. 85 (1971), 33-38.

Kooles, J. J. "The Map Collection in the M. E. Saltykov-Shchedrin Public Library at Leningrad." Imago Mundi, vol. 20 (1966), 79-81.

Layng, Theodor E. "Problems in the Map Room." Canadian Library, vol. 18, no. 2 (1961), 63-66.

Marshall, Douglas W. "The Division of Maps, William L. Clements Library, University of Michigan." S. L. A., Geography and Map Division, Bulletin No. 89 (1972), 41-47.

May, Betty and Karen Lockhead. "The National Map Collection of Canada." S. L. A., Geography and Map Division, Bulletin No. 85 (1971), 2-12.

Meynen, Emil, ed. Kartensammlung und Kartendokumentation. Schriftenfolge herausgegeben von Emil Meynen. Bundesanstalt für Landeskunde und Raumforschung, Bad-Godesberg: 1966- .

Mueller, Anne. "The Map Collection of the Los Angeles Public Library." S. L. A., Geography and Map Division, Bulletin No. 43 (1961), 17-19.

Ristow, Walter W. "Map Librarianship." Library Journal, vol. 92, no. 18 (1967), 3610-3614.

Ristow, Walter W. "Map Collections in the Soviet Union and the Democratic Republic of Germany." S. L. A., Geography and Map Division, Bulletin No. 84 (1971), 20-23, 39.

Scheffler, Emma M. "Maps in the Illinois State Archives." Illinois Libraries, vol. 44 (June 1962), 418-426.

Skelton, Raleigh A. "The Map Room, British Museum." The Geographical Journal, vol. 126, no. 3 (1960), 367-368.

Special Libraries Association. Geography and Map Division. Map Collections in United States and Canada: A Directory. 2d ed. New York, 1970.

Starr, Dorothy. "Detroit Public Library Map Room." S. L. A., Geography and Map Division, Bulletin No. 79 (1970), 34-35.

Stephenson, R. W. Federal Government Map Collecting: Brief History. S. L. A., Washington, D. C. Chapter, 1969; 60p.

Stevens, Stanley D. "Planning a Map Library? Create a Master Plan." Special Libraries, vol. 63, no. 4 (1972), 172-176.

Tessier, Yves. "The Map Library of L'Université Laval."
    Special Libraries, vol. 61, no. 3 (1970), 131-132.

Thatcher, E. P. "The Map Library of the University of
    Oregon." S. L. A., Geography and Map Division, Bul-
    letin No. 43 (1961), 20-21.

Wallis, H. "The Role of a National Library." Cartographic
    Journal, vol. 3, no. 1 (1966), 11-14.

Warren, K. F. "Introduction to the Map Resources of the
    British Museum." Professional Geographer, vol. 17,
    no. 6 (1965), 1-7.

Winearls, J. "Map Libraries in Canada." The Cartographer,
    vol. 3, no. 2 (1966), 161-165.

Woods, Bill M. "Recommendations for a Map Collection at
    the Chicago Undergraduate Division, University of Illi-
    nois." Illinois Libraries, vol. 39 (March 1957), 74-78.

Woods, Bill M. "Map Librarianship: A Selected Bibliogra-
    phy." New Jersey Library Association, 1970; 18p.

Woods, Bill M. "Map Librarianship." S. L. A., Geography
    and Map Division, Bulletin No. 23 (1956), 9-12.

Yonge, Ena L. "Map Department of the American Geograph-
    ical Society." Professional Geographer, vol. 7, no. 2
    (1955), 2-5.

INDEX

Abbeville 32
Abrams, E. F. 535
Académie Royale des Sciences 60
Aeronautical Charts 91
Aeronautical Charts and Information Center 216
Akademiia Nauk SSSR 530
Alexander, Gerard L. 530, 537
Alonso, Patricia A. G. 533
American Congress on Surveying and Mapping 523
American Geographical Society 533
American Geographical Society, Map Department 530
Analemma 189
Anaximander 2, 38, 40
Anaximenes 2
Ancient map 37
Anderson, O. C. 533
Andregg, C. H. 530
Andrews, William Loring 19
Angle measurement 60
Antiquarian map trade 227-230
Appendix Theatri A. Ortelii et Atlantis G. Mercatoris 29
Arabs 6, 45
Arcano del Mare 35, 59
Area names 354
Aristotle 2
Army Map Service 211
Association of American Geographers 530

Atlante Veneto 32
Atlantic Neptune 35
Atlantis Appendix 29
Atlas 21, 29, 193, 475
Atlas Maior sive Cosmographia Blaviana 29, 59
Atlas Novus 29, 31
Atlas Russicas 60
Aumen, W. C. 156
Aune, Quintin A. 527
Avedon, Don M. 535
Azimuth 69

Babylon 1
Babylonians 38
Bagrow, Leo 523
Bahn, C. I. 208, 364
Balchin, W. G. 530
Baldock, E. D. 1
Barrow, William J. 535
Bartlett, Dorothy W. 531
Bartz, B. S. 527
Behaim 53
Bennett, Charles F. 531
Bergen, John V. 537
Berghaus, Heinrich 36
Bertelli 52
Best, Thomas D. 525
Bianco, Andrea 48
Bibliography 523-540
Biruni, al 46
Blaeu, William Jansjoon 11, 29, 31, 35, 58, 59
Boah, R. I. 385
Bedleian map 53
Boggs, Samuel W. and

541